JESUS
in the Church's Gospels:

*Modern Scholarship and the
Earliest Sources*

JOHN REUMANN

FORTRESS PRESS   PHILADELPHIA

To the Memory of my Mother
(† 9 June, 1966, Göttingen)
and for Rebecca, Amy, and Miriam,
that Jesus may be confessed as Lord
in their generation, as in our parents' day

ACKNOWLEDGMENTS

The quotation from *The Prophet from Nazareth* by Morton Scott Enslin (copyright © 1961 by Morton Scott Enslin) is used by permission of McGraw-Hill Book Company.

The quotations from *Through the Valley of the Kwai* by Ernest Gordon (copyright © 1962 by Ernest Gordon) are reprinted by permission of Harper & Row, Publishers, Incorporated.

The quotation from *Time, The Weekly News Magazine,* is quoted with permission.

Biblical quotations from the Revised Standard Version
of the Bible, copyrighted 1946 and 1952 by the
Division of Christian Education of the
National Council of the Churches of Christ in the
United States of America, are used by permission.

Contents

Introduction

There are many books about Jesus of Nazareth—what he did and what he said—and more are being written every year.

This one is offered in order (1) to provide some idea, in light of the current status of historical study, of what we can know about Jesus and his teaching according to the oldest and best sources available today; and (2) to suggest why it should no longer be possible to present as serious history the traditional "lives" of the sort which deal with Jesus "from the cradle to the grave" (or the Annunciation to the Ascension)—the type of which Albert Schweitzer remarked, "When one knows two or three of them, one knows them all";[1]—and (3) to indicate why even the teachings attributed to Jesus need to be sifted critically so as to separate what might actually have been spoken by Jesus from that which stems from the early church.

Unlike some presentations, however, we shall be concerned here to see value not only in what comes from the historical Jesus himself but also in the materials which bear the stamp of the Christian community and of the evangelists, produced under the aegis of the risen Christ. For in actuality, to put the matter as sharply as possible, none of the material available comes direct and purely from Jesus; all of it owes something to the early church. Thus, in seeking Jesus, we must reckon with "Jesus in the church's gospels."

There are, of course, many reasons why books about Jesus are still being written. For one thing, even in a "world come of age," and especially in churchly circles, there remains a piety and veneration for the man from Nazareth. And as always there also exists, still today, even in circles often far removed from the church, a curiosity about and interest in this figure and a certain fascination with his life and teaching. Further there is the fact that new sources bearing on the origins of Christianity and on the outlook of the age in which Jesus lived have become available in the last two decades, notably the Dead Sea Scrolls from Qumran in Palestine, and the *Gospel of Thomas* and a whole gnostic library from the Nile Valley in Egypt. There is also the fact that new methods have arisen in the last generation or so for examining the old, long-known sources, including the biblical documents. On the basis of these methods and the newly recovered sources, some scholars have claimed new insights into the age-old story of Jesus. Sometimes "the new" is a delusion and is historically unlikely; sometimes it is of real importance.

It is the contention of this book that life-of-Jesus research has turned a corner and can no longer proceed in certain of the ways familiar to many readers, especially in the Anglo-Saxon world and particularly in America. For critical study has made impossible much that passed for current coin in the realm of gospel study and many of the opinions about Jesus. And while writer after writer has repeated the cliché that "it is impossible to write a biography of Jesus," books which attempt just that have continued to appear.

If a biography is impossible, then it is time to suggest what can appear with good scholarly conscience in its stead, even if this be only a series of vignettes about Jesus and occasional snatches of his teaching, and even if it must deal more often with the portraits of Jesus from this evangelist or that early Christian source than with "Jesus as he was."

Above all, it is time that scholars try to show, especially for the average reader, with as much clarity as possible and on the basis of the New Testament text itself, why some of the traditional reconstructions about Jesus are untenable, even if this means saying, "We do not know what happened historically," instead of putting another romanticized and psychologized construct in place of what the evangelists themselves have presented. If we cannot any longer say "what happened" at many points in Jesus' lifetime, at least we can try to explain how such a view about the biblical accounts has arisen; we can suggest why such and such a detail was not likely historically, and where in primitive Christianity certain elements in the story can be fitted.

All this is to say that this book appears in the wake of "the New Quest of the historical Jesus." By that expression is meant the movement launched over a decade ago by critical scholarship as an attempt to recover something of the Jesus of history, following more than a century of efforts by the "Old Quest" to find Jesus "as he really was," and a generation or so which attempted few treatments of the historical Jesus since it was widely held that a biography of any sort was impossible (on these movements, see below, pp. 39-41). But this book appears some fifteen years after the inception of the New Quest, and with an awareness that in many ways this New Quest has by now fragmented into half a dozen directions.

The present volume appears also as an effort especially for readers in the American scene and as an effort which views previous endeavors with American eyes. That phrase needs explanation. I mean more than that every retelling of the story of Jesus is always done for a specific time and place and in its idiom. I mean more specifically in this instance with eyes which look appreciatively at contributions to the study of Jesus in English and other languages, especially German and French, both on the continent and in the British Isles (as well as in America), but with a mind which refuses to endorse completely either the conservative stance that has marked much of Anglo-Saxon work or that radical bent which both in the "no biography" approach and in phases of the New Quest has marked work in Germany especially. For in life-of-Jesus study, as soon becomes apparent, there is a gap between much Anglo-Saxon and much German work which is greater than the thirty miles of English Channel which separates England from the continent. Americans have usually been acquainted (often, only) with the British approach, and the radical scholarship from Germany sometimes comes as a distinct shock. Nowadays, however, there are encouraging signs that American scholars are in a position to be heirs of both approaches and to make judgments and contributions of their own. If our stance is often closest in this book to that of certain German scholars such as Rudolf Bultmann and Günther Bornkamm, it is, hopefully, not without appreciation for the often traditional approach in Britain and a reflection of some of its merits. Hopefully, too, this book will provide some indication of how the tide is moving, as one observer sees it, in Protestant and Roman Catholic, not to overlook Jewish and secular, scholarship. At times my endeavor has been not so much to present results (for clear-cut conclusions are not always possible) as to show why and how one arrives at particular findings.

Traditionally, such a study as we are taking up has been entitled "The Life and Teachings of Jesus," and has often been based exclusively on the four gospels, Matthew, Mark, Luke, and John, and on a harmonization of them of one sort or another at that. Today it is recognized, however, that one must also draw upon whatever other sources may be available. Accordingly this book will at times refer to Christian writings outside the New Testament gospels, to Jewish sources (including the Dead Sea Scrolls), and to the newly available *Gospel of Thomas,* when there is pertinent material in these documents.

We have asserted that it is widely recognized nowadays, following more than a century of intensive study, that a "life" of Jesus in the conventional sense of a biography cannot be written. It should now be explained that this is so because of (1) the nature of the sources and also, in my opinion, because of (2) the nature of the man who is the subject of study.

In spite of the new sources available, it has become increasingly evident that for historical knowledge of Jesus one is dependent chiefly on the New Testament gospels, and particularly on the first three—Matthew, Mark, and Luke. These gospels, it is now apparent too, were not intended to provide "biographies" of Jesus. Too much of his life is omitted (about twenty-eight out of the thirty years). What is told is often rearranged or put into different sequences by the evangelists, so that sometimes the exact order of events is, to say the least, problematical. All the material about Jesus is presented from the viewpoint of the believing Christian community in the years after the resurrection, and that fact makes a difference. What we get therefore in our gospel sources are sketches, vignettes of a man, but the man whom followers worshiped as lord. We thus see Jesus in the New Testament as faith chose to present him, in accord with faith which saw him as crucified and risen lord.

As for the man himself, we must remember that he is to this extent different from the subject of other "biography." He is regarded by those who tell of him as alive after death, and as enthroned over the world and men. One is telling not just of a man Jesus, as a "biography" would, but also of God and his acts in and through Jesus—and this amounts to a "theology."

All this holds for the teachings of Jesus, in their own way, as well as for his "life." For what Jesus said is likewise reported from the standpoint of the early church, and his teachings are regarded as·the work not merely of a man but of the lord, now risen and exalted. And they are presented in the context of the life of the early church.

It is not therefore a "biography" in the usual sense which is possible from our sources, but "Jesus in the church's gospels."[2] This phrase, which I stress, suggests a double thrust. (1) We can to an extent try to depict Jesus "as he was," before the resurrection, historically—insofar as this is possible. (2) We also find him proclaimed as lord in the gospel sources—set forth as the early Christians wished him to be seen, as one who proclaimed God's will and as himself a proclamation about God for men.

As already remarked, our particular basis for exploring this double portrait will be the "Synoptic Gospels"—those first three gospels, Matthew, Mark, and Luke, which, when printed in columns alongside one another, exhibit close parallels and give a common or "synoptic" overall view of Jesus. The Fourth Gospel is certainly not without value historically and theologically and will be referred to from time to time, but its portrait of Jesus is so different at many points as to require separate treatment. This emphasis on the Synoptics for historical purposes is, I think, justified in light of most current biblical scholarship, though, of course, nowadays no one writes off the Fourth Gospel as just a later theological construct. John's historical traditions must at times be assessed as superior to those in the Synoptics, and on some chronological matters, for example, I would prefer John. Hence the occasional references to John, in spite of the relatively greater weight on the Synoptics, and the preference for Synoptic traditions on some matters, and Johannine on others.

A word about the order in which the topics relating to our subject will be treated. First something must be said about the world in which Jesus lived and about the sources available to us concerning him. Then we must face the question of how much historical knowledge is really possible concerning this man from Nazareth whom Christians came to worship as lord. As "test areas" two examples have been chosen, one from Jesus' "life" (the story of the Passion), and one from his teachings (the Lord's Prayer). Then the crucial matter of the resurrection of Jesus is considered. Only at this point is a brief note appended on what most "lives" of Jesus begin with: the birth stories and an "outline" of his career. And only after the discussion of the Passion and resurrection will the attempt be made to explore Jesus' message (about the kingdom of God), as presented in preaching, parables, and miracles; his "ethics"; his "person," as expressed in various titles like "Christ"; and finally the matter of Jesus and his followers, that is, the links connecting this man to the later church and to men today.

This arrangement, as can readily be seen, seems to "stand on its head" the usual sequence of a "life" of Jesus from the manger to the tomb. Anyone who seeks the conventional arrangement can find it, of course, in many other books about Jesus (see the list at the end, "Some Books for Further Reading"). Or one can read the gospels for himself. But these very gospels, he will find, themselves exhibit a variety of sequences. Mark, for example, omits all mention of Jesus' early years. Each of the evangelists begins differently and has his own emphases. And the gospels generally (as well as the New Testament as a whole) stress Jesus' death and resurrection above all else. Therefore, for this presentation, we shall put the emphasis not on the reconstruction of a chronological "life," but on what the New Testament itself regards as central: namely, Jesus considered in the light of his cross and resurrection.

Albert Schweitzer, who studied many previous "lives" of Jesus —and found them all wanting—wrote some sixty years ago, "There is no historical task which so reveals a man's true self as the writing of a Life of Jesus."[3] This is certainly true. One fears that "lives" of Jesus sometimes tell us more about the would-be biographer than about Jesus! For all too often the writers mold Jesus in their own image. The images of Jesus presented to the public, even in the name of "scientific scholarship," have been many and varied.

In writing about Jesus, therefore, there is a further difficulty, already suggested, namely, Jesus himself. The writer may start out to query the sources for what they will tell him about Jesus. Inevitably he discovers, however, if he is at all willing to listen, that the sources also question him. To be sure, Jesus was a real man, and can be the object of historical investigation and even the "subject" of a book. We should, we think, be able to treat him as we treat other topics, in an "I-to-it" relationship, where I investigate the "subject" (Jesus) as an "it." But in the process, one finds, Jesus Christ, the lord, almost inevitably takes the measure of the historian too. He confronts us. He questions us. The relation becomes one of "I" and a "Thou." Jesus Christ speaks, through Scripture, as God's word to us.

This experience I, too, have found to be true. Accordingly I underscore three convictions which stand out. One is that if we would know about Jesus—and in turn about God (whom Jesus claimed to reveal)—then we must go to Scripture and its proclamation. The claim is that in Jesus, God revealed himself as he has nowhere else, and that the Bible has something to tell men about God revealed in Jesus Christ which will be found in no other place. Significantly, even when it is said "God is dead," men still look to Jesus of Nazareth as a clue for meaning.

But, secondly, we must use the historical approach in studying Scripture. This is necessary because the revelation came in history and is witnessed to in historical documents. This means use of the so-called historical-critical method of study. If that approach seems negative at times, it is because the historian's job is to ask questions, to be skeptical, to demand proof—in order to help us see what we can know, and prove, historically—and what we cannot. If some readers find it surprising that we cannot always come up with historical answers from the sources, even in the Bible, that may simply be because the average person today does not know the problems connected with historical study in general.

To illustrate: the writer Edgar Allan Poe died in 1848. A Baltimore physician who attended him at his death later went around giving lectures on how Poe died; this eyewitness loved to portray Poe quoting long selections from his poems on his deathbed, his final word a dramatic "Nevermore!" But a letter of this physician, written in 1848, has recently come to light. The letter omits any such details. Which account is correct? The historian's job is to probe and see what the facts really are, what Poe did in fact say. But such a thing is not always easy to settle. The details about Poe's death involve happenings only a century ago, with a document available as evidence which was written the same year that the event took place. One can guess at the problems for the historian with events which happened almost 2,000 years ago and which were not recorded until fifty years after they occurred—as is the case with the story of Jesus. No wonder a historian must at times say, whether he is dealing with Edgar Allan Poe or Jesus of Nazareth, "We do not know."

Nonetheless, and this is the third point, we ought to go to the Bible with a certain expectation—expecting it to speak to us anew in our day. For such is the nature of the Bible. Such has

been the common Christian experience. Such has been my experience. When one studies Scripture in depth, when (perhaps
even because, I suggest) one treats it critically, then one sees new
things and finds new insights. He is himself addressed by God
and the Gospel.

A few technical matters. It is suggested that readers make use
of a copy of the Bible as they read this book, to check for themselves some of the biblical references and see firsthand what is
being argued. It has not always been possible in the book to quote
in full the passages which clinch or amplify a point, but merely
to provide the biblical references. For such study the Revised
Standard Version is especially recommended. In the book the RSV
has generally been quoted, though occasionally other renderings
are introduced (see the list of abbreviations on p. xvi, or the list
"Some Books for Further Reading," pp. 492-93), and at times the
author has provided his own translation in order to make a
point clear.

It is particularly suggested that readers employ for study of
certain passages a "harmony of the gospels" which prints Matthew, Mark, and Luke (plus perhaps also John) in parallel columns (several editions are cited in the bibliography). Only when
the three or four versions of the text are seen side by side can one
appreciate some of the problems of agreement and disagreement
in the scriptures themselves. In order to facilitate such direct
comparison of the Synoptics we have occasionally printed important passages in this way in the book. On this device depend
many of the observations offered about the Synoptics.

Needless to say, it is impossible within the bounds of any book
of reasonable length to state in each case why the author accepts
an incident or saying (or a certain form of it) as authentically
from Jesus but regards some other story or form as secondary. I
have tried to provide enough sample cases in which details are
offered, however, so that the reader can see something of the
method involved, even if he does not always agree with the conclusions. I have also sought to treat several key passages in greater
detail by reverting to them in more than one connection. Thus,
for example, the pericope about Peter's Confession at Caesarea
Philippi is treated with regard not only to Christology but also to
discipleship and the church. Ideally other passages ought to be

analyzed in similar depth, but often only conclusions or summary judgments could be given.

By and large an attempt has been made to provide in the body of the book a continuous text which can be read through without need to refer to footnotes. In that way one can follow the line of argument and general sequence of views without checking the notes, which are grouped at the back of the book (pp. 336-485).

The footnotes are intended to do at least two things. (1) They provide the customary documentation for quotations and opinions, and for references in the primary and secondary sources. (2) An attempt has also been made to supply supplementary material in the notes which amplifies what has been said in the body of the book, or which corrects false impressions which can arise, or which even provides reference to dissenting voices. In many instances an attempt has been made to survey the spectrum of opinions on a question, indicating some authority who favors each position, while also explaining the view which the author takes. I am conscious of the fact that one duty of a teacher, like a good reporter, is to indicate accurately the various options on certain issues, but he also, as a scholar in his own right, ought to make clear where he stands and why. In this task the notes are often an aid, to show the options and explicate certain judgments.

The matter of bibliography in a book on Jesus is a genuine problem. How far ought one to go in citing references? On every question much has been written. In general I have tried to confine myself, for one thing, to the literature in English, though where a definitive treatment exists in German or French, or where the English literature is deficient on a point, I have not hesitated to cite an article or book in some other language. (As for the biblical languages, words in transliteration have been introduced only where necessary.) As a rule I have also tried to cite items which are readily accessible, particularly in paperback editions. From commentaries, representative, rather than exhaustive, citations have been provided. In many cases, rather than overload the notes I have indicated dictionary articles or treatments such as those in "Facet Books" which provide additional bibliography.

Something should be said about the list of books for further reading in comparison with the bibliographical references in the notes. On pp. 492 ff. there is provided first of all a series of titles for primary source material on the life of Jesus, for commentaries on this material, and for general surveys. Then follows, chapter by chapter, a bibliography on topics covered in the book. Usually a brief comment is added on the nature of the work noted. All titles in this list of books have been chosen with the general reader in mind who might wish additional material on a subject. The books have been selected, therefore, in terms of their availability (all on this list are in English and are of reasonably recent date or have lately been reprinted) and for their readability. They have not necessarily been selected for their full compatibility with my own conclusions in the body of this book, since often the positions which I have taken depend on specialized literature, perhaps not available in English. I regard this reading list as providing a reasonably respectable (though not definitive) group of titles to which one might turn, on aspects of the present book which interest him.

For documentation of my own opinions and for the often more scholarly literature one must turn to the footnotes. There, particularly with regard to terms like "Christ" or "Son of man" or subjects like "church" or "the Holy Spirit," a fuller listing occurs, often including works of more advanced level. Even so, I have tried to avoid mentioning every last article which might be cited, especially in the German literature. Obviously, in the process, some titles which ought to have appeared have been sacrificed.

A glossary of key terms used in the book, such as may not be familiar to some readers or which are used in a particular sense here, is given at the end of the book, pp. 486-91. These definitions will explain, for example, how I am using "eschatology" and "apocalyptic," "Essene" and "Essenic," and the distinctions made between "the Gospel" and "the gospel tradition," or "*kerygma*" and "Jesus-material."

There remains the pleasant task of expressing appreciation to the many without whose help this book would not have come to be. In 1959–60 it was my privilege to study at Cambridge University on a Faculty Fellowship of the American Association of Theological Schools, and in 1965–66 at Göttingen University as a Guggenheim Fellow. I owe a debt far greater than the notes to this book reveal, to the professors to whom I listened in those years—C. F. D. Moule, and Harald Riesenfeld who was at Cambridge in 1959; Hans Conzelmann, Eduard Lohse, and Joachim Jeremias—and also to my "Doctor-Father," Morton S. Enslin, now of Bryn Mawr College, whose independent scholarship and personal encouragement I have treasured over the years. Their ideas and even some of their phrases, I fear, have been absorbed into my own thinking. This is to confess a debt of gratitude, even though, I am sure, I have, at more than one point mis-understood such scholars and on occasion, of course, have differed from each one. I am sure, too, that other friends will shake their heads over this point or that, "If only he had seen my article or had considered. . . ." I can only say that on many much-debated topics, such as Synoptic source criticism or the impact of form criticism, I have had to make my decisions as I see the issues and the evidence today. That often means that when one accepts one view he must reject, often reluctantly, another theory, especially if the whole is to hang together with any consistency.

While I have treated the Synoptic Gospels in lectures at the Lutheran Theological Seminary, Philadelphia, several times in the past six years, the first version of this book was written during 1965–66, chiefly in Germany, specifically for use in the Adult Sunday Church School curriculum of the Lutheran Church in America. To officials of the denomination's Board of Parish Edu-cation I wish to record my particular thanks for the freedom so readily granted to experiment with a departure from the tradi-tional in a course[4] used throughout the denomination in 1966–67 and for permission to submit the manuscript (which was larger than that format could accommodate) to Fortress Press for con-sideration for publication in this expanded form. Helpful sug-gestions have come from a number of friends who read the manu-script, including Harold Remus and Philip R. Hoh, during 1966–67, when the manuscript was to a considerable extent rewritten.

Thus, as always, in historical study of the Bible, we stand upon the shoulders of others. To many persons whose opinions are reflected in the book without any reference to their names, thanks must be expressed also. And to those with whom I have on occa-sion differed (the reasons in these cases being set forth usually in a bit more detail than normal), appreciations are also due. The aim throughout has been, however, amid all the views which have been advanced, to let the text speak for itself.

Finally it must be added—as is readily apparent from the history of life-of-Jesus research—that this book, like others that have preceded it, is in no sense to be regarded as the "last word" on Jesus of Nazareth. For he will continue to speak to men—which is as it should be with Jesus in the church's gospels.

JOHN REUMANN

Philadelphia, Pennsylvania
31 May, 1967

Abbreviations

NEB	*The New English Bible*
KJV	King James Version
RSV	Revised Standard Version
par.	parallel or parallels in the Synoptic Gospels
Ant.	*Jewish Antiquities* by Josephus

1

The Man from Nazareth in Galilee

How and where does one begin to tell the tremendous story of Jesus Christ, the man from Nazareth in Galilee?

The Gospel of Mark, the first such story to be written out (at least, the first to come down to us), opens with the enigmatic phrase, "The beginning of the good news about Jesus Christ . . . ." But even after reading the opening verses of Mark, one finds it hard to tell precisely what Mark regarded as the starting point. Was it the appearance of John the Baptist, or Jesus' own appearance, or the message Jesus preached, or his death and resurrection, or something much earlier, the Old Testament prophecies? If Mark posed something of a dilemma here even for his earliest readers, how much more are we at a loss today, separated by so many centuries from the lifetime of Jesus?

But suppose you wanted to tell the story of Jesus to a child, or to a friend who knew little about him, or to a student from another land, of some other religion. Where would you begin?

A logical starting point might be with Jesus' birth (though Mark's Gospel never mentions it), followed by an account of his life, incident by incident. However, it is often difficult to determine what the proper order of all the events reported in our gospels should be. Indeed, it is a question whether they can all be fitted together chronologically.

Another way of telling the story of Jesus would be to commence with the most important part. That surely would involve the cross and resurrection. Our gospels spend the most space and put the greatest emphasis on these significant events at the close of Jesus' earthly career. Paul, like all the other early preachers, always told primarily about Christ crucified and risen.

Someone else might suggest that the starting point should lie at the beginning of all things, in the heart of God, who created all that is. The cross and empty tomb, Jesus' birth and whole career, go back "before the foundation of the world"—"Ere the worlds began to be," as the Christian poet Prudentius put it in the fourth century. The first poet to write in the English language, Caedmon, began his epic about God and Christ in this way:

> Now must we praise the author of the heavenly kingdom, the Creator's power and counsel.

Still others, their eyes on history, could insist that the emphasis should be on the story of Jesus Christ through the centuries. A thrilling tale it is, of how the man from Nazareth was confessed as the Christ, his influence growing through the ages. For his followers came to regard him, not as a man whose career ended on a cross, but as one who lives and reigns as Lord.

Finally, it might occur to someone, in telling about Jesus, that he should begin with what Jesus means in his own life. Paul, from that moment on Damascus Road, always thought of Jesus this way—as "the Son of God who loved *me* and gave himself *for me.*"

These few examples perhaps already suggest that, in telling the story of Jesus Christ, it makes a difference where we start, and that our whole perspective on the picture of Jesus may vary with the standpoint we take. We are not the first people to be confronted with this question, however. In the first century, within a generation of the lifetime of Jesus, Christians were already faced with this very problem. In the New Testament we have four examples of different starting points, in the gospels of Matthew, Mark, Luke, and John. Each of these is worth considering for its particular emphasis.

Luke begins in the manner of historians of his day. He commences with a "prefatory note" or introduction to a friend or patron named Theophilus (Luke 1:1-4), telling how he has tried to trace out sources and set things into an orderly account. Some have called Luke the "first Christian historian," because he puts events into a framework of world history. His gospel comes closest of any in the New Testament to what we would call a "life" or even a "biography" of Jesus. It emphasizes who Jesus was in history.

Mark and John both begin their gospel accounts with more theological prologues. Of the two, John's is the better known (1:1-18): "In the beginning was the Word. . . ." This theme of a word which was with God, a word through which God expressed himself, is an idea which was known both to Greek philosophy and the Wisdom literature of the Old Testament. John connects it with the historical appearance of Jesus, who made known what God was really like.

Mark's opening verses (1:1-13) are less readily spotted as a prologue, but in their own way they are just as theological as

John's. Like John 1:1-18, Mark 1:1-13 tells us that Jesus fulfilled the ancient expectations of the Old Testament, that John the Baptist had prepared the way for him, and that Jesus, though tested by Satan (1:12-13), was destined to triumph—heaven is with him (1:11). The very phrase used by the heavenly voice, "my beloved Son" (Mark 1:11), happens to represent the same Hebrew expression which appears as the climax of John 1, "the only Son" (vs. 18). Thus, Mark and John both are telling us who Jesus is, in relation to God, before they recount the story of his ministry. John starts with the word in heaven; Mark begins either with John the Baptist or the Old Testament, depending on how we punctuate his opening verses.[1]

Thus Luke emphasizes Jesus' place in history, while Mark and John stress theologically who he is. All three gospels present a real man, who actually lived, tangible and visible, in our world— yet a man whom faith sees as related to God the Father as no one else had ever been.

But what shall we make of the beginning in Matthew? Surely this is the dullest opening of any gospel, with its lead sentence, "The book of the genealogy of Jesus Christ," followed by sixteen verses of names, each connected by the word "begat." "Aminadab begat Naasson"—what is inspiring or significant about that? Worse yet, Matthew has been put at the front of the New Testament, so that the collection of Christian Scriptures begins with some forty-one names in an unglamorous genealogy.

In fairness to the author, however, we must recognize that in his day genealogies were not regarded as quite so dull or unglamorous. Ancestry and bloodlines counted. Paul once referred to himself as "of the tribe of Benjamin," a Hebrew born of Hebrews (Philippians 3:5), and he could probably, with some great pride, have reeled off his genealogy. The "Priestly Writer" in the Old Testament devoted many verses to genealogical listings (Genesis 5; 10; 11:10-32, for example). In order for a man to be able to serve as a priest or Levite in the temple at Jerusalem, it was important for him to be able to show who his forebears had been and that his blood was pure (see Luke 1:5 and Leviticus 21:14). Some scholars think it probable that genealogical records were kept not only privately by Jewish families but also in official archives in Jesus' day. Thus these lists had importance— both for family interest in the past and for current legal purposes.

Such documents might carry considerable authority in disputes under Jewish law.

More relevant in Matthew's opening genealogy is the "christological" interest. We have already seen how the other evangelists open their accounts by using some title like "Christ" or "Word" or "Son" for Jesus. Naturally each of these titles honoring Jesus had its own particular meaning, a meaning which deserves further investigation. Here we may simply note that Matthew's opening verses are built around two titles, "Christ" and "son of David." The first sentence, before the genealogical listing begins, describes him as "Christ" and "son of David." The genealogy then falls into three parts, each with fourteen names:

from Abraham to *David the king* (14 generations, vss. 2-6);

from *David's son*, Solomon, to Jechoniah and the Babylonian Exile (14 generations, vss. 6b-11);

from the exile in Jechoniah's time to Joseph, "the husband of Mary, of whom Jesus was born, who is called *Christ* (14 generations, vss. 12-16).

There are all sorts of puzzles about the details of this list, not the least of which is the fact that the last section contains only thirteen names—unless Jechoniah is to be counted twice or unless (more possibly) Matthew intended "Christ" to be counted as a name by which Jesus would later be confessed (Matthew 16:16).

But the really striking point is how Matthew arranges this list of ancestors to emphasize David (vss. 1, 6, 17) and "Christ" (vss. 1, 16, 17). Here are titles which Matthew will reiterate throughout his gospel (for "son of David," see 12:23, 21:9, and 21:15, for example) so that we get his point: Jesus is the son of David and the Christ. Thus Matthew in chapter 1 is telling us who Jesus is, just as chapter 2 tells us whence he came (note the geographical designations—Bethlehem, Egypt, Bethlehem, Nazareth—each one of which is connected with an Old Testament quotation). In this way Matthew begins his story, as do the other evangelists, by setting before readers the fact that Jesus is a man in history (from Bethlehem, Nazareth, etc.), yet one who rates the significant title of Christ.

The emphasis, that Jesus was a figure who actually appeared on the stage of human life, a man who lived in a specific time and place, is thus to be found in Matthew's genealogy, as well as in chapter 2 and the other gospels. Indeed, that is perhaps the special value which Matthew's opening verses have for us today: to portray Jesus as a man of a specific time and place in history.

The Kingdoms of This World

While Matthew fixes his eyes primarily on this man Jesus, he also has a genuine concern for men and women with their day-to-day yearnings amid the kingdoms of this world. So also the other evangelists, especially Luke. They write for a human audience, and they write against the backdrop of history. Bethlehem, Egypt, the deportation to Babylon (Matthew 1:17); Caesar Augustus, Quirinius the governor of Syria (Luke 2:2)—these are things of which history is made, and in such details the story of Jesus is rooted. Luke stresses world history particularly, Matthew the history of Israel.

The pattern in Matthew 1 is almost inescapable, even for the most casual reader: three time-spans of fourteen generations each. The evangelist is connecting Jesus with Israel's history, from Abraham through David, to the fall of Jerusalem in 586 B.C., down to the time when Jesus lived. Here is one reason why Matthew's Gospel has been put at the head of the New Testament canon: the opening verses point back to the Old Testament and the whole history of Israel as the proper background for the subject of the new writings, Jesus Christ. Lines can be drawn, the New Testament claims, from Abraham to Jesus (John 8:58; Galatians 3:16), from David to him (Acts 2:25-31), and even from the figures like the "Son of man" in the very latest books of the Old Testament such as Daniel (see Acts 7:55-60). The lines connect the past history of Israel to Jesus, and Matthew seeks to make that clear at the outset.

To understand Jesus of Nazareth, it is therefore necessary to know something of the whole Old Testament. His knowledge of the Old Testament suggests that Jesus had himself been reared on the Hebrew Scriptures with their accounts of how God had rescued his people Israel from bondage in Egypt and led them in the Exodus, through the wilderness, into the promised land of Palestine. He was familiar with the epic of faith involving the patriarchs Abraham, Isaac, and Jacob, prior to the sojourn in Egypt. Like any Jewish boy, he would have known the subsequent story of nationhood, the period of the judges, then the kings Saul and David, the glorious time of Solomon's monarchy, followed

by the sad, depressing tale of how first Israel in the north and
then Judah in the south fell away from God, fell to conquerors,
and were dragged off into exile. Doubtless his sessions at the
synagogue school in Nazareth acquainted him also with the words
of the prophets and with all the moods of the Hebrew psalms
and sacred writings.

But even more likely to have left an impression on any boy in
Galilee was the more recent history of his people and his land,
the final third of the forty-two generations of which Matthew
speaks, "from the deportation to Babylon" to the present day. To
us this period is comparatively little known, especially the period
after the last of the Old Testament canonical books was composed, but for anyone of Jesus' generation these centuries were
probably just as vivid as the great times previously. We may guess
that the history of the so-called Intertestamental Period (the decades between the Old and New Testaments, from perhaps 165
B.C. or so until the beginning of Jesus' ministry about A.D. 27)
left its marks on every Jew and his life to an even greater extent
than the previous centuries had. Usually the marks were scars, for
this period had been one of captivity and oppression more than
one of glory. What happened in these dark and somber times?
What events, so obscure to us today, would have been etched
vividly in the mind of a Jew in Jesus' times?

The exile in Babylon after the fall of Jerusalem in 586 lasted
a generation. Then the Persians, who in 539 had overthrown the
Babylonians, permitted a small number of Jews to return home
to Palestine. Ezra the scribe and Nehemiah the governor restored
some semblance of religious life in Jerusalem. Not free, but at
least under a benevolent conqueror, Israel's faith blossomed a bit.
Then in 332 B.C. new rulers appeared, the Greeks. Alexander of
Macedonia destroyed the Persian empire, and, upon his death,
his territories were divided by his generals into three spheres, each
ruled by a Hellenistic king. The ruling house in Egypt was called
the Ptolemies; that in Syria, the Seleucids. As might be guessed,
Palestine was a prize in between Egypt and Syria, over which
Ptolemy and Seleucid fought. Again, not free—and this time in
the grip of Greek rulers who sought to impose their way of life
and even their religion on the Jews. These rulers sought to make
their Greek way of life as attractive as they could to the peoples
whom they had conquered, building model cities and promoting

Hellenistic fashions and values. Many of the conquered people were impressed by Greek culture and openly adopted it, but many Jews despised these foreign ways.

Then came a brief time of bloodshed and glory for the Jews. One of the Seleucid rulers went too far. Antiochus IV, "God Manifest," as he liked to be known, attempted to take over the temple at Jerusalem for pagan rites; he sought to prohibit circumcision and other religious practices of the Jews, and had his soldiers ferret out their sacred books. At this moment, when the very heart of Old Testament faith was threatened, a heroic revolt, touched off by a country priest named Mattathias and carried to victory under his five sons, expelled the Seleucids from the land. The Jews now set up an independent state—the first since 586 B.C. and the last until the birth of modern Israel in A.D. 1948. Judas, a son of Mattathias, of the house of Hashmon, was the great leader in the struggle. From his nickname, Maccabeus, or "Hammerer" (against the Gentiles), came the term "Maccabean," often applied to this revolt and period. From the name of the family (Hashmon), out of which came the rulers for the new Jewish state, arose the adjective "Hasmonean," also applied to the dynasty and age (roughly the century 165–63 B.C.).

Unfortunately, however, even though a Jewish ruler now occupied the throne, all was not well. A thirst for power, quarrels over the temple priesthood, party rivalry, and even unspeakable cruelty marked the century of independence when the Hasmoneans ruled Palestine. The Jewish state, begun with such high hopes when the temple had been purified in 165 B.C. from the desecrations of Antiochus, came to an end amid bickering among Jewish factions when one group invited in the Romans to restore order. Pompey, a Roman general, took Jerusalem in 63 B.C. He entered even the Holy of Holies (expressing amazement that it was empty, with no statue), and, before he went his way, appointed puppet rulers to govern for Rome.

Palestine was now, for all practical purposes, under Roman control. For a while, Maccabean figureheads were still kept in power. Then from about 37 B.C. until his death in 4 B.C., Herod, that remarkable politician, ruthless yet efficient, ruled in Rome's name. Some of his numerous sons (legitimate and otherwise) still held positions of power as princes in Jesus' day, but in A.D. 6 Caesar shifted the rule from native "royalty" in Judea, Idumea,

and Samaria to professional governors or *procurators,* the best
known of whom was to be Pontius Pilate, who governed the
troubled land in the year that Jesus died.

Such had been the sequence of overlords—Babylonians, Persians, Greek-Egyptian Ptolemies, Seleucids, and Romans, to say
nothing of Hasmonean tyrants or Parthian invaders (an army
from Parthia to the east held Jerusalem briefly in 40-39 B.C.).
Little Palestine was not often numbered among the kindoms of
this world, but was frequently ground under their heels.

And where was God, who had been with the fathers in the
past? True, some saw his hand gloriously at work in the Maccabean revolt. But other pious Jews, offended at the pomp and
power of the later Hasmoneans, retreated to an austere life of
their own at a desert place called Qumran, sometime in the second
century B.C. Still other Jews simply hung on, waiting for an intervention from God. Would he again "turn many of the sons
of Israel to the Lord their God"? (Luke 1:16). When would he
scatter the proud and visit and redeem his people (cf. 1:51, 68)?
Perhaps the most sincere of the Jews devoted themselves to deep-
ening their religious practices, inherited from their ancestors and
centered in the law (or *Torah*). And some, of course, just drifted
on, concerned mainly with eking out a living, enough food for
the day or the morrow—no time for "ultimates" in life.

Such, in broad outline, was the scene as it might have been
viewed by a boy growing up in Nazareth of Galilee about A.D. 7,
or the year 760 A.U.C., as the conquerors referred to it, *ab urbe
condita,* "from the founding of the city" of Rome.

Palestine, Cockpit of History, in Jesus' Day

It is to the pulsebeat and chronology of Rome's great empire
that Luke gears the date for the start of Jesus' ministry. At 3:1-2
he synchronizes the appearance of John the Baptist (who drew
Jesus forth from Nazareth to the Jordan River and started him
on his work of preaching and teaching) in this way:

> In the fifteenth year of the reign of Tiberius Caesar, Pontius Pilate
> being governor of Judea, and Herod being tetrarch of Galilee, and
> his brother Philip, tetrarch of the region of Ituraea and Trachonitis,
> and Lysanias tetrarch of Abilene, in the high-priesthood of Annas
> and Caiaphas. . . .

John's coming is tied to the date of the emperor's accession, and
the rule of four of his local subordinates, and the term of the

high priest in Jerusalem as well. This complex way of counting means a date in A.D. 26 or, more likely, a year or so later,[2] but even more important, it reminds us how Jesus' life was lived under Roman rule and how intricately his destiny was to be bound up with political and religious officials in Palestine.

There could have been worse fates than to live in the empire at this time. In many ways, life was more comfortable than it was to be for the next eighteen centuries in Europe. Roads, aquaducts, theaters—the Romans built these everywhere. Travel was usually safe. Augustus had reorganized the government. A great festival known as the "Secular Games," for which Horace wrote his ode the *Carmen Saeculare*, was held in 17 B.C. to mark the new era of prosperity. A beautiful little "Altar of Peace," erected in Rome between 13 and 9 B.C., symbolized a rare interlude in world history when war was for a moment banished from the scene.

Caesar's administrative reorganization was felt in Palestine upon the fall of Herod's son, Archelaus. Actually, though we usually do not have that impression, Herod the Great, cruel as he was, must be assessed as an able ruler—he had to be, to hold power over thirty-five years in turbulent Palestine. Some have termed him "Israel's greatest king,"[3] and in his own mind he regarded himself as a defender of Jews throughout the world and desired to enrich the culture of Palestine.

Herod's son Archelaus, who succeeded him, though with more limited power as mere ethnarch (and not king) of Judea, had little of his father's political skill and was deposed and banished by Caesar, his territory henceforth attached to the province of Syria and governed by a procurator. Other sons, Herod Antipas in Galilee and Philip to the east, still ruled in Jesus' time.

It was Herod Antipas—who built a Greek city (on a former cemetery) by the Sea of Galilee, a city which he named Tiberias (in honor of the emperor)—with whom Jesus, like John the Baptist, came into conflict. John was put to death by Antipas for condemning the way this prince had divorced his wife and taken Herodias away from her husband, his own half brother (see Mark 6:17). This same Antipas, Jesus called a "fox," one of the sharpest epithets recorded from his lips (Luke 13:31-33). Their paths later crossed in Jerusalem, where Jesus refused to answer his questions and Herod Antipas treated him with contempt mingled with curiosity (Luke 23:6-12).

Thus Jesus was not immune from or unaware of the political currents and personalities of the day. He did not live in a vacuum. Throughout his ministry he seems to have been aware of what went on in the halls of government, and even to have expressed himself at times on questions such as the payment of taxes to Caesar or the nationalist determination to revolt against Rome (Mark 12:14-17).

The political boundaries which Rome imposed on Palestine did not, however, fully accord with the geographical or economic divisions in the land or with the religious distinctions which had grown up.

Geographically, Palestine, a country not quite the size of Los Angeles County, California, consists of a variety of landscapes. It begins along the Mediterranean Sea with a narrow coastal strip of often fertile land, widest and most prosperous in the south, but virtually edged out of the picture around Mount Carmel and modern Haifa, where the mountains come crowding right up to the sea. North of this mountain spur some plains suited for farming again appear along the sea. Then to the east of this coastal plain comes the hill country, limestone ridges, often gently rolling, usually less prosperous. Next is the backbone of the land, the mountains, such as Jerusalem is situated on. In the extreme north, these mountains rise to a height of 9100 feet in the case of snowcapped Mount Hermon, beyond Caesarea Philippi. In the more level country of Galilee, a "mountain" like Tabor is less than 2000 feet, but stands out because of the flat plain around it.

To the east of the mountainous backbone of the land comes a great depression which gradually deepens as it slopes to the south. This depression begins near Caesarea Philippi in the north. Its several little streams broaden into a swampy lake called Huleh, which the Israelis have now drained. From this lake the water, now the Jordan River, flows for about a dozen miles, then empties into another lake, the "Sea of Galilee" (or Gennesaret). From here the Jordan River flows south again, meandering its way to the Dead Sea (1285 feet below sea level), that brackish, salty lake from which no river ever escapes into the surrounding hills and parched desert wastes. To complete the picture, we have further east, beyond the Jordan, a high plateau or tableland. It is known to us as the Decapolis or "League of Ten Greek Cities" in the north, and as Perea in the south. Jesus' ministry was concentrated in Galilee, save for trips southward to Jerusalem. For these he seems to have taken a route east of the Jordan (Mark 10:1), though Luke reports a rambling journey through the central part of the country, including Samaria (Luke 9:51—18:14), and John places one incident by the well of Sychar in Samaria (4:4ff.). On rare occasions, Jesus seems to have gone northward from Galilee into less Jewish country near Tyre and Sidon (Mark 7:24-31). But it is a rather amazing fact that, according to the gospels, his ministry was confined to Jewish cities and towns. He never went near Tiberias (the city which Antipas built), nor Scythopolis, nor even Sepphoris, which was only four miles or so away from Nazareth. In terms of the geographical evidence we must conclude that Jesus' ministry was pretty much what he once said it was: primarily (Matthew 15:24 says "only") to the "lost sheep of the house of Israel."

Economically there were factors in the picture, too, which show up in Jesus' ministry. Palestine was not a rich country. It lacked any mineral wealth. There was often not enough rainfall. But given peace and diligent attention, the land could be generally self-supporting. Olives, grapes, figs grew in abundance; there was some wheat and barley and garden vegetables, plus cattle and sheep. (Swine, of course, were rare, but note the story about a herd of pigs in the Decapolis, near Gergesa, Mark 5:1-13). In famines, grain had to be imported, as Herod did in 24-23 B.C. An abundance of fish was caught in the Sea of Galilee, and from a town called Taricheae dried and pickled fish were exported all over the empire.

Some slaves worked on the land. Jesus' parables refer to them, as well as to free laborers. Craftsmen and businessmen congregated in the towns and cities, but generally the pace of life was rural, not urban. The geographical situation of Palestine, particularly of Galilee, made it a bridge for trade from north to south and east to west, but often Jewish religious restrictions prevented the sincerely religious man from engaging in such activities. Jews were forbidden to practice usury (though elsewhere in the ancient world, interest rates ran 12 to 36 percent). Men who worked as tax collectors were regarded not only as unpatriotic (because they served a foreign government) but also as moral outcasts (cf. Matthew 21:31). Yet Jesus' ministry brought him into contact with such "publicans," and one of them, Levi (or Matthew; see

Mark 2:13-14 and Matthew 9:9) is listed among his disciples. Jesus told stories about laborers in a vineyard grumbling over wages (Matthew 20:1-16), and even about a "dishonest steward" who is in some ways set up as a model for the disciples (Luke 16:1-9)! Jesus must be credited with, if not an economic interest, as least keen observation of business life in Palestine.

While economic conditions in Palestine were bearable for most of the population in Jesus' day, the line between survival and death must often have been very thin. A poor harvest or a rise in taxes might well mean starvation for some. A growing population aggravated problems, for while many Jews emigrated overseas, many more returned to the Holy Land. Josephus gives the (probably fantastic) figure of three million people resident in Galilee alone. Modern scholars have suggested figures of under one million all the way to seven million for the entire land. But the overpopulation (in proportion to the limited resources) threatened disaster.

The "straw that often broke the camel's back" was taxation. The demands of the Roman government and the moneymaking syndicates to whom it farmed out the opportunity of collecting taxes (at a commission plus, often, a percent which found its way into the collector's pocket) were bad enough. But there were also religious dues, so that the Jew faced a double system of taxation. In addition to the tithe, there was also a second tithe, an offering of first fruits from a crop, the temple tax, a payment (equal to two week's wages) due when a first child was born, thankofferings, etc.—a dozen items, which added to Roman demands, might have taken 40 percent of an already precariously stretched income.

Some experts think these taxes led to a decline in farming and a general restlessness in the land. Others would go even further and suggest that poverty turned some men to brigandage (robbers existed in Palestine in the period, cf. Luke 10:30), others to schemes for driving the Romans out or to hatred of the priests and their demands, and still others to dreaming of a wonderful time when God would right all these wrongs. It is oversimplification to say that apocalyptic dreams arose from poverty. But many a Jew who heard the cry "Hosanna! Blessed is the kingdom of our father David that is coming!" might put a more political and economic interpretation on it than we are accustomed to. It was neither the first nor the last time in history that economic poverty erupted into political outcry, fanned by religious hope.

Religiously there were divisions in the land which show them-selves during Jesus' ministry. The most obvious one, a division into Judea, Galilee, and Samaria, is familiar to most. Judea was the southern area around Jerusalem. Its tone of life was set by that great city with its temple. Here clustered priests and Levites, rabbis and scribes, and many a pious soul who, no matter where he was, could not forget the promise that Jerusalem was the place where Yahweh dwells (Psalm 135:21), the city of the great King (Matthew 5:35), the place to be set above one's highest joy (Psalm 137:6). Jesus' judgment was to be different: he called Jerusalem a city that kills the prophets and stones those sent to her; for him it was a place of death (Luke 13:33-34). But we must remember that it was in this city that the gospel of Jesus as the risen Christ was first preached, and the early adherents in-cluded not just Galileans but also Jerusalemites.

Galilee was another story. This northern province even in Old Testament times was not always fully "Israelitized." Its very name means the "circle or district of the Gentiles." It had been con-quered by the Maccabees and "re-Judaized" only in 80 B.C., and like many another place at a crossroads of the world had a racially mixed population. It had many a devout inhabitant, some even chauvinistic in their faith, but also many more who were inclined to be careless about the punctilious rules of religion which the ex-perts in Jerusalem proposed. Rabbis like Johanan ben Zakkai and Akiba, who taught in Galilee in the first century A.D., seem glad to have been able to leave its provincial towns when the chance came to settle in Jerusalem, where the subtleties of their teaching about the law would be properly appreciated. "Can anything good come out of Nazareth?" (John 1:46) and ". . . no prophet is to rise from Galilee" (John 7:52) were sneers that Galileans might expect.

If that sort of haughty tolerance marked Jerusalem's view of Galilee, the attitude toward Samaria, the central section of the land, was one of downright hatred. Samaritans, who claimed to stem from the Israelites of the once great Northern Kingdom (which fell in 722 B.C.), felt they were loyal worshipers of Yah-weh. The Jews looked on them, however, as a mixed breed, cor-rupted by centuries of intermarriage with foreigners, and as a people who had corrupted in turn the revelation of the Old

Testament. There was a long history of rivalry. The Samaritans, refused permission to worship at Jerusalem, had built a temple of their own on Mount Gerizim. They venerated their own version of the Pentateuch (Genesis-Deuteronomy), written in their own form of script and including variant readings which favored their particular views. The situation had grown so bad that John could sum it up with the terse comment, "Jews have no dealings with Samaritans" (4:9). In the face of such animosity, it is highly significant that in Luke's Gospel the leper who gives thanks is a Samaritan and the hero of a parable is the Good Samaritan (17:16; 10:33); such an attitude was unusual. More typical of the hatreds of the day is the jibe directed at Jesus, ". . . you are a Samaritan" (John 8:48).

Political, geographical, economic, religious conditions—we cannot read the gospel story of Jesus without meeting these elements on every page. "Herodians" are mentioned, men who were partisans of the Herod family (especially Herod Antipas) and that dynasty's line of thought. "Scribes" are met at many turns in Jesus' life. They are not simply secretaries or men who can write, but "doctors of the law," experts at teaching and interpreting the Old Testament codes and the legal judgments which had grown up around them. Often these scribes belonged to the Pharisee party, but they could be associated with other groups as well. Scribes occupied many of the seventy-one seats in the highest Jewish governing body at Jerusalem, the Sanhedrin, membership in which included also priests (from a few aristocratic families) and "elders" or leading laymen.

In looking at the Palestinian world in Jesus' day we run the danger of trying to catalog every type and group with which he might have had contact. Time and our sources do not permit this. But there were four groups which must not be overlooked if we want a balanced picture of the people Jesus met. One of them is the Essenes, never actually mentioned in the New Testament by name, but long known to students of the period from references outside the Bible. Now that ruins of an Essenic center at Qumran and scrolls from their library have been found, we can put together a picture of these pious Jews who rejected the Maccabean state and the priesthood at Jerusalem and went out into the desert to develop a "true Israel." They pored over the Scriptures, adhered to strict religious disciplines, and longed for a day when

God would lead the forces of righteousness to victory. Their fervent way of life has been called "Judaism at its 'boiling point,' " but also "Judaism straining at the leash of the Law."[4]

Jesus seems not to have been in direct contact with this group that set itself apart from the world and the mainstream of Jewish life, though John the Baptist may have had connections with Qumran in his younger days. The Dead Sea Scrolls often provide illuminating parallels to things in our gospels, but there is a basic antithesis in the attitude each takes toward the law. Qumran practiced a "super-piety," with more restrictive rules about the Sabbath than any other Jewish group, and elaborate ritual to bring forgiveness for sins. Jesus violated such Sabbath rules and dared to pronounce forgiveness in God's name with no "if's" or "but's" attached. Professor Ethelbert Stauffer goes so far as to say that, if Jesus had fallen into the hands of this group, "they would have murdered him as ruthlessly as did the Pharisees."[5]

The second group, the Zealots, needs only brief mention. They were a "political action group" dedicated to freeing Palestine from its conquerors, even by military revolt. They numbered in their ranks *sicarii,* or "dagger-men," who with no thought of their own lives would murder any opponent. The movement doubtless goes back to "those who were zealous for the law" in Maccabean times. The earliest political zealot of any prominence to which we have reference today may have been a revolutionist named Judas of Galilee (see Acts 5:37; there is also a reference in Josephus, the Jewish historian); this Judas led an insurrection when the Romans made a census in A.D. 6 or 7. The Zealots emerged with disastrous influence in A.D. 66, when they pushed the Jews into a war with Rome that ended with the burning of Jerusalem. Somewhat to our surprise, however, "a member of the Zealot party" (as the NEB phrases it), a man named Simon, is listed as a disciple of Jesus (Mark 3:18; see also Luke 6:15 RSV.).

The Sadducees were a group with whom Jesus had little in common. They seem to have taken their name from Zadok, a priest in David's time. First appearing in the second century B.C., they gradually gained control of the Jerusalem priesthood. Economically, they represented the wealthy aristocracy, a few rich families who shared among themselves the office of high priest, which was sometimes sold to men lacking the legal and moral qualifications for it (no wonder the Qumran group spoke of the

"wicked priest" at Jerusalem). Politically the Sadducees learned
how to play ball with foreign conquerors, and often were the
most "hellenized" of Jews (no wonder the pious often hated
them). Religiously, they were "old-fashioned conservatives," wanting nothing but the law[6] as the basis of religion, and a largely
uninterpreted law at that. For the Sadducees did not try to update
the law to meet new needs, as the Pharisees were doing, by appealing to oral traditions as equally sacrosanct alongside the written word, nor did they flee from the "modern world" to a desert
refuge where the law might more readily be obeyed, as did the
Qumran pietists. Instead of such retreat from life or reapplication
of the revealed law to areas of life not explicitly treated in Scripture, the Sadducees were happy to leave these areas untouched,
closing their eyes to change, while maintaining that they were ad-
hering to the letter of Scripture. Perhaps the best we can say for
them is that they had a sort of hardheaded "common-sense religion" which preserved their private privileges—until the war of
A.D. 67-70 wiped them from the pages of history. Jesus never
says a good word about them, and seems to have little in common
with them.

The Pharisees, last but most important, are the group which
seems to appear in the worst light in the New Testament. It is
true that Jesus often differed sharply with them. But it is also a
fact that in many ways he stood closer to the Pharisees than to the
Sadducees, Zealots, or Essenes. His frequent contacts with them,
and perhaps differences which arose later on, may be what makes
the contrast so stark.

No one really knows the origin of the name "Pharisee." It may
mean "separated ones" (separated from Gentiles, or from the
common people, or from the priests). It could mean "interpreters"
(of Scripture). Or it has been proposed that it was originally a
nickname, "Persianizers," because the group absorbed certain ideas
during the period of Persian rule. Certain it is that the Pharisees
go back two or three centuries prior to Jesus' day and that by his
time they formed a devout association, esteemed by much of the
population, perhaps more so than any other group. If the Pharisees appear to be legalistic, it is because they were dedicated to
applying the age-old law of Israel to every area of life and under
conditions markedly different from those obtaining in the days of
Moses and the subsequent centuries when the law originated.

These Pharisees had also developed a hope in a future resurrection, and much that is finest in Judaism later on is attributable to the Pharisees. Out of their faith came rabbinic Judaism after the destruction of Jerusalem in A.D. 70. They have been called the "progressives," in contrast to the Sadducean conservatives. Attempts have been made to see an economic contrast between wealthy, landed families (the Sadducees) and an energetic commercial class (the Pharisees). But the religious side probably should be kept most prominent. The Pharisees represented living faith in contrast to the "ossified orthodoxy" of the Sadducees.

It would be false to the facts to make a single, monolithic "party" out of any of these groups. Pharisees were divided, for example, into liberal and conservative wings, under Hillel and Shammai, respectively. None of these groups comprised an absolute majority in Judaism. It has been estimated that the Pharisees totaled only some 35,000, or at most five percent of the Jewish population, the Sadducees and Essenes only two percent altogether.[7]

These were the groups in Jesus' world with which he rubbed shoulders and traded arguments, the groups which he influenced and by which he in turn was influenced. For if we take seriously the fact that Jesus was a real man, who lived in the world at a specific time and place, then we must allow that influence on him from many elements in that world is possible.[8] All this is implied in a statement that Jesus' ministry was at a time when Tiberius Caesar was in his fifteenth year upon the throne and Caiaphas was high priest, in a land where, more than once in the past, historical decisions had been reached which affected later centuries, as if Palestine were a cockpit, controlling the course of the world.

This is so in this instance because, as Luke 3:2 reminds us, it was at this time and place that "the word of God came. . . ."

The Gospel and Our Gospels

Some Christians so much emphasize the Bible as the "Word of God" (an understanding which may be perfectly valid from the standpoint of faith)—and those who are not so convinced react by shunting aside the term—that we are in danger of overlooking a simple fact: the Bible itself talks about the word of God. It does this frequently and with all sorts and shades of meaning.

Luke 3:2 says, for example, ". . . the word of God came to John [the Baptist] the son of Zechariah in the wilderness." That reminds one of the phrase which stands at the beginning of so many books of the Old Testament prophets—"The word of the Lord came to Ezekiel," or "The word that came to Jeremiah from the Lord: 'Stand . . . and say, Hear the word of the Lord' " (7:1-2), or "The oracle of the word of the Lord to Israel by Malachi." The Book of Acts regularly made its theme the word of God. Paul's motto and joy was ". . . to speak the word of God without fear" (Philippians 1:14). John's starting point in his story about Jesus is the Word which was with God.

In view of such emphases in Scripture, there is truth in the contention that no one will ever understand the Bible without knowing what Scripture means by "the word of God." No one will comprehend the gospels' picture of Jesus without attention to this phrase, not merely because the Fourth Gospel (and the epistles) refer to Jesus as the Word, but because his own teachings reproved men of the day for "making void the word of God" by tricks they practiced (Mark 7:13), and spoke of the blessedness of those who "hear the word of God and do it" (Luke 8:21), and compared his mission to sowing the word in the hearts of men (Mark 4:14).

"Word" is a tricky word to comprehend, however, because it has so many meanings. Basically it refers to a message, whether spoken (the way Jesus preached his word, Mark 2:2) or written (as the Old Testament message which had been recorded and could now be referred to in scriptural form, Mark 7:13). Sometimes this message or word was so impressed on the prophet or preacher that his very life and being was virtually inseparable from what he proclaimed. Jeremiah's sufferings came because of what he preached; his sufferings in turn became a part of his

message. Ezekiel and Hosea acted out in their own experience
what came to be presented as a message from the Lord, or, if you
please, they set forth a message that had taken shape in their personal experiences. To this extent, the word of the Lord had been
personalized, even prior to Jesus' day.

What gives "the word of the Lord" its particular character in
biblical thought, however, is the fact that it is "of the Lord." It
comes from God, and is about God, and is, in its power and effec-
tiveness, even accompanied by God or his Spirit. All this gives
the word of the Lord (or word of God) a special quality, according to the biblical writers. For them it is an extension of God
himself, powerfully at work, creating, reproving, renewing, sustaining. One can even say that the word of God, while nominally
a message, couched in words, is also an action. The phrase is a
sort of shorthand expression for "God at work." The Old Testament can say that creation took place "by the word of the Lord"
(Psalm 33:6), that all his revelations (through the prophets, for
example) came "by the word of the Lord," and that Yahweh's
word will accomplish that for which he sends it (Isaiah 55:11).

It is not surprising, therefore, when his contemporaries sensed
the power of God at work through Jesus, that they spoke of how
"his word was with authority," referring both to what he said and
what he did (Luke 4:32, 36). They felt his word was like that
of prophets and men of God in olden times. After the resurrection, followers openly spoke of Jesus as the Word of God (John
1:1-18), the message they preached as "the word," and even the
Christian movement itself as "the word" (Acts 6:7; 12:24;
19:20). No wonder Christians since then have viewed the word
of God as something central for their faith and have identified
the Word with Jesus Christ himself, as well as with the message
about Christ and the Scriptures which record that message.

If you had asked an early Christian what his religion was all
about, chances are he might have said, "the word of God," for the
phrase was a technical term in the early church for the Christian
message. If you had pressed him further, he would have identified
this word—a message, but also a powerful redemptive action—
with Jesus of Nazareth. Then he would have poured out the
whole story to you of who Jesus was, what he said, and what he
did. Especially he would have emphasized to you the part about
Jesus' cross and resurrection. The word of God that early Chris-

tians proclaimed concerned, as I Corinthians 1:23 puts it, "Christ crucified"; Acts 17:18 puts it, "Jesus and the resurrection." This is what John, the author of Revelation, went to prison for, "the word of God and testimony about Jesus" (Revelation 1:9).

Thus, if we today want to study about Jesus, we must do so in a sense via "the word of God." This means not merely that we have to approach the man of Nazareth through " Holy Scripture," the New Testament writings which Jesus' followers later came to regard as word of God. It means also that we have access to him only through source material which the people who transmitted and compiled it regarded as tinged with "word-of-God" quality, with all that phrase implies in biblical thought.

The Earliest Message about Jesus

What are the sources available for getting at the life of Jesus? The truth is, there is virtually no material from the pagan historians of the first century such as Tacitus, or Suetonius, or the Jew Josephus—just enough to make clear, to even the most skeptical historian, that Jesus of Nazareth actually lived and died.[1] From the rabbinic writings (written down a century or more later, to be sure, but preserved in oral form from an earlier date) can be culled some half a dozen references which tell us that much and a bit more, including the fact that "Yeshu of Nazareth" had disciples and was put to death at Passover time.[2] Islamic literature preserves some late traces, of interest to experts. The apocryphal gospels and recent gnostic finds (like the *Gospel of Thomas*) are filled with legends and overlaid with ideas of all sorts from alien hands, although here and there one may find a saying or a story with a claim to authenticity. Archeology has yielded evidence about the Christian movement in the first two centuries, but virtually nothing on Jesus himself, save perhaps two inscriptions in burial chambers found in 1945 at Talpioth, near Jerusalem; the brief Greek inscriptions contain the name "Jesus"—and either a lament over the death of a man of that name or a prayer addressed to him in behalf of someone else, "Jesus, let (him who rests here) arise." The inscriptions are thus ambiguous, as archeological evidence often is, and still under debate. All of this nonbiblical material assures us that Jesus of Nazareth really lived and died, but leaves, of course, a matter like the resurrection or the miracles unproven one way or the other.

We are left thus with the New Testament itself as the chief source from which to learn more about Jesus. The epistles, particularly those of Paul, might seem the obvious place to turn since these are the oldest written Christian documents we have. Paul's earliest letters go back within twenty years of the crucifixion. But though the epistles can tell us far more about Jesus than we might suppose,[3] they are concerned with the faith and life of the early church rather than with the career of Jesus. Above all, the epistles are open to the objection that they seem frightfully "theological" and apt to present what they say about Jesus from a theological, rather than a historical, point of view.

The four gospels seem to meet one of the objections which could be posed against the epistles as a source on the life of Jesus: they are, in form and content, far more detailed about Jesus' words and activities than any epistle is. But the gospels are also far more vulnerable than the epistles on another count: they were written at a later date, and hence are at a greater remove from the lifetime of Jesus. At the best, the oldest written gospel comes from the sixties, thirty years after the cross, and the canonical gospels more likely date between A.D. 70 and 100 than before that time. Moreover we have already seen that, like the epistles, they were subject to theological interests: each gospel begins in a different way and stresses particular theological titles for Jesus.

Thus it appears that, taken as they stand, the New Testament documents all give us evidence recorded only some two or three decades (or more) after Jesus lived. More important, all these gospels and epistles bear the stamp of what the early church would call "the word of God," a conviction that God was at work not merely during Jesus' ministry, but in his followers ever since. If we are historically minded, this may be a disappointment and even a shock: we can get no closer to Jesus, apparently, than the "theologically charged" Christian records from A.D. 50–100.

The situation is not quite so gloomy as it may seem, however, for thanks to modern study of the Bible we can now edge back closer to Jesus' own lifetime. One way to do this is by "listening in" on the earliest Christian preaching and confessions about Jesus. We must remember that long before Paul or Mark wrote, Christians were proclaiming orally the story of Jesus, a message that they called "the word of God," first in Palestine and then throughout the entire Eastern Mediterranean world.

Peter's sermon at Pentecost, in Acts 2, provides us with an example of early Christian preaching about Jesus. The address takes its starting point, as good preaching often does, from the current scene. Peter explains that his listeners are mistaken in what they think is happening: this isn't drunkenness, but an outpouring of God's Spirit. What is more, he uses an Old Testament text (Joel 2:28-32) to make his point. Judging from other sermons reported in Acts, this sort of introduction must have been fairly common: to start from a misunderstanding and weave in a scriptural text.

It is the body of the sermon which especially catches our attention in this case, however. Peter's real subject is Jesus of Nazareth, "a man . . . whom you crucified, whom God raised up." Peter tells us just a little about Jesus' ministry, its mighty works and wonders (Acts 2:22), far more about his death and resurrection (2:23-32), a bit about his exaltation at God's right hand as lord (2:33), and how the risen Christ has sent the Holy Spirit, whose coming is a sure sign of the New Age about which Joel has prophesied. There is a final appeal, for decision, to repent— the way preaching that has conviction should close, with a call to act (2:38-40).

With the analysis of this "word" (2:41) still in our mind, we may next turn to a similar scene in Acts 10. Peter's sermon at the house of the centurion Cornelius has sometimes been called a sort of "Gentile Pentecost," for the scene ends with the Holy Spirit being poured on the non-Jews who heard Peter's word (10:44). We can skip over Peter's introduction, which again is tailored to the current scene (10:34-35). The heart of Peter's sermon this time too is what he says about how the Jews in Jerusalem put Jesus to death, but God raised him up (10:39-40). There is, as in chapter 2, a brief resumé of Jesus' ministry—how, after baptism, he "went about doing good and healing." Again there is greater emphasis on his death and the fact that he is alive. There is a tie to the Old Testament ("the prophets bear witness," 10:43, just as chapter 2 made use of Old Testament materials), and before the closing appeal is made, one further step is taken, not found in the Pentecost sermon, namely a claim that Jesus Christ will one day judge the living and the dead. There are other parallels between the sermons, such as the fact that both of them speak of a need to witness for Jesus Christ (10:42; 2:32; cf. Revelation 1:9).

It is clear, however, that we have a common pattern in the sermons in Acts (a pattern, incidentally, which reappears in chapter 13, at 3:12-26, 4:8-12, and elsewhere). Now, of course, Luke, the final editor, may have imposed a certain uniformity on this material when he edited it about A.D. 90. Some scholars would even make him entirely responsible for these sermons. But other experts are convinced that he is using much earlier sources, some of these sources (chapter 10 is particularly cited) going back to the Aramaic language, which the earliest Christians spoke. For that reason it has been contended that we have in Acts an outline of the earliest message about Jesus, going back to the thirties and forties A.D.

Can such a possibility be checked in any way? Yes, through certain passages in Paul, where the apostle seems to be quoting earlier material which has come to him from the same Aramaic-speaking church whose message is reflected in Acts. I Corinthians 15:1-11 is the best example. Paul wrote this letter about A.D. 55 or so, but he claims here that this is the Gospel as he preached it when he first came to Corinth half a dozen years before (15:1). What is more, Paul claims that this is the message which he holds in common with other early Christian preachers, "Whether then it was I or they, so we preach . . ." (15:11). Most important, Paul avows that this summary of the Gospel is not only what he and other early Christian preachers were accustomed to deliver, it is also the Gospel which he "received," i.e., which was handed on to him by those who were followers of Jesus even before Paul was converted (15:3). Paul employs here a technical phrase which Jewish rabbis used to designate careful transmission of a message, orally, with complete fidelity, over the years. Thus we have every reason to believe that Paul's summary message is the one circulating in the church in the thirties and forties, perhaps from within a year or so of the crucifixion itself.

As for content, Paul's message agrees with that in Acts in basic outline:

Christ died for our sins in accordance with the Scriptures;
he was buried;
he was raised on the third day in accordance with the Scriptures;
he appeared to Cephas, then to the twelve, and to other witnesses.

The stress is on Christ's death and resurrection, the forgiveness of sins, and Christ's present power.

Other passages in Paul can be analyzed and put together to give a coherent picture of "the word" or "Gospel" which Paul and others were preaching in the earliest church. In the opinion of many experts this common message running through the Pauline epistles and Acts went something like this:

> What the Old Testament Scriptures promised is being fulfilled: a New Age has dawned through the mighty acts of God.
> He who has spoken and acted in so many ways in the past, especially in Israel's history, has now once and for all time revealed his final purpose, through Jesus of Nazareth, a man of David's seed, baptized by John,
> who did mighty works by the power of God,
> whom men crucified—he died and was buried—
> but whom God raised up on the third day
> and exalted to his right hand (all as the Scriptures say),
> declaring him Christ and lord and judge-to-come.
> These things we witness to you and call upon you now to accept what God has done in Jesus: repent, believe, be baptized, find life and forgiveness and the gift of the Spirit in him.

Here then is the earliest message about Jesus recoverable from our sources. It gives a picture of him as a man in Palestine whose ministry led to a cross, but whom God raised and exalted, so that now he is lord—confessed and proclaimed as the Christ, the object of worship and subject of teaching among his followers. This picture of Jesus Christ is obviously not "untheological"; but can any picture of Jesus omit portraying the relationship to God, since some such relationship is involved in all of Jesus' message? This summary stresses God's working in Jesus' career, but then Jesus' every statement assumed God's hand at work. However, this summary portrait of Jesus in this earliest message of the New Testament is a crucial step back toward the man himself because it comes from a date closer to Jesus' lifetime than the gospels or even the epistles. And it is this message about Jesus, or *kerygma* ("proclamation"), to use the technical Greek term that Paul employs, which, in fact, served as a sort of "filter" through which all memories of the historical Jesus have come down to us. The *kerygma* provides a framework within which all other pictures of him, sketched by Paul, or Mark, or Luke, are set. We have here the Gospel (or central message) before the gospels (or individual presentations of Jesus). If we want to take up any story or saying of Jesus preserved by the early Christians, we must first focus our eyes on this picture in the Gospel (or *kerygma*), a picture familiar to all early Christians.

The most important thing about this central Gospel or *kerygma* is that it provides a basic unity for the entire New Testament. For here is the message that stands behind every New Testament book. No matter how much these books may differ in situation, expression, or emphasis, they presume a common Gospel. This Gospel is a key to unity amid the diversity which may strike us as we read the separate books of the New Testament.

The Rise of the Gospels

When early Christians went forth telling their "good news" about the "Christ event," what God had brought to pass in the life, death, and resurrection of Jesus, they did so at first by word of mouth, eagerly and almost breathlessly, in sermon and conversation. Only after a time did they begin to write their message down. Why did Christians make this transition from oral report to written material, and when? And how did written "gospels" emerge as specific representations of "the Gospel"?

The story is an intricate one spread over some six or seven decades, but recent scholarship helps us piece it together. To put the answer as briefly as possible: Christians began to write letters, sermons, collections of material about Jesus, and eventually larger literary works as soon as the need arose to do so. By A.D. 50, we know, Paul was writing letters back to congregations which he had founded, to encourage them or answer their questions. Acts 15:22-29 reports that church leaders in Jerusalem, on one occasion at least, issued a letter or decree about a problem then vexing Christianity, that of the terms on which non-Jews should be admitted to the new faith. Needs of this sort account for a shift to writing.

Another factor over the years was the "thermometer of eschatology"—expectations about when Jesus would come again. These must have risen and fallen with contemporary events. At times the expectation was at fever pitch, as some people looked for Jesus to reappear immediately on the clouds of heaven (see II Thessalonians 2:1-12, where Paul seeks to calm such feelings). At other times Christians were coming to realize that Christ's return must, for the present, be in the form of the Spirit and that a longer future than had been expected stretched before them in the world.

As this conviction grew, there would have been more incentive to gather material about Jesus for coming generations. At all times and in all places in this exciting first century, Christians would have been eager for additional information about Jesus. Reports of what he said or did would have been retold by adoring lips and applied in the life of the Christian community.

We have already noted a gap between Jesus' lifetime and Paul's letters, the oldest written documents in the New Testament; however, we have also seen how that gap is bridged in part by the Gospel (or *kerygma*), the earliest message about Jesus. But is there any other link connecting Jesus' lifetime with the later New Testament writings?

A second bond which provides continuity between Jesus and our gospels and the other New Testament writings is the "gospel tradition," a name given to a host of stories about what Jesus did and reports about what he said. One must remember that "tradition" meant originally "that which is handed down," and specifically what is passed on by word of mouth. That sense fits perfectly here, in the period of the decades prior to the time when written gospels or other Christian documents began to appear. It is called the *"gospel* tradition" in this case because the material involved circulated with the Gospel and conveyed to people a fuller content of what the Gospel was all about.

One should not be disturbed, as some Christians might be, that it is necessary to use the term "tradition" to describe the manner of formulation of the Christian message for this early period. Paul himself employs the term to describe his teaching at this time, as we noted above in discussing I Corinthians 15 and as we can see if we look at II Thessalonians 3:6, for example.

What should be a cause of concern, however, is the possibility that this tradition might have become separated from the Gospel, with which it originally circulated. In that case, stories concerning Jesus and sayings of his would have been interpreted apart from the basic message of what God has done in Jesus Christ. Then there would be the risk of seeing Jesus simply as a "great man" or "noble teacher," apart from the "framework" or "setting" which early Christians assumed, the setting of Jesus of Nazareth as crucified and risen lord. The "gospel tradition"—or "Jesus-material," to give another name to the accounts about the man of Nazareth and what he taught—has much more to tell us about

Jesus than the basic Christian proclamation could include (just as the full account of a battle or a baseball game always includes much more detail than the headlines or summary on page one can). But in studying the "Jesus-material" (or "gospel tradition") as a second link with the historical Jesus, we must always be careful to view it and its parts in light of the Gospel, if we are to be true to the intentions of our sources.

Perhaps the matter can be made clear this way. Philippians 2:6-11 is a magnificent summation of what God did in Jesus Christ: "though in the form of God, . . . he emptied himself, taking the form of a servant . . .; he became obedient unto death, on a cross; therefore God has highly exalted him and bestowed on him the name . . . Lord. . . ." If you put the words "I believe" in front of them, the verses would make a splendid confession of faith. If you write them out as poetry (the form many experts think the verses originally had), 2:6-11 would make a striking hymn (which some scholars think it was). But would Philippians 2:6-11 ever be enough to tell the full and vivid story of the man from Nazareth? Would the verses not rather, taken by themselves, allow the Gospel to be made into a myth, about a heavenly creature who came down briefly to earth and then ascended again?

The same thing is true of the summary of the Gospel which Paul quotes in I Corinthians 15:3 ff. It is a mere skeleton. So also with the sermons in Acts. They tell us a modicum about Jesus—he "went about doing good," he healed many, he died at Jerusalem, God raised him up. But these "headlines" are really invitations to learn more about his ministry and miracles, the passion story, and the throbbing heart that gave new life to all of this, the resurrection. Most certainly anyone who heard and accepted all this would want to know, too, what Jesus had taught, so that he could apply it to his life. It is the gospel tradition or Jesus-material which does all these things. By telling more about Jesus it supplemented the dramatic announcements of the Gospel with the necessary detail. It put "flesh" on the "skeleton," as it were, and clothed the bare outline.

Right here we have a clue as to why the written gospels eventually came to be composed: the Gospel and the "Jesus-material" must be viewed together. The bare Gospel taken by itself (as at Philippians 2:6-11) could dissolve into a vague myth. The bare outline of the *kerygma* at I Corinthians 15 or the sermons in Acts

might lose touch with Palestinian reality. The teachings of Jesus
and the ethic which the Gospel demands might be lost sight of,
if all one ever heard was the terse summary of the Christ event.
On the other hand, if the Jesus-material circulated by itself, Jesus
might appear simply as a wandering rabbi, a prophetic teacher,
a wise man, or wonder-worker. The result would be moralism
without Gospel, and the picture of Jesus would lose touch with
the reality of God which had been so basic for Jesus and which
came to a climax when God did not abandon him in death but
raised him up (Acts 2:31-32).

To put it another way, if we had only the epistles of the New
Testament, we would run the risk of losing a crucial part of the
picture of Jesus, his earthly life and teachings. If we had just the
Jesus-tradition, we might miss the overarching purpose and actions
of God. Therefore, it came to be seen that, if the full understanding of Jesus Christ was to be preserved, Jesus-material must remain incorporated within, and be set forth in, the Gospel framework. The result was a literary type which the world had never
seen before—the gospel form, which we encounter in the New
Testament.

We have said that the course of the gospel tradition or Jesus-
material is a complicated one, leading from the ministry of Jesus
to the time when the material was incorporated in our written
gospels some thirty-five to sixty years later. Actually there are four
steps involved, as we shall see. Throughout the whole period,
however, we must remember that the Jesus-material did not exist
in a vacuum but was being put to daily use. Over the decades
from A.D. 30 to 90, the stories about Jesus and sayings from him
were being utilized by Christians within the Christian community
for needs that faced them every day.

We must reckon with the fact that, during this time, the gospel
tradition was not an ossified mummy, kept in a glass case in a
museum. It was a living thing, ever growing and maturing and
finding its true strength. The early Christians did not lock up the
Jesus-material on file cards and in reference works for future
generations. Instead they employed what they knew of Jesus'
words and activities in their task of telling others about him, in
ministering to one another, in shaping their prayers, worship, and
daily life. Not "biography, for the sake of biography," but the
word-of-God quality for life! They were not interested in analyz-

ing the wire, but in benefiting from the electric current which flowed through it.

One must even say that it was the experience of early Christians in these decades that, though they had no inspired scriptures of their own as yet (apart from the Old Testament inherited from Israel), they were conscious of the power of the Holy Spirit shaping and applying anew the Jesus-material—until at last an evangelist (also under the Spirit, Christians would say) put the gospel tradition (about what Jesus said and did) together with the Gospel (about what God was doing through Jesus), to form our written gospels.

To picture something of this exciting process, let us imagine the period when the transition was being made from the life of Jesus to the written gospels which tell us about it, as a chart spread out before us marked at twenty-year intervals. Jesus' ministry probably ran from A.D. 27 or so until his death in A.D. 30 (the most likely date). By the year 50 the first written documents from Christian hands, the letters of Paul, are beginning to appear. Twenty years later comes that most decisive and tragic of dates, the fall of Jerusalem, in September, A.D. 70.

Long before this, Christianity had already begun to spread far outside Palestine, into the Gentile world. It had made the transition from the Aramaic language which Jesus spoke and the first Christians as well, to the Greek which was used all over the world. Now, after 70, ties with Judaism would be increasingly tenuous, and Christianity would become more and more a Gentile affair. It is at just this point, more likely a little before 70 than after it, that the gospel form, a written book combining the outline of the basic Gospel message with some of the Jesus-tradition, first appeared.

The Gospel of Mark, the book which represents this momentous step, should probably be dated about A.D. 67. It is toward the end of the next twenty-year period, about A.D. 90, that Matthew and Luke appear. It is hard to be dogmatic about which one was completed first, though Matthew is likely the earlier of the two. John's Gospel can be dated not much after Matthew's and Luke's, sometime in the nineties. We must remember that "books" like this, hand-copied at a time long prior to the invention of the printing press, scarcely had a publication date in the modern sense. An evangelist might complete his gospel book one year but then add further material which he came across a few years later; more years might go by until additional copies were made and circulated, and perhaps even at that point a few more details might be added to the contents.

The picture can be sketched in chart form (but remember that the Gospel message was the "framework" or "filter" through which all the Jesus-material moved) such as appears on page 31. It can be seen at a glance how the Gospel provides a basic image of Jesus which pervades all the writings of the New Testament and how this Gospel carries us back to the common apostolic picture of Jesus from the resurrection on. It is also to be noted that the gospel tradition or Jesus-material provides a second link carrying us back to Jesus within this framework.

Against this background, the four stages of development from Jesus to our written gospels can now be described.

(1) *During Jesus' own lifetime,* so far as we know, *no written records* were kept about him by friend or foe. Perhaps there was a file on his case in Pilate's archives or at the temple, but if these ever existed, they were destroyed long ago, most likely in A.D. 70. Jesus could write (John 8:6, 8), but all his teaching was oral, though often in a poetic form in Aramaic which made it easy to memorize. It has been suggested that when Jesus sent the seventy disciples out on a preaching mission (Luke 10:1 ff.), they perhaps wrote down their instructions. But the biblical records never say this. It appears that all knowledge of what Jesus said and did was transmitted by word of mouth from the time of his ministry on. Just as reports about him might have gone from one bazaar or village to another during his lifetime, so also after his death and resurrection. Only now it was men and women who believed in him as *risen* lord who transmitted these reports.

(2) *From A.D. 30 to 50 or 90* and even beyond, the gospel tradition was spread by *word of mouth.* There was little impulse as yet to write for posterity; instead believers felt impelled to speak the news as quickly and widely as possible. Stories about Jesus usually circulated in this period singly; only in time were some of them strung together into longer narratives (except for the long Passion account which was a unit from the beginning). So also with the sayings. They were retold separately, pretty much as remembered—a parable, a rebuke to Pharisees, a little maxim

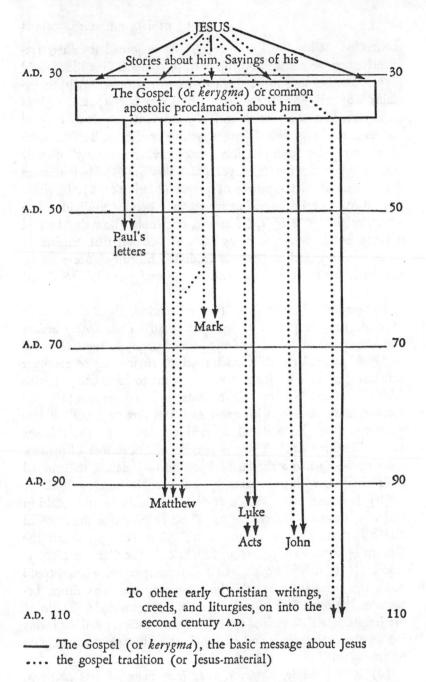

JESUS

Stories about him, Sayings of his

A.D. 30 ─────────────────────────────── 30

The Gospel (or *kerygma*) or common
apostolic proclamation about him

A.D. 50 ─────────────────────────────── 50

Paul's
letters

Mark

A.D. 70 ─────────────────────────────── 70

A.D. 90 ─────────────────────────────── 90

Matthew

Luke

Acts   John

To other early Christian writings,
creeds, and liturgies, on into the
A.D. 110   second century A.D.   110

───── The Gospel (or *kerygma*), the basic message about Jesus
.... the gospel tradition (or Jesus-material)

DEVELOPMENT FROM JESUS
TO THE GOSPEL BOOKS

about God. When stories or sayings were joined together, frequently they were linked on the basis of content. One idea would suggest another and make them easier to remember. All this explains why our gospels sometimes link together separate sayings from Jesus in a new context and why different gospels may report the same teaching with different setting or details. To illustrate: Matthew reports the injunction "forgive when you pray" directly after he gives the Lord's Prayer (Matthew 6:14); Mark attaches it to a section on the power of prayer (Mark 11:25). In either place it makes good sense, but we are hard pressed to decide when Jesus "originally" said it. Of course, one could allow that he said it twice, but there are so many cases of this sort that consistency in maintaining such a position leads to absurdity.[4] More likely, the varied arrangements go back to the oral period, after Jesus' day.

To complete the picture of this oral period, three things must be said. (a) People in antiquity had an *extraordinary ability* (which we lack in this day of the printed page) *to remember oral material,* particularly if it had rhythm, rhyme, or some other structure (as some of Jesus' sayings appear to have had). Jewish rabbis transmitted orally their intricate explanations about the law for a century or two, with great care and accuracy, until it was permitted that the material be written down, in the *Mishna* (second century A.D.). There is reason to believe that Christians, some of whom had a similar background in Judaism, transmitted their materials with some accuracy over a much shorter period.

(b) It is well established that oral material, told and retold in this way, *takes on definite forms.* These forms make the material easier to remember and protect it against change. When the Grimm brothers were collecting folk tales in the German countryside in 1810, they discovered that illiterate peasant women could retell the same story exactly the same way countless times, because of the form in which the story was transmitted.[5] Certain of the Jesus-materials—such as miracle stories—took on definite forms too in the oral period, and that helped make for more accurate transmission.

(c) It is possible, however, that Jesus-material was *changed, added to, or, some critics think, on occasion even created* in this oral period. We have seen that the material was being used by Christians in their churches, for practical purposes, in the interests of faith. We must therefore be alert to the possibility that in the oral period the early church reworked material to make it more meaningful. Surely the meaning of the cross was being spelled out and its ramifications explored in new and more significant terms in this period. It is likely that Jesus' life and teachings were likewise finding new and deeper interpretations in this same period. John's Gospel has Jesus promising, "When the Spirit of truth comes, he will guide you into all the truth" (John 16:13). There are few areas where the early Christians can have expected the Spirit to have deepened the meaning more than in the gospel tradition in this period after the resurrection and Pentecost.

(3) *About* A.D. *50 to 70, written sources* begin to appear. Obviously there were written materials in addition to the letters of Paul (and others) known to us. Second Timothy 4:13 refers to "books and above all the parchments" in a passage which many who treat the Pastoral Epistles as post-Pauline compilations regard as a genuine fragment, and some think Paul includes there not just the Old Testament but also some primitive account of the Passion or a collection of Jesus' teachings. Other scholars think that by A.D. 50 there was in written form a narrative of Jesus' trial and death, perhaps several of them, and a collection (or collections) of the sayings of Jesus such as might have been used in catechetical instruction or for reading as lessons at Sunday services. Some critics have even supposed that an early draft of Mark was circulating in the fifties. Those who have studied the matter have found it convenient to use letters to designate these supposed sources which may have been circulating in writing in the interval between the early oral period and the written gospels. Most commonly the following sources are supposed:

Mk—an early version of the Gospel which was later expanded into the Gospel of Mark which we know in the canon.

Q—an arbitrary symbol for a "sayings source" or collection of Jesus' teachings utilized by Matthew and Luke but not by Mark; perhaps there were even several such collections, one used by Matthew, one by Luke.

M—a special source presupposed for all or some of the material which turns up only in Matthew.

L—a special source presumed to lie behind material found only in Luke.

When Matthew, Mark, and Luke are printed side by side, as in a gospel harmony, these "sources" show up in a very striking way. Marcan material practically always reappears in Matthew or Luke or both. Q is material found only in Matthew and Luke, not Mark. M and L turn up in one gospel only. Charts on the Synoptic Gospels can also illustrate this point. It is sometimes very important, in reading a gospel passage, to pay attention to what source is involved, for Mk, Q, M, and L each has its own characteristics.

(4) Finally there is the work of the *evangelists* themselves. They gathered the source material and oral traditions together, combining Jesus-material with the basic Gospel message. The result is a unified account which combines reports about Jesus' ministry and teaching with the story of his suffering, death, and resurrection. We must not imagine these editors as mere "paste-pot-and-scissors" men, gluing together a few verses from here and a thought from there. They were men of the Spirit, too, each with a creativity of his own. Mark, Matthew, Luke, and John each chose to begin somewhat differently (as we have seen in our study of introductions), each emphasized those facets of Jesus' life and teachings which best fitted the needs of his church and his readers. That is another reason why each gospel will differ, and a reason why we must pay attention to the tendencies of an evangelist-editor when we study a passage in his gospel.

Superimposing what we have now noted on our previous chart, we get a fuller picture of the growth of the gospels (see page 35). Complicated as all this may look, it is actually a simplified picture of what some scholars have proposed, as they try to account for all the facts in the development of the gospels.[6] One can read all sorts of inferences from such a chart of development. For example, Matthew may be seen as the work of an evangelist who draws on Mark, on a collection of sayings (Q) which he shares in common with Luke, and on a certain amount of material which no one else has in the entire New Testament (M). Or one can see how John develops the Gospel and the Jesus-tradition in his own way, independent of Matthew, Mark, or Luke.

It is also possible to take a story about Jesus or a saying of his and try to trace its transmission from original eyewitness accounts, through the oral period, into a written source, and then its use by an evangelist.[7] This is the way Luke 1:1-4 describes the process of writing a gospel from the origins in Jesus' day to the third

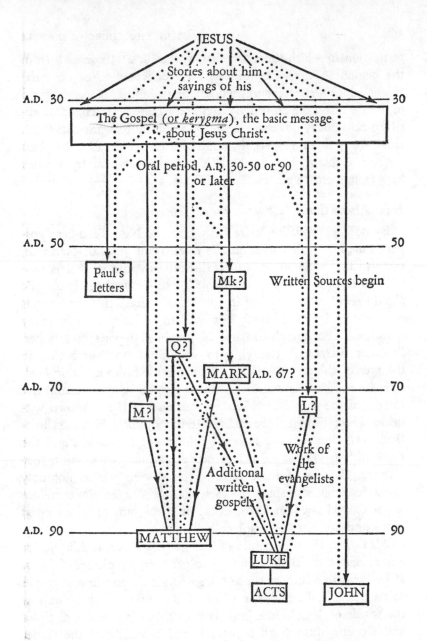

JESUS

Stories about him
sayings of his

A.D. 30 — — — — — — — — — — — — — — — — 30

The Gospel (or *kerygma*), the basic message
about Jesus Christ.

Oral period, A.D. 30-50 or 90
or later

A.D. 50 — — — — — — — — — — — — — — — — 50

Paul's
letters

Mk?   Written Sources begin

Q?

MARK A.D. 67?

A.D. 70 — — — — — — — — — — — — — — — — 70

M?   L?

Additional   Work of
written   the
gospels   evangelists

A.D. 90 — — — — — — — — — — — — — — — — 90

MATTHEW

LUKE

ACTS   JOHN

THE GROWTH OF THE GOSPELS

generation in which the evangelist works: ". . . those who from the beginning were eyewitnesses . . . delivered to us . . . the things which were accomplished among us" until "it seemed good to me . . . to write an orderly account," Luke says. The most exciting possibility, however, is the opportunity to work backward, from the written gospels, through the earlier decades, to Jesus himself. Knowing how our gospels took shape, we can try to work back from them, to glimpse Jesus as he was.

How Much Can We Know about Jesus?

By now, appreciating more fully how the New Testament gospels, our only real sources on the ministry of Jesus of Nazareth, came to be composed, we can realistically inquire what it is possible to learn and what it is impossible to know about Jesus. We should recall what was said in the Introduction,[8] that the gospels were not designed to satisfy our modern curiosity with its many questions. The gospels are not biographical reports but, rather, "witness literature," testifying to who Jesus was—or better, in the eyes of the early Christians, who regarded him as living lord, who he *is*. We know also that these gospels bear the stamp not merely of the man from Nazareth but also of the unknown witnesses who transmitted the units of testimony about him, the Christians who compiled the material into larger collections, and the evangelists who arranged it into gospels, all under the Spirit, they claimed. Because of these factors, the gospels tell us not only about Jesus but also about the early church. We see him therefore as the Gospel saw him, as the evangelists saw him, as faith viewed him—and not just "biographically."

All this in the very nature of the gospels makes it difficult for any reader of the Bible nowadays to get a simple picture of Jesus. If he turns to Matthew 10, to take a single chapter in one gospel as an example, he finds the voice of the early church as well as the words of Jesus. Here Jesus is commissioning twelve disciples and sending them forth to preach and heal. Yet if the reader compares the names of the twelve at Matthew 10:2-4 with similar lists at Mark 3:16-19 and Luke 6:14-16, he finds not only differences in order but also in names. Is "Matthew the tax collector" the same as "Levi the son of Alphaeus," whose call to follow is described at Mark 2:14 and parallels? Do these lists reflect varying traditions within the early church? The reader will be per-

plexed to hear the warning that the disciples will be dragged before rulers of the *Gentiles* (Matthew 10:18), when 10:5 has
warned them *not* to go among the Gentiles. The modern reader
will scarcely know what to make of the fact that the disciples are
told they "will not have gone through all the towns of Israel,
before the Son of man comes" (10:23), and then the twelve are
reported as returning to Jesus and resuming their discipleship,
with no visitation from the Son of man occurring (see Matthew
11:1 and 12:1 and Mark 6:30). Finally he will be at a loss about
what to do with the fact that some of the verses fit nicely into the
time of Jesus' earthly ministry but others of them seem to refer
to situations in the early church. Such problems make it hard to
arrive at a very satisfactory reconstruction of how Jesus sent forth
the twelve, let alone what was in his mind at the time.

Matthew 10 is, of course, a very complex chapter, put together
by Matthew from materials out of Mark, *Q,* and *M,* for Christians of his day. Very careful study would be needed to thread
our way through it, to try to ascertain what each section means.
But in spite of such difficulties—and the chapter is noted merely
as a sample illustration—men have long supposed that they could
use the gospels as sources to work out a picture of Jesus for themselves.

It is easy to recall the many forms which replicas of Jesus have
taken in art. These range from the paintings in the catacombs
(which make him look much like the pagan deity Apollo) and
the formalized but haunting mosaics at Ravenna where a majestic
Christ reigns supreme, to agonizing crucifixes from the Middle
Ages (where the emphasis is on the suffering man), to modern
sketches of Jesus in Bermuda shorts. There have been all sorts of
attempts to make Jesus "contemporary," including Renaissance
scenes where a landscape in Burgundy or Umbria appears at the
background for a nativity scene, with the local prince or bishop
bearing gifts to the Christ-child's crib. Perhaps we have also seen
sketches of Jesus as a native Christian artist in China or Africa
depicts him—with slant eyes or black skin.

All of us can appreciate how readily artistic representations of
Jesus in painting or sculpture reflect the artist's own times and inclinations. But is it always realized that word-pictures of Jesus
often betray the same influences? Every "life" of Jesus ever written has been colored by the writer and the times in which he

lived. It is important to realize this, since books about Jesus often
have a great influence on us, sometimes an even greater influence
than the New Testament itself. Yet these books by modern authors—be they Fulton J. Sheen or Fulton Oursler or Ethelbert
Stauffer—inevitably reflect the philosophy and faith of the biographers and read the New Testament through their particular eyes.
This is not to say that we dare cease from attempting to visualize
Jesus, nor even that we should refrain from reading this writer's
effort or that one's. But it does mean that we must keep alert
to the fact that throughout history Jesus has more than once been
depicted in strange ways and misleading forms, thanks to the pre-
sumptions or prejudices of the writers. The best defenses against
such subjective views about Jesus are to study the gospels themselves carefully and to know something about how "lives of
Jesus" have varied over the years.

As early as the second century after Christ, men began to try
to portray Jesus "as he was" (or as men wished him to be). Thus,
for example, a convert from Mesopotamia named Tatian combined the four gospels into a single account called a "harmony"
about A.D. 160. This practice of constructing gospel harmonies has
continued to our own day. Some people may be familiar, for example, with "the History of the Passion" read in certain liturgical
churches during Lent. Such a harmonization has the advantage of
fitting together all the accounts into a composite whole. Its dis-
advantage is that it frequently must obscure or misinterpret or
leave out what one evangelist says in order to make it agree with
what another gospel has. In Tatian's case there were also other
factors at work, for he had certain moralizing tendencies. He
favored monasticism and was against marriage, and so did not
scruple reading his own opinions into the harmony he made from
the biblical accounts.

The Middle Ages knew a picture of Jesus that often depended
on legends and traditions from outside Scripture[9] and that knew
even the biblical sources often only secondhand and in translations. The Renaissance and Reformation encouraged a more historical approach to Jesus, sweeping away many of the accretions
of the centuries, as did Rationalism later on. Luther protested
against those medieval representations which made Jesus a stern
judge or a forlorn figure on the cross or depicted him "vested in
a choir cope and golden crown" at the expense of his humanity.

It was the human, historical side of Jesus which was increasingly emphasized, although at times, especially under the rationalists, this was in deliberate opposition to any notion of his relationship to God.

Real study of the life of Jesus came only in the eighteenth and nineteenth centuries. H. S. Reimarus, a teacher of oriental languages in Hamburg, Germany, left at his death in 1768 a manuscript so controversial it could be published only posthumously and anonymously, as "Fragments of an Unknown Author," seen through the press by the poet Lessing between 1774 and 1778. This manuscript claimed that Jesus had aimed at political power and died a failure, crying, "My God, my God, why hast thou forsaken me?" (Mark 15:34). His disciples, however, were, according to Reimarus, crafty fellows, who did not want to go back to working for a living; so they stole the corpse, invented the message that he was risen, and started a church.

Nineteenth-century "lives of Jesus" often went even further. One of them has Jesus as the tool of the secret society of Essenes who revived him after his "death" and allowed him to make "resurrection appearances" from time to time. Another one explained the miracles as natural happenings—Jesus shared his lunch, so did everyone else in the crowd, and thus all the five thousand were fed. Others "psychologized" Jesus and tried to explain what emotional experiences led him to think of himself as "Messiah." A Frenchman, Renan, wrote an appealing account which employed "aesthetic feeling" as a fifth gospel source. David Friedrich Strauss brought out the most famous of all these "lives of Jesus" in 1835-36 when he depicted most of the New Testament narratives as "myths" invented by the early church. One of his chapters was headed irreverently, "Sea Stories and Fish Stories." The book caused a storm which raged the rest of his lifetime and posed questions which are still with us. In essence, Strauss asked how much of the Jesus portrayed in the New Testament can be termed historical.

Of course, there were other, more traditional "lives" written during this period. Some of the more sensational examples are emphasized here because they were the ones which garnered the most attention. If biblical criticism sometimes seems "radical" today, it is worth noting that the "good old days" of a century ago produced some "wild men" more daring in many ways. It is also worth pointing out that the "Quest for the historical Jesus," as this nineteenth-century movement was called, with its probing search for "the real Jesus," was a pursuit carried on not only by liberals and rationalists but by conservative, devout Christian scholars also, by Catholics as well as Protestants. Indeed, many conservatives were led to more careful study of the gospels precisely to answer the claims advanced in some of the "liberal" lives. One thing that became clear to all involved was that the earliest and most reliable sources would have to be picked out in order to get back to the "original" picture of Jesus. Because certain of the more radical "lives" worked on the assumption that Matthew was the oldest gospel (and therefore the correct starting point), other scholars, often conservatives, began to experiment with other views. It was at this time that evidence was accumulated, and the conviction grew, that Mark was the first gospel to be composed. The nineteenth century did not give us any commonly agreed portrait of Jesus, but it did pioneer in isolating the sources (*Mk, Q, M, L*) with which most students of the Synoptic problem operate today.

This nineteenth-century "quest" ended in failure, though, with regard to its prime goal, a "life" of Jesus. Hence in the opening decades of the twentieth century the quest was replaced by a mood of increasing resignation that no biography of Jesus and no analysis of his "spiritual development" were possible. Scholars like Rudolf Bultmann still studied the "Jesus-material" intensively and wrote on the man and his teachings, but the old, easy optimism about the historian's ability to control the facts and get back to the past "objectively" was gone. Moreover, it was now recognized that there ran through the New Testament records a far heavier emphasis on the Gospel or apostolic *kerygma* than the nineteenth century had supposed, and it became apparent that the church's influence on the Jesus-material was greater than had previously been allowed. Finally, there was a new element injected into the picture by Albert Schweitzer in his now famous book, published in 1906, *The Quest of the Historical Jesus*. He pointed out how most of the nineteenth-century writers ignored "eschatology," that expectation of the end of human history which colored so much of what Jesus said. Matthew 10:23, with its expectation that the "Son of man" would come on clouds of heaven during Jesus' lifetime, even before the disciples had completed their preaching tour of Palestine, was the basis on which Schweitzer began his own reconstruction of Jesus. Schweitzer's portrait of Jesus, not unlike that of Reimarus in 1778, is now recognized as a one-sided caricature too. For Jesus was not just a "wild-eyed eschatologist" any more than he was merely a "noble teacher." But Schweitzer had called attention to a question which no study ever dare overlook: How does expectation about God's "ultimates" run through all that Jesus said?

Today there are some scholars, of course, who go on in the "Old Quest," seeking to psychologize the life of Jesus as men did in the nineteenth century. Others are pessimistic about the historian's ability to tell us anything very much about the "real Jesus." In the last decade or so a movement has sprung up, however, which takes a position somewhere between these two positions. This movement realizes that we cannot write a biography of Jesus as the nineteenth-century scholars hoped to do. But it also affirms that in the interest of faith, as well as for the sake of historical study, we must come to see the person about whom the Gospel speaks as a genuine human being, with a life and teachings of his own.

The "New Quest," as this approach has come to be called, accepts the fact that we must operate within the framework of the Gospel or apostolic *kerygma* and must move back through this earliest preaching about Jesus to the man of Nazareth. We may not sidestep this basic Gospel portrait which we find impressed on every story and assumed in every saying from Jesus.[10] At the same time, it is hoped, we can employ the "Jesus-material," in light of the Gospel, to find, not a different picture of Jesus, but the same one in greater depth and detail. In this way the "New Quest" is committed both to use the tools of modern historical scholarship and to perceive the "word-of-God" quality in the New Testament sources. A book by Günther Bornkamm, of Heidelberg, entitled *Jesus of Nazareth*, has been widely hailed as representative of this approach.

In the pages which follow we shall generally reflect this view: that we must try to see something of Jesus historically, although aware that we can (and ought) never shake off the theological perspective of the New Testament, and that we must not presume to fictionalize a biography of Jesus the way nineteenth-century writers often did. The Norwegian resistance-leader and bishop,

Eivind Berggrav, once warned, "Each of us has his own image
of Jesus, or he has no Jesus at all." That is true. Study of Jesus
as he stands behind the Gospel is required lest the figure of Christ
turn into a phantom. But our image of Jesus must be shaped by
the New Testament records, and that means, because of their nature, by both faith and history. For again and again we shall find
that both the testimony of faith and the facts of history are mingled in our accounts.

Unquestionably, then, our gospels do reflect some historical interest and do give us some historically usable material about Jesus.
Where perspectives differ from one gospel to another, it may be
because the writers stood in different situations or chose to select
different facts. Theologically there was a common Gospel, but its
rich contents could be developed along different lines at various
times and places. To see how these various factors worked together in the composition of the gospels, we shall investigate in
the following pages a number of incidents and teachings from
Jesus' career, to see what can be learned about Jesus. For example,
chapters 3 and 4 will treat two places where our records are rather
full and the matters most important. The one, a narrative section,
is the Passion. The other, dealing with the teaching of Jesus, concerns the Lord's Prayer. The same mingling of history and theology that we shall look for in these examples can be seen even
more briefly, however, in a problem which we take as an example
here, the problem of an "outline" for the ministry of Jesus.

The common apostolic Gospel spoke of how Jesus went around
teaching and healing and then died at Jerusalem. Mark's Gospel
develops that outline along simple geographical lines: a ministry
in Galilee (chapters 1-9), and then the Passion journey to Jerusalem (chapters 10-16). Luke follows the same outline but with
considerable freedom. He omits Mark 6:45 through 8:26 (a sort
of repetition of certain types of happenings in Galilee) and inserts a "travel section" or journey through Samaria (Luke 9:51—
18:14). Luke thus has a three-part geographical outline: Galilee,
Samaria, Jerusalem. Matthew takes the basic outline found in
Mark and inserts into it five great discourses or addresses by Jesus
where he employs his M and Q material. Each discourse ends with
the same formula, "And it came to pass when Jesus had ended
these words . . ." (see 7:28; 11:1, 13:53; 19:1; 26:1). Thus
the Synoptics use a common outline; each develops it differently:

MARK	LUKE	MATTHEW (5 discourses)
	Galilee	<Sermon on the Mount (chaps. 5-7)
Galilee		<To Disciples (chap. 10)
		<Parables of the Kingdom (chap. 13)
	Samaria	
Jerusalem	Jerusalem	
		<On Humility (chap. 18)
		<Eschatology (chaps. 24-25)

John, as is well-known, follows a completely different outline, according to which Jesus makes many trips to Jerusalem (as early as chapter 2:13-25) at every festival, and appears in Samaria quite early in his ministry (chapter 4).

Now which outline is historically the one to be preferred? Did Jesus preach in Jerusalem only during the final week of his life (as the Synoptics imply) or several times during his career (so John)? Related to this is the problem of the length of Jesus' ministry. Was it one year or so (as may be inferred from the Synoptics) or three years at least (so John)? Even if all these matters could be fitted together, we have nagging problems such as the date of the cleansing of the temple; was it early in the ministry or during "Holy Week"? (Contrast John 2:13-17 with Mark 11:15-18; even within the Synoptics, Matthew 21:1-17 has it on "Palm Sunday," but Mark 11:12-18 puts it on the next day.) It once was fashionable to prefer Mark over John on such details, but now it is recognized that on such details John may at times be correct. The upshot, however, is that on many such historical matters we cannot attain a conclusive answer and must simply assume one of the conflicting views to be correct—or perhaps that both views have something to be said for them. For the Synoptics may have conflated Jesus' ministry and compressed it, in order to concentrate everything on the final trip to Jerusalem, while John may have spread out his materials in order to make certain parts more dramatic.

Dates, places, historical details, then, we cannot always pin down. Something of the person of Jesus and what he said we can hope to find in the Gospel and the gospel tradition. It is proper that we begin at the heart of that Gospel, where the gospel tradition is fullest, namely, at the Passion of Jesus.

3

"The Christ Must Suffer Many Things"

To test how much we can learn about Jesus of Nazareth from our gospels, no better place exists than the Passion accounts. For in the chapters about the suffering and death of Jesus, the evangelists deal with the last days and hours of his life in greater detail than they do in any other part, recounting the happenings almost minute by minute. Here the gospels also connect incidents about Jesus more completely and afford fuller insight into their meanings than for any other segment of his life. At this point our historical sources in Matthew, Mark, Luke, and John are richest. In fact, there is almost an embarrassing richness of material, for one of the problems which anyone faces in reading the gospels is to try to fit together all the details of the four Passion accounts into a "seamless whole."

Thus, while the story of Jesus' last days in Jerusalem should be the place where we can tell "what happened" with greatest accuracy, the fact is that the very detail of the gospel sources poses problems when we try to reconstruct the narrative, let alone ascertain what may have gone on in the mind of Caiaphas, Pilate, Judas, or even Jesus himself.

Moreover, every account which we possess of Jesus' legal trials, sufferings, and death has come to us from the hands and hearts and lips of Christians who believed that God was at work in these things and that He had not abandoned Jesus, even in these terrible experiences, but had raised him from the dead, to reign as living lord. We might expect one sort of account of Jesus' last days from his enemies or from a Roman stenographer at Pilate's court, but a different sort of retelling of the Passion narrative from Christians who believed that this death upon a cross had worked their salvation. That was exactly what happened. When Paul (or other early Christians) told of Jesus' Passion, it was in light of a faith that "the Son of God . . . loved me and gave himself for me" (Galatians 2:20). Thus there is always the dimension of faith in our gospel records. Hence, in studying the Passion to discover "what happened," we must reckon with the interpretations and insights of believers who felt something wondrous had happened to them because of the death of Jesus.

Thus, while the Passion account can be read as an exercise in "what happened" historically, these chapters also bring us theologically to the center of the gospels, and indeed of the whole New Testament. D. E. Nineham, who has published a commentary on Mark for lay people, likes to describe Mark's Gospel, in a homely phrase, as "rather like a tadpole—a large head with a comparatively short tail." He goes on to explain:

> The head of the Gospel is . . . the Passion Narrative—the account of the last few days in Jerusalem when Jesus suffered and died. Here is the heart of the Gospel, its center of gravity . . . not only has Mark given to the passion the position of pre-eminence and climax in the Gospel—he has selected and arranged the rest of his material that, for all its importance, it is seen to be subordinate to what happened in Jerusalem . . . practically everything . . . is in some way introductory to the passion of Jesus; the aim throughout is quite single-minded—to help the reader see Jesus on the Cross.[1]

What Nineham says of Mark applies to the other gospels too. In each of them—Matthew, Luke, and John—the Passion is not "a tail that wags the dog," but "the head of the tadpole," around which the rest of the structure takes shape. The gospels are pre-eminently about "Jesus on the cross."

This judgment of a New Testament historian concerning the gospels is also shared by theologians when they appraise Christianity as a whole: the Passion and death of Jesus (interpreted, of course, by faith, in light of the resurrection) is the heart of the Gospel. To keep the "tadpole" analogy, it is the head of the Christian religion. It is the source for Christianity. Emil Brunner wrote, "He who understands the Cross aright . . . understands the Bible, he understands Jesus Christ." Luther referred to the text about the cross, "He bore our sins" (Isaiah 53:4; I Peter 2:24; cf. Matthew 8:17), as "the foundation upon which stands the whole of the New Testament or the Gospel, as that which alone distinguishes us and our religion from all other religions."[2] This is likewise the view of the New Testament, that Jesus' suffering which culminates in a cross, is the touchstone, the heart of it all.

The Death of Jesus as the Center of the Gospels

That the death of Jesus was the center of the Gospel (or kerygma), we have already seen. Paul and the other early missionaries came preaching "Christ crucified" (I Corinthians 1:23).

Their effort was to publicly portray or placard before men's eyes "Jesus Christ on the cross" (Galatians 3:1)—just as Professor Nineham says was to be the aim of the later evangelists.

If we turn to the gospel tradition (or "Jesus-material"), the picture is much the same. It is not merely that the kerygma, with its emphasis on the cross, provided a foundation or frame for all the "Jesus-material." There was also, as far back as we can see in primitive Christianity, some sort of sustained and continuous account of Jesus' arrest, his condemnation by the Jewish Sanhedrin and the Roman governor, and then the journey to the cross, and finally his death. Such a "core" narrative about the most important sequence of events in world history, so far as early Christians were concerned, would have been told and retold, with ever new appreciation and insights. Some who have studied the matter in great detail are convinced, in fact, that several such cycles of Passion narrative were in existence, in each of the great centers of Christianity, long before Mark wrote down a single word. One cycle might have narrated the Passion as it was recollected at Jerusalem, another as it was recited at Antioch, or Ephesus, or some other Christian center. The possibility that these several Passion cycles existed, even prior to the time of the evangelists, would help explain why our written gospels differ in emphases and details, as we shall see.

A clear example of how the gospel tradition of Jesus' sayings has preserved a Passion account is the series of Passion "predictions" at Mark 8:31; 9:31; and 10:33-34 (with parallels in Matthew and Luke).[3] That there are three of them reflects a favorite numerical pattern from the ancient world. That they are spaced at about equal intervals (in our numbering, about a chapter apart) is probably the work of Mark. (It is just coincidence, however, that the modern verse numbers in each chapter, 31, 31, 33-34, form a pattern.) We are scarcely accustomed to thinking of these verses as Passion *narratives* because they appear on Jesus' lips as *predictions;* 8:31, for example, says:

> He began to teach them [the disciples] that the Son of man must suffer many things, and be rejected by the elders and the chief priests and the scribes, and be killed, and after three days rise again.

But if the longest of the Passion "predictions" at 10:33-34 is read with attention to the key words (italicized below), it becomes apparent that we have a skeleton outline for the events of the last days of Jesus' life:

> Behold, we are going up to *Jerusalem;* and the Son of man will be *delivered* to the *chief priests and the scribes,* and they will *condemn* him to death, and deliver him to the *Gentiles;* and they will *mock* him, and *spit upon* him, and *scourge* him, and *kill* him; and after three days he will *rise.*

The gospel tradition, like the basic Gospel, was thus concerned with Jesus' Passion.

Finally, the evangelists, in putting the Gospel and the "Jesus-material" together, likewise made the death of Jesus central. The Passion can be seen to be the chief thing in the outline of the gospels even statistically. Roughly a sixth to a third of each gospel is devoted to Jesus' last days in Jerusalem, so that, as it has been claimed, the gospels are essentially Passion stories with extended introductions. Matthew provides an excellent example of the proportions according to which an evangelist assigned space to what he deemed significant. All the centuries prior to Jesus are hurried over in part of a chapter (Matthew 1:1-17). Jesus' birth and infancy are covered in a chapter and a half (1:18—2:23). The year or more of his public ministry in Galilee (including Matthew's extensive collections of sermons and teachings) occupy sixteen chapters (chapters 3-18), and the journey to Jerusalem takes up two more. But eight chapters (chapters 21-28) are then devoted to the final week in Jerusalem (some of them very long chapters, at that), and the closer we come to the end, the more detailed the account becomes. Matthew 26 and 27 (the longest chapters in the book) give us an almost hour-by-hour account from the time of Jesus' arrest until his burial. It is not enough to say that Matthew had inherited an abundance of material on the Passion. He himself, like all other early Christians, saw the cross as central. The very statistics of the structure of his gospel make clear where he wants to put the emphasis.

The same thing is true as far as climax goes. Our gospels are constructed so as to reach their dramatic climax in the cross. Surely a high spot (if not *the* climax for all the Synoptics) is the confession of the Roman centurion on guard duty at Calvary, "Truly this man was God's son" (Mark 15:39 and par.). In fact, Mark makes the crucifixion scene so important that he drops the curtain on his story with virtually no emphasis on the resurrection appearances (see 16:8, the end of Mark in the oldest manuscripts).

The Gospel, the "Jesus-material," and the evangelists, then, all make the cross central. To this list could be added other elements which stress the same centrality of the cross of Jesus Christ: the early Christian creeds (note how the Second Article of the Apostles' Creed centers in Jesus' suffering and death); the sacraments (we are baptized "into his death," Romans 6:3; the Lord's Supper proclaims Jesus' death, I Corinthians 11:26); and even ethics and daily life—the disciple is not greater than his master, he who would follow Jesus must deny self and *take up his cross* (Mark 8:34); Paul's existence was dominated by the motto, "I have been crucified with Christ" (Galatians 2:20), and the Christian missionary is one who is "always carrying in the body the death of Jesus" (II Corinthians 4:10). In short, wherever we look, the centrality of the cross is to be seen. It is the starting point even for a study of the life of Jesus, both historically (in terms of fullest sources) and theologically (in terms of central meaning).

Two points need to be kept in mind, however, when examining the Passion accounts and their meaning. The one is rather obvious and has already been alluded to: the story of Jesus' suffering and death is always told *in the light of the resurrection.* What is said of the last days and hours of Jesus' earthly life is told with the full confidence that he now shares eternal life with God and reigns supreme. This conviction, that Jesus is lord and has triumphed even over death, is never allowed, however, to turn the Passion story into mere "play acting," as if Jesus were a "divine robot," "going through the motions" of suffering, and pretending to die. A stark realism, that here a genuine man was put to death on a cruel instrument of torture, deserted by his friends and tempted to deny his God and his mission, appears again and again in our gospel records, even though all this is being recounted from the later perspective of the resurrection. The only way to read these records is as the story of a real human being who "has suffered and been tempted," who tasted "the suffering of death" (Hebrews 2:18; 2:9)—even though faith sees, better than any contemporary of his, who he was and that God "saw him through" the uttermost extremities of human existence.

The other point is less obvious and requires some explaining. It is the fact that early Christians felt they had to *explain the death* of Jesus, whereas they simply *declared the resurrection.* This view is in sharp contrast to the modern notion that the Passion is something which can be factually recounted but one must struggle to explain the resurrection. We are so familiar with the idea that *"Christ* [i.e., the Messiah] died," we are scarcely aware how unexpected and offensive such tidings were to Jewish ears and how nonsensical to the Greek mind. How could the death of a man in Jerusalem be "good news?" Especially when he was merely a poor Jew from Galilee, or was one said to be the Messiah but had died in a way in which usually only slaves and rebels were put to death—on a cross. To proclaim such a ludicrous figure as "the one ordained by God to be judge of the living and the dead" (Acts 10:42) or as the lord of all "through whom we exist" (I Corinthians 8:6) demanded some pretty tall explaining. The whole business would be something like trying to proclaim as savior today some wild-eyed pretender from an "underdeveloped country" or an unlettered rabble-rouser who had been hit by a garbage truck and died ignominiously.

A Jew of the day might have asked, "How could the messiah come from Nazareth? Why did God let Jesus die if he was messiah?" The Gentile might say tauntingly, "If Jesus is all you say, why did he live in Palestine, of all places? On what grounds could such a person as this teacher be condemned to death? And how could a crucifixion effect such results as you claim—forgiveness of sins, and all that?" Such were the sort of questions which early Christians faced and to which they had to reply. To the *risen Lord* each of them could testify from his own experience. The *crucified Jesus* was a fact of history which they had to explain. So it was that kerygma to a limited extent, and the gospel tradition and the evangelists to a greater degree, bent their efforts to retelling the Passion story in such a way that would help answer these questions and overcome objections. When we "listen in" on New Testament witness about the cross, it is not, then, just historical reporting that we hear. Men are talking about what is central for their faith, in such a way that the questions of "unfaith" are clarified.

At this point we need to remind ourselves that the gospel narratives about Jesus' Passion and death are not just another chapter of "Profiles in Courage"—although magnificent courage was exhibited by Jesus. Nor are we afforded a glimpse of just another in the long series of martyrs who were faithful to God—though Luke in particular likes to bring out similarities between Jesus'

death and that of other martyrs (compare Luke 23:34 with Acts
7:60). We are not even simply viewing "the greatest tragedy of
the ages." The gospels intend us to see that Jesus' death "made
things different" between God and man, so that in the drama of
the cross a new way of access to the Father was created (Romans
5:2; Ephesians 2:18), through the blood of Jesus shed for men.
The technical name for this is "atonement," and, just as in Paul's
letters or Acts, so in the gospels the concern is to show how God
and man were made to be "at one" through Jesus' death. We
must remember, however, that nowhere in the New Testament is
the meaning of the cross confined to any single "doctrine of atonement"; at best there are pictures, such as the image of "justification" in terms of a law court (Romans 3:21-26) or "reconcilia-
tion" in terms of personal relationships (II Corinthians 5:17-21).
In the gospels we must expect these "pictures" to be worked into
the narrative itself. But there will be hints of the meaning of
Jesus' death, woven into the Passion narrative as early Christians
told it.

Before turning to the detailed Passion narratives in our New
Testament gospels, we may help ourselves to see the forest as a
whole (before looking at the individual trees) if we note something in general about early Christian accounts of Jesus' suffering
and death. I Corinthians 15:3b-5 has rightly been called the oldest
written account, because it provides a balanced (four-line) poetic
structure that goes back prior even to A.D. 55 when Paul wrote
these words in Greek, goes back seemingly to the earliest Aramaic-
speaking Christians in Palestine.[4]
The passage runs:

> [We believe]
> that Christ *died* for our sins in accordance with the scriptures,
>   that he *was buried*,
> that he *was raised* on the third day in accordance with the scriptures,
>   and that he *appeared* to Cephas, then to the twelve.

It can be seen at a glance that each line has a key verb in it
(italicized above) (died, was buried, was raised, appeared), and
that lines one and three balance each other neatly (each has "according to the scriptures" while "for our sins" parallels the phrase
"on the third day"). Somewhat to our surprise we see that almost
nothing is said about the "when" or "by whom" or even "how"
Jesus' death occurred; it is the "why" that matters: Christ died

"for our sins," in accord with God's will (this is the import of "according to the scriptures"). This summary of the Passion, it may be further noted, connects it with the resurrection (nothing is said of Jesus' life and ministry), and it affirms that *"Christ* [the Messiah] *died,"* a teaching familiar perhaps to our ears but strange to hearers then, for the idea of the death of the messiah for sins is difficult to find in the Old Testament—yet here it is said to be "in accordance with the scriptures." We can suppose that Paul and his hearers had certain Old Testament chapters in mind, and that, as the Passion narrative was later retold, there would be attempts to draw out this scriptural background in more detail. It can also be guessed that such a skeletal outline of the Passion would raise questions such as "when" and "at whose hand" Christ died.

The Passion predictions in the Synoptic Gospels (noted above) told of Jesus' death in more detail and in a way intended to answer some of these questions. If all nine forms of these predictions are put together, we get a more complete outline of the Passion. "Jerusalem" is mentioned as the place. It is explained that the Son of man *"must"* suffer— literally, "it is necessary that . . . ," implying a divine necessity, as part of God's plan, discerned in the Old Testament prophets (cf. Luke 18:31). His enemies are named as "chief priests and scribes" and as "the Gentiles" (Romans).

A fuller outline, drawing on the Marcan predictions, appears as follows:

	FIRST PROPHECY	SECOND PROPHECY	THIRD PROPHECY
Handed over to chief priests, scribes	—	Mark 9:31	Mark 10:33
Jewish trial—"rejected"	Mark 8:31	—	—
"condemned"	—	—	Mark 10:33
Handed over to the Romans	—	—	Mark 10:33
"Suffer many things"	Mark 8:31	—	—
Maltreated (mocked, scourged, etc.)	—	—	Mark 10:34
Executed (by the Romans)	Mark 8:31	Mark 9:31	Mark 10:34
Resurrection	Mark 8:31	Mark 9:31	Mark 10:34

Here is a basic account as it might have been told by some of the earliest Christians: "At Jerusalem, according to God's plan, the

Son of man is handed over (or betrayed), rejected by the Jewish leadership; he is maltreated and is killed by the Romans, but God raises him up on the third day."

It will be noted, however, that even this relatively fuller account would prompt still more questions. Who arrested Jesus? What of his betrayer? (Only Matthew 27:3-10 tells us of the death of Judas as part of the Passion narrative.) What were Jesus' legal trials like? (Only Luke 23:6-16 has a hearing before Herod Antipas, only John 19:1-15 a private interview with Pilate.) It was in the interest of answering such questions that each evangelist drew in whatever material was available to him and framed his story of the Passion, to meet the needs of those who would read his gospel. We may therefore expect that in our finished gospels each evangelist will reflect his own use of the Old Testament (especially strong in Matthew), his own apologetic interests (Matthew tends to be anti-Jewish at points), his own dramatic touches (compare Luke 22:43-44 or John 13:30), and at times didactic pointers which interest him (Luke 23:34 is an example par excellence of what forgiveness should be).

Thus we find our gospel stories of Jesus' Passion to have been built up from a basic proclamation about Jesus' death which goes back to the kerygma, plus Passion narratives which were part of the "Jesus tradition," plus other sayings and stories which the evangelists each know, plus, finally, reflections from the Old Testament and influences from the world in which the evangelists lived. We must not expect Matthew to tell his story just as Mark does, nor Luke as either of them, to say nothing of the Fourth Gospel.

A chart will help us see the overall picture before we look more closely at the Jewish and Roman trials and the crucifixion scene. The Synoptic Gospels narrate these incidents:

	MARK	MATTHEW	LUKE
The arrest of Jesus	14:43-52	26:47-56	22:47-53
Jewish Trial			
Jesus before the Sanhedrin	14:53-65	26:57-68	22:54*a*, 63-71
Peter's denial	14:54, 66-72	26:58, 69-75	22:54*b*-62
Delivered to Pilate	15:1	27:1-2	23:1
(Death of Judas)	——	27:3-10	——

Roman Trial

Jesus before Pilate	15:2-5	27:11-14	23:2-5
(Before Herod)	——	——	23:6-16
Sentenced by Pilate	15:6-15	27:15-26	23:17-25
Mocked by soldiers	15:16-20	27:27-31	——

Calvary

The road to the cross	15:21	27:32	23:26-32
The crucifixion	15:22-32	27:33-44	23:33-43
The death of Jesus	15:33-41	27:45-56	23:44-49
The burial of Jesus	15:42-47	27:57-61	23:50-56
(The guard at the tomb)	——	27:62-66	——

A broad agreement is apparent. But certain incidents (in parentheses above), like the "Death of Judas," appear in one gospel only. Even where all three gospels roughly parallel each other, there are often differences within a section. For example, Luke avoids any mention of a trial before the Sanhedrin at night and recounts Peter's denial before the Sanhedrin trial, not after it. If John's witness is added, the same sort of result occurs again: some broad agreements, and some even sharper differences, if not contradictions.

Even when all four accounts are utilized to the fullest extent, riddles and unanswered questions remain. A famous problem is that of date.[5] Many scholars feel that April 7, A.D. 30 fits all the evidence best as the time of the first Good Friday. But Ethelbert Stauffer's "life of Jesus" argues for April 3, A.D. 33, and others would place the crucifixion as early as A.D. 27 or 28. A similar chronological problem is the hour of the day when Jesus was placed upon the cross. Mark 15:25 says, "it was the third hour [9 A.M. by the Jewish reckoning], when they crucified him." John 19:14 maintains it was not until about the sixth hour that sentence was passed, i.e., around noon, a chronology followed to this day in widespread Good Friday three-hour services, from 12 to 3 P.M. Various attempts have been made to explain or reconcile the two statements. A distinguished Roman Catholic scholar has become convinced that the best solution is to regard 15:25 as a later insertion into Mark.[6] The truth of the matter is that it is hard for us to be dogmatic about chronological details, even in this best documented day in Jesus' life, since the earliest sources were interested in the "what" and not the "when."

The same thing holds for many of the other questions which we should like answered—the charges against Jesus, the trial procedure, the motives of Judas, and even the much debated legal question of whether a Jewish court had the right to put a man to death or whether only the Roman rulers could do that. At points we find it hard to tell where the prisoner Jesus was taken and when, and which of the mockery scenes occurred when. To all of these questions an attempt can be made by historians to give answers, but many times the evidence is fragmentary or the outcome remains uncertain. Such difficulties make it hard to deal with the further problems of guilt and even of anti-Semitism which have cropped up in many discussions of Jesus' Passion.[7]

Aware of such problems, however, and of how our Passion accounts were composed, we need not despair as we approach the center of early Christian witness and the richest, most detailed parts of the gospel records. However, we need to keep in mind that these witness accounts were not compiled to answer our historical questions, but to tell of "Jesus our Lord, who was put to death for our trespasses and raised for our justification" (Romans 4:25). They want us to see "Jesus on the cross," even if we cannot make out all the historical circumstances which led him there; they wish us to understand the cross, so that we understand the Bible and Jesus Christ.

The Arrest of Jesus and the "Jewish Trial"

With the seizure of Jesus by a crowd from the chief priests and elders at night in the garden called Gethsemane, just outside the walls of Jerusalem, the great epic of the Passion begins. A sustained narrative, with the Synoptic Gospels and John agreeing more closely than at any other point, the story moves on through Jewish and Roman trials to the dramatic crucifixion scene. We are accustomed to read along with this, as background, the narratives about Jesus' last meal with his disciples in the Upper Room and the scene of prayer in Gethsemane. But since the earliest Passion accounts seem to have begun with the arrest, there is reason to reserve these other passages for detailed treatment later on (see chapters 4 and 10) and to begin here with the arrest.

The action that follows is quite simple when reduced to its bare outline. The captive is first taken before the Jewish officials. They reach their decision against him and send him on to Pilate, who is in Jerusalem at Passover time. The Roman governor delivers him to be crucified, a Roman means of executing criminals, and the death penalty is swiftly inflicted. But when we look in detail at the accounts in our gospels, questions begin to arise. The most obvious one is: Why two trials, one ecclesiastical (by Jewish officials) based on charges of a religious nature, the other political (by the Roman governor) based on political charges? Further historical problems emerge in connection with each trial, but it is quite clear that the four gospels agree in assuming two such legal procedures, each involving a series of hearings or sessions, for the man from Nazareth.

It must be remembered that Palestine in A.D. 30 was a captive land. The independent Jewish government which had existed in Maccabean times had been swept away in the Roman occupation. Even the measure of autonomy which Herod the Great had enjoyed was now replaced by the rule of a Roman procurator, technically the *praefectus provinciae Judaeae,* subordinate only to the legate of Caesar in Syria; this procurator had power of life and death over those who dwelt in the province of Judea. Of course, the Roman government wisely allowed the local, native officials certain power and used existing political instruments, such as the Sanhedrin, an aristocratic Senate of priests and elders in Jerusalem which had possessed great authority among Jews from its inception about 200 B.C. Understandably the prisoner Jesus, charged with offenses against the Jewish law, would first and especially be subject to the decision of the Jewish Sanhedrin, but this body in turn was dependent, at least to some extent, on the support and concurrence of the real ruler of Palestine, Rome's representative, the governor.

At this point we are confronted with one of the still unresolved debates which plague the study of the trial of Jesus. Did the Sanhedrin have the power, at this time, to impose and carry out a death sentence? The Synoptics imply, and the Fourth Gospel plainly says, that it did not. When, according to John's Gospel, Pilate tells the Jews, "Judge Jesus in accordance with your law," they reply, "It is not lawful for us to put any man to death" (John 18:31). Here it is presupposed that Rome reserved this right for itself, through its governor; the Sanhedrin thus could not inflict the sentence of death on its own. On this basis, it is presumed that Jewish officials found Jesus worthy of death, but could not execute him. Pilate had to pronounce the death sentence, and so the Jewish leaders cleverly shifted the charges from religious ones (which Pilate might not bother with) to political ones of which any representative of Caesar had to take cognizance. Hence the two trials.

However, in the last fifty years, some scholars have interpreted the evidence differently. The Frenchman Juster argued in 1914 that the Sanhedrin did have the right to inflict the death penalty. In 1931 the German historian Hans Lietzmann combined this claim with the fact that there are some obvious difficulties in our accounts of the Jewish trial and the fact that Jesus was put to death in a Roman way, not by the Jewish method of stoning; Lietzmann claimed therefore that there never was any Sanhedrin trial—Jesus was seized, condemned, and executed solely by the Romans. On this view, the report of the Jewish trial in Mark 14:55-65 and par. is unhistorical. In a book published in 1961 a refugee scholar from Czechoslovakia now living in London, Paul Winter, carried Lietzmann's line of argument further and suggested a motive for the fabrication of the Sanhedrin trial. Christians in the fifties and sixties, he said, wanted to whitewash the Romans and transfer responsibility for Jesus' death to the Jews. The basis was not anti-Jewish feeling, however, but pro-Roman inclinations. Christians wanted to achieve a more cordial relationship with Roman officials. One way of gaining this was to exonerate the actions of the Roman governor Pilate, and this was done by suggesting that he was pushed to his decision by the Jewish priests, who had already tried and condemned Jesus.

Needless to say, there have been objections to this theory by other experts in Jewish law and in Roman government. The discussion is very complicated on the key question of whether the Sanhedrin could inflict the death sentence or not. To sample the evidence: in sources available to us there are four possible cases of executions under the authority of the Sanhedrin, but each one is susceptible to alternate interpretations.

1. Stephen was stoned after a hearing before the Sanhedrin (Acts 6:12—7:60). Or was this a lynching by mob action (see 7:54, 57-58)? Or was it a case of the Sanhedrin overstepping its legal competence? Or had the Sanhedrin received authority from Pilate to proceed against Christians in this way, perhaps due to the fact that Pilate was at that time on good terms with Caiaphas, the Jewish leader? All these explanations of the stoning have been proposed.

2. James the brother of Jesus was stoned to death in a persecution of Christians under the high priest Ananus in the year 62, according to the Jewish historian Josephus (*Ant.* 20.200)—but this occurred during a period of disorder, after the death of Porcius Festus, when there was no Roman governor in the land, and Ananus was later deposed because of this deed.

3. James the brother of John was killed about A.D. 44 (Acts 12:2), and Jewish sources say a priest's daughter named Imarta bath Tali was burned for unchastity[8]—but both incidents occurred under King Herod Agrippa I (A.D. 41-44) when for a brief time there was a "Jewish state."

4. The Sanhedrin had the right to execute on the spot any Gentiles caught violating the temple grounds, as an inscription proves[9]—but this refers to Gentiles committing a well-defined sacrilege, not to Jews guilty of some other crime.

Along with these four cases is to be considered an incident during the period when Albinus was procurator (A.D. 62-64). A "prophet of doom," named Jesus, son of Ananus (not the high priest mentioned above), was taken into custody by the Jewish leaders, scourged, and then turned over to the Romans, presumably to be executed. This incident, reported by Josephus in his *Jewish War* 6.300-309, suggests that the Jews lacked power to condemn a man to death and carry out the execution. Also injected into the discussion is a statement preserved from Jewish tradition in the Talmud to the effect that "forty years before the destruction of the temple, jurisdiction over life and death was taken away" from the Jews. The number "forty" is an inexact, round number, probably meaning a generation, but the reference to the destruction of the temple in A.D. 70 makes the statement sound more precise chronologically. Some investigators think the statement refers to what happened in A.D. 6, roughly a generation before A.D. 70: the Jews lost their full juridical power when Judea became a province in the Roman empire, governed by a procurator.

Finally other pieces of evidence have been adduced in order to support the claim that John 18:31 is factually correct, and that the Jews did not, in Jesus' day, have the right to execute the death penalty. The story of the woman taken in adultery, reported in many manuscripts at John 7:53—8:11, is one case claimed as relevant. (Even though the story may not have originally stood at that point in John's composition, the pericope is an early tradition of some importance.) The story concerns a married woman (not an engaged girl, in the opinion of several exegetes) and describes a scene on the way from a court hearing, after she has been condemned to die; the court members are leading her out to her execution, in accord with Jewish custom. The question addressed to Jesus when this procession meets him—"Teacher, this woman has been caught in the act of adultery. Now in the law Moses commanded *us* to stone such. What do you say about her?" (John 8:4-5, italics added)—is then, on this interpretation, really one about the legal rights of the Jews under the Roman occupation. Opponents are attempting to put the teacher from Galilee on the spot, just as with the question about the tribute money (Mark 12:41-44 and par.): "this they said to test him, that they might have some charge to bring against him" (John 8:6). If Jesus says the sentence should be carried out by the Jews, then he is unmasked in Roman eyes as a revolutionist, advocating defiance of Roman authority. If he says no, that they should not execute her, then he would make himself unpopular with his own people. In this way John 7:53—8:11 is assumed to show that the Jews did not have the *ius gladii* or "power of the sword" during the lifetime of Jesus—if the story, attached at this point in some manuscripts and to the Gospel of Luke in others, can be assumed to reflect accurately historical details from the period.

The last bit of evidence we note here on this debated issue is a reference in a Mishna tractate, the "Fasting Scroll" (*Megillat Taanith*), a Jewish document that tells when fasting is commanded and when it need not be observed. The scroll explains that Elul (= August/September) 22 is a national holiday, on which there need be no fasting, because "on the seventeenth of the month the Romans withdrew from Jerusalem" (a reference to the surrender of the Roman cohort in Jerusalem to Jewish forces in September of A.D. 66), and then more specifically because "on the twenty-second of the month the killing of evildoers began again"—i.e., on Elul 22, the Jews again had power to execute those who broke the law, after having been deprived of this power during the whole period from A.D. 6 to 66. So runs another argument for the correctness of the contention of John 18:31 that at the time of Jesus' trial it was not lawful for Jewish authorities to execute someone who broke their laws.

To sum up a net impression from all these clues, we may say that the evidence does not demonstrate in a clear-cut way that the Sanhedrin had power to put offenders to death. More likely, Jewish officials seized such power in isolated cases, but were subject to the Roman governor when he was there. This is to say that in the case of Jesus there no doubt was a Jewish trial or hearing of some sort, followed by a Roman trial where the official sentence was pronounced, because only the governor had such power. We may conclude that some Jewish officials reached a decision that Jesus should be killed, but the execution was carried out by the Roman rulers, and that, perhaps for political reasons rather than any religious accusations which were of concern to Jews. But there are clearly problems in determining exactly what happened at each stage of the trials.

A bird's-eye view of the steps from the time of the arrest of Jesus until he was turned over to Pilate will help us follow the sequence and spot the problems. Major changes made by Luke and John in the sequence reported by Mark and Matthew are indicated by arrows.

	MARK 14	MATTHEW 26	LUKE 22	JOHN 18
Jesus arrested	vss. 43-52	vss. 47-56	vss. 47-53	vss. 2-12
				13-23 to Annas
To the high priest	53-54	57-58	54a	24
The priests seek evidence	55-56	59-60		—
"He destroys the temple"	57-59	60-61		cf. 2:19
The high priest gets a "confession"	60-62	62-64	(67-70)	—
The verdict: death	63-64	65-66	(71)	—
Jesus is mocked	65	67-68	63-65	—
Peter's denial	66-72	69-75	54b-62	18:15-18, 25-27
			Trial, 66-71	
The morning session	15:1	27:1-2	cf. 22:66-23:1	18:28

As can be seen immediately, Mark and Matthew agree closely. They state that a night trial before the Jewish Sanhedrin followed Jesus' arrest. The trial ended with the verdict "He deserves death," after the high priest himself had confronted Jesus and succeeded in getting him to utter "blasphemy." However, both Mark and Matthew suffer from the difficulty that, after this decision has been reached at night, the council or Sanhedrin seems to meet again, as soon as it was morning, to decide on Jesus' death.

7 Luke has what in many ways is a much more logical picture. The prisoner is arrested and mocked by the soldiers during the night hours, during which time also Peter denies that he knows Jesus. Then, "when day came" (22:66), the Sanhedrin met and tried Jesus. Luke thus has only *one* session of the Sanhedrin and avoids a night meeting. He also abbreviates the Jewish trial considerably, though he then gives the Roman trial and its charges in greater detail. Some claim that Luke has simply used his common sense and retold the Jewish trial along the lines of historical probability. Others feel he had a more accurate special source which is to be preferred to what Matthew and Mark report here.

John blurs the Jewish trial even more. Jesus is not taken to the Sanhedrin (as in Mark and Matthew), nor is he held captive by soldiers all night (as in Luke), but he is brought first to the home of Annas, the father-in-law of Caiaphas (18:13), then to the high priest Caiaphas (18:24), then to the governor at the praetorium (18:28). In this way any trial before the full Sanhedrin seems excluded. In fact, the chief interrogation (18:19-23) seems to take place before Annas and not before Caiaphas at all, and Peter's denial occurs at the home of Annas, not in the courtyard of the high priest Caiaphas. Luther noted these discrepancies and was inclined to prefer the Synoptic version. To get a smoother order of events, he even proposed rearranging the order of the verses in John (as one Syriac manuscript was subsequently discovered to have done!).[10]

It is, one must admit, impossible to fit all the evidence in the gospels together without preferring one version over another at certain points. A working conclusion might be that after Jesus was arrested he was subject to examination by Jewish officials, in something like a grand jury action, but we must be very hesitant about pinpointing precisely at what hour this occurred or about listing who was involved. Now on to the details which we can recover from this confused night that began in a garden and ended on the way to a Roman judge.

The basic account commences with the betrayal of Jesus. The Synoptic versions present a series of vivid, disjointed impressions of the action, such as often characterize unexpected events at night. Evidently, Judas knew where Jesus would go to pray when he left the Upper Room, and led a crowd armed with swords and clubs, sent by the chief priests, scribes, and elders. The garden on the Mount of Olives, east of the city wall, may have been a favorite retreat for Jesus and his friends (cf. Luke 22:39). Judas approached Jesus with the usual greeting of a disciple to his rabbi—a kiss. Only this time it was the symbol to his new henchmen, "This is the man, seize him."

The evangelists show us Jesus reproaching his enemies for one brief moment: "Have you come out with weapons, at night, to take me as if I were a robber, when I was accessible day after day in the temple?" But he submits with the words, "Let the scriptures be fulfilled," as if to tell us that the hand of God is foreshadowed even in this. For a moment there is a show of force. One of the men with Jesus—Mark has the curious phrase, "One definite man, someone," as if he knew it was Peter but doesn't want to identify him—strikes off the ear of the slave of the high priest. Luke makes it the *right* ear, and John gives the slave's name as Malchus (18:10). John also states that Peter struck the blow. Matthew adds a word of reproach to the swordsman (26: 52-54), and Luke reports that Jesus healed the ear (22:51)—the only such miracle in the whole Passion narrative. But the net result is that the disciples, all of them, forsake Jesus and run away. (The evangelists are quite candid in portraying the actions of the disciples.)

Mark alone inserts at this moment a perplexing comment that there was one young man following Jesus who didn't get away so easily (14:51-52). The crowd seized him, but he wriggled out of the linen cloth they grabbed, and ran away unclothed. All sorts of symbolic meanings have been seen in the incident—a reference to the "Day of the Lord" (cf. Amos 2:16, where it is said that on that day "he who is stout of heart . . . shall flee away naked"), or a figure of the resurrection (Jesus was wrapped for burial in the same kind of linen cloth, Mark 15:46, but escaped from his captor, Death, leaving the cloth behind, cf. John 20:6). All sorts of guesses have been made identifying the young man as John, or James the brother of Jesus, or young John Mark at whose mother's house the Last Supper may have been eaten and who could have followed Jesus into the night. If this last guess is correct, Mark would have been a witness to Jesus' arrest.

It is worth asking who it was that seized Jesus in this way. The Synoptics speak of a crowd with swords and clubs sent by the temple officials. John, however, refers to "a band of soldiers"

(18:3) and even to their captain (18:12). This has led to the supposition that Roman soldiery as well as a Jewish mob was involved in the arrest. The word translated "band of soldiers" meant specifically a cohort, the tenth part of a legion, though its normal complement of 600 men seems exceptionally large for such an action and the word could also be applied to the temple police. We dare not think of the group which took Jesus captive as just a mob. At the least, temple police with swords were there (cf. Luke 22:4, 52), and it is even possible the Romans had been tipped off and were involved. (It is striking that Pilate was ready and available to hear the case early the next morning. Perhaps he knew more of the matter than we commonly suppose.)

What Judas betrayed is also a topic which has intrigued readers of the Passion story. Albert Schweitzer thought it was a secret teaching of Jesus that he claimed to be the messiah. Others feel it was Jesus' words about destroying the temple, which crop up during his trial. Some claim that Judas simply offered Jesus' enemies a place and opportunity where he could be seized without causing a commotion. Judas' motives are wrapped in even greater obscurity. Greed for money is often cited as a reason (Mark 14:11). But the attempt has also been made to portray Judas as a loyal follower of Jesus who was dissatisfied because his master's cause wasn't progressing rapidly enough. He thought that if he could put Jesus "on the spot" and force his hand, then Jesus would work some spectacular miracle that would win the day— and Judas would be a hero for having promoted this. Unfortunately our gospel records are not interested in such matters of motive and psychology, and the only answer ever really given is a theological one advanced by Luke 22:3, "Satan entered in Judas called Iscariot." Here again it is assumed that more than human powers were contending in the Passion drama.

One other word ought to be noted in the scene where Jesus is taken captive. "Have you come out as against a *robber?*" Jesus asks (Mark 14:48). His question implies that he is being treated like one, even though his conduct as teacher in the temple was just the opposite. The Greek word here can denote "revolutionist" or "rebel," and raises the possibility that Jesus was regarded in Roman eyes as a political menace, the sort of revolutionary leader in which Palestine abounded.

Jesus was led away to a hearing by Jewish officials. As previously explained, it is hard to tell where this trial took place and whether it was by night (Mark, Matthew) or at daybreak (Luke). Mark 14:53 says he was taken "to the high priest," with whom "all the chief priests and the elders and the scribes were assembled"—i.e., the Sanhedrin. Matthew 26:57 identifies the chief priest as Caiaphas, but John 18:12 ff. places the interrogation before Annas, his father-in-law. If we harmonized all these accounts, the result would be a preliminary hearing before Annas, a trial before Caiaphas and the Sanhedrin at night, and a further Sanhedrin session at the crack of dawn, although even this combination would still disagree with what Luke describes, namely a *single* session when it was day. All this is a staggering amount of legal hearings to crowd in between midnight and 6 A.M., and those who wish to fit all the accounts together are forced to make the night session a sort of "preliminary hearing" and the dawn session the official action when all the Sanhedrin members were present. A difficulty with this is that Mark and Matthew present all their details of the Jewish trial under the *night* meeting, whereas Luke places the examination of Jesus in the *daytime* session. And if we move the Jewish trial too late in the day, we crowd the schedule for all the events which must take place before Jesus is nailed to the cross at 9 A.M. or noon.

There are still further problems in our accounts. A good many features in the Synoptic story of the trial do not fit with what we know of Jewish legal procedures at this time. According to Jewish sources, a trial involving the death penalty could take place only by day, never at night. The sentence could be pronounced only at a second session, the next day (and the Jewish day began at sundown). The Sanhedrin's regular meeting place was in a hall at the temple, but it is unlikely that the strictest leaders of the nation would have assembled there on the eve of a festival—or anywhere else if it was the sacred night of the Passover as Mark 14:12-16 reports. Finally there is the statement that Jesus is convicted on the grounds that he has uttered blasphemy by claiming to be the messiah (Mark 14:64). But in Judaism, it was no crime to claim to be messiah; blasphemy was strictly a matter of misuse of Yahweh's name—a charge which was not leveled against Jesus.

Of course, all our Jewish sources on these points come from a later date in the second century A.D. or so, and the attempt has been made to claim that in Jesus' day the Sadducees ran things under a different set of rules from those later recorded by the Pharisees and their descendants. But, if anything, Sadducean customs may have been more strict, not less, on such points. It has also been argued that there were two Sanhedrins—one political, a Roman tool, which condemned Jesus; the other religious, which had nothing to do with the trial. But this distinction is unconvincing. Nor is there any real claim in the New Testament reports that Jesus' case was regarded as so extraordinary that the Sanhedrin willfully departed from its own rules. We are left with the conclusion that our New Testament accounts do not square with Jewish legal practice as we know it.

A final difficulty which has often been discussed is how the New Testament evangelists could have known what went on within the walls of the Jewish courtroom. None of them were eyewitnesses. At best Peter was cringing in a dark courtyard outside. A traditional answer has been that some Sanhedrin member like Joseph of Arimathea or Nicodemus, who were friendly to Jesus and perhaps later became Christians (cf. Mark 15:43, John 3:1), passed on word of what happened. This is highly conjectural, and if such is the correct explanation, these reports from inside the Sanhedrin, recounted orally over the years, must still have been subject to many influences and even changes until written down in our gospels in the variety of forms which we must try to fit together. An alternate theory is that the accounts of the Jewish trial arose wholly within the post-resurrection church, without any "historical source"; this theory, of course, holds especially for those who deny that there ever was a Jewish trial. A minimal admission by those who posit such a trial is that our gospel records of Jesus' trial reflect at many points the views of the Christian community, and these records do not answer satisfactorily all the questions which we may care to put.

What stands out is that the gospels all want to portray Jesus as what they believed him to be—messiah and Son of God—throughout his interrogation by the Jews, and they want to show the responsibility of the Jewish authorities in putting him to death. Mark 15:1 may give the tersest and most basic account:

> And straightway, early in the morning, the chief priests together with the elders and the scribes, indeed the whole Sanhedrin, held a council session; having bound Jesus, they led him away and turned him over to Pilate.

Details which expand on this brief summary are, for the reasons outlined above, difficult for the historian to recover.

At certain points, however, a few historical notes do illumine the biblical text for us. Annas was high priest from A.D. 6/7 to 15, Joseph Caiaphas from about 18 to 36. The office was traditionally supposed to be for life (Numbers 35:25), but in Jesus' day tenure depended on Roman favor.[11] Annas and his son-in-law must have mastered well the art of getting along with their Roman overlords. The priestly family of Annas and Caiaphas was doubtless involved in Jesus' trial somehow.

The trial was marked by the appearance of false witnesses (Mark 14:55-56). The old Jewish rule that a crime must be proved on the evidence of two or three witnesses (Deuteronomy 19:15) was evidently followed. About 100 B.C., the practice had arisen of interrogating these witnesses *separately*, so as to avoid collusion between them (such as Daniel exposes in the story of Susanna in the Apocrypha, verses 28, 34, 45 ff.). Some rabbis like Johanan ben Zakkai were famous for their acute cross-examination of witnesses. On the assumption that the Marcan account of the trial is basically accurate, it has been argued that at Mark 14: 56-59 it was members of the Sanhedrin itself who exposed the falsity of this witness against Jesus,[12] for Jesus himself was silent throughout the trial (14:61). The gospels never openly claim that the Sanhedrin conducted a "kangaroo court," or was unfair. Mark may here reflect the fact that some witnesses against Jesus were refuted by the council members themselves.

The charge at Mark 14:58 (par. Matthew 26:61) is harder to deal with: "We heard him say, 'I will destroy the temple of God and build it in three days.' " Mark calls it "false witness" which "did not agree." But Jesus *did* say something of this sort (see Mark 13:2; 15:29; Acts 6:14). John 2:19-22 interprets such a saying as referring to "the temple of his body" and the resurrection, and perhaps to his body the church, which would replace the old temple of the Jews in Jerusalem (cf. Ephesians 2:19-22). We are dealing here with something the historical Jesus said about a physical temple of stone, the fuller meaning of which was seen by the early church after the resurrection. It scarcely provided a legal basis for a verdict of guilty.

The verdict came, according to our accounts, only after the high priest took matters into his own hands and asked, "Are you the Christ, the Son of God?" Jesus' answer is ambiguous:

Mark 14:62	Matthew 26:64	Luke 22:70
I am	You have said so	You say that I am

However, it is declared blasphemous, and he is judged worthy of death.

Before he is led off to Pilate we are treated to a scene where apparently the members of the Sanhedrin and their attendants mock Jesus, spit on him, and slap him. Of the several times that Jesus is mocked in the Passion narrative, this is the one where he is treated as a prophet and scorned. They blindfold him (Luke 22: 64) and then say, "Prophesy! Who is it that struck you?"

In looking at these verses on the Jewish trial we have bypassed the well-known story of Peter's denial, which is intertwined with it, either before or after the Sanhedrin trial. All four gospels have the story and agree that three times Peter denied knowing Jesus and that then a cock crew,[13] reminding him of a prophecy by Jesus predicting his unfaithfulness. Luke 22:61 heightens the drama by having "the Lord" look on Peter in this moment of anguish. It seems idle to labor the point that Mark refers to *two* cock crows, and that the gospels vary on who quizzes Peter. While this story is scarcely essential to the Passion narrative itself, and does not help us learn what went on inside at the Jewish trial, it is the sort of picture of the "Prince of the Apostles," Peter, that later Christians would scarcely invent. Many students of the gospels feel that here, if anywhere, we have a genuine reminiscence from Peter.

Memories of eyewitnesses (Peter's denial, perhaps John Mark in the garden of Gethsemane), staccato impressions of the arrest, reports of the Jewish trials and hearings not written up until some time after they occurred, all of this passed on some fifty years by Christians and used in preaching and teaching about their lord, and then combined in varying ways by four different evangelists —such are our Passion accounts. It would be a rash man who would put his finger on each item and say "historical fact" or "false." What comes through unquestionably is a powerful picture of the man from Nazareth, deserted by his friends, hailed before the highest authorities of his people, yet still comporting himself with quiet dignity and authority. This, in spite of the many details which historical study must leave unsettled.

The aims of the gospels in these accounts are (1) to confess Jesus as messiah and Son of God and (2) to portray the involvement in his fate of the Jewish leaders (specifically the chief priests, scribes, and elders; the Pharisees are virtually never noted). All too often, subsequent Christians have failed to make this first confession their own, and have overstressed "Jewish guilt" in such a way that anti-Semitism resulted and persecution so harsh as that under the Nazis became possible.

In the New Testament there is already some tendency to stress the innocence of Pilate and the Romans at the expense of the Jews. The Synoptics usually implicate only the priestly rulers in Jerusalem, whereas the Fourth Gospel tends to lump "the Jews" together as a group. Later documents like the *Gospel of Peter* exonerate Pilate completely and heighten Jewish guilt. In still later tradition Pilate becomes a saint, and the Jews are charged with "deicide"—that terrible word which Thomas Aquinas among others used, "murderers of God." Medieval liturgies spoke of "the perfidious Jews," and Chaucer's *Canterbury Tales* portray some of the rampant anti-Semitism which arose based on exaggerations of the Passion story. All too often hatred generated by *religious* views in the Passion narrative about the *Sanhedrin* has been transferred to the *political, economic,* and *social* realms and directed against *all* Jews.

For the New Testament, especially for Paul's theology, the ground at Calvary is equal and all men stand condemned. It is a terrible perversion of the Gospel to suppose that by passing guilt for the cross off onto the Jews one somehow exonerates oneself of sin. It is likewise a travesty of justice to assume that the involvement of a handful of Jews in Jerusalem could condemn all Jews in the world in Jesus' day, let alone all Jews of subsequent generations. The Second Vatican Council wrestled with many unfair stigmatizations of the Jews in Roman Catholicism. Protestants, at least those accustomed to careful historical study of the Bible, have come to see that the New Testament scarcely allows men today to draw facile conclusions about "Jewish guilt," and that the tendency to magnify Jewish responsibility is a later development that scarcely fits the original facts.

In view of the centuries of partisan abuse that misunderstandings of the Jewish trial of Jesus have brought about, one concrete resolve that ought to occur to every fair-minded person, let alone every disciple of Jesus of Nazareth, is to make redress for false hatreds of the past. The Passion story is no invitation to anti-Semitism, even though some Jews were involved in Jesus' death. For so, too, were some Romans.

The Trial before Pilate

The Roman or political trial of Jesus of Nazareth, which led directly to his crucifixion, is, while not without its enigmas for the historian, generally clearer and less controversial than the Jewish trial. There is, in addition, a certain fascination for readers in the three characters who cross the path of Jesus in this part of the story—Pontius Pilate, the Roman governor; Herod Antipas, the tetrarch of Galilee, who happened to be in Jerusalem at the time; and a mysterious fellow prisoner called Barabbas.

The gospel accounts of the happenings move forward in little segments of a few verses at a time, in a sometimes repetitious, almost jerky way, reminding one of "home movies." It is the sort of composition one expects when little units of human experience and bits of reflection have been handed down separately for some years. In places, of course, we sense the outline of the earliest, basic, "core" account. Elsewhere we are conscious of elaborations which spell out this point or that in more detail. This basic core account is usually reflected in several gospels, and in some instances, the questions from Pilate and the answers by Jesus are given in virtual verbatim agreement by all four evangelists. Elsewhere a detail or incident may be given by one gospel alone. The fact that only one source reports it does not necessarily mean, however, that something is historically suspect any more than several accounts (which may have simply borrowed from the earliest one) guarantee a thing as fact. Each case must be weighed separately.

How the series of incidents during the trial before Pilate fall together can be seen from the following conspectus:

	MARK 15	MATT. 27	LUKE 23	JOHN 18
Jesus delivered to Pilate (discussed above, at the end of the Jewish trial)	vs. 1	vss. 1-2	vs. 1	vs. 28
Here Matthew inserts the death of Judas	——	vss. 3-10	——	——
The trial before Pilate	vss. 2-5	vss. 11-14	vss. 2-5	18:29—19:15
Here Luke inserts a story of how Jesus was sent to Herod Antipas	——	——	vss. 6-16	——
The "Barabbas incident"	vss. 6-15a	15-26a	17-25a	18:38b-40
The sentence of death	15b	26b	25b	19:16
Jesus is mocked by the soldiers	16-20	27-31	——	19:1-3

One can easily see that all four gospels agree in broad outline. That Matthew chooses to insert in his narrative the death of Judas is no serious interruption to the flow of the story; Matthew is relating an incident of special interest to himself and his audience. Only Luke among the other evangelists chose to say anything about the fate of Judas, and he did so in the Book of Acts (1:18-19), offering a somewhat different version of the story. That Luke inserts a hearing before Herod Antipas is more of a problem, however, and one wonders why the other three gospels overlooked this part of the story. Luke also, it will be noted, omits any mocking of Jesus by the soldiers after he has been sentenced, though Luke had reported such mockery elsewhere.[14] There are several scenes of mockery in the Passion narrative and the natural place, according to Roman practice, would have been after Jesus had been sentenced.

If one looks carefully, it will also be seen that John locates the mockery of Jesus by Pilate's soldiers (with a crown of thorns, etc.) at an earlier point (19:1-3) than the Synoptics do which have it after the sentencing. The sentencing in John occurs only at 19:16, and the verses between the mocking and the sentencing are taken up by a long dialogue involving Pilate, the Jews, and Jesus (19:4-15). As anyone knows who has ever read the Johannine Passion account, the trial before Pilate is much longer in John, with more wordy discussions, than in the Synoptics (John 18:29—19:15, contrasted with Mark 15:2-15; John has twenty-seven verses compared with thirteen in Mark, even though John tells the Barabbas incident much more briefly). In the Synoptics, we mark Jesus' silence again and again—"Jesus made no further answer" (Mark 15:5). By contrast, in John there are long discourses between Jesus and Pilate—on kingship, 18:33-37; on authority, 19:8-11. It is not enough to chalk such differences up to the fact that John and the Synoptics often do not agree in their presentations of Jesus. We shall seek reasons why each emphasizes what he does.

In light of this general analysis, we may now proceed to see what the biblical verses say, step by step, about the Roman trial.

"Now Jesus stood before the governor" (Matthew 27:11). We are not told where in Jerusalem Pilate held court, and the best archeologists are divided on the precise location. John 18:28 refers to the "praetorium" or governor's residence. Actually the seat of government was not in Jerusalem, but at Caesarea on the coast. Pilate came to the Holy City only on ceremonial occasions like Passover, when there might be trouble from Jewish fanatics. Where did he reside in Jerusalem on such occasions? The great tower fortification, the "Antonia," overlooking the temple from the northwest, is one possibility, and a large ancient paved area (complete with marks in the stone from games the soldiers played) has been uncovered which fits the description of "The Pavement" or Gabbatha at John 19:13. A site favored by perhaps even more exegetes is the former palace of Herod, some distance to the west but not far from the traditional site of Calvary.

The man before whom Jesus stood arraigned is likewise something of a puzzle, even though biblical references can be supplemented by other source material[15] and now even by an inscription from Caesarea mentioning his name. We know more about Pontius Pilate than about most similar officials in Caesar's provincial administration, and he has been the subject of a number of legends. He took office as procurator of Judea about A.D. 26 and held it until 36, a fairly long period for such a tempestuous post. In spite of the stormy sailing which marked Pilate's governorship, he must have had a certain amount of ability (and some friends at Rome) in order to hold the post so long.

As governor, Pilate was confronted with a restless people, their various parties reflecting a spectrum of views; with economic problems; the need to preserve good relations with his superiors in Rome as well as with the leaders of his subjects; and ambitious princes of the Herodian dynasty who ruled enclaves in the province. The last two matters may be illustrated by reference to Antipas and Sejanus. Herod Antipas, who governed Galilee, the area from which Jesus came, had ambitions of his own and enjoyed a certain favor with the Emperor Tiberius himself; at times, as on the "issue of the gilded shields" (see below), Antipas and Pilate took opposite sides, and there is reason for Luke's remark (23:12) that the two men were "at enmity with each other" in A.D. 30.

Sejanus was an even more ambitious official in Tiberius' court. He was apparently plotting to seize power in the empire for himself early in the thirties, for Tiberius was a virtual recluse on the island of Capri. Sejanus enters our story because he seems to have been responsible for Pilate's appointment as governor. Pilate may thus be regarded as Sejanus' representative in Palestine. Now Sejanus was a notorious anti-Semite, and we may picture Pilate in the difficult position of pushing his master's anti-Jewish program as governor of Palestine, while at the same time having to live with the local Jewish authorities on whom stability in the land depended. A theory has recently been advanced by Ethelbert Stauffer[16] that Pilate was pushed by the Sanhedrin authorities into executing Jesus because Pilate's personal position was so precarious. It is a fact that Sejanus' machinations were discovered, and Tiberius had him put to death in October, A.D. 31. Thereafter, Pilate's position as a partisan of Sejanus would have been very delicate, and, it is reasoned, he had to "play ball" with the Jerusalem officials and do what they wanted. A weakness in this theory is that it requires a date in April, 32, for the crucifixion (which is less likely as the year than A.D. 30 or even 33), but the web of evidence allows us to see Pilate as a politician very much enmeshed in agonizing dilemmas.

It would have taken a political genius to ride out the storms which faced the governor in Palestine from A.D. 26 to 36. Pilate's handling of incidents of which we have knowledge suggests that he was a man of only ordinary gifts and was, furthermore, weak and inconsistent, unable to make up his own mind. The "incident of the military ensigns" is a case in point. Out of respect for Jewish scruples against carved representations of human beings in the Holy City, previous procurators had forbidden troops to carry banners into Jerusalem with such figures on them. Pilate determined to send troops in with the offensive ensigns, but, typically, he did so by night, with ensigns covered over. The Jewish protest was nonetheless so great that he had to order the offending units back to Caesarea. On another occasion he tried to hang golden shields inscribed with the names of Caesar and Pilate in Jerusalem. A protest led by Antipas went to the emperor himself, who ordered Pilate to remove them. When poor Pilate tried to give Jerusalem a better water supply, which was badly needed, he stirred up another hornet's nest of opposition by using temple revenues for the project. This time he did not back down, but let his troopers massacre those who protested. Luke 13:1 speaks of some luckless Galileans "whose blood Pilate had mingled with their sacrifices."[17] Eventually Pilate was sent back to Rome for punishment by the Emperor after his soldiers slaughtered some Samaritans in A.D. 36. Reportedly, he then committed suicide.

Historically, then, Pilate was a man of many weaknesses, although he was able to survive in a difficult post for ten years. Vacillation, not principle, marked his career. Oddly enough, Christian tradition has dealt kindly with Pilate. He received a place in the church's creeds (as early as I Timothy 6:13) as a chronological "peg" for dating the death of Jesus. The Coptic Church claims that Pilate and his wife (named Procula, according to legend) died as Christians, and Ethiopia venerates him as a saint. But this is later romanticizing. The judge who looked on Jesus was a run-of-the-mill provincial ruler, perhaps with some prejudices against the perpetual religious bickerings of "these bothersome Jews," and an increasingly difficult position as regards their leaders.

The Synoptic account of the hearing is quite simple. It is assumed in Mark and Matthew that the chief priests have decided on a political charge against Jesus and have told Pilate of the charge. (Luke 23:2 lists three specific political charges.[18]) The governor asks, "Are you the King of the Jews?" As at Matthew 26:64 (in his response to the high priest), Jesus answers with an enigmatic, "You have said so"—a reply which can mean "Yes" or can imply, "*You* say so, *I* don't." All four gospels have this question by Pilate and this answer. More charges follow (Mark 15:3). When Jesus gives no answers, Pilate remarks about his silence and wonders over it (15:4-5). We have already called attention to "the silence of Jesus" as a theme during these trials (cf. Mark 14:61; Luke 23:9), and contrasted it with the dialogue reported in John. The facts are that Mark and Matthew stress his silence, Luke notes it only in the hearing before Herod, and John has Jesus speak with Pilate but never to the Jews. One possibility is that Isaiah 53:7 (cf. Acts 8:32) is behind this "silence" theme in the Synoptics:

> He was oppressed, and he was afflicted,
>   *yet he opened not his mouth;*
> like a lamb that is led to the slaughter,
>   and like a sheep that before its shearers is dumb,
>   *so he opened not his mouth.*

Perhaps Jesus himself had this verse in mind, it has been claimed; but in that case it is hard to account for all the dialogue reported in John, if that is at all historical. It is more probable that the Synoptic version is influenced by Isaiah 53 and that John has expanded the words of the historical Jesus in the spirit of the risen Christ, to give us a picture of what Jesus Christ means by his kingdom and authority.

At this point Mark, Matthew, and John go right on to the Barabbas incident, but Luke inserts a passage (23:6-16) on how Pilate sent Jesus to Herod Antipas, on the grounds that as a Galilean he belonged under Herod's jurisdiction. Herod Antipas had ruled Galilee throughout Jesus' ministry. His marriage to Herodias, after divorcing his first wife, not only brought him trouble with his ex-father-in-law, a Nabatean king, but also, as we have seen, denunciation by John the Baptist, whom he executed (Mark 6:14-29). According to Luke 13:31, he had designs on Jesus' life too. But Antipas also was possessed of a curiosity to see Jesus, of whom he heard from members of his own staff (Luke 8:3); he hoped that he might see his subject from Nazareth perform a miracle (Luke 23:6-8).

According to Luke, Pilate shipped Jesus off to Antipas for a double purpose. As a gesture of kindness, in sending this man whom Antipas was anxious to see, the action might heal the breach that divided Pilate and Antipas. In this he was successful, for Luke says they "became friends with each other that very day" (23:12). But more important, Herod Antipas might settle for him this annoying case on which the Jews were pressing him (23:5). In this Pilate was unsuccessful, for Herod was foxy enough not to do Pilate's "hatchet work" for him. He sent Jesus back to Pilate with the message that he found nothing deserving of death in him. Presumably his desire to kill Jesus (13:31) had given way to greater caution: let Pilate solve his own problem.[19]

It is curious that no other evangelist reports this incident. Luke, however, seems to show particular interest in Herod Antipas in a series of verses (3:1, 19; 8:3; 13:31) which come from his own hand or from his L source. This particular story fits in well with Luke's theme, which he stresses in Acts, that Christianity is no menace to the empire—just as officials find Paul innocent of such charges (Acts 16:35-39, 18:15, 25:25; 26:31), so here Antipas finds Jesus not guilty of the accusations. On the other hand, Antipas does let his soldiers mock Jesus (Luke 23:11), and this fits in with the little picture in a prayer at Acts 4:25-28, to the effect that in Jerusalem ". . . there were gathered together against . . . Jesus . . . both Herod and Pontius Pilate, with the Gentiles and the peoples of Israel," in fulfillment of Psalm 2:2:

The kings of the earth [like Herod] set themselves in array,
and the rulers [like Pilate] were gathered together,
against the Lord and against his Anointed [Christ].

Here we have the idea of Old Testament prophecy fulfilled. Indeed, some commentators regard the whole scene in Luke as built
up from the Old Testament verses; others think that Luke's "special source" here preserves authentic detail. A final decision depends in part on how one evaluates the *L* source and whether one
thinks there was enough time during the early morning hours to
accommodate the hearing before Antipas.

All four gospels now report the effort of Pilate to stave off a
decision about Jesus of Nazareth by offering to free some prisoner,
evidently hoping that either the Jews will ask for Jesus and take
him off his hands or, in obtaining the release of someone else, will
forget about Jesus. In accordance with custom at the feast, the text
says, the governor will release any prisoner the crowd desires.
He asks them whether they want "the King of the Jews" (Mark
15:9). They call, instead, for a man named Barabbas, a "notorious
prisoner" (Matthew 27:16), "who had committed murder" in a
recent revolt (Mark 15:7). Pilate tries again to get them to select
Jesus, but they call for Barabbas' release and demand that Jesus
be crucified. Pilate complies.

The makeup of the crowd is hard to ascertain. Either the group
is dominated by friends of Barabbas or the populace has changed
in its attitude toward Jesus since the triumphal entry a few days
before (if we accept that scene at face value). Or is this a mob
of retainers and supporters of the priests (Luke 23:1), whom the
chief priests stir up and persuade to do what they want (Mark
15:11)?

The most striking detail is that at Matthew 27:17 a variant
reading (see the RSV note) reports that the full name of the
other prisoner was "*Jesus* Barabbas." The choice, translating the
names, is then between "Jesus 'Son-of-the-father' [Bar-Abba]" and
"Jesus who is called messiah." The reading is given in only a few
manuscripts, but the *New English Bible* and *Today's English
Version* of the New Testament (1966) have adopted it on the
grounds that the reference to another man named Jesus is more
likely to have been dropped by pious copyists than to have been
added by them. At Colossians 4:11 a case occurs where a man
named Jesus Justus is mentioned, and the name "Jesus" there has

been dropped by some copyists. "Jesus" was a fairly common name in the Jewish world of the day, and it seems more likely that two men named Jesus were involved than that Matthew added the name to heighten the irony.

To readers the most disturbing feature about the incident may be that outside the New Testament we cannot document the "custom" here described. The Roman historian Livy speaks of cases where there was a mass amnesty or parole of prisoners by the Romans at a festival, and attempts have been made to trace such acts of clemency back to Babylonian times. A papyrus from Egypt (A.D. 85) describes how the governor tells a prisoner that he deserves a good scourging but then says, "I will give you to the people"; but this appears to be a single, exceptional case, not a custom. Roman law seems to have allowed only the emperor or senate to set free a man already condemned; governors do not seem to have had that power. A pronouncement by the rabbis hints that prisoners released from jail after the lambs were slaughtered for Passover might nonetheless partake of the Passover meal—suggesting that there were enough such cases to call for a rule—but the relevance of such a pronouncement to our story depends on a chronology according to which the Passover meal has *not* yet been eaten. In short, to sum up a confusing matter, we have no exact "parallel" to any such custom, only the New Testament's word for it. It is distressing therefore that the evangelists do not make clear whether the crowd could choose *anyone* it wished or whether Pilate limited their choice to *two names* (contrast Matthew 27:15 and 17), and whether the crowd came prepared to invoke the custom (Mark 15:8) or Pilate had to remind them of it (John 18:39). All sorts of "explanations" have been proposed.[20] None of them settles the matter fully.

Pilate's sentence, to which he is finally pushed, is tersely given: ". . . having scourged Jesus, he delivered him to be crucified" (Mark 15:15*b*). The wording fits technical Roman procedure, since crucifixion was regularly preceded by a brutal whipping with thongs studded with bone and pieces of metal that cut into the flesh. The closing verses of the section (Mark 15:16-20) show the soldiers engaged in the sort of horseplay, mocking Jesus, that is common around a barracks when undisciplined savagery can be vented on a defenseless man. There is something, however, to be said for the theory that Jesus is here mocked as a *king*, with purple robe, crown, and reed scepter, just as in connection with the Jewish trial he was mocked as a *prophet* (Mark 14:65).[21] The crown of thorns probably was more an instrument of mockery than of torture, since it appears to have been made of thistly branches, not plants with bayonet-like thorns—but the terms are too inexact in Greek to allow botanists to tell.

One feature not always noted is that Luke and John can be read to suggest that *the Jews*, not Roman soldiers, crucified Jesus:

> Pilate "released the man . . . whom they [the Jews] asked for; but Jesus he delivered up *to their will* . . . *they* led him away . . ." (Luke 23:25-26).
> Pilate said to them, "Shall I crucify your King?" The chief priests answered, "We have no king but Caesar." Then he handed him over *to them* to be crucified. So *they* took Jesus . . . (John 19:15-16).

In each case, the antecedent is "the Jews," though from Mark and Matthew we are accustomed to the clearer presentation in which the soldiers of the governor do the crucifying. Perhaps the impression is merely the result of careless phraseology, but other details suggest that in the gospels written after Mark there was a further tendency to emphasize Jewish guilt and the innocence of the Roman empire.

Matthew reflects this tendency by inserting the detail of how Pilate "washed his hands" of the matter (a Jewish custom, see Deuteronomy 21:6; Psalm 26:6) and by inserting in Mark's account the terrible cry attributed to *all* the people, "His blood be on us and on our children!" (Matthew 27:24-25). Or does Matthew want to suggest the irony that Jesus' blood must be on *all* who wish to be saved (cf. 26:28)?

Luke emphasizes Roman innocence by showing Pilate's attempts to let Jesus go and by insisting that the Jewish leaders and crowd pushed him on against his will. He has Pilate thrice declare Jesus innocent (23:4, 14, 22); Herod finds no fault deserving death in him (23:15); Pilate proposes a light whipping, as a substitute for death (23:16, 22). John suggests that Pilate tried to avoid killing Jesus by turning the matter back to the Jews for some milder punishment (18:31), as well as by declaring Jesus innocent (18:38) and by seeking to arouse the crowd's sympathy for the forlorn Jesus (19:5, "Behold, the man"). In all the gospels there is the Barabbas episode. In these ways a favorable picture of Pilate is suggested.

Our examination of the texts has suggested, however, that Jewish involvement, certainly beyond a few priestly leaders, was less than is sometimes felt, and Roman involvement was greater than is often supposed. There can be no one "scapegoat" on whom to blame the evil that led to the cross.

Our examination of the Roman trial has tended to focus attention on Pilate. A picture emerges not of a wicked man, but of a weak one unable to act consistently according to principle. It is easy both to feel sympathy and to condemn the man, caught as he was in a desperate situation yet failing to act justly.

But Pilate and the historical problems connected with the trial and ethical reflections about the governor are not what the evangelists meant us primarily to see in the Passion story. They point to Jesus and the cross, where, in their view, lies the hope for all the world's Pilates and Judases and Simon Peters—and for Barabbas, the one person who could literally say, "Jesus of Nazareth died in place of me."

At the Cross

The story of the crucifixion of Jesus is told by the four evangelists with considerably more reserve than we are accustomed to. We may be used to the dramatic license of the preacher, drawing out every moment of the agony on Good Friday, or to an artist's representation which depicts the suffering in gory colors or with graphic realism. There is, of course, a genuine human appeal in the crucifixion scene as presented in the gospels, but the suffering and agony are not belabored.

Reasons for this are not hard to find. The evangelists and their readers lived in a world all too familiar with the bloody details of execution on a cross. They didn't need instruction in the practice.[22] Therefore the gospels do not dramatize the matter the way a modern writer, such as J. B. Phillips, feels compelled to do. He begins the scene in one of his plays with two soldiers talking at Calvary, in this way:

OLD SOLDIER. What's the matter, Sergius my lad? You're looking a bit green and no mistake. . . .
SERGIUS. I'm all right. It's just that it's my first—my first—
OLD SOLDIER. Your first crucifixion, eh? (Heartily) We-ell, don't worry. I've seen hundreds. . . .[23]

This might be taken for granted by first-century hearers.

Then, too, our gospels were written, not to convey emotional descriptions of an execution for the dramatic impact on an audience that might be roused to pity thereby, but primarily for usage among Christians, in preaching, teaching, and worship. Furthermore, our gospel accounts came into being *after* the resurrection and reflect the post-resurrection situation in which Christians lived. The story of the cross was being told by men who knew that its apparent finality was not the end to Jesus of Nazareth and who believed that its agony and suffering had meaning in God's eternal plan. We must also remember that our descriptions of the crucifixion were finally edited at a time when Christianity had split decisively from Judaism and was seeking to make its way into the Roman world.

Under these conditions our four gospel accounts were put together for us. But they were based on earlier reports which went back to Jerusalem on April 7, A.D. 30 (or whatever year one decides on for the date of the crucifixion). But who had been there to provide the witness? What reflections had deepened the reports of these witnesses over the intervening years? We must reckon with the fact that on that night the disciples had long since fled (Mark 14:50; Matthew 26:56). Even Peter, who had followed part of the way (Mark 14:66-72), was not there. We are dependent, as in the earliest resurrection accounts, on a group we have not noticed before in the Passion narrative—the woman from Galilee, who kept watch over some of the happenings at the cross (Mark 15:40-41, 47). John's Gospel says "the disciple whom he loved" was also present (John 19:26), but the precise identity of this figure remains a mystery. Traditionally he is identified with John, the son of Zebedee, but others have felt Lazarus was intended, or an idealized representation of the "true disciple." There were also enemies and bystanders present, some of whom, it can be conjectured, later became Christians and contributed accounts of what happened. The impression one gets in reading the crucifixion narrative is of a series of brief scenes and fragmentary reminiscences—which is exactly what one might expect from the sort of witnesses we can presume to have watched the happenings. The Galilean women might contribute some details, a converted Jew from Jerusalem still others. Over the years these were woven together into the accounts which have come down to us.

One other outstanding influence on this part of the Passion narrative must be noted—the Old Testament. The people who first told of the death of Jesus were religious people. Their religion was that of the One Book, the Old Testament (interpreted now, of course, through what had come to pass in Jesus Christ). Almost inevitably their language reflected the thoughts and phrases of the Old Testament. Just as John Bunyan cast his book *The Pilgrim's Progress* in biblical language, so the early Christians showed their roots in the ancient Hebrew Scriptures.

It is a fact that the Greek world had its pictures of an innocent and righteous man who is unjustly put to death. Plato has a remarkable passage about the just man who is "scourged, tortured, bound in chains, his eyes burnt out, until, after suffering every kind of abuse, he is crucified."[24] But in the Old Testament the story of such a righteous sufferer is an even more common literary and religious theme. In certain psalms, like Psalm 22, there appears a regular "plot line" about the good man who suffers for his fidelity to God but who also looks to the Lord for vindication; so also with "the Servant" in Isaiah 53. Such Old Testament references were known to Jesus and to Jews of the day, including his enemies. It is not intrinsically impossible that some of the ancient Hebrew turns of phrase could have been on the lips of the original participants in the Passion drama. These chapters in the Old Testament were even better known to early Christians who meditated on the Passion in the light of them. Accordingly we can expect to find the influence of the Old Testament increasing as the story of the cross was retold over the years, and as the evangelists pored over the Old Testament passages, seeking further insights. The gospel accounts of the crucifixion, which are post-Easter accounts, told in retrospect, recollecting the happenings from many angles, will thus have an Old Testament cast to them.

A final preliminary observation is necessary. It concerns the sayings of Jesus reported in this part of the narrative. Here, as nowhere else in the Passion, according to the Synoptics, Jesus speaks—frequently. But what were his "last words"? For, as is well known, seven "words from the cross" are recorded in the four gospels, which, at three-hour services on Good Friday, are somewhat artificially grouped in a chronological order.

There are many historical questions which can be raised about

these "last words." Who heard them and preserved them? Who
stood close enough to hear the death gasps of Jesus? Was it the
women?[25] More important is the point that no one gospel records
all seven words. Mark and Matthew agree in reporting a single
saying. Luke has three more, all of which occur in Luke only.
John has three words, none of them found in any other gospel.
The customary arrangement of the seven is rather arbitrary at
points; no one can tell absolutely what the "original" order was.
Most significant is the fact that each evangelist intends a single
saying to be the climax of his account. When we read the seven
words in a gospel harmony, we may be missing the impact which
the evangelist intended his saying or sayings to have. In fairness
to each individual gospel, therefore, we should try to hear each
saying exclusively in its setting in that gospel, and not transfer
it to a composite picture which no New Testament writer intended.
Gerhard Gloege writes of the seven sayings:

> Every word leads its own life, basically. The whole Jesus is some-
> where in every word. And every word helps the bloody events on
> Golgotha to take on a new aspect for us. We should try to read and
> understand each Gospel on its own first of all, as if there were no
> second, third or fourth Gospel beside it. Only then do we hear the
> full tones which the chorus of voices singing antiphonally—or poly-
> phonally—makes it possible to hear.[26]

In what follows, we shall listen for the solo voice in each gospel,
not just to the full chorus.

The structure of the Passion sections on the crucifixion is a
familiar one. The Apostles' Creed proclaims how Jesus "*suffered*
at the time when Pontius Pilate ruled, was *crucified, died,* and
was *buried.*" We shall examine each of these steps in turn, as the
gospels do. First is the suffering on the way to Calvary. Then
the *crucifixion* scene is described. Next comes a presentation of the
death of Jesus. Last, but not to be overlooked (for it was already
an article enumerated in the little creed at I Corinthians 15:4),
is the *burial.*

In a sense, all the stages thus far examined—the arrest, the
two trials, the several scourgings—present Jesus' suffering. But the
road to Calvary brings him to the climax of his sufferings. The
basic Passion account contained the statement that "they led him
[Jesus] out . . . to the place called Golgotha . . . and they crucified
him" (Mark 15:20*b*–24*a*). The pain and torture of the journey

to "the place of the skull" is not spelled out, but a single incident reported in all three Synoptic Gospels makes plain the suffering involved. Jesus was tottering so badly from his ordeal that the soldiers in charge commandeered a passing civilian, Simon of Cyrene, to carry the crossbeam for Jesus. It was Roman practice for the condemned man to carry his own cross, but the army also had the right to impress a person into service (cf. Matthew 5:41). Jesus' cross-bearer was not Simon Peter, or any other disciple, but a total stranger (some have even thought him a Negro because he came from Cyrene in North Africa, but there was a large Jewish colony there, and so the man was probably Jewish). However, if the date was Passover,[27] one wonders what a Jew was doing "coming in from the country" (Mark 15:21). The passage is one of the few in Mark where a person's proper name is given (outside of the twelve disciples). The description of Simon as "the father of Alexander and Rufus" in Mark has aroused further curiosity, and the usual answer is that "Rufus" is the man mentioned in Romans 16:13 as "eminent in the Lord." That would mean that Simon became a Christian after this experience, and his son was a leader whom Paul knew.

John tantalizes us with the statement that Jesus "went out, *bearing his own cross*, to . . . Golgotha" (19:17). Some commentators rationalize the two accounts and claim that Jesus started out bearing his own cross (as in John) but later transferred it to Simon. But no gospel writer says this, and it is better to interpret John's account as it stands. John wants to picture Christ as all-sufficient, even at this tragic moment (he stresses Christ's glory here rather than the humanity of Jesus), and perhaps he has deliberately omitted any reference to Simon of Cyrene in order to thwart certain "heretics." For when John wrote, gnostic groups were claiming that Jesus had not died on the cross, but that *Simon was crucified in his place.*

Luke adds a detail here, just as he later supplements the basic account of the crucifixion scene. Luke 23:27-32 tells how a multitude of people, especially women, followed Jesus, weeping. Because he calls them "daughters of Jerusalem" (23:28), they are presumably not the women from Galilee. Speaking prophetically, he urges them to weep rather for themselves, their children, and their city. The time will come, he says, when they will wish they had never been born. For if this is what happens to an innocent

man (like Jesus), then what can a guilty city expect? (Cf. also
Luke 19:41-44.) The whole little speech is full of Old Testament
phraseology (see Zechariah 12:10-11; Hosea 10:8; Ezekiel 20:
47).

Next we see the *crucifixion scene* itself. The site was a skull-
shaped hill called in Aramaic "Golgotha." (The Latin translation
for "skull," *calvaria,* gives us the word "Calvary.") The basic
account simply said, ". . . there they crucified him" (Luke 23:33).
Mark adds a detail as to time, "it was the third hour, when they
crucified him," i.e., 9 A.M. (Mark 15:25). As already noted, this
conflicts with John 19:14, where Jesus is condemned by Pilate
about noon. Accordingly, some critics regard the verse in Mark
as a later addition.[28] It is a fact that neither Matthew nor Luke
repeat Mark's phrase about the time. We are free therefore to
imagine the execution as lasting from noon to 3 P.M., if we are
willing to disregard this verse in Mark. It is the other expansions
and details which are more interesting than those concerning time
and place.

Mark and Matthew tell how, at the outset of the ordeal at
Golgotha, Jesus was offered wine mixed with some drug to deaden
the pain. He did not accept it. The offer was a gesture of compassion. Guilds of women who thus ministered to suffering criminals are known to have existed at Jerusalem. Their motto was
Proverbs 31:6:

> Give strong drink to him who is perishing,
>   and wine to those in bitter distress.

All four gospels report how the soldiers, who were entitled
to the prisoners' few possessions as a reward, divided up Jesus'
clothing by lot. Presumably there were five items of dress and
four soldiers. Each got something, and dice were thrown for
Jesus' tunic. Behind all the accounts looms Psalm 22:18, which
John in fact quotes (19:24) and regards as fulfilled completely
in both of its lines:

> They parted my garments among them,
>   and for my clothing they cast lots.

All four gospels likewise report an inscription placed over
Jesus' head, giving the charge against him, in accordance with
Roman practice. The inscription read, according to the gospels:

MARK 15:26	MATTHEW 27:37	LUKE 23:38	JOHN 19:19
	This is Jesus		Jesus of Nazareth,
The King of	the King of	The King of	the King of the
the Jews.	the Jews.	the Jews —	Jews.
		this fellow!	

As can be observed, even though there are minor variations in the way the wording is reported Jesus is being put to death as a "king" who might threaten Caesar. John seems to suggest that Pilate had some revenge on the Jewish priests with this phrase— "You wanted Jesus crucified as a would-be king? Very well, I dub him 'the king of you Jews'" (cf. John 19:21-22).

In the Middle East (and in the United States until at least the nineteenth century) executions were public events, and attracted a crowd. The government thus not only provided "entertainment" for some of the viler members of society but also took this as an opportunity to give an object lesson in what happens to those who break the law. Jesus' execution was no exception. Passersby (Mark 15:29), "the people" (Luke 23:35), and, rather surprisingly at Passovertime, the chief priests and Jewish rulers (Mark 15:31) were there. They are said to have made jests at Jesus and mocked him. Mark seems to present this mockery in three stages:

1) *those who passed by* derided him (15:29);

2) *the chief priests with the scribes* mocked him (15:31);

3) *those crucified with him* also reviled him (15:32).

Note that those who abuse Jesus are seemingly all Jews; the Romans present will respond differently. Further, the abuse by these Jews is presented in language drawn from the Old Testament; for example:

PSALM 22:7	MARK 15
All who see me mock at me,	the chief priests mocked him (vs. 31)
they make mouths at me,	those who passed by derided him,
they wag their heads. . . .	wagging their heads (vs. 29)

PSALM 22:8	MATTHEW 27:43
He committed his cause to the Lord,	He trusts in God;
let him deliver him,	let God deliver him now,
let him rescue him, for	if he desires him. . . .
he delights in him!	

Jesus' response is—silence, as during so much of his trial.

At least, that is true in Mark and Matthew: Jesus does not speak. According to Luke, he breaks silence twice during this period, both times in connection with his "enemies." Almost at the beginning of the crucifixion scene, Luke 23:34 has the words of Jesus: "Father, forgive them; for they know not what they do." It has long been debated whether the "them" refers to the Roman soldiers gambling beneath the cross, or to the Jews who were putting him to death in ignorance. Probably the intention was to cover both groups, and ultimately all men. In Acts the sermons given by Luke take up the theme that the Jews acted out of ignorance (3:17; 13:27), and the first martyr Stephen prayed a prayer which was similar in spirit (for Saul and his other murderers): "Lord, do not hold this sin against them" (Acts 7:60). Oddly, some copies of Luke's Gospel omit 23:34, perhaps because the special source. The effect of his account is to show Jesus not merely copyists in their day could not believe that Jesus would have prayed for forgiveness for the Jews.

The other Lucan addition is the word to the penitent thief: "Truly, I say to you, today you will be with me in Paradise." This little section, Luke 23:39-43, is similar to other Lucan stories about forgiveness for people who repent (see 7:36-50; 18:9-14; 19:1-10). It is cast in typically Semitic, Jewish terms, including the words *amen* ("truly") and "Paradise," and is meant to offer the man more than he asked for: not just some future kingdom, but immediate transfer to the realm of God. Luke has throughout the crucifixion scene departed from the bare presentation in the other Synoptics, so much so that scholars postulate that he had a as a dying man, but as a model for martyrs like Stephen (cf. Luke 23:34 with Acts 7:60) and for all Christians, and as offering immediate access to God, even to a penitent thief.

The actual *death of Jesus* is tersely described at Mark 15:37: he "uttered a loud cry, and breathed his last." Strictly speaking, Mark and Matthew do not tell us what that "loud cry" was. The only word they report from the cross came sometime earlier: "My God, my God, why hast thou forsaken me?" (Mark 15:34). We get the point of these words, which were spoken in Aramaic (so Mark) or Hebrew (Matthew), only if we know they are the opening verse of Psalm 22, and then only if we read the entire psalm. It begins in despair (22:1) but ends as a song of trust in

God, that He will care for the righteous man in his extremity (see 22:19-31). Pious Jews recited these words when catastrophes threatened, and it is likely that Jesus had in mind the entire psalm or even spoke it in a low, inaudible voice. Such is the picture the evangelists encourage, and it is probably right to take the use of Psalm 22:1 not only as signifying that Jesus' sufferings have reached their nadir at this point—abandonment even by God— but also as a confession of faith that God will yet vindicate him.

The other sidelights on Jesus' death can be quickly noted. A bystander mistakes the Hebrew word *Eli* ("My God") as a call for *Eli*jah, who was looked on as a helper in time of need. ("I will send you Elijah the prophet before the great and terrible day of the Lord comes," Malachi 4:5). Someone—Jew or soldier? —out of compassion or hostility we cannot tell (compare Luke 23:36-37 with Mark 15:35-36)—offers him wine vinegar.[29] Jesus' side is pierced, to see whether he is dead (John 19:34). The women continue their vigil (Mark 15:40-41). Elijah does not come, but the evangelists report some symbolic, apocalyptic happenings of the type traditionally associated with the Day of the Lord, in order to indicate, through these phenomena, as Jesus dies, that his cross means a new era for men. There is darkness over the land (as at Exodus 10:21-22; Amos 5:18, 20; 8:9), and the veil in the temple, which blocked from view the heart of the sanctuary, is torn in two from top to bottom—symbolizing, in Christian eyes, the access now opened by Jesus' death to the heart of God. The gospels here are saying, in the strange language of apocalyptic and under the guise of narrative, what the Letter to the Hebrews declares in other terms: "We have . . . a hope that enters into the inner shrine behind the curtain . . ." (6:19), a ". . . new and living way which he [Jesus] opened for us through the curtain . . ." (10:20). Matthew even includes a strange little narrative about an earthquake and a resurrection of Old Testament saints (27:52-53) which presages Jesus' own resurrection. Above all, there is the confession of the Roman centurion, the climax of the Passion: "Truly, this man was God's son" (Mark 15:39, par. Matthew 27:54).[30] Christians saw deeper meaning in the phrase "Son of God" than any pagan would. It was a term by which they confessed what Jesus meant to them. In this phrase we sense the primary purpose of the whole Passion narrative: to confess and tell about Jesus as the Christ of God.

One final scene remains, *the burial of Jesus*. It had to be included, first because it was part of the story and was necessary as a step to the testimony about the resurrection; in order to affirm that Jesus was risen, Christians had to be sure to assert that he had died and been buried. Then, too, against gnostic notions, later on, that Jesus had not really died, it was necessary to insist that he was unquestionably "dead and buried." The fact that he was buried by a pious Jew, who had not been a member of the inner circle of followers of Jesus, namely, Joseph of Arimathea, stamps the story (Mark 15:42-47) with the stamp of authenticity. No member of the twelve, not even the women from Galilee, but a man who was at best a secret pupil of Jesus, dared the fury of both Jews and Romans by entombing the crucified Nazarene.

The evangelists do not moralize on this point. They have reached the end of the earthly life of Jesus, but in such a way that the stage is set for what was really the beginning of the Gospel, God's action in raising him from the dead. The women watch where he is laid (Mark 15:47); they will go there on Easter morn. But at the tomb the story of Jesus' human career ends.

We began this chapter by asking how much we can learn about the historical Jesus from the detailed narratives of the Passion, taking it as a test case on historicity. There *are* points where the gospels put us in touch with Jesus "as he was" and with the actual happenings. But we end up seeing as much and more of how the early church looked on Jesus as the Christ and on his cross as the fulfillment of God's ancient plan. This is especially evident, as we have noted, in the frequent references made to the Old Testament in this closing section of the Passion narrative. These references include:

Isa. 53 (prominent in our minds, but not actually quoted here; Luke 22:37 quotes Isaiah 53:12, "he was reckoned with transgressors," at an earlier point; and Mark 15:28 [see RSV footnote] is an addition found in later manuscripts only)

	MARK	MATT.	LUKE	JOHN
Ps. 22:18	15:24	27:35	23:34*b*	19:24
(garments divided)				
Ps. 22:7	15:29	27:39	23:35	—
(wagging their heads)				

Ps. 22:8 ("let God deliver him . . .")	—	27:43	—	—
Ps. 22:1 ("My God, my God . . .")	15:34	27:46	—	—
Ps. 69:21 ("vinegar to drink," cf. Psalm 22:15)	15:36	27:48	23:36	19:29
	cf. vs. 23	cf. vs. 34		
Ps. 31:5 ("Into thy hands . . .") (a substitute for use of Psalm 22:1)	—	—	23:46	—
Ps. 38:11 ("my kinsmen stand afar off")	(cf. 15:40)	(27:55)	23:49	(cf. 19:25)
Deut. 21:22-23; Exodus 34:25 (the body shall not remain on the cross all night)	15:43-46	27:57-60	23:50-54	19:38-42

The impression left with those who pored over these Bible verses was that Jesus' death had not been merely some miscarriage of justice, or the tragic end of a great man, but represented God's will (cf. Acts 2:23; 4:28). The evangelists may tell of the cross at times in a didactic way, sometimes in an apologetic way—teaching us this or explaining that. But primarily they speak about it as a confession concerning Jesus Christ and what God was doing in him. They believed that "in Christ, God was reconciling the world to himself," "making peace by the blood of his cross." Therefore they tell of the Passion as "a preached message rather than a literal report."[31] They do not "chronicle" Friday, April 7, A.D. 30. They present it transformed as a Friday that can be called "Good"—for "us men, and our salvation," as the church's creed was later to phrase it.

This cannot be counted as loss—unless, contrary to the intent of the gospels, we want to limit ourselves to the biography of a man of the past, instead of the Gospel of a lord who lives. But will not the matter be different with our other test case, the area of Jesus' teachings? How could they feel the hand of Easter? With this in mind, we turn to his teachings, after which we shall examine the resurrection itself.

4

The Lord Taught Them to Pray

The teachings of Jesus have been funneled to us through the disciples and witnesses of the early church. That is significant.

As far as we know, Jesus himself wrote nothing.[1] It was his disciples who preserved, transmitted, and eventually wrote down some of the things he said. Their accounts, as we know, come to us in gospels written about a generation—some forty to seventy years—after the Passion and resurrection of Jesus Christ. This simple fact, that Jesus' teachings have come down to us in this way, has two immediate corollaries which are of immense significance as we consider the sayings which have been preserved for us.

First of all, powerful factors were at work to preserve what Jesus had taught *in the form in which he had spoken it.* Pupils of a great teacher are often wont to repeat what he said in exactly the way he said it, reiterating his pet phrases and even reproducing his characteristic mannerisms. In the Orient, it had for centuries been the custom to preserve teachings in oral form, without writing them down, but without altering them either. The ancient mind had an amazing ability to memorize thousands of lines of poetry, or column after column of laws, and then to transmit these intact. It was an ability which our reliance on the printed word has virtually destroyed. We are so dependent on "looking it up" in a book that we have lost any idea of how much the mind can memorize. Judaism recognized this human capacity to memorize and used it to advantage in passing on the teachings of its rabbis orally. Not merely the law, but interpretations of it, and comments on the interpretation by a series of rabbis were all passed on accurately for several generations without being written down. It is therefore no great stretch of historical imagination to suppose that Jesus' teachings could have been transmitted from A.D. 30 until the end of the century by word of mouth with little or no alteration, and some scholars in Sweden have recently stressed this point.[2]

In support of this view the following arguments, among others, have been advanced. First, to those who revered his words and passed them on, Jesus was a figure of authority. He was the teacher who had replaced the rabbis and overshadowed even Moses. As the "one teacher" (Matthew 23:8), he was to be obeyed. This reverence for what Jesus had said would work to cast a protective fence around his words, guarding them against accidental or malicious change. Furthermore, it has been argued, again by some of the Swedish scholars, that Jesus taught his disciples in the manner of the rabbis of the day—i.e., by rote memorization; that would mean that he drilled into them what he wanted them to learn, and they repeated it aloud until they were letter-perfect at the teachings of the master. It is apparent in many cases, too, that Jesus' teachings were cast in poetic form, with rhythm and even rhyme at times—all features which would make material easier to memorize. All in all, an impressive case can be made for the view that Jesus' teachings could have been passed on with great accuracy from the days when he spoke in Galilee until some evangelist recorded them for us.

Balancing this, however, is a second fact: the early church which handed down the sayings of Jesus and finally recorded them in the New Testament *viewed everything in light of Easter and under the tutelage of the Holy Spirit.* This means, in the light of the changed situation which Easter brought, and after the coming of the Holy Spirit who was believed to be teaching and guiding the Christian community. This new light made a difference in how some of the sayings of Jesus were understood. In commenting, for example, on Jesus' words about destroying the temple (cf. Mark 14:58; John 2:19), the Fourth Evangelist says quite plainly that it was only *after* Jesus was raised from the dead that the disciples "remembered that he had said this" and grasped its full meaning (John 2:22).[3] So also with other of his teachings; what he said could be grasped only after the Spirit was given (John 7:39). After all, was it not the Spirit who would guide men "into all truth"? He would "bring to remembrance" what Jesus had said, he would bear witness to Jesus, setting the world straight on what his coming had meant, taking what was Jesus' word and declaring its full meaning to those who were "in Christ" (cf. John 14:16-17, 26; 15:26; 16:12-15). What John's Gospel thus makes explicit is implicit in the other gospels: the Spirit of the risen Christ, after Easter, was the "lens" through which the sayings of Jesus were viewed; the Spirit provided for early Christians new interpretive insights and greater depths which were to be probed in Jesus' teachings. Under the Spirit, the church, employing the sayings of Jesus, sought to assert the mind of Christ.

Did all this happen the day after Easter? Was it confined to a brief period in the decade of the thirties? Scarcely. According to the New Testament writers themselves, the work of the Holy Spirit was not just a sudden, singular thing, confined to Pentecost Sunday. Two decades or more after Easter, Paul claimed to have "visions and revelations of the Lord" (II Corinthians 12:1; cf. Galatians 2:2; Acts 16:7; 27:23-24). In the nineties the author of the last book in the Bible, Revelation, describes how he was "in the Spirit" and saw visions of God and the Lamb and their will for the world. All through these decades Christians believed that the Spirit of the Lord was at work in their midst (II Corinthians 3:12-18). This being so, one can scarcely exclude the creative breath of this Spirit from touching on something so important in the church's life as the "Jesus-material" or tradition of what he had said and taught. Early Christians assumed the Spirit's activity here as well as elsewhere. Further, any sort of doctrine of "inspiration"—about the working of the Spirit—with regard to the New Testament writings must also allow for the creativity of the Spirit in the work of the evangelists. Contrary to later views, they were not just "scribes" or "reporters," but men who preached the Gospel in the very way they set forth the Jesus-material. And to preach the Gospel meant, for these people, to speak in and under the Spirit. Thus, the light of Easter and the early Christian understanding of the presence of the Spirit led to a difference not only in how Jesus' words were understood, but also indeed in which words were chosen to be passed on and recorded in a gospel.

Moreover, the Jesus who had spoken these words was now regarded as more than a teacher in Galilee. He is now for believers the lord, who lives—and still speaks. His words spoken in the flesh are not simply to be collected in a code or revered as antiques, but are to be applied in contemporary life. And the lord himself, it was understood, would through his Spirit guide his followers into an understanding of the words for a new day. For early Christians the Jesus-material was "alive," capable of application, of adaptation, and even of growth. The Lord Jesus could speak through his prophets in the church (Acts 11:27-28; 13:1; I Corinthians 12:28-29; cf. I Peter 1:10-11). All this adds up to a powerful case for the possibility that Jesus' teachings in the New Testament period were not regarded as static but as dynamic, full of new insights beyond what men had comprehended when the man from Nazareth first spoke. Simply to "pass on" the teachings of Jesus, untouched by the new insights of the post-Easter Gospel, would be treason to the Lord Jesus!

Two factors, then, are at work with regard to the teachings of Jesus in the New Testament: a staunch *fidelity* to what he had said, and an amazing *freedom* in handling his words, under the Spirit, in a more meaningful way.[4] The first force, if left to itself, would have led to a stagnant literalism—we would have the words of a dead teacher, nothing more. The second element by itself would breed chaos—freewheeling interpretations piled one upon the other, until one would despair of ever knowing anything at all of what Jesus said. The two together, however, combine to give us Jesus' teachings in the New Testament gospels as what the early Christians regarded as word of God; the teachings are faithful in spirit to what Jesus had said, but are presented now in light of the cross and resurrection and the coming of the Holy Spirit.

Partisans of each of these factors have, of course, often overstated their case. Sometimes the stamp of the post-Easter church and its Spirit-filled creativity are stressed so much that one wonders if there is any saying which the critics still care to attribute to Jesus of Nazareth. Other writers stress so much the "simple teachings" of the historical Jesus that the Gospel of the Passion and resurrection, and the work of the Spirit seem overlooked. Still others seem to overlook the long process of how the "Jesus-material" came to us. In practice, how did the two factors work out as influences?

An excellent testing ground, where we can observe both of these factors at work, is Jesus' teaching on prayer, and particularly the prayer which the Lord taught his disciples to pray. For we deal here with words which Jesus gave to his disciples during the earthly ministry, words which include no reference to the cross or resurrection, nor any phrases common in later Christian prayers such as "in Jesus' name" or "by the Spirit." Yet the very name used for it today, the *Lord's* Prayer, suggests that the prayer is looked upon as the work of someone who is more than a teacher, as does the fact that these words are prayed mainly by persons who confess Jesus as the Christ and savior. In this prayer, and some verses connected with it in the gospels, we can seek to trace out how something Jesus actually said can be painstakingly recovered in its original form, and also how Jesus' words developed, with new additions, after the Spirit was given to those who called him lord.

A Prayer for Disciples

The Lord's Prayer is recorded at two places in the New Testament, but in forms that differ in minor and major ways.

MATTHEW 6:9-13	LUKE 11:2-4
[9] Our Father who art in heaven,	[2] Father,
Hallowed be thy name.	Hallowed be thy name.
[10] Thy kingdom come,	Thy kingdom come.
Thy will be done,	
On earth as it is in heaven.	
[11] Give us this day our daily bread;[a]	[3] Give us each day our daily bread;[a]
[12] And forgive us our debts,	[4] and forgive us our sins,
As we also have forgiven our debtors;	for we ourselves forgive every one who is indebted to us;
[13] And lead us not into temptation,	and lead us not into temptation.
But deliver us from evil.[b]	

Those who are accustomed to the King James Version of the Bible from 1611 will notice some few differences between the Lucan and Matthean forms of the prayer (Luke lacks the doxology, for example, even in the KJV). The Revised Standard Version of 1946 (quoted above), which is based on even older manuscripts, the best ones available, brings out such differences more sharply, for instance in the way that God is addressed (Matthew has "Our Father who art in heaven," Luke simply "Father").

An examination of the context in Matthew 6 and Luke 11 shows further that each evangelist gives the prayer in a different setting. Matthew's longer, more formal version is presented as part of the "Sermon on the Mount" (as we call it), three chapters (Matthew 5-7) where Jesus' teachings are grouped together in a large block. Luke gives the Lord's Prayer not only in a simpler,

[a] Or, *our bread for the morrow.*

[b] Or, *the evil one.* Other authorities, some ancient, add, in some form, *For thine is the kingdom and the power and the glory, for ever. Amen.*

briefer form, but also in a more natural, less formal setting. Luke does not include it in his "Sermon on the Plain" (6:17-49). Rather, one day, while Jesus is praying, his disciples ask him for a prayer which they can use. Jesus responds with the words recorded at 11:2-4. Luke thus provides a shorter version of the prayer, given in a "life-setting"; Matthew presents a longer version, as part of a more formal presentation of Jesus' teachings.[5] One could claim, of course, that Jesus taught the prayer twice, on different occasions, but that still would not account for the variations of wording in several of the petitions. Presumably Jesus, if he was at all concerned to provide a prayer which disciples would use repeatedly, a prayer with definite form, rhythm, and perhaps even rhyme, would employ one, single, set form of prayer which was both memorable and memorizable, and not confuse the disciples with varying wordings. People therefore want to know, if possible, what words go back to Jesus' own lifetime and ministry, and how the more formal additions grew up which we find especially in Matthew.

Some of those who have made a careful study of the Lord's Prayer are convinced that it is possible to work back from the two versions in Matthew and Luke to something like the "disciples' prayer" which Jesus originally gave.[6] Of course, we must reckon with the fact that we are looking at the prayer in English, while the New Testament has it in Greek, and Jesus originally would have taught it in Aramaic. There are also questions about the channels through which the Lord's Prayer came down from Jesus' day to the time of the gospels—presumably it was through the Q strata of material, since Mark does not include the prayer— and about the influence which Christian usage had on the prayer, during these years of transmission, for we are dealing with words that men prayed, not that they embalmed. However, careful study (which includes attempts to render the prayer back into the Aramaic language that Jesus spoke) has led to the conclusion that Luke's Gospel preserves the oldest form so far as *length* goes, but that Matthew has preserved the original so far as *wording* is concerned. The prayer that Jesus taught during his ministry was short and terse, as in Luke; for details on the precise wording Matthew is often more helpful. The whole story of the Lord's Prayer from the day that Jesus first spoke it until our gospels recorded it in two forms might be summarized something like this.

One day, while Jesus was praying "in a certain place," one of
his disciples asked, "Lord, teach us to pray, as John [the Baptist]
taught his disciples to pray" (Luke 11:1). It is a good guess that
the place where this occurred was Bethany or somewhere on the
Mount of Olives, perhaps at Gethsemane. It is true that chapter
11 is part of the "Samaritan section" of Luke's Gospel, but the
last site mentioned is a village where, it is said, Mary and Martha
lived (10:38-42). New Testament tradition is that their home
was in Bethany (John 11:1 ff.), and so it is not impossible that
the place where Jesus taught his disciples to pray was near
Bethany and Jerusalem, not in Samaria. Various Jewish groups,
like the Essenes at Qumran or a brotherhood of Pharisees, are
likely to have had distinctive prayers of their own. Apparently
John the Baptist had provided a characteristic prayer for those
who heeded his preaching (cf. Luke 5:33). Not unnaturally,
Jesus' disciples wanted one too, which would embody the picture
of God and of the kingdom and of life that Jesus was proclaiming. For prayers reflect what men hold dear.

Other passages in the gospels make it possible to try to present
a fuller picture of Jesus' own practices in prayer. Luke, especially,
portrays him as a man who spoke constantly with God, at both
important and unimportant moments in his life (cf. Luke 3:21;
4:42; 6:12; 9:29). Mark sums up Jesus' miraculous power over
the fiercest of demons by quoting his words that such conquest
comes about "only through prayer" (9:29). Jesus must have
given the impression of a man who lived by prayer. Taking all
these references together, perhaps it is not too far from the truth
to think of the disciples at Luke 11:1 as talking in much the way
that J. B. Phillips pictures them in a play about Jesus. One of
them complains that he would be too tired to go off and pray
in a free moment as Jesus does. Another gives the rejoiner, "But
he gets his strength from prayer," and then goes on, "it's his *will*
that gets strengthened." When Jesus comes back from praying,
Judas is portrayed as saying, "We shall see a man—tired maybe,
but a man . . . *renewed inside,* and the new strength will shine in
his eyes."[7] This reconstruction is, of course, fiction, but the impression Jesus made was real. Men wanted to pray to God as he
did. Hence, they asked, "Teach us to pray."

Jesus provided a very simple pattern for prayer. If we follow
the form in Luke but employ some details from the wording in

Matthew (and allow for the differences between Aramaic, Greek,
and English), we may presume that the prayer went something
like this:

Dear Father,
Hallowed be thy name;
Thy kingdom come;
Our bread for tomorrow, give us today;
And forgive us our debts, as we also here and now
    forgive our debtors;
And let us not fall into temptation.[8]

The prayer is the essence of simplicity, direct, fervent, personal.
There is a clear structure: (1) the address to God as "Father";
(2) two "thy"-petitions, for God's name and kingdom; (3)
two "our"-petitions, about what is necessary for us here and now,
today, namely, bread and forgiveness; and, finally, (4) a concluding request, which may strike us as abrupt but which actually
rounds out the prayer. We may imagine that Jesus' followers soon
made this prayer their own and prayed it frequently, both during
his earthly ministry and after the resurrection. They rendered it
into the Greek in which we have it in the New Testament, while
subsequent followers have translated it into the hundreds of languages and dialects in which the Lord's Prayer has been said over
the centuries.

The first disciples who said this prayer were Jews, men familiar
with a long heritage of prayer and worship. They had their customary formulations which they employed when they prayed.
Thus, for example, the opening word "Father" (or "Dear Father") employed by Jesus would have seemed to Jewish ears a
presumptuous and overfamiliar way of addressing God. Therefore,
in spite of the daring way in which Jesus had characteristically
begun his prayer, some of his followers later on—and they were
probably the Jewish-Christians among whom Matthew's Gospel
originated—expanded the opening to the more formal phrase,
"Our Father, who art in heaven" (Matthew 6:9).[9] In this way
they emphasized God's majesty (instead of the intimacy which
Jesus' term suggested) and the "corporate" or group aspect of
prayer. The prayer now seemed more appropriate for formal use,
as in a church assembly.

So also with the ending. A doxology was soon added (recorded
in Matthew 6:13 in some manuscripts, but not in Luke), "For
thine is the kingdom and the power and the glory, for ever.

Amen." Such closing words were customary in the Old Testament
and Judaism. David's prayer at I Chronicles 29:11-12 runs,
"Thine, O Lord, is . . . the power, and the glory . . . thine is the
kingdom." It is usually stated that the doxology must have been
added by Jesus' followers only after the resurrection, since it
occurs only in certain manuscripts of Matthew. But if it were
so late an addition, it is odd that there is not more of a "Christian" tone to it, with some phrase like "through Jesus Christ our
Lord." Since Jesus was just as familiar with Jewish habits of
prayer as his later followers were, it is not impossible that Jesus
himself used this doxology at times—even though the version at
Luke 11 lacks the words.[10]

Two other additions are made in Matthew. After the two
"thy"-petitions, Matthew adds a third (6:10b):

Thy will be done, on earth as it is in heaven.

Here we have an explanation to clarify the second petition, "Thy
kingdom come." The kingdom comes as God's will is done, as
Luther emphasized in explaining this third petition of the Lord's
Prayer in his *Small Catechism*. And just as this petition has been
added in Matthew for clarification at the end of the "thy"-
petitions, so also, at the end of the "our"-petitions, Matthew adds
(6:13b) what becomes the seventh petition in his prayer:

But deliver us from the evil.

The interpretation is doubtless correct which takes the last words
as a reference to "the evil one," i.e., Satan (compare Matthew
13:19 with Mark 4:15).[11] Satan is to be seen behind the "tempta-
tions" of the sixth petition, from which men seek to be delivered.
Thus again the addition in Matthew serves to clarify something in
the briefer form of the prayer in Luke.

With these additions Matthew provides a version of the Lord's
Prayer which is fuller and more formal, the kind that disciples
might better pray together in a group, with some phrases now expanded and clarified. Note that there is a structure to Matthew's
prayer that is even more artful and "liturgical" than that in Luke:

ADDRESS:	Our Father who art in heaven,
THREE "THY"-PETITIONS:	1. Hallowed be thy name.
	2. Thy kingdom come.
	3. Thy will be done, on earth as it is in heaven.

FOUR "OUR"-PETITIONS: 4. Give us this day our daily bread;
                          5. And forgive us our debts,
                             As we also have forgiven our debt-
                             ors;
                          6. And lead us not into temptation,
                          7. But deliver us from evil.
DOXOLOGY: For thine is the kingdom and the
(in some manuscripts)   power and the glory, for ever.
                             Amen.

This is the form, with its seven petitions (considered a "perfect number" in antiquity), which came into general use. It is the form with which most Christians are familiar. It seems to represent an expansion of the words taught by the historical Jesus (as reported in Luke 11), but an expansion under the Spirit, an expansion which is also part of the New Testament and without which the prayers of Christians would be immensely poorer. The most amazing thing about this expansion is that it remains *true to the original words and intent of Jesus' prayer.* What is added is intended to clarify what is already there or to fill it out in accord with Jewish practice. There is nothing about the atonement, or Christology, or even the Holy Spirit, but only about God and his kingdom and his power to deliver men. We must conclude that the longer form of the Lord's Prayer represents a further working out of Jesus' own words, not a falsification of them. The early church, in its new situations, remained true here to the "Jesus-tradition."

We have now looked at the structure and development of the prayer and noted petitions three and seven and the doxology. There are still some problems in the remaining petitions when we compare Matthew and Luke, as well as some general questions. Perhaps the most jarring difficulty is that so little in the Lord's Prayer, whether we examine it in the shorter or longer form, is original with Jesus. It has already been pointed out that the address in Matthew and the doxology parallel Jewish forms. But the same thing is true of the rest of the prayer, even in Luke. Virtually every detail in the prayer that Jesus taught can be duplicated in the sayings of rabbis and Jewish teachers of the day. Indeed, one expert in the Talmud was able to patch together solely from Jewish sources a prayer which says the same things as the Lord's Prayer.[12] We must face the fact that Jesus' prayer is

far from original. Indeed, not only this prayer but much of what
he taught finds parallels in the sages of the Jews and of other
peoples, often decades or centuries earlier.

Many Christians (and non-Christians who look on Jesus with
respect) are surprised to learn that such parallels exist to what
Jesus said. In part, this is because they have failed to see Jesus in
historical perspective, in the world of his day. Yet such is precisely what we should expect to find: Jesus lived at a specific time
and place in history and expressed himself in the idiom of that
day. In part, the shock of discovering the "non-originality" of
Jesus' teachings may stem from the common conception of Jesus
as "the Great Teacher," "great" being taken to mean "unique."
Against this conception stands the judgment, expressed bluntly
by one scholar, "There is not a single one of Jesus' ethical teachings of which it could not be said, a priori, that it has any claim,
as an individual precept, to absolute originality."[13] Perhaps that is
overstating it, but the general point is correct. This applies also
to the Lord's Prayer. But is this loss? We have already learned
that for early Christians the Gospel and the gospels centered in
the cross and resurrection, not in the ethics of a "Great Teacher."
It is true that Jesus was a teacher and that he announced the will
of God, but our gospels never claim that his importance lay in
any "unique ethical teachings." Therefore one must expect much
of what he taught to come right out of the world of his day. It
is who Jesus was, and what he did, and often how he said a thing
that put an edge on what he said, and made it distinctive.

Having thus acknowledged that Jesus' teachings will in many
ways run parallel to Old Testament and Jewish thought and that
many of the things he said will not prove to be "original," we
must add that along with the parallels which can be found, some
differences from the teachers of his day can be pointed out. In
the case of the Lord's Prayer, the general characteristics which
mark it as distinct are the directness of the prayer, its succinctness,
and the underlying conviction that God is at work now, in Jesus'
day. A. R. George speaks of the Lord's Prayer thus:

> In one sense it is not original, for the separate clauses can all be
> paralleled from Jewish sources. . . . But the choice and arrangement
> of these petitions and their brevity make a powerful impression of
> originality.[14]

That patchwork prayer culled from the rabbis runs to 157 words.
Compare that with the total of only 68 for the Lord's Prayer in

its Matthean form (including the doxology)! Even Jewish scholars who have examined the matter agree that Jesus' teachings were terse and incisive compared with those of the rabbis.[15] "The originality of Jesus consists in this," Wellhausen stated, "that he had the feeling for what was true and eternal amid a chaotic mass of rubbish."[16] Jesus' originality thus lay not so much in *what* he taught as in *how* he said it and in his conviction that God was *now* at work. For Jesus spoke of God with new directness and of the intervention of God's kingdom with new certainty.

The wheat, gleaned from so much chaff, an urgency of the presence and the will of God—how does all this apply in specific terms to the Lord's Prayer?

The Lord's Prayer and the Praying Lord

It has been suggested that the "original" elements in the Lord's Prayer are three: the way Jesus speaks of the kingdom; the manner in which he addresses God; and, in some ways, the concept of forgiveness. To claim here an element of originality does not mean, of course, that people prior to Jesus had not spoken of these themes or prayed about them; for centuries Jews had. It simply means that Jesus gave new emphasis and eschatological conviction to what had been said before and thus spoke of God and his kingdom and forgiveness differently. Indeed, his words take us, at times, to the very heart of the Gospel.

First, the kingdom. The disciples were to pray, "Thy kingdom come." Matthew adds, as an explanation, "by thy will being done." There is also a further reference to the kingdom in the doxology: "for thine is the kingdom . . . for ever." It is quite clear here that the kingdom belongs to God, but Jesus envisions it as coming into the world of men. Much more will be said on this topic when we examine the full evidence from the preaching and parables and miracles of Jesus, for "the kingdom of God" was the chief theme of his ministry (see chapter 6). But even at this point, in light of the references in the Lord's Prayer, it can be seen that three things characterize the kingdom.[17] (1) *It already exists.* For the Old Testament and late Judaism, God's kingly, sovereign rule is, like his power and glory, a fact "from everlasting to everlasting." Independent of man, it exists (as the explanation at Matthew 6:10*b* implies) "in heaven," the transcendent realm beyond earth, where God is and whence he rules the world. That "God

is king" is part of the basic situation which the Old Testament
and Jesus presuppose. (2) This existing kingdom *"comes."* Men
are to pray for its advent in their lives. Jesus' basic message was
that God's rule was in fact "breaking in," then and there, during
his ministry.[18] Matthew interprets this to mean specifically that
God's dominion becomes real to men when they do his will. (3)
This kingdom *is to come.* There will be a future fulfillment. The
prayer is *not* one of thanks that the kingdom *has* come. Even
after the resurrection, in the "new era of the Gospel," Christians
did not change the prayer of Jesus to claim that the kingdom had
already arrived. They continued to pray, "Thy kingdom come,"
looking forward to a future consummation when God would be
all in all (I Corinthians 15:24-28). In the way it centers on the
kingdom of God, the Lord's Prayer is characteristic of Jesus'
message as a whole.

Secondly, Jesus' term for God. The prayer as given in Luke
began simply, "Father." In all likelihood the word in Aramaic
was a term which the Greek New Testament employs several
times, the term *Abba.* According to Mark 14:36, for example,
Jesus prayed in Gethsemane, *"Abba,* Father . . . ." That Aramaic
word made a strong impression on early Christians, even those
whose language was Greek, for we find them using it to refer to
God long after Christianity had left Palestine and spread hundreds
and thousands of miles beyond into the Greek-speaking world. To
the Galatians, Paul wrote, "God has sent the Spirit of his Son into
our hearts, crying, *'Abba!* Father!' " (Galatians 4:6). Christians
as far away as Rome knew this same cry, *"Abba!* Father!" (Romans 8:15). The word must have become ingrained in the prayers of Christians who otherwise knew no Aramaic—much as
people today employ a Hebrew term like "Amen."

The most probable explanation for this widespread early Christian usage of *Abba* is that it came from Jesus himself.[19] He spoke
to God as Father (cf. Matthew 11:25; 26:39, 42; Luke 23:34,
46; John 11:41, etc.), and the word in his native language was
Abba. The startling thing is that this is perhaps the one word in
the Lord's Prayer which a Jew of Jesus' day would *not* have used.
We must make no mistake about the matter. Men had for centuries spoken of God as "Father"—Sumerians and Greeks, as
well as Israelites. The Old Testament compares God to a father
(though rather rarely, and avoiding the pagan idea that God had

physically begotten man, as in so many myths). Israel confessed of God, "Thou art our father" (Isaiah 63:16). The word used for "father" in Hebrew was *ab*, and Jews would speak of God as "our father" (*abinu*, as at Matthew 6:9). But the form *abba* had a special sense. It was the word a child used for his earthly father, a sort of diminutive, the first word a baby might stammer. *Abba* was thus used in the sense of "Daddy," but of course, no Jew would ever think of addressing Yahweh on his throne in such terms. That, however, is, it seems, just what Jesus did. He took this intimate, homely word out of daily life and used it to address the Lord of the heavens. We need a term in English which will suggest this warm, intimate association without flippancy or sentimentality. Perhaps "Dear Father" will do.[20]

Thus, as his regular practice, according to our gospel sources, Jesus spoke to God in terms of unique intimacy that no one else of his day would venture. The word *Abba* tells us how Jesus thought of God—as a dear father, even though a king. It gives us some hint also of how Jesus thought of himself—as one in a personal relationship with God, as son. Above all, it is the word that Jesus shared with his disciples for their use: "When *you* pray, say: '*Abba*, Father . . . .' " Jesus was opening the way for a new relationship with God for his followers. They are adopted sons. Jesus' prayer thus stressed the "vertical" relationship for them—with God. In time his followers came to realize the "horizontal" implications too: all who call God "*Abba*" are bound together in this new relationship and want to pray, "*Our* Father. . . ."

Thirdly, forgiveness. Matthew has:

Forgive us our *debts,* as we also have forgiven our *debtors.*

Luke reads:

Forgive us our *sins,* for we ourselves forgive every one who is *indebted* to us.

In Jesus' original prayer, it is the terms "debts" and "debtors" which were doubtless used, for in Aramaic sin is spoken of as a "debt." Matthew has rendered this Aramaic term quite literally, but Luke has perhaps gotten the sense better with his word "sins," although he makes the neat distinction that we sin *against God* but are debtors to our *fellowmen.* At Matthew 6:14-15 the same Aramaic term for "debts" is probably rendered by the Greek word for "trespasses," and so we can say that there are at least three different ways in the New Testament of expressing the same underlying term:

the Aramaic term (*ḥobḥa*)

literally "debts" (Matthew 6:12) or "sins" (Luke 11:4) or "trespasses" (Matthew 6:14)

Which term is used today—and usage by Christians in praying the Lord's Prayer has varied considerably from denomination to denomination—depends on what people have become accustomed to in years of worship, and on which gets across the meaning best to modern man (hence the willingness to experiment with new translations of the Lord's Prayer).

The really difficult thing about this petition, in the eyes of many Christians, is that it makes it sound as if God's forgiveness depends on their *first* forgiving their fellowmen. This is especially true in Matthew:

Forgive us . . . as we *have forgiven* our debtors.

Does this mean that one must first forgive in order to merit God's forgiveness?[21] If so, it would be contrary to the sequence in the Gospel as other parts of the New Testament clearly set it forth; for example, the epistles say, "forgive one another, as God in Christ forgave you" (see Ephesians 4:32; Colossians 3:13). Yet Jesus here seems to be laying down a condition to experience the grace of God: first, forgive, then be forgiven. If so, Jesus' teaching would even be a step behind that of Judaism, for the rabbis taught that God forgives unconditionally.[22] Is this one place where, in contrast to the rabbis, Jesus was "original," but with an "originality" that is retrogressive when compared with the norm in Jewish thought?

To help us understand this petition, three things must be said.

(1) The phrase "as we *have forgiven* our debtors" represents a literal translation of an Aramaic verb form which means "as we *herewith forgive* our debtors."[23] Luke has correctly caught the sense when he makes a change in tense: "for we ourselves *forgive* everyone who is indebted to us." The prayer is a pledge to forgive *all* men, *here and now*, and in the future, as we stand and ask for God's forgiveness. A fair rendering might be, "Forgive us, O God, as we also here and now forgive those who have wronged us."[24]

(2) Secondly it must be remembered to whom Jesus addressed these words. This is a *disciples'* prayer, for followers who already know of God as *Abba* and who have experienced something of his power and goodness. It is not that their prayer "primes the pump" and "starts the action" so that God then forgives them. Rather God and the Gospel stand prior to their prayer. Their actions and prayers are a response. First he has given; in response to his goodness, they forgive. This prayer can be understood only by those who know the Gospel of Jesus.

(3) This interpretation fits well with the general message of Jesus: God acts and man is to respond. For example, in the parable of the Unmerciful Servant (Matthew 18:23-35), the servant is first forgiven an enormous debt by his lord. It is his failure to respond by forgiving a fellow servant an infinitesimal amount which brings condemnation on him. "Should not you have had mercy on your fellow servant, *as I had mercy* on you?" (18:33).

Jesus' teaching here, that the forgiven must forgive, is not only good theology, however. There is also a profound psychological point involved. Who can accept forgiveness if he is not ready to give it to others too? Do people not sometimes in life block God's gifts to them by a refusal to open their hearts and pass these gifts on? (Cf. I John 3:16-17; 4:10-11, 19-21.) This failure to forgive others, if habitual, will be a barrier preventing even God's forgiveness from getting through. And so there must be "wire-cutting," on both sides, in some of the "barbed-wire entanglements" which mar so many human relationships—lest we barricade ourselves in "self," so that even God is blocked out.[25] "Forgivingness"—absolutely, to all—is part of Jesus' prayer. It repeats the Old Testament message of the loving-kindness of God, but with a demand for personal response which no man can evade.

The remaining petitions of the prayer are less strikingly original, and owe even more to the Old Testament and to the Judaism of Jesus' day. The first petition, "Hallowed be thy name," is much like the part of the *Qaddish*, a synagogue prayer which Jesus doubtless knew. It ran:

Hallowed and exalted be God's great name in the world which he created according to his will.

This prayer then went on to speak of God's kingdom, just as the Lord's Prayer does, asking that God would act "speedily and soon." God's "name" means, in Old Testament terms, his person, his inner being. To "make holy" his name or person implies that He should hallow it by mighty acts which cause men to reverence him, and also that men should hail him as the only God, by the way they live.

The fourth petition (in Matthew's numbering) has caused all sorts of difficulty for interpreters. Matthew begins, "Give us today . . . ," but Luke has (literally), "Keep on giving us day by day." Matthew's wording is probably more original and closer to Jesus' Aramaic, but Luke made it into a general truth, applicable to experience over a long period of time.[26] The real difficulty lies in the phrase "our daily bread." So we translate and say it, rather glibly. (And actually the rendering is not a bad one, when all is considered.) But the fact is that scholars are not sure what the word we render as "daily" comes from or exactly what it means. There are no other certain examples of this word from all the literature of antiquity.[27] Hence the experts are reduced to guessing, from scraps of evidence, as to the precise sense. The most likely answer is that it means "bread for the morrow, give us today"— i.e., give us enough to see us through the next step on the way.

A further problem of interpretation is what Jesus meant by "bread." It is reassuring to discover that the term implies, first of all, everything that men need physically for sustenance in life (and that means a great deal more of "things" in twentieth-century America than it did in first-century Palestine). It is reassuring, because Jesus here seems concerned with down-to-earth things at the very start of the "our"-petitions. We must not make God so "spiritual" that such economic factors are excluded from our prayers. But "bread" in antiquity had an even more profound meaning. Men spoke of the "bread of life" which would sustain man more than just physically. In John's Gospel, Jesus is himself identified as the bread of life which "gives life to the world," the bread which, specifically through the Spirit and through Jesus' words, means true life (see John 6:22ff.; especially verses 32-35, 51, 63). The Lord's Prayer here does not mention even indirectly the "bread" in the Lord's Supper, as the Middle Ages thought it did,[28] but surely it prays for more than physical sustenance; it asks God for the life that can come into our existence only from God—through the Spirit and through Jesus' words. What ought to astonish us is that Jesus taught his disciples to pray for such "bread"—which his Jewish contemporaries expected only in the "last times"—*here and now*, in the present, "this day," "daily," "each day."

The sixth petition, "Lead us not into temptation," requires comment at two points. The verb might suggest that God can lead men into temptation. That is denied by James 1:13 and by Jewish thought in Jesus' day: God does not tempt any man.[29] The sense is rather, "Do not bring us to the test," or as an ancient variant in a prayer from King's College Chapel, Cambridge, has it, "Suffer us not to be led into temptation." But what is the "temptation" or "the test"? The term may well include the daily difficulties and dangers which confront any righteous man. As a saying in the Apocrypha put it:

> My son, if you come forward to serve the Lord,
> Prepare yourself for temptation. (Wisdom of Sirach 2:1)

But surely Jesus' words referred to more than just routine encumbrances which plague all men. The term he used is one that in writings of the day referred to trials of the last times (Mark 14:38), *the* Test, the final great trial—the danger of falling away from God. Matthew means us to see this sense when he adds, "Deliver us from the Evil One." God is here pictured as the one who holds all things in his power, including men who call him *Abba* and trust in him. But they must not presume they stand, least of all by themselves—lest they fall before the onslaughts of evil. That is the kind of world in which they live. And on that note, the prayer of Jesus returns those who hear and pray it to stark reality: it fixes their eyes on God but amid the testings of the world.

It is sometimes said that this prayer of Jesus can be used in a variety of ways. People can pray it formally, together in church, with a set form of words in an agreed translation. Or it can be spoken by individuals in a more intimate form. One can take each of its master thoughts and meditate on them in one's own words, for one's own situation. The New Testament itself, it can be said, encourages such flexibility in using the Lord's Prayer. For Luke presents it in a simple form, Matthew more liturgically. The latter gives a literal wording, the former paraphrases to get the sense. Indeed, Christians of the first century or two were even more flexible than this. Instead of "Thy kingdom come," some copies of the prayer have, "Thy Holy Spirit come upon us and cleanse us," or in the first petition, "Hallowed be thy name upon us"—phrases which were particularly applicable when the prayer was used at a baptismal service.[30] Matthew has used the Lord's Prayer as a contrast to prayers which "heap up empty phrases" and "many words" (6:5-8). Luke employs it as the sort of prayer that gives men confidence to speak to God. God will hear, and answer prayer (11:5-13). The important thing, for all these early scribes and evangelists, is that men pray to God along these lines. Jesus has provided a pattern for prayer—but not a straitjacket to confine men's words.

Even more important, Jesus offered in his own life an example of persistent prayer which encouraged men to follow his lead. In setting the stage for the question at Luke 11:1, "teach us to pray," we remarked that Jesus' own practice doubtless inspired his followers to ask for a pattern for their prayers. Without doubt, Jesus was a man of prayer all his life, but there is one particular scene in the gospels which has special ties with the Lord's Prayer. It is the picture of Jesus in Gethsemane. Here we see the praying lord, and there are close connections, not always fully appreciated, with the Lord's Prayer.

"The night in which he was betrayed" began with a meal. From the Upper Room in the southwestern part of Jerusalem, where they had eaten together, Jesus and eleven of his followers then made their way through the darkened streets across the Kidron Valley to a garden on the Mount of Olives where Jesus was accustomed to go (Luke 22:39). There had been prayers together and a hymn in the Upper Room (Mark 14:26), and even as they went, Jesus talked in Old Testament terms (Mark 14:27=Zechariah 13:7). But now there was to be even deeper prayer, in solitude, in the kind of "private place" that Jesus recommended for such prayers (Matthew 6:6). Peter was full of boastfulness: come what may, *he* would not fall away, he assured Jesus: "If I must die with you, I will not deny you" (Mark 14: 29, 31). Jesus spoke prophetically when he reminded Peter that this was exactly what he would do: ". . . before the cock crows twice, you will deny me three times." At that moment Peter was forgetting the petition in the disciples' prayer which said, "Suffer us not to be led into temptation," for we are weak. Confident of his own ability, he courted testing—and he fell away, denying his lord.

It is in the garden of Gethsemane itself, however, that the parallels between the Lord's Prayer and the praying lord really become clear. Jesus leaves the main group of disciples while he goes on further into the night with Peter, James, and John, to pray. He bares some of the anguish of his soul to them (Mark 14:34)—Luther said, "No one ever feared death so much as this Man"[31]—and then he went on a stone's throw further, alone, to pray. Three times he speaks virtually the same prayer, and returns each time to find his friends, not in prayer, but slumbering. It is the content of Jesus' prayer which interests us here.

Abba, Father, all things are possible to thee; remove this cup from me; yet not what I will, but what thou wilt. (Mark 14:36)

True, the three gospels report the three prayers with slight variations in wording. But the general thrust is clear. What does Jesus say? (1) "Remove this cup from me." One's "cup" is one's lot in life, the disaster (Isaiah 51:17) or good fortune (Psalm 23:5) which lies ahead of one. Here it denotes the ordeal awaiting Jesus at Jerusalem. The verb "remove" happens to be the same basic one in Greek that we render as "lead" in the sixth petition of the Lord's Prayer:[32] "*remove* this cup from me," "*lead* us not into temptation." Jesus knows the dangers of such a test. Unlike Peter, he does not rush to meet it, trusting in himself. He hesitates before facing the ordeal. At this moment, says Karl Barth, "the bill is being presented" for the world's redemption.[33] Jesus is counting the cost—but with trust in God. (2) "All things are possible in thee." Here Jesus' words are akin to the doxology, "Thine is . . . the power and the glory." (3) "Yet not what I will, but what thou wilt." This is the third petition of the Lord's Prayer put into personal terms, "Thy will be done." (4) Finally, there is the key word, "Abba, Father," with which the Lord's Prayer and the prayer in Gethsemane both begin. Here is expressed that relationship of trust and confidence that would see Jesus through all the tribulations of the Passion ordeal ahead.

We must say that the prayer of Jesus in Gethsemane remarkably reflects the content of the prayer that Jesus had taught his disciples to pray. The praying lord and the Lord's Prayer become one. We find not merely a pattern for prayer but a man who actually does pray thus and who lives as he prays. Jesus puts the contents of the prayer he had taught into words that fit the situation of the moment in his life. And in this way we learn here, not merely how Jesus may have prayed in a given instance, but how a Christian ought to pray.

Rather surprisingly, as we looked at the sayings of Jesus to learn something about the man from Nazareth, we have discovered that we are also (thanks to the technique of the evangelists and the nature of the gospel material) looking at our own human situation and learning something for our lives, in this case regarding prayer. We examine the Lord's Prayer and discover *both* a form of prayer which (so far as we can tell) the historical Jesus taught *and* a version of the prayer that his followers developed under the Spirit in their actual praying. We look at Jesus in Gethsemane and discover, while we are trying to reconstruct the picture of Jesus in the garden, that a gospel message slips in about how one ought to pray (which was something the evangelists probably intended the scene to teach).

Historians must ask searching questions about this Gethsemane scene. Who was there to record Jesus' words if the disciples were asleep? Since Mark, Matthew, and Luke differ in their accounts of what he said, how can we be sure of the precise wording? Also, is it not possible that the wording, as we have it, has been influenced by the Lord's Prayer, so that the scene is meant to show us how to pray, as much as how Jesus actually prayed?

By now, such questions should be apparent and familiar to us. We know that the gospel records, even when they report the sayings of Jesus, are not tape recordings or machine-gun camera photographs of what happened or was said in Jesus' ministry. They are gospel proclamations of the Jesus-material, directed at followers and would-be followers of Christ. The men who were responsible for passing on to us the scene at Gethsemane were not interested as much in chronicling Jesus' words to God on April 6, A.D. 30, as in teaching men to pray as the Lord desired.

To answer the questions, then, as directly as possible, with which we began this study of Jesus' Passion and the Lord's Prayer: yes, we can know *something* of the Jesus of history (not in spite of, but *because of* modern research). We can see *some events* in his life take shape, we can hear *some things he said*, perhaps even in the very Aramaic language that he spoke. But the answer is "No" to any biography of Jesus, "No" to any psychological study of him, "No" to any uncritical acceptance of *every* word in the four gospels as an utterance during the *historical* ministry. We cannot expect to recover what Jesus said or did with absolute accuracy.[34] Not only the narratives about Jesus but the words of his lips are touched by the Gospel faith of the early church and (early Christians believed) by the Spirit of the Lord. The voice of the earthly Jesus is blended with the voice of the heavenly lord—until, for the early church, the words become the Word of God.

Such a view of Jesus Christ in our New Testament gospels depends, of course, on the assumption that the resurrection bulked as large in early Christian thought as we have been claiming. How stands it with the resurrection of Jesus in the light of historical research today?

5

God Raised Him from the Dead

In the cathedral church at Haderslev, Denmark, near the main entrance, in the south aisle, hangs an unusual painting. Seen from one angle, as you move down the aisle, it portrays the crucifixion. Move on a bit and view it again, and this "perspective painting," framed within its ornamented pilasters, has become a portrayal of the resurrection. The position and condition of Jesus have changed. The colors shift from somber blacks and grays to a more brilliant array. Even the audience changes; at least the figures in the resurrection scene are no longer bowed down in grief, they look upward in joy and awe.

The painter's trick perspective may strike art connoisseurs as just a step removed from those pictures of Jesus where his eyes follow the viewer across the room. But whatever the verdict on the technique, this Danish artist has captured a profound point in the New Testament's picture of Jesus Christ: cross and resurrection belong together. Jesus is seen as the one who died at Calvary and who was raised again by God. The features of the crucified Nazarene and the exalted lord are blended together on the same canvas. Good Friday and Easter are superimposed on each other. To express it, with regard to the New Testament, in terms which we have used before, crucifixion and resurrection, thus superimposed, provide the kerygmatic frame of reference within which all the material about Jesus was transmitted, the "lens" through which all is viewed:

Jesus our Lord,
put to death for our trespasses,
raised for our justification. (Romans 4:25)

We have spoken of Jesus' death in great detail and have seen how the Gospel centered in it. At the same time it has been noted that the Gospel is always an understanding of Jesus and his death in the light of the resurrection. It has been claimed that the resurrection of Jesus and his exaltation as lord is the interpreting fact for all that early Christians told of Jesus' works and words. "Be it known to you all . . . that . . . Jesus Christ of Nazareth . . . God raised from the dead" (Acts 4:10). Here is the supreme miracle which dazzled even Jesus' closest followers and left his disciples with the awed confession, in the words of Psalm 118:

23, "This is the Lord's doing; it is marvelous in our eyes" (cf. Mark 12:10).

Before going any further, we must now take time to examine what the New Testament writings, and especially the gospels, say about the resurrection of Jesus Christ. What is the "evidence," what are the problems, and how do the biblical accounts stand up in light of modern historical study? In what ways is the resurrection projected into the picture of the historical Jesus in the church's gospels? Is it correct that the resurrection is an indispensable starting point for consideration of Jesus and his message as portrayed in these gospels?

The Resurrection and Its Interpreting Role

It has already been emphasized that the kerygma or basic proclamation of earliest Christianity drew its impact not merely from a statement that Jesus of Nazareth had been crucified but from what was inseparably bound up with this "death notice": namely, the announcement of the unparalleled news that this Jesus has been raised up by God from the dead and exalted to God's right hand. The sermons in Acts are filled with this news (Acts 2:24, 32; 3:15, 26; 4:33; 5:30). The earliest letter which we have from Paul (and that means the oldest Christian document preserved today), I Thessalonians, has this same theme—"we believe that Jesus died and rose again" (4:14), Jesus "whom he raised from the dead" (1:10). Throughout primitive Christianity ran a common message: Jesus lives as lord, because God raised him up.

We have also emphasized repeatedly that this message stands behind every epistle, every gospel, and every other writing in the New Testament. It is the assumption behind every section and verse of these documents. This conviction—that God has raised Jesus from the dead, has exalted him as lord over all the world, and has revealed him to his church as the Living One—

> sustains all the statements of the New Testament. Without the certainty of Easter there would be no New Testament—not one single line. . . . It is not the message of Christmas but the preaching of the Resurrection that stands at the beginning of the history of the Church. If there were no Easter there would be no Christian Church.[1]

No Easter message, then no New Testament or church. But how does the New Testament spell out this message? What accounts does it give of that underlying message, "Christ is risen"?

It needs to be said immediately that the New Testament writings, chiefly the gospels, abound in accounts of Jesus' resurrection, but that these accounts vary in their perspective and emphases. We have already dealt with I Corinthians 15:4-8 and verses like Acts 2:23-24 as typical announcements of what God has done following Jesus' death. How do the gospels elaborate on this?

In a sense Mark's Gospel does not. It ends abruptly with the story (16:1-8) of how the women went to the tomb early in the morning of the first day of the week to complete the last faithful rites of loving hands, embalming Jesus' body. Instead, they find the body gone, hear an announcement from "a young man . . . dressed in a white robe" that Jesus is risen—and then retreat in astonishment and fear. This is the way the oldest manuscripts conclude. But many readers have not been content to think that Mark would have wished to end his gospel this way. In the second century A.D., scribes added a "short ending" as well as a longer one (16:9-20 in later numberings) put together from details in other gospels and early Christian literature.[2] All sorts of explanations for the abrupt ending at vs. 8 have been proposed—e.g., that Mark's original ending was somehow lost, or that he planned or actually wrote a second volume (which we do not have).

But if one reads the Gospel of Mark through as a unit, preferably at a single sitting, one begins to see that the seemingly abrupt ending at 16:8 is not so strange after all and is in fact quite effective as literature and witness.[3] Mark 1:1 gives the title of the book as "The Beginning of the Gospel of Jesus Christ." When he reaches the end of the book (16:8), the reader senses that, in a way, the real beginning comes only with the resurrection, thanks to which Jesus is seen as the Christ, there is a Gospel message, and the Gospel is going forward and has reached him as he read the book. Mark has presented, on every page, the picture of a man through whom God worked extraordinarily; it is unthinkable that God should abandon this Jesus at death, especially after, Mark tells us, Jesus had taught that God would raise him up (8:31; 9:31; 10:34). The literary ending is, therefore, ironic. How stupid, readers will say, to stand silent and afraid, as these women did, in the face of such news, uncommunicative and awed by fear. For the news that Jesus lives and reigns as lord has been announced (16:6; 1:1; 12:10-11; etc.). Perhaps Mark even intended readers to infer that the women were silent only for a time, that they soon told what they had heard. The evangelist's implication would be, "Go and do thou likewise."

But not every gospel need close with the sort of dramatic irony which Mark used. Matthew and Luke availed themselves of some of the many reports about the resurrection which were circulating in the Christian world, to bring their gospels to the conclusions they sought. Matthew not only has Mark's story of the women at the empty tomb (28:1-8) but he adds that Jesus himself then appeared to them (28:9-10).[4] He also reports a story that was circulating among the Jews (28:11-15), to the effect that the Roman guards were bribed to spread a tale that the disciples stole the body during the night. Matthew, as a Jewish Christian, was presumably in a position to hear such a tale. In reporting it, he refrains from any long list of refutations against it, but makes the notation that the story stemmed from the chief priests and was made possible by bribes. Matthew is confident that no one could really believe this incredible alternative to what seemed so certain to him: that God had raised Jesus up. The Matthean Gospel then concludes with a majestic, panoramic scene in Galilee where the risen lord, whom men now worship, commissions his followers to "go into all the world" with his message and authority and accompanied by his presence (28:16-20).

Luke has resurrection appearances too, but a completely different series from those in Matthew. Like Mark, he recounts the visit of the women to the empty tomb, though his list of the women involved is longer (24:1-11; vs. 12 is an addition found only in later manuscripts, derived from John 20:3-10).[5] Then Luke has a lengthy and vivid account of how the risen Jesus appeared on the road between Jerusalem and Emmaus to two disciples, one of whom is Cleopas and the other possibly Simon Peter (24:13-35).[6] The two no sooner hurry back to Jerusalem to report this unbelievable news to the other disciples than Jesus appears to all of them there (24:36-49).[7] Here he commissions them for their future work, though the power of the Spirit will not be given until later, according to Luke-Acts (Luke 24:49; cf. Acts 1:4; 2:1 ff.). Luke lets the curtain fall on his gospel with a brief note about Jesus' departure at Bethany (or his ascension, if we add what some manuscripts do, as in the RSV footnote). The closing note is of the inevitable response to all this: great joy, and

praise to God (24:50-53). Of course, this closing is but the end
of "Act I"; the stage is set for the curtain to rise on "Act II" and
the further story, in the Acts of the Apostles.

When we examine all of these resurrection accounts (and even
if we add those in John and the references elsewhere in the New
Testament), several obvious features stand out.

1. There is *no actual description* of the resurrection itself. That
remains for noncanonical and specifically gnostic documents to
provide later on, and then with fantastic details, as in the *Gospel
of Peter,* where the cross follows Jesus from the tomb and the
resurrected Christ towers higher than the heavens. The New
Testament claims the resurrection was an act of God, but it nowhere attempts to describe it. What Phillips Brooks wrote of the
nativity applies even more to the resurrection of Jesus Christ:

> How silently, how silently,
> The wondrous Gift is given![8]

Silently, unseen, undescribed. God's greatest act is felt in its effects, not chronicled in its details. The God of revelation remains
hidden, and there is reserve, precisely at the greatest unveiling of
his power.

2. *The action is God's.* This means that the resurrection was
not a feat performed by Jesus himself. Nowhere in the New
Testament is it said that Jesus rolled the stone away, though
modern Christians sometimes seem to have a picture of Jesus
resuscitating himself, tidying up the tomb (cf. John 20:7), and
making his way to God. As a matter of fact, the regular New
Testament formulas are "God raised Jesus" or "Jesus was raised
up by God." Such expressions occur some thirty times. The only
exception is I Thessalonians 4:14 (and perhaps John 10:17-18),
and even there the overall emphasis is still on God's action (cf.
I Thessalonians 1:10 and John 10:18, "from my Father"). The
resurrection is to be seen in continuity with God's previous mighty
acts, as the work of God, in the view of the New Testament.

3. The resurrection appearances are described in *short individual narratives,*[9] *without any common framework.* In the Passion story, we learned, there was a common outline, however
much each evangelist might add to or vary it. With the resurrection there is a common message that "Jesus is risen," but for the
most part each writer reports different resurrection appearances;
there is no general framework into which these separate narratives

can be set as was the case with the incidents in the Passion.[10] This, it has been pointed out, stems from the fact that the Passion had to be explained and so a common narrative framework was important, whereas every apostle and every apostolic witness knew the risen Christ and took the resurrection as the starting point for what he said.[11] To explain why Jesus died, a general outline of what had occurred was a necessity; to declare that He lived, each witness chose those accounts about the resurrection which were most meaningful to him and to his audience.

When we examine the several resurrection accounts more closely, however, questions about detail and problems of "what happened" soon appear. To list these is nothing new. Two hundred years ago the rationalist Reimarus compiled a collection of "contradictions" and "improbabilities," to which little more can be added today. The most noticeable discrepancies include (a) the matter of place. Matthew has the final appearance of Jesus and the "Great Commission" in Galilee (28:16-20). Luke places the farewell and ascension at Bethany, near Jerusalem (24:50-53; Acts 1:1-12). John, as if to do justice to both views, has the appearances in Jerusalem (chapter 20) and then an epilogue by the Sea of Galilee (in chapter 21). There is (b) the question of who went first to the empty tomb. John says it was Mary Magdalene, apparently alone (20:1 ff.). Matthew refers to "Mary Magdalene and the other Mary" (28:1). Mark notes three women— "Mary Magdalene, and Mary the mother of James, and Salome" (16:1).[12] Luke has a reference to "the women who had come with him from Galilee" (23:55), and identifies them as "Mary Magdalene and Joanna and Mary the mother of James and the other women" (24:10). Besides questions of place and people, there are also lesser problems, such as (c) how many angels were present at the empty tomb? Matthew says one ("an angel of the Lord," 28:2); John says "two angels in white" spoke to Mary Magdalene (20:12). Luke agrees basically with John ("two men . . . in dazzling apparel," 24:4), while Mark with his reference to "a young man" seems to line up with Matthew.[13] Over the years, Christians as well as agnostics, scholarly experts as well as simple readers, have debated these points. Some of the answers given by Christians, like the one that "if two angels were present, then there was one present" (thus making all accounts "correct"), have often been as rationalistic as the objections of men like

Reimarus.[14] All in all, it must be admitted, even by the staunchest believer, that there are problems connected with the resurrection if one looks at it historically. If the cross is, as it has been called, "a mighty question mark against the sky,"[15] the resurrection, when examined in the light of reason and subjected to the historians' scrutiny, poses a greater question-mark.

In the opinion of the early Christians, however, the resurrection of Jesus Christ poses a question mark that is even greater in another sense, and that is the question of faith. For them it poses a question to everyone who hears the message that "Jesus is risen from the dead": namely *do you believe?* For, in spite of all the historical problems and all the logical and rational improbabilities, in spite of all the centuries of human experience that death is the end to every human life, these early Christians wanted to say to men, as they preached their message, "Do you believe that there is a God who has power over death, and that in this one case, that of Jesus of Nazareth, God exerted his power to raise him up and give him a position of honor?" Their kerygma then went on to ask, "Will you commit yourself to a God who acted thus in Jesus' case and will do similarly for those who believe in him?" As one of Paul's letters reminded his readers, "God raised the Lord and will also raise us up by his power" (I Corinthians 6:14). Such a Christianity proclaimed the resurrection and knew its power. It made no thorough attempt to explain "what happened," but believed and proclaimed "the God . . . who gives life to the dead" (Romans 4:17). Hence, the New Testament insists the act was God's, but avoids descriptions of the "how"; it offers only varied impressions of the results, from a number of angles.

Yet through the centuries because of all the problems of apologetics and questions posed by reason about the resurrection of Jesus, men have sought to see if anything can be said to clarify some of the "contradictions" and "improbabilities"—with or without removing the miracle. For example, to the question of the place where the resurrection appearances are to be localized, it has often been deemed a likely answer that, according to the oldest accounts, Jesus appeared first in Jerusalem (even Matthew does not deny that, see Matthew 28:9-10), and then in Galilee. Even Luke has a vestige of these post-resurrection appearances in Galilee at Acts 1:11 (in the phrase "Men *of Galilee*") and probably otherwise omits them in order to keep all appearances at Jerusalem and thus to lead into his story in "Volume 2," where the Gospel spreads forth from Jerusalem, not Galilee (see Acts 1:8).

The matter of the women at the tomb is more difficult, but it is clear that running through all the accounts is the fact that it was women who first discovered something had occurred, and that Mary Magdalene is the prime figure in all four gospels. It has been suggested that these initial witnesses are never mentioned in a list like that at I Corinthians 15:4-8 because in the Jewish world the testimony of women had no legal value. (Therefore only the appearances to men are listed in I Corinthians, as a series of witnesses who might convince in accord with Old Testament requirements.) Further, then, in this case, the accounts of the experience of the women might have been less carefully preserved; details in their narrative, like that of the number of angels at the tomb, would have been subject to variation. So runs one explanation.

If we ask what in the New Testament can be considered as direct "proofs" for the event behind the message which these varied reports present, the answer is twofold. First of all, in order of occurrence in the gospel accounts, comes the empty tomb. All four gospels agree in saying that the tomb was empty, save for grave cloths (John 20:6-7). It is often stated that Paul did not know of an empty tomb. It is true that (like many other things about Jesus) the empty tomb is never mentioned in Paul's letters. However, the sequence in I Corinthians 15:3-4, "died . . . was buried . . . was raised," suggests that Jesus' resurrection left the tomb empty, and Paul's Old Testament understanding of the body as a necessary external expression of one's essential "personhood" argues in the same direction.[16] Moreover, as a Pharisee Paul had been familiar with the idea of a bodily resurrection even before he became a Christian. We can therefore hold that Paul and all four gospels agree on an empty tomb. It further can be claimed that even Jesus' enemies admitted that the tomb had been robbed of its body and was empty. That was precisely the "explanation" which Jewish officials spread, according to Matthew 28:13. The difference was that these officials did not see it as an action of God. Rather, they said, "His disciples came by night and stole him away." The fact that such a story was circulating suggests, however, that even opponents did not deny the body was gone.

In spite of all this possible evidence, one must take note how the argument of the "empty tomb" is employed. Even in the New Testament the empty tomb by itself proves nothing, since it can be explained as the result of God's action or as the result of body-snatching by friends or as a result of confusion about the location of the tomb. The New Testament is itself aware of this point. For, according to the Synoptic accounts, the immediate result of finding the tomb empty (even when coupled with the angelic words) is fear and trembling (Mark 16:8; Matthew 28:8). Mary Magdalene's first reaction to an empty tomb is to suppose the gardener has taken the corpse and placed it somewhere else (John 20:13-15).

Therefore the second element, *the appearances of the risen Christ,* looms more important than the empty tomb and was the convincing factor. Jesus "appeared" or "was seen," he spoke and ate with his old companions. Chapter 15 of I Corinthians lists six cases of such appearances—to Cephas (Peter), James, Paul, the twelve, to "all the apostles," and "more than five hundred brethren at one time," most of whom were still alive when Paul wrote twenty-five years later. As already noted, Matthew reports appearances to the women and the eleven; Luke, to the women, to Cleopas and Peter (or another disciple), and to the eleven; John, to Mary Magdalene, the ten, the eleven, and in Galilee. As also previously stated, it is impossible to fit all these into a single, overall sequence or to harmonize the separate accounts. Nonetheless the appearances of Jesus, for a time after his death, provided convincing proof to those who saw and those who believed their testimony, that "God has raised Jesus from the dead." This for them explained the empty tomb.

Of course, one can argue for a resurrection without an empty tomb, just as one can allow for an empty tomb within a resurrection.[17] Even the implications of *both* an empty tomb and the stories about resurrection appearances can be circumvented. Along with the "explanations" already noted in passing, the following theories have been propounded at one time or another:

a) The whole thing was a deliberate invention, a story made up by the disciples who had enjoyed the days of itinerant preaching with Jesus and, knowing a good thing when they had it, did not want to give up such an existence and go back to work. So they invented their various resurrection accounts.

b) The disciples stole the body, either for reasons indicated under the previous theory, or because they revered Jesus so much that they wanted to provide proper burial for his body.

c) The authorities or someone such as the gardener moved the body. On this view, the women and the disciples actually found the tomb empty and so are not to be blamed when they thought they saw Jesus alive.

d) The women went to the wrong tomb. According to this interpretation, it was early in the morning when the women came, on a hazy day. These women had had only a quick look at the grave at sundown on Friday. So it was that they went to the wrong sepulcher, where a helpful gardener tried to explain, "If you are seeking Jesus, he is not *here* (in this tomb)," and then (pointing), "See the place where they laid him . . . over there." The women misunderstood this and started the rumor of an empty tomb.

e) Jesus swooned on the cross and was buried while still alive; the coolness of the tomb roused him and he made an escape.

f) Visions were involved, either subjectively (for which "hallucinations" would be a more honest term), or objectively—it has sometimes been said that God sent "a telegram from heaven" to the disciples.

To each of these theories (and to the various combinations and variations of them which have been proposed), objections have in turn been listed by Christian believers who want to sustain the miraculousness of the biblical account, and by historians who work through the probabilities and improbabilities of each answer, and even by critics hostile to the idea of a resurrection who, however, want to discredit other theories so that their own explanation may stand.

To the first two theories outlined above, it is, for example, answered that a deliberate plot would be hard to pull off among so many as five hundred or even a dozen men and to sustain over a twenty or thirty year period. Also, in this case, the "witnesses" (or conspirators) might be expected to have a basic, agreed story, rather than so many independent accounts about their "experience." And if they were lazy frauds to begin with, they would scarcely have faced the dangerous life they did as missionary preachers and would scarcely have taught the high ethics that their writings contain. And psychologically, could men as fright-

ened and scattered as the disciples reportedly were at the time of
the crucifixion have invented such a hoax at such a time? Body-
snatching is the last thing of which the disciples were capable
that weekend, it is maintained; it is not the thing with which a
moral religion like New Testament Christianity would have begun.

Theory c) faces the question, "Who moved the body and why?"
Answers vary, but such a person, if hostile, could have put a
stop to the Christian movement just by producing the body or
by relating his story. If friendly to Jesus and the movement which
arose, he must presumably have been a person who would profit
from the rise of the new religion. And who, it is asked, did profit
in terms of this world's goods in first-century Christianity?

Theory d), it is observed, must omit the words "He is risen"
in the speech assigned to the gardener, and does not, without further theorizing, reckon with the reported appearances of Jesus.
As for e), the records insist that Jesus really died. Such an explanation, that he swooned, seems not to have appeared in antiquity
but only under eighteenth-century rationalism, where "friends" of
Christianity wanted a rational explanation which would still allow
the "event" to stand. To it the nineteenth-century skeptic and
critic, David Friedrich Strauss, replied that, on the supposition
that Jesus survived his ordeal on the cross and was resuscitated
and then cared for by friends or fellow plotters, Jesus

> should have been not seldom, but constantly, with his disciples, who
> were those from whom he could the most immediately expect such
> tendance. For where are we to suppose that he dwelt in the long
> intervals between his appearances? in solitude? in the open air? in
> the wilderness and on mountains? That was no suitable abode for an
> invalid, and nothing remains but to suppose that he must have been
> concealed among secret colleagues of whom even his disciples knew
> nothing. But thus to conceal his real abode even from his own dis-
> ciples, to show himself to them only seldom, and designedly to pre-
> sent and withdraw himself suddenly, would be a kind of double
> dealing, an affectation of the supernatural, which would exhibit Jesus
> and his cause in a light foreign to the object itself so far as it lies
> before us in our original sources of information, and only thrown
> upon it by the dark lantern of modern, yet already obsolete, con-
> ceptions.[18]

As for the theory of subjective visions, it makes the resurrection occur because people wanted it to happen. But, it is objected,
did they want or expect it? A resurrection of Jesus is precisely
what disciples, who had run away, and the women, who were col-

lecting embalming ointments, were seemingly *not* expecting or even remotely hoping for. Moreover, in the history of religions such visions are common with individuals but are less likely in groups of eleven or five hundred, it is claimed. As for an "objective vision," a solution embraced by some supporters of the Bible, the very phrase seems a contradiction in terms. And if one explains that God could send "a telegram from heaven," one might as well argue that he could raise Jesus from the dead. The notion of "psychological visions" may be attractive to the modern mind, but, as an explanation, it scarcely does justice, even in its "objective" form to the New Testament presentation.

So runs the debate—only a small portion of which, in its long history, has been summarized here.

There are thus all sorts of "explanations" available for the resurrection—if one wants one. In some theories, it is even allowed that "something happened," but this "something" is then rationally explained. But the New Testament Gospel, without any description or explanation, simply declares, *God* did this. One is left with a choice between this explanation, which must stand without any direct "historical" proof, and rational explanations, which do not always satisfy all the evidence, let alone the spiritual longings of many men.

In such a situation the indirect evidence which the New Testament offers for the resurrection of Jesus has often been appealed to, as of considerable import. There is (1) the fact that early Christian preaching proclaimed Jesus as *the Lord.* In the very place of his shame and death, soon after it happened, preachers are saying, "God raised him up . . . [and] . . . made him Lord" (Acts 2:24, 36). (2) From the time of the earliest church at Jerusalem, there was a *Lord's Supper.* This meal assumes the presence of the risen Jesus. (3) There developed a new *Lord's Day* to mark the resurrection of Jesus. So great was the resurrection emphasis that the centuries-old practice of a divinely ordained Sabbath was set aside by Christians for a new Lord's Day. (4) A *Lord's Book* arose, both in the sense that the Old Testament was interpreted about and around Jesus, and that a New Testament literature appeared with him as its theme. Every one of these developments must somehow be explained. The simplest explanation, in the opinion of many, is that the resurrection of Jesus Christ provided the basis. In this sense there is proof in history for the resurrection: that is, only such an event can explain the sequel, the church and Christianity.[19]

There is just one other thing to add about the resurrection itself, to keep the record straight. What happened to Jesus is *not,* in the New Testament accounts, like the experience of Lazarus whom Jesus raised from the dead (John 11)—for Lazarus, we may assume, later died again. It is not even like Old Testament stories where some worthy like Enoch (Genesis 5:24) or Elijah (II Kings 2) was "translated" to heaven or like Jewish legends in which Moses, for example, was "assumed" into heaven. Jesus was not simply restored to life or just wafted up to heaven. He was exalted and received lordship, a place at God's "right hand," and a role in his rule of the universe such as was never claimed for any Old Testament worthy. Indeed, one book in the New Testament, the Epistle to the Hebrews, can so emphasize Jesus' exaltation that it virutally never mentions the resurrection.[20] Such an emphasis is one-sided, but it at least corrects the tendency to talk about a resurrection without seeing it as exaltation of Jesus of Nazareth to lordship. But the sermons in Acts (2:36; 2:33; 5:30-31) are clear on this point. Jesus is not merely restored to life, but is also glorified. He is triumphant.

Here surely is something that only faith can know. No historical method can demonstrate, or can be expected to demonstrate, that Jesus is lord. Historically speaking, it may be that a resurrection is the best explanation for the rise of the Christian church— more than one skeptic who set out to disprove the resurrection of Jesus found himself convinced on these grounds; but we have also seen that other "explanations" are available for those who want them. A Heidelberg historian, Hans von Campenhausen, has claimed recently that an empty tomb is quite likely on historical grounds[21]—but alternate "answers" about that tomb are possible, if one desires them. But to "know Christ" as living and know the "power of his resurrection," as Paul puts it (Philippians 3:10)— that is an experience of the exalted lord which effaces all other arguments and dispels the doubts. It did for Paul, the other apostolic witnesses, the evangelists, and the multitude of nameless men and women whose faith has left its stamp upon the New Testament documents. They bid men to see the "historical Jesus"— and all of life—from this perspective.

The Resurrection Light in Jesus' Life

Christians are accustomed to take a view of the resurrection such as the New Testament offers and look *forward* with it, applying it to their life and the world since Jesus' day. They claim that the resurrection has "made a difference." They see the resurrection as God's victory over death and sin. They feel that a new age has begun and look forward to the final and complete fulfillment someday. Meanwhile they live in an "interim" between Jesus' resurrection and the final triumph, between D day and V day. To borrow another simile, from Karl Heim, this interim corresponds to the

> interval, long or short, between the lightning-flash and the roll of thunder, which is its actual consequence. The Resurrection is the flash of divine lightning, which strikes down the powers of darkness, and makes it impossible for them ever to win the victory in this universe. But then comes the long pause before the 'victory roll' of divine thunder. We live and witness in that interim period.[22]

It is the lightning-flash of the resurrection which for the Christian believer illumines the steps of his way until the final thunderous triumph. Easter illumines things from A.D. 30 on.

There is truth in this simile, for the New Testament does develop the idea that all Christian life is lived in the light of Jesus' resurrection. But there is also another sense, not so readily perceived, in which the gospels allow the resurrection lightning-flash to illumine things: they let the lightning-flash project *backward* as well as forward. They let the light shine backward to illumine Jesus' life and ministry and teachings as portrayed in the gospels.

This was inevitable. For Christians, from Easter on, knew Jesus as risen lord. Even his most intimate acquaintances from the years in Galilee could not presume on any past familiarity; they of all people recognized Jesus now as something far more than a prophet or teacher, as One whom they worshiped (Matthew 28:17; Acts 7:59-60) and proclaimed as Christ and lord. And as they told the old stories of what Jesus had said and done, it was always in the afterglow of the lightning-flash. They were not telling reverent anecdotes about a dead man; rather, they were relating their experiences with him in light of the supreme experience, namely, living fellowship with him who sat at God's right hand, with him who had not left them comfortless, but who accompanied them in spirit, always and everywhere, to the close of the age (Matthew 28:20). Small wonder then that their witness to Jesus of Nazareth was tinged with the colors of the Easter dawn. Their accounts could not help but reflect some of the lightning-flash. The new element, namely, that "Christ lives," projected itself back into the old stories men recounted about him.

In this way all material in our gospels reflects the resurrection and its glow. In Gloege's words, the light of Easter "is shed on every part of the Gospels," and he quotes the great German pietist scholar of the early eighteenth century, Bengel, to the effect that these books "breathe resurrection."[23] However, this general point must be qualified by saying that the reflection of the lightning-flash occurs more sporadically and with varying degrees of brightness in the Synoptics and more constantly and with a greater intensity in the Gospel of John.

For the Synoptic evangelist-editors seem to have been more scrupulous than John in remembering that they are telling a story of events prior to the resurrection, even though these three evangelists too are of course committed to a view of the resurrection as the starting point for all of their interpretations. It is only occasionally, though, that the Synoptics let the light of the resurrection shine intensely during Jesus' ministry. By contrast, John portrays the ministry much more in triumphant "resurrection terms." What he regards as the ultimate truth, that "Jesus is the Christ, the Son of God," who lives and now offers life (20:31), he is not afraid to let shine through his account of the historical ministry. After all, so far as he was concerned, he was not writing a biography about who Jesus *was,* but witness literature about who he *is*—lord and Christ.

This resurrection light in Jesus' life can be perceived, for example, in certain titles that are applied to Jesus in our gospels. The names of Jesus and the claims for him found in the Synoptics and John are, of course, a large area of study (see chapter 9). Here we shall simply note an example or two to illustrate the tendency of our gospel accounts to take names for the Lord Jesus familiar from use in prayers and worship after the resurrection and to project them back into stories of the period prior to A.D. 30. It is as if in the story of George Washington and the cherry tree we interject a title describing him as what we later know him to be, the "Father of his Country." The boy who chopped down the cherry tree was not yet the hero of the American Revolution or the first president, but we can see how the retelling of such a story in later years could fall into using such language. How does this sort of thing show itself in the gospel accounts about Jesus?

During his years in Galilee and the days in Jerusalem, how did men address Jesus when they spoke to him? Doubtless they used his actual name, "Jesus of Nazareth" (Luke 18:37), or "Jesus, son of Mary" (Mark 6:3), or some description like "the carpenter's son" (Matthew 13:55), or "the teacher" (*rabbi*, Mark 5:35), or "the prophet" (Matthew 21:11). There is no record that men ever called him "Son of man" or, in his contacts with the public, "Son of God" or even "Christ." All of these are titles which developed, at best, from use only within the group of disciples during his lifetime, and perhaps only after the resurrection; they were not everyday epithets for the historical Jesus.

With the word that we translate as "lord" the story is a little more complicated. When we say "lord," we usually think of some ruler enthroned in splendor or at least of some great personage, perhaps a member of the nobility, for example, in England. It must be remembered, however, that the Greek word here, *kyrios* (which we may recognize in the phrase still used in some churches, *kyrie eleison*, "Lord, have mercy"), could also mean nothing more than "sir" or "mister." To this day it is the word that a Greek would use in addressing a man on the street in Athens: "*Kyrie,* my good man. . . ." Therefore, without going into the further question of the Aramaic which stood behind this Greek, we may simply note that often in our gospels Jesus is addressed by his contemporaries as *kyrie*, "sir," "mister," or is spoken of as "lord" in an everyday sense. For example, the Syrophoenician woman says, "Yes, Lord" (Mark 7:28, RSV; NEB, "Sir"; cf. Matthew 8:2, 6, 8, 21, 25; or Luke 10:1, 40-41). During Jesus' lifetime *kyrie* was nothing more than a polite form of address. After the resurrection, however, Christians used this word as the supreme confession of who Jesus is—"Jesus Christ is lord (*kyrios*)," as at Philippians 2:11 or I Corinthians 12:3. Among Greeks and Romans *kyrios* was a title claimed for gods in various cults and even for the emperor (see I Corinthians 8:5-6). It was the word which in Christian copies of the Greek Old Testament was to be employed for "Yahweh."[24] In ascribing lord-

ship to the risen Jesus, as *kyrios*, Christians thus gave him a name
or title "above every name"; they were placing him in a class
with God.

Now when did early Christians believe Jesus had entered into
this position of lordship, when did he receive the title *kyrios*?
Philippians 2 says that after his death God exalted him and gave
him the name of lord (*kyrios*, 2:8-11)—i.e., at the resurrection.
So also Acts 2:36; at the resurrection "God has made him . . .
Lord . . . this Jesus whom you crucified." After the resurrection
therefore the term *kyrios* took on new meaning for Christians.
Where it had simply meant "mister" or "sir" in Jesus' lifetime,
Christians now saw reflections of Jesus' new heavenly lordship.
The fact of the matter is that when Mark tells the story of Jesus,
he is rather sparing of such uses of *kyrios*, but in Matthew, Luke,
and John the number of such examples grows. The resurrection
light is steadily expanding its beams on the gospel accounts. At
some points we can see how one evangelist has employed Jesus-
material without retouching it, while another writer adds the term
"lord," apparently conscious of its deeper, post-resurrection sense.
For example, Mark's very vivid account of the healing of a leper
begins, "If you will, you can make me clean" (1:40); Matthew
8:2 and Luke 5:12 have, "*Lord*, if you will, you can make me
clean." In the story of the stilling of the storm, we read that the
disciples said:

"*Teacher*, do you not care if we perish?" (Mark 4:38);
"*Master, Master*, we are perishing!" (Luke 8:24);
"Save, *Lord*; we are perishing." (Matthew 8:25).

In each incident, of course, the word *kyrios*, in the sense "sir" or
"mister," could have been used originally. Our point is simply
that as the stories (miracle stories in these cases) were retold in
the early church the deeper significance of the word as "lord" was
seen and sometimes brought out—resurrection light falls on these
narratives. Luke (or his special source)[25] in the narrative sections
especially liked to bring in this term and imply a picture of Jesus
as the lord, with power and authority. "The Lord" did this, "the
Lord" said that (see Luke 7:13; 10:1). Features of the heavenly
lord are commingled with accounts of the earthly Jesus.[26]

Another example where exploration reveals the light of the

resurrection projected back into Jesus' life involves the word "glory." Originally, of course, in Old Testament thought, "glory" belongs to God. He is the God of glory (Exodus 24:17; Psalm 29:3; Acts 7:2), and in the New Testament it was by the glory of God that Jesus was raised from the dead (Romans 6:4). Then something begins to happen to this word which was originally applied to God. Stephen's vision beholds Jesus encompassed within God's glory (Acts 7:55, Stephen saw "the glory of God, and Jesus standing at the right hand of God"). The Christian explanation as to how Christ has entered into this glory is that God "raised him from the dead and gave him glory" (I Peter 1:21). Hence, after the resurrection Jesus could even be spoken of as "the lord of glory" (I Corinthians 2:8; James 2:1)—i.e., he shares the glory which in the Old Testament belongs to God. Such language we are accustomed to in the epistles. Does it occur in the Synoptics? Generally the first three gospels are quite reserved in this respect. They employ the term chiefly with reference to future glory, the glory to be revealed at the time when the Son of man "comes in the glory of his Father" (Mark 8:38 and par.). With the exception of one other scene, to be discussed in a moment, the only remaining example in the Synoptics is in Luke, in connection with the wondrous tale of Jesus' birth. There, we are told, when the angels sang, "the glory of the Lord shone around them" (2:9); God's glory, meaning his power and presence, was manifested at Jesus' birth.

It is in John's Gospel that glory is magnified during Jesus' ministry; it becomes a key theme in the presentation by the Fourth Evangelist. The first "sign" that Jesus did, the miracle at the wedding feast at Cana, "manifested his glory" (2:11). Presumably so also did his other wondrous deeds. Particularly, however, in the greatest deed of all, the cross, was Jesus glorified and his glory manifested (see 12:23, 28; 13:31; 17:1, 4-5). It is fair to say that John views the cross more as triumph than as a place of suffering and defeat. To this degree John makes the cross rather than the resurrection the moment of triumph and glory. He further projects the glory back over the whole ministry until it is possible to say, in looking at the story of Jesus' life, "We have beheld his glory" (1:14). Seemingly, glory has been transferred from God to Christ, and from the resurrection period to the earthly ministry.

While recognizing what the Fourth Gospel has done, we must add two things about its portrait of Jesus. (1) John has not transformed his theology into a "theology of glory" (which talks of power and privilege, not mission and suffering), the way later eras of church history have often tried to do. He retains a "theology of the cross." That is, his theology centers in the cross; agony and suffering are not passed over. Indeed, it is precisely there, in the cross, that God's power is seen to be at work, and this power is designated by the biblical word "glory." It is clear that John lets more of the resurrection light shine back on Jesus' lifetime than does any other evangelist, but it is not true that he shortchanges either the Passion or the resurrection. (2) When John does speak of "glory" during Jesus' lifetime, it is a glory which could be seen only with the "eyes of faith." Jesus manifested glory by what he did at Cana, but it was only the disciples who saw the meaning and glory, and they beheld it only by believing in him (2:11). It was a matter of believing, John implies, not just seeing, to be able to behold the glory of God (11:40; 11:4). One should add that this faith and hence the vision of glory and comprehension of what Jesus was doing came only after the resurrection; that John says too at times (see 2:22; 7:39). Even the statement, "We have beheld his glory" (1:14), can be said only in retrospect, as a consequence of the resurrection.

It was mentioned that there is one scene during the ministry in the Synoptics where Jesus' glory appears more fully. That scene is the transfiguration, and it represents another sample case where we can ask about "resurrection light." More than one critic has called these verses on the transfiguration "a misplaced resurrection scene." What are the bases for this view, what are the facts, and how can it all be assessed?

Matthew, Mark, and Luke all report the incident directly after Peter's confession at Caesarea Philippi and the first Passion prediction and some words about discipleship (Mark 8:27—9:1, par.). All three accounts tell us how Jesus took the "inner three," Peter, James, and John, from his group of twelve, and led them to a high mountain. There Jesus was "transfigured" or "transformed" before them, his face and garments brilliantly white. Together with this new and changed Jesus appeared two patriarchs from Old Testament times, Elijah (symbolizing the proph-

ets), a man who had gone heavenward in a chariot of fire instead
of dying (II Kings 2:11), and Moses (symbolizing the law), a
man whose grave no one knew (Deuteronomy 34:6). Luke alone
states what they talked about, namely, the departure or "exodus"
which Jesus would accomplish at Jerusalem (Luke 9:31). Luke
adds that the disciples, who had been drowsy, now saw the glory
of the scene and Jesus' special glory (9:32). In all three accounts,
Peter stammers something about how good it is to be there and
wants to build three shelters for the three transfigured figures. A
cloud swallows up the group, and there is a voice, "This is my
beloved Son; listen to him." Then the touch of Jesus snaps the
three disciples from their mood of fear and awe (Matthew 17:6-
7), and they see "Jesus only." Mark and Matthew add that Jesus
commanded them to silence about the incident.

Readers have long been puzzled about what to make of this
narrative. A place where it occurred is hard to fix. Mount Tabor
in Galilee is the traditional site, but Mount Hermon is much more
impressive as a mountain and lies near Caesarea Philippi; some
prefer it. Others are reminded of the mountain of the Great Commission in Matthew 28:16. Fixing the time poses problems too,
even though Mark and Matthew begin their accounts with the
words, "after six days." One problem is that Luke says instead,
"about eight days after these sayings." The question arises, "six
(or eight) days" after what event or what dialogue? Is it the
sayings at Mark 8:34—9:1, or the confession at Caesarea Philippi, or what? Usually such phrases of time appear only in the
Passion and resurrection narratives. John omits such a story,
though he has a scene at Jerusalem where a voice from heaven
speaks, glorifying Jesus (John 12:28-30). The Second Epistle of
Peter also refers to the scene on "the holy mountain" where God's
glory was revealed with the words, "This is my beloved Son, with
whom I am well pleased" (II Peter 1:16-18). The business about
the booths may reflect a connection with a Jewish festival when
people were to live for seven days in shelters or huts in commemo-
ration of the Exodus (Leviticus 23:39-43), or it may just be the
notion, "It's good we three are here to build shelters for you."
The cloud is a common Old Testament symbol for the presence of
God, and the words from heaven, similar to those at Jesus' baptism (Mark 1:11, par.), derive from Psalm 2:7; Isaiah 42:1,
and elsewhere in the Old Testament. A most significant clue for

interpretation in Luke is his reference to Jesus' "exit" from the world at Jerusalem and the future glory which is now glimpsed for a moment. Such comments on details are easy to make. What shall we make of the total scene?

In many ways the transfiguration account does tie in with scenes of Jesus' resurrection glory. There are all the usual historical problems connected with such an account—was it a dream while the disciples slept, or a vision while they were awake, or what? To some extent has the the later glory of the risen Christ slipped back into an earlier experience? Or was the experience entirely a post-Easter one? It is easier to ask such questions than to answer them, and all sorts of theories have been proposed. One is the possibility, which many prefer who wish to see the transfiguration as an event in Jesus' lifetime, that Jesus, on one occasion during his earthly ministry, as he talked of God and his glory, raised the vision of his closest followers to behold him in a new way, as the revealer of a message that ranked with that of Moses and Elijah. To add that Peter and the others grasped this message more fully, as to its real meaning, only after the resurrection, is simply to follow what Mark (9:9-10) and Matthew say. In this way an experience during the lifetime of Jesus is preserved behind the story as it is recounted in our post-resurrection gospels.

We have now seen how, in the titles ascribed to Jesus, in the idea of glory, and at the transfiguration, something of the resurrection light is apparent in our gospel accounts of Jesus' ministry.[27] The power of the resurrection is thus seen in "preview form," as it were, during his lifetime. Even more often, of course, the gospels speak of post-Easter appearances of the glorious, risen Christ. A final question now to be posed is how long these appearances of the risen Jesus to men on earth went on. To put it another way, how long did the peculiar resurrection light burn so brilliantly? We have observed it flaming forth at Easter and occasionally on prior occasions in the gospels during Jesus' ministry. By the end of the first century no "resurrection appearance" was to be expected any more (though Christians did claim continuing fellowship with the Lord Christ). For some nineteen hundred years Christians have not presumed to look for such occurrences as took place for a time after Passover in A.D. 30. The question is, How long, according to early Christian documents, did these appearances go on after Easter, before the later customary means of contact with Christ (through word, the Spirit, sacraments, and prayer) became the norm for Christians?

A conclusive answer is not easy to derive from even just the biblical evidence—let alone statements outside of Scripture. In I Corinthians 15, the list of six appearances gives no dates for any of them. The striking thing is that Paul includes his own experience on the Damascus Road with the other resurrection appearances he cites (I Corinthians 15:8, with a reference assumed to Acts 9:1-9). This would mean a "resurrection appearance" at the time of Paul's conversion, a year, or as much as five years, after Jesus' death. Yet, according to Acts 7, at the martyrdom of Stephen, some time after Easter (a few months? a year?), Jesus is depicted as by now exalted at God's right hand, where the dying Stephen beholds him (7:56). In John 20 this exaltation seems to take place on the same day as the resurrection, and it is then that the exalted Jesus gives the Spirit to his disciples (20:19-23). He also appears to them a week later when Thomas is present (20:26-29); still later there is a scene in Galilee where Jesus is again present (chapter 21). Shall we picture Jesus as immediately exalted to heaven and then coming down from heaven to appear to Peter, James, and the others at Jerusalem or in Galilee immediately after his resurrection, and then making a similar appearance to Paul but several years later near Damascus?

Somewhat differently from these biblical accounts, the gnostic gospels of the second century presume that Jesus stayed on earth for a year or more after his resurrection (for twelve years, some say), imparting secret doctrines—an idea which shows how fuzzy ancient Christianity could become about how long Jesus continued to make appearances on earth among men.[28]

To take up the last biblical bit of evidence, Luke, as is well known, posits a period of forty days after Easter until the ascension, ten days after which the risen Christ poured out the Spirit (Acts 1:1-11; cf. Luke 24:50-53). Luke's version has become normal in the church's calendar of Easter-Ascension-Pentecost, but the other pieces of evidence in the New Testament and other early Christian writings do not fit at several points with Luke's pattern. The difficulties with Luke's picture are (1) he does not give the impression that the resurrection appearances during the forty days are "from heaven" as the other accounts do; (2) Paul's Damascus

Road experience would fall into a different category from the appearances during the forty days—and this would contradict the impression from I Corinthians 15, where it is classified with them; (3) Luke postpones till Pentecost what John presents as an experience on Easter Day, namely, the giving of the Holy Spirit. We might chart the evidence this way:

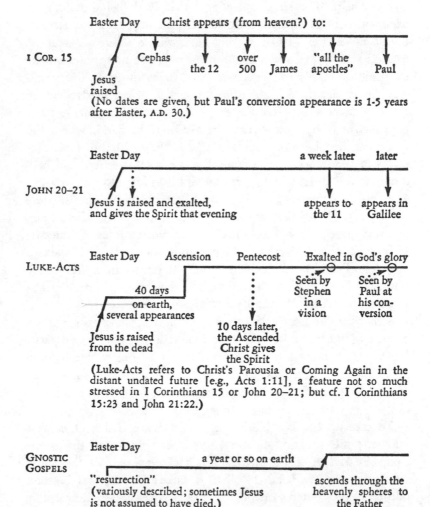

(No dates are given, but Paul's conversion appearance is 1-5 years after Easter, A.D. 30.)

(Luke-Acts refers to Christ's Parousia or Coming Again in the distant undated future [e.g., Acts 1:11], a feature not so much stressed in I Corinthians 15 or John 20–21; but cf. I Corinthians 15:23 and John 21:22.)

Perhaps all this points to the fact that the resurrection appearances are separate tales which never can be put into an ordered framework. Perhaps there is wisdom in the view that Luke has strung out, in a chronological framework, events that John has compressed into a briefer time—and it may be that any "original" sequence of experiences was somewhere between what Luke and John offer—i.e., each evangelist has reshaped the chronology. But one thing must be said in favor of Luke's picture of the ascension (which only he gives us).[29] For all the difficulties which its "geography" causes the modern mind (How can "heaven" be "up"?), Luke does give one profound answer: there was an end to the sort of appearances that the original disciples knew. Jesus will not desert his followers. He will be with them in other ways from now on. But the sort of appearances granted for a brief time has ceased. The ascension thus provides what has been called "an acted declaration of finality" to the resurrection appearances.[30] In a dramatic scene outside Jerusalem, Jesus writes "finis" to that kind of manifestation which is henceforth at an end (save for one extraordinary appearance to Paul). Christians are not to hanker after such visits from Jesus. From now on, for the interim (however long that may be), the contacts must be through prayer, through the Spirit and Jesus' words, and through the proclamation in its several forms (including sacraments) of the word of God. "Do not cling to me," Jesus says, "in the form in which I was" (cf. John 20:17). Henceforth believers must know Jesus not "after the flesh," as a man of earth, from a merely human point of view or by worldly standards of understanding, but as the lord (cf. II Corinthians 5:16)—and that means as risen and exalted, not just as a historical figure.

Here is the difference which the resurrection makes. It renders dubious any mere quest for the Jesus of history, for one discovers through historical studies that the records are constantly illuminated by the resurrection light. It demands commitment to a Jesus who is lord, and not just a human figure, for the resurrection has stamped Jesus in the New Testament records as not just a figure of the past but one of continuing significance. It provides us with the Gospel, since, in the words of the Archbishop of Canterbury, "The Gospel without the resurrection was not merely a Gospel without its final chapter; it was not a gospel at all."[31]

What is more, the resurrection made possible the gospels in the particular form they took, as works of history and of the witness of faith. It has, through these gospels and the Jesus they present, furthered communion between men in later centuries and Jesus the lord, in a way whereby (Christians believe) he speaks and men give heed, whereby they pray and he will hear. This is so, claims the New Testament, *if* men respond to the apostolic announcement that "God raised Jesus from the dead." And if one says "Yes" and wants to hear the ancient words of Jesus speak in their bipolar character as historical records and as Word of God, what do they say?

A NOTE ON THE "OUTLINE" OF JESUS' LIFE
AND THE NATIVITY STORIES

Since our presentation will now move back from the kerygma of the early church (about the death and resurrection of Jesus) to the kerygma (about the reign of God) which Jesus himself proclaimed during his ministry and, in light of this message about the kingdom, to Jesus' other teachings and some of his actions, a word is in order here as to why so little is being said about the "outline" of Jesus' life. For most "lives" of Jesus begin with his birth and infancy and then describe the development of his thought and unfold his career in some sort of chronological outline.

It is—or, for historical critical scholars, should be—impossible today, in the face of modern biblical study, to go on making the biographical constructs about Jesus such as some writers in the eighteenth and nineteenth centuries loved to indulge in. For all too often these "lives" simply reflected the outlooks (and prejudices) of the respective biographers. Frequently one reconstruction flatly contradicted another, and they canceled each other out. There are, however, more substantial reasons which lead to reservations about attempting to outline the life of Jesus than merely the singular lack of success which attended the nineteenth-century quest for a "biographical Jesus."

One obvious reason for hesitance about making a chronological outline is the disagreement already within the New Testament sources on such matters. John's chronology, as is well known, is not that of the Synoptics.[32] The Fourth Gospel has Jesus make several trips to Jerusalem in the course of his ministry; the Synoptics present just one, at the final, fatal Passover season. The Fourth Gospel suggests a public ministry of three years or so (three Passover festivals are mentioned, 2:13; 6:4; and 11:55); the Synoptics note only one Passover, the final one at the time of Jesus' death, and even if the reference to grain growing in the grainfields which is now recorded at Mark 2:23 be taken to refer to the springtime of the previous year, with Jesus' baptism (Mark 1:9) having occurred a few months previously, the longest ministry one can posit on the basis of the Synoptics is only a little over a year—but not three years. There are further disagreements over the dating for specific incidents, such as the cleansing of the temple; the Synoptics locate it during Passion week, John puts it at the beginning of Jesus' three-year ministry (John 2:13-22).

Moreover, even the Synoptics sometimes disagree among themselves. Luke inserts a "Samaritan" or "Travel Section" (9:51— 18:14). Matthew rearranges passages in Mark and inserts additional material of his own to create great blocks of teaching material or discourses by Jesus, like the Sermon on the Mount (Matthew 5–7). The three Synoptics differ as to where they locate specific incidents within the lifetime of Jesus—for example, whether the temple cleansing took place the same day as the triumphal entry (so Matthew) or the next day (as in Mark)—just as they do, we have seen, in the sequence of happenings and the trials during the Passion (discussed in chapter 3), and elsewhere.

It was once thought necessary, and possible, to harmonize these varying chronologies. Usually this harmonization was at the expense of the Johannine account, on the grounds that John was "theological" (and therefore not "historical"), while Mark, the oldest gospel, must be "historical." Nowadays it is recognized that Mark too is "theological," and that it is possible the Fourth Gospel may preserve sound historical traditions at places and reflect accurate details at points where Mark may not. Accordingly it may be that Jesus' ministry was longer than that depicted in the Synoptics and that John has tended to stretch it out over an even longer period of time in order to follow a pattern determined by the calendar of Jewish festivals like Passover; this would mean a ministry somewhere between one and three years in length. However, we cannot be sure about such matters, because the sources disagree.

A second reason for being more hesitant than many scholars have been about claiming one of the chronologies in our gospels as historical (or even one of them with slight modifications) is the growing feeling that even the most "historical" appearing one may derive from the early church and its preaching, and not from a concern for chronology. We have already indicated that the

Johannine outline has long been regarded as "too theological" and that recent research, while granting that John may be right at some points historically, suggests the chronology of the Fourth Gospel is built up around some calendrical or liturgical pattern.[33] In this situation some writers have therefore, as we have noted, preferred Mark.[34] It is not too much to say that most recent lives of Jesus are constructed around a chronological outline which derives basically from Mark, perhaps as corrected at a few points by John, and amplified with incidents inserted into this framework from the other gospels. However, it seems increasingly apparent to many observers that the Marcan outline is nothing else than the outline of the kerygma writ large and filled out with examples under each of its points. Thus the sequence found in a sermon such as that by Peter at Acts 10:36-43 (baptism—Galilean ministry, especially involving healing miracles—Jerusalem—death and resurrection) is very much the sequence found in Mark's Gospel. And since all the Synoptics basically follow Mark's outline, they too are reflections of the kerygma structure.[35] It is not, of course, impossible that the actual career of Jesus did include precisely the elements proclaimed in the kerygma and perhaps even in the order recited there, and that, to say the least, his public ministry first centered in Galilee and his life ended in Jerusalem. However, the arrangement seems too pat when all contact with Judea and Jerusalem is avoided until the final Passover journey (even Luke and certainly John break away from that sort of outline). The Marcan outline, derived from the kerygma, seems too much like a dramatic simplification made for preaching purposes for us to allow it to be taken as straight historical chronology.

A third reason for avoiding the traditional chronological outline of Jesus' life is that most writers, having taken over or set up a sequence of "what (they think) happened when" in his career, then go on to construct a course of psychological development which they believe occurred in the mind of Jesus. Sometimes these writers lay stress on the pressure of certain external events which they think shaped the development of Jesus' self-consciousness. Thus, John the Baptist's preaching is often taken as the "spark" which set Jesus thinking about his destiny; a vision at his baptism confirmed his hopes; first the success and then the rejections which he met in his ministry caused him to frame and then revise his plans, it is said. Albert Schweitzer's reconstruction is a classic example of this approach, showing how Jesus is supposed to have come to the realization that he must go to Jerusalem and die in order to "trigger" the final explosion which would bring all history to an end.[36] Sometimes these modern writers stress, not the pressure of external events in shaping Jesus' plans, but Jesus himself as the mastermind who plotted his plans and molded men to carry them out. An extreme recent example of this approach is Hugh Schonfield's book, *The Passover Plot,* in which Jesus is depicted as a Machiavellian schemer who sought to fake his own death by a drug-induced coma and then to stage a "resurrection."[37]

The trouble with these psychological reconstructions—"fiction" one is tempted to call them when one measures them alongside each other and then in comparison with the records—is that they assume the records were interested in providing this sort of psychological analysis of Jesus (what early Christian told of his lord in that way?) or assume that modern investigators can put together a psychological portrait of Jesus on the basis of the records we have. Usually these attempts simply do not reckon critically enough with the gospel sources, and they mistake ideas from the evangelists or the early church for bona fide musings of Jesus himself. In particular they assume it is possible to draw up a historical, chronological outline on the basis of which a psychological reconstruction can be made. The oftentimes bad psychologizing is exceeded only by the bad historicizing, and what interpreters get is a reflection of Mark's or Luke's Christology—or of the modern writers' own imagination—instead of the self-consciousness of Jesus which they seek.

At this point the investigator must simply be reverently agnostic and admit we cannot know the precise historical course of Jesus' life, let alone the psychological development which went on in Jesus' mind. Such a position does not deny that we can know something about certain incidents in his life; perhaps we can even suggest a certain progression from Galilee to Jerusalem. And surely, from such a position, critical scholarship can and must carry out its necessary, though negative, task of showing where each of the fictional reconstructions of Jesus' life and mind has gone wrong. But, in positive terms, who can tell us historically of the sequence of events in any "Samaritan ministry" or of a "Perean period" beyond the Jordan (cf. Mark 10:1, par. Matthew

19:1-2), or of an extended ministry at Jerusalem? Who can guarantee for us that the hostility against Jesus was built up at the start of his ministry the way Mark 2:1—3:6 reports and then was "in suspension," so to speak, until the Passion began (Mark 11:1 ff.), as over against the possibility that Mark has, for dramatic purposes, grouped together at the start of his gospel some stories about conflicts between Jesus and his enemies which originally had a setting in his ministry later on.[38] In short, it is not simply a matter of caution, but a necessity compelled by the sources, to eschew an outline which arranges the incidents of Jesus' ministry into a chronological framework.

This stance just indicated does not exclude completely, it needs to be added, the possibility that we can on occasion glimpse something of Jesus' own view on a subject or grasp his set of mind on this point or that.[39] We thus repudiate the possibility of recovering his "messianic consciousness" or even his particular "self-consciousness," but we can hope to see something of his understanding of life—how he looked on existence under God and life in a time when God's reign was drawing near. We ought not expect a Christology or even a "messianology," but it is likely that Jesus did give serious thought to what he was proclaiming in his words and deeds, and what it all meant, and even that he was aware that his course of action could mean death for him—in that case, what did trust in the God he proclaimed, imply?

That far we can try to go, on the basis of the sources, critically examined, but what we are denying is the possibility, so dear to most lives of Jesus, of tracing the development of Jesus' views and then of psychologizing this development. For in the material about Jesus, contained in the gospels, the resurrection light shines through in case after case. The kerygmatic outline provides a preacher's sketch, not a historian's chronology. The Christology involved is the early church's confession, not memoirs from a disciple's hand apart from Easter, let alone "the diary of Jesus' innermost thoughts" during his lifetime.

The implications of the position which has been adopted here come out nowhere more clearly than with regard to the nativity stories, those passages about the birth and infancy of Jesus which most Christians associate with the Christmas season. True, two gospels start with such material (or properly, Matthew presents his nativity story after an opening genealogy, and Luke records his nativity section after his opening "historian's preface"). However, the proper historical and theological evaluation of such stories requires that they be examined in the light of Easter and of the church's confession with respect to who Jesus really is. The following observations may be made:

(1) The traditional Christmas story cannot be the starting point for telling the life of Jesus historically or of his development psychologically, since what Matthew and Luke report about his birth and infancy was not, during his ministry, public knowledge (cf. Luke 2:19, 51b), on the basis of which the reports and assessments of him arose; by the time we get the materials in the form in which we have them today, they are tinged with resurrection light. For the "Christmas story," as we have it recorded in our gospels, represents accounts from the viewpoint of believing Christians after Easter. (2) The Gospel can be presented without any reference to the birth stories. The kerygma did not include them, nor did Q. Mark, the oldest gospel, does not have them. John has a prologue on the word instead. As a holy day, the nativity is a late development (third or fourth century A.D., with either December 25 or January 6 celebrated as the date at first); contrast this with Easter which is the great Christian festival from the outset.[40]

(3) Christmas and Christmas customs, we need to remember, have always been subject to many romantic influences and have tended to assimilate pagan practices (which, in turn, are then "Christianized"). Examples are easy to note; even the date of December 25 was originally a day of the sun god.[41] (4) The whole New Testament insists on the full humanity of Jesus and assumes he was born, grew up, etc., on earth, though no details are given (Galatians 4:4, "born of woman," refers to his birth as a human being, not to a virgin birth). Few areas, however, were later subject to more legends than the infancy of Jesus (e.g., the New Testament Apocrypha).[42]

(5) Matthew and Luke do present material about the birth which deserves attention. It derives from the special sources of Matthew and Luke, M and L respectively. If one seeks for historical origins, it us usually said that—if there are firsthand sources to be reckoned with—Mary conveyed the information to Luke, though Luke also seems to have had a series of stories about John the Baptist which he has woven in with those about Jesus; moreover, the origin of some of the hymns in Luke 1–2 has been

much debated. All the stories show a heavy influence from the Old
Testament and doubtless bear the stamp of countless retellings
within Christian circles.

Matthew begins with a genealogy (1:1-17) which we have
previously considered.[43] The structure of the rest of Matthew 1–2
is built around Old Testament quotations (note the phrase, "fulfilled what was spoken by the prophet(s)," at 1:22; 2:5, 15, 17,
and 23). To a great extent the fulfillment of prophecy governs
the course of the narrative. The incident of the Magi (NEB,
"astrologers") at 2:1-12 is meant to show how the East paid
homage to Jesus; he is to be lord of all the world (cf. 28:19-
20).[44] The "Slaughter of the Innocents" by Herod (2:16-18) is
in keeping with that tyrant's character, but no non-biblical source
refers to it. The flight into Egypt (2:13-15) and the return to
Nazareth (2:19-23) both fit Old Testament prophetic passages
(though an exact source for 2:23 is hard to find). All these incidents occurred a considerable time after Jesus' birth. The nativity
occurs at 1:18-25. Matthew specifically calls Mary a virgin mother,
using Isaiah 7:14 (in the Greek, not the Hebrew) as the basis for
the presentation. Otherwise Joseph plays a more prominent part
than in Luke (see Matthew 1:19, 20, 24-25). Verse 25 states, as
13:55-56 also affirms, that Mary and Joseph later had other children. The name "Jesus" is significant (1:21).

Luke interweaves material on John and Jesus (1:5-25 with
26-38; vss. 57-80 with 2:1-20). The many hymns (1:14-17;
1:46-55 = the Magnificat; 1:68-79 = the Benedictus) reflect Old
Testament patterns (cf. I Samuel 2:1-10, e.g.) and were probably
used in early Christian worship before Luke recorded them. Luke
likes to pair and contrast men and women (Zechariah's unbelief
and Mary's faith; Simeon and Anna). The birth story (2:1-20)
explains that the parents were at Bethlehem because of a census.
Rough parallels to such a provincial census exist, but historians
cannot document such a census taken in the whole empire at this
particular date from any known source outside the Bible.[45] Luke
presents the child as virgin-born at 1:27 and 1:35.[46] Such statements in Luke (and Matthew) are assertions of faith, affirming
who Christians believe Jesus is, i.e., the son of God (see Luke
3:38).[47] Mark 1:1 makes this same confession without any
(virgin) birth stories. Note the other titles of Jesus at Luke 2:11
(a concatenation of christological terms, "savior," "Christ,"

"lord") and the momentary shining through of God's glory. The nativity stories thus tell readers who Jesus is. To this extent, all the nativity stories seek to describe what early Christians believed about Jesus.[48] The stories might be called "Christology in picture form."

6

The Good News of the Reign of God — Preaching and Parables

Ask any hundred New Testament scholars around the world, Protestant, Catholic, or non-Christian, what the central message of Jesus of Nazareth was, and the vast majority of them—perhaps every single expert—would agree that his message centered in the kingdom of God. Such unanimity of opinion may seem rare among biblical experts nowadays, when so many conflicting ideas are voiced about most issues. Yet such is the case. The ancient sources in the gospels, especially the Synoptics, give such an answer.[1] The modern investigators agree.[2] The "good news" which Jesus announced had to do with God and his kingdom.

An early Christian in Corinth or Rome in the fifties or seventies of the first century would have agreed. He was familiar with the term "good news" or Gospel and knew from the Jesus-material (and from any written gospels which might have been available to him by then) that the great theme which his lord had proclaimed during the ministry on earth was the kingdom of God. True, by now the term was not used as frequently as Jesus had employed it. For Roman police officials and spies would be suspicious of a term like "kingdom"—it might mask a threat to Caesar's empire—and Jewish and pagan informers were all too quick to denounce Christians to the authorities. Hence the kingdom about which Jesus spoke had come to be expressed in a host of other terms and themes which made more sense to people who did not know Semitic backgrounds and the Old Testament roots for the biblical idea of "God's kingdom." Paul, in his letters, employed terms like "righteousness" and "peace" and "joy" to show what the kingdom meant (Romans 14:17). Indeed, the earliest apostolic preaching could set forth its message without any reference to the kingdom of God. But at the least early Christians would have recognized the term as the special theme of Jesus.[3]

But today when we hear about Jesus' message of the kingdom of God, it sounds strange to our ears and prompts a multitude of questions. This is not surprising, for we are twenty centuries removed from a message that already had a strange ring and had to be translated into new terminology soon after the resurrection, that is, in the earliest decades of Christianity. Further, we usually lack the knowledge of Old Testament and Semitic ways of thought, which for the Greek-speaking Christians too were strange already in the first century. We find it hard to pierce through to the meaning of the parables, which Jesus especially used in speaking about the kingdom. We wonder how to relate the kingdom to the church (without realizing that Christians of the first century were already struggling with that problem, and have left some answers in the New Testament). In short, what did "kingdom" mean for Jesus and his hearers? What does the term say to men nowadays who still pray, "Thy kingdom come"? Is it something men build? How does a person respond and live who wants to be loyal both to Jesus' teaching about the kingdom and to the Gospel about "Christ crucified and risen"? One thing is clear: Jesus' central teaching, ancient as it is, is no museum piece, but prompts lively questions, which great names like Schweitzer and Bultmann have debated (and men continue to discuss) in our century.

The Gospel of Jesus about the Kingdom of God

There is a tremendous danger for modern men that Jesus' teachings and message, as they are heard read in little snatches in church on Sundays or are scanned piecemeal by individuals, will seem isolated from each other and atomistic. An item here, a ray of light there, a truth somewhere else, but seldom anything to integrate all of Jesus' teachings into a whole that makes sense as a totality and can be analyzed in its parts on some consistent basis. That is why it is so important to see that Jesus had a central message, and that it was about God's kingdom. For it is this theme of the kingdom which integrates all of Jesus' words and deeds.

That claim is a fact for which readers do not need to take the word of some expert. They can check it for themselves in the Synoptic records. For whether one turns to the preaching of Jesus (and in connection with it what is often called his individual teachings) or to the parables (which bulk so large in the Jesus-material), or to the miracles (which always trouble moderns, not only as to whether they happened, but also as to what they have to do with Jesus' basic message), one finds that the theme is the kingdom of God, a unifying emphasis around which all that Jesus said and did can be arranged. Mark's Gospel opens, after its brief prologue (or as the climax of this prologue),[4] with a terse statement of good news, intended to set the tone for the entire book:

Now after John was arrested, Jesus came into Galilee, preaching the gospel of God, and saying, "The time is fulfilled, and the kingdom of God is at hand; repent, and believe in the gospel."

(Mark 1:14-15)

What Jesus preaches centers in the kingdom. Both Matthew (4:12-17) and Luke (4:14-21, 43), each to be sure with his own emphases, begin their gospel accounts of Jesus' public ministry on the same note: Jesus began to preach, "The kingdom of heaven is at hand" (Matthew 4:17); "I must preach the good news of the kingdom of God . . . for I was sent for this purpose" (Luke 4:43). Many manuscripts add at Mark 1:14, Jesus preached "the gospel of the kingdom of God." His message was not about himself but God, God and his kingdom.[5]

Alongside the preaching of Jesus, place his parables. It is not necessary to go through the much discussed problem of what a parable is in order to be able to see that Jesus' parables center in the kingdom of God. "To what shall we liken the kingdom of God?" "The kingdom is like. . . ." So the parables often begin. They talk of God in terms of a king who does this or that. They compare the kingdom of heaven to objects and happenings in everyday life. Even those parables which do not specifically use the word "kingdom" seem to set forth some aspect of it. God's kingdom is the subject of Jesus' most characteristic manner of speaking, the parables.

As for the miracles, while many people have seen in them mere magical tricks to make converts, or humanitarian gestures by Jesus showing his compassion for men, or special devices by God to prompt the initial stirrings of faith which led to Christianity, it must be claimed that the miracles relate to the kingdom, too. So modern biblical scholarship insists. The miracles are not "divine showmanship," or "messanic Band-Aids" for a few of humanity's woes. The miracles are meant as demonstrations of the power of the kingdom about which Jesus preaches and speaks in parables. Jesus claims his miracles are signs of the coming of the kingdom of God (Matthew 12:28, par. Luke 11:20). They are, as one biblical theologian calls them, "enacted proclamations that the kingdom of God has come."[6]

Preaching, parables, miracles—all point to the kingdom as Jesus' single, great theme. As E. F. Scott put it, "Thus everything in Jesus' thought is connected with his idea of the Kingdom. This is the key at once to his ethic, to his theology, to his social teaching, to his inward religion."[7]

But what did the term "kingdom" mean? That has been under debate for a long time. Some have conceived of the kingdom of God in utopian terms, as a sort of distant millennium which God would one day bring about, a sort of "heaven" such as Revelation 21–22 describes. Others have claimed that the kingdom of God is something present now, and it comes about, such men have often added, through human endeavor. From the time of Augustine on, and especially in the Middle Ages, it was common to equate the kingdom of God with the church. Luther identified it with the forgiveness of sins (cf. Colossians 1:13-14). Pietism often saw the kingdom present where certain rules of conduct or moral patterns were observed. Sectarian groups have attempted to set up the kingdom of God on earth through their missionary programs or by claiming that the Second Coming has occurred and the kingdom is being manifested in their special group. The Russian novelist Tolstoy sought to bring it about by a literal obedience to the Sermon on the Mount.

Much of nineteenth-century theology conceived of the kingdom as an evolutionary process, which modern progress was bringing to its proper climax. A great deal was heard then (and still is heard in some circles of American Protestantism) about "building the kingdom of God" by doing this or that. It became a social gospel program. Albert Schweitzer helped smash such notions at the turn of the century, at least in Europe, when he pointed out that much of Jesus' language smacks of the strange world of Jewish apocalyptic and that Jesus did not teach a kingdom men would build over the centuries but a single, shattering action of God which would create his kingdom at the same time as it ended all world history.

Since Schweitzer's day his key word "eschatology" (i.e., what relates to the "last times") has been widely heard in connection with the kingdom. The views that (1) Jesus saw this kingdom as fully realized in his own day and that (2) he viewed it as something around the corner but still in the future have each had their champions. Attempts have been made, notably by Rudolf Bultman and his pupils, to trace out what Jesus' announcement about the kingdom meant in terms of human existence, so that Jesus' message might be preached meaningfully to men today.

Christological aspects of the kingdom have been studied, too, as
have the ethics of the kingdom and the grace it offers. Oscar Cullmann has tried to state the difficult relation between "the kingdom
of God" and "the kingdom of Christ" which is implied at times
in the epistles and other post-resurrection writings of the New
Testament.[8] Luckily we need not evaluate where each of these
views may be right or wrong before considering the meaning
which Jesus gave to the term. Rather, keeping in mind this mass
of theories, we shall look at his words and their background,
seeking to find an understanding of the kingdom which can serve
as a criterion for the varied, later interpretations.

Any early Christian, we said, would have recognized that Jesus'
message about the kingdom was his proclamation or kerygma.
Mark, in fact, in his assertion that "Jesus came . . . preaching
[kēr_yssōn]" (1:14) uses the Greek root that provides the word for
"apostolic proclamation" (kerygma). Jesus had a message to
preach, but his kerygma was different from the later proclamation
of the apostles. This is, of course, because the great events of cross
and resurrection occurred in between his proclaiming and theirs.
The church had "Christ crucified and risen" to preach, but it is
a tribute to its faithfulness to the historical Jesus that the church
did not discard Jesus' kerygma. The church in its gospels reports
that Jesus came preaching the kingdom of God.

Jesus' message, prior to the resurrection, on the other side of
the empty tomb, is thus different from that of Christians on this
side of Easter. It was also different, at least in emphasis, from the
message of those who had gone before him, like John the Baptist
and the Old Testament prophets. Luke felt this difference so
keenly that he never allows John the Baptist to refer to the kingdom. It was a fact, however, that Jews and the Old Testament
had spoken of this theme long prior to Jesus. Matthew feels this
continuity so strongly that he has John the Baptist preach the
same message which Jesus proclaimed shortly thereafter, "Repent,
for the kingdom of heaven is at hand" (Matthew 3:2; cf. 4:17;
contrast Luke 3:3 and 4:43).[9] Luke thus stresses Jesus' message
as something new; Matthew, as good news in continuity with the
past in God's revelation. We must say that Jesus' theme of the
kingdom represented nothing new to Jewish ears; but what he said
about it and its imminence—the announcement that it was "at
hand"—represented something new and startling.

The proper starting point for understanding Jesus' message is therefore the Old Testament. This is true even of the term *euangelion*, the Greek word translated "gospel." Any early Christian would have recognized *euangelion* as the word for the "good news" which he had accepted about Jesus Christ. Any citizen of the Roman empire would have known the same word as meaning "a reward to a messenger for bringing good news" or as the term state officials used for some announcement about Caesar. But the real background for the idea of "preaching the gospel" or "announcing good news" lies in the Old Testament. There this term is associated with God and his good news and, what is more important, with his kingdom.[10]

It is the Second Isaiah who especially used such language more than five centuries before Jesus' day. He pictured a herald bringing "good tidings to Zion" (40:9), a herald who hurried on before the people returning to Jerusalem from their exile in Babylon. In a famous passage, Isaiah depicts the people of Jerusalem straining their eyes, as they stand on the wall, to catch a glimpse of this herald on a mountain peak; they break forth into song:

How beautiful upon the mountains are the feet of him who
    brings good tidings,
  who publishes peace, who brings good tidings of good,
  who publishes salvation, who says to Zion,
      "Your God reigns." (Isaiah 52:7)

Here, in a few short lines, the theme of a herald who brings "gospel," about peace and salvation, is bound together with the theme "God reigns" or is king. God has asserted his lordship, the herald's message announces, by working comfort, redemption, and salvation for his people (52:9-10). In this case the "gospel" and redemption have to do with the return from the Babylonian Exile. In other instances, similar language is used to describe an earlier "exodus," not from Babylon but from Egypt, and what Yahweh had done then. Psalm 68:4-14 speaks in such terms about how God "leads out the prisoners to prosperity," from Egypt to Canaan, and how a great host "bore the tidings" (68:11) of what Yahweh the king had done (cf. vss. 7-10, 14). Israel thus had a "gospel" message about the First Exodus (from Egypt) and the Second Exodus (from Babylon).[11] This language, announcing good news which God has wrought, could also be applied to an individual's experience, as when he is delivered from sickness or some other

trouble; the psalmist speaks of telling "the glad news of deliverance in the great congregation" (Psalm 40:9). On the basis of
such experiences in men's lives and the nation's history, another
psalmist could urge not only Israel but all the world to burst forth
with joy because a new age has come:

> O sing unto the Lord a new song; sing . . . , all the earth!
> . . . tell of his salvation from day to day,
> Declare his glory among the nations,
>   his marvelous works among all the peoples! . . .
> Say among the nations, "The Lord reigns." (Psalm 96:1-3, 10)

All these examples from Isaiah and the Psalms use the same
word (which we commonly translate as "gospel") to describe an
announcement about an action of God for man's salvation. When
therefore Jesus is depicted in the New Testament as preaching a
gospel about the kingdom of God, he stands in a long train of
witnesses to God's redeeming actions in the past. Jesus of Nazareth was renewing an age-old message about God as one who acts
to save. It may have been noted that in these Old Testament passages God is described as king (Psalm 68:24) or as "reigning"
(Isaiah 52:7, literally, "being king"). And so there is an even
closer connection between the Old Testament and the New: Jesus'
proclamation was a continuation of an Old Testament theme about
God's kingship. He shares the conviction which witnesses in ancient Israel voiced about the Exodus, and the return from Babylon,
and in some of their individual experiences: God is manifesting
his power as king, and that is "good news." According to Luke
4:16-19, Jesus even began his ministry with a public announcement that he was following in the footsteps of the herald in
Second Isaiah: Jesus announced in the synagogue at Nazareth,
"The Lord . . . has anointed me to preach good news . . . to proclaim release . . . to proclaim the year of the Lord's favor"
(Luke 4:18-19 = Isaiah 61:1-2). Hence Jesus preached that the
time set by God had come, the kingdom was about to be made
manifest.

Jesus' term does not mean a geographical kingdom like Great
Britain or medieval France or the state which Herod ruled. It
certainly does not mean a territorial, political organization set up
for the purpose of government. "Kingdom of God" rather denotes kingship—that God is king; as in Old Testament thought,
he reigns. Of course, God's rule takes form in the world of time

and space, but most modern scholars are agreed that it denotes God's reign rather than his realm, his kingship rather than a kingdom.[12] Commentators prefer to use some word like "regime" or "God's sway" or "sovereignty" to denote God's being king. Our literal and conventional rendering is so well established, however, that even translations like that of J. B. Phillips and *The New English Bible* prefer to keep the customary phrase "kingdom of God"; they rely on further knowledge about biblical thought on the part of readers to make clear what the meaning is.

That "kingdom of God" denotes God's kingship and kingly power is shown frequently and clearly by Old Testament usage. There some verbal expression, such as "Yahweh reigns" or "the Lord is king," is much more common than the noun phrase, "kingdom of God," but the meaning is the same. It is simply that the Hebrew language seems to prefer such dynamic, verbal expressions. Here are some examples of the concrete way in which the Old Testament speaks of God's kingship:

> The Lord sits enthroned as king for ever. (Psalm 29:10)
> The Lord will reign for ever and ever. (Exodus 15:18)
> I will extol thee, my God and King. . . .
> All they works . . . all thy saints . . . shall speak of the glory
> of thy kingdom, and tell of thy power,
> to make known to the sons of men thy mighty deeds,
> and the glorious splendor of thy kingdom.
> Thy kingdom is an everlasting kingdom,
> and thy dominion endures throughout all generations.
> (Psalm 145:1, 10-13)

The emphasis is similar in Psalms 47, 93, 95–99, which are compositions which were probably read each year at Israel's New Year festival and which announced dramatically God's enthronement as Israel's king for the coming year.

In these Old Testament references, just as in Matthew's version of the Lord's Prayer, God's "being king" or his kingdom is spoken of sometimes as an eternal, almost timeless sovereignty, sometimes as a reign that is already present (Psalm 99:1, "The Lord reigns"), and sometimes as a future event to be realized "some day":

> The Lord of hosts will reign . . . in Jerusalem . . . he will manifest his glory. (Isaiah 24:23)
> The kingdom shall be the Lord's. (Obadiah 21)

Occasionally this future hope is combined with a confession that Yahweh is king now:

The Lord is our king: he will save us. (Isaiah 33:22)

As times grew darker for Israel, however, as Jews were persecuted for loyalty to God and his law (as in the Maccabean period), as Roman rule continued, hope for an assertion by Yahweh of his kingly power grew more and more intense. There were poignant longings for him to assert his kingship in the world, his power to save. In apocalyptic circles fantastic imagery often flourished—for example, of an age when every grape vine would have a thousand branches, each branch a thousand clusters, each cluster a thousand grapes, and each grape would produce a hundred and twenty gallons of wine—a prodigious hope especially in a "dry and thirsty land."[13]

Hence, when Jesus came announcing the kingdom, there was the danger that some would take his message in such fantasy-terms, or that others would see it as a call to arms against the Roman overlords in Yahweh's name, or simply as a timeless truth that God rules in heaven. The fact is that Jesus' message skirted all these extremes. It proclaimed an age-old theme out of Israel's scriptures, but it had a fresh urgency. For Jesus said, according to Mark's summary of his message, "The time is *fulfilled*, the kingdom of God *is at hand*." What did the herald mean by such an announcement?

Characteristics of the Kingdom

In contrast to all the talk in apocalyptic circles about a future kingdom or an "age to come" and in contrast to occasional references to the kingdom of God in the rabbinical writings,[14] Jesus spoke frequently and with dramatic certainty about God's kingship as about to be manifested here and now. He saw as "good news," "close at hand" and "upon you," what others dreamed about or spoke of as a "yoke" to be accepted. Although Jesus employed an ancient term in speaking of the kingdom of God, his freshness in handling it created the air of "authority" or "distinctiveness" or "directness" which his contemporaries were quick to see. The phrase came to be stamped with new meaning and emerges as a "Jesus term"—one that he used in an inimitable way.[15] The little kerygma of Mark 1:14-15 sounds "like the title of a programme."[16] What was the divine program, the realization of which Jesus proclaimed was beginning to be set in motion?

In general, what stands out is (1) the nearness of the kingdom in Jesus' view. It is "close at hand." There is a famous debate over whether the verb at Mark 1:15 should be rendered, "The kingdom of God is at hand" (KJV, RSV) or "The kingdom is upon you" (NEB). The final decision here depends on some details of linguistic usage and on an examination of other sayings of Jesus as scholars try to determine whether he regarded the kingdom as present or future.[17] But at the least, one must say that if Jesus did not regard it as present, he certainly looked for it in the immediate future. Its nearness is the most striking feature of what he says about the kingdom. God and his reign—and therefore salvation—are near, near enough to attain.

Three other general characteristics can be listed briefly, even though each one of them demands detailed justification as we study the sayings of Jesus later on.

(2) Jesus assumes the kingdom is something given by God. It is not man's creation or something human beings build, step by step. Albert Schweitzer may have overdone the apocalyptic emphasis and may have made Jesus' message center too much around a divine thunderclap which would dissolve all history and bring the kingdom in the twinkling of an eye, but Schweitzer was on sound biblical grounds in rejecting the widespread notion of the kingdom as something men build.[18] All too often an image has been employed which likens the kingdom to a Pacific coral reef, built up over the centuries—each individual, each generation makes a contribution until the whole evolves. The image is wrong. The kingdom comes more like a typhoon or volcano. Suddenly, it's there, and the action is not man's. The kingdom of God has a miraculous, supernatural character. It is something God the Father gives (Luke 12:32; Matthew 21:43). Man simply receives it, as a child receives a gift (Mark 10:15).

(3) This kingdom of God about which Jesus speaks transcends the nationalist limits which many Jews of his day put on it, and at times there are hints that it is universal in nature.

There were Jewish groups, like the Zealots, of course, who looked on the Romans and most other foreigners as enemies; Yahweh was king of Israel alone. That meant a narrow view of his kingship. The apocalyptic groups, like Qumran, tended to

narrow the circle even more. Not all Israel was worthy, but only
the little conventicle which truly kept the law and observed all
the proper requirements of piety. That made God king of a still
smaller group. The Pharisees did seek proselytes from among non-
Jews, and had a missionary outreach, but conversion and the new
religion for these proselytes was often along strictly legalistic
lines.[19] That meant that God's kingdom was being worked out
in terms of law and even casuistry.

It is difficult, however, to claim that Jesus' message of the kingdom in his lifetime manifested a universal outreach. Jesus was
scarcely ever, if at all, outside of Palestine. His mission was historically to "the lost sheep of the house of Israel."[20] But even in
this setting Jesus' message showed a much more universal concern
than that of Zealot, apocalyptist, or Pharisee. He avoided nationalist, warlike limitations in his outlook. His interest was never
confined to one small "holy" group, and he condemned legalism
and pettifogging rules and practices. He welcomed outcasts, tax
gatherers, sinners. When he occasionally came into contact with
non-Jews, he eventually heeded their pleas. A *"Q"* saying at Matthew 8:11 (par. Luke 13:28-29) emphasizes, "Men will come
from east and west, and from north and south, and sit at table
[in Jewish thought, a significant expression of fellowship] in the
kingdom of God." Compare also the parable of the Great Supper
(Luke 14:15-24, par. Matthew 22:1-10), where God's kingdom
is likened to a case where the chosen guests failed to come and
instead outsiders from the streets and lanes ended up "eating
bread in the kingdom of God." It remained for the Great Commission in the post-resurrection period to set forth the ultimate
ideal of the universal outlook, "Go . . . and make disciples of all
nations" (Matthew 28:19-20). Historically it took considerable
effort on the part of Paul and others to convince some of their
fellow believers that a Gentile mission fitted the intent of Christ.
But there were already seeds of a more universal outlook in Jesus'
message about the kingdom, especially when compared with some
contemporary Jewish views.[21]

(4) Finally there is the question to what extent the coming of
God's kingdom, now or soon, with its worldwide dimensions, was
somehow associated with the appearance of Jesus of Nazareth himself on the stage of history. Jesus voiced his message with directness and distinctiveness. "Kingdom of God" becomes a "Jesus

term," intimately associated with him. His preaching, parables, and miracles were manifestations of the coming kingdom. He spoke of God so intimately, as *Abba,* that some connection seemingly must exist between the sovereign kingship of God and the person of Jesus, and, one supposes, there must be some connection between what he did and the salvation which the kingship of God implies.

Subsequently, Christians have become accustomed to say that "Jesus brought the kingdom" or was "himself the expression of God's reign," or at least, as generations have sung in the *Te Deum,* Jesus "opened the kingdom of heaven to all believers" by his cross and resurrection, when he had "overcome the sharpness of death." But such are to a great extent the expressions of post-Easter faith and theology. There *should* be a connection, believers think, between Jesus himself and God's kingdom, but such links are notoriously hard to find in the words of Jesus. The problem ought be kept in mind during any examination of the evidence. Jesus preached God as king. But did he, directly or by implication, also make a claim for himself which linked his own person to the sovereignty of God which was coming on the scene? Did he by his actions associate the coming of the kingdom with his own lifetime, or with himself?[22]

A good place to begin if one wishes to see the relationship between Jesus and the kingdom is in a comparison between Jesus and John the Baptist. Much that has just been said about the kingdom of God as Jesus proclaimed it also seems true for the preaching of John the Baptist. John came announcing, "Repent, for the kingdom of heaven is at hand" (Matthew 3:2, though both Mark and Luke omit any such message on the Baptizer's lips). He spoke in apocalyptic terms of "the axe . . . laid to the root of the trees," ready to cut, and of a judgment with fire, as the actions of a God who is able to work miraculous salvation or to execute wrath (Matthew 3:7-10, par. Luke 3:7-9). In his ethical advice John counseled tax gatherers and soldiers—certainly outcasts from Judaism and likely (in the latter case) pagans (Luke 3:10-14). Thus John spoke of the kingdom as near, God-given, and for more than Jews. One thing is lacking, though, in comparison with Jesus: nowhere in our records is it suggested that the coming of God's kingdom is bound up with John's words and deeds. He points ahead to someone mightier than himself (Mark

1:7-8). It is nowhere recorded that John the Baptist worked
miracles, which were signs of the kingdom. Nowhere does John
refer to any casting out of demons (as Jesus does), as a token
that "the kingdom of God is upon you." John practices a water
rite to prepare men for the kingdom; he does not act as if it were
already "breaking in" through his ministry.

This difference between John and Jesus as regards the kingdom
has been described dramatically as the difference between "the
eleventh and the twelfth hours." Now the clock has struck, "the
shift in the aeons is here."[23] If we ask "how," the answer is, in
Jesus' words and deeds. As he himself claimed, reflecting words
from Isaiah 35, in the fact that "the blind receive their sight, the
lame walk, lepers are cleansed, deaf men hear, the dead are raised,
and the good news is being preached" (Matthew 11:2-6, par. Luke
7:18-23; cf. also Luke 4:18-19). Significantly, those words were
addressed to John the Baptist and suggest a difference between the
two men of which both were conscious. This dividing line is even
clearer in a saying preserved at Matthew 11:11, par. Luke 7:28—
John is greatest of those "born of women" outside the kingdom,
but "who is least in the kingdom" is greater than he! This implies that John is on the other side of a dividing line, and that
the kingdom is seen to be tied up with Jesus' own ministry. An
examination of the relation of Jesus and John, as regards the kingdom, thus gives some evidence that the coming of God's reign
is associated with a man, Jesus of Nazareth, as never before in history. It is in the miracles, or mighty deeds of God through Jesus,
that we shall find this claim even more decisively reiterated (see
chapter 7). The answer which ultimately satisfies the situation is
that in the work and words of Jesus there was an "indirect Christology" implied—this man acts for God and his kingdom; after
the resurrection, the early church was to draw this out more fully
and directly and make the Christology explicit.

Two characteristics of Jesus' view of the kingdom have so far
been mentioned only in general terms. A more precise formulation of what Jesus taught is required. The one is the crucial question of whether Jesus regarded the kingdom as present or future
in his lifetime. We have tended to say both elements are true.
Now it is time to see if and how the scriptural evidence supports
such an answer. In some ways Mark 1:15, which seems the clearest statement, is the toughest place to begin. The verb which we

are accustomed to translate, "the kingdom *is-at-hand*," is a form
in Greek that means literally, "has drawn near." However, such a
perfect tense in Greek regularly has a present implication, and the
"battle of the philologists" centers on whether this should be
brought out by a phrase like "is near at hand" or in a stronger
phrase, such as "has already come."[24] Experts have ransacked
Greek literature for examples which might shed light on the
usage in the gospels; they have also tried to reconstruct what the
original Aramaic might have been. Let it be said that the RSV/
KJV formulation, "The kingdom [has drawn near and therefore]
is at hand," probably commands the support of most scholars who
have studied the problem. But so important a translation as *The
New English Bible* inclines toward a more emphatic position: the
kingdom is not just close at hand, it is "upon you."

If we turn to other sayings of Jesus, the matter gets even more
complicated. Both views, that the kingdom is present and that it
is future, appear. In the Lord's Prayer we have already noticed
in connection with the petition, "Thy kingdom come," a sense in
which the kingdom is regarded as present as well as senses in
which it is looked upon as eternal and future. Mark 9:1 is a verse
which is the despair of commentators; Jesus says:

> "Truly, I say to you, there are some standing here who will not
> taste death before they see the kingdom of God come with power."

The parallels in Matthew 16:28 and Luke 9:27 each change the
wording and the meaning slightly, but the general purport is
certainly to regard the coming of the kingdom as future in relation to that moment of Jesus' life.[25] On the other hand, Jesus, in
a dispute with the scribes, claims that he is casting out demons
with God's help; he then draws the conclusion that men should
thereby know that God's kingdom has come upon them (Matthew
12:28, par. Luke 11:20). Likewise at Luke 16:16: ever since
John the Baptist, Jesus says, the kingdom of God has been
preached, during his ministry, and men are storming their way
into it.[26] In these and other instances Jesus' words regard the
kingdom as present.

As can be guessed, when the sources present unresolved problems, men have offered explanations to smooth out the conflict.
Tempting as such solutions may seem, we ought to reject the
"psychological," "biographical," and "realized eschatology" answers. The "psychological" answer says that Jesus' opinion shifted

back and forth from moment to moment, and that our biblical material reflects his vacillation. The "biographical" answer holds that Jesus changed his opinion from one period to another in his life, so that chronologically what the "young Jesus" said differs from the view of the "mature man." The trouble with both these answers is that they assume the gospel records can be used to provide psychological explanations or to reconstruct biography. Furthermore, the evidence does not fall into a neat pattern so that one position can be attributed to the "young" Jesus in Galilee and another to the maturer man in Jerusalem. Both views appear throughout, practically side by side.

"Realized eschatology," an explanation associated with the name of the British professor C. H. Dodd, has enjoyed much vogue.[27] It insists that Jesus regarded the kingdom as present, and that the "futurist" sayings were added to his words by the early church.[28] Naturally, it is possible that the early church added or heightened certain emphases in Jesus' words, and Dodd has done a great service in calling our attention to the fact that the novel note in Jesus' message was his reference to the kingdom "here and now." Dodd rescued the word "eschatology" from relegation at the end of things to a place of primacy in Jesus' lifetime: it was *then* that God's ends were being realized. But it is going too far to attempt to eliminate every statement about the future kingdom from the authentic words of Jesus. Some of the renderings in *The New English Bible* (a project for which Professor Dodd has been General Director) seem to strain too much to make Jesus' statements fit with "realized eschatology" alone (cf. Mark 9:1 in NEB, which speaks of "the Kingdom of God already come in power").

There is furthermore a neat trap awaiting us if we make the kingdom wholly present during Jesus' ministry: why, then, the cross? If all has come to pass during the ministry, why is any death necessary? That connection, between Jesus' death and the manifestation of God's kingly, saving power, is worked out only in further sayings of Jesus, where he uses certain titles or makes claims about himself, and in the post-Easter church, as in the Pauline statement that God by the cross brought us into the kingdom of his Son (Colossians 1:13). "Realized eschatology" is only a partial truth which enables us to take seriously the future promises to be fulfilled. Like the Old Testament picture of God's reign, Jesus sees a present and a future side to the kingdom.

Both aspects, then, must be left standing as part of Jesus' message. For him, God's reign is being actualized in men's lives, but there is more to come. The present fulfillment presages future fulfillment. The promise of a future kingdom, where God shall be sovereign alone, is united with present fulfillment when one man, Jesus of Nazareth, realizes what God's kingship means and lives by his power. Such is what made Jesus' ministry and presence so significant. Through him God was at work. It is a time of salvation.

The other feature in Jesus' view of the kingdom which requires more careful statement is the question of whether this kingdom is sudden or gradual in its coming. Both positions have their champions, who for their views can cite valid evidence. On the one hand, in the Old Testament and Jewish thought the kingdom is usually conceived of as coming suddenly. John the Baptist took over this idea, and so did Jesus. There is no notion of a gradual evolution (or of a calendar according to which its advent can be spelled out).[29] A famous, though often misunderstood, little incident from Jesus' life makes this point clearly:

> Being asked by the Pharisees when the kingdom of God was coming, he answered them, "The kingdom of God is not coming with signs to be observed; nor will they say, 'Lo, here it is!' or 'There!' for behold, the kingdom of God is in the midst of you."
>
> (Luke 17:20-21)

Older interpretation took the final phrase to mean "within you" (as in the RSV note)—suggesting that the kingdom is something within each individual's heart. Dodd and the school of "realized eschatology" interpreted it to refer to the presence of the kingdom right now—as the NEB has it, "In fact the kingdom of God is among you." However, the sense that seems closest to what Jesus meant and to a reply to the question of the Pharisees is that the kingdom of God comes without any signs to be observed; no timetable, no gestures to call attention to it. Suddenly, it's there. One exegete paraphrases, "Not 'Here it is' or 'There'; for, look, God's kingdom is given into your hands!"—thus making the point that it is God's gift as well as something sudden.[30]

The strand of evidence which cuts in the opposite direction, however, is a series of parables in which the kingdom of God is compared to something that grows or multiplies—for example, a seed (Mark 4:30-32, 26-29), leaven (Matthew 13:33, par. Luke

13:20-21), the work of a sower planting seed (Mark 4:1-9).
These "parables of growth"[31] seem to suggest that the kingdom is
like a living organism which matures slowly over the years. We
might be inclined to say that Jesus planted the seed and that the
kingdom has been growing over the centuries; but how would
that fit with the other verses about the suddenness of its coming?
C. H. Dodd, in the 1930's, offered an interpretation which carried the process several steps further back. The sowing, he said,
was done by the Old Testament prophets and John the Baptist;
therefore in Jesus' ministry the harvest was already beginning to
appear. The kingdom was there—realized eschatology!

One must object that modern categories are being imposed if
"growth" in these parables is taken to mean evolution or human
achievement. For even in the parable of the Seed at Mark 4:26-
29 it is God who causes the growth (the farmer sleeps; the seed
grows "of itself," literally "automatically"). Furthermore, the
real point in these parables is not so much growth but contrast.
They would better be called "parables of contrast," contrast between humble beginnings and the future results. In this case there
is a real application to Jesus' ministry. Everything during the ministry looked insignificant. In Bornkamm's words, "An unknown
rabbi . . . in a remote corner of Palestine? On his cross the sport of
passers-by? Is this the kingdom of God? The shift in the ages?"[32]
No greater contrast could exist between this and the results, Jesus
raised and exalted, a new age begun. There is a contrast. But
there is also involved in parables like these a certainty about results—certainty because in these humble beginnings, in the words
and deeds of the man from Nazareth, God is at work. Read in
such ways, these parables do not depict a slow evolution or clash
with the idea that the kingdom is God's doing, coming with suddenness. Rather they contrast present and future, and strike a note
of certainty that God will do what is promised.

Perhaps the word "certainty" is a clue to the interpretation also
of verses like Mark 9:1 and passages like it ("before these bystanders die, the kingdom will have come"). In Jewish apocalyptic such terms of "nearness," immediacy, and suddenness express
a conviction of certainty.[33] The speaker is so sure *that* such and
such a thing will occur that he says it will be immediate and
sudden. His conviction *that* God will act is so great that he voices
it in terms of when and how. Such language, we must remember,

was common in Jesus' day, and some of his sayings are cast in apocalyptic mold. "Decoding" them, we have an emphasis on the certainty of God's action. Perhaps "suddenly or gradually?" is the wrong question. Both types of language seek to emphasize certainty about God's kingdom—he will bring it to be.

In his preaching Jesus was certain, then, that God was about to usher in his reign into the lives of men. Hence Jesus called on them to repent, that is, to turn in a new direction, to God. He spoke of God's concern about sin and of his salvation which was now at work as the forgiveness of sins (Mark 1:14-15). To see what more he meant by the kingdom of God, it is necessary to turn to the parables, which seem both to conceal and reveal what the reign of God offers.

"Many Things in Parables"—The Offer of the Kingdom

Jesus, says Mark, with reference to the crowds who followed so eagerly to hear his message, "taught them many things in parables" (4:2). Then after a sample of three such parables, only one of which he bothers to explain (4:3-32), Mark adds, "With many such parables he spoke the word to them . . ." (4:33). Matthew puts it even more strongly: "he said nothing to them without a parable" (13:34). Altogether, some fifty to seventy parables (depending on how one counts them) appear in the gospels. Most of them, in one way or the other, concern the kingdom. The parable was seemingly Jesus' favorite form of communication about his chief theme, the kingdom. Therefore, if we would know what he said about the reign of God, it is necessary to penetrate into the meaning of the parable form.

This is no easy task. For a parable was originally designed to make men think. And Jesus' parables, for better or for worse, have made men think—think along all sorts of lines, some right (more or less), others contrary to Jesus' intended meaning. The "many things" of which Jesus spoke have been interpreted in many ways, some of them quite arbitrary and fantastic. It is a merit of modern scholarship that it has peeled away a number of these false accretions. It has used its critical tools to help recover Jesus' voice in the parables. Here, as perhaps almost nowhere else, we hear his historical words. Above all, critical study has helped us see that the parables, even though they refer to many things, deal with one chief thing, the kingdom of God.

What is a parable? Literally the word means "a placing of
one thing alongside another," for comparison. Aristotle, in his
Rhetoric, spoke of such juxtaposition for the purpose of comparison and illustration. Many people think of Jesus' parables as setting alongside of each other some detail or incident out of human
life and a truth about heaven. Hence parables are popularly de-
fined as "earthly stories with a heavenly meaning." But that definition is all too general and is open to serious misunderstanding. A
"heavenly meaning" can be quite vague and remote from us,
whereas Jesus' parables spoke directly to immediate human situations. "Heavenly meaning" smacks of a realm of "general spiritual
truths," whereas Jesus spoke quite specifically about God and what
he was about to do. Above all, the notion of "heavenly meanings"
has often led to a search for fanciful applications of the details
in the parables. All too frequently the parables have been allegorized to make them say what the interpreter wanted them to.

It is not too much to say that for about nineteen of the twenty
centuries of Christianity the parables have been widely and devas-
tatingly misunderstood. Men treated them as hunting grounds for
whatever doctrines they wanted to find—by allegorizing the details.[34] The inn where the Good Samaritan took the man who fell
among thieves was given a "heavenly meaning"; so were the oil
and wine which were poured into his wounds. On this basis the
beast on which the Samaritan had ridden (Luke 10:34) had to
have a special meaning, as did the birds which lodged in the shrub
that grew from a mustard seed (Mark 4:30-32). As recently as
a century ago, a book which our grandfathers regarded as standard,
Archbishop Trench's *Notes on the Parables,*[35] was by and large
allegorizing them the same way they had been handled in the
Middle Ages and in the thousand years of allegorizing before that.

It was a German professor in Marburg, Adolf Jülicher, who
about 1890 decisively stated the case that parables are not like
allegories where there are many points of contact between the two
things being compared; a parable has only one, central point of
comparison between the "earthly story" and the real subject about
which Jesus intends to make a point.[36] The difference between a
parable and an allegory can be sketched as in the chart on page 161.
Jülicher made the mistake, however, of presenting the point of
comparison in a parable as a "general truth." His ethical maxims
were often just pious platitudes. The parables in this mode of in-

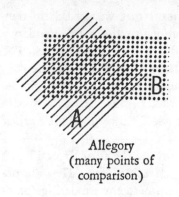

Allegory
(many points of
comparison)

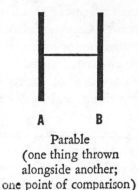

A   B

Parable
(one thing thrown
alongside another;
one point of comparison)

terpretation often did not pack much punch. Other investigators, therefore, while holding on to the truth which Jülicher discovered (that parables are not allegories), have stressed the parables' quite specific reference to the kingdom. In particular the analysis by C. H. Dodd[37] emphasized that the one point of comparison regularly concerned the kingdom or kingship of God. A lifelong study of parables by another professor in Germany, Joachim Jeremias of Göttingen, who grew up in the parsonage where his father was chief Lutheran pastor in Jerusalem, has performed especial service in penetrating back behind the present and later forms of the parables to the original meaning in Jesus' lifetime.[38] Of course, not everyone is of one mind on all matters of interpretation; for example, some experts feel that Jesus could have used a touch of allegory here and there, as the rabbis did.[39] But there is widespread agreement on how to work back to the historical Jesus and his message in parables about the kingdom of God.

We shall examine the results of that investigation first, but then we shall also pay attention to some insights from the parables as the early church and the evangelists have put them together for us. In this way it is possible to do justice to each part of the "double setting" which the parables can have: (1) an initial, original meaning, during the ministry of Jesus; (2) a further, post-resurrection meaning in the early church, as the evangelists have recorded them for us.[40]

Before we dig into what the parables of Jesus said about the kingdom as part of his original message, some preliminary observations are necessary. The first is that prior to Jesus' day there was already a long history of the use of parables in the Old Testa-

ment and among the Jews. This means that we should rid ourselves of Greek and Western definitions of the parable and pay
attention to Semitic backgrounds. Here were Jesus' roots. The
Hebrew term (*mashal*) which we render "parable" actually covered a variety of literary forms. These included proverbs, simple
comparisons, and longer parable-stories. Because of this a maxim
like Luke 4:23, "Physician, heal yourself," can literally be called
a "parable" (RSV "proverb").

More important is the fact that some of the formal parables in
the Old Testament are set in scenes of controversy. They are devices in a "war of words," and several of them are daring forays
in a life-and-death struggle. II Samuel 12:1-14 is the famous story
by Nathan about a rich man with many flocks who steals the one
ewe lamb of a poor neighbor. David's indignation burns at such
a thing. Then, his guard down, David is told by Nathan, "You
are the man—that's just how you behaved with Uriah's wife,
Bathsheba." Later Joab "gets through" to David with a similar
sort of parable (II Samuel 14:1-11). At Judges 9:7-21, Jotham
tells a parable about the trees—and then has to run for his life
when the point of his story is grasped.

These Old Testament examples lead to a second observation,
that for Jesus, just as in these earlier cases, parables were weapons.
They were ways of "getting through" with a message to which
men might not listen otherwise. They were instruments for debates, just as with the rabbis.[41] They were weapons of defense
against charges made about Jesus, and weapons of attack to press
home his views. This was an aspect of the parables which was not
understood even by Jülicher: that they must be viewed, not as
teaching timeless truths, but as quite specific advances and defenses by Jesus as he proclaims the kingdom and skirmishes with
the scribes and Pharisees over the message he has been commissioned to proclaim. Jesus' stories, which often seem to us moderns
rather harmless literary gems, thus turn out to be "parables of
conflict"—not that they describe a conflict so much as they were
themselves part of a conflict. Jesus answers his critics. Jesus states
his message in a way that will "get through," in parables. Sometimes our gospels preserve this original "conflict" setting, sometimes they do not.[42]

That prompts another important observation. It is the simple
fact that Matthew, Mark, and Luke do not always give the para-

bles with their original setting and meaning; often the parables in our gospels have been "worked over" to draw out new and further meanings. It is easy to prove this to oneself. Sometimes the same parable is used differently in different gospels. It has a different setting, it makes a different point when the several gospel settings are compared. An obvious example is Jesus' parable about a lost sheep. Luke 15:1-10 has Jesus address the parable of the Lost Sheep to opponents who have been criticizing Jesus because he receives sinners and eats with them (15:1-2). Matthew, on the other hand, inserts the story in a chapter addressed to the disciples on discipline within their community (18:12-14). Luke has thus given us a setting in Jesus' life (as an answer to critics), defending his outreach to outcasts by saying, "That's the way God is— he seeks the lost." Matthew employs the parable to teach Christians the need for seeking out pastorally any brother who has strayed from the fold. Now we could rationalize and say that the historical Jesus told the parable both ways. But the one version (in Luke) fits into his life quite well, while the other (in Matthew) applies to later, post-resurrection problems.[43] Further, there are so many examples of this sort of revision and reworking that we find it hard to claim that Jesus told so many parables in two ways. There appears to have been a definite tendency to reapply some of Jesus' parables after the resurrection in order to get new meanings from them. In fact, Professor Jeremias has formulated some "laws" on the development in the parables from Jesus' lifetime to the primitive church (see below, pp. 181-85).

All this allows us to tackle one of the most puzzling features about the parables—their purpose. Why did Jesus say so many things in parables? It would seem common sense to reply, "Because he wanted to 'get through' to men," or "Because it was an Old Testament and Jewish device," or "Because the parable was an effective way to answer opponents." However, the Gospel of Mark has an explanation which seems to defy common sense. According to Mark 4:12, Jesus speaks in parables "*in order that* they [men outside the kingdom] may indeed see but not perceive, and may indeed hear but not understand; *lest* they should turn again and be forgiven." According to this verse, Jesus used parables to keep men from getting his message; the secret about the kingdom of God is only for those "to whom it has been given" (4:11). Some commentators have seized on these words to say, Here is

the Pauline idea of predestination—Mark thinks that Jesus' message is only for a few for whom it was predestined; the parables
will conceal it from the rest. Most scholars are convinced, however, that such a reflection of predestination was not Jesus' aim
(although Mark evidently understood it as such). Jesus used parables to help men understand, not to shut them out from his good
news.

It must be observed that Mark 4:12 is a quotation from Isaiah
6:9-10. Study of Isaiah 6 shows that the words there are part of
Isaiah's call from God, where the *purpose* of his work is stated
in terms of its *results*: his work will have the outcome that men
will see but not perceive, hear but not understand the message.
In Hebrew, result and purpose can be expressed the same way
grammatically, and so one explanation is to claim that Mark 4:12
is simply picturing the result of Jesus' parables as their purpose.
But it is further to be observed that Matthew puts Mark's point
quite differently: according to Matthew 13:13, Jesus speaks in
parables "*because* seeing they [men] do not see, and hearing they
do not hear, nor do they understand."[44] Matthew implies that
Jesus employed parables because men did not grasp his message;
the picture-language of parables might help them. A second solution is therefore to claim that Matthew has correctly understood
what Mark has put incorrectly. A more technical solution is the
view that Jesus' original Aramaic meant basically what Matthew
has, but was also capable of translation into the Greek found in
Mark. In this view, Matthew has rightly phrased what Mark mis-
translated. More drastic is Jeremias' solution: Jesus once said what
Mark 4:12 has, but *not* with reference to the parables. They were
thus not intended to obscure things for men, but to clarify.

It must be granted that no one solution has been accepted by
everyone with regard to the problem of Mark 4:12, par. Matthew
13:13. There is wide agreement, however, that Mark does not
correctly state Jesus' purpose in telling parables. Jesus' stories were
to set forth his message, not to confuse men. Plainly, even in
Mark, the aim of the parables (4:11) is to tell about the kingdom
of God and the secret that Jesus was to announce: the kingdom
is at hand.

These difficulties and backgrounds acknowledged, we can now
try to see just what the parables say about the kingdom. There

is in them, everyone agrees, a message and a theology about God and his kingship. Professor Jeremias has outlined the thought of Jesus' parables under the following headings.[45] (1) Now is the day of salvation. "The time is at hand." The program of the kingdom (Isaiah 35:5-6) is being fulfilled (Luke 7:22, par. Matthew 11:5). "The kingdom is upon you," it is a time for joy (cf. Mark 2:19). (2) God's salvation, his mercy, goodness, and love for sinners, are being exhibited. The kingdom and all it means are being offered to lost men who need salvation. Publicans, harlots, and gross sinners understand the grace in this, even if Pharisees do not. Jesus' parables proclaim what God is really like: a loving Father who receives the worst prodigal "back home" (Luke 15: 20-24), a God who rejoices when a single sinner is recovered from his wandering (Luke 15:7, 10). (3) There is the assurance that God's power will bring the kingdom to pass, in spite of the seemingly small beginnings in Jesus' ministry. Here fit all the parables about "growth" in Mark 4 and Matthew 13. The real point is the contrast between the insignificant beginnings in the ministry of Jesus and his band of followers and the certain harvest which God will bring about.

Alongside these notes of joy and confidence, another note in the parables is that of (4) crisis. Catastrophe is imminent, for the coming of God the king means judgment as well as salvation. Hence Jesus speaks of salt which has become useless and is trodden under foot (Matthew 5:13). He speaks not only in terms of a "New Exodus" and salvation but also of the possibility that a new deluge and a new catastrophe like Sodom and Gomorrah are at hand (Luke 17:26-29). This crisis especially threatens those who think they are secure, like the rich farmer who was really a fool (Luke 12:16-20), and the religious leaders (Matthew 21: 43-45). Because men are obstinate, even in the face of God's judgment, there are those for whom the coming of the kingdom means catastrophe. Hence some of the parables suggest that (5) it may already be too late in such cases. Luke 13:6-9, the parable of the Fig Tree, holds out just one more chance. The parable of the Householder who has closed his door (Luke 13:24-30) and that of the Great Supper (Luke 14:15-24, cf. Matthew 22:1-10) say that for some it is already too late. For other men, however, Jesus' call to the kingdom became a spur to action. The coming of God's salvation challenged them to respond. Some parables thus (6) demand resolute action while there is time. In this category fit those about the Unjust Steward (Luke 16:1-8) and the Rich Man and Lazarus (16:19-31). Jesus calls for firm measures of response while there is time. For those who respond, other parables of Jesus speak about (7) discipleship, specifically the joy and service and love and practice of forgiveness to be found in those who have experienced the coming of God's kingship and salvation. These seven categories cover most of Jesus' parables, but a few of his statements involving parable-like comparisons also touch on (8) the way of the Son of man (e.g., John 12:24, his glory is like that of a grain of wheat which must die before it can bear fruit) and on (9) the consummation (e.g., Matthew 13:24-30, 47-48: God's kingdom for the present allows the tares and wheat to grow together, the bad with the good, but one day God will judge).

The last two categories proposed by Professor Jeremias we shall examine later on[46]; it is the first seven particularly which expand the message about the kingdom. These seven points A. M. Hunter has attempted to boil down to four: (1) the coming of the kingdom; (2) the grace of the kingdom; (3) the crisis of the kingdom; and (4) the men of the kingdom.[47] Enough has already been said about (1) the chief feature of Jesus' message, the nearness of the kingdom, even in the small beginnings in Jesus' lifetime, and about (3) the crisis for men which God's coming as Judge a.d Savior always implies. More needs to be said about the "grace" of the kingdom and then about its practical consequences, that is, what the men and women of the kingdom are like in their daily life.

The analyses by both Jeremias and Hunter agree that Jesus' message about the kingdom stressed the "grace" of God's salvation.[48] Mercy, goodness, love for sinful men are what God is setting forth. The words of Jesus proclaim this, his actions spell it out. We are here at the center of the Gospel, God's free offer of salvation to men. "Grace" is the term used especially in the epistles to describe this, but God's "graciousness" or "favor" is a common Old Testament theme with which Jesus was fully familiar. It is "love in action," in word and deed. We can readily see it in the cross, we can see it obviously in a kingdom that is completely "God-given," we can perceive it in the way Jesus receives and accepts and even eats with "sinners" (Mark 2:16).

That is grace and mercy manifest. But do the parables ever teach such a theme? The answer is yes, as two examples will show.

We must remember that "religious people" of the day, like the scribes and Pharisees, criticized Jesus for consorting with such irreligious folk as publicans and harlots (who sensed the crisis Jesus was talking about and gladly heeded the offer of the kingdom). How did Jesus reply to such critics? Sometimes he rebuked them—they are like disobedient children who say "No" to God (Matthew 21:28-32; 22:1-14). More positively, he defended his actions and the understanding of God involved by saying, in effect, "Your idea of God is all wrong, this is what God is like, the kingdom of God is like . . . ." Then came a parable.

One of the parables which replies to these critics and tells what God is like is the one we call the "Laborers in the Vineyard" (Matthew 20:1-16). It is a well-known parable and in liturgical churches is read annually on Septuagesima Sunday, but the point of the parable is not always clearly understood.[49] The parable is not about "fair labor practices," or even about the "laborers in the vineyard." Its real subject is the "Good Employer," a figure under which Jesus speaks about God.[50] The whole point is the goodness of the employer (20:15), his generosity. He has had compassion on the unemployed and their families. He has given something not bargained for, something not even promised, beyond men's wildest dream: a share in the kingdom, entirely out of his own graciousness. That is what God is like, Jesus says, "Your Father is merciful" (Luke 6:36). God is all goodness. Do not murmur against him. Accept his free offer. And indirectly Jesus is saying that he himself is acting just the way God does, by consorting with sinners and accepting them. His answer to his critics is to say that God and his kingdom and salvation are like that.

In a few other instances Jesus makes a different type of reply. He assumes the offer of God's kingdom and points to the way people have responded who appreciate that offer of grace. On one occasion, for example, a Pharisee named Simon, a man of stern rectitude, invited Jesus to dinner (Luke 7:36-50). Simon was doubtless one of those people who "thought he had it made" to such an extent that he seldom bothered to forgive others—and in turn found it increasingly unnecessary to ask for God's forgiveness for himelf. He was a walking specimen of what Jesus'

teaching on "forgivingness"[51] had warned against. Accordingly
Simon was greatly disturbed when a woman who was plainly a
sinner interrupted the meal to anoint Jesus' feet with precious
myrrh. Simon expected Jesus, as a prophet, to know what kind of
woman she was and rebuke her. What Simon did not know is
that this woman had previously accepted Jesus' message of God's
mercy, of salvation freely given in the kingdom. She had now
come to express her gratitude, in her own way, by a simple but
costly action, with tears of joy and lavish love.

Jesus explained to Simon, "Her great love proves that her many
sins have been forgiven." Then he warned him, "Where little
has been forgiven, little love is shown" (Luke 7:47, NEB).[52]
To illustrate that point, Jesus told a parable about Two Debtors
(Luke 7:41-43). One owed fifty denarii, the other ten times as
much. Their creditor forgave them both. "Which of the two will
love him more?" Simon, with his pragmatic mind, answered,
"The one to whom he forgave more." But Simon missed the
point that the woman who anointed Jesus' feet had experienced
just such magnanimous forgiveness—she was responding. Simon
had felt forgiveness so little that his attitude toward Jesus and
others was thoughtless and unloving. No water for Jesus' feet,
no warm greeting. Above all, Simon missed the point in the
parable that *both* men had been forgiven freely, absolutely. He
and the woman of the streets both needed to have a debt canceled. Where is there such a creditor as that? Why, he is like the
Generous Employer of Matthew 20. God it is who is being described, God who forgives all men, Pharisee and harlot alike, absolutely, completely.[53] In Professor Jeremias' words, "Clearly
Jesus was speaking about God, of his inconceivable goodness. 'Do
you not understand, Simon? This woman's love, which you despise, is the expression of her boundless gratitude for God's inconceivable goodness. Wronging both her and me, you are missing
God's best gift!' "[54]

It may be significant that such parables as these two are both
omitted in a later gnostic collection in the *Gospel of Thomas*. It
is significant that the church's gospels preserve them for us, for
they set forth the essence of the Gospel, the gracious forgiveness
of God, his free offer of salvation, in and through Jesus of Nazareth. It will be observed that the parable of the Two Debtors is
set within a story about how forgiven sinners respond. That brings

us to the other element we shall single out in Jesus' parables about the kingdom, the obedient response of which Jesus speaks.

"Many Things in Parables"—The Demands of the Kingdom

The church, said Dietrich Bonhoeffer, the German theologian who was martyred by the Nazis at the close of World War II, all too often offers "cheap grace."[55] The church peddles the sacraments; it mouths a sentimental message about God as love in some vague sense, missing both the element of judgment (which God's presence always implies) and the costliness of the cross as the expression of that love. All too often it has been easy for Christians to assume that grace is cheap. If God's like that, all goodness and love, why bother to obey? "God will forgive, that's his business."

If Christians since the resurrection fall into the fallacy of "cheap grace," how much easier was it to do so during the period of Jesus' ministry? For there had been no cross as yet to which one could point and say, "The cost was not cheap." Other dangers also lurked then to a proper response toward Jesus' message. There were some men, for example, of apocalyptic outlook, who sat back and said, "God will do all," and promptly abandoned the world of men and went off to their own monastic colonies of would-be saints, like that at Qumran. They drew a line between themselves and the "wicked" world and confined themselves to a few "brethren" of similar outlook, thus avoiding any response in the world at large. Then there were doubtless others, we can imagine, publicans and harlots, who accepted Jesus' offer as a kind of "insurance policy"—and forthwith went on with their graft and harlotry. Without some sort of response in the world— when viewed just as a free offer where you "sign your name" and then forget about anything more—Jesus' message of the kingdom would become a travesty on the Holy God. It would be a meaningless fiasco of "cheap grace."

But anyone who heard Jesus' preaching or listened to his parables could scarcely make this mistake. His kerygma was charged with terms like "repent" and "believe." His teachings talked about how the men of the kingdom live. A call to obedience as an aspect of faith and the demand that followers match their lives to the will of God are what strike one again and again in the sayings of Jesus. Professor Jeremias' outline of what the parables say goes on, after the initial emphasis on God's mercy and an assurance of God's power now and in the time to come, to a second emphasis on man's response and responsibility in the face of God's coming.[56] Resolute action is called for, before it is too late—or else the coming of the kingdom will mean ruin and catastrophe. The word that sums up this response is "discipleship," to be realized in the world of here and now.

A. M. Hunter also finds that the parables have a lot to say about the men of the kingdom.[57] Those who have made the decision and said "Yes" to God's offer now find discipleship under God's kingship their challenge. There is a "pattern" or "design" for life which appears in Jesus' teachings.[58] Naturally, full consideration of all this will take us into Jesus' "ethics" or way of life for men under the reign of God (see chapter 8). On that subject there is much to be learned from sayings of Jesus which are not in parable form. Here we shall look simply at what certain of the parables say about this "response" side of Jesus' message concerning the kingdom of God. For the coming of the kingdom carries a demand[59] to fit one's life to the will of him who has given salvation. Where much is given, much is required. Where much has been forgiven, much love and forgiveness ought to be shown, in response. This, too, the parables teach.

It goes almost without saying that Jesus assumed the kingdom of God should absorb the whole man. It challenges everything that is in a man and exhorts him to give everything he has in response to a God who has freely given salvation and a new relationship with himself as Father and sovereign lord. Jesus committed himself this way in utmost obedience to the Father and in unstinting service to his fellowmen. He expected his disciples to do the same when they heeded the announcement about the kingdom. The demand of the kingdom was self-surrender, then a life of forgiveness, service, and love. The result is not abject slavery but joyous living. It means, not a life that is like a series of hurdles to reach a goal, but a glad pilgrimage after one has unexpectedly been set on the right road and given direction and company, and the assurance he needs for the journey. Professor Jeremias speaks of the "overpowering" and "overwhelming" joy at the "glad Good News"; its effect "fills the heart with gladness; it makes life's whole aim the consummation of the divine community and produces the most whole-hearted self-sacrifice"—the kind of joy which Zacchaeus experienced when salvation came to his house (Luke 19:1-10), the kind of whole-hearted self-sacrifice which the woman who had been a sinner expressed at Simon's house (Luke 7:36-50).[60]

We need not belabor with examples the initial, characteristic features of Jesus' demand, now that the kingdom or salvation is at hand. It begins with a response of faith, faith in God. "Believe in the Good News" of God (Mark 1:15). "Have faith in God" (Mark 11:22). Trust that God is able. This call for faith in God is an exclusive one: God alone, no other lord, no rivals. It is an "either/or," not a case of "both God and something else." "No one can serve two masters. . . . You cannot serve God and mammon" (Matthew 6:24, par. Luke 16:13).

Note that the disciple's relation to God is here cast in terms of "serving." The new relationship to God which is marked by the response of faith therefore also involves serving. Later interpretation has so often denatured faith and robbed it of its biblical meaning of obedience as well as trust, that perhaps one other word ought to be added to make clear what Jesus meant. That word is "action." The children of the kingdom are to have faith in God; that also involves obedient serving; that in turn means joyous action.

We find this latter idea expressed in two brief parables of Jesus about a hidden treasure and a pearl:

> "The kingdom of heaven [i.e., of God] is like treasure hidden in a field, which a man found and covered up; then in his joy he goes and sells all that he has and buys that field. Again, the kingdom of heaven is like a merchant in search of fine pearls, who, on finding one pearl of great value, went and sold all that he had and bought it." (Matthew 13:44-46)

In both cases a man happens on a treasure not of his own creation. There it is, suddenly confronting him. In the first instance, a laborer, working in the fields, happens on a trove of coins or jewels which had been buried in some past century. In the second, a wholesale merchant stumbles onto an especially valuable pearl. In each case there is an instantaneous and total response; the men give everything they have for the treasure which has crossed their paths. We would expect the point to be the need for absolute self-surrender to the kingdom, "Give everything you have," and that element is indeed involved. But even more, there is a note of joy. The fulness of each man's response is the reaction engendered by the joy that comes when the long-sought discovery is made.

Put all of these features together and you begin to get an idea of the sort of response to the kingdom of which Jesus speaks: a joyous, serving, active faith, where a man surrenders himself to God and his goodness. Such a definition is reminiscent of the sort of faith about which Paul and Luther later spoke and in which they and countless others have lived. And why should there not be such a connection? For the chief source whence Paul and Luther derived that understanding of faith was Jesus Christ.

But left to men's hands and minds, such a stress on actions and the performance of service to fulfill the will of God could lead to an overemphasis on what the servant does. If one concentrates too long on the duties and demands, he will soon lose sight of the initial gift. That is an inevitable temptation. This is what happened with the Pharisees at times. Eyes were fixed on the prescriptions of the law and on their own performances. The God whose will was involved could be increasingly overlooked. Man's actions would then become correspondingly important, even as a means to salvation. Religion then became a parade of legalistic duties, salvation a "do-it-yourself" process. Men ran the danger of becoming hypocrites or "play-actors," "grand-standing" their religion. Jesus had severe criticism for such an outlook (e.g., Matthew 5:21—6:18; 23:1-36).[61] But Jesus' own disciples ran the danger of falling into the same pattern: their own works, intended as a response to God's goodness, might come to be looked upon as a means of salvation and a claim on God.

At times, therefore, Jesus addresses his parables to such an attitude of self-righteousness that may lurk among his disciples. His words about the Servant's Wages or Reward at Luke 17:7-10 are an example:

"Will any one of you, who has a servant plowing or keeping sheep, say to him when he has come in from the field, 'Come at once and sit down at table'? Will he not rather say to him, 'Prepare supper for me, and gird yourself and serve me, till I eat and drink; and afterward you shall eat and drink'? Does he thank the servant because he did what was commanded? So you also, when you have done all that is commanded you, say, 'We are unworthy servants; we have only done what was our duty.' "

The words could originally have been addressed by Jesus to the crowd or even to opponents, for the expectation of attaining righteousness by one's works was widespread in Judaism. But Luke seems to regard them as addressed to the disciples (17:1, 5); since he uses the specific, later term "apostles," Luke may be suggesting that the parable was one that the later leaders of the church should take to heart.[62] The story is a curious one about a farmer who has just one slave. Can you imagine that master saying, when the slave has finished his chores in the field, "Now sit down and I'll serve you supper"? Rather, he'll expect him to go on with his duties in the house as well. A slave doesn't deserve thanks for doing what he has been commanded to do.

So it is with you who are God's servants. When you have carried out all God's orders (if you ever get that far), do not presume to think that God is in your debt and you have earned your relationship with him. Say, rather, "We are servants and deserve no credit; we have only done our duty" (17:10, NEB).[63] Whatever your sacrifice, whatever your achievement, you remain the servant, not the lord. What you have received—the treasure, the pearl, the kingdom, salvation—is God's gift. Luther realized this when he said repeatedly, with respect to God, "We are beggers." We depend on God's goodness and grace, even after long years of faithful service under him. Because of this emphasis, Jesus was able to talk about response to God in the most strenuous, "activist" terms, without letting his followers fall into the delusion of self-righteousness or the idea that they had been saved by their own works.

Jesus' demand for a decision, for a response to the message of the kingdom, thus meant (1) a joyous, serving, active faith, but (2) the exclusion of notions of self-righteousness. The initial gift and the sustaining grace are God's. But in what specific ways was man to respond to the kingdom? One element we have already found prominent in the prayer Jesus taught his disciples: forgivingness.[64] The practice that Jesus urges in his prayer—that disciples who have experienced something of God's kingdom and salvation should in turn pledge and practice forgiveness—finds lodgment in his parables too. The parable of the Unmerciful Servant (Matthew 18:23-35) is a good illustration. Matthew employs it to answer the question of how often one should forgive. The human mind always wants rules or limits. "Shall I go up to seven times in forgiving a Christian brother who sins against me?" Jesus replies, Not seven but seventy-seven—symbolically an unlimited number—as often as the person asks for forgiveness (Matthew 18:21-22, par. Luke 17:4). But the parable itself goes deeper than that. As Jesus recounted it, the story hinted of a Final Judgment by God. There was a warning that God would hold accountable those who trifle with the gift of forgiveness, those who do not deal with others as God has dealt with them—forgivingly, with love.

The parable, as Jesus unfolds it, compares the kingdom of heaven to an accounting (as in Matthew 20:1-15)—the king is settling accounts with his servants (18:23).[65] The story is set in a Gentile land, probably involving a satrap or governor of the king in some eastern empire, for non-Jewish customs appear (for example, the sale of a wife and children for debt, 18:25). This satrap, an official of some importance, owes the king an astronomical sum, ten thousand talents. The note in the RSV that a talent was worth about one thousand dollars, while a denarius was worth about twenty cents, gives the right proportions, but does not begin to suggest the staggering size of the debt. Ten thousand was the highest number used in ancient counting, and a talent the biggest unit of currency. Sale of himself and his family wouldn't begin to cover the debt. The satrap throws himself at the mercy of his lord, promising to pay all (as if he ever could). The lord of that servant, out of pity, forgives him the debt completely. "The King's mercy far exceeds the plea of his servant,"[66] which was merely for a postponement of the payment.

But then comes a second scene. Another servant, subordinate to the satrap, owes him one hundred denarii. He promises to repay it all—something quite possible; he begs with the very words the satrap has just used in pleading with the king (vss. 26, 29). But the satrap refuses, grabs him by the throat, and has him thrown in jail. Unmindful of the mercy he has received—or perhaps desirous to show his petty authority—he reacts just the opposite from his lord. Luckily other servants have observed the events and tell the king. He summons the satrap who had received such immense forgiveness and couldn't pass it on, and sentences him to jail—literally to the "torturers" (RSV note), "till he should pay all his debt"—an impossibility, never to be achieved.

Jesus is plainly depicting here the God whom he sets forth elsewhere as a forgiving Father. This God forgives, far beyond the pleas of his servants—on the basis of no "collateral," no human achievement, but solely out of his goodness. This utter grace applies to the Last Judgment too. The reckoning will show God's mercy. But there is the warning that those who have received the forgiveness of the kingdom are to share it. In their relationships with others, there is to be no stubborn "standing on one's rights" for disciples; when a brother seeks it, forgiveness is to be granted. If you act as if you've never heard of forgiveness, then God will act that way with you too. "So also my heavenly Father will do to every one of you, if you do not forgive your brother from your heart" (vs. 35). Jesus expects his disciples to practice forgiveness, because they have received it and because it is the king's will for them. Failure to do so is an abuse of the Good News.

The case is very similar with love. Disciples have experienced God as *Abba*, a heavenly Father who cares for them. They have come to know his care and hence that their lives are kept securely, in the hands of God (see Matthew 6:26-30). "Brother, He's got you 'n' me, in his hand;" is a disciples' song. They know that which—after the cross—the epistles will speak of so frequently as "the love of God." So it is that Jesus demands a response of love from those who follow him—love for God, but above all, love at its most practical, love for one's fellowman. Again of course the human mind asks for limits or rules. How much? How far? Jesus answered that question a number of times, especially in a celebrated parable about the Good Samaritan (Luke 10:25-37).

As the account runs in our gospels, a lawyer, apparently disturbed by Jesus' preaching, asked him to select the greatest commandment in the law (Mark 12:28, par. Matthew 22:36). Jesus directed him to love, to show love for God and for his neighbor (Deuteronomy 6:5 and Leviticus 19:18). In Jesus' answer there was also an emphasis on action: *"Do* this, and you will live" (Luke 10:28). Not theoretical speculation but active discipleship. But the lawyer wanted to know more: How far must this go? 'Who is my neighbor?" (10:29). Jews generally included in this category all their fellow countrymen and even converts who had embraced the faith of Israel. Some Pharisaic circles may have limited neighborliness to those of their own group, however, and Qumran actually taught hatred for the "sons of darkness," i.e., those outside the sect. How far is love to extend—to "our own kind"? to those of the same faith as we? to all men?

Jesus then, according to Luke, told a story, probably based on an actual happening along the Jerusalem-Jericho road. It is a story which has become a classic, about a robbery victim on that road. After a priest and a Levite appear and pass by on the other side, leaving him lying in his blood, the audience probably expected the third traveler to be a Jewish layman. But anyone with "anti-clerical" feelings was in for a surprise. Jesus' "hero" is a Samaritan—a member of that hated race which had crowned a long series of indignities against the Jews by defiling the temple at Jerusalem just a few years before. (Samaritans had dumped dead men's bones in the courtyard during the sacred Passover season.) In the face of current racial bitterness, Jesus' story doubtless has a "bite" to it. But it was not just to teach that people in minority groups can be better fellows than our own clergymen that Jesus told this tale. He was answering the dilemma about how far the disciples should practice love. The question had been put in objective terms, "Who is my neighbor?" Jesus shifted it to a subjective one, "Who proved to be the neighbor?" That is to say, we must not think of people as "objects" with regard to whom we "fulfill commands." We must act as persons, which means we must let others confront us as persons not as objects. To the question about the limits of love and responsibility, Jesus replies in effect, "Stop asking for a rule. Put yourself in the place of the suffering, helpless man. Ask, 'Who has need of me?' And then go to work! For God's sake, for the sake of the love you know from him, practice love, share it with those who need you."

A joyous, serving, active faith; the practice of forgivingness; love unlimited, realized in life, yet without any notion of self-righteousness or rules to be fulfilled in order to earn status with God or man—such is the response of disciples to the kingdom and the salvation which Jesus' parables envision. Is it realistic for men today?

Once in a while we hear that it is. Ernest Gordon, a Scotsman who was captured by the Japanese in Malaya and who spent most of World War II in the notorious prison camp on the River Kwai, reports something of the problem—and the possibilities—concerning forgiveness in a prisoner-of-war camp. He writes:

> When we said the Lord's Prayer in the prison camp, we stumbled over the phrase, "And forgive us our trespasses as we forgive those

who trespass against us." This was not only because some [of] us were of Scottish background, and accustomed to using "debts" and "debtors." It was because it meant asking forgiveness for the Japanese.

We had learned from our Bible reading that Jesus had his enemies just as we had ours. But there was this difference: He loved his enemies.

He prayed for them. Even as the nails were being hammered through his hands and feet, he cried out, "Father, forgive them, for they know not what they do."

We hated ours. We had spent a good deal of time in plotting for them a rich variety of satisfying punishments. We could see how wonderful it was that Jesus forgave in this way. Yet for us to do the same was beyond our attainment.[67]

But later on, Gordon reports, the love of God touched these prisoners, and other things happened. Once, on the way to Bangkok by rail, they saw railway cars packed with Japanese wounded on the way back from the Burma front—no medical treatment, wounds were inflamed, full of pus and maggots. The British soldiers went to help these wounded wayfarers with canteens, rags, and rations. An Allied officer reprimanded them as fools. "Have you never heard," the reply to him came, "the story of the man who was going from Jerusalem to Jericho?" There was a blank look, and after the story of the Good Samaritan was recounted, the officer protested, "But that's different. . . . That's in the Bible. . . . These are our enemies."

"Who is mine enemy?" Gordon demanded. "Isn't he my neighbor? God makes neighbors; we make enemies. . . . Mine enemy *is* my neighbor!"[68]

On another occasion, it was these prisoners, who had learned something of discipleship and forgiveness from their Bible study, who actually prevented the Allied liberator-troops from killing the prison guards on the spot.[69]

So runs the experience. The demand becomes a possibility, when men know Jesus Christ. The teachings of the parables find practice here and now in life. But that happens because the parables which Jesus spoke during his ministry were preserved and used after the resurrection in the Christian church. What Jesus said regarding the offer and demand of the kingdom was passed on in the new situation after Easter. But, of course, not always without change. What happened to the message of the kingdom after A.D. 30?

"The Kingdom" in the Church—A Chapter of Parables

The fate of the parables after Jesus' death is something we seldom stop to consider. If Jesus had died a quiet, natural death, a few of his parables might have been transmitted along with the parables of other rabbis. We would know of them today only if we dug into rabbinical literature.

But when it was proclaimed and believed that God had raised Jesus from the dead, two things happened to the parables. On the one hand, they were preserved the more carefully because they were now more important than ever before. Jesus the lord had spoken them. On the other hand, the parables were now subject to new applications and change for the simple reason that they were now being told and applied in a new situation. The time when God would in his kingdom bring the salvation about which Jesus had preached was now seen to be even more intimately connected with Jesus than men had supposed. His death and resurrection were regarded as the places where that salvation had been wrought and where God's sovereign power had flashed forth. The Gospel was still about God and his kingly power, but now it took the specific form of a proclamation of what He had done in Jesus of Nazareth. There was the same offer of grace, there was still a demand for a response of faith and love. But the Jesus-material was now set in a new framework, the framework of Christ proclaimed as lord.

How fared the parables in this period of change? What happened to them in the oral period, in the age of the gospel sources, and through the work of the evangelists? It is only when we inquire into these matters that we begin to understand more fully the parables as they stand in our gospels.

In general the parables were transmitted and used like any other Jesus-material. To an extent they suffered less change than some of the sayings and the narratives for the simple reason that the parables were a form peculiar to Jesus in Christian circles, for we almost never find parables in the epistles and other literature of the New Testament period.[70] Nonetheless, Jesus' parables did undergo change and development. New applications, under the Spirit and in light of the resurrection and especially in expectation of a "Second Coming" of Jesus, were inevitable. The Jesus-material was collected, reworked, and assembled in various arrangements, to make it more relevant for Christians who now thought, not in

Hebraic, Old Testament terms, but increasingly in Greek terms; who saw their kerygma not in terms of the kingdom of God, but of the King's power revealed in the work of his beloved Son; who saw their problem, not as impending crisis and immediate judgment, but as the need for help in "getting through" and continuing in faith until the Final Judgment. C. Leslie Mitton notes, for example, how what he calls "parables of urgency"—which originally described the urgent or crisis situation caused by Jesus' announcement of the kingdom—were changed and renewed in sense during the decades between Jesus' death and the writing of our gospels:

> As the message of Jesus was passed on in the Church, after His death and resurrection, these parables of urgency came to be interpreted not so much in the circumstances of the ministry of Jesus as in the circumstances of the preachers' own day. The parables, for instance, which call for watchfulness and prompt decision (for example, the Parables of the Ten Virgins and the Thief at Midnight) came to be related to the current expectations that the Second Coming of Christ was soon to take place.[71]

It is with these new meanings, these "current expectations" of the fifties, sixties, and seventies A.D., that we are now concerned. We shall find that they speak to us with a message, the message which the evangelists intended, just as much as the original parables of Jesus do. Readers today are not poorer but the richer for this work of modern scholarship in laying bare a "double setting" for the parables, for now we have the meaning from Jesus' ministry (as outlined above) and additional insights from the time of the risen Christ in the early church.

If one wants to see how the parables of Jesus suffered change when separated from the Gospel, it is possible to do so in the *Gospel of Thomas*.[72] This document, assembled about A.D. 140, under gnostic and ascetic influences, from earlier collections of sayings attributed to Jesus, demonstrates what could happen to the Jesus-material outside the framework of the kerygma. The Gospel, from the viewpoint of what became normative Christianity, is here made cockeyed and slanted, the parables often distorted, sometimes unrecognizable, Jesus scarcely the figure to whom readers of the New Testament are accustomed. A few of the parables in *Thomas* are little different from those in our gospels. Many more exhibit subtle alterations. Certain ones border on the fantastic and, by subsequent standards, the heretical.

To illustrate, the version of the parable of the Sower in *Thomas* is similar to that at Mark 4, and shows little change from the familiar New Testament version.[73]

> Jesus said: "Behold, the sower went forth, he filled his hand, he sowed [seeds]. Some fell on the road; the birds came and gathered them up. Others fell on the rock and did not send a root down into the earth and did not send an ear to heaven. And others fell among thorns; they choked the seed, and the worm ate it. And others fell upon the good soil; and it brought forth good fruit to heaven—it bore sixty-fold and one-hundred-and-twenty-fold." (*Thomas* 9)

Thomas differs more in his version of the Great Supper (*Thomas* 64; Matthew 22:1-14 and Luke 14:15-24).[74] As in the canonical version, people give a series of excuses when they are invited to the banquet the master is giving. One excuse which *Thomas* adds, "I have bought a village; I go to collect the rent," has a distinct Egyptian coloring, for in Egypt wealthy men did purchase whole villages. Another excuse is rephrased to reflect the ascetic outlook opposing marriage which is so common in *Thomas*. Whereas Luke 14:20 has, "I have married a wife, and therefore I cannot come," *Thomas* substitutes, "My friend will celebrate a wedding, and I am to direct the banquet." *Thomas* does not stress as much as do the canonical versions the closing detail about going out into the highways and hedges to invite others to the banquet, but *Thomas* does add, "The buyers and the merchants shall not enter 'the place' [= kingdom] of my Father." This addition reflects the detail in the original parable that some men were too busy with their business to accept the invitation, but it also is part of a prejudice against tradesmen which appears elsewhere in *Thomas*.

Thomas is even more "gnostic" when he retells the parable of the Lost Sheep (cf. Matthew 18:12-14, par. Luke 15:3-7):

> Jesus said: The kingdom is like *a shepherd* who had a hundred sheep. One of them went astray; *it was the largest*. He left the ninety-nine [and] sought for the one until he found it. *After he had tired himself out*, he said to the sheep, *I love you more than the ninety-nine*. (*Thomas* 107)[75]

Gone is the element of rejoicing over the lost which has been found (Luke 15:5-7). Some of *Thomas'* other changes (in italics above) are just matters of common sense, like calling the man "a shepherd" or saying he got tired from the search for the lost sheep. But other additions reflect gnostic ideology. The lost sheep represents the gnostic man, "larger" (more important) than any

other, and the one whom the master loves more than any other
—i.e., the gnostic is the one who counts in God's sight. Extremely
gnostic or at least esoteric in tone are sayings like these:

> The kingdom of the Father is like a man who wanted to kill a
> powerful man. He drew the sword within his house and ran it
> through the wall, so that he might know whether his hand would be
> strong enough. Then he killed the powerful man. (98)

> Simon Peter said to them, "Let Mary go away from us, for women
> are not worthy of life." Jesus said, "Lo, I shall lead her, so that I
> may make her male, that she too may become a living spirit, like you
> men. For every woman who makes herself a male will enter the
> kingdom of heaven." (114)[76]

When we compare these sayings with those in three Synoptic
Gospels, we can readily see how the Jesus-material suffered change
as it was used and reused. At times, *Thomas* may, of course, preserve original reflections of what Jesus said. Other times we can
put our fingers on definite changes which have been made.

In the case of the parables it is possible to work out these
changes with some exactitude, for we sometimes have two, three,
or four versions of the same parable in the Synoptics and *Thomas*.
By careful study of the details and comparison with what we
know of Jesus and what we know of the habits of each source
and each evangelist,[77] It is even possible to map out patterns of
change which take place within the parables. Professor Jeremias
has done this brilliantly for the parables in the Synoptics and
Thomas by listing seven "laws of transformation" which applied
as the parables of Jesus were told in the early church and eventually written down by the evangelists.[78] We will note some of
these transformations, which anyone can readily check for himself
in the biblical text.

As parables were retold there was, for one thing, a tendency to
embellish them or add details. For example, in the parable of the
Talents (Matthew 25:14-30) three men receive money from their
lord—five, two, and one talent respectively. In Luke (19:11-27)
there are ten servants, each of whom receives one pound from his
lord, but only three of them play any further part in the story. It
is commonly said that whereas Matthew's parable reflects the in-
equality of "talents" in life, Luke has chosen to stress "equal
opportunities"—each man gets the same amount. There is yet
another version, further embellished, in the *Gospel according to
the Hebrews,* which says the one servant was rewarded, the one

who had hidden his talent was rebuked, but the third who had "wasted his master's money with harlots and flute-girls" was "shut up in prison."[79] This version has given Jesus' parable a new moral: what is really abominated is using the money on "loose women."

Another tendency was to transform the parables of Jesus from announcements about the kingdom and its demands to exhortations for members of the early church. This is a perfectly understandable change. For a fellowship of Christians it was no longer necessary to go on announcing to them week after week that the kingdom was at hand; but Christian believers did require encouragement and exhortation to do this or that in their daily life. Reference has already been made[80] to the parable about the Lost Sheep in Luke (15:3-7) as an answer by Jesus to those who criticized him for associating with tax collectors and sinners who were "unclean" and did not conform to the regulations of the law (15:1-2). Matthew has presented this as an exhortation to Christian disciples to seek out any lost brother who has strayed from the fold (18:12-14). Jesus' picture of God (as one who seeks the lost) and his defense of his ministry have become in Matthew an encouragement for Christians in their duties of discipleship.[81] This same parable also illustrates a tendency to "reaudience" the parables, that is, to change the audience to whom a story is addressed. Here the shift is from Jesus' critics to his disciples.

We have already noted how the early church sometimes allegorized the parables of Jesus, expanded the conclusions (cf. Matthew 20:16), and collected them into groups. These features will be illustrated shortly from Matthew 13, but first it is worthwhile discussing the effect of one other change from Jesus' day to the time of the gospels. That change is the new situation in which the church found itself. Not only was the church now living "after Easter," but it had also taken a giant step from Palestine to the Greco-Roman world. That step sometimes made desirable certain changes in the content of the parables. Why, for instance, do Luke and Matthew differ slightly in their description of the house of a foolish man?

> "And every one who hears these words of mine and does not do
> them will be like a foolish man who built his house upon the sand;
> and the rain fell, and the floods came, and the winds blew and beat
> against that house, and it fell; and great was the fall of it." (Matthew
> 7:26-27)

"But he who hears and does not do them is like a man who built a house on the ground without a foundation; against which the stream broke, and immediately it fell, and the ruin of that house was great." (Luke 6:49)

Matthew is describing a scene in Palestine, where a house can be built on rock or sand and where a sudden cloudburst may create a "flash flood." But outside Palestine, conditions are different, and Luke pictures Hellenistic building techniques, where a house might be built with a cellar (cf. 6:48); instead of a flash flood, a stream overflows its banks and causes a flood. It is not hard to see that Matthew preserves the language Jesus would have used, whereas Luke (or his source) has put it into terms which Gentiles would understand.[82] Anyone who knows much about the idioms which modern missionaries must use in translating Scripture for remote tribes in South America or Africa can appreciate the changes here necessitated.[83]

The missionary outlook of the early church was another element in the changed situation which sometimes has repercussions in the parables. In Jesus' lifetime there was virtually nothing said directly about a universal mission, but after the resurrection many came to believe that the early church was committed to evangelizing the world. We can read between the lines of a parable, or really two parables, preserved in Matthew 22, to see how this commitment affected what Matthew records and how he says it. Matthew 22: 1-10 is the parable of the Marriage Feast which is similar to Luke 14:16-24. Plainly, Matthew has some strange details. In his account, the people who refuse invitations to the wedding feast kill the king's messengers, in return for which the king has troops destroy those murderers and their city. Strange conduct over a spurned invitation to a wedding feast! (Doubtless Matthew saw here an allegorical reference to the Jews' refusal of God's invitation to the "messianic banquet" and the subsequent destruction of Jerusalem by the Romans in A.D. 70.) Even stranger is the detail that the servants of the king then go out into the streets of the city (after it had been destroyed) and invite "both bad and good" to the wedding feast. Then comes the most curious addition, in verses 11-13, which only Matthew has: the king tosses out of the banquet hall one guest who has no "wedding garment" on—as if people picked up off the streets of a destroyed city could be expected to be attired in wedding garb! Matthew has plainly conflated another parable with the one preserved at 22:1-10 (par. Luke 14:16-24), and has allegorized the whole. What were his intentions here?

Read in the light of conditions in the church of Matthew's day, the answer appears to be as follows. The Jews, it was held, had refused God's invitation to a "messianic wedding feast." They have received their just punishment (cf. Matthew 24:2). Now the church, made up of those who have responded to God's call, is to go into all the world, seeking all men, both bad and good (cf. 28:19-20). But in a missionary church some people may gain entrance who do not measure up to the demands. They abuse free grace. They do not live and act responsively. For these people, Matthew says, there will be a judgment one day where they will be condemned by God the king. Matthew adds one of his favorite mottos, "Many [really, all men] are called, but few are chosen"— not all will measure up (22:14). Matthew is here standing by the idea of a Gospel of free grace and a worldwide preaching of it. But he also insists, through this parable, that converts must match their lives to this Gospel. It is the same message as Paul's in Romans 6: those who are baptized must not just go on sinning but are to live out a life of grace. Some would even go so far as to see the "wedding garment" as the gift of justification (to use Paul's terms) which is to clothe believers in the justified life.

A particular feature in the church's situation which affected its use of the parables was the "delay of the parousia." As is well-known, the early church expected Jesus to come again on the clouds of heaven. This "Second Coming"(or *parousia,* to use the Greek word for "coming") led to a quite intense expectancy at times (see I Thessalonians 4:13—5:11 and II Thessalonians 2: 1-12).[84] Naturally, early Christians wanted the parables to speak to their concern about why the Second Coming had not occurred as yet, and five parables[85] as they now stand in our gospels deal with this subject. However, Jeremias is doubtless correct that such parables, if Jesus told them, originally referred to the crisis caused by the ministry of Jesus. We take the shortest of such parables as an example:

> . . . if the householder had known in what hour of the night the thief was coming, he would have watched and would not have let his house be broken into. Therefore you also must be ready. . . .
> (Matthew 24:43-44, par. Luke 12:39-40)

The little story probably derives from an incident in a village where a burglar broke into a house by digging through a mud wall. Jesus used it to warn men to be ready, to be alert, to respond in face of what could be a catastrophe which he saw coming, namely, the kingdom and God's judgment. Early Christians saw the kingdom and judgment as coming for their world in the parousia of Jesus. Accordingly they took this figure of the thief in the night and applied it to Jesus Christ. Thus, I Thessalonians 5:2 says:

. . . the day of the Lord will come like a thief in the night.

The risen Christ himself says, at Revelation 16:15 and 3:3:

Lo, I am coming like a thief.
I will come like a thief, and you will not know at what hour I will come upon you.

The imagery of a parable told during Jesus' ministry thus appears here in words of the risen Christ, applied quite unexpectedly to Jesus, so that *he* is the burglar in the night! Our gospels reflect this post-Easter point of view when they place the parable about the Thief at Midnight (one of the least likely "christological images" that one could imagine) in a discourse about the Day of the Lord (Matthew 24:42), when the Son of man will come (Luke 12:40). The message of the parable has been made to speak to the delay of the Second Coming; it counsels, "Be ready."

Plainly, things have happened to Jesus' parables as the several evangelists retell them. One should not lament too much the fact that Matthew and the others have brought new meanings out of Jesus' words, for to the early Christians these re-applications were also insights provided by the Holy Spirit and the risen Christ. Indeed, one can claim, some of these new insights might be just as relevant, or even more so today, as the original point which was made by Jesus in his lifetime. A good example is the "doctrine of the church" which Matthew presents through the parables of Jesus. In the parable of the Wedding Feast it has been observed how Matthew speaks to the church of his day about what the church should be. Matthew does the same thing elsewhere, notably in chapter 13.

Matthew 13 is a collection of some seven parables, built up from Mark 4 but with the use of a little Q material and a great deal of special Matthean (M) material. The result is a chapter of parables about the kingdom—underlying which is a picture of the church. Here is the structure, showing how Matthew has built up his chapter (italics indicate the parables in Matthew's collection; arrows show how the "explanation" to a parable may appear several units later; broken lines indicate a parallel which appears at another point):

MARK	CONTENTS	MATTHEW	
4:1-9	*Parable of the Sower*	13:1-9	
4:10-12	Purpose of the parables,	13:10-13	
──	in fulfillment of Isaiah 6:9-10	13:14-15	
──	Consequent blessedness of the disciples	13:16-17	(*Q*)
4:13-20	Interpretation of "the Sower"	13:18-23	
4:21-25	Purpose of the parables	──	(cf. 13:12)
4:26-29	Parable of the Seed Growing Secretly	──	
──	*Parable of the Wheat and the Tares*	13:24-30	(*M*)
4:30-32	*Parable of the Mustard Seed*	13:31-32	
──	*Parable of the Leaven*	13:33	(*Q*)
4:33-34	Jesus' use of parables	13:34-35	
──	Interpretation of "Wheat and Tares"	13:36-43	(*M*)
──	*Parables of the Treasure and the Pearl*	13:44-46	(*M*)
──	*Parable of the Dragnet*	13:47-50	(*M*)
──	*"Parable" of the Householder*	13:51-52	(*M*)

Even though this chapter is a most artful and complex arrangement, it is not too hard to see what Matthew has done. The three parables in Mark (Sower, Seed Growing Secretly, and the Mustard Seed, the second of the three being omitted) have been expanded by use of other material into a collection of seven,[86] all of them concerning the kingdom of heaven. Matthew gives allegorical explanations to two of the parables—the Sower (as Mark had already done), and the Wheat and the Tares (for which Matthew seems responsible). It is in his interpretation of the Wheat and the Tares that Matthew speaks most pointedly to the readers of his gospel in the church of his day.[87] Since we have already explored some of the other parables in this chapter to see what they meant during Jesus' ministry,[88] we shall now concentrate on Matthew's allegorical explanation of the Wheat and Tares as a key to what he is saying to the church throughout the chapter.

Curiously, Matthew's interpretation (13:36-43) ignores what was the point of the original parable (13:24-30), namely, patience (see 13:30—the servants are not to try to dig out the weeds or tares but are patiently to let them grow together until the harvest). Rather, Matthew's explanation provides an elaborate allegory where seven specific points are allegorized (vss. 37-39):

(1) he who sows the good seed is the Son of man;
(2) the field is the world;
(3) the good seed means the "sons of the kingdom";
(4) the weeds are the "sons of the Evil One";
(5) the enemy who sowed them is the Devil;
(6) the harvest is the "close of the age";
(7) the reapers are angels.

There is added an apocalypse about "the close of the age" when the angels of the Son of man will gather all evildoers from the kingdom and throw them into a "furnace of fire," while "the righteous" (like those in the "wedding garments" at 22:11-13) "will shine" like the sun (cf. Daniel 12:3) in the kingdom of their Father.

The striking thing is that an overwhelming number of the phrases in verses 37-43 of chapter 13 are terms which never appear otherwise on the lips of Jesus in our gospels but which are characteristic of Matthew the evangelist. Professor Jeremias has listed thirty-seven such "Mattheanisms."[89] For example, "The field is the world" (which reminds one of John Wesley's famous missionary motto, "The world is my parish") scarcely fits the historical period of Jesus' ministry but does characterize the post-Easter situation (cf. 28:19). The "kingdom" of "the Son of man" is found only here and at 16:28, and sounds like a phrase which Matthew has coined. So also with "the sons of the kingdom" (elsewhere only at Matthew 8:12) and "the kingdom of their Father" (found otherwise only at 26:29). "The close of the age" (vs. 40; 13:49; 24:3; 28:20) also is a phrase found only in Matthew.

If all these bits of evidence are put together, it adds up to a strong case that Matthew is the author of the interpretation of the parable at 13:36-43. The verses do not fit the period of the historical ministry but of the church in Matthew's day (i.e., the "sons of the kingdom") and its worldwide task ("the field is the world") and its apocalyptic interest ("the close of the age").

But all this may still not be too meaningful unless we observe the picture of the church conveyed in these verses.[90] (1) The church for Matthew is the kingdom of the Son of man. If we want to know where some early Christians thought the kingdom was to be found, the answer is, for Matthew's Gospel, in the community of those who acknowledge Jesus as lord and Son of man. At the parousia this kingdom of the Son of man will be replaced by the kingdom of God the Father (13:43). But (2) this church is not perfect or completely good. It is made up of "both bad and good" (22:10). It is an assembly of righteous men and evildoers. To rigorists and puritans who wished to purge the membership rolls and root out all who do not conform to a certain code of conduct, Matthew replies, "Let both grow together until the harvest" (13:30). It is not your job to make such decisions. Some day, at the parousia, God will judge. For its journey through this world, the church is a "mixed society" embracing of all sorts of people.[91] But (3) to people inclined to take advantage of God's grace, Matthew keeps warning that God will judge and hence (4) response, discipleship matters. There must be a "wedding garment" (22:11-13). There must be fruitbearing (21:43); wheat, not weeds. Finally, remember that (5) this church, made up of all sorts of people, has a missionary task in all the world. The world may be large, Matthew says, the age in which we live difficult, but God is with his people until the end of the world, until "the close of the age" (28:20).

So it is that in these parables, and especially where Matthew interprets what he sees in them, we have an exciting doctrine of the church: the church is God's reign manifested in Christ as Son of man, among all sorts of people, who seek as disciples to carry out a universal task under God the Savior and Judge. Of course, Matthew cannot come out and say this in so many words. He must weave it in via parables and under allegorical explanations. He must allow the risen Christ to speak under the figure of the historical Jesus. How else could he do it, using as he does the gospel-form? But Matthew has done it, and the words speak to disciples as the word of God.

An obvious conclusion, necessitated by such findings, is that not every word in the gospels assigned to Jesus Christ can be regarded as having been spoken by the historical Jesus during his earthly ministry. In some verses we have rather the voice of the early church or of the evangelists as they comprehended the mind of

Christ now risen and exalted. That does not mean that such passages as transcend the historical ministry are valueless. Quite the contrary, they speak too as God's word. The matter might be summed up thus: An interpretation to a parable, like the allegorical one to the Sower, or on the Wheat and Tares, may still be true to the mind of Christ and be inspired by the Spirit of God. All that is necessary is that "we might have to give up saying, 'Thus *said* the Lord' "—but "it will not necessarily mean that we should be wrong in believing 'Thus *saith* the Lord.' "[92]

A Problem Parable: The Unjust Steward

By this time, all the parables may appear to readers as problems. What with the possibility of "double settings"—one meaning in Jesus' lifetime, a second in the early church—allegorizations by the evangelists, "reaudiencing" and all the other steps of transformation, plus the necessity for those studying the parables today to be informed about many of the customs and practices of Jesus' day assumed in his parables, it is not easy to get to the point of these passages.

But then no one ever said it was easy. Jesus, in using parables, assumed that his audience would lavish some thought on the presentation which he so artfully put together. Those who had ears to hear would hear—and think and understand. The "time fuse" on a parable might take a little while to burn down, but sooner or later there would be an explosion or a flash—a flash of light and comprehension, wholehearted response; or an explosion of angry rejection. Likewise Matthew assumed that his readers would notice how he was using traditional words along with new expressions and would in time grasp the meaning it was now necessary to put across.

Parables are thus meant to be understood—not, necessarily, on the spur of the moment, but soon, after a little thought. For people today, twenty centuries and thousands of miles removed from the world of the parables, the process takes a little longer and requires some study and often a good guide or commentary. But even if one takes all these aids into consideration, there is one parable which has nonetheless regularly defied interpretation—or at least the attaining of agreement as to any one interpretation. That parable is the Unjust Steward (Luke 16:1 ff.). It bristles with more than the usual difficulties, one of them being that Jesus seems to praise a crook and make him the hero of his parable, and another being the fact that there are so many lines of application which Luke has supplied that it is a problem to know what is the point and main teaching.

So hard is this parable to understand that the compilers of the Lutheran *Service Book and Hymnal* decided a few years ago to follow a change adopted by Episcopalians and allow an alternate to Luke 16:1-9 and the parable of the Unjust Steward as the Gospel Lesson to be read in church on the Ninth Sunday after Trinity.[93] One reason given for this change was that the parable of the Unjust Steward is just too difficult to comprehend. However, new light from research into the world of Jesus' day and what has been learned of how the parables fared in the early church open the possibility today, as perhaps never before, since the time when Luke put the material together, for discovering the original meaning and the later applications of this story of a dishonest steward. It now seems apparent that one difficulty with the old Gospel Lesson assigned for the Ninth Sunday after Trinity was that it went on two verses too many—or stopped four verses too soon. It can also be said that only when one is willing to look for reapplication of Jesus' parables in the early church will one understand all verses that cluster around Luke 16:1-7.[94]

To begin with, this Lucan parable (it has no parallel in any other gospel, including the *Gospel of Thomas*) is not directly a parable of the kingdom. It does not begin with the familiar formula "The kingdom of God is like. . . ." But it does deal indirectly with the kingdom, as does almost everything that Jesus said; on that, most commentators are agreed. A. M. Hunter, for example, feels it applies to "the men of the kingdom" and tells how they will act in life, namely, prudently and wisely (16:8). His view is that the parable was addressed to disciples (16:1), and thus counseled them on the kind of life necessary for people who have heeded the announcement of "kingdom come." Joachim Jeremias, on the other hand, has a different interpretation. He claims the parable was originally addressed to the unconverted crowds during Jesus' ministry and dealt with the crisis which was at hand, the crisis of the coming kingdom. The steward in the parable had acted resolutely when confronted by a crisis. People who hear Jesus' announcement about the kingdom should act just as resolutely in their time of crisis now.[95]

That two distinguished interpreters of the New Testament thus disagree about the audience addressed and the subject or central point of this parable is to be explained by the fact that they are each looking at a many-sided parable from different angles. Both men are right on the basis of the frame of reference which each has chosen. For Professor Hunter has by and large looked at the parable as it now stands, in its churchly setting. Therefore he gives it the meaning which it had for Luke. Professor Jeremias has sought in the parable the meaning which it had originally, i.e., the meaning during Jesus' ministry. To put the matter another way: we have here a case of how a parable from Jesus was re-applied in the early church. According to one of the "laws of transformation," what was originally a parable of crisis during Jesus' ministry later became a device for exhorting disciples to a prudent kind of life.

Coupled with this question of which setting one emphasizes for the parable is the tricky question of how one is to divide the verses following Luke 16:1. Liturgical tradition has drawn a line after 16:9; that was the ending for the Gospel Lesson for the Ninth Sunday after Trinity. The RSV also has a new paragraph start at that point, with 16:10. But from the standpoint of sense and content, that is almost certainly wrong. The sense would demand that reading and studying of this passage ought to go on through 16:13. Actually the next two verses also continue the subject of the parable in that they report how Pharisees, who were opponents of Jesus, heard these words and scoffed, and 16:19-31 goes on further with the subject of money in the parable of the Rich Man and Lazarus.[96] But the verses down through 16:13 are the ones directly dependent on the parable of the Unjust Steward. There is an additional question of precisely how far the parable itself extends, whether through verse 7 or to include verse 8 as well. As we shall see in a moment, this is no idle quibble, for much turns on how verse 8 is interpreted.

The verses themselves are easy enough to understand, with a few exceptions. However, comment on them can enrich our understanding at several points. Luke says that Jesus spoke "to the disciples" (16:1a). However, this whole section of the "Samaritan ministry" is rather confusing if one asks whom Jesus is addressing at any given moment. At 14:25 he speaks to "great multitudes" who accompanied him. According to 15:1, which gives the next detail as to audience, tax collectors, sinners, Pharisees, and scribes were drawing near to hear him. At 16:14, we are told, the Pharisees heard "all this" that Jesus had said in verses 1-13. It would appear that, according to Luke's setting, a large group of persons who were not disciples of Jesus heard his parable about the Unjust Steward; some of them were friendly and on the verge of responding favorably, others were hostile. Luke's phrase, "to the disciples," is simply his way of indicating that the parable has meaning or meanings for the followers of Jesus too— even though it was originally spoken to a mixed audience, including opponents and an uncommitted multitude, as well as disciples.

The story in the parable fits Galilee, where there were many large estates belonging to rich, absentee landowners and run by stewards. The owner, in this case, hears rumors about his agent and decides to "sack" him. The steward faces a crisis: too weak physically to dig, too strong morally to beg, what shall he do now for a livelihood? In the short time left to him before he must turn over his account books, he calls in certain debtors and changes the amounts which the records say they owe to his master. The bill of the man who owes 100 measures of olive oil is cut to 50; that of a man who is in debt to the tune of 100 measures of wheat is cut to 80. The figures represent huge amounts, the yield of almost 150 olive trees or 100 acres of wheat land. In each case about 500 dinars' worth was removed from the bill— the equivalent of ten years' salary for the average working man. Probably similar actions were taken with other debtors, one by one. The parable closes with the words, "The master commended the dishonest steward for his prudence," and a cryptic comment that "the sons of this world are wiser . . . than the sons of light" (16:8).

The "hero" of this story is termed a "dishonest steward" (vs. 8), but people seldom stop to ask where his dishonesty lay. Usually it is assumed that he was dishonest in what he did for his master's debtors. Yet that cannot be correct, for "the master commended the dishonest steward." J. B. Phillips was so struck by this problem, he reports,[97] that in his translation he was much tempted to follow the clever suggestion (though he did not adopt it in his final rendering) of punctuating verses 8 and 9 as questions, so that they would read:

"Did the master commend the dishonest steward?"
"Do I tell you, 'Make friends for yourselves by means of unrighteous mammon'?"

In each case the answer would be expected, "No," and Jesus' own interpretation would come in verses 10 ff. But this solution, while attractive and possible, has convinced few readers.

It is more to the point to observe that the only real charge against the steward is in verse 1: he was accused of "wasting his master's goods." We are not told whether the charge was true or false, for that does not matter for the rest of the plot.

What about this business of changing the bills of his master's debtors? Recent research[98] has suggested that the man was doing nothing dishonest but was perfectly within his rights. Under Jewish custom and law an agent such as this steward had the legal power to do such things in his master's name. It was also the practice that such agents got no regular salary but were permitted to make a profit for themselves on transactions in the master's name. Very probably the agent was engaged in making loans at high interest rates. Such usury was forbidden to Jews, but there were ways around the law, as this steward (let us call him "Benjamin") knew. One practice was to have a man write, "I owe Benjamin 100 measures of wheat." There is no reference to interest here. The trick was that Benjamin gave the borrower only 50 or 80 measures to begin with. When the borrower paid back the 100 measures recorded on the bill, the agent then had a profit of 20 or 50 measures for himself. This amounted to "interest."

In our story, when the steward cut down the bills from 100 to 80 or 50, he was not then cheating his master; he was simply forgoing the profit he would have realized if he had been allowed to stay on in his job. By so doing, he was "feathering his nest" with these debtors. For such a favor, they would gladly receive him into their homes (vs. 4). No wonder the master commended the steward who had been accused to him. Clever rascal! When he saw a crisis coming, he responded with alacrity and acted with prudence. The audience might have expected a rebuke. The master in the parable (and Jesus in his story) commended him. Phillips has caught the flavor when he refers to "this rascally steward," instead of "the dishonest bailiff" (NEB).

The meaning which Jesus had in mind, then, was this: every-one of you who hears my message about the kingdom is faced with a crisis just as much as that steward was. Where now you hesitate, or doubt, or waver—act! Act as resolutely as this steward did. Boldly stake all on the kingdom![99]

For such an interpretation of the parable's meaning in Jesus' ministry there is one further detail in verse 8 which is crucial, even though it is seldom noted. Actually, it is the key which opened the door to further interpretations of the parable in the early church. In verse 8, who is "the master"? Literally, the Greek says, *"The lord* commended the dishonest steward." Our first guess might be, the master of the household, the lord in the parable, the rich man of verse 1, and that is probably correct for the original story. The story concluded on the note that the rascally steward's employer praised him; he knew an astute trick when he saw one! However, this word "master" or literally "the lord" could have other meanings for Luke and early Christians. "The Lord" could mean, of course, God, as at Luke 2:9 or 14:23. But this parable is not about God. Jesus does not describe him as a rich, absentee landowner. The other possibility and the one which was a likely influence on Luke is that "the Lord" could denote Jesus. We have already noted[100] how Luke especially lets this "post-resurrection" phrase penetrate back into the story of Jesus' earthly ministry; cf. 10:1 or 12:42, or, in a similar parable situation, 18:6. It is likely therefore that Jesus' original story concluded with the words, "The master [*kyrios*] of this rascally steward praised him for his prudence." Then Jesus waited for his hearers to "catch on" and apply the point of such resolute action to the crisis of the kingdom.

After the resurrection, however, these words at 16:8a came to be understood as a reference to Jesus, with the sense, "Why, the Lord Jesus commended the steward for his prudence! What shall we Christians make of that?" In short, "the lord" had one meaning in the original story, and another in the early church, as we might expect in versions before and after Easter.

Now the cryptic ending of the original parable invited additions which would draw out the meaning more precisely. Jesus' own parables did not usually append such morals, but closed quickly and strikingly, the way 16:8a does. However, in Luke 16:8b-13 a whole series of additions, from the Jesus-material and out of a Palestinian setting, are attached to the original parable. We may sketch the outline thus and then comment on each addition (lines from one section to another represent verbal links, which are listed at the right and will be discussed below):

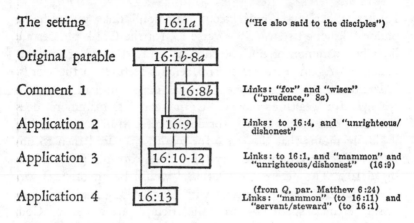

The setting   `16:1a`   ("He also said to the disciples")

Original parable   `16:1b-8a`

Comment 1   `16:8b`   Links: "for" and "wiser" ("prudence," 8a)

Application 2   `16:9`   Links: to 16:4, and "unrighteous/dishonest"

Application 3   `16:10-12`   Links: to 16:1, and "mammon" and "unrighteous/dishonest" (16:9)

Application 4   `16:13`   (from Q, par. Matthew 6:24) Links: "mammon" (to 16:11) and "servant/steward" (to 16:1)

The latter half of verse 8 is a comment on the fact that the Lord Jesus picked such a man as this rascally steward as hero of his parable:

> . . . for the sons of this world [or this age] are wiser in their own generation than the sons of light. (16:8b)

The verse has a strong Semitic cast. "Sons of light" and "sons of this age" are phrases found in the Dead Sea Scrolls. The comment sounds like a Palestinian proverb, "The worldly are more astute than the otherworldly in dealing with their own kind" (NEB). "Wiser" (16:8b) involves the same Greek root as "prudence" (8a). Note that the proverb concerns their relation with each other ("in their own generation") and does not have to do with their relationship to God. The verse is commenting that the astuteness and resolution with which men of this world proceed in their relations with each other (e.g., in business) can rate our admiration. Jesus' original parable said the steward acted wisely in his crisis. The comment, however, contains the wish that Christians would act wisely and as boldly in their lives as do "worldly" people.

The next comment (16:9) obviously harkens back to verse 4 of the parable:

> "And I tell you, make friends for yourselves by means of unrighteous mammon, so that when it fails they *may receive you into the* eternal *habitations.* (16:9)

"And the steward said . . . 'I have decided what to do, so that people
may receive me into their *houses* when I am put out of the stewardship.' " (16:3-4)

Further, the phrase "unrighteous mammon" links up with the
phrase "dishonest steward" in verse 8*a*, for the Greek phrases are
literally "mammon of unrighteousness" and "steward of unrighteousness." Again there are several Semitic features in the words.
"Mammon" was originally an oriental deity but had become a
synonym for wealth or money. "Unrighteousness mammon" does
not mean that money is evil, nor does it refer to ill-gotten wealth;
it simply means that the quest for wealth may lead men to unrighteous actions, until the very thing itself corrupts (cf. I Timothy 6:10). The "eternal habitations" would be an oriental way
of speaking of dwelling-places with God. Along this line, Professor Jeremias speculates that "the friends" are angels of God,
and that the whole expression is therefore a way of saying, "Use
your money wisely, in the sight of God, so that when money no
longer avails—that is, in the Day of the Lord—God may receive
you into an eternal home."[101] This could seem to mean an admonition to almsgiving and generous stewardship of wealth, and Jesus
did speak on such subjects at times (Matthew 6:2-4). The verse
would then make Jesus sound like a teacher of wisdom, giving
advice on wise use of money. Perhaps that is how some early
Christians understood the verse, and Christians through the centuries have often needed a jarring reminder that one's "response"
to God includes the use of temporal possessions and the stewardship of money.[102] But one must be careful not to slip from this
"demand" into a notion that such use of wealth "buys" salvation
or "feathers a nest" in heaven. Elsewhere, Jesus insists that alms
should be given without notoriety; any "reward" from God will
be a matter of surprise, not the result of an "insurance policy
philanthropy"[103] (Matthew 6:2-4). Indeed, the great Synoptic picture of the Final Judgment at Matthew 25:31-46 rules out any
self-seeking almsgiving; it is spontaneous, unconscious acts of
kindness which count ("Lord, when did we see thee . . . ?").

Jeremias ventures the intriguing suggestion that verse 9 was
originally directed to tax collectors (cf. Luke 15:1).[104] They had to
work with "unrighteous mammon" every day. Very well, Jesus
is saying, "Use money prudently—none of it sticking to your
hands or slipping into your pockets. Use it in such a way that

'when money is a thing of the past, you may be received into an eternal home' " (NEB). One cannot be positive that the words originally had that setting, but it is attractive to think so. The application of the verse to the stewardship of money is a reminder that disciples who are engrossed in the kingdom of God still live and labor in the realm of mammon. God's gift of salvation has its implications even here.

The third application, which is about faithfulness in life, is much easier to understand:

10 "He who is faithful in a very little is faithful also in much; and he who is dishonest in a very little is dishonest in much. 11 If then you have not been faithful in the unrighteous mammon, who will entrust to you the true riches? 12 And if you have not been faithful in that which is another's, who will give you that which is your own?" (Luke 16:10-12)

This application connects with verse 1 of the parable. The steward wasted his master's goods; the master, having found him unfaithful in such small things, does not want to go on entrusting him with bigger things. Note that verses 10-12 make no use of the rest of the parable but require only the connection to verse 1. Note also that the steward is now, in this application, no longer a model to be imitated in his resolute action; he is not a figure whom the master can commend. He is here (as in verse 1) a warning of what *not* to do: Don't be unfaithful the way this man was. Stewards are to be found faithful (I Corinthians 4:2; Luke 12:42, II Timothy 1:11-14). These verses, 10-12, have their own little structure. The words "unrighteous mammon" link them to verse 9. The general theme of faithfulness in life is stated in verse 9. Then two particular applications are made: to "mammon" and "true riches" (vs. 11), and to "that which is another's" and "that which is your own" (vs. 12). Fidelity with all that is entrusted to us is the point.

The final application comes in a saying at verse 13 which Matthew has made part of his Sermon on the Mount (6:24):

"No one can serve two masters; for either he will hate the one and love the other, or he will be devoted to the one and despise the other. You cannot serve God and mammon.

Again there is a link to a previous verse (16:11) through the word "mammon," as well as to 16:1-8a through the word "servant" (which in Greek, *oikētēs*, is related to the term *oikonomos*, which is translated as "steward"). The point is a blunt "either/ or": either God or mammon must be lord of a man's life. The unrighteous steward served unrighteous mammon, according to this interpretation; the trustworthy steward will serve God.

In 16:8*b*-13 four comments on or applications of the original parable (16:1-8*a*) have now emerged. All of these applications seem to go back to Palestinian soil; they may also go back to Jesus himself. But there is good reason to suppose that none of these four applications was the one original point of the parable. For each picks out a distinct feature or detail in the parable and builds on it, with each application leading on to the next. F. C. Grant has likened verses 9-13 to "the notes of an early church preacher or teacher, who used the parables for Christian . . . exhortation."[105]

However, in these applications which the evangelist has included, one can find meaningful lessons; each makes a point. But historically one would find it hard to hold that all these verses were spoken in just this order on one single occasion by Jesus. Parables do not work like that. But critical analysis helps to recover an original parable from the historical Jesus, which has been reapplied in several ways by early Christians, its eschatological call gradually being transformed into a hortatory admonition. Outlined it would look something like this:

Original parable	16:1-8*a*	Act resolutely in the crisis now!
eschatological application	16:8*b*	Be as (eschatologically) prudent as worldly people are in their dealings with one another.
hortatory admonition	16:9	Use your means wisely, generously.
	16:10-12	Be faithful in life.
	16:13	It is either God or mammon.

In this way a parable of Jesus which might have spoken only to a limited time and place has been made to speak over the centuries.

7

The Mighty Works of the
Reign of God

The miracles performed by Jesus of Nazareth are like "little lightning-flashes" in our gospels. They presage the great lightning-flash" of the resurrection. They illumine the ministry with momentary demonstrations of God's power. The wondrous signs which God works through Jesus are like knockings at the gate. They show that the reign of God, which only God can inaugurate, is at the door. Such a view of these mighty works is what recent biblical scholarship has emphasized, in contrast to older approaches which often centered in how the miracles are to be explained—or explained away.[1]

Miracles—the Kingdom Comes with Power

All too often, and especially in the last century, readers of the gospels have felt that Jesus' miracles stick out like a "sore thumb." Even those readers most open to such stories about Jesus have failed to see how miracles relate to the central message of the kingdom of God which he set forth in proclamation and parable. It is a great gain, therefore, that modern scholarship views the miracles in relation to the kingdom. The simple fact that Jesus himself associated these happenings with the advent of God's reign—and therefore with salvation, and judgment—should guard against wrong notions about the purpose of these mighty acts.

Because, however, the miracles have been separated from Jesus' message about God and his reign, all too often discussion has dwelt solely on such problems as, "What happened? How can we explain it?" Severed from Jesus' general message and viewed in terms which ignore their first-century Gospel setting, the miracles have frequently been the basis for sharp attacks on Christianity. A pagan philosopher, Celsus, in the second century A.D. attacked Jesus on the grounds that he was a magician who had learned "tricks" from Egyptian sorcerers in his youth.[2] In the seventeenth and eighteenth centuries, the rationalists made Jesus' miracles the focal point of their attack on traditional Christianity, as when Hume rejected any transgression of a "law of nature."[3] The nineteenth century deified "laws of nature" (as it understood them) even more. Miracles, regarded as contrary to such "laws," were "excess baggage," an embarrassment that ought to be dropped from Christianity. Matthew Arnold, the poet, flatly asserted, "Miracles do not happen," and held that the Bible would continue as a source of life and joy only if its world of "illusion, rumor, and fairy-tale" were removed.[4]

Such an attitude still dominates the thinking of many today. The forward march of science seems to have excluded God and the miraculous more than ever from the picture (though actually scientists today are far less likely to talk in terms of rigid, unbending "laws of nature" than in the nineteenth century). Biblical criticism has aggravated the problem by forcing us to see some of the difficulties in the New Testament accounts themselves. Matthew, for instance, sometimes has *two* men healed where the Marcan account has just one (compare Mark 5:1-20 with Matthew 8:28-34; or Mark 10:46-52, the story of Bartimaeus, with the account about "two blind men" at Matthew 20:29-34). Or again, in the story of the healing of blind Bartimaeus, Mark and Matthew place the incident *after* Jesus' departure from Jericho; Luke 18:35 has it as Jesus "drew near" to Jericho. Such discrepancies are easy to collect if one reads the gospels with a critical eye and asks, "What happened?" The records do not always agree.[5] Indeed, it seems that every one of the sorts of "transformation" which Professor Jeremias has documented for the parables occured also with the miracle tales in the early church. As stories of Jesus' mighty works were told and retold, they too were often embellished or reworked, and they were certainly collected together into little groups or sequences such as we have in our gospels today (cf. Mark 4:35–5:43 and Matthew 8–9).[6]

Any study of the miracles ought therefore to begin with a frank admission that these stories have caused difficulties for many persons and that in today's world the very notion of a miracle worked by God will seem to many a "fairy tale." It no longer suffices to say to these people, "You must believe it because the Bible says so." Their own experience and their notion of the world seems to exclude "miracle." Moreover, the biblical accounts themselves appear contradictory. In these few pages it is, of course, not possible to deal with every intellectual, apologetical problem of modern man or with every biblical account exegetically. But a few remarks may put the miracles of Jesus into a proper perspective, appropriate for their study today.

To begin with, there seems no question that, in the eyes of his contemporaries, Jesus did work miracles. This is the unanimous report of all four gospels and of Acts (see Acts 10:38), and of all the sources like *Q, M,* and *L* behind them. There is no "early strand" of Jesus-material which is devoid of miracles. It may be that some of these miracle stories have been heightened in the retelling and that some are later additions to the Jesus-material, and that some sources are more likely to play up miracles than others. But a Jesus-minus-miracles is not supported by the sources, and such a figure receives little comfort from critical scholarship. Perhaps the most surprising confirmation of this point is the fact that included among Jewish references to Jesus in the rabbinic writings is the statement that he was a wonder-worker or "sorcerer"—i.e., he performed what contemporaries regarded as miracles.[7]

Next, it is necessary to put this observation into further historical perspective by adding that in the ancient world most people believed in miracles.[8] Pagans told of miracles performed by Pythagoras and Simon the Sorcerer (see Acts 8:9-24) and by a man whom some worshiped as a god, Apollonius of Tyana.[9] These tales are often similar to those about Jesus in our gospels. Jews recounted the miracles of certain rabbis; of one holy man who lived about A.D. 70 it was said, "Woe to the man who meets a water-snake! But woe to the water-snake which meets Rabbi Hanina!"[10] Thus, Jews and pagans alike had their accounts concerning wonder-workers.

This brings us to a third point. Inasmuch as there are miracle stories about Jesus similar to those about other men of his day, one may ask whether there is anything that distinguishes such tales in the Jesus-material from their counterparts elsewhere in antiquity. It must be recognized that by themselves Jesus' miracles prove nothing, for such stories are told of a number of people in antiquity. And Jesus made no claim for himself and his person directly on the basis of his mighty deeds; he never said, "My miracles prove that I am the messiah." Further, his miracles must be called ambiguous in that they could be interpreted in various ways. During Jesus' lifetime people had differing explanations for the fact that "things happened" through him. Some concluded that Jesus was a prophet, others that God had "visited" his people (to put it in Old Testament language; see Luke 7:16; cf. 1:68

and Exodus 4:31). But enemies said, "He works miracles, all right, but by the power of Beelzebul." The net result is that Jesus' contemporaries believed he did work miracles, but they explained his deeds in different ways—as acts of God, or of Satan. He left an impression of abnormal authority, but this authority was part of the controversy carried on about Jesus: was he "God's man" or a man in league with the demons? His miracles are in this way like the resurrection: one can confess them to be acts of God or explain them in some other way.[11]

At this point the question of presuppositions on the part of the interpreter arises. One's opinion about any given miracle story will depend to a great extent on how one thinks about God and the world. If it is insisted that the world is a "closed universe" where only inevitable "laws of nature" operate, then the whole notion of a miracle worked by God historically is excluded.[12] If, on the other hand, it is allowed that "God is able" (Mark 10:27b; Luke 1:49)—able to work in his own universe—then, even though one may not wish to give absolute credence to every such account from antiquity, it is possible to look at each miracle story and assess it on its merits by certain criteria, rather than on the basis of a foregone conclusion.

But what tests are there which are helpful for assessing miracle accounts on their respective merits, provided one is willing to grant that such actions are not sheer impossibilities? At least three tests suggest themselves which may be used with the miracles of Jesus.[13]

(1) There is the test of sources. Is the account from an early or a late source, from a reliable or utterly unreliable source? Obviously one is more likely to be impressed by a reference in an early gospel like Mark or in a source like Q than by an interpolation such as Mark 16:17-18 or by a detail in some later source like the *Gospel of the Nazarenes*.[14] One is likely to be even more impressed by "multiple attestation"[15] in several good sources which are independent of each other than by a reference in just one source. Moreover, canonical limits, or a "critical canon" which may be set up within the New Testament canon, obviously play a role in such decisions for some investigators too.

(2) The test of probability also plays a part. Whether investigators realize it or not, all of them are likely to operate with "degrees of probability." While there is, of course, in a strict

sense, no such thing as a "big" or a "little" miracle (either it is a miracle or it is not), modern minds balk at some things as less likely than others. Certain miracles are considered "explainable" and therefore likely, others are not. Or some miracles have been accepted by certain investigators just because they seem inexplicable.

Often investigators combine these two standards, "sources" and "probability," in order to set up "degrees" of miracles, as to which they will accept and which they will not. Investigators have thus sometimes made distinctions involving miracles in the New Testament and those in the Old; "legends" outside the Bible, as they are prone to term them—for example, the account about the boy Jesus making clay pigeons which come alive[16]—and biblical accounts; events at the shrine of Our Lady of Lourdes in the past century in contrast with events of two thousand years ago; healings at a Hindu temple or fire-walking in Polynesia as compared with happenings at a Christian shrine; a miracle attributed to voodoo magic and something which can be credited to nature or to the God proclaimed in Scripture. Investigators draw their lines at one place or another, and—the point is—their criteria will doubtless include such matters as the source which describes the purported miracle, and the degree of probability within the known world and the religious and philosophical frame of reference of the investigator. In many cases personal experience becomes the touchstone. Yet even experience may not be the final guide. It is worth recalling C. S. Lewis' story about the only person he ever met who claimed to have seen a ghost—her experience still left her unconvinced. In such cases, "Seeing is not believing."[17] Of course, there is also the danger that people will limit what they conceive to be possible for God or in a narrative on the basis of their own restricted experiences; for this reason George Boobyer warned that "where unusual religious activities are concerned, ordinary experience can too easily be made normative."[18]

Important as these two criteria are, they ought never to be the final word in treating the miracles attributed to Jesus. For there is (3) the most important test which, theologically at least, ought to be decisive: it is congruity of the account with the character of God and Jesus as it is known, apart from this or that particular miracle. One must ask of a miracle in the gospels (or, for that matter, in some noncanonical source) whether it accords with what is otherwise ascertainable about the nature of God or the person of Jesus. Does it fit with the general impression one has of him? Does it reveal that "God is able"? that he is loving? that he is Father and lord? that he is judge? Does it fit with Jesus' demonstrably central message about the kingdom? Here is a reason why one must acknowledge some miracles as lying at the heart of Jesus' proclamation, and declare others, like that where the boy Jesus makes clay birds which come to life and fly away, as frivolous and unrelated to the kingdom.

This key element, of agreement with the otherwise revealed nature of God and the character of Jesus, is vividly portrayed in a scene which all three Synoptic Gospels record. Mark pictures the Galilean ministry, not as one grand "success story," but as including a current of opposition from the outset. Where God's sovereignty is proclaimed, human obstinacy opposes it. This opposition comes even from Jesus' friends and family (Mark 3:21, 31-35).[19] It comes most vehemently through men who see Satan, not God, at work in Jesus' ministry.[20] "He is possessed by Beelzebul,[21] and by the prince of demons he casts out demons," they say.

Jesus replies to this charge that he is exorcizing demons with the aid of the chief of demons by saying that this would mean "civil war" within Satan's kingdom. This would be like a kingdom or a household divided against itself—it would fall. Jesus rejects the notion that he works with Satan's power. If not the devil's power, then whose? There is only one other possibility, and in a saying preserved in Q but not in Mark, Jesus presses home the point (Matthew 12:28, par. Luke 11:20). It is by God's power that he drives out demons. And "if it is by the Spirit of God [Luke has 'the finger of God']²² that I cast out demons, then the kingdom of God has come upon you." Jesus' claim is that his miracles are a sign that God is at work, his reign drawing near— so near that in the miracles it "has come upon you."

A dramatic little picture clinches Jesus' claim about what is happening. No one, he says, could ever set foot in the house of a strong man or plunder the palace of an armed man unless he had first overcome that man. The "strong man" is Satan, who has "bound" many people, through demons, illness, and sin. As you can see, Jesus implies, men are now, as a foreshadowing of the coming reign of God, being set free from Satan, sins are being forgiven, demons driven out. These miracles can mean only one thing: that the One who is stronger than Satan, namely God, has taken the field.

Thus Jesus relates his miracles to the kingdom. The miracles are to be attributed to God and are announcements that God and his salvation are entering into the world of men. By working miracles Jesus was doing something which set him off from John the Baptist (see John 10:41)[23] and the leaders at Qumran. By claiming that his miracles were lightning-flashes of God's coming kingdom, he was differentiating himself from rabbis and pagans alike who were also credited with miracles. The purpose of the miracles was to present the kingdom come with power. What was the content of these mighty acts?

The Miracles of Healing

All in all, some thirty-seven miracles of Jesus are reported in our canonical gospels, twenty-two in Luke, twenty-one in Matthew, nineteen in Mark (thus making the Synoptics rather similar in the amount of emphasis on this point).[24] By comparison, there are only eight in John. (John prefers to narrate only a few examples but then employs each as the basis for some further teaching. For example, in chapter 6 the feeding of the five thousand is followed by a discourse on the bread of life.)

It is customary to classify the various miracles of Jesus as (1) "healing miracles" and (2) "nature miracles." The latter deal, not with persons, but with something in nature such as a fig tree or a storm at sea. They are sometimes referred to as "creation miracles." The miracles of healing may in turn be subdivided into a larger group in which there is the expulsion of a demon, and a smaller number in which there is a death involved and then a restoration to life, plus cases where some illness like blindness, paralysis, or "leprosy" (a broad term used to cover all sorts of skin diseases) is involved. Some prefer to distinguish healings of body and healings of mind.

It must be remembered that all classifications are somewhat arbitrary.[25] For, in biblical thought, man is a part of creation and, with it, stands in contrast to God. The biblical view of man does not make distinctions between "body" and "mind" the way we often do. In fact, when Jesus healed a paralytic, his first words were, "Your sins are forgiven" (Mark 2:3-12). Furthermore, it

is likely that for people of Jesus' day every disease and even
death were considered the work of Satan's demons, not just the
obvious cases where an exorcism was involved. Death and illness
were considered part of that "bondage" from which only God
could set men free (see Luke 13:16). It must be added, however,
that in the gospel presentations Jesus does not subscribe to the
common opinion that every illness or misfortune was directly connected to that man's specific sins (see Luke 13:2-5 and John
9:3). While he did hold that all men are subject to sin, disease,
and death (Luke 13:3, 5), he made no simple equation saying
that *this* sin had led to *this* illness.

But all these types of miracles attributed to Jesus have one
thing in common: an action of God through Jesus is assumed, a
mighty act in the world here and now. In almost every case, too—
the cursing of the fig tree seems an exception (Matthew 21:
18-19)—these miracles seem to reflect God's purpose for good
and are congruent with his character as a gracious father. Finally,
though this may be hardest to show in the nature miracles, there
always is reference to some critical happening or meaning in human lives and history. If all this is put together, a definition for
"miracle" results; as H. H. Farmer phrased it, a miracle is "a
significant and critical event or combination of events in a human
situation into the causation of which God's good purpose, acting
relevantly to that situation, enters as an indispensable factor."[26]
That would apply to an answer to prayer; it also fits Jesus' miracles, by and large. It does exclude, however, poetic notions of "the
miracle of a snowflake" or "the pattern of hoar-frost on the
kitchen-window," for these are not significant in the human situation. They are not miracles in the biblical sense.

To return to classification of the miracles, it is a fact that New
Testament miracle stories regularly have a definite three-point
structure to them. (1) The situation or condition of the person
is described. (2) A method of cure is narrated. (3) The miraculous recovery of the person or correction of the condition is attested. For illustration, compare Mark 1:30-31: (1) "Simon's
mother-in-law lay sick with a fever"; (2) Jesus took her by the
hand and raised her up; (3) "the fever left her; and she served
them." But it is also a fact that pagan miracle stories have the
same general outline. So do the testimonials for health foods and
wonder drugs.[27] How else could a healing be described?

More noteworthy than either classifications or attempts at definition, however, is the terminology used by the gospels.[28] It has
been pointed out that John likes to call Jesus' miracles "signs" in
the sense that men of faith see what they point to (John 2:11;
6:26), whereas the Synoptics speak of signs mainly in a bad
sense, as that which opponents demand as proof (Matthew 12:38-
39).[29] Somewhat surprising is the fact that our gospels virtually
never use the normal term of the ancient world, *miraculum*,
"something astonishing," or an equivalent term to designate what
Jesus did. Only at Matthew 21:15 does the phrase "wonderful
things" occur, and then it results in indignation on the part of
the priests and scribes—"when the chief priests and the scribes
saw the wonderful things that he [Jesus] did, . . . they were in-
dignant." "Strange things" occurs just once (Luke 5:26), and
then on the lips of the crowd. "Portents" and "prodigies" are
never used in the gospels except in a derogatory sense (see John
4:48 for an example).

This survey of terminology leaves us with the conclusion that
the Synoptics prefer to call Jesus' miracles "deeds of power." The
Greek word employed, *dynamis* (from which the English words
"dynamic," "dynamo," and "dynamite," etc., are derived), is the
same term which we have already met in the doxology to the
Lord's Prayer—"thine is . . . the power"—where it is significantly
paralleled with "the kingdom." The concept is basic to the Old
Testament idea of God, where repeatedly there is reference to
how he has shown his power in this event or that (cf. Deuteronomy 3:24; Exodus 15:6; Isaiah 40:26; Jeremiah 32:17). He is
"the God of power," and in Jewish usage "the Power" could
even be used as a paraphrase for "God." Thus at Mark 14:62
"the right hand of Power" means "the right hand of God."

Jesus' miracles are thus outward expressions of the power of
the Power; "the energies of God are stored in them."[30] When we
are reminded that this same term "power" is used by Paul with
reference to Jesus' resurrection (Romans 1:4) and for the Gospel
as "the power of God for salvation" (Romans 1:16), we begin
to see that the biblical term for Jesus' miracles is not meant to
smack of "the wondrous" or "the amazing," but to reflect the
power of God, which is the theme of the Gospel.

What men call "miracles" may thus be wondrous signs, but
only to those who have eyes to see and ears to hear—just as with

the miracle, the resurrection, which was not apparent to all men, but only to chosen witnesses (Acts 10:40-41). To other men the miracles may be startling and may even call for explanations of some sort. But they are significant, as revelations of God's power and character, only for those who see and hear with faith. This applies first of all to the resurrection of Jesus, and then to the miracles reported during his ministry. If one allows the resurrection miracle as a necessary explanation to account for the rise of the Christian church,[31] then one ought not to be surprised if antecedent examples of God's power and control in the world appear during the historical ministry. Miracles and the resurrection thus cohere, and both are congruent with the biblical concept of God and with Jesus' preaching of the kingdom. This does not mean that investigators who accept all this may not still want to measure and assess individual miracles on the basis of other tests. But it does insist that "mighty acts of power" are precisely what should be expected, by the man of faith, in connection with God's revelation of his kingly power.

Such an approach, of course, puts a heavy stress on faith,[32] and it must be admitted that, as a Pauline phrase puts it, "faith is not every man's thing" (II Thessalonians 3:2, Luther's rendering). But this element of faith on the part of men was intrinsic to Jesus' miracles. In fact, the degree to which Jesus' miracles are made to relate to human faith according to the Synoptic Gospels is always rather shocking to readers of the Bible today. At his hometown of Nazareth, for example, Jesus, we are told, could do no mighty work or deed of power because of the unbelief there (Mark 6:5-6). For in the afflicted person who comes to him Jesus looks for faith in God. Sometimes the very petition which people direct to Jesus reflects their implicit trust that God's power is working through him. Other times Jesus asks more pointedly "Do you believe . . . ?" (John 11:26), or even "Do you believe that I am able to do this?" (Matthew 9:28). More often he comments, "Your faith has made you well" (Mark 5:34). Sometimes he even seems to test the persistency of this faith (cf. Matthew 15: 22-28). Once, at least, Jesus refers to the faith not just of the sick person but of his four friends who let him down through the roof to Jesus (Mark 2:5). This is not so much a matter of "vicarious" faith, where one man's belief substitutes for another's, as a case where a broader personal relationship is involved, beyond just the patient himself. Elsewhere Jesus comments that his own disciples could not cast out a demon because they were men of little faith (Matthew 17:19-20). Disciples, sufferers, and their friends were thus all involved in a "web" of faith.

All this means that Jesus' miracles, as acts of God's power, presuppose the faith of the participants. More specifically, it means a personal relationship with God, a relationship which makes one's existence sure and wholesome and open to God. Such an emphasis helps distinguish Jesus' miracles from all forms of magic and the performances of other wonder-workers of the day, as does also the fact that Jesus did not use spells and incantations but worked his cures and salvation by his powerful word.[33]

There is one other general consideration which applies to all the healing miracles. It pertains to their purpose. Often it is said that Jesus healed the blind, lame, and sick on humanitarian grounds. True, the gospels often say that he was "moved with pity" (Mark 1:41) or "had compassion" on the multitude (Matthew 14:14; Mark 8:2). Such a motivation also fits in with the general character of God as loving and merciful. But as a total explanation for the miracles, this idea fails at one key point: if Jesus' aim was merely humanitarian, then why did he cure so few of the blind and lame and sick in Palestine? To put it another way, why has God not worked miraculous healings of all sick people since Jesus' day? A better explanation, therefore, is that Jesus' healings were not just motivated by pity for people, but must be connected with his unique central message of the kingdom. The miracles are "lightning-flashes" of God's power, signifying the overthrow of Satan and the fuller manifestation of God's sovereignty which is soon to come.

Against this background consider as a typical example of healing miracles attributed to Jesus the story of the woman with a hemorrhage and the raising of Jairus' daughter (Mark 5:21-43 is the most vivid of the three Synoptic accounts). The passage is a "double" miracle story. For while Jesus and a crowd are on their way to the house of Jairus, a ruler of the synagogue, whose daughter is on the point of death, there comes a woman who had suffered from a flow of blood for a dozen years. She implores Jesus' help. She has the faith that just the touch, even of his garment, will cure her. He heals her and then restores Jairus' child to life.

It is easy to point out problems in the narratives. The statement that the woman "had suffered much under many physicians, and had spent all that she had, and was no better but rather grew worse" (Mark 5:26) is changed by Luke in a famous editorial alteration to read, she "could not be healed by any one" (8:43); it was changed because, some say, Luke was a physician and wanted to omit this slur on his profession. Mark has Jairus say, when he first contacts Jesus, "My little daughter is at the point of death" (Mark 5:23); but according to Matthew, he said, "My daughter has just died" (9:18).[34] Matthew simply has Jesus take the child by the hand and raise her up (9:25); Mark 5:41 preserves an Aramaic phrase, *"Talitha cumi,"* which Jesus spoke, while Luke translates this for his readers, "Child, arise" (8:54). It is obvious that we today cannot tell precisely what happened every second. It is also apparent that in some of the accounts of Jesus' miracles we can see parallels to Old Testament or pagan miracle stories. It ought also be added that the restoration to life here at Mark 5:41-42 is not like Jesus' own resurrection in that it is never said that Jairus' daughter (or the son of the widow at Nain, Luke 7:11-17, or Lazarus in John 11) will not die; they experience a restoration to "life" for the remainder of their natural lives, but not a resurrection into eternal life. A careful reading of Mark 5 shows too that Jesus makes no claim for himself on the basis of this miracle (in fact, Mark 5:43 has him command silence), nor does the evangelist use it as a "proof" for Jesus' divinity.

But all these observations avoid what was the crucial question for the early Christians and the evangelists. It was not simply, "Did it happen like this?" but, directed to the hearers and readers, "Do you believe that God has the power to do such things and that Jesus of Nazareth was the one in whom he historically revealed this power?" The resurrection of Jesus himself is, of course, the touchstone as to whether one believes in a God like this or not. But the miracles, in their own way, pose the same question: the power of God . . . breaking in . . . here and now. Is God's sovereign reign being revealed as life, healing, and salvation?

Mark and Luke have a special way of presenting this point in the story of the woman with the hemorrhage. Jesus, they say, perceived that "power had gone forth from him," when the woman was healed. Luke has the same idea elsewhere too (6:19).

Once he explains the matter by saying that "the power of the Lord was with Jesus to heal men" (Luke 5:17). God's power, the power of the kingdom, at work to save—in Jesus. That is what the miracle stories present.

Nature Miracles

The "creation miracles" pose basically the same question: Does God's power extend into the workings of his own universe? Did it do so in specific ways during Jesus' ministry? But special problems enter in here, which make for difficulties not encountered in the healing miracles.

For one thing, the nature miracles deal with inanimate things and operate on the subhuman level. It is harder to think of God being concerned in a miraculous way about "things" than it is to know him as One who cares for all men. Then, too, some of the nature miracles partake of the nature of legends and folklore —a coin found in a fish's mouth, the wind and waters stilled at a man's command. It has been argued, with some reason, that these miracle stories grew up only in later years, after Jesus' day, in the Hellenistic church, and do not go back even to the earliest years of the Christian movement in Palestine at all.[35] Further, these nature miracles are harder to associate with the advent of the kingdom. Above all, there is sometimes the matter of purpose. The miracles wrought in nature do not seem to tie in as readily with the good purpose of a benevolent God. To curse a fig tree because it has no fruit at the time of year when "it was not the season for figs" (Mark 11:13-14) seems capricious in the extreme, and to shrivel it away to its roots for that reason does not seem to fit in with the God whom Jesus normally proclaimed.

There are more than a half-dozen stories which fit into this category of "nature miracle." Among them are the stilling of a storm (Mark 4:35-41, par. Luke 8:22-25, and Matthew 8:18, 23-27); the walking on the water (Mark 6:45-52, par. Matthew 14:22-33); the feeding of the five thousand (the one miracle story found in all four gospels); the feeding of the four thousand (Mark 8:1-10, par. Matthew 15:32-39); the miraculous catch of fish (Luke 5:1-11); the coin in the fish's mouth (Matthew 17:27); and the fig tree.

Because of the particular difficulties about these narratives, all sorts of explanations have been offered. Recognizing that similar stories about other great men appeared in the ancient world, some have assumed that pagan legends were transferred to Jesus by adoring followers in the Greek world in the decades after the resurrection. Thus Plutarch tells a story of a storm at sea where Caesar calmed his crewmen by saying, "Don't be afraid, you are carrying Caesar. . . ."[36] A Christian writer of the second century, Aristides, recites stories which claim that the gods Asclepius and Serapis walked on the sea.[37] Further afield, in India, there is a story that a disciple of Buddha walked across the surface of a river as long as he meditated on Buddha; when he stopped meditating, he began to sink, and saved himself only by becoming enwrapped in his meditating again.[38] There are similarities of theme, though details surely differ. When Peter, for example, tries to walk on water, it is not meditation but the Lord who saves him (Matthew 14:30-31). Christology, not just piety, is involved in the retelling of this tale. It was the conclusion of Bultmann, who amassed many parallels and analogues to the New Testament miracle stories and who studied this material with utmost thoroughness, that such stories can scarcely be reckoned the source for any gospel tale,[39] though they do illustrate the atmosphere which existed in the world of the day. Hence the nature miracles in the gospels cannot be chalked up simply as Christian borrowings of pagan tales.

Related to this point is the fact that such miracle stories existed long prior to Jesus' day in the Old Testament and in Jewish circles. Some have seized on this point, however, and would explain the miracles attributed to Jesus as New Testament versions of Old Testament tales.[40] Again there are points of similarity involved. Moses provided manna in the wilderness (Exodus 16); Jesus feeds crowds of five thousand and four thousand in the wilderness, and John's Gospel draws parallels and contrasts (see John 6, especially verses 30-34). The feeding of a hundred men from twenty barley loaves, in II Kings 4:42-44, has also been compared with Jesus' feeding miracles. It is a fact that there are parallels between stories where Elisha restored to life the son of a Shunammite woman (II Kings 4:32-37) and where Jesus gave life back to the son of a widow woman at Nain (Luke 7:11-17). Elisha also healed a leper (II Kings 5, the Naaman story); so does Jesus (Mark 1:40-45; Luke 17:11-19, where foreigners are involved, just as in II Kings 5). But all these similar stories about nature (and healing) miracles prove nothing. We have already seen[41] how New Testament stories may well be told in Old Testament language. Old Testament influence doubtless affected the accounts of Jesus' miracles. But Old Testament narratives scarcely suffice to explain all the miracle stories told about Jesus.

A third line of explanation involves psychologizing. It rests on the objection that the nature miracles are pointless when compared with the healings of Jesus, because they do not affect persons. Accordingly, some interpreters have tried to treat the nature miracles so as to make their point "people-centered." A clever example is the way one famous preacher handled the stilling of the storm. He suggested that Jesus' words, "Peace! Be still!" (Mark 4:39), were directed not to the wind and the waves but to the fearful hearts of the disciples. Jesus calmed them so that they actually thought the storm had ceased, for they now felt safe.[42] So also with explanations to the feeding miracles which maintain that the miracle was not the multiplication of barley loaves and fishes, but a miracle in human hearts—Jesus persuaded men to share what they had, and so no one went hungry.[43] Appealing as this idea may be to modern minds, it is scarcely what the first-century Christians assumed.

The miracle least susceptible to this approach is that of the fig tree (Matthew 21:18-22). Here there seems to be no "good effects" on men. A tree is withered up because it did not bear fruit. As an explanation, however, some propose that this "miracle story" is simply an expansion of a parable which Jesus once told about a fig tree:

> "A man had a fig tree planted in his vineyard; and he came seeking fruit on it and found none. And he said to the vine dresser, 'Lo, these three years I have come seeking fruit on this fig tree, and I find none. Cut it down; why should it use up the ground?' And he answered him, 'Let it alone, sir, this year also, till I dig about it and put on manure. And if it bears fruit next year, well and good; but if not, you can cut it down.' " (Luke 13:6-9)

Some would claim that out of this parable about God's judgment on Israel for its "fruitlessness" the early church created a miracle story which teaches the same lesson, though in harsher terms. Others would hold that Jesus himself "acted out" this parable, just as Old Testament prophets often did; hence, the miracle story.

Still another way of handling nature miracles is to see "allusions" in them to "symbolic truths." The tales themselves are regarded as pictorial ways, such as a storyteller might adopt, of presenting deeper truths. To take two examples. It is pointed out that
in the Old Testament "the sea" is often a symbol for chaos and
opposition to God (e.g., Genesis 1:2; Psalm 65:7; Isaiah 51:9;
Psalm 77:16-20). Thus in the Book of Revelation, heaven is said
to be a place where there is no sea (21:1). On this basis it is stated
that Jesus' walking on the water and his stilling of the storm at
sea mean the control by God through Jesus of this age-old enemy,
the sea, and all it stands for.[44] Not the incident but an allegorical
significance is made central. Similarly with the feeding miracles.
It has been pointed out that some of the vocabulary in the story
of the feeding of the five thousand also occurs in the Last Supper
scene and later in connection with the Lord's Supper (compare
Mark 6:41 and John 6 with Mark 14:22 and I Corinthians 11:
24).[45] From this it is concluded that the real meaning of the
feeding stories is to be found for us in the "bread from heaven"
of the Lord's Supper. Such an "allusive" sense to the miracles
may have occurred to some early Christians, but it is doubtful that
they saw in them only the basis for an allegory.

A final type of interpretation is to make these miracles the basis
for some teaching, so that the point of the miracle is seen in a
doctrine of Jesus or of the evangelist. We have already observed
that the Fourth Gospel tends to do this; there is a connection, for
example, between the presentation of Jesus as the light of the
world (8:12) and the miracle where Jesus gives light and sight
to a man blind since birth (9:1-41). Mark has a similar arrangement when he places the story of the healing of a blind man
(8:22-26) just prior to the scene where Simon Peter's eyes are
opened by revelation and he confesses Jesus as the Christ (8:27-
29). Again, there may be something to this point, that the miracles can serve as a basis for teaching, but it is questionable if that
was the original intent of the individual miracle story.

Quite apart from these various explanations, we move closer to
the intent of the Synoptic narratives when it is noted that these
nature miracles were not so much a separate category in the eyes
of early Christians as an extension of the same power of God
which was exhibited in the healing miracles, now seen in other
areas. In fact, the nature miracles, use some of the same terms as

8

The New Way of Life under
the Reign of God

The preaching of Jesus, the parables he told, and the miracles he worked all proclaim a single theme: the coming of the kingdom of God. That means the coming of God himself, in salvation and judgment. Through the deeds and words of this man from Nazareth, God's sovereign reign and power are being set forth for men. There is a gracious offer, the possibility of a new relationship with God. Yet all this calls for response, as the parables make clear. Life is offered, but a new way of life is demanded on the part of those who become disciples. Forgiveness is announced, but repentance is called for too. Salvation is "in the air" and "on the way." However the very presence of Jesus' message also brings a crisis; it warns of a judgment that is taking place now, as well as of a future judgment.

We must now ask what this proclamation by Jesus meant to men of his day in terms of their daily lives and their future fates. What was the "ethics" of Jesus like? How did one "respond" to his message and then how did one live, during that period when Jesus was preaching in Palestine?

Of course, we know that after the resurrection the proper response to the Christian message was to repent and be baptized and then to live by faith in the risen lord, as a part of his body (I Corinthians 12:12-27), the church (Acts 2:38, 44-47; 6:7). But before the cross, during Jesus' earthly ministry, there was no such "pattern of response." To a preacher like John the Baptist one responded with repentance, baptism, and reform of morals (Luke 3:3, 10-14). But it is far from certain that Jesus baptized during his ministry.[1] There was no "church" to which to become attached. A small band of disciples followed him about, but Jesus did not ask even that of everyone; some he enjoined to stay where they were (cf. Mark 5:19-20), to watch, to wait, to testify to what the Lord had done for them.[2] But how were they to live, with what manner of life? Was Jesus a "reformer of morals"? A teacher of ethics? We are likely to understand Jesus' teaching to contemporaries on these topics (and its meaning for us) only we first ask how people during this earthly ministry looked on

the healing miracles do. In telling the sea to "be still" (Mark 4:39), Jesus uses exactly the same words as were employed in rebuking a demon (1:25). Likewise the structure of the healing miracle stories can be duplicated in the "creation miracles": there is the situation, the "cure," and the result (see Mark 4:37-38, 39a, 39b-41, the stilling of the storm at sea).

This clue, that nature miracles and healing miracles went together in early Christian thought, points on to what is at stake theologically in these accounts. In the biblical view, man and nature are not separate categories but a unity. It is not man versus nature (and versus God), but God standing over against man-and-nature as their Creator. Thus, when man "falls," creation "falls" too (Genesis 3:14-24); when man is "redeemed," then creation will follow him into the redemptive process too (Romans 8:19-21). So it is that the Bible speaks of a "new heaven and a new earth" as the goal of redemption, and not just of "saved souls." If man and nature are thus a unity, so far as salvation goes, it should not surprise us that flashes of God's power as revealed through Jesus might appear in the inanimate world as well as among the persons of his day.

What often offends modern readers is the concreteness of the "nature miracles" in the gospels. Did Jesus really stop a tempest on the Sea of Galilee? Had he really been sure that there was a coin in the fish's mouth—if there was such a happening? At that point no one, not even the most conservative commentator, can ever offer any convincing or final historical proof. Each interpreter draws the line where he wants, on the grounds of history and faith; his own experience in the world and his awareness of God's power; his own assessment of the sources, "possibility," and congruity with God's know character.

This present study of the miracles can best close (1) by observing how the New Testament evangelists sometimes edited the miracle stories so as to bring out a point which the evangelist wants to leave with his readers; and (2) by looking at a saying from Jesus himself.

Matthew provides several fascinating examples of how an evangelist arranges and shapes miracle stories so as to make a new point for readers of his day. In chapters 8 and 9 Matthew has grouped together no fewer than ten miracle stories, some of which he takes over from various places in Mark, some of which come

out of Q, and one of which is unique to Matthew. No doubt
Matthew has grouped these stories together here, just as he has
concentrated teachings of Jesus in chapters 5–7, in order to show
that Jesus is the messiah in deed (chapters 8–9) as well as in
word (chapters 5–7).[46] But he also employed this assembly of
miracle tales to serve another purpose, the fulfillment of an Old
Testament theme. As Matthew comments:

> This was to fulfil what was spoken by the prophet Isaiah, "He took
> our infirmities and bore our diseases." (8:17 = Isaiah 53:4)

Matthew has thus employed the miracles to show what was clear
to Christians after Easter: that Jesus is the Christ who fulfills the
Scripture passages about "the Servant" in Isaiah 53. In this way the
miracles have become direct testimony, after Easter, as to who
Jesus is.[47]

The other example is the way Matthew handles the story of
the storm at sea (8:23-27).[48] All three gospels describe how
Jesus and his companions are endangered by a storm at sea. Matthew alone emphasizes that it is specifically his disciples who have
followed him into the ship. ("Disciple" and "follow" are words
which Matthew stresses in this passage.)[49] The storm is described
by Matthew in terms which normally are employed for the great
apocalyptic "storm" which one day will sweep over the world
(the word for "storm" at 8:24 is the same as that at Mark 13:8
for "earthquake"). The most startling change is in what the disciples say:

> Mark 4:38, "Teacher, do you not care if we perish?"
> Luke 8:24, "Master, Master, we are perishing!"
> Matthew 8:25, *"Save, Lord; we are perishing."*

Jesus is addressed with a term which later Christians employed to
express his heavenly lordship. In fact, the cry, "Save, *Kyrie,"*
sounds as if it could come right out of the church's liturgy. When
we add the fact that from early times the ship was a symbol for
the Christian church, then we begin to get an impression of the
powerful message which Matthew's version leaves. The church is
a storm-tossed ship amid the waves of the world. Even the disciples who loyally follow their lord can grow fearful. But Jesus
Christ is with them. Therefore they need not be afraid, their lord
has all power and authority (compare Matthew 28:18, 20*b*). The
miracle has become a lesson for disciples in the church after the
resurrection.

That is the way an evangelist uses the miracle stories. But what
of the historical Jesus? Even John the Baptist was puzzled by the
deeds and words of Jesus. Hence John asked, "Are you he who is
to come, or shall we look for another of a different sort?" Jesus
gave an enigmatic answer (Matthew 11:4-6, par. Luke 7:22-23):

> Go and tell John what you hear and see:
> the blind receive their sight, and the lame walk;
> lepers are cleansed, and the deaf hear, and the dead
>   are raised up;
> and the poor have good news preached to them.
> And blessed is he who takes no offense at me.

These words point plainly to Jesus' message of good news and to
his miracles. To understand the meaning, we must know that the
phrases about the blind, the lame, and the deaf, and about the
good tidings for the afflicted come out of the Book of Isaiah (35:
5-6; 61:1), where they are pictures of the coming age when God
will restore his glory in the world. Jesus' words and deeds thus
unite in the claim that God's kingdom is coming soon. The message is being proclaimed, the lightning is flashing.[50]

"But give us *proof* of this," men kept asking. Jesus refused
any such signs. "No sign shall be given," he replied, "—except
the sign of the prophet Jonah." What is that? According to Matthew, it is the resurrection of Jesus (Matthew 12:40):

> For as Jonah was three days and three nights in the belly of the
> whale, so will the Son of man be three days and three nights in
> the heart of the earth.

But that is a sign which applies only after the resurrection. Luke
has something different from this Matthean interpretation. Luke
says simply—and surely this, rather than the Matthean version,
is the voice of the historical Jesus (Luke 11:30):

> For as Jonah became a sign to the men of Nineveh [who re-
> pented at the preaching of Jonah], so will the Son of man be to
> this generation.

The sign—is Jesus himself, and his preaching. Occasionally the
scene is illumined by the lightning-flash of mighty deeds. But it
is so only for those who look with faith. To other eyes the miracles simply obscure their vision even more; they attribute them to
Beelzebul. Who *is* this Jesus, and what does the coming of the
kingdom he announces mean to men?

Jesus as Teacher and Prophet

At this point we are not asking how Jesus came to be regarded, after the resurrection, as "Lord and Christ." We are not inquiring how he spoke of himself, nor even how a few of his closest followers may have spoken about him in exceptional moments during the ministry (on these matters, see chapter 9), but only about how friends and foes generally thought of him in Galilee and Jerusalem in A.D. 29-30. To this question there is a clear answer. During his earthly ministry Jesus was looked upon by those who heard and saw him as a prophet and a rabbi (that is, teacher). They spoke of him in precisely these terms, and the gospels, even though written at a later time by Christians who accorded Jesus much more exalted titles, preserve these descriptions.

To some people it may be somewhat disappointing that Jesus was thought of as "only a teacher" during his ministry, or that certain scholars paint him as "just a prophet," reserving his other titles for the time after Easter. This sounds like a "least-common-denominator" Jesus; he is "reduced" to rabbi and prophet. But in part any disappointment is assuaged when it is discovered what these terms meant to people of Jesus' day. For they give Jesus a significance far greater than might be supposed for the period prior to the cross.

It has already been noted how Jesus' mighty deeds hinted of a link between himself and the kingdom. He worked "by the Spirit of God." His preaching and his own person together were "the sign of Jonah." Hence it was that people began to look on Jesus as himself somehow connected with the coming salvation of God which he was announcing. They used the two terms "teacher" and "prophet" to describe the impression which Jesus made on them. Though we may not suspect it at first glance, these titles do, in fact, do justice to a connection between Jesus and the coming of the kingdom.

First let us ask what the term "prophet" would have meant to Jesus' contemporaries. The report that was going the rounds after one of his miracles was, "A great prophet has arisen among us" (Luke 7:16). People said he was "a prophet, like one of the prophets of old" or even like Elijah (Mark 6:15). The disciples summed up popular opinion by saying that Jesus was being likened to Elijah, Jeremiah, and John the Baptist—all of them prophets (Matthew 16:14). A passing remark by a Pharisee (at

Luke 7:39) accords with this outlook: Jesus is presumed to be a prophet. Adversaries had to tread cautiously because the multitudes in Jerusalem regarded Jesus as a prophet (Matthew 21:46). As if to bear this out, the Passion narrative once presents Jesus being mocked as a prophet (Matthew 26:68). Compare also the opinion of disciples on the Emmaus Road, after Jesus' death but before they know of the resurrection: Jesus "was a prophet mighty in deed and word before God and all the people" (Luke 24:11). Jesus, therefore, seems to have been widely regarded as a prophet from the Lord.[3]

But there is more to the picture. To some, he was not just "*a* prophet" but "*the* prophet." The crowds at Jerusalem on "Palm Sunday" hailed him as "the prophet, Jesus from Nazareth of Galilee" (Matthew 21:11). This phrase does not mean simply "a well-known prophet out of Nazareth," but *the* prophet "who comes in the name of the Lord" (21:9). This same phrase occurs several times in John's Gospel, at 1:21; 6:14; 7:40; and 7:52.[4] Some people were saying, "This is really *the* prophet" (7:40).

To appreciate the importance of these references, we must grasp two things. The one is that Jews of Jesus' day believed to a considerable degree that prophecy, inspired by God, had ceased but that it would return at the coming of the "new age." Already in the Old Testament there are passages about the cessation of prophecy (see Zechariah 13:2-6 and Psalm 74:9). The hope for its revival is depicted in passages like Malachi 4:5-6 (the closing words in the Old Testament canon of Christians, that Elijah will come) and Joel 2:28-29 (quoted by Peter at Pentecost as a proof that the new age had come, Acts 2:17-18). A vivid reflection of this dearth of prophets and prophecy is the fact that when Judas Maccabeus recaptured the temple at Jerusalem from the pagans, the defiled altar stones were stored away "until a prophet should come to tell them what to do with them" (I Maccabees 4:45-46).[5] At Qumran, the sect's leader was sometimes regarded as a prophet, but here too there was expectation of a future prophet who would come.[6] Generally Palestine was waiting for a "new time" when God would send prophets. The impression made by vivid spokesmen for God, like John the Baptist and Jesus, is partly explicable against this background.

The other point is that Deuteronomy 18:15 had promised through Moses that in the last days "the Lord your God will raise up for you a prophet like me from among you." This hope had become very precious over the years when it was believed there were no prophets and the Holy Spirit was no longer active in Israel. Men were looking not just for *a* prophet but for *the* prophet, that is, the prophet like Moses. It is precisely this hope for "the prophet like Moses" which Jesus fulfilled, according to one of Peter's sermons after the resurrection (Acts 3:22-26).

We get a picture of how intense this hope was in Jesus' day from certain references in Josephus. A man named Theudas (see Acts 5:36), who claimed to be a prophet, said that he would repeat the "miracle of the Exodus" by dividing the waters of the Jordan in two (*Antiquities* 20:97-102). An Egyptian who gained a reputation as a prophet (cf. Acts 21:38) got thousands of people from Jerusalem to follow him out into the wilderness, where he said he would work redemption.[7]

People thus hoped "the prophet" would bring God's new age of redemption. When Jews applied this term to Jesus, it was a title of no mean importance. They were thinking of him as the one who might bring age-old promises to pass, with the inauguration of the new age.

There is one ominous note to add. Prophets in Old Testament times had often been rejected, scorned, and even put to death. Jesus knew how many of these prophetic predecessors had been martyred. According to a *Q* passage, Jesus once said to the Jews that God sent prophets "whom your fathers killed"—a whole series of them, from Abel to Zechariah; then, speaking as a prophet himself, Jesus warned that "the blood of all the prophets . . . may be required of this generation" (Luke 11:47-51, par. Matthew 23:29-36).[8] On another occasion, as he was making his way toward the Holy City, he remarked ironically, "It cannot be that a prophet should perish away from Jerusalem" (Luke 13:33). "Jerusalem," he laments, "killing the prophets and stoning those who are sent to you" (13:34, par. Matthew 23:37).[9] Perhaps even the words at Mark 10:45, about giving "his life as a ransom for many," are to be understood against this background of *prophet-martyrs*.[10]

It is possible that Jesus himself may have thought of his role in just such terms.[11] True, no saying of his ever calls him a prophet directly (Mark 6:4 is a proverb which he quotes). But sayings like Luke 13:33 imply that he regarded himself as one of this venerable company of prophet-martyrs. John's Gospel clearly describes him as *the* prophet, as does the sermon at Acts 3:22-26. Curiously, later Christianity paid little heed to this theme. As the church became more "clericalized," Jesus was far more often thought of as "priest" or "king" than as "prophet." But for the earliest Christians, as well as during his lifetime, Jesus was regarded as fulfilling a prophet's mission and at times the not insignificant role of "*the* prophet."

The story is similar, if less dramatic, with the term "*teacher.*"[12] The word is used almost fifty times in the gospels. Over forty of these refer to Jesus, and almost thirty of them are cases where people address him with the term (e.g., Mark 9:17; note also 9:5 [RSV note]). Unquestionably, they regarded him as a teacher. One of Mark's first descriptions of Jesus tells how "on the sabbath he entered the synagogue and taught" (1:21). In a Matthean summary of Jesus' work in Galilee, teaching is actually mentioned ahead of preaching and healing (Matthew 4:23). Some Christians today have an innate suspicion of any picture of Jesus as a teacher. They fear that it will make him "merely a teacher," like Confucius or some philosopher. Their immediate reaction is to say, "He was much more." True as this may be for faith since the cross and Easter, the fact of the matter is that Jesus was unquestionably regarded as a teacher during his lifetime, and the New Testament gospels have faithfully preserved this emphasis even after the resurrection.

"Jesus the teacher" must be viewed, however, squarely within the context of teaching in the Judaism of Jesus' day. The word which the New Testament applies to Jesus—*didaskalos,* "teacher" —is also employed of John the Baptist (Luke 3:12), Nicodemus (John 3:10), and the Jewish teachers in the temple (Luke 2:46). Jesus is sometimes specifically called "rabbi" (John 1:38; the Hebrew word involved here meant "great" or "exalted one," and was often applied to teachers).[13] In form and content, Jesus taught much as did the rabbis of the day.[14] He used parables, he expounded Old Testament passages, he did much of his teaching in synagogues. Like the rabbis, he had disciples. To the crowds he appeared as another among the many teachers in the land. Men came to him with personal problems and questions about the biblical law (see Mark 12:14, 32; Luke 12:13).

This background in Judaism for the term "teacher" is very different from the notion dominant in the Greek world. To the Greeks a teacher was one who develops a pupil's intellect or draws out through systematic instruction some skill which is there by nature. In the Old Testament, teaching concerns not just the mind or intellect but the *whole man,* and has above all to do with presenting God's will as it has been revealed. Mark 12:28-34, where Jesus answers the question, "Which commandment is the first of all?" provides an insight into what "teaching" meant in a Jewish environment; here the law is applied to the whole man—all his heart, soul, mind, and strength—and the teaching involves proper exposition of Scripture. The teacher is a spokesman for the Lord "who knows the thoughts of man"; he expounds the words of God who "teaches men knowledge" (Psalm 94:10-11).[15]

Against this background it must be asked, Did Jesus' teaching differ from that of his many predecessors in Israel and his Jewish contemporaries? Often it is difficult to discover any difference in content. At times Jesus gives the impression of being a "teacher of the wisdom of the Lord," very much like earlier sages, and even for the early church he was God's wisdom (I Corinthians 1:30) and the teacher of true knowledge (Matthew 23:10, NEB; Colossians 2:2-3). It is no solution, in a quest for some "uniqueness" about Jesus in this area, to claim that he taught such wisdom in public but "unique doctrines" in secret, for the gospels scarcely attribute any such body of esoteric teachings to him. A further fact to be reckoned with is the point that Jesus' ethical teachings did not by themselves cause his fate. Conceivably Jesus might have set up a "school" where the finer points of interpretation of the law were discussed—in which case he might have lived out his life in tranquility and honor, like Hillel. Yet Jesus, who appears as a teacher, was crucified.

To some extent the explanation lies in the fact that (1) Jesus, while he still made the Old Testament law his starting point, went beyond this and claimed to voice the will of God. In this way he often sharply criticized current teaching (and teachers) in Palestine. The way he "radicalized"[16] and heightened the intent of the Old Testament earned him enemies. (2) He related his teachings to the kingdom message which his preaching and miracles set forth.[17] The "ethics" of Jesus assumes the nearness of God and his sovereign power; this context for his teaching distinguished

him from his contemporaries and even from John the Baptist.
(3) Jesus refused to intellectualize his teachings, as some of the
rabbis did. Their emphasis on study seemed at times to make
obedient doing secondary to study,[18] and the complexities of the
law overawed many a man. Jesus made his message speak to the
"common man" in terms of his daily life, without hedging it in
with multitudes of legal details. (4) Finally, Jesus' own person
seems to have made a difference. It is not always *what* he says that
differs but *who* says it that makes it mean something more. Here
speaks the man who knows God as Father and sets forth the
Father's will with absolute assurance. Men "were astonished at his
teaching, for he taught them as one who had authority, and not
as the scribes" (Mark 1:22). This "authority" which marked his
preaching and mighty deeds, and which some scholars regard as a
hallmark of the historical Jesus, also appears in Jesus' teachings
at times.[19]

It is not surprising that Jesus came to be regarded as "greater
than Solomon" (Luke 11:31), as "*the* teacher," the one teacher
who reveals God's will (Matthew 23:8; 26:18). When he spoke,
it was "firsthand"—for God—and men listened. What did he
say?

The Development of the Sermons of Jesus

A number of problems make it difficult for readers today to
discover and understand the teachings of Jesus as they are embodied in his sayings and sermons.

One is the fact that they are scattered in a seemingly disorgan-
ized way throughout four different gospels. They seem to have an
"occasional" nature, reporting helter-skelter what Jesus said on
this occasion or that. Often they consist of single, isolated sentences, given without context, or worse yet, in different contexts
in different gospels.[20] Only at times are they grouped into collections or arranged by categories about a given theme.

But this last fact points to a second difficulty. These teachings,
like all the Jesus-material, were passed along for several decades
by word of mouth and then assembled in written collections (Q)
for several more decades before the evangelists recorded them for
us. There is every probability that the sayings were revised, "re-
audienced," and reapplied in this transmission process from Jesus
to the written gospels.[21] These initial difficulties, of scattered, "oc-

casional" sayings and changes and reworkings as they were passed
along, can be seen plainly in the material in that richest collection
of Jesus' teachings, the Sermon on the Mount (Matthew 5–7),
and its much shorter parallel in Luke, the Sermon on the Plain
(6:17-49).

Third, there is difficulty regarding what is to be considered the
central theme in Jesus' teachings. Though we have already explained how the kingdom of God was the overall subject of Jesus'
message, other themes, particularly from his ethical teaching, have
been stressed by some. One could say, he taught about God and
about man ("theology" and "anthropology" or "existence"), but
such terms are too general; *how* did he look on God and man
and how did he relate them? It has therefore been argued that
Jesus' teachings centered in God's providence.[22] True, he talked
about how God cares for men, as well as for the birds of the air
and the flowers of the field (e.g., Matthew 6:25-34), and a great
deal of his teaching derives from the fact that men need not be
anxious when they know such a God. But "providence" as a theme
makes Jesus sound more like a Greek philosopher than a prophet
who proclaimed the kingdom, and an emphasis on the "security"
of faith can blunt the frequent demand upon men also found in
Jesus' teachings. Still others would stress love as the heart of Jesus'
ethical instruction.[23] Jesus did call for love for God and love for
man. Love sums up the law (Matthew 22:34-40). There is no
case where love is not commanded. This emphasis on love has
obvious appeal today—indeed, a "demand to love" has become
almost too commonplace as a theme. With reference to Jesus'
teachings, it must be asked, however, whether "love," important
as it is, covers all that Jesus touched on. Is it perhaps a modern
tendency to try to subsume all under "love"?

We have already made clear that Jesus' ethical teachings must
be seen in association with his general message about the kingdom.
Teaching is not to be separated from preaching. The "ethics" assumes the proclamation of the kingdom. What is demanded of
men assumes the action of God and his gift of the kingdom—
that is, of himself, his power and presence. This general condition
is made clear in the summary verse at Matthew 4:17: "Repent,
for the kingdom of heaven is at hand." The ethical response of
repentance follows because the reign of God has come. Jesus'
ethics are for the men of the kingdom.

While the proclamation of the reign of God must be assumed as the setting and basis for Jesus' ethical teaching, it may be pointed out that a connection between the kingdom and ethics is not made in so many words in every specific case. He does not regularly say, "Do this because the kingdom is at hand." We must infer such a setting.

There is a fourth difficulty, about which most people do not pause to think: while the kingdom is the assumption which underlies all of Jesus' teachings, how, one must ask, are the individual themes of his teaching linked together?[24] Jesus spoke about God (and his kingship), about "eschatology" (the coming of the kingdom or of the Son of man), and about "ethics" (do this, love your neighbor, etc.). Yet almost never are these categories bound together in a single sentence or paragraph. What interconnection exists?

A common answer is that Jesus' eschatology underlies his ethics. "Because the end is near, act thus and so." A word of caution is necessary at this point, however. Albert Schweitzer took up this idea of an "eschatological ethics" and carried it to its logical conclusion.[25] Jesus, he said, expected the end of the world during his lifetime, perhaps during his ministry, certainly right after his death. Therefore, according to Schweitzer, Jesus' ethics were intended just for this brief interim, a period of several weeks or so. Luke 6:30 would be advice for such a time: "Give to every one who begs from you; and of him who takes away your goods do not ask them again." This makes of Jesus' teachings "an ethics for heroes," at the end of the world, but with no permanent value for us since Jesus' day. Most scholars are agreed that Schweitzer's theory of an "ethic for the interim" is a misunderstanding of Jesus' intent. But the theory warns us not to tie ethics too closely to eschatology, for the gospel texts do not always support such an interpretation. In the Sermon on the Mount, e.g., nothing is said about the "world's end" or an "interim." Coming catastrophe is not made the basis for obedience.[26] Jesus' teachings hold good whether the end is near or far away. God's will in the last hour remains what it has always been. There is more to Jesus' teachings than just advice for the "crisis" when Jesus came or at the end of the world.

Another famous answer is that of Rudolf Bultmann. He maintains that what holds Jesus' views of God and eschatology and the healing miracles do. In telling the sea to "be still" (Mark 4:39), Jesus uses exactly the same words as were employed in rebuking a demon (1:25). Likewise the structure of the healing miracle stories can be duplicated in the "creation miracles": there is the situation, the "cure," and the result (see Mark 4:37-38, 39a, 39b-41, the stilling of the storm at sea).

This clue, that nature miracles and healing miracles went together in early Christian thought, points on to what is at stake theologically in these accounts. In the biblical view, man and nature are not separate categories but a unity. It is not man versus nature (and versus God), but God standing over against man-and-nature as their Creator. Thus, when man "falls," creation "falls" too (Genesis 3:14-24); when man is "redeemed," then creation will follow him into the redemptive process too (Romans 8:19-21). So it is that the Bible speaks of a "new heaven and a new earth" as the goal of redemption, and not just of "saved souls." If man and nature are thus a unity, so far as salvation goes, it should not surprise us that flashes of God's power as revealed through Jesus might appear in the inanimate world as well as among the persons of his day.

What often offends modern readers is the concreteness of the "nature miracles" in the gospels. Did Jesus really stop a tempest on the Sea of Galilee? Had he really been sure that there was a coin in the fish's mouth—if there was such a happening? At that point no one, not even the most conservative commentator, can ever offer any convincing or final historical proof. Each interpreter draws the line where he wants, on the grounds of history and faith; his own experience in the world and his awareness of God's power; his own assessment of the sources, "possibility," and congruity with God's know character.

This present study of the miracles can best close (1) by observing how the New Testament evangelists sometimes edited the miracle stories so as to bring out a point which the evangelist wants to leave with his readers; and (2) by looking at a saying from Jesus himself.

Matthew provides several fascinating examples of how an evangelist arranges and shapes miracle stories so as to make a new point for readers of his day. In chapters 8 and 9 Matthew has grouped together no fewer than ten miracle stories, some of which he takes over from various places in Mark, some of which come

out of *Q,* and one of which is unique to Matthew. No doubt
Matthew has grouped these stories together here, just as he has
concentrated teachings of Jesus in chapters 5–7, in order to show
that Jesus is the messiah in deed (chapters 8–9) as well as in
word (chapters 5–7).[46] But he also employed this assembly of
miracle tales to serve another purpose, the fulfillment of an Old
Testament theme. As Matthew comments:

> This was to fulfil what was spoken by the prophet Isaiah, "He took
> our infirmities and bore our diseases." (8:17 = Isaiah 53:4)

Matthew has thus employed the miracles to show what was clear
to Christians after Easter: that Jesus is the Christ who fulfills the
Scripture passages about "the Servant" in Isaiah 53. In this way the
miracles have become direct testimony, after Easter, as to who
Jesus is.[47]

The other example is the way Matthew handles the story of
the storm at sea (8:23-27).[48] All three gospels describe how
Jesus and his companions are endangered by a storm at sea. Matthew alone emphasizes that it is specifically his disciples who have
followed him into the ship. ("Disciple" and "follow" are words
which Matthew stresses in this passage.)[49] The storm is described
by Matthew in terms which normally are employed for the great
apocalyptic "storm" which one day will sweep over the world
(the word for "storm" at 8:24 is the same as that at Mark 13:8
for "earthquake"). The most startling change is in what the disciples say:

> Mark 4:38, "Teacher, do you not care if we perish?"
> Luke 8:24, "Master, Master, we are perishing!"
> Matthew 8:25, *"Save, Lord; we are perishing."*

Jesus is addressed with a term which later Christians employed to
express his heavenly lordship. In fact, the cry, "Save, *Kyrie,"*
sounds as if it could come right out of the church's liturgy. When
we add the fact that from early times the ship was a symbol for
the Christian church, then we begin to get an impression of the
powerful message which Matthew's version leaves. The church is
a storm-tossed ship amid the waves of the world. Even the disciples who loyally follow their lord can grow fearful. But Jesus
Christ is with them. Therefore they need not be afraid, their lord
has all power and authority (compare Matthew 28:18, 20*b*). The
miracle has become a lesson for disciples in the church after the
resurrection.

That is the way an evangelist uses the miracle stories. But what of the historical Jesus? Even John the Baptist was puzzled by the deeds and words of Jesus. Hence John asked, "Are you he who is to come, or shall we look for another of a different sort?" Jesus gave an enigmatic answer (Matthew 11:4-6, par. Luke 7:22-23):

> Go and tell John what you hear and see:
> the blind receive their sight, and the lame walk;
> lepers are cleansed, and the deaf hear, and the dead
>   are raised up;
> and the poor have good news preached to them.
> And blessed is he who takes no offense at me.

These words point plainly to Jesus' message of good news and to his miracles. To understand the meaning, we must know that the phrases about the blind, the lame, and the deaf, and about the good tidings for the afflicted come out of the Book of Isaiah (35: 5-6; 61:1), where they are pictures of the coming age when God will restore his glory in the world. Jesus' words and deeds thus unite in the claim that God's kingdom is coming soon. The message is being proclaimed, the lightning is flashing.[50]

"But give us *proof* of this," men kept asking. Jesus refused any such signs. "No sign shall be given," he replied, "—except the sign of the prophet Jonah." What is that? According to Matthew, it is the resurrection of Jesus (Matthew 12:40):

> For as Jonah was three days and three nights in the belly of the whale, so will the Son of man be three days and three nights in the heart of the earth.

But that is a sign which applies only after the resurrection. Luke has something different from this Matthean interpretation. Luke says simply—and surely this, rather than the Matthean version, is the voice of the historical Jesus (Luke 11:30):

> For as Jonah became a sign to the men of Nineveh [for they repented at the preaching of Jonah], so will the Son of man be to this generation.

The sign—is Jesus himself, and his preaching. Occasionally the scene is illumined by the lightning-flash of mighty deeds, but this is so only for those who look with faith. To other men the miracles simply obscure their vision even more; they attribute them to Beelzebul. Who *is* this Jesus, and what does the coming of the kingdom he announces mean to men?

The New Way of Life under the Reign of God

The preaching of Jesus, the parables he told, and the miracles he worked all proclaim a single theme: the coming of the kingdom of God. That means the coming of God himself, in salvation and judgment. Through the deeds and words of this man from Nazareth, God's sovereign reign and power are being set forth for men. There is a gracious offer, the possibility of a new relationship with God. Yet all this calls for response, as the parables make clear. Life is offered, but a new way of life is demanded on the part of those who become disciples. Forgiveness is announced, but repentance is called for too. Salvation is "in the air" and "on the way." However the very presence of Jesus' message also brings a crisis; it warns of a judgment that is taking place now, as well as of a future judgment.

We must now ask what this proclamation by Jesus meant to men of his day in terms of their daily lives and their future fates. What was the "ethics" of Jesus like? How did one "respond" to his message and then how did one live, during that period when Jesus was preaching in Palestine?

Of course, we know that after the resurrection the proper response to the Christian message was to repent and be baptized and then to live by faith in the risen lord, as a part of his body (I Corinthians 12:12-27), the church (Acts 2:38, 44-47; 6:7). But before the cross, during Jesus' earthly ministry, there was no such "pattern of response." To a preacher like John the Baptist one responded with repentance, baptism, and reform of morals (Luke 3:3, 10-14). But it is far from certain that Jesus baptized during his ministry.[1] There was no "church" to which to become attached. A small band of disciples followed him about, but Jesus did not ask even that of everyone; some he enjoined to stay where they were (cf. Mark 5:19-20), to watch, to wait, to testify to what the Lord had done for them.[2] But *how* were they to live, with what manner of life? Was Jesus a "reformer of morals"? A teacher of ethics? We are likely to understand Jesus' teaching to his contemporaries on these topics (and its meaning for us) only if we first ask how people during this earthly ministry looked on him.

Jesus as Teacher and Prophet

At this point we are not asking how Jesus came to be regarded, after the resurrection, as "Lord and Christ." We are not inquiring how he spoke of himself, nor even how a few of his closest followers may have spoken about him in exceptional moments during the ministry (on these matters, see chapter 9), but only about how friends and foes generally thought of him in Galilee and Jerusalem in A.D. 29-30. To this question there is a clear answer. During his earthly ministry Jesus was looked upon by those who heard and saw him as a prophet and a rabbi (that is, teacher). They spoke of him in precisely these terms, and the gospels, even though written at a later time by Christians who accorded Jesus much more exalted titles, preserve these descriptions.

To some people it may be somewhat disappointing that Jesus was thought of as "only a teacher" during his ministry, or that certain scholars paint him as "just a prophet," reserving his other titles for the time after Easter. This sounds like a "least-common-denominator" Jesus; he is "reduced" to rabbi and prophet. But in part any disappointment is assuaged when it is discovered what these terms meant to people of Jesus' day. For they give Jesus a significance far greater than might be supposed for the period prior to the cross.

It has already been noted how Jesus' mighty deeds hinted of a link between himself and the kingdom. He worked "by the Spirit of God." His preaching and his own person together were "the sign of Jonah." Hence it was that people began to look on Jesus as himself somehow connected with the coming salvation of God which he was announcing. They used the two terms "teacher" and "prophet" to describe the impression which Jesus made on them. Though we may not suspect it at first glance, these titles do, in fact, do justice to a connection between Jesus and the coming of the kingdom.

First let us ask what the term "prophet" would have meant to Jesus' contemporaries. The report that was going the rounds after one of his miracles was, "A great prophet has arisen among us" (Luke 7:16). People said he was "a prophet, like one of the prophets of old" or even like Elijah (Mark 6:15). The disciples summed up popular opinion by saying that Jesus was being likened to Elijah, Jeremiah, and John the Baptist—all of them prophets (Matthew 16:14). A passing remark by a Pharisee (at

Luke 7:39) accords with this outlook: Jesus is presumed to be a prophet. Adversaries had to tread cautiously because the multitudes in Jerusalem regarded Jesus as a prophet (Matthew 21:46). As if to bear this out, the Passion narrative once presents Jesus being mocked as a prophet (Matthew 26:68). Compare also the opinion of disciples on the Emmaus Road, after Jesus' death but before they know of the resurrection: Jesus "was a prophet mighty in deed and word before God and all the people" (Luke 24:11). Jesus, therefore, seems to have been widely regarded as a prophet from the Lord.[3]

But there is more to the picture. To some, he was not just "*a* prophet" but "*the* prophet." The crowds at Jerusalem on "Palm Sunday" hailed him as "the prophet, Jesus from Nazareth of Galilee" (Matthew 21:11). This phrase does not mean simply "a well-known prophet out of Nazareth," but *the* prophet "who comes in the name of the Lord" (21:9). This same phrase occurs several times in John's Gospel, at 1:21; 6:14; 7:40; and 7:52.[4] Some people were saying, "This is really *the* prophet" (7:40).

To appreciate the importance of these references, we must grasp two things. The one is that Jews of Jesus' day believed to a considerable degree that prophecy, inspired by God, had ceased but that it would return at the coming of the "new age." Already in the Old Testament there are passages about the cessation of prophecy (see Zechariah 13:2-6 and Psalm 74:9). The hope for its revival is depicted in passages like Malachi 4:5-6 (the closing words in the Old Testament canon of Christians, that Elijah will come) and Joel 2:28-29 (quoted by Peter at Pentecost as a proof that the new age had come, Acts 2:17-18). A vivid reflection of this dearth of prophets and prophecy is the fact that when Judas Maccabeus recaptured the temple at Jerusalem from the pagans, the defiled altar stones were stored away "until a prophet should come to tell them what to do with them" (I Maccabees 4:45-46).[5] At Qumran, the sect's leader was sometimes regarded as a prophet, but here too there was expectation of a future prophet who would come.[6] Generally Palestine was waiting for a "new time" when God would send prophets. The impression made by vivid spokesmen for God, like John the Baptist and Jesus, is partly explicable against this background.

The other point is that Deuteronomy 18:15 had promised through Moses that in the last days "the Lord your God will raise up for you a prophet like me from among you." This hope had become very precious over the years when it was believed there were no prophets and the Holy Spirit was no longer active in Israel. Men were looking not just for *a* prophet but for *the* prophet, that is, the prophet like Moses. It is precisely this hope for "the prophet like Moses" which Jesus fulfilled, according to one of Peter's sermons after the resurrection (Acts 3:22-26).

We get a picture of how intense this hope was in Jesus' day from certain references in Josephus. A man named Theudas (see Acts 5:36), who claimed to be a prophet, said that he would repeat the "miracle of the Exodus" by dividing the waters of the Jordan in two (*Antiquities* 20:97-102). An Egyptian who gained a reputation as a prophet (cf. Acts 21:38) got thousands of people from Jerusalem to follow him out into the wilderness, where he said he would work redemption.[7]

People thus hoped "the prophet" would bring God's new age of redemption. When Jews applied this term to Jesus, it was a title of no mean importance. They were thinking of him as the one who might bring age-old promises to pass, with the inauguration of the new age.

There is one ominous note to add. Prophets in Old Testament times had often been rejected, scorned, and even put to death. Jesus knew how many of these prophetic predecessors had been martyred. According to a *Q* passage, Jesus once said to the Jews that God sent prophets "whom your fathers killed"—a whole series of them, from Abel to Zechariah; then, speaking as a prophet himself, Jesus warned that "the blood of all the prophets . . . may be required of this generation" (Luke 11:47-51, par. Matthew 23:29-36).[8] On another occasion, as he was making his way toward the Holy City, he remarked ironically, "It cannot be that a prophet should perish away from Jerusalem" (Luke 13:33). "Jerusalem," he laments, "killing the prophets and stoning those who are sent to you" (13:34, par. Matthew 23:37).[9] Perhaps even the words at Mark 10:45, about giving "his life as a ransom for many," are to be understood against this background of *prophet-martyrs*.[10]

It is possible that Jesus himself may have thought of his role in just such terms.[11] True, no saying of his ever calls him a prophet directly (Mark 6:4 is a proverb which he quotes). But sayings like Luke 13:33 imply that he regarded himself as one of this venerable company of prophet-martyrs. John's Gospel clearly describes him as *the* prophet, as does the sermon at Acts 3:22-26. Curiously, later Christianity paid little heed to this theme. As the church became more "clericalized," Jesus was far more often thought of as "priest" or "king" than as "prophet." But for the earliest Christians, as well as during his lifetime, Jesus was regarded as fulfilling a prophet's mission and at times the not insignificant role of *"the* prophet."

The story is similar, if less dramatic, with the term *"teacher."*[12] The word is used almost fifty times in the gospels. Over forty of these refer to Jesus, and almost thirty of them are cases where people address him with the term (e.g., Mark 9:17; note also 9:5 [RSV note]). Unquestionably, they regarded him as a teacher. One of Mark's first descriptions of Jesus tells how "on the sabbath he entered the synagogue and taught" (1:21). In a Matthean summary of Jesus' work in Galilee, teaching is actually mentioned ahead of preaching and healing (Matthew 4:23). Some Christians today have an innate suspicion of any picture of Jesus as a teacher. They fear that it will make him "merely a teacher," like Confucius or some philosopher. Their immediate reaction is to say, "He was much more." True as this may be for faith since the cross and Easter, the fact of the matter is that Jesus was unquestionably regarded as a teacher during his lifetime, and the New Testament gospels have faithfully preserved this emphasis even after the resurrection.

"Jesus the teacher" must be viewed, however, squarely within the context of teaching in the Judaism of Jesus' day. The word which the New Testament applies to Jesus—*didaskalos,* "teacher" —is also employed of John the Baptist (Luke 3:12), Nicodemus (John 3:10), and the Jewish teachers in the temple (Luke 2:46). Jesus is sometimes specifically called "rabbi" (John 1:38; the Hebrew word involved here meant "great" or "exalted one," and was often applied to teachers).[13] In form and content, Jesus taught much as did the rabbis of the day.[14] He used parables, he expounded Old Testament passages, he did much of his teaching in synagogues. Like the rabbis, he had disciples. To the crowds he appeared as another among the many teachers in the land. Men came to him with personal problems and questions about the biblical law (see Mark 12:14, 32; Luke 12:13).

This background in Judaism for the term "teacher" is very different from the notion dominant in the Greek world. To the Greeks a teacher was one who develops a pupil's intellect or draws out through systematic instruction some skill which is there by nature. In the Old Testament, teaching concerns not just the mind or intellect but the *whole man,* and has above all to do with presenting God's will as it has been revealed. Mark 12:28-34, where Jesus answers the question, "Which commandment is the first of all?" provides an insight into what "teaching" meant in a Jewish environment; here the law is applied to the whole man—all his heart, soul, mind, and strength—and the teaching involves proper exposition of Scripture. The teacher is a spokesman for the Lord "who knows the thoughts of man"; he expounds the words of God who "teaches men knowledge" (Psalm 94:10-11).[15]

Against this background it must be asked, Did Jesus' teaching differ from that of his many predecessors in Israel and his Jewish contemporaries? Often it is difficult to discover any difference in content. At times Jesus gives the impression of being a "teacher of the wisdom of the Lord," very much like earlier sages, and even for the early church he was God's wisdom (I Corinthians 1:30) and the teacher of true knowledge (Matthew 23:10, NEB; Colossians 2:2-3). It is no solution, in a quest for some "uniqueness" about Jesus in this area, to claim that he taught such wisdom in public but "unique doctrines" in secret, for the gospels scarcely attribute any such body of esoteric teachings to him. A further fact to be reckoned with is the point that Jesus' ethical teachings did not by themselves cause his fate. Conceivably Jesus might have set up a "school" where the finer points of interpretation of the law were discussed—in which case he might have lived out his life in tranquility and honor, like Hillel. Yet Jesus, who appears as a teacher, was crucified.

To some extent the explanation lies in the fact that (1) Jesus, while he still made the Old Testament law his starting point, went beyond this and claimed to voice the will of God. In this way he often sharply criticized current teaching (and teachers) in Palestine. The way he "radicalized"[16] and heightened the intent of the Old Testament earned him enemies. (2) He related his teachings to the kingdom message which his preaching and miracles set forth.[17] The "ethics" of Jesus assumes the nearness of God and his sovereign power; this context for his teaching distinguished

him from his contemporaries and even from John the Baptist.
(3) Jesus refused to intellectualize his teachings, as some of the
rabbis did. Their emphasis on study seemed at times to make
obedient doing secondary to study,[18] and the complexities of the
law overawed many a man. Jesus made his message speak to the
"common man" in terms of his daily life, without hedging it in
with multitudes of legal details. (4) Finally, Jesus' own person
seems to have made a difference. It is not always *what* he says that
differs but *who* says it that makes it mean something more. Here
speaks the man who knows God as Father and sets forth the
Father's will with absolute assurance. Men "were astonished at his
teaching, for he taught them as one who had authority, and not
as the scribes" (Mark 1:22). This "authority" which marked his
preaching and mighty deeds, and which some scholars regard as a
hallmark of the historical Jesus, also appears in Jesus' teachings
at times.[19]

It is not surprising that Jesus came to be regarded as "greater
than Solomon" (Luke 11:31), as "*the* teacher," the one teacher
who reveals God's will (Matthew 23:8; 26:18). When he spoke,
it was "firsthand"—for God—and men listened. What did he
say?

The Development of the Sermons of Jesus

A number of problems make it difficult for readers today to
discover and understand the teachings of Jesus as they are embodied in his sayings and sermons.

One is the fact that they are scattered in a seemingly disorgan-
ized way throughout four different gospels. They seem to have an
"occasional" nature, reporting helter-skelter what Jesus said on
this occasion or that. Often they consist of single, isolated sentences, given without context, or worse yet, in different contexts
in different gospels.[20] Only at times are they grouped into collections or arranged by categories about a given theme.

But this last fact points to a second difficulty. These teachings,
like all the Jesus-material, were passed along for several decades
by word of mouth and then assembled in written collections (Q)
for several more decades before the evangelists recorded them for
us. There is every probability that the sayings were revised, "re-
audienced," and reapplied in this transmission process from Jesus
to the written gospels.[21] These initial difficulties, of scattered, "oc-

casional" sayings and changes and reworkings as they were passed along, can be seen plainly in the material in that richest collection of Jesus' teachings, the Sermon on the Mount (Matthew 5–7), and its much shorter parallel in Luke, the Sermon on the Plain (6:17-49).

Third, there is difficulty regarding what is to be considered the central theme in Jesus' teachings. Though we have already explained how the kingdom of God was the overall subject of Jesus' message, other themes, particularly from his ethical teaching, have been stressed by some. One could say, he taught about God and about man ("theology" and "anthropology" or "existence"), but such terms are too general; *how* did he look on God and man and how did he relate them? It has therefore been argued that Jesus' teachings centered in God's providence.[22] True, he talked about how God cares for men, as well as for the birds of the air and the flowers of the field (e.g., Matthew 6:25-34), and a great deal of his teaching derives from the fact that men need not be anxious when they know such a God. But "providence" as a theme makes Jesus sound more like a Greek philosopher than a prophet who proclaimed the kingdom, and an emphasis on the "security" of faith can blunt the frequent demand upon men also found in Jesus' teachings. Still others would stress love as the heart of Jesus' ethical instruction.[23] Jesus did call for love for God and love for man. Love sums up the law (Matthew 22:34-40). There is no case where love is not commanded. This emphasis on love has obvious appeal today—indeed, a "demand to love" has become almost too commonplace as a theme. With reference to Jesus' teachings, it must be asked, however, whether "love," important as it is, covers all that Jesus touched on. Is it perhaps a modern tendency to try to subsume all under "love"?

We have already made clear that Jesus' ethical teachings must be seen in association with his general message about the kingdom. Teaching is not to be separated from preaching. The "ethics" assumes the proclamation of the kingdom. What is demanded of men assumes the action of God and his gift of the kingdom— that is, of himself, his power and presence. This general condition is made clear in the summary verse at Matthew 4:17: "Repent, *for* the kingdom of heaven is at hand." The ethical response of repentance follows because the reign of God has come. Jesus' ethics are for the men of the kingdom.

While the proclamation of the reign of God must be assumed
as the setting and basis for Jesus' ethical teaching, it may be
pointed out that a connection between the kingdom and ethics is
not made in so many words in every specific case. He does not
regularly say, "Do this because the kingdom is at hand." We must
infer such a setting.

There is a fourth difficulty, about which most people do not
pause to think: while the kingdom is the assumption which underlies all of Jesus' teachings, how, one must ask, are the individual
themes of his teaching linked together?[24] Jesus spoke about God
(and his kingship), about "eschatology" (the coming of the kingdom or of the Son of man), and about "ethics" (do this, love
your neighbor, etc.). Yet almost never are these categories bound
together in a single sentence or paragraph. What interconnection
exists?

A common answer is that Jesus' eschatology underlies his ethics.
"Because the end is near, act thus and so." A word of caution is
necessary at this point, however. Albert Schweitzer took up this
idea of an "eschatological ethics" and carried it to its logical conclusion.[25] Jesus, he said, expected the end of the world during his
lifetime, perhaps during his ministry, certainly right after his
death. Therefore, according to Schweitzer, Jesus' ethics were intended just for this brief interim, a period of several weeks or so.
Luke 6:30 would be advice for such a time: "Give to every one
who begs from you; and of him who takes away your goods do
not ask them again." This makes of Jesus' teachings "an ethics for
heroes," at the end of the world, but with no permanent value for
us since Jesus' day. Most scholars are agreed that Schweitzer's
theory of an "ethic for the interim" is a misunderstanding of
Jesus' intent. But the theory warns us not to tie ethics too closely
to eschatology, for the gospel texts do not always support such an
interpretation. In the Sermon on the Mount, e.g., nothing is said
about the "world's end" or an "interim." Coming catastrophe is
not made the basis for obedience.[26] Jesus' teachings hold good
whether the end is near or far away. God's will in the last hour
remains what it has always been. There is more to Jesus' teachings
than just advice for the "crisis" when Jesus came or at the end
of the world.

Another famous answer is that of Rudolf Bultmann. He maintains that what holds Jesus' views of God and eschatology and

ethics together is the view of "existence" involved. The understanding of human existence can be said to be the same in what
Jesus teaches about God the Father, the crisis of "kingdom come,"
and the ethical demand on men. But the trouble is, again, that
the texts themselves in the New Testament do not make either
this connection or the "concept of existence" explicit.[27]

Perhaps the best answer to these problems of what is "central"
and how Jesus' various teachings are linked together is simply to
say that at this point, as in so much else in his work as teacher,
Jesus was conforming to the style of Jewish teachers of the day.[28]
As the words of the rabbis have come down to us, they are often
a mixture of parables, sayings, debates, and comments on comments. They, too, are likely to skip back and forth from the "doctrine of God" to "moral teachings," to remarks about the future
age to come, to interpretations of the law.

Jesus' teachings, then, are not systematic in arrangement, nor
are they comprehensive in content, covering each topic exhaus-
tively. They assume Jesus' view of God and God's eschatological
action in bringing the kingdom in the near future. Underlying
them is a common understanding of man's existence. But these
things will not be explicitly stated in each instance. His teachings
spoke to men in specific, current situations, but they did not necessarily have value only for that moment; they continue to have
validity beyond any "interim"—after the resurrection and, with
adjustment, even for new and changed situations in the present
day.

To anticipate one other general question: if it is asked where
Jesus' ethical teachings make their greatest contribution or have
their clearest "insight," the answer must be that they focus, constantly and as no contemporary or prior teachings had, on the
will of God. They often begin with the earlier formulations in
the Old Testament law about the will of God, but they constantly
put these into even sharper and more radical terms. Or they transcend rabbinic debate about what a command means, or go back
behind the law's statement to the will of the Creator. For example,
when the Pharisee asked for an exposition of Moses, Jesus went
back behind Moses to "the beginning of creation" and the will of
God (Mark 10:2-9). This will of God is set forth by him with
authority, the authority attached to revelation. "You have heard it
said by them of old, . . . but *I* say to you. . . ." The will of God

addresses men with an authority and absoluteness which asks not "something" of him but for the man himself. It strikes down all attempts to distinguish intentions and actions or to play off against each other "willing" and "doing," for act and intent are both involved. "God does not demand this or that of me; he demands me."

This sort of ethical teaching is embodied especially in the two great "sermons" in the Synoptic Gospels, the one on "the Plain" (Luke) and the other on "the Mount" (Matthew). Next to the parables, these are doubtless the best known, most important—and most misunderstood—of the words of Jesus. Mahatma Gandhi thought that the whole message of Jesus was contained in the Sermon on the Mount.[29] The historian Gordon Rupp is nearer to the truth when he contends that "the theology of the Sermon on the Mount is far more intricate than that of the Nicene and Athanasian Creeds."[30] For the part of Jesus' message which is contained in these sermons has had a complex history and has been variously interpreted.

It will help to clear the ground by noting briefly some of these theories of interpretation.[31] Schweitzer, as we have seen, made them "martial law" for a crisis—without any ongoing meaning for normal times. Others have taken them to have just the opposite import: these sermons are to be literally obeyed, as the laws or blueprint for society in every age. Matthew 5:33-37 enjoins, "Do not swear [an oath] at all"; hence one does not take an oath in court. Gandhi tended in this direction. So did Francis of Assisi, the Anabaptists of Luther's Day, and the Russian novelist, Count Leo Tolstoy. These people believed they could run their lives and even the world on the basis of the Sermon on the Mount. They supposed that ultimately men could fulfill its demands. But of one New Testament scholar who took this view, Rudolf Bultmann once asked the penetrating question, "Who ever fulfilled the Sermon on the Mount? Will [Professor X] claim that he fulfills the demands of the Sermon on the Mount? Or does he assume that some other man does? Then why not?"[32] Of course, no man ever has. And if everyone tried to live life according to its precepts, society would be wrecked. Police, law courts, oaths, all instruments of justice would be ignored.[33] Yet some people long for such a "utopia" (literally, "no-place"). Tolstoy lamented that if it weren't for his wife or children or family ties, he might have lived literally according to the Sermon on the Mount—thus blaming others for his failure—and toward the end of his life he left all such ties in an attempt to practice his theory.

One result of such attempts at literal obedience is that, in light of Matthew 5:21-28 (the words about not even hating the brother or lusting in the heart), we must end up confessing that we have sinned; in the words of Romans 3:12, "No one does good, not even one." Who can claim to have loved enemies and persecutors, the way Matthew 5:44 demands? That brings us to another view of the sermon: as a standard we can never fulfill, it simply makes us aware of our sins. It convicts us of our sins and shows the need for a savior, as Paul says.[34] The trouble with this view, long dear to many Protestants, is that the sermon itself never speaks of "unfulfillability." There is no indication that Jesus did not intend his words to be taken positively, any more than the text suggests that Jesus intended his words to be a blueprint for Palestinian (or American) society.

Other escapes from this dilemma have been sought. Roman Catholics have traditionally solved it by saying that these strong precepts such as Matthew 5:30 (about cutting off whatever causes one to sin) are not for all Christians but only for the "spiritually elite"; the sermon's words hold for monks and saints, the average Christian can rest content with the lesser requirements of the church. Again, there is not a word of this in the Sermon itself.

Yet another solution—and many find it congenial—is to regard the Sermon as "an ethic of intention." It tells us the intent of God's will, without meaning that we must take the precepts literally. "It tells us, not what we must do, but what we must be." "Attitudes, not acts." "Direction, not directions."[35] These are ways of putting this view. Matthew 5:32, "Every one who divorces his wife, except on the ground of unchastity, makes her an adulteress," is taken to proclaim the sanctity of marriage, not to legislate a rule on divorce. Such interpretation makes the sermon usable today, but runs the danger of watering it down to harmless platitudes.

It may be noted that each interpretation of the Sermon presumes a certain view of Jesus:

Schweitzer's "interim-ethic": Jesus = an apocalyptist;

A law to be fulfilled: Jesus = a "new Moses," a teacher of Torah;

An unfulfillable demand: Jesus = a preacher who convicts us of our sins;

A "second-stage" ethic for the elite: Jesus = a "retreat master" for the "spiritual development" of monks;

An ethic of intent: Jesus = a molder of character.

All these views cannot be right. Some, like the "monastic" view, seem contrary to the general spirit of the New Testament. Others get off the track when they add the word "only" or claim the sermon is "only law" or "only direction." No single view suffices for the whole sermon.[36]

The reason lies in the fact that the Sermon on the Mount (or Plain) is not a single piece but rather a remarkable construction of material from the Jesus-tradition. As such, it calls for careful analysis. Anyone who has examined Matthew 5–7 and Luke 6 with care is aware of this composite nature from several obvious facts. For one thing, there are sections which reflect Jesus' basic message; yet other sections are more commonplace and find parallels in Jewish teachings of the day. Even the Golden Rule, by which some set such store, is found in Rabbi Hillel (20 B.C.), in a negative form:

> What is hateful to you, do not do to anyone else. The whole law is contained in this sentence. All the rest is only commentary.[37] (Cf. Matthew 7:12)

Then, too, Matthew's Sermon on the Mount is obviously an expanded version of Luke 6:20-49, the "Sermon on the Plain." And some of the material with which Matthew expands Luke's sermon is found in Luke in quite different contexts,[38] while others of Matthew's additions bear the stamp of Matthew's own outlook and are unique to him (e.g., 5:17-20).

From all that we have previously learned about the Jesus-material, the following are probable conclusions about how the "Sermon on the Mount" in Matthew 5–7 has grown up.

(1) Matthew has added certain verses and phrases to an existing sermon, just as he did with the collection of parables in Matthew 13 and with the Lord's Prayer. One need read no more than a few verses in either sermon to see that Matthew has such additions.

MATTHEW	LUKE
Blessed are the poor *in spirit*, ...	Blessed are you poor, ...
(5:3)	(6:20)

Blessed are those who hunger and thirst *for righteousness,* . . . . (5:6)	Blessed are you that hunger now, ... (6:21)
Seek first his kingdom *and his right-eousness,* . . . . (6:33)	Seek his kingdom, ... (12:31)

(2) Luke 6:20-49 preserves an earlier form of this sermon, perhaps as it was already in the Q document. But (3) the Lucan form is also a combination of a number of sayings and brief units from Jesus which seemingly were separately transmitted in the oral period. This can be seen by observing how the second person plural is used for a few verses, then the second singular, then the plural, then the third person, and so on. The easiest way to prove this to oneself is to read through the King James Version and observe the use of "ye" (second person plural) and "thou" and "thee":

Luke 6:20-28, "ye"
    6:29-30, "thee"
    6:31-38, "ye"
    6:39-40, third person
    6:41-42, "thou."

We have here a series of separate teachings, not a continuous and single "sermon."

(4) Behind these separate teachings and the sermon compilations stands Jesus, the teacher. He said such things in his teachings, though on many separate occasions. The early church and the evangelists gathered these teachings in the two forms in which they now exist, to provide a powerful "sermon of the Messiah."

It is possible to add that these collections of Jesus-material in Q and Luke 6 and Matthew 5–7 were doubtless used for catechetical purposes. Here was Jesus the teacher speaking to the early church. One may add, too, that Jesus no doubt actually did give "sermons" in the course of his ministry, and that one may even have been on a "level place" (Luke 6:17), another on a little hill (Matthew 5:1). The two compilations which the evangelists give us do include examples of things he said. But one may not suppose that they are tape-recorded versions of one or two continuous sermons. Gloege writes unequivocally and correctly of the Sermon on the Mount, "Jesus never delivered it as it stands."[39] Calvin, four hundred years ago, recognized the point. Modern biblical study, on the part of both Protestant and Roman Catholic scholars, enables us to picture thus the development of the sermons:

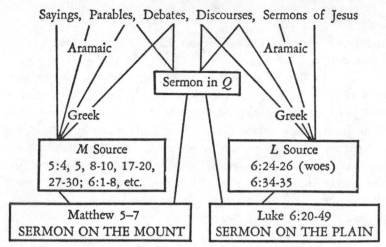

DEVELOPMENT OF THE SERMONS
ATTRIBUTED TO JESUS IN MATTHEW AND LUKE

It cannot be assumed with Q material, of course, that each item included in the sermon in Q has ended up in Matthew's sermon or Luke's, or that each item in the sermons provided by Matthew and Luke was originally in an earlier sermon. But the chart does help depict general lines of development, though each saying or unit of material must be traced out along its own lines of transmission, so far as the sources permit.

The Sermon on the Plain

Of the two sermons provided in the Synoptic Gospels, Luke's version is more likely closer to an actual sermon of Jesus—though even the finished product in Luke owes much to the early church. Luke 6:20-49, after the descriptive setting by Luke in verses 17-19, may be outlined thus:

(1) Four beatitudes (6:20-23; Matthew has nine).

(2) Four woes (6:24-26; Matthew's rough parallel occurs in chapter 23, the woes against the Pharisees).

(3) Love for enemies (6:27-36; cf. Matthew 5:39-42, 44-48).

(4) Against judging other men (6:37-42; cf. Matthew 7:1-5).

(5) Fruitbearing as a test of goodness (6:43-46; cf. Matthew 7:16-21 and 12:33-35).

(6) ˙Be hearers and doers of the word (6:47-49; cf. Matthew 7:24-27, the conclusion of the sermon).

Much of the sermon is quite familiar. "Do good to those who hate you. . . . Forgive. . . . The good man out of the good treasure of his heart produces good. . . . Hear my words and do them." In interpreting and applying these words, one must remember, however, that "something had preceded" these imperatives. Those who heard knew that before he set demands before them Jesus had first taught them, "God has forgiven you, God who cares for men has shown you mercy, he has done good for you."[40]

Just in case this Gospel setting for Jesus' exposition of God's will is not clear, note how the sermon, in Luke as well as in Matthew, begins with "beatitudes."[41] These are statements about how blessed (or "happy" in a religious sense) are those to whom these words are directed. To the disciples Jesus said (Luke 6:20-23):

"Blessed are you poor, for yours is the kingdom of God.
"Blessed are you that hunger now, for you shall be satisfied.
"Blessed are you that weep now, for you shall laugh.
"Blessed are you when men hate you, . . . your reward is great in heaven. . . ."

We miss the point of these verses unless we see them as prophetic promises of salvation from God. Poor, hungry, sorrowful, hated—that describes man's situation now. Fulfillment, joy, reward, the kingdom—that describes what God offers. Each statement might be turned around to read, heaven will reward you, God will bring joy and fullness, he will give you the kingdom (cf. Luke 12:32).[42] The most surprising thing about these promises is that Jesus views them as resulting in a present blessedness. "Blessed *are* you. . . ." Note especially the opening words of the sermon: "Yours *is* the kingdom of God."

Because God has blessed men with the kingdom—the gift of salvation and himself—he can address the men of the kingdom with an ethic of the will of God.

The Sermon on the Mount: The New Life and the New Righteousness

It is Matthew, with his more richly developed presentation of Jesus' teaching and his expanded sermon, who brings out most fully the disciples' new way of life. To men who know the dawning of the kingdom, as a time of salvation and of the coming of God, Matthew presents the "absoluteness" of Jesus' demand, with utmost stringency. Matthew heightens to the greatest possible de-

gree the necessity for "fruitbearing." He does this especially
through the use of key words like "righteousness" and "perfection." At the same time Matthew's treatment illustrates how early
Christians sought to respond to the spirit of the risen Christ in
adapting the ethical demand of the historical Jesus to the situation
in which they found themselves—after the resurrection, but as still
erring human beings in the world. Matthew thus shows us both
the rigor in Jesus' ethic of the will of God and a certain compassion for disciples living amid the depressing grays and blacks of
human existence in a sinful world.

We must begin any survey of Matthew's Sermon on the Mount
by reminding ourselves that, both in the original setting of the
teachings in Jesus' lifetime and their use in the church of Matthew's day, we are dealing with an ethic which has certain characteristics.

(1) It is a disciple's ethic. This means that it is not directed
to the world as a blueprint for running governments or welfare
programs, but to disciples whose sins have been forgiven, who
live under God's reign, for their personal relationships. Because it
speaks to disciples, the sermon can base its appeal on what they
know of the heavenly Father (5:48). It can therefore move from
what they *are,* by God's grace—"You *are* the salt of the earth"
(5:13); "You *are* the light of the world" (5:14)—to what they
ought to do in view of this new situation in life, namely, do "good
works" which proclaim glory to the Father in heaven (5:16). The
rest of the sermon unfolds example after example of what the
disciple's new way of life may be like, in view of the nearness of
God and coming of his salvation and because of the present and
future blessedness which his beatitude-promises provide.

(2) However, Jesus' teachings, even as compiled in the Sermon
on the Mount, must be reckoned a defective ethic. It has "holes"
in it, great areas of human life which are not touched. True, it
touches on hate, lust, retaliation, and anxiety; it deals with sex,
divorce, truthfulness, prayer, charity, and open-mindedness toward
the other fellow. But vast problem areas of modern life, where
moderns might wish Jesus had spoken an authoritative word, never
entered the horizon of speaker or hearers in first-century Palestine.
Indeed, many of the problems of Jesus' own day are not treated
in the sermons or anywhere else in Jesus' teachings. There is nothing about slavery or private property. To modern minds, the most

glaring omission is the lack of any "social ethics" or concern with communal problems which arise out of social life. Yet one cannot prove that Jesus lacked interest in such matters; it is simply that in his situation, as a subject in a minor Roman province, with no say in government, and with other interests of his own, he did not prescribe a "program" for such matters.

Modern-day followers are not, of course, thereby exempted from wrestling with such problems, but they cannot solve their problems merely by citing a verse from Jesus. If that seems to leave them to their own resources—plus the insights of the Holy Spirit and the "mind of Christ"—then they are simply in the same situation as Paul and all the other Christians after the resurrection. For in dealing with some of the thorny problems confronting him at Corinth, Paul had to confess that he had no commandment from the Lord, either of the earthly Jesus or the risen Christ (cf. I Corinthians 7:6, 12, 25; contrast 7:10); but he did speak as one who had the Spirit of God (I Corinthians 7:40; 7:25; 2:16). All this means that even the Sermon on the Mount is a defective, incomplete ethic, not covering all phases of life today. Christians since the resurrection have had to construct an ethics for personal life and society by drawing on far more than just the words of the historical Jesus.

(3) Dare it be suggested, on the basis of these facts, that in Matthew's Gospel one can already see the moral and social teachings of Christianity as a developing ethic? Certainly this was true for Paul. In new situations in Corinth, Ephesus, and elsewhere, he had to develop the ethical implications of the Gospel and of the will of God as expressed in the Old Testament and in the Jesus-material. The same holds true for believers today. Christians, individually and in groups, must seek to work out what the Gospel and God's will mean for personal existence and society as they face new problems like a world population explosion, a hydrogen bomb holocaust, and international cooperation for interplanetary exploration. And it was true for Matthew and the Christians for whom his gospel was composed in the eighties or nineties A.D.

Recall what Matthew was seeking to do: to take the teachings which Jesus had spoken sixty years before, in specific situations in Palestine, and make them address people in other lands and situations after the resurrection. The ethics of the men of the kingdom had somehow to be made applicable for members of the church.

The demand for response made on the disciples who heeded Jesus' tidings that the kingdom was coming had to be made just as vivid for believers in Matthew's day. Jesus spoke of a good tree bringing forth good fruit. Matthew, who knew that by God's goodness salvation had now come, wanted to make clear that Christian disciples should bring forth fruit ("good works") in their lives.

Professor Jeremias has coined a phrase which links Jesus' message and Matthew's concern (it is a theme also found in Paul, cf. Galatians 5:6); he employs the phrase "living faith" or "faith which is lived out in life."[43] Just as Jesus looked for faith as a response to his miracles,[44] so also with the ethical teachings. They spell out for the life of the disciple the will of God which he has come to know in faith. Application, in life, by faith, of God's will, opens the way to a fruitfully developing ethic.[45] Out of good and honest hearts, disciples seek to do God's will to his glory among men.

Discovering how Matthew gets across a defective but developed ethic for disciples in the Sermon on the Mount is a fascinating area which modern biblical scholarship has helped make clear. We have already noted how Matthew groups together the teachings of Jesus in chapters 5-7 and ten miracles of Jesus in chapters 8-9; if we read the chapters together, as Matthew intended, his arrangement keeps us from making Jesus "just a teacher" or "just a miracle-worker." We are further forced to see how both these activities relate to the kingdom when we observe the introductory and closing phrases which Matthew employs to set off the block of five chapters. At 4:23-25 and 9:35-38 he uses some of the same phrases (italicized below) to tie all this together within a neat framework:

> 4:23 "He went about all Galilee, *teaching in their synagogues and preaching the gospel of the kingdom and healing every disease and every infirmity* among the people." (Great crowds followed him, 4:24-25.)
>
> > Chapters 5-7, the Sermon on the Mount—Jesus the Teacher, depicted as "the Messiah of the word."
> >
> > Chapters 8-9, ten miracle stories—Jesus the Prophet who works the mighty deeds of God's new age, depicted as "the Messiah of the deed."
>
> 9:35 "Jesus went about all the cities and villages, *teaching in their synagogues and preaching the gospel of the kingdom, and healing every disease and every infirmity.*" (Crowds followed him, "like sheep without a shepherd," 9:36.)

The reader has here a magnificent picture of Jesus and his activities which proclaim the kingdom. And when chapter 9 closes with Jesus saying, "The harvest is plentiful, but the laborers are few; pray therefore the Lord of the harvest to send out laborers into his harvest," the reader may well be moved to pray in response, "Send me." Very well, Matthew goes on in chapter 10 to offer instructions for disciples sent forth to witness to the world.

If Matthew's setting for the Sermon on the Mount is so carefully worked out, then the structure he has given the sermon deserves careful attention too. While scholars differ over this detail or that, it is clear that the general outline is built up like his (after the physical setting for the sermon is described at 5:1-2):

I. *The Gospel setting* for the sermon (5:3-16):
   A. Nine beatitudes about the men of the kingdom (5:3-12)
   B. The disciples of the kingdom as salt and light in the world (5:13-16)
II. *The ethical theme*: the greater righteousness demanded of the men of the kingdom (5:17-20)
III. *The new way of righteousness in life*—six *contrasts* with the old way taught by the scribes (5:21-48):
   murder and hate (5:21-26)
   adultery and lust (5:27-30)
   divorce and remarriage (5:31-32)
   truthfulness and the swearing of oaths (5:33-37)
   retaliation and helpfulness (5:38-42)
   love for enemies, by sons of their Father in heaven (5:43-48)
IV. *The new way of righteousness in life*—three *examples* concerning pious practices valued by the Pharisees (6:1-18):
   the giving of alms (6:1-4)
   prayer (including the Lord's Prayer as an illustration, 6:5-15)
   fasting (before God, not men, 6:16-18)
V. *The new way of righteousness in life*—advice for disciples (6:19—7:27): on true treasure (6:19-21)
                 the "sound eye" (6:22-23)
                 serving one master (6:24)
                 anxiety (6:25-34)
                 judging (7:1-5)
                 profaning the holy (7:6)
                 God and prayer (7:7-11)
                 the Golden Rule (7:12)
                 the "narrow gate" (7:13-14)
                 fruitbearing (7:15-20)
                 self-deception (7:21-23)
                 hearing and doing (7:24-27)
Closing comment (7:28-29; cf. 11:1; 13:53; 19:1; 26:1)

Matthew addresses the sermon to the disciples (5:1), but the crowds also hear (7:28). That is true to the facts, in that Jesus originally gave his teachings openly, but it was only the followers who had accepted the message of the kingdom who could really understand. Thus it is that the first part (5:3-16) repeats the "Gospel basis" for what follows. The theme verse at 5:20 demands of those who have heard the good news a response in righteousness which is greater than that of the scribes and Pharisees (who provide the foil in sections III and IV respectively).[46] The aim of Jesus is not to destroy the Old Testament revelation of God's will (he often takes it as his starting point), but to bring it to its fullness. The contrasts between the old and new (5:21-48) and with Pharisaic practices (6:1-18) are easy enough to see in Matthew (Luke lacks such a structure in his outline). But part V is almost impossible to outline with any continuity. Chapter 6:19-34 deals with worldly possessions and needs. Chapter 7 stresses judgment, 7:13-27 providing four warnings about final judgment. Verses 15-20 and 21-23 go together, warning that you will know men "by their fruits" (7:20) but also that in some cases you will *not* know them by their fruits (7:21-23). The Golden Rule provides one sort of conclusion, but the final admonition in the sermon is against trying to separate hearing and doing (7:24-27).

Some of the teachings in the sermon we have already examined, for example the Lord's Prayer, the beatitudes, and forgivingness. Out of the many little sections which call for special study, three details will be examined here, plus Jesus' general teaching about love which underlies so much of what he says.

One prominent term which cannot escape notice in Matthew is "righteousness." The outline above made it the theme of the sermon (5:20), a new and better righteousness. At 5:6, 5:10, 6:1 (RSV, "piety"), and 6:33 there are further references to righteousness. The remarkable thing is that in all these instances it is only Matthew who has the word "righteousness." Either Luke lacks the verse or Matthew introduces the word into a Lucan sentence.[47] Elsewhere, again in passages which appear only in his gospel, Matthew refers to "the way of righteousness" (21:32) and to how Jesus fulfilled "all righteousness" (3:15). The conclusion is inevitable that this is a favorite Matthean theme. He alone emphasizes it, among the Synoptics.[48]

We must not confuse this usage of Matthew with Paul's phrase, "the righteousness of God." In Paul, the term denotes God's saving righteousness which delivers men (Romans 1:17). In Matthew it denotes conduct which is right and pleasing before God, which fulfills his will. There is a "way of righteousness" in which John the Baptist walked (21:32), which Jesus fulfilled totally (3:15), and in which disciples are to walk. It is a "piety" (6:1) which must exceed that of the scribes and Pharisees (5:20). Disciples are to hunger and thirst after righteousness (5:6), even though it brings persecution on them. The most amazing verse, however, is 6:33, where Matthew inserts the words "and his righteousness" into Jesus' saying (from Q, Luke 12:31), so that it reads, "Seek first [God's] kingdom *and his righteousness*." This implies that righteousness, like the kingdom, belongs to God and is a gift from him. But once this gift is given, then righteousness —in the sense now of right conduct according to the will of God —becomes of prime importance for men of the kingdom; it is to be sought in life. By his use of the word "righteousness," Matthew conveys the double aspect of Jesus' message about God's gift and demand.

The story is similar with Matthew's oft misunderstood term "perfect" in his disciples' ethic. He takes one's breath away when he writes of the standard for discipleship: "You, therefore, must be *perfect*, as your heavenly Father is perfect" (5:48). Luke has simply "Be *merciful*, even as your Father is *merciful*" (6:36). Many prefer Luke's rendering as the more realistic, and it is even possible that both "perfect" and "merciful" are "translation variants" of the same Semitic word employed by Jesus.[49] But a reference to "perfection" is no accident in Matthew. At 19:21 he has Jesus say to the rich young ruler, "If you would be perfect," whereas Mark and Luke has simply, "One thing you lack." It should be noted that Matthew's word "perfect" can also be rendered "mature" (see Colossians 4:12), and that the goal may therefore be called "maturity." But Matthew means more than that; he means a character like God's, loving and bounteous (cf. 5:43-48). Unrealistic? Impossible? But Matthew, it must be remembered, is presenting a disciple's ethic, an ethic of the will of God. God wills sons who are like their heavenly Father.

However, is there ever any relief in Matthew from such a high and rigorous ethical demand? Yes, at a place in the sermon where one might not expect it, with regard to divorce. There is little question that Jesus taught as a general principle there should be no divorce (Mark 10:2-12).[50] When the Pharisees pointed out that Moses allowed divorce (Deuteronomy 24:1), Jesus directed them back to God's will from creation (Genesis 1:27; 2:24), and concluded against divorce on any grounds:

> "Whoever divorces his wife and marries another, commits adultery against her; and if she divorces her husband and marries another, she commits adultery." (Mark 10:11-12)[51]

Luke has the same principle (16:18). But Matthew, as is well-known, twice lists an exception to this principle. He adds the words "except on the ground of unchastity" in the Sermon on the Mount (5:32) and also at 19:9, the Matthean parallel to Mark 10:11, the passage on divorce.

If it is claimed that the historical Jesus taught both things, one involves him in hopeless contradiction (no divorce, yet one allowable exception). It is far more likely to assume that Matthew adds the exception based on the experience in the Christian community over the decades since Jesus spoke. Paul seems to have made a similar exception in Corinth, allowing separation when the non-Christian partner desired it (I Corinthians 7:15). It is often said that there is here a sort of "legalism" entering into the church, which allowed exceptions to Jesus' simple but strict teachings. Perhaps. But it is also to be presumed that the exceptions were likewise held by the early Christians to represent the mind of Christ among his people; these cases show a willingness to recognize that God's will (no divorce) must always be worked out in ambiguous and difficult human situations. Matthew's "exception" allows the absolute principle to stand as norm, but recognizes exceptional instances. This, too, is part of the Sermon on the Mount.[52]

Oddly enough, love enters into the sermon in Matthew in only one obvious reference: "Love your enemies" (5:44).[53] It might also be deduced from 6:24 that men are to love and serve God while despising mammon. Everyone would assume, however, that love—for God and the neighbor—underlies what Jesus says here and elsewhere.[54] In this connection there is a verse, outside Matthew 5–7, that calls for comment: "You shall love your neighbor as yourself" (Mark 12:31)[55] Like much else in Jesus' ethic of the will of God, this precept derives from the Old Testament

(Leviticus 19:18). But in Jesus' usage it was not a command to love oneself. Not: first, love yourself, then the neighbor, then God. Rather, Jesus was implying that by nature each individual knows all too well how to love himself, how to serve and honor self. Very well, treat your neighbor that way, serve God with the devotion which you're naturally inclined to give to self. In this way Jesus was answering the perpetual question, "How much shall I love? How far must love go?" with an answer which no human being could mistake or over which he could quibble: as much as by nature you are accustomed to love self, just that much are you to love the neighbor.[15]

An absolute standard is thus set up which everyone by nature knows. An absolute ethic is set forth, often with the help of the Old Testament revelation but also on the basis of Jesus' own authority. A call for righteousness and perfection, like God's—but tempered with an awareness of man's situation in the world. Such is Jesus' ethic, in the gospels.

The Crisis of Judgment—Rewards and Punishment

Jesus often spoke of God's coming judgment. Did he pose this as a threat, in order to get men to obey God's will? He also used the term "reward" and sometimes employed phrases about future punishments. Were these spurs to good deeds, to motivate men ethically?

There is no question that the note of judgment appeared in Jesus' teachings again and again. It was no doubt far more frequent in what Jesus said than it is in sermons today. Modern man, perhaps in reaction to much preaching of the past, does not like to hear about a divine judgment of the living and the dead. But Jesus uncompromisingly referred to judgment. This does not mean he ruthlessly denounced sin as his chief topic on every occasion, and he certainly did not write off men, even the worst of them, as "hopeless sinners." (Indeed, his ministry seemed directed especially to those whom the society of the day felt to be least promising—the "lawless" Galileans, the tax collectors, the prostitutes.) But God as judge, and the related assumption of a resurrection where men would stand before the judgment seat, and then the corollaries of reward and punishment—features which are regularly found in the literature of late Judaism—all are part of the picture in Jesus' teachings.

It could not be otherwise when Jesus talked about the coming of the kingdom. For that meant the coming of God, and God's presence inevitably means judgment as well as salvation. Because of this, Jesus said, "Repent" (Mark 1:15). His parables called upon men to decide. His ethics confronted them with a demand. His proclamation and his own appearance caused a crisis—a "judging" or even a "division" (Greek *krisis*)—so that men had to reach a decision and act, in view of the impending salvation and judgment by God. The time is short. The door to life is narrow, the way hard (Luke 13:24, par. Matthew 7:13-14). There is no leisure for even the most pressing duties of normal life, such as waiting to bury one's parents (Matthew 8:22). Discipleship must be immediate. There can be no looking back; a man must keep his hand on the plow, if he is fit for the kingdom of God (Luke 9:62). That is why discipleship is such a great decision to make. "Count the cost," "consider the need to renounce all." So say Jesus' parables (Luke 14:26-33).

This idea of God's presence as judgment and demand runs as a constant theme through what Jesus says. He does not regard this judgment as an inflexible working out of certain laws in human experience. Jesus did not have in mind the notion expressed in a later proverb, "The history of the world is the judgment of the world." Rather, much more in harmony with the Old Testament, he viewed the divine judgment, for one thing, as something future and catastrophic, at the "end of the world." It is not the unfolding of some cosmic law in human experience, but a final scene before the throne of God, after "history" has come to an end. In this picture, God is the judge (only after Easter are there occasional references to the Son as sharing in the judgment; cf. Romans 14:10 with II Corinthians 5:10). And God's judgment will be all-knowing, all-encompassing, and supremely just.[57]

The Old Testament writers had prophesied and at times longed for such a "Day of the Lord," a day when the Lord of hosts would act (Malachi 4:3). "This world" and its kingdoms would no longer be separated from "that world" of God and his kingly power. The apocalyptists painted, in sometimes garish colors, scenes of how the righteous ones would feast and the wicked would get their due reward of punishment (cf. Isaiah 24–27; Zechariah 12–14; Joel 3; Malachi 4). John the Baptist stood in this prophetic-apocalyptic succession when he warned the Pharisees and Sadducees of "wrath to come." He saw God's judgment as an "axe . . . laid to the root of the trees" (Matthew 3:10) and as a winnowing process in which wheat for the granary is separated from the chaff which is to be burned (Matthew 3:12).

Similar expressions about a future judgment by God appear in Jesus' utterances. The very notion of the kingdom includes a "harvest time" when the reapers will gather the wheat into the Lord's barn but bundle the weeds to be burned (Matthew 13:24-30; cf. 13:36-43, where Matthew develops the idea further in an allegorical explanation, with verse 43 a reflection of Old Testament apocalyptic in Daniel 12:2-3 and Malachi 4:1-3).

The chief difference between Jesus' teachings and many traditional apocalyptic pictures of a future judgment is that with Jesus this judgment is also a matter of the "here and now." The judgment has also become present. "The time is fulfilled." The demand is now. Now is the time of decision. We have already seen how Jesus' views the kingdom as both future and present. This automatically makes judgment before God a present matter as well as a future one. Men are judged by the way they respond at the present to the words of Jesus. One of his most difficult sayings to interpret makes this much clear, at least: that man's eternal fate at the Last Judgment depends on how he responds to Jesus and his message in the here and now:

"Whoever is ashamed of me and of my words in this adulterous and sinful generation, of him will the Son of man also be ashamed, when he comes in the glory of his Father with the holy angels." (Mark 8:38)

This is Jesus' view of "this generation," this age—"sinful." Here the certainty of judgment is announced (Matthew 16:27 adds that the Son of man "will repay every man for what he has done"). Here is the basis on which men will stand or fall: their attitude toward Jesus and his words.[58]

The new or "unique" element is not the condemnation of this age as hopeless, or the idea of judging what men have done—the Old Testament spoke of these things. The new thing is the way the judgment is, in effect, decided now by one's attitude toward Jesus. He is himself "the sign of Jonah" and the basis for judgment. Thus he himself is the "crisis," or division, which causes the separation between "believers" and those who refuse to believe. The result, as a saying of Jesus puts it, is "a man set against his father," "daughter against mother," foes in one's own household, a house divided three against two, as men and women make their decisions (Matthew 10:34-36, par. Luke 12:51-53). Hence we can understand the dramatic image that at the judgment, of two men in the field or two women at a mill, one is taken and the other left (Matthew 24:40-41, par. Luke 17:34-35).

It is John's Gospel which brings out most vividly the coming of Jesus Christ as a crisis and division or separation among men. The light shines in the darkness. People either receive him or they do not (John 1:5, 9-13). Upon their decision hangs their fate. Indeed, it is decided already, in the way they heed Jesus. "Truly, truly, I say to you, he who hears my word and believes him who sent me, has eternal life; he does not come into judgment, but has passed from death to life" (John 5:24). This Johannine saying moves eternal life up to the present and virtually eliminates any future judgment. (Some scholars feel that the occasional references in John to a future resurrection are actually additions [e.g., 5:28-29, in contrast to 5:24-25], though there is no manuscript evidence for such a view.[59] John has little to say about the future judgment, however, and clearly emphasizes a present "separation" based on response to Jesus' word.) It may be said that in the gospels as a whole, one's future fate at the Last Judgment is determined by one's attitude and response now to Jesus and his word. John may have heightened this a bit and seems to have in mind the way men respond to the preached word about Jesus in the church, but something of the same sort was doubtless true during his lifetime. Jesus' coming presented itself as a crisis of judgment to men.

Jesus, then, in his person and teaching, betokened God's judgment. Response now to him anticipates the future outcome before God. Man is confronted with a time when all earthly security is lost—only God matters, and what he offers. And God's judgment offers reward and implies punishment. On such topics, Judaism, following the Old Testament, had its own ideas. Jesus' words sometimes reflect these views, to the embarrassment of modern Christians. But what he says is not always what some people think he said, as closer examination shows.

Jesus' teaching about punishments is easily disposed of, for little is really said on the topic in the gospels. This is also true of

the Bible as a whole. The spotlight is not on the punishment of
sinners but on the blessings of the saved. One might say that at
the heart of biblical revelation is God; gathered round him are
the hosts of the redeemed; only occasionally and peripherally is
there reference to those who in life have seemed far from God
and reference to their ultimate fate. The light streams from God
but only occasionally does it enlighten us about those who have
never heard the Gospel message or who seem to defy it. The biblical picture is a positive one, about salvation; it rarely speaks of the
negative side, or "damnation," in specific terms.

Certainly this is true of the Old Testament. Here the focus is
upon Abraham and Israel and, later, on the "remnant" or "true
Israel." Only occasionally is there something said about the Israelites who have departed from God or about the other nations
of the world. When there are visions of God's judgment in apocalyptic writers, the description is usually in picture and symbol, not
prose or factual reporting. What is said is chiefly "backlighting"
for the portrait of how God will save his own. This is clearly
illustrated in biblical teaching about the general resurrection. Some
passages (e.g., Isaiah 26:12-19; Ezekiel 37:11-14) tell of the resurrection of Israel only, because here is where the interest is;
others deal with a "double resurrection" of all men, both good
and bad (Daniel 12:2), though even here the focus is on Israel.[60]

Jesus, like the Pharisees, assumed a general resurrection of all
men (Mark 12:18-27). He assumed that there would follow a
judgment of all men by God (Matthew 25:31-46). But we can
scarcely work out a definitive statement on the fate of nonbelievers
from the few allusions in his words. A few passages suggest punishment for them—but not with the notion that they will be
"purged" of sin by sufferings in any "purgatory." Other verses
might hint that sinners will be "extinguished" or blotted out—
but not with such clarity that one can claim that "eternal extinction" is the fate of the wicked. Still other passages hold open the
possibility that all men might someday be saved by God—at least
a "universalist" reading of the New Testament evidence has found
supporters in both ancient and modern times.[61] But the little
phrases in Jesus' sayings on which theories have been built are
often in picture language (about a "heavenly meal," or "Gehenna"
as "a place of burning.") Many of them are commonplace figures
out of Jewish apocalyptic. Certainly details in a parable cannot be

pressed. A few of the verses involved are "tag lines" which the
early church seems to have inserted among Jesus' sayings in the
gospels.[62]

To sum up: Jesus took seriously a judgment by God (Matthew
10:28, par. Luke 12:5). The Judge of all the earth has all power.
Man is rightly challenged by what lies ahead. But there is no
systematic picture of "hell," no detailed discussion of punishments. And while the judgment is a part of Jesus' message, there
is no attempt to ground ethics therein; it is not, "Do this, or
else. . . ."[63]

More frequently, though, Jesus does speak of rewards (Matthew
5:12; 6:1, 4, 5, 6) and of "treasures in heaven" (Matthew 6:20;
cf. 6:33).[64] It may be observed that most of these references are
peculiar to Matthew (there are three times as many as in Mark
and Luke combined), but enough occur in the other gospels and
sources to make it clear that we have a term which Jesus used,
even though it is Matthew and his gospel for Jewish Christians
which make the most of the theme.[65] Note these examples from
the Synoptic tradition:

> Your reward is great in heaven. (Luke 6:23, par. Matthew 5:12)
> Whoever gives you a cup of water to drink because you bear the
> name of Christ, will by no means lose his reward. (Mark 9:41; cf.
> Matthew 10:40-42)
> Love your enemies, and do good, and lend, expecting nothing in
> return; and your reward will be great, and you will be sons of the
> Most High. (Luke 6:35)

Such references have always caused difficulties for those Christians who regard salvation as completely and totally a gift from
God. Yet here Jesus speaks frankly of rewards. Such verses are
all too frequently ignored or "swept under the rug," in order
that Paul's doctrine of "grace alone" can be preserved without
any conflicting notion of rewards. The startling thing is, however,
as anyone discovers who goes through Paul's letters, that Paul,
too, talked of a judgment based on works and expected a reward
from God for his work as a Christian missionary. (Cf. Romans
2:6-11; II Corinthians 5:10; I Corinthians 3:6-9, 10-15). Paul,
it must be concluded, taught *both* salvation (justification) by
grace alone through faith, *and* a judgment based on works alone.
The problem is not just with Jesus' words, therefore, but with
Paul as well.

One answer in this situation is to claim that in Paul and Jesus we have at this point still a holdover from Jewish teachings. Both of them taught in an atmosphere where "works" and "reward" were stressed, and so they almost inevitably employed such terms. (This would also explain why a Jewish-Christian gospel like Matthew especially abounds in the term "reward." It was the language the hearers expected.) When Jesus was asked by the rich young ruler, "What good *deed* must I *do,* to have eternal life?" he answered him in terms of his own world: "Keep the [Old Testament] commandments" (Matthew 19:16-22). Similarly, he said to a scribe, "Do this, and you will live" (Luke 10:28). Even Paul still used the language of Judaism about "rewards" and "works" at times. Thus Jesus and Paul, it is said, accommodated their expressions and reflected the outlook of their hearers, even though they basically conceived of salvation as a gift from God. But this answer, correct as it may be, does not fully satisfy. If they basically did not agree with it, why did they use such a terminology?

Another solution is to hold that Paul and Jesus taught a judgment based on works where all men will be found guilty before God—but that then God, of his grace, will have mercy and save those who had heeded the Gospel offer.[66] That may work for Paul (cf. Romans 3:19-21 and Galatians 3:22), but not so clearly for Jesus. Too many texts are "left over" and do not fall into the pattern.

We have previously seen that Jesus presented salvation as a gift of God, not something man earns.[67] Keeping this in mind, we may put what Jesus said concerning reward into perspective if several points are noted. Jesus and Paul presume a judgment based on works. Whether a man stands or falls depends on his relation to Jesus and the Gospel. Salvation is a gift. The kingdom and eternal life are things one "inherits," not things one earns (Matthew 19:29; 25:34). But beyond this there *is* the possibility of reward from God for work as a faithful steward. This Paul expects (I Corinthians 3:8, 14). Jesus' parables suggest the same idea (Matthew 25:14-30, especially verses 21 and 23). This is not salvation based on works but something on top of salvation—recompense for faithful service. It is not wages laboriously earned and then grudgingly paid, but reward for the servant which is joyously granted. God's nature is to give justly and liberally to those who are his own.

The meaning and import of what Jesus says—which in the history of the church has often slipped over into a doctrine of "righteousness by works," instead of reward for the righteous servants in the kingdom—requires keeping the following things in mind.

(1) Jesus' words about reward are addressed, not to the unsaved man, but to disciples who already know the Gospel of the kingdom. The beatitudes speak of reward (Matthew 5:12, par. Luke 6:23) for those who have already accepted God's offer. It is the kingdom which brings all other things (Matthew 6:33). So also Paul: it is the Christian who has experienced a new relationship with God by grace alone who can presume that God will reward what he has built on the foundation of Christ.

(2) Disciples know that they are always in a servant-master relation. They are not laborers who earn a wage, but servants—one of Jesus' parables says they are always "unworthy servants" (Luke 17:9-10)—servants whose recompense arises out of the goodness of their Master, once they have been taken into his service.[68]

(3) Their "reward" comes precisely for what they do without any eye to a reward. When Luke 6:35 refers to reward, it is with regard to actions done in response to God's goodness, because he is kind and merciful, not to actions performed to "see what we can get in return." When you lend, the verse says, "expect nothing in return." This notion, that it is unpremeditated, spontaneous, unselfish actions which God will reward, is precisely what appears in the "parable"[69] of the Last Judgment at Matthew 25:31-46— the righteous do not know when they have fed, clothed, or comforted Christ, because they were simply helping people in the world with no thought of reward (verses 37-40).

(4) The reward is eschatologically future. It "will be great" (Luke 6:35), it lies "in heaven" (Matthew 5:12). (5) If it is asked precisely what the reward is, Jesus never spells it out in dazzling specifics, the way apocalyptic sometimes did. It is made just concrete enough to prevent men from "spiritualizing" it into vagueness (cf. Matthew 10:40-42; 19:29). But ultimately the reward is simply—God himself, and life and fellowship with him. All the talk about "a prophet's reward" or "a righteous man's reward" boils down to receiving Christ and him who sent him— i.e., God (Matthew 10:40). The "reward" of the righteous at the

Last Judgment is to inherit (not earn) "the kingdom prepared for you"—and the kingdom means the presence of God himself (Matthew 25:34). Reward involves being "sons of the Most High" (Luke 6:35).

This picture of God as the reward for disciples who have by grace entered into a new relationship with him is borne out by some of the Old Testament references to reward. For example, after God called Abraham and as he entered into a covenant relationship with him, the Lord said, "Fear not, Abram, I am your shield; your reward shall be very great" (Genesis 15:1).[70] Reward arises from God and the relation which his grace establishes, and in some passages is nothing else than God and his giving of himself. As Isaiah puts it:

> Behold, the Lord God comes with might,
> and his arm rules for him;
> behold, his reward is with him,
> and his recompense before him. (40:10; cf. 62:11)

God's coming means salvation—and judgment—and, for those who have unostentatiously done his will, the reward of God himself. Early Christians thus held fast paradoxically to the idea of salvation as an absolute gift of grace, and to a trust that in the Lord their labor was not in vain (I Corinthians 15:58); God will himself reward what they have done in the service for which his gift of salvation has freed them. The reward is not the motive for ethics. God is (Luke 6:35-36). But they knew from Jesus that the God who offers salvation also watches over human life and is not unmindful even of the cup of cold water given in his name.[71]

All this deals with Christian disciples. What of those who never heard the Gospel? They cannot be judged on the basis of response to Jesus and his word. Matthew seems to have been aware of this question when he framed the eschatological discourse in chapter 25 of his Gospel. The parables about the Ten Maidens and on the Talents (25:1-30) deal with believers. They are to be ready for the coming of the Lord (verses 1-13), administering as faithful stewards and servants what God has entrusted to them (verses 14-30).

But in the allegorical parable about the Sheep and Goats (25: 31-46) Matthew seems to deal with the fate of non-Christians. The verses, because of the difficulties they pose, have rightly been

called the "Everest of Synoptic criticism."[72] We have already
referred to several details, and it may be that the parable (which,
as it stands in Matthew, is now allegory—it is the only parable of
Jesus where "the king" is not God but the Son of man) originally
dealt with disciples and their works. But as it stands, the judgment pictures "all the *nations*" (verse 32) gathered before the
king's throne. That means, all the pagans, all the Gentiles. How
are they judged? On the basis of the light they had, and specifically on the basis of the way they treated the Lord Christ in the
person of "the least of these my brethren."[73]

The picture suggests that pagans will be judged—in cases where
they have not heard the Gospel of Jesus—on the basis of what
they did in life. How did they treat their fellow men? "The least
of these my brethren" is open to two different interpretations. It
may mean the Christians. In that case, men would be judged on
how they treated Christ's followers. More daring is the view that
it means all the despised, rejected, suffering outcasts of society—
with these destitute, disenfranchised people Christ identifies himself, even as the historical Jesus did in his table fellowship with
the tax collectors, harlots, and outcasts. Pagans are judged by the
way they treated such persons when they had the chance.

Jesus in the Synoptic Gospels thus teaches a judgment, for all
men. It is based on works. For pagans it rides on the question of
how, according to the light they had, they dealt with Jesus' lesser
brothers, in the church and in the world. For disciples, their relation to God through Jesus and his message means the certainty[74]
of hope and grace. And they know God not merely as gracious
but also as just. Hence they can serve in the world, day by day,
knowing that the reward of God is part of his promise.

Luther recognized all this and went even further in a postscript
to his commentary on the Sermon on the Mount. He was even
willing to use the traditional word "merit" for the fruit that
follows faith, *provided* one remembers that we are discussing the
fruit that follows grace and the forgiveness of sins[75]—*provided*
we are clear that the Sermon on the Mount, like all of Jesus'
ethics, is not about "how men become Christians" but concerns
"what believing disciples do."

9

Stony Ground—and the
Claim of Jesus Christ

"Some seed fell on stony ground" (Mark 4:5). These words in the parable of the Sower, certain scholars think, may have been spoken by Jesus with reference to his own experiences during his ministry.[1] The phrase may thus reflect a time when his efforts were meeting with little success. For Jesus had come proclaiming the Gospel of the reign of God, through his words and deeds. But men often closed their ears to the news of "kingdom come" and resisted its implications for their lives; they saw instead Beelzebul at work in Jesus' activities. He had taught and prophesied a new way of life under the reign of God, but most men loved instead the old. And so there was opposition to the message—and to the man himself from Nazareth. "No prophet is to rise from Galilee," they sneered (John 7:52).

One writer has put the connection between the message and this opposition as tersely as this: "Jesus used parables and Jesus was put to death."[2] The preaching, the parables, and the mighty works themselves led in only one direction—to a cross. For even his most innocent-sounding stories could prick to the sensitive core beneath hardened, stony hearts and lead, in some cases, not to repentence, but to animosity. Antagonism and hostility which eventually burst forth into a cry of "Crucify!" are frequently observed in the gospel stories about Jesus. Even so "charming" a tale as that about the Good Samaritan (Luke 10:30-37) could cause hatred to well up, for Jesus was touching on a sensitive area of religion and race relations when he made a Samaritan the hero. An Englishman has written:

> Once in America I heard a wonderful lecture on the parables of the gospels. The lecturer described how the priest and the Levite passed by on the other side, and it was left to one of the despised and hated Samaritan race to do what all must recognize to be a plain duty of ministry to the wounded man. Then he added, 'Murmur among the crowd: We'll get this guy one day'.
> And they did.[3]

All too often we picture Jesus simply as a wonderful teller of tales or as "Jerusalem's most popular dinner guest."[4] We miss the point that Jesus' stories packed a punch which offended many who heard them. The startling new hospitality which he practiced at that most sacred of Semitic occasions, the dinner table and its fellowship, by eating with sinners and publicans, caused people to regard him as a menace to law and custom. He embodied a claim which fell on stony ground, ground that bore no fruit (Matthew 21:34, 43). In time the rocky ground choked off the man and his message. The opposition, which gathers all through Jesus' ministry, has its moment of triumph on a hill one spring day outside Jerusalem—upon a cross.

"Why did he have to die?" That is a question we humans often ask in life. Precise answers in this case or that are often shrouded in mystery. When we ask, "Why did Jesus die?" the problem becomes even more complex, for it touches, in the view of the gospels, on the ultimate will of God himself. The early Christians who wrote the gospels were convinced that the cross was the result not only of human passions and rising hatred, but also of the divine purpose and plan in the Passion.[5] We may, in purely human terms, try to trace out the cause and shape of opposition to Jesus. Behind it all are claims about Jesus which his opponents sensed, and, ultimately, a claim about the purpose of God. In these matters we are studying ancient history from the lifetime of Jesus, but we soon see that we are also examining the experience of the early church.

The Opposition to Jesus

That certain men, for varying reasons, opposed Jesus all through his ministry, there can be no doubt. In Palestine, seething with so many opinions, so serious about religion, divided into so many different camps, it was inevitable that any man of conviction who rose above the crowd would arouse opponents. And Jesus was a man who had "God and God's business constantly in his mind."[6] What Karl Barth has called his "attack of grace"[7] mobilized the defenders of the Jewish law against him.

But precisely who these opponents were and why they so stoutly opposed Jesus with a hatred to death, is more difficult to determine from the biblical records.[8] We have already seen[9] that in the accounts of Jesus' trial and death it is sometimes simply "the Jews" who are designated as the enemies responsible (John 18:12; 19:7, 12); more often "the chief priests and the elders and the scribes" (Mark 14:43, 53) or the Sanhedrin (or council, Mark

14:55) are specifically mentioned. It is noteworthy that the official Jewish leaders are thus made responsible (though we have seen that their part is probably played up and that of the Romans is played down). Rather startling is the fact that the Pharisees are rarely mentioned by name among the enemies of Jesus in the Passion narrative,[10] especially when we discover that the Pharisees were foremost among Jesus' opponents in the earlier parts of his ministry. In contrast with the Passion, where the hierarchy of priests and elders dominates the scene, we must examine two other places in the gospels where opposition to Jesus comes to the fore: namely, in Jerusalem prior to the arrest and trial, and in Galilee early in the ministry.

The opposition to Jesus in Jerusalem is described in Mark 11–12 and parallels. According to the Synoptic Gospels this period in Jerusalem lasted three or four days from "Palm Sunday" until "Holy Thursday," though there are hints in the Synoptics, and the Fourth Gospel plainly states, that the ministry of Jesus in Jerusalem was somewhat longer. It is in this period that some seven stories are set, depicting conflict between Jesus and his various opponents (Mark 11:27–12:44).

The Jerusalem ministry commences with the triumphal entry and the applause of the crowd (Mark 11:1-10). There follow the triumphs of the cleansing of the temple (11:15-19) and the "enacted parable" of the Withered Fig Tree (11:12-14, 20-25). The result seems to be astonishment; people are spellbound at his words and deeds (11:18), just as they had been in Galilee (1:22). But underneath this surface mood runs an undercurrent of fear and opposition (11:18), again just as in Galilee (3:6). The real issue is the authority by which Jesus acts thus (11:28): Is it from Satan (and therefore a delusion), or is it power from God? The scenes of the temple cleansing and the Fig Tree are meant to show us that Jesus does act authoritatively. Then Mark (and he is followed in most details by Matthew and Luke) gives us seven quick scenes showing the opposition which these claims to authority evoked. The well-known stories are listed on page 254.

As can be seen at a glance, Mark ties the seven incidents together —questions and answers, parables, comments—in pell-mell fashion. Matthew inserts some additional parables (21:28-32, the Two Sons; 22:1-14, the Wedding Feast)[11] and greatly expands

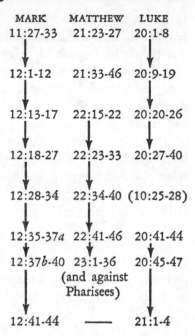

	MARK	MATTHEW	LUKE
1. A Question about Authority	11:27-33	21:23-27	20:1-8
2. Jesus' Parable about the Wicked Husbandmen	12:1-12	21:33-46	20:9-19
3. A Question about Tribute to Caesar	12:13-17	22:15-22	20:20-26
4. A Question about the Resurrection	12:18-27	22:23-33	20:27-40
5. A Question about the Great Commandment	12:28-34	22:34-40	(10:25-28)
6. A Question about the Messiah as David's Son	12:35-37a	22:41-46	20:41-44
Warnings against the Scribes	12:37b-40	23:1-36 (and against Pharisees)	20:45-47
7. In Praise of a Widow and Her Gift	12:41-44	——	21:1-4

the words of warning against the scribes to include the Pharisees, using the closing words of his chapter (23:37-39, against Jerusalem) to lead directly into his discourse (chapter 24) on the destruction of the temple at Jerusalem, the center for the scribes and Pharisees. Luke has the same arrangement of the seven incidents as Mark, except that he has told the story about the Great Commandment at a much earlier point (Luke 10:25-28).

These seven "conflict stories," involving a game of question-and-answer between Jesus and his opponents in Jerusalem, are familiar enough.[12] The scene is the temple, where Jesus is walking about and teaching (Mark 11:27; Luke 20:1). (Teaching among the rabbis, we must remember, often took the form of dialogue and questions and answer.) No further details of setting are given. Mark plainly means to show, however, that these exchanges in the temple courts concern six key issues of the day: divine authority, the relation of Israel to God, the relation of Israel to Caesar, the future resurrection, the greatest commandment in the law, and the Messiah. In a sense, of course, all of these have to do with law, for the Pentateuch and the other Old Testament books were regarded by most Jews as authoritative revelation on such matters.

At the very outset Jesus seems to claim an authority which allows him to act in ways that run counter to Old Testament law and the manner in which its defenders understood it. "By what authority are you doing these things, or who gave you this authority to do them?" (Mark 11:28). The question may refer to the way Jesus has just cleansed the temple, or, more likely, to the whole career of Jesus. He answers by impaling them on a counter-question about John the Baptist's authority (which they had also refused to recognize); but in the dilemma Jesus poses for them he claims that his own authority is "from heaven"—that is, from God! He acts with divine warrant; that is apparent in the scenes which follow.

The parable of the Wicked Tenants threatens that "the vine-yard of the Lord" will be taken away from Israel and given to "others" who will render fruits to God (Matthew 21:43), if the people of the day do not heed God's address to them. Some critics think that this parable virtually "signed Jesus' death warrant," with its implication that he is the "son" and "heir" (Mark 12:6-7); the result was an attempt to arrest him then and there.[13] We may call this parable a "No" from God to the proud claims of many religious Israelites of the day, while the attempt to seize Jesus is a "No" from Israel to him.

Next Jesus is asked a trick question. "Is it lawful to pay taxes to Caesar or not?" If he says "No," he will, of course, seem a suspicious character or revolutionist in the eyes of Rome; if, on the other hand, he answers "Yes," then he will lose the support of many Jews who groaned under the weight of Roman taxation. The men who asked the question are variously described as "Pharisees" and "some Herodians" or as "spies, who pretended to be sincere" (Luke 20:20). Their question, however, is typical of the Zealots, that revolutionist group of Jews who held "no king but Yahweh," and who wanted to pay no taxes to Rome.[14] Jesus' striking answer, "Render to Caesar the things that are Caesar's, and to God the things that are God's," avoids the trap and speaks a "No" to such Zealotism at the same time as it is a "Yes" to God.

Then comes that complex question about the woman who had been married to seven brothers successively.[15] At the resurrection, whose wife will she be? The Sadducees who asked it did not believe in a resurrection anyway (Mark 12:18), and Jesus, in proclaiming the power of God and asserting that relations in the life to come are completely other than what they have been in this life,[16] says "No" to the Sadducees and their casuistic reasonings.

The next question comes from men who loved the Scriptures even more than the Sadducees, the scribes, who debated which of the 248 commandments and the 365 prohibitions in the Pentateuch was the most important. Jesus' answer is a "No" to their legalistic quibblings in that he directs them simply to "love God and love your neighbor as yourself."[17]

A final question, this time posed by Jesus, puts all these critics to silence; he asks them how the expected Messiah could be regarded as a son of David (and thus inferior to David) when David had presumably called him "lord" (and therefore his superior) in Psalm 110. The enemies were reduced to silence, and it is little wonder that all three evangelists report here a section that begins (Mark 12:38), "Beware of the scribes . . . ," when the scribes of Jerusalem have opposed Jesus in these ways. Lest it seem, however, that Jesus' words in Jerusalem are only condemnations, there is a closing scene (Mark 12:41-44). Jesus speaks approvingly of one widow who gives everything she has, her whole living, as a gift to God. That is faith: saying "Yes" to the "Yes" of God.

We may now list in summary the opponents who speak against Jesus in the conflict stories just described.[18] He says "No" to:

1. the Zealots and their wishes (Mark 12:13-17);
2. the Sadducees and their hypocrisy (Mark 12:18-27);
3. the Pharisees and their legalism (Mark 12:28-34).

The opponents are most frequently designated as Pharisees and scribes, though Sadducees and Herodians are mentioned too. The chief priests and the elders are referred to only once (Mark 11:27), even though the scenes take place in the temple at Jerusalem. Thus it would seem that while the Pharisees are virtually never mentioned in the Passion narrative itself, they are the chief enemies of Jesus during the Jerusalem ministry, but that the chief priests and their helpers who play the leading roles in the arrest and trial are almost never mentioned among Jesus' enemies prior to that time.

This impression about the opponents of Jesus can be checked in one final place. Mark 2:1—3:6 is another collection in which half a dozen "conflict stories" have been grouped together in a similar way. Again Mark and Luke agree in arrangement, while Matthew divides the material somewhat differently.[19]

	MARK	MATTHEW	LUKE
1. Controversy over how Jesus forgives sins and heals a paralytic man	2:1-12	9:1-8	5:17-26
2. Jesus calls a tax collector (Levi)[20] to follow him	2:13-14	9:9	5:27-28
3. At dinner Jesus is criticized for eating with such tax collectors and sinners	2:15-17	9:10-13	5:29-32
4. A question about fasting	2:18-22	9:14-17	5:33-39
5. A controversy over how Jesus' disciples pluck and eat ears of grain in a field on the Sabbath	2:23-28	12:1-8	6:1-5
6. Jesus is condemned for healing a man with a withered hand on the Sabbath in a synagogue	3:1-6	12:9-14	6:6-11

The place is Capernaum in Galilee, and the incidents are set in various locations there—in a house, in a synagogue, alongside the Sea of Galilee, and in nearby grainfields. We need to note four things.

(1) At times certain mysterious titles like "Son of man" or "the bridegroom" crop up in what Jesus says to his opponents:

The Son of man has authority on earth to forgive sins. (Mark 2:10)
The Son of man is lord of the sabbath. (Matthew 12:8)
Can the wedding guests fast while the bridegroom is with them? (Mark 2:19)

Such titles seem to hint that a claim is being made for Jesus, and it is just such titles which we shall study later to see the assertions about Jesus at which some men took offense.

(2) These six incidents again deal with key issues of the day in the Jewish world: how sins are forgiven; religion and people in jobs of dubious propriety and "cleanness," people therefore

with whom no religious person ought to have anything to do; food regulations and table fellowship with such outcasts; pious practices like fasting; the law's requirements on keeping the Sabbath; and the very purpose of the Sabbath itself. In each case Jesus' words and actions run counter to the way the scribes and Pharisees interpreted the Old Testament law.

(3) The opponents of Jesus are rather clearly and consistently identified. They are "scribes" (Mark 2:6; Luke 5:21 adds "and Pharisees"), or "scribes of the Pharisees" (Mark 2:16), "the Pharisees" (with disciples of John the Baptist too, according to Mark 2:18), and "the Pharisees" by themselves (2:23-24) or with the Herodians (3:6). It is scribes and Pharisees, not priests, who comprise the opposition in Galilee.

(4) After each incident there is increasing opposition to Jesus, a rising crescendo of hatred, which closes with these enemies plotting Jesus' death. The very verbs which Mark and Luke choose show this change.[21] At the beginning (Luke 5:17), the Pharisees and teachers of the law are simply "sitting by." Soon there are questionings in their heart about the way Jesus acts (Mark 2:6). The people are awed at what Jesus does (Luke 5:26), but the scribes and Pharisees murmur against him and his disciples (5:30).[22] Bested twice more in their controversies with Jesus, they end up "filled with fury," making plans to destroy him (Luke 6:11). It has been observed that it would make abundant sense to move directly from this point in Mark's Gospel—"The Pharisees . . . held counsel . . . how to destroy him" (3:6)—to the beginning of the Passion narrative (14:1): "the chief priests and the scribes were seeking how to . . . kill him."[23]

It is now clear that opposition to Jesus' message and to the man himself runs throughout the gospels. During his ministry in Galilee and Jerusalem it is the scribes and Pharisees who are his regular opponents. In the Passion drama, however, it is the chief priests and the elders who send him to the cross. Here lies the problem: Why this shift in those singled out by the gospels as the opponents of Jesus?

Some have claimed that the "controversy stories" in Mark 2–3, 11–12, with their battle-lines drawn against the Pharisees rather than the priests, reflect more of the time around A.D. 70, when the gospels were being written, than the period of Jesus' own lifetime.[24] While Jesus himself no doubt did debate with Pharisees on certain points, he also seems to have stood close to them at other points.[25] The early church, however, found itself increasingly in opposition to the Pharisees and their descendants in rabbinical Judaism. After A.D. 70, when the temple was destroyed, there were no more priests; it was the Pharisees and the rabbis who constituted, and hence were identified with, the Jewish opposition to Christianity. The long tirade in Matthew 23 against the "scribes *and Pharisees*" who "sit in Moses' seat" doubtless reflects the changed situation. It is a fact that, in some of the controversy stories we have just examined, the Pharisees' criticisms are directed against the followers of Jesus (and hence the early Christians), rather than against Jesus himself (see Mark 2:18, 24).

But making allowance for this fact that the gospel records perhaps play up opposition to the Pharisees during Jesus' ministry more than might have been the case, we may say, nonetheless, that the picture in the New Testament makes sense to a modern historian. What Jesus said and did brought him onto a collision course with many religious positions of the day. His teaching differed from that of Sadducee, Zealot, Essene—and, at points, that of the Pharisee. He often clashed with precisely the most "religious" elements he met in Galilee and Jerusalem, the scribes and Pharisees. The official leaders in Jerusalem, the temple priesthood and the Sanhedrin, included, of course, representatives of several of the groups with which Jesus came into conflict. It was not some single party, like the Pharisees, but the administrative leadership in Jerusalem, in association with the Roman rulers, who had the final say. The cross cannot be regarded as the work of some particular Jewish group. It is the local manifestation in the circumstances of A.D. 30, of a more universal rejection of the divine "attack of grace," a hatred in every human heart of "one who had God constantly in his mind." No historical study about the enemies of Jesus should tempt modern readers to suppose that "we" can be excluded from the "they" in the question of the Negro spiritual, "Were you there when *they* crucified my Lord?" "We" were there—in Galilee, in Jerusalem—and not simply in the ranks of followers.

One final thing emerges from any study of Jesus' opponents. Men stood against him not merely because of what he said but because of what he did. His proclamation included acts contrary to

Sabbath-laws, it involved meals with social outcasts, glad accept-ance of "unclean men" in his disciple band. The most indelible impression of Jesus left by his enemies is the horrified remark, "This man receives sinners and eats with them" (Luke 15:2). In this way particularly Jesus himself embodied what he preached: a reign of God where sinners are mercifully accepted as they are, into table fellowship. Thus Jesus himself is tied up with the claims he made. He himself is intimately associated with the coming new age. For men rejected not merely his message, but the man from Nazareth himself.

The Claim of Jesus: Is He "Messiah"?

One of the most famous New Testament verses is the saying from the cross at Luke 23:34, "Father, forgive them; for they know not what they do." The verse is a reminder that, to a cer-tain extent, men acted in ignorance with regard to Jesus and did not realize what they were doing when they put him to death. There is another sense, however, in which it can be said of the enemies of Jesus that they did know what they were doing. Mor-ton S. Enslin has advanced the thesis that

> All who heard Jesus understood him. His enemies sent him to the cross, not because they did not know what he meant, but because they did. His first followers braved the same opposition which had cost him his life and sounded his word at home and abroad because they knew what he had meant and had accepted it as the very word of God.[26]

There is a great deal to be said for such a view. Pharisees and scribes, priests and elders, Sadducees, Herodians, and the com-mon people of the land—enough of what Jesus intended got through to them, as to his own disciples, that they could deter-mine in their own minds to be for Jesus or against him, to follow him or to oppose him and send him to the cross.

But how much did these men who heard him during his life-time know of any claim that Jesus made for himself? To what extent were they aware of titles which Christians today take so much for granted, such as "Messiah" or "King"? Jesus' message centered in God as Father, not in himself or his own preroga-tives as Son. He taught the reign of God, not the kingship of Jesus. Christians today are so accustomed to viewing Jesus in the glorious resurrection light and after nineteen centuries of confes-sion of him as lord that they find it hard to think of him apart from any of the traditional titles. Yet if one is to see him in any sense as he was during his earthly life (and indeed if believers are to appreciate the very titles with which Christian piety is accustomed to adorn his person), then one must make the effort to trace the rise of certain titles claimed for Jesus in the New Testament. The obvious one with which to begin is that which always comes first to mind in connection with the word "Christian": the title "Christ."

The term "Christ"[27] comes from a Greek work (*christos*) which means "anointed." As such, it is a translation of a Hebrew word (*mashiach*) which also means "anointed," from which is derived the term "Messiah" in English. Thus "Christ" and "Messiah" are simply words from the two principal biblical languages, both meaning exactly the same thing, an "anointed" person.[28]

Often the word "messiahship" has been used to refer not only to Jesus' status as "anointed" but also to cover all the other titles like "Son of man" and "Servant" which might be applied to him, and "messianic" has been used to refer to all expectations about Jesus and a future "golden age" to come.[29] Study of the terms "Messiah" and "Christ" will gain in precision, however, if we restrict ourselves to passages where the Bible actually uses the word "anoint" or some derivative; the other titles will be examined later in this chapter.

The first thing that a Christian studying the Old Testament must get straight is that there was no single unanimous "Jewish doctrine" of the Messiah (or the Christ) upon which Jesus could have drawn in his day.[30] The term occurs only some thirty-nine times in the entire Hebrew Scriptures. It was usually not a title, but a description. Thus it could be applied to kings: Saul, David, and all the latter's successors were "anointed" of the Lord (David, e.g., is designated "Yahweh's anointed" at II Samuel 19:21). Rather surprisingly a Persian king, Cyrus, is once called "the Lord's anointed" too (Isaiah 45:1), meaning that he had been designated for a special work. The term was likewise applied to priests; according to the law, Aaron and his sons were to be anointed (Exodus 28:41; Leviticus 4:3). One verse (which is repeated twice in the Old Testament) uses the term also to describe the patriarchs as prophets:

"Touch not my anointed ones,
   do my prophets no harm!" (Psalm 105:15 = I Chronicles 16:22)

The prophet Elijah was commissioned to anoint Elisha as his successor and to anoint new kings in both Israel and Syria (I Kings 19:15-16). It would appear that, in the world of the Old Testament, "messiah" or "anointed one" was scarcely a technical term, any more than "president" need be today.

It is the background of "anointing" in ancient Near Eastern kingship which has especially interested certain investigators recently.[31] Among Israel's neighbors the king was regularly regarded as the anointed representative of the gods. Some scholars have made much of the fact that at certain periods and in certain circles in Israel God's reign was viewed as manifested through an anointed ruler, and that in certain psalms (for example, Psalm 89:1-4, 19-20, 26-29) or in Isaiah 9-11 there was a vivid hope for a new and blessed era under some (anointed) "son of David." It is worth pointing out, however, that in all such Old Testament references to a "messiah" figure (or anointed king) this messiah is always viewed in the context of the reign of God and as subordinate to him. To put it another way, any talk of the "messiah" is in a "kingdom context," and he is at most Yahweh's "executive officer."

Even more noteworthy is the variety of views appearing in the Old Testament and other Jewish writings about "messiah" figures. It was perfectly possible, of course, to speak about the kingdom or reign of God without any reference to an anointed agent who would bring it about (though one could never speak of the "messiah" apart from the kingdom). The *Assumption of Moses,* a document probably written during Jesus' lifetime, envisioned first a messenger coming, then God himself bringing the kingdom. Here "the Eternal God" rises from his throne to begin his reign.[32] This view is in line with the picture at Malachi 3:1 and 4:5 in the Old Testament. At other times it was thought that an anointed son of David (a "Davidic messiah") would usher in the reign of God. Isaiah 9:6-7 depicts such a king in terms that have become familiar through Handel's *Messiah,* and so also does the *Psalms of Solomon,* a document of Pharisaic origin and dated about 50 B.C.[33] Yet there were times when the interest was in an anointed priest rather than an anointed king. During the Exile and afterward, kings from the line of David were no more, and priestly rulers were the hope of Israel.[34] For example, a very obscure reference at Daniel 9:25 to "an anointed one, a prince," and then in verse 26 to "an anointed one" who "shall be cut off" was originally intended to refer in verse 25 to a leader in the restored Jewish community in Palestine in the 530's and 520's B.C.—either a governor, Zerubbabel, who was of Davidic descent, or more likely his colleague, the high priest Joshua (cf. Zechariah 3–6)— and in verse 26 to a later high priest, Onias III, who was deposed in 175 B.C. and murdered. Thus the reference was to an anointed priestly ruler.[35] If the book of Enoch is pre-Christian, to sample one final view, then some Jews in the Intertestamental Period expected a chosen Messiah from heaven called "the Son of Man."[36]

It will be noted that in the Old Testament at times there is expectation of an anointed king and at times of an anointed priest. Prophets, we have said, could be anointed too. All this constitutes the background of the surprising passages which have turned up in the Dead Sea Scrolls about "the coming of the prophet and the anointed ones [plural] of Aaron and Israel."[37] The people at Qumran seem to have looked for two "messiahs" (in addition to a prophet): a "messiah [anointed one] of Aaron," a priestly figure, and, subordinate to him, a "messiah of Israel," a lay or political leader.[38] It is possible that some Jews of Jesus' day expected a single messianic figure to come from heaven, while others may have thought some gifted human leader would be raised up. If you had asked the "man in the street," in Jerusalem, he would have probably had in mind a political king, the military-leader type who would drive out the Romans,[39] most likely a descendant of David, for the scribes insisted that "the Christ [or Messiah] is the son of David" (Mark 12:35). The question about the tribute money (Mark 12:13-17) was the sort that would stir up hopes in many a Jewish heart for just that sort of military deliverer.

Faced with such variety in concept and connotations of the term "messiah,"[40] could Jesus have found the title very serviceable for his own ministry and work? The fact is that the early church, after the resurrection, did give the title "Messiah" (or in its Greek form "Christ") to Jesus. One of the earliest Christian confessions was, "Jesus is the Christ" (I John 2:22; 5:1).[41] Early preachers like Paul sought to show that "this Jesus, whom I proclaim to you, is the Christ" (Acts 17:3). John's Gospel was written so that men might "believe that Jesus is the Christ . . ."

(20:31). Acts 3:20 speaks, in the excellent phrase of *The New English Bible*, about "the Messiah [whom God] has already appointed, that is, Jesus." We must realize, though, that the early Christians were not simply taking over some one Old Testament idea of "messiah" and molding their proclamation about Jesus as Christ to fit it; they were rather giving this title "anointed one" (Messiah, Christ) new meanings derived from their actual experience with Jesus. Thus they could refer to "the Christ, Jesus" (Acts 5:42), or "Christ Jesus" (Acts 24:24), or "Jesus Christ" (Acts 10:36), all in the same book of Acts. It appears that in time "Christ" became, not a title, as it originally was, but "Jesus' last name," so to speak—as Christians today sometimes regard it. The word "Christian" itself comes, of course, from "Christ," and means, literally, one who believes that Jesus is the Messiah.[42]

But could Jesus have used this title, prior to the resurrection, during his ministry, when we recall all the wrong kinds of meanings it might have conveyed to hearers? More important, what evidence is there that he did or did not employ the title? The arguments advanced by even the conservative New Testament scholar Ethelbert Stauffer are impressive in showing that Jesus did not claim in his lifetime to be the Christ, let alone define what the term might mean to him.[43] For example, Jesus never seems to use "messiah" of himself (though the evangelist Matthew attributes it to him in a verse like 23:10). And in what is generally regarded as the oldest source, *Q*, there are no messianic affirmations about Jesus. But such general arguments will scarcely suffice without looking at the two scenes where Jesus is directly offered the title "messiah."

The first scene is that dramatic moment which the Synoptic Gospels portray at Caesarea Philippi when Peter makes his confession, "You are the Christ" (Mark 8:27-33, par. Matthew 16:13-23 and Luke 9:18-22). The passage has engrossed readers down through the centuries because of the words addressed to Peter in the Matthean version, ". . . you are Peter, and on this rock I will build my church . . ." (16:17-19). The thorny problems about Peter's authority and the founding of the church in this passage (on which the Church of Rome has set such store) will receive detailed discussion later on.[44] Here we concentrate on Peter's confession and Jesus' response.

Alone with his disciples, to the north of Galilee, on the shaded, well-watered slopes of Mount Hermon, as the story is retold, Jesus quizzes his disciples on the opinions men hold currently about him. Some, the disciples report, identify Jesus with John the Baptist, others with Elijah or one of the prophets. Thus, in the eyes of the crowd, Jesus reminds them most of a prophet, but no one seems to be calling him in public a messiah or anointed one. Then Jesus asks the disciples directly, "But who do you say that I am?" The Synoptic accounts continue as follows:

MARK 8:29-31	MATTHEW 16:16, 20-21	LUKE 9:20-22
Peter answered him, "You are the Christ."	Simon Peter replied, "You are the Christ, the Son of the living God."	And Peter answered, "The Christ of God."
And he charged them to tell no one about him.	Then he strictly charged the disciples to tell no one that he was the Christ.	But he charged and commanded them to tell this to no one,
And he began to teach them that the Son of man must suffer many things, . . . be killed, and after three days rise again.	From that time Jesus began to show his disciples that he must go to Jerusalem and suffer many things, . . . be killed, and on the third day be raised.	saying, "The Son of man must suffer many things, . . . be killed, and on the third day be raised."

While details in wording may differ, all three accounts agree that Peter called him Christ or Messiah. But Jesus does not praise him for this. Instead, he orders silence about the matter. Then he goes on to talk instead of the *Son of man* (not the messiah) and of suffering. Jesus' emphasis on the Son of man and suffering is so pronounced that Peter even tries to rebuke him (Mark 8:32), and Jesus then has to rebuke Peter, "Get behind me, Satan! For you are not on the side of God, but of men."

This incident at Caesarea Philippi can be read as a downright rejection of the term "Christ" by Jesus, if the right words are emphasized: *Peter* said, "You are the *Christ*," but Jesus warned them against saying this and began to speak of the *Son of man* instead. However, "rejection" may be too strong a word. It would be better to say that Jesus is reserved about the title "Christ," and prefers "Son of man."[45]

The other noteworthy scene where the title "Christ" is thrust
upon Jesus occurs during his trial before the Sanhedrin. Its climax
comes when the high priest asks:

MARK 14:61	MATTHEW 26:63	LUKE 22:67, 70
"Are you the Christ, the Son of the Blessed?"	"Tell us if you are the Christ, the Son of God."	"If you are the Christ, tell us. . . . Are you the Son of God, then?"

However the exact question may have been worded, Jesus is being
challenged to claim or reject the title of Christ. According to
Mark 14:62, Jesus said simply, "I am." That should end the
matter; in this one supreme moment, according to Mark, he confessed to being the Christ. But Matthew has a slightly different
answer: "You have said so" (26:64). That, too, at first seems
an affirmative answer, and many scholars take it that way. Luke,
however, has a more noncommittal answer, "You say that I am,"
and a closer look at Matthew reveals that the Greek reads literally,
"*You* [singular emphatic] have said [so]," implying "*I* do not say
so." Thus there are some who prefer Matthew's version, with the
interpretation, "*You* say so, not *I*; I don't admit to what you mean
by 'messiah.' " Luke's version also contains this implication, "*You*
[plural, emphatic] say that I am" (22:70). The construction here
is similar to that in Matthew in that it emphasizes the word
"you." In fact, even in Mark some commentators prefer a variant
reading which says, "You [singular, emphatic] say that I am," thus
combining what is found in other manuscripts of Mark with the
Matthean version.[46]

More important, just as at Caesarea Philippi, Jesus here goes
on to speak about the Son of man. In all three gospels he adds,
"You will see the Son of man sitting at the right hand of Power
[of God], and coming with the clouds of heaven" (Mark 14:62*b*).
Thus whether Jesus said "Yes" or "No" to the high priest's
question, he immediately dropped the term "Christ" and preferred to go on speaking about the Son of man. This is the significant point for our study.

At the least, one must say that during his ministry Jesus was
reticent to accept the title "messiah" when it was offered. He
never claimed it and at key moments seems to reject it or at least
wishes to talk in other terms. "Son of man" seems to have been
a greater favorite on his lips. In any case, Jesus' usage—or lack
of it—left leeway enough that, after the resurrection, the early

church could take up the title of Messiah or Christ and apply it, now purified of many of its past meanings, to him. Early Christians used the word "Christ" in light of what they knew about Jesus of Nazareth, and in light of their experience that he was now exalted as Lord; they did not make their proclamation of Jesus as Christ conform to a rigid doctrine of the Messiah.[47]

The Mysterious "Son of Man"

At the supreme moments in his life Jesus speaks about the Son of man. This is true at Caesarea Philippi, and it is also true at the trial before the high priest. Mention the term "Christ," and Jesus speaks of the Son of man.

In the four gospels the phrase "Son of man" occurs some eighty times. It figures in John just as significantly as it does in the Synoptics. What is more, the title is spread throughout all the sources usually posited for the gospels, namely Q, Matthew's special source, and Luke's L source, as well as Mark. The really striking thing, however, is that this term "Son of man" is never used by anyone else but Jesus. It is never employed by either friend or foe in addressing Jesus; it is not even used by the evangelists in narrative sections. It occurs solely on the lips of Jesus himself. When we add that "Son of man" never occurs in any of the letters of Paul, nor in any of the other New Testament epistles, and that it is found just once in the New Testament outside of the gospels (Acts 7:56),[48] then it is apparent that we have discovered (and it is statistically verifiable) a title seemingly unique to Jesus in early Christian usage: he alone employs the term. For that reason "Son of man" has been called "Jesus' own chosen, favorite messianic term."[49]

The phrase itself is an awkward one which sounds much more felicitous in English than in the Greek of the New Testament. "Son of man" is the rendering followed by virtually every English New Testament. German is able to form a single word, *Menschensohn,* but the Greek reads literally, "the son of the man," a remarkably harsh-sounding combination which must have grated on Greek ears. But that is what the gospels have as a literal translation of a Semitic phrase which occurs in the Old Testament in both Hebrew and Aramaic. That the Semitic original may have varied connotations is clear and forms part of the problem of the meaning of "Son of man."

It is probably best to get a bird's-eye view of gospel uses of
this term before tackling the Old Testament background and the
problems of interpretation. This is helpful, if for no other reason
than to see what everybody agrees on, prior to getting into an
area where there is at present probably more difference of opinion
than anywhere else in gospel studies.[50] But even before survey-
ing New Testament uses it is worth pointing out what every
writer in recent years insists upon: "Son of man" does not denote
simply Jesus' humanity as over against his divinity. That impression is sometimes given in hymns of the Christian church. "Beautiful Saviour" seems to contrast "Son of God and Son of Man,"
and S. C. Lowry's poem begins:

> Son of God, eternal Saviour,
> Source of life and truth and grace,
> Son of Man, whose birth incarnate
> Hallows all our human race. . . .[51]

Such may have been the notion of nineteenth-century hymn
writers, but we know now that "Son of man" was one of the most
pretentious terms anyone in the ancient world could use;[52] it
often suggested divinity and supernatural power, not just "humanity." When one reads it in the New Testament, one should keep
in mind overtones of a mysterious, almost awesome "Son of man"
behind at least some passages.[53]

All of the references to the Son of man in Mark, Matthew,
and Luke can be grouped under three headings.[54] The experts are
agreed on this classification, no matter how they may differ in
theory when they come to interpretation of the passages in the
three groupings. Placing the passages in these three categories will
help us get a clear picture of what the Synoptic Gospels say about
the Son of man—or properly, what they say Jesus said, since in
every instance the phrase is on his lips. In virtually every case, too,
it will be noted, Jesus speaks of "Son of man" in the third person: "The Son of man . . . *he* will do this or that." The connection between "I" (Jesus) and the Son of man (in the third person) is made directly only in a few cases, and then only in later
manuscripts. Thus at Mark 8:27, at Caesarea Philippi, Jesus asks,
"Who do men say that I am?" Matthew 16:13 words the question
as, "Who do men say that the Son of man is?" (RSV). Later
manuscripts of Matthew have combined both forms to read,
"Who do men say that I, the Son of man, am?" (RSV note).

But that is a later combination made long after Matthew's time. Matthew 16:13 views Jesus as the Son of man, but the formulation is plainly the evangelist's wording. Jesus' own question (Mark 8:27) seems not to have used the phrase, let alone to have applied it to himself. Hence the point stands, as part of the mystery, that Jesus talked often about the Son of man, but in the third person, without explicitly identifying himself as Son of man.

The first category into which "Son-of-man sayings" fall has to do with the Passion. In these sayings the Son of man is mentioned in connection with humiliation, suffering, and death, and with the announcement that God will raise him up. Typical are the three Passion predictions at Mark 8:31, 9:31, and 10:33-34 (and parallels), which have already been examined in our study of the death of Jesus in chapter 3.[55] At Caesarea Philippi, for example, after Peter's confession, Jesus began to teach his disciples:

> "The Son of man must suffer many things, and be rejected by the elders and chief priests and scribes, and be killed, and on the third day be raised." (Luke 9:22; cf. Mark 8:31)

Mark 10:45 also belongs in this category:

> "The Son of man came not to be served but to serve, and to give his life as a ransom for many."

Such sayings emphasize suffering and service. They describe what has been called the "Via Dolorosa" or way of sorrows of the Son of man.[56] The striking thing, statistically, is that all these Son-of-man Passion sayings occur in Mark (and of course in Matthean and Lucan parallels which draw on Mark). This type of saying never occurs in the Q source, though perhaps that should not surprise us, since Q is reputed to have been a collection of sayings and not to have had a Passion account.

A second classification into which a sizable number of Son-of-man sayings fits deals with the parousia, the future coming, of the Son of man on the clouds of heaven in great glory. These parousia sayings are familiar from certain well-known New Testament passages which speak in these terms, for example:

> "And there will be signs in sun and moon and stars, and upon the earth distress . . . men fainting with fear. . . . And then they will see the Son of man coming in a cloud with power and great glory." (Luke 21:25-27)

The "Little Apocalypse" (in Mark 13, par. Matthew 24 and Luke

17 and 21) is filled with references to such a "coming of the Son
of man." We have also heard such language in Jesus' answer to
the high priest:

> "You will see the Son of man sitting at the right hand of Power,
> and coming with the clouds of heaven." (Mark 14:62)

It likewise occurs directly after Peter's confession at Caesarea
Philippi, when Jesus speaks of how "the Son of man is to come
with his angels in the glory of his Father" (Matthew 16:27; cf.
Mark 8:38). This sort of language, about angels, glory, heavenly
signs, and a last judgment as history draws to a close, is the speech
of Jewish apocalyptic, the "revealing" of the final act in God's
program for the world. It is a type of thinking which flourished
late in the Old Testament and especially in the dark days of the
Intertestamental Period. In the Synoptic Gospels, sayings about
the parousia of the Son of man occur in both Mark and the Q
source. The odd thing, statistically, is that they never are combined with the Passion sayings. That is, sayings about the suffering, death, and resurrection of the Son of man never speak of his
future coming in great glory, and, vice versa, the parousia sayings
never mention the Passion of the Son of man. To put it another
way, class I sayings (on the Passion) and class II sayings (on the
parousia) are never mixed.

The third class of Son-of-man sayings, the least important
group in many ways, is miscellaneous in nature. Sayings are
classed here which have to do with neither the suffering nor the
future coming of the Son of man. Most of them have in common
the fact that they refer to the present situation of the Son of man
or his earthly activity, in contrast with sufferings to come or future
glory. For that reason, and to make them easy to remember alongside the Passion and parousia sayings, those in class III are sometimes referred to as "present Son-of-man sayings." Typical examples include:

> "Foxes have holes, and birds of the air have nests; but the Son of
> man has nowhere to lay his head." (Luke 9:58, par. Matthew 8:20)
> "John [the Baptist] came neither eating nor drinking, and they
> say, 'He has a demon'; the Son of man came eating and drinking,
> and they say, 'Behold, a glutton and a drunkard, a friend of tax
> collectors and sinners!' " (Matthew 11:19, par. Luke 7:34)
> "The Son of man has authority on earth to forgive sins." (Mark
> 2:10)
> "The Son of man is lord even of the sabbath." (Mark 2:28)

All of these examples refer to the Son of man in the present moment, at the time of speaking, in his humble life on earth, criticized by opponents, yet with an aura of authority nonetheless. This third class of Son-of-man sayings is the least troublesome to interpret. But even here, though the emphasis is on humility and humanity, there is an air of mystery which the term never loses. Furthermore, there are difficulties when some of the sayings in this group are compared with class II sayings.

Such are the ways in which Jesus uses "Son of man" in the Synoptic Gospels. The Fourth Gospel, in using the term, does not alter the situation radically. On Jesus' lips the phrase refers to suffering ("the Son of man [must] be lifted up" on a cross, 3:14) and to glory ("now is the Son of man glorified," 13:31, though it will be noted that John sees this glory in the cross and resurrection, rather than at some future coming).[57] John's Gospel develops the idea that the Son of man carries out God's judgment (5:27), and also gives a picture of the Son of man as a bridge between heaven and earth, a sort of "Jacob's ladder" let down from God to man (1:51; 3:13; 6:62). All this compounds the mystery of the term Son of man.

The one significant place in all the New Testament outside the gospels where the phrase "the Son of man" occurs is at Acts 7:56.[58] There Stephen, the martyr, cries out to his opponents just before he is stoned to death, "Behold, I see the heavens opened, and the Son of man standing[59] at the right hand of God." Here, plainly, in a moment of triumphal vision, Stephen has identified the risen, exalted Lord Jesus with the Son of man. Paul, it has been stated, never uses the title "Son of man." That is correct so far as the literal phrase "the Son of the man" goes, for Paul's Greek readers would scarcely have understood such a Semitic turn of phrase. But it is possible that Paul alludes to the Son-of-man figure when he refers to "the last Adam . . . the man . . . of heaven" (I Corinthians 15:45-49). His image is of the Man, the perfect man, yet one who also is from God in heaven (as in John's picture of the Son of man).[60]

The Jesus of the gospels, then, used "Son of man" in three ways. But the term was not used in a vacuum. For example, Daniel 7 and Jewish apocalyptic had used the phrase. Since it seems that Jesus was drawing on the Hebrew Scriptures and not just on some general concept of Man or Son of man in the ancient Orient,[61] can a precise Old Testament background be found? Here opinions vary. At least three backgrounds in the Old Testament have been suggested, and some students of the problem make use of additional, noncanonical Jewish writings which Jesus might have known. The best thing we can do at this point is to list the possible backgrounds for "Son of man." Then we can analyze the various solutions proposed to unravel the mystery.

It is apparent, to take the simplest background first, that "son of man" in Hebrew can be simply a poetic expression for "man" or "mankind." Note the parallel meanings in the verse at Psalm 8:4 (quoted at Hebrews 2:6):

> What is *man* that thou art mindful of him,
> and the *son of man* that thou dost care for him?

Here "son of man" equals "man." So also Psalm 144:3 or 146:3. The plural "sons of men" would mean "men," and that is how Scripture sometimes employs the phrase (Psalm 12:1, 8; Ephesians 3:5). There are times when this Semitic mode of expression takes on a further meaning. At Psalm 80:17 the parallelism in the lines,

> But let thy hand be upon *the man of thy right hand,*
> the *son of man* whom thou hast made strong for thyself,

suggests a particularly honored man. On the other hand, at Job 25:6 man and the son of man are described as "a worm." In these cases the term gets its meaning from the context. This background is little help in determining what Jesus meant.

Therefore the book of Ezekiel has been proposed as background.[62] Some eighty times the prophet Ezekiel is addressed as "son of man." For instance, God says, "Son of man, stand upon your feet, and I will speak with you" (2:1), or, "son of man, prophesy" (36:1). The term here may, of course, denote the frailty of man in contrast to the Lord God, as in the Old Testament generally:

> God is not man, that he should lie,
> or a son of man, that he should repent. (Numbers 23:19)

But in Ezekiel "son of man" also denotes man taken into God's service, frail man subject to God, but used as His prophet. When we recall that Jesus did strike his contemporaries as a prophet, then this background in Ezekiel seems a possibility.[63]

Perhaps even more scholars, however, are impressed with Daniel 7 as the background.[64] Daniel 7:13 is, after all, quoted in Revelation and at Mark 14:62 when Jesus speaks of the Son of man "coming with the clouds of heaven." The class II Son-of-man sayings are apocalyptic, and that is the mood of Daniel 7, as well as of a number of noncanonical Jewish writings which refer to the Son of man. To appreciate the connections between Daniel and the New Testament one ought to read through the entire majestic vision of that chapter, especially Daniel 7:13-22. Those connections are part of one of the possible explanations about the mysterious Son of man [65] The variety of backgrounds and of uses may well mystify readers today. They probably mystified the contemporaries of Jesus too, for on one occasion the crowd, according to the Gospel of John (12:34), asked point-blank, "Who is this Son of man?"

Jesus and the Son-of-Man Figure

Jesus never directly answered the crowd's question about the identity of the Son of man (John 12:34-36). For believers today there is no "orthodox" position on the Son-of-man question stated in Christian creeds (though there are traditional ones in various circles), and salvation does not hinge on belief that Jesus called himself the Son of man. The title, oddly, never found its way into any creed—the closest is in the New Testament at John 9:35 when the blind man who has been healed but then expelled from the synagogue is asked, "Do you believe in the Son of man?" The compilers of neither the Apostles' nor the Nicene Creeds saw fit, however, to include the phrase "Son of man" as part of a Christian statement of faith.

What does "Son of man" mean when it is found in the gospels? We have listed at least three possible areas of origin in the Old Testament (Psalms, Ezekiel, Daniel 7) and three classes of Son-of-man sayings on the lips of Jesus (about the Passion, the parousia, and the present). The half a dozen or so major theories which have been proposed over the years take divergent views on the matters of origin and usage. Before plunging into the various theories, we may deal briefly with the class III sayings.

These sayings about the Son of man at the present time in Jesus' ministry can in some cases be satisfactorily explained, and excluded from our problem, by noting that "son of man" may simply mean "man" or "mankind." There is nothing mysterious here. At Psalm 8:4 "son of man" has exactly the same meaning as "man." Such an explanation can be applied to Mark 2:28, for example:

"The son of man is lord even of the sabbath."

This need not mean anything more than that man is sovereign even over the Sabbath day. Indeed, Mark 2:27 seems to imply such a sense when it states:

The sabbath was made for man, not man for the sabbath.

"Son of man," then, would have no special meaning in verse 28, it means the same thing as in verse 27, "man."[66]

One explanation for the whole Son-of-man mystery is but a step beyond the fact just pointed out, that "son of man" can mean "mankind" or "man." In Aramaic, according to some experts in that language, the phrase can also mean "this man," in the sense of "one" (*on dit, man sagt*) or "I."[67] It can be simply an elaborate or circuitous way of speaking of oneself through the use of the third person. On this view, Jesus' use of "Son of man" is not mysterious or "messianic" in any sense. It is just a cryptic way of saying "one" or "I."[68] Perhaps this was the idiom Matthew had in mind when he wrote, "Who do men say that the Son of man is?" instead of what Mark had, "Who do men say that I am?" The equation "Son of man" = "I" does work in some cases, especially with the class III sayings about the present moment. "The Son of man has nowhere to lay his head" could simply mean "I have no place I can call my own." But while this explanation is attractive in some instances, it will scarcely fit all cases, especially the sayings about the Passion and the parousia. Few students of the Bible are convinced the problem is solved if "Son of man" is stripped of all Old Testament background and is viewed as merely a way of expressing the first-person pronoun. The problem is more complex than that.

It will be recalled that one of the oddities about the Son-of-man material is that the two types of Passion and parousia sayings are never mixed.[69] No verse has Jesus speaking in the same breath about the sufferings of the Son of man and the glories of the future coming of the Son of man. Many scholars have been impressed by this fact and have therefore framed theories that one class or another of the sayings was created by the early church and not spoken by the historical Jesus at all.

One such theory—and it is a second explanation of the Son-of-man problem—assumes that Jesus spoke the Passion sayings but that the apocalyptic (class II) Son-of-man sayings were placed on his lips by his followers in the early church.[70] It is argued that there is reason to believe that the three Passion predictions, in which Jesus speaks of how the Son of man must suffer many things (Mark 8:31; 9:31; 10:33-34), could go back in essence to Jesus' own thought and expectation. This theory accepts these verses but is suspicious of those that talk so much about angels, heavenly signs, and a future parousia. Such were the interests of Jewish apocalyptic, but, it is asked, was Jesus really wrapped up in these things? We know, on the other hand, that at times the young church was greatly influenced by apocalyptic thought. Paul's letters are full of it (e.g., II Thessalonians 2:1-12). We know it affected some of Jesus' parables and gave them new meanings.[71] Could not apocalyptic, the argument runs, have also infiltrated the gospels and affected even the sayings of Jesus? This view is presented for example, by John A. T. Robinson, author of *Honest to God,* who once wrote a book claiming that Jesus never taught a Second Coming, the doctrine was read back onto his lips.[72] This second position holds that the Passion sayings are authentic, the ones about the parousia not.

A third widely-held position among scholars reverses this view. This third explanation holds that the parousia sayings (class II) are authentic, but the Passion sayings not.[73] On this reading of the evidence, the verses about the Son of man's suffering, dying, and being raised on the third day are regarded as inventions of the early church after the resurrection. Jesus did not predict his Passion, but the Christians proclaimed it, after the fact, in these Son-of-man sayings. On the other hand, the class II, parousia sayings— or some of them—are accepted as things Jesus actually said. According to this view, Jesus did talk about a mysterious Son of man coming on the clouds of heaven. It is at this point, however, that an unexpected twist is introduced. Proponents of this view hold that in referring to the Son of man Jesus had in mind, not himself, but someone else. That is startling, if one is accustomed to regard Jesus as the Son of man and the phrase as a substitute for "I." There are a few verses, however, which make one pause and think. Mark 8:38 (par. Luke 9:26) is the best example, especially if certain words are italicized. Jesus says:

> For whoever is ashamed of *me* and of *my* words . . . , of him
> will the *Son of man* be ashamed, when *he* comes in the glory of
> *his* Father. . . .

Now it does seem as if Jesus is here making a distinction between
himself ("me and my words") and the Son of man. Proponents
of this view sometimes also add the "psychological argument"
that no "sane man" could ever have thought of himself as coming
on the clouds of heaven in the future. They save Jesus' sanity by
assuming that he had someone else in mind as Son of man. The
relation of Jesus to this mysterious Son of man is very close,
however, since, when the Son of man appears, one's fate will be
determined by how one has responded to Jesus and his words. It
was after the resurrection, on this view, that the momentous step
was taken when Stephen, in that moment of vision, identified the
Son of man with Jesus (Acts 7:56). Ever since then, the theory
goes, Christians have regarded Jesus as the Son of man. This
third theory enjoys the support of Rudolf Bultmann and has been
worked out in detail by certain of his pupils in Germany. Some
recent treatments by British scholars have endorsed the view.
Certain American New Testament scholars have employed the
"psychological argument" in support of such a theory.[74] But by
no means all of the critical scholars are convinced.[75] The theory
labors under the assumption that Jesus was much involved in
apocalyptic speculations but never spoke of his own fate and death.

The clearest evidence that no one theory rules the roost is the
fact that other explanations continue to be put forth. If the last
two are not startling enough, a fourth view may well be. It holds
that Jesus never spoke about the Son of man. The average reader
may wonder what prompts anyone to claim this, when the four
gospels have "Son of man" on Jesus' lips over eighty times. The
explanation depends on a fact that alert readers may have noticed:
none of the Son-of-man sayings which we have been discussing
ever mentions the kingdom of God. This is surprising, but true.
Of course, a connection has sometimes been created. Luke 17:20-
25 speaks of the kingdom, and then of the coming of the Son of
man and his prior suffering, but here several separate sayings have
probably been welded together by Luke.[76] The truth therefore is
that in the Synoptics there are verses about a Son of man who has
no kingdom, and verses about a kingdom which has no Son of
man. Now it is unthinkable to deny, say supporters of this view,

that Jesus proclaimed the kingdom of God; therefore, they conclude, it is the Son-of-man element which must have been introduced into his sayings later on. The logic is powerful, but it is an
argument from silence and has not convinced a large number of
scholars to date.[77]

At this point some readers may be weary of all theories and
may want to ask, "Why not simply assume that all of the Son-
of-man sayings were actually spoken by Jesus?" There are scholars
who hold just that view.[78] They regard "Son of man" as Jesus'
favorite title, an incognito among men which conceals as well as
reveals. However, we have learned enough to know that "Son of
man" may have different connotations in different types of sayings.
And so we must be more precise, in the interests of finding out
what Jesus meant in each case. We must also seek a more precise
background and should demand, if possible, some link between
"the Son of man" and "the kingdom." Is there any theory which
meets with some success in answering these questions?

We shall assume, because of the widespread evidence in the
New Testament sources, that Jesus did on occasion use the term
"Son of man," and that his usage roots in the Old Testament and
intertestamental Judaism. Where we come out in treating the New
Testament depends to a great extent, however, on where we choose
to begin in the Old. The late T. W. Manson, a British scholar,
long championed the book of Daniel as a basis for Jesus' use of
Son of man, and his theory (which we shall follow at many
points but modify as well) helps answer certain of the obvious
problems—though scarcely all details of the mystery.[79] A basic
question is whether Jesus' use of the term stems from apocalyptic
or not. On this score, there is much to be said for Manson's view
of Daniel 7 as the origin of Jesus' usage, rather than Ezekiel or
just the Psalms.

In Daniel 7, the prophet or seer has a dream in which four
animal-like figures appear, a lion, a bear, a leopard, and a monster
with horns and great iron teeth. These represent four empires
which have oppressed Israel, the people of God.[80] In sharp contrast to these animal figures, a fifth figure in human form appears, "one like a son of man" (7:13, i.e., a human being). This
son-of-man figure, after being overwhelmed by the fourth beast
(cf. 7:19, 21-22, 25), rises on the clouds of heaven to the throne
of God (who is called the Ancient of Days), and God grants him

dominion, glory, and kingdom (7:14). What does the vision mean? The son-of-man figure, it can be deduced from 7:18, 22, and 27, here represents "the saints of the Most High," who have held on in the war waged against them. To put it in historical terms—for Daniel was writing at the time of the Maccabean revolt, about 165 B.C.—the saints of the Most High God, represented by the son-of-man figure, were those Israelites loyal to the Lord who would suffer martyrdom rather than fall from their faith under a foreign oppressor. The vision assures them, under the guise of the image of the son of man, that they will be exalted to God's glory and receive the kingdom in God's good time.[81]

In Daniel 7, therefore, the son of man is a figure who experiences martyrdom because he is faithful to the Lord; but thanks to God, he is vindicated, exalted, and receives glory and kingship. This imagery made a great impression on the Jews, right down into the Christian era. An apocalypse from the first century A.D., IV Ezra, speaks of "the Man on the clouds of heaven," and a section of Enoch (written perhaps even later) views the Son of man as a supernatural, chosen messiah, who comes to be with the people of God.[82]

What does all this have to do with Jesus? In using "Son of man," he would certainly have been employing a title that was splendidly ambiguous. Each hearer might take from it what he wanted (as scholars do today), while at the same time the phrase gave expression to certain aspects which Jesus wished to convey. Since it means "one" or "I," he could use it to speak of himself, but in the third person. He could use it to mean "man" or "mankind," but at the same time to suggest the world of angels and God and divine judgment. It had a proper prophetic note from its use in Ezekiel, and from its apocalyptic background it struck a note of ultimacy, that God's hour was at hand. It was a term with a personal and individual sound to it—for how many other men used "Son of man" during this period to refer to themselves? It seems characteristic of Jesus. At the same time it was actually also a "corporate" term, for in Daniel it referred to a group of people, summed up in a single figure. There are those who think that "Son of man" at times has corporate connotations when Jesus uses it, referring to Jesus and his disciples,[83] much as Paul might use the phrase "in Christ" for all the company united with the Lord.

The Daniel background adds to the Son-of-man idea a "plot," an outline of happenings: it is the pattern of martyrdom, then exaltation; suffering, then victory.[84] That is just what occurred with Jesus—the "Son of man must suffer many things, be killed, and on the third day be raised." It is a plot suggested in a number of Old Testament passages and one that caught the eye of early Christians.[85] Further Daniel 7 uses the language of apocalyptic to describe the eventual glory of the Son-of-man figure; so do the Son-of-man sayings—"on a cloud, at the right hand of God, with power and great glory." Most of all, Daniel 7, alone among scriptural references, links the kingdom and the Son of man, for God gives kingship to the Son-of-man figure. Such are the implications when Jesus uses the term too: for the great boon he announces is the coming of the kingdom of God, a coming with which his words and deeds and even he himself are intimately associated. "Whosoever is ashamed of me and my words . . ."— that is the criterion for the future: response to Jesus. Yet like the words of Daniel, he too promises "a kingdom which the Father has appointed" for him and which he covenants with "those who have continued with [him] in [his] trials" (Luke 22:28-30). On all these counts, the Son-of-man title fits into the total gospel picture of Jesus.

We can scarcely answer all the problems about the Son-of-man verses.[86] Several of the theories have elements of appeal. At the least, one ought to be aware of the main lines of usage in the Son-of-man sayings, and where and why there is debate over this feature or that. The Danielic background can enrich one's understanding of the whole concept. All this information, however, cannot and ought not to strip away the proper mystery about the term. The use of it on Jesus' lips points to his role in God's drama of salvation: he undergoes suffering but clings fast in faith to God, who will bring the glory. We must not forget that prominent in the references is the fact that the Son of man, august as he is, is portrayed as serving.

The Servant of the Lord

One of the most moving and impressive figures in all of Scripture is "the Servant of the Lord." He appears in the pages of the Old Testament, especially in the "Servant Songs," scattered through Isaiah, chapters 40–53. In certain New Testament epistles and in Acts this "Servant of the Lord" is identified as Jesus Christ. Some people think that the Servant, and especially the "suffering Servant of the Lord," whom Isaiah 53 depicts, dominates the gospels as well. It has been claimed that "Servant" was Jesus' favorite term for describing his mission and work. But although the idea of a "serving lord" and a "serving church" are rich in meaning for us today, the biblical verses involved are difficult to interpret.[87] We begin with the Old Testament background.

It was a new and important step when the author of the songs in Isaiah 40–66 spoke of the nation, Israel, as "servant of the Lord." During the Babylonian Exile, about 540 B.C., the Second Isaiah, as this author is often called, announced that God had not forgotten his servant Israel (or "Jacob," as the nation is referred to at Isaiah 41:8) but had a major task for the people who were still loyal to God (Isaiah 41:8-10; 44:1-2; 48:20). In four poems, often called the "Servant Songs,"[88] all marked by the use of the phrase "my servant," the prophet then reported the Lord's words. (1) At 42:1-4, God introduces the servant as "my chosen, in whom my soul delights," who will bring "justice" (or true religion) to the nations. (2) At 49:1-6, the servant is commissioned to be "a light to the nations." (3) The servant meets opposition, however (50:4-11). (4) The climax comes in 52:13–53:12. Here, in words familiar from their use on Good Friday, the servant—who now seems an individual rather than the nation—is "rejected by men"; the "man of sorrows" suffers, is "numbered with the transgressors," and is put to death. Yet his death makes "intercession for the transgressors." The Suffering Servant is "an offering for sin" who makes "many to be accounted righteous."

This unidentified "Servant" in Isaiah is in the New Testament, after the resurrection, equated with Jesus Christ. Philip the Evangelist on the road to Gaza meets an Ethiopian treasury official who is puzzling over the servant-figure in Isaiah 53. "Was the prophet speaking about himself or some one else?" he asks. Philip uses that opening to apply the verses to Jesus (Acts 8:26-38). First Peter 2:21-25 employs whole sentences from Isaiah 53 to describe the Passion of Jesus who "bore our sins," while we were "straying like sheep."[89] Philippians 2:7 speaks of how Christ Jesus took on "the form of a servant."[90] Above all, the early Christian sermons in the book of Acts, especially those by Peter, portray Jesus as the "Servant of the Lord" (3:13, 26).[91]

Some scholars, following hints in the gospels, trace the use of the servant-figure back, not just to Peter or some other early Christian after the resurrection, but to Jesus himself during his ministry. Jesus, it is claimed, thought of himself in "Servant terms" and understood the "Son of man" in terms of the Servant of Second Isaiah. Certain verses from the gospels can even be combined to yield a picture of the Son of man much like that of the "Servant Songs":

> [The Son of man] must suffer many things, and be rejected (Mark 8:31), and be treated with contempt (9:12), and be delivered into the hands of men, and they shall kill him (9:31; cf. 10:33-34); he came not to be served but to serve [i.e., be Yahweh's servant], and to give his life as a ransom for many (10:45).[92]

Was Jesus thinking of himself as the Servant? Do we have here a "window into his mind"?

We have previously seen the difficulties involved in handling any saying about the Son of man. There are other problems, too; for example, the debate as to when this combination of "the Servant" with "the Son of man" first took place. Was it after the resurrection (as in Acts 8:26-38)? Or was Jesus the original mind who first linked the two?[93] Or, as a few scholars believe who have explored hints in Jewish literature, was the connection made prior to Jesus' day, so that Jesus was fulfilling an expectation about a "servant-messiah" current in some Jewish circles?[94] To complicate matters still more, the Old Testament background in the "Servant Songs" is not so clear as it appears at first glance.

In the Old Testament the term "servant" could simply mean a slave, perhaps in a temple (Joshua 9:23), or a servant of the king.[95] Those who worship a god are called his "servants" (Psalm 113:1; II Kings 10:23); "servants of Yahweh" thus stood in opposition to "servants of Baal." It was understood that God will care for his servants (Isaiah 65:13-14). The phrase "servants of the Lord" could be applied to the prophets (Amos 3:7), to patriarchs like Abraham or Moses (Numbers 12:7; cf. Hebrews 3:5), or to kings, like David. While individuals or certain groups in Israel could be called "God's servants," every Israelite in a sense was a "servant of the Lord," and the name "Obadiah" (borne by thirteen individuals in the Old Testament) meant originally "servant of Yahweh." It must be added that to be a servant of the Lord meant duties and obligations, and privilege and protection. There is thus ample background for Second Isaiah's use.

Three things stand out as problems, however, about references to "the servant" in Isaiah 40–53.[96] One is authorship. While some modern scholars have felt that the "Servant Songs" were written by a different hand than the nearby chapters, there is more tendency now to credit the four songs to Second Isaiah himself. But no one is sure who this "Second Isaiah" was. A second problem is whom the author had in mind as "the servant." Many verses suggest that he saw the nation of Israel or some fraction of the nation as God's servant. Jewish interpretation has followed that line. But 49:3-5 says the "servant" has a mission *to* Israel, and chapter 53 points to an *individual* as servant. Accordingly others have tried to identify some individual as the servant, perhaps the prophet himself or the Persian king Cyrus who is called the Lord's "messiah" or "anointed" (Isaiah 45:1). A common answer is that the poet was thinking at times of the nation of Israel as God's servant and at other times of an individual who summed up and represented the whole nation, as a "corporate personality."[97]

A third fact is that Isaiah's "Servant-figure" seems to have attracted little attention after 540 B.C. Later Old Testament writings seem not to refer very often to either Israel or to an individual as "The Servant." The Targum or translation of Isaiah 53 into Aramaic, the common language of Jesus' day, does, it is true, identify the Servant with the messiah, but it also carefully transfers all notion of suffering away from him to Israel or the Gentiles. It is thus not possible to find much clear expectation of a "suffering servant-messiah" in Jewish documents prior to Jesus' time, and even the Dead Sea Scrolls have not helped here.[98] It appears that "the Servant" was a part of the Old Testament in "deep freeze," awaiting development at some later time. It is important to note, too, that no one in Jesus' day spoke of the "Servant Songs" in isolation as we do; these poems were simply regarded as a part of the entire book of Isaiah. Strangely, they wielded remarkably little influence. We must be careful not to try to make Jesus fit a "servant image" which moderns have carved out of the Old Testament.

Yet the New Testament sermons and epistles do view Jesus as the Servant and specifically as the "suffering servant." First Peter, which stresses the sufferings of Christ (2:21), blends Isaiah 53 with a picture of the Passion to show the meaning of the death of Jesus: "By his wounds you have been healed" (2:24). Using Second Isaiah, Peter connects the sufferings of Jesus with the forgiveness of men's sins more clearly than even Luke and Paul. The pertinent verses in Acts and Philippians reflect the fact that Greek writers had a difficult time translating the Hebrew term "servant." Sometimes a word that suggests "slave" rather than "servant" is used (*doulos*, Philippians 2:7), at other times a term that can mean "son" as well as "servant" (*pais*; cf. Acts 3:13, 26). Thus early Christians plainly thought of Jesus as the Son who became a servant, indeed who assumed the form of a slave, and died on the cross to redeem men. He fulfills the Suffering Servant passages in Isaiah.

But how much did Jesus himself use "servant imagery"? The answer is that he employed it much less than we suppose. Even if we include what the evangelists wrote, along with what Jesus said, the net impression is at best of Jesus as servant but not as suffering servant.

Rather surprisingly, only one direct quotation from a "Servant Song" turns up on Jesus' lips in our gospels. It is Luke 22:37: "I tell you that this scripture [Isaiah 53:12] must be fulfilled in me, 'And he was reckoned with transgressors.' " That is not the most likely verse from Isaiah 53 which Christians today might choose to describe the work of Jesus. Luke apparently quotes it to explain why Jesus' disciples had swords and looked like transgressors when he was arrested (22:36, 52).

The words spoken by the heavenly voice at Jesus' baptism (Mark 1:11, par. Matthew 3:17 and Luke 3:22) echo Isaiah 42:1 and 44:2, "with thee I am well pleased." Perhaps these words, which also are spoken at the transfiguration (Matthew 17:5), are meant to identify Jesus as the Servant mentioned at Isaiah 42. However, the heavenly voice also reflects Psalm 2:7, "You are my son," and we must remember that the words are addressed *to* Jesus, not spoken by him.[99]

Therefore we are left with just a few sayings which may reflect Servant passages. Mark 2:20 has been claimed as a reflection of Isaiah 53:8, "The days will come when the bridegroom is *taken away*" (the Servant was "*taken away* from the land of the living"). When Jesus in the Upper Room speaks of "my blood of the covenant, which is *poured out for many* for the forgiveness of sins" (Matthew 26:28), some sense a reference to Isaiah 53:12, where the Servant was said to have *"poured out* his soul to death" for "the sin *of many."* These are tantalizing clues, but scarcely clear until they are pointed out—and then, in each case, highly debatable.

The famous Son-of-man saying at Mark 10:45 is the hardest one to settle as to whether or not it alludes to the Suffering Servant of Isaiah. Its wording, "The Son of man came not to be served but to serve, and to give his life as a ransom for many," seems to come right out of Isaiah 53:10-12, where the Servant "makes himself an offering for sin," for "many." Unfortunately a careful examination of the Hebrew and Greek texts reveals that the connections are not so close in the original languages as they are in English.[100] Related to this saying is Luke 19:10, "The Son of man came to seek and to save the lost," where "Son of man" has been connected with a phrase, not from Isaiah, but from Ezekiel 34:16. It is possible that yet another saying of Jesus stands behind all these verses, for in the Upper Room, at Luke 22:24-27, Jesus "lectures" his disciples about greatness in the kingdom of God and reminds them that he is among them as "one who serves." John's Gospel dramatizes the teaching at this point: Jesus washes the disciples' feet (John 13:1-17), serving them literally.[101]

The longest quotation from a "Servant Song" in any gospel comes at Matthew 12:18-21. The words are not, however, on Jesus' lips but represent a comment by the evangelist on certain events:

> This was to fulfil what was spoken by the prophet Isaiah [42:1-4]:
> [18] "Behold, my servant whom I have chosen,
> my beloved with whom my soul is well pleased.
> I will put my Spirit upon him,
> and he shall proclaim justice to the Gentiles.
> [19] He will not wrangle or cry aloud,
> nor will any one hear his voice in the streets;
> [20] he will not break a bruised reed
> or quench a smoldering wick,
> [21] till he brings justice to victory;
> and in his name will the Gentiles hope."

Matthew sees the incidents from Jesus' life which he has just been reporting in chapters 8–12 as fulfillment of these words. The fact that Jesus would not argue with his enemies but withdrew (12:15) is taken as fulfilling the words, "He will not wrangle . . . ," and the next line, no one will "hear his voice in the streets," applies to the fact that Jesus ordered those whom he healed "not to make him known" (12:16). That Matthew intended to identify Jesus as the Servant is further made evident at 8:17. There Matthew quotes Isaiah 53:4, "He took our infirmities and bore our diseases"; this Matthew sees fulfilled in the various healing miracles he reports in 8:1—9:33. Plainly, for Matthew, Jesus fulfills the Servant's role in these ways, but strikingly, nothing at all is said about a *suffering* servant. The words in Isaiah 53 on suffering are not employed.[102]

What do we make of all these references? Jesus appears as "one who serves." He practiced and taught a life of service. He ministered to human needs. Yet he uses the technical "Servant-language" of Second Isaiah much less than one expects. According to the Synoptic accounts, Jesus elsewhere did quote from the book of Isaiah. In answer to John the Baptist, he recalled Isaiah's words to describe his work (Matthew 11:4-6, par. Luke 7:22-23), and he read Isaiah 61:1-2 in the synagogue at Nazareth to describe his mission (Luke 4:16-21). Elsewhere Jesus referred to Old Testament figures like "the shepherd" to describe himself (Mark 14:27 = Zechariah 13:7), but for some reason he did not employ —at least widely—the servant-of-the-Lord image. The most likely reason is that "the Servant" was not a widely appreciated figure in Jesus' world.

One must therefore say that while Jesus did spend himself in serving, it was only later on that his followers rediscovered the words of Isaiah, which took on new meaning in light of the actual life lived by Jesus. Romans 5:18-19 speaks of him as the "One Man for all men," whose obedience led to many being accounted righteous; the words are influenced by Isaiah 53:11, but the portrait in Paul's mind is that of Jesus who died upon the cross.[103]

What Jesus did as "one who served" has left a far greater impression on the gospels and in the lives of Christians than any quotes he employed out of the "Servant Songs." This point is brought home by a startling fact in the book of Acts. Three times phrases from Isaiah are quoted to describe a missionary task. Acts 13:47 is from a "Servant Song" (Isaiah 49:6):

> I have set you to be a light for the Gentiles, that you may bring salvation to the uttermost parts of the earth.

Acts 26:17-18 reflects Isaiah 35:5 and 42:6-7:

> I send you to open the Gentiles' eyes, that they may turn from dark-
> ness to light. . . .

Acts 28:26-27 quotes the words of Isaiah 6:9-10, which begin,

> Go to this people, and say. . . .

The striking thing is that all these verses from Isaiah, with their
Servant-language, are applied to Paul, not Jesus. Paul, a servant
of Jesus Christ, had learned that following Christ means carrying
out the servant's role. That is something the church and disciples
were meant by the New Testament authors to learn—and practice.

The Son—of God!

Jesus of Nazareth made an impression on his followers which
led them to refer to him in their gospel-witnessing not only as
messiah, Son of man, and servant of God, but also as the Son of
God.[104] This latter term is a principal element in the confession
which in the form of a "fish" later Christians carved on the walls
of the catacombs; the symbol derives from the first letters of the
Greek words for "Jesus Christ, Son of God, Savior"—*Iēsous
Christos Theou Huios Sōtēr*, spelling the Greek word *ichthus*,
"fish." "Son of God" is a phrase which, while experiencing certain changes in meaning, has survived to the present with probably
more influence than any other title ascribed to Jesus; in this way it
differs from "Son of man," which was little used after Jesus'
day.[105] On the other hand, "Son of God" differs from "Servant"
and "Christ" in that one finds it used not only by others about
Jesus but also, in one form or another, on the lips of Jesus himself. In short, we have in "Son of God" a phrase which can be
seemingly traced back to Jesus (as "Christ" cannot) and which
has exerted profound influence over Christians down to our times.

Unfortunately, this title for Jesus which continues to have such
importance is capable of misunderstanding today in at least three
ways. For one thing, when some, especially those outside the
church, hear the claim that Jesus is the Son of God, they are apt
to think of it in crass, physical terms. They call to mind the birth
stories and think of some of the old pagan myths about the gods'
begetting offspring of human mothers. The expression "Son of
God" has a biological ring to it. Secondly—and this is the danger
for people inside the church who hear traditional creeds recited
habitually—"Son of God" calls to mind metaphysical terms like
"substance" and similar words deriving from Greek philosophy.

The phrases of the Nicene Creed, "the only-begotten Son of God, . . . Begotten, not made, Being of one substance with the Father," tempt one to interpret the New Testament affirmations about Jesus in the categories of Greek philosophy. As if this were not enough, there is the persistent danger, thirdly, that moderns will nullify the intent of Scripture when it calls Jesus "Son of God" by means of a widespread notion that "after all, men everywhere, all men, are by nature sons of God." Careful analysis of what the New Testament means by "Son of God" is needed lest one sell its meaning short as pagan myth, philosophical abstraction, or pious platitude. The New Testament meant something else than such things.

Previously we have seen that one of the Greek words for "servant" (*pais*) which was applied to Jesus could also mean "son."[106] Thus at Acts 3:13 Peter's sermon can be said to deal with "God's servant Jesus" or with "God's son" (RSV note, "Or *child*"). We learned also in our study of the prayer which Jesus taught his disciples that he addressed God intimately as "Father" —that is, in the language of a son.[107] The church which Jesus had taught to pray "Abba! Father!" (Romans 8:15) came to think of Jesus as the Son of the Father. There is no question but that early Christians soon came to regard the man from Nazareth as Son of God (cf. Acts 8:37).[108] The title appears in all the strata of the Synoptic Gospels, Mark, *Q*, *M*, and *L*, as well as in John.

The first gospel to be written has "Son of God" only some five times, but all these occasions in Mark are significant. The very title of the book, according to some manuscripts, is "The Beginning of the Gospel of Jesus Christ, the Son of God." Twice demonic spirits confess him as "Son of (the Most High) God" (3:11; 5:7). The climax of the Jewish trial comes when the high priest asks Jesus (14:61), "Are you the Christ, the Son of the Blessed?" (which is a Semitic paraphrase for "Son of God"). The climax of the entire book is the words of the Roman centurion at 15:39, "Truly this man was the Son of God!"[109] No one could read the Gospel of Mark without becoming aware of this basic point of witness, that Jesus is God's Son. This emphasis grows in the later gospels. John's whole purpose is to show that "Jesus is the Christ, the Son of God" and that life may be had, by believing, in his name (20:31).

Now the very emphasis on this point in Mark and his successors has led some scholars to be suspicious of the title, regarding
it as an accretion originating in the Greek-speaking church. They
point out that "son of God" was a common title in the pagan
world. The kings of Egypt had claimed to be descendants of the
sun-god Ra. During Jesus' lifetime, Caesar Augustus was using
the phrase "son of God" on his coins and inscriptions, claiming
to be *"filius divi."* Later Roman emperors gloried in the claim of
divinity. Many were the legends about men who had been made
divine, and every city had its shrines for deified men. Such were
the connotations of "son of God" in the Greco-Roman world, and
some investigators suspect that the gospels, written in such a
world, applied the well-known pagan epithet to Jesus as part of
their efforts to honor him.[110]

In view of such suspicions, it is particularly important to note
the Semitic background of the phrase "Son of God," for this
title does appear in the Old Testament with various meanings.[111]

(1) "God's son" can be applied to the nation of Israel. Moses
was told to tell Pharoah, "Thus says the Lord, Israel is my first-
born son" (Exodus 4:22). That is the meaning of the famous
verse at Hosea 11:1, where God says, "Out of Egypt I called my
son." Hosea's reference was to the Exodus when God called his
"son," the Israelite people, out of captivity. (This is the verse
which Matthew later reapplies to Jesus, Matthew 2:15.) Hosea
even goes on to picture his people as a child whom God has
cradled in his arms, cared for, and taught to walk (11:3, 8).

(2) More specifically the Old Testament can apply "Son of
God" to the king, as the leader and symbol of the nation of Israel.
The king is the anointed ruler whom God has chosen and whom
he even deigns, according to the ancient formula used at royal
coronations, to call his son. Second Samuel 7:14 enshrines the
promise of Yahweh to David, delivered through the prophet
Nathan, "I will be his father, and he shall be my son." Psalm
89:19-20, 26-29 reflects this promise to David, who calls God
"my Father" (verse 26), and Psalm 2:7 records this decree of
the Lord with a formula for the adoption of the king by God,
proclaimed at his enthronement: "You are my son, today I have
begotten you."

(3) Such language can also be applied to other figures besides
Israel and its king, figures who have some special commission

from God. For just as use of "son of God" denoted a special position and task for the nation and king of Israel, so the same phrase could be employed for others entrusted with some particular status and task. The expression "sons of God" seems to have been used sometimes of the ministering angels of the Lord (Daniel 3:25, 28). Thus, according to the book of Job, the "sons of God" (or angels) are said to have shouted for joy, "when the morning stars sang together" at the creation of the world (38:7); they are also described as presenting themselves before God on certain days as a sort of court (1:6; 2:1). The very obscure passage as Genesis 6.2 seems to refer to angels as sons of God who transgressed from their appointed tasks. A much debated question is whether Jewish writings prior to Jesus' day ever referred to the messiah as "son of God." It is much debated—and most experts have given a negative answer—because there is lacking precise evidence to tell how early the "royal psalms" like Psalm 2 with their Son-of-God language (2:7) were applied to the messiah. A fragment from the caves of Qumran has been reported, however, which uses "son [of God]" in a messianic sense.[112] All in all, it would seem that one need not go to the Greek world to find a background for New Testament usage of "Son of God." The title already existed in the Hebrew writings, applied to Israel, its king, to angels, and probably to the messiah. Indeed, any righteous Israelite could be called a son of God, a God who "will love you more than your mother does" (Sirach 4:10).

The most important thing to note in this Semitic background for "son of God" is the meaning of the phrase. These Old Testament references have nothing to do with a physical begetting, as in pagan myths, like those about Heracles as son of Zeus by the mortal woman Alcmene, or Achilles as son of a sea-goddess, Thetis, and Peleus, a mortal man. For the Lord to have intercourse with a female consort or a human being was absolutely repugnant to the Hebrew faith.[113] The references also have nothing to do with "being," "substance," or any of the other terms of Greek metaphysics. The Hebrew usage denotes a moral relationship rather than a physical or metaphysical one. Its meaning was functional, that is, it referred to a nation's or an individual's functioning in a close personal relationship with God. This moral side may be seen in the phrase "son of Belial" (I Samuel 2:12, KJV), which refers, not to physical descent, but to a wicked na-

ture (RSV, "worthless men"). The functional aspect comes to
the fore in the Semitic phrase found in the New Testament, "sons
of the bridechamber"; that means wedding guests (Mark 2:19,
compare KJV and RSV). Thus, against this background, to be
"son of God" would mean to stand in a moral and functional
relationship to God, not to be biologically generated by God or
compounded of the same "substance."

Specifically, in light of the Old Testament examples, to be
designated "son of God" means being chosen or elected to a task,
thus participating in the work of God; it implies also obedience,
the obedience of a son to a father. Such filial obedience, unfortunately, is what at times the nation of Israel and its kings, and
at times even the angels lacked. Jesus did exhibit such obedience,
and every time the term "son of God" is applied to him in the
New Testament the idea is nearby that he was obedient, even to
death. "Son though he was, he had to prove the meaning of
obedience through all that he suffered" (Hebrews 5:8, J. B.
Phillips). To be the Son of God means to obey the Father's will.
The discipline involved in being God's son is vividly portrayed
at Hebrews 12:5-11. So, the epistles.

But in the Synoptic Gospels are there any expressions of this
idea of the obedience of a true son, chosen to carry out the
Father's will, in passages which go back to Jesus himself and not
just to the declarations of the early church? We have already referred to Jesus' use of "*Abba,* Father," in addressing God.[114]
Professor Joachim Jeremias, who has devoted intensive study to
this word, believes that no one in Judaism dared speak to God
in this intimate way until the eighteenth century A.D. and that we
have here a daring innovation on Jesus' part, possible only for
one who believed he stood in a unique relationship to God.[115] If,
the argument runs, we had only the one prayer of Jesus in Gethsemane as evidence, "Abba, Father, . . . what thou wilt" (Mark
14:36), we would, by these few words alone, be compelled to
conclude that Jesus' understanding of himself was as God's
chosen, obedient son. He is "the Son."

There is also a series of sayings from Jesus which begin with
the verb "I came":

I came not to call the righteous, but sinners. (Mark 2:17)
I have not come to bring peace, but a sword. (Matthew 10:34)
The Son of man [= I] came to seek and to save the lost.
(Luke 19:10)

Let us go . . . that I may preach . . . for that is why I came out.
(Mark 1:38)

Opinion is divided about these verses, but some commentators
sense that they express not only a consciousness of his mission on
Jesus' part but also a hint about his origins: he had come from
God and stood in a special relationship to him.[116] Here would
then be the idea of sonship, an idea which the supposedly "more
developed theology" in the Gospel of John expresses quite clearly:
"I came from the Father and have come into the world" (16:28).
"Do you say . . . 'You are blaspheming' because I said, 'I am the
Son of God'?" (10:36).

In addition, the gospels contain places where Jesus is called
"Son of God" by others. The demons call him that (Mark 3:11;
5:7), and so does a voice from heaven at his baptism and again
at the transfiguration (Mark 1:11; 9:7).[117] In the temptation
narrative Satan begins his onslaught with the words (Matthew
4:3, par. Luke 4:3), "If you are the Son of God, . . ."—expressing, not doubt that Jesus stood in a unique personal relationship with the Father, so much as the desire to make him disobedient to that sonship. These passages are meant to show us that the
"supernatural world"—demons, the devil, and God—recognizes
Jesus as Son of God in the Old Testament sense of chosen, conse-
crated, and obedient.

All of this is indirect evidence, however, involving what others
say, or using related terms like "Father." Are there any places
where Jesus in the Synoptics calls himself "Son," if not, in the
fuller term, "Son of God"? Three appear worth investigating.

Mark 12:6 (par. Matthew 21:37; Luke 20:13) occurs in the
parable of the Wicked Tenants, which we have already noted in
connection with Jesus' debates with his opponents.[118] To the un-
grateful farm workers who have beaten up his messengers and
refused to give him his due, the master sends last of all "his son"
(so Matthew; Mark 12:6 and Luke read, his "beloved son").
It is difficult to hold that Jesus used originally the full phrase
"beloved son," since the Matthean version does not have the adjective "beloved," which sounds like allegorical detail from
preachers who retold the parable in the early church. But can we
cross off the entire parable as a creation of the early Christians? In
favor of its authenticity is the fact that the parable in vss. 1-9
contains no reference to the resurrection of the Son, which one

would expect if this parable were composed after Easter. A. M. Hunter is possibly right in claiming that this parable is autobiographical, with the man who told it as the central figure.[119] Here, in a last appeal to Israel in the crisis which his coming brings, the one who calls God "*Abba*, Father" recognizes the full danger to which his obedience as a son will bring him. He goes on along the way of the Son of God, like the messengers (prophets) before him—to death (compare Matthew 23:34-37, par. Luke 11: 49-51, 13:34). In this parable Jesus could have alluded to himself as "the son."

The most disputed passage in which Jesus speaks as Son is the *Q*-saying at Matthew 11:25-27, par. Luke 10:21-22:

> I thank thee, Father, Lord of heaven and earth, that thou hast hidden these things from the wise and understanding and revealed them to babes; yea, Father, for such was thy gracious will. All things have been delivered to me by my Father; and no one knows the Son except the Father, and no one knows the Father except the Son and any one to whom the Son chooses to reveal him.

In the Fourth Gospel such language would sound at home, but in *Q*, that earliest collection of Jesus' teachings, the verses have been called "a thunderbolt fallen from the Johannine sky."[120] Fifty years ago the saying was under grave suspicion as a creation of the early church. A noted Jewish commentator, usually very generous in his comments on Jesus, confessed he would like to prove these words spurious, since if it could be shown that Jesus really uttered them, orthodox Christianity would receive notable encouragement.[121]

The tendency in recent years in many circles has been to defend the words as genuinely from Jesus.[122] One must not, of course, take "Father" and "Son" in a later, Greek sense. One must remember that the word "reveal" fits in with Jesus' general message, announcing the reign of God soon to be established. Clear evidence that these words need not be a Hellenistic innovation is the fact that centuries before, in the Semitic world, the Egyptian Pharoah Akhenaten (Amenophis IV) said in his "Hymn to the Sun" (fourteenth century B.C.), "No other knows thee except thy son Akhenaten." In Jesus' own time the Teacher of Righteousness at Qumran claimed in a similar way to have knowledge from God, by revelation.[123] These Semitic parallels are grounds for claiming that a man in Palestine in the first century A.D. could have spoken

this way. If Jesus did, then we have here his "prophetic consciousness" raised to a higher degree; his consciousness of vocation and
obedience to his mission (expressed in prayer by the word "Abba") is now more clearly expressed. One can even note in these
verses what Stauffer has called "a declaration of war" on Qumran
and all others like the Teacher of Righteousness who claimed to
reveal God.[124] Jesus' words may parallel theirs in some ways. But
his words are noteworthy for suggesting that he uniquely claims
to be announcing God's plan and will. Jesus alone does this, as
Son.

If Jesus in this way occasionally hinted at his own role as God's
obedient spokesman, as Son, it remains true that he was nonetheless reserved in describing this role and anxious to limit it to
God's reign and the immediate implications thereof. Jesus did not
present himself as a "know-it-all" about anything and everything,
as a final key verse shows. Mark 13:32, speaking of the dates
when Jerusalem would fall and when God's final plan would be
put into effect, says, "Of that day or that hour no one knows, not
even the angels in heaven, nor the Son, but only the Father." If
the passage we have just discussed is dismissed by some scholars
because in it Jesus lays claim to special knowledge, this verse in
Mark is, ironically, dismissed by others even though in it Jesus
professes ignorance! For here Jesus denies he knows the date for
what will come to pass. However, still other scholars, including
some of the radical ones of a generation ago, have regarded Mark
13:32 as a "pillar" on which a "life of Jesus" might be erected,
just because of its admission of ignorance; the verse is so daring,
they said, that no early Christian would have thought of inventing
it.[125] We may note that Jesus in this verse uses the title "Son,"
but to affirm his ignorance about certain things.

Could the historical Jesus have spoken this way? Yes, we may
answer, if we are convinced that he, while genuinely a man, was
one who knew God so intimately as to call him *"Abba."* Confidence that these three passages stem from Jesus of Nazareth is
strengthened by the fact that in all three of them he is called
simply "the Son," whereas in the preaching of the early church
he is referred to as "Son of God" (Acts 8:37 or Romans 1:4,
e.g.); and by the fact that the preaching of the early church connects the title "Son of God" with specific Old Testament verses
(usually Psalm 2:7 or II Samuel 7:14) and with the resurrection

(Romans 1:2, 4), whereas these three passages are not Old Testament citations and there is no talk of the resurrection, even in the parable of the Wicked Tenants.[126] Thus, Jesus seems to have spoken of himself as "the Son," though the fuller concept of "Son of God" had to wait until after the resurrection for development.

All in all, the gospel evidence allows the conclusion that Jesus did regard himself as the Son, in the Old Testament sense. In public utterance, he preferred the ambiguous but significant title "Son of man." He never used the word "Christ" of himself, and he exhibited a claim to the title of "God's Servant" more through his whole life and death than by use of specific citations from Isaiah. The impression he left with many contemporaries was that of prophet and teacher, but in an authoritative sense. All these titles, often little used during his lifetime and vaguely perceived during his trial as a claim made by Jesus, flowed together after the resurrection to give believers a fuller picture of the meaning of his coming. While some of the words may go back historically to Jesus, one dare not underestimate the resurrection and the coming of the Spirit as the real factors in developing an understanding of Jesus' person and work—what is called "Christology."[127]

In this chapter by no means all the later titles for Jesus have been taken up. Already in the New Testament the confession that "Jesus is the Lord" was a keystone for faith, for example.[128] But we have seen the general course of development and have examined the titles that are particularly important in the gospels.

After the resurrection the early church was faced with a choice. On the basis of their experiences with Jesus of Nazareth and now with the risen lord, Christians had to decide between "Jesusolatry" (an adulation of the man and hero worship of him) and "Christology" (a doctrine of his work and person in relation to God's purpose and all that that implies).[129] For the most part they chose Christology—not simply a worship of the man Jesus, but the spelling out of his meaning as Christ, lord, Son of God, and all the other titles men have laid at his feet. The process has gone on over the centuries—through great councils at Nicaea and Chalcedon, in the language of poets and hymn writers, in the devotion of countless believers. It will reach its final goal—the New Testament declares, in its moments of eschatological vision—only when people of every tongue and nation own him as king of kings and lord of lords. Meanwhile, today it reaches its personal climaxes each time we grope for words—out of the ancient creeds, from the New Testament, or from personal experience—to declare him what he is for us.

10

Promises and Puzzles— Jesus and His Followers

"Jesus came preaching the kingdom of God—and the church resulted!" So runs a stinging and oft-repeated taunt against New Testament Christianity.

Anyone is apt at times to sympathize with such a contrast between "the man from Galilee" and the church in the form in which it is known today, organized and institutional. Even the most loyal church member must be tempted on occasion to see a tension between the reign of God as Jesus proclaimed it and the acknowledgment of God's lordship as it has been developed in the church. This contrast points up one of the most baffling puzzles in gospel study: Did Jesus "found" a church?

To state the matter in the boldest, most negative terms, only one of the four gospels ever even uses the word "church." That gospel is the most "ecclesiastical" of the four, Matthew, and both its references are disputed as to authenticity. The one, Matthew 18:17, seems to be part of a section of rules for church discipline which grew up long after Jesus' death. The other is the famous verse made so controversial by Roman Catholic use and emblazoned on the dome of the Pope's church, St. Peter's, in Rome, "You are Peter, and on this rock I will build my church . . ." (16:18). In the face of such a situation, it is indeed debatable whether during his ministry Jesus established a church in any historical sense.

Related is the problem of Jesus' view of the future. Did he envision a short or long interval before the consummation of the world? An interval long enough to establish a church? Let alone, a "time" or "age" of the church in the world, lasting for decades or centuries? This puzzle, too, has divided scholars and puzzled Bible readers over the years.

We have already learned, however, to make distinctions between Jesus' ministry and the period after the resurrection. We have often had to set in contrast the periods before and after that great turning point, the resurrection, before and after the coming of the Holy Spirit. And so here, too, with the church. Perhaps one must look for its birth, not during Jesus' ministry, but only after Easter, with the gift of the Holy Spirit. Perhaps the best one can expect are links between the lifetime of Jesus and the "age of the church," so that there is some sort of continuity between disciples who followed Jesus and members who live in his body, the church, so that there is a continuity between certain promises of his and the fulfillment in subsequent experiences. In this chapter we shall look at several such "links." But first we must examine a number of passages where Jesus is presented as speaking of what lay ahead for the followers he had gathered, and for the world.

Jesus and the Future

The Synoptic Gospels are shot through with passages about the future. Sayings on the lips of Jesus look beyond his death to his resurrection or vindication by God. Words of his refer to catastrophes on earth and persecution for the disciples. Discourses deal with the coming of the Son of man and the "end of the age." Needless to say, there has been debate for more than a century over which of these are authentic and whether Jesus looked for a consummation to all history within his lifetime, or for a brief interval before the end, or for a period of church history, or for thousands and thousands of years of the historical process before the climax comes.[1]

We have already met with Albert Schweitzer's view that Jesus expected the world to end during his ministry (Matthew 10:23) or at least shortly after his death (Mark 9:1).[2] Reference has also been made to the attempt by J. A. T. Robinson to claim that Jesus never taught a "Second Coming"—that all such references are creations of the early church, and that verses like Mark 14:62 or 8:38 refer to Jesus' *going* to the Father, not his coming again (cf. Daniel 7:13)[3] It is well-known from church history how various Adventist and similar religious groups, on the basis of sayings from Jesus and other biblical passages, have constructed "timetables" for the end of the world, supposed to occur, for example, in 1914, 1959, or 1990. They seek to "decode" Jesus' words to reveal the date of "Armageddon" (Revelation 16:16)[4]—in spite of the promise that Christ will come like a thief in the night (Revelation 16:15), not on the basis of some well-announced travel plan. It is likewise well-known how other groups have often attributed to Jesus (on even less biblical grounds) an optimistic hope for continuing evolution in the world until the kingdom is achieved among men, painlessly and antiseptically.

With so many theories competing, it is no wonder that Jesus' view of the future is a matter of considerable confusion. A variety of opinions often flourishes where there are few facts. Such is the case here, for there is far less solid evidence about what the historical Jesus thought concerning the future than is often supposed, and at certain points one must simply be content to say, "We do not know what Jesus thought on this or that."

Perhaps as good a place to start as any is to recall that during his lifetime Jesus was regarded as a prophet.[5] That means, in biblical terminology, primarily a "forth-teller" of God's will, not a "fore-teller" of the future. However, the two aspects are often related, and forthright statement about what God was going to do in the near or distant future was regularly a part of a prophet's role. One may say that for Jesus this sort of "discerning of the times" under the hand of God had to do especially with the fall of Jerusalem. The Synoptics depict him as predicting that the Jews, running an ofttimes proud, determined course, restive and rebellious, would collide with Rome's power, and the result would be destruction for the Holy City and death and captivity for many of the people. We need not invest Jesus with any "divine" nature to make plausible the probability that he could have foreseen such a national catastrophe. Anyone with discernment and a willingness to "count God in" so far as the world's activities go, might foresee such a result. Indeed, some of the rabbis in the fifties and sixties saw it too and warned against the "collision course."[6]

It is likewise not impossible that Jesus, aware of how prophets for God had suffered in the past, mindful of the experience of John the Baptist, and acutely conscious of the experience of opposition which he was himself encountering, might have spoken also of opposition for his followers. This might include suffering and, in the future, even martyrdom. Those who chose to be disciples of his must be told what following him might entail.

To this picture may be added—though the evidence is less accessible and tangible—that Jesus claimed some insight into God's overall plan. At the least this means he could have seen the great drama and sweep of Israel's history in the past and might have believed that God by revelation had enabled him to see how he and his message were part of the continuation and fulfillment of this unfolding plan. It might mean also that he even saw something of how his own work and death, as well as a period beyond, until the judgment and consummation, fitted into God's plan. Such a cryptic statement as, "This generation will not pass away till all has taken place" (Luke 21:32, par. Matthew 24:34; Mark 13:30), hints that Jesus might have entertained such thoughts, but unfortunately we are not told what "all" means or what "all these things" (Mark 13:30) includes. Indeed, just two verses later comes a disclaimer that Jesus knew every detail (Mark 13:32). Hence, one must be cautious, to say the least, about claiming that Jesus during the years on earth was cognizant of all God's plans, even though his prophetic announcements do reveal a conviction that God's plan was being manifested in the kingdom.

This "prophetic consciousness" of Jesus was also intensified by the apocalyptic element so common in his day. While in the centuries prior to Jesus prophets were widely reputed to have ceased in Israel,[7] Judaism nonetheless had its apocalyptic seers, like the author of Daniel, who carried on certain of the functions of classical prophecy. At Qumran there were those who had visions of the future like that described in the "Scroll of the War between the Sons of Light and the Sons of Darkness."[8] Apocalyptic played a part not to be minimized in early Christianity (cf. II Thessalonians 2:1-12, or the book of Revelation).[9] There is every likelihood, therefore, that Jesus' own outlook included some apocalyptic aspects. Certainly his sayings as recorded for us do speak of catastrophic happenings and of a dramatic "end of the world" accompanied by lightning-flashes, flames of fire, and judgment. Some scholars have tended to make Jesus *only* an apocalyptist. Some have argued, on the other hand, that Jesus' teachings were later made "more apocalyptic" in the early church.[10] The actual evidence suggests that Jesus employed some apocalyptic imagery, but the early church may have enhanced this feature in some of its portraits of him (cf. Revelation 1:12-18).

Generally, with regard to Jesus' teachings about the future, the following conclusions stand out. (1) There was a remarkable reserve on his part compared to apocalyptists before him and some of the prophets in primitive Christianity. He said, "Of that day or that hour no one knows, not even the angels in heaven, nor the Son, but only the Father" (Mark 13:32). This word about the time of the parousia has been called "a pillar passage" on which any "life" of Jesus must be constructed, for it denies omniscience to Jesus in a way which seemingly no early Christian would have dared invent.[11] (2) The teachings of Jesus can be expected to employ many conventional apocalyptic symbols about angels, earthquakes, and dire predictions on "the days to come," just as in the intertestamental writers.[12] On occasion these phrases may be additions from the early church, but some of them could come from Jesus himself. In either instance these phrases are, according to apocalyptic convention, symbols and not literal descriptions or precise "timetables." (3) In such teachings attributed to Jesus it is necessary to ask whether the reference is to events which occurred at the fall of Jerusalem in A.D. 70 or to an ultimate and final consummation, expected in the future. These two topics are often blurred together in the gospel accounts.

The prime example in the gospels where we have a considerable compilation of materials about "the end" is Mark 13 and its parallels. Most of the contents of this chapter has been incorporated by Matthew in an even longer discourse beginning at 24:1. However, Matthew has also built up his "discourse about the end" by adding to what was found in Mark some materials from Q and M. In particular, he has supplemented Mark 13 by adding a series of parables (24:37 ff.), including those in chapter 25 where, we have seen,[13] his parables speak to the question of Christians and the parousia (25:1-30) and to the problem of pagans and the Last Judgment (25:31-46). However, Matthew has also seen fit to transfer part of Mark 13 to another discourse, Matthew 10: 17-21 (par. Mark 13:9-12), where it is part of a missionary discourse in chapter 10. In Luke, the materials from Mark 13 appear at two different points: some in Luke 21:8 ff., some in 17:22-37. Luke thus has Jesus discuss the "last things" both in Jerusalem (chapter 21), as in Mark and Matthew, and on the way through Samaria (17:22 ff.).

When one thus sees how the apocalyptic material of Mark 13 turns up at several places and in different guises in the various Synoptic Gospels, one can appreciate the fact that Mark 13 is one of the few individual chapters in the Bible on which an entire commentary has been composed.[14] Its contents bristle with difficulties. For example, what is the setting? Mark places the discourse "on the Mount of Olives opposite the temple," with Peter, James, John and Andrew present, an "inner group" out of the twelve (13:3). Matthew has the same setting but all the disciples seem to be present (24:3) for this private discourse. Luke, however, places the teaching in the temple (where Luke sets all of Jesus' teaching in Jerusalem; cf. 19:47, 20:1; 21:1-8); further- more, he makes no indication that these are private teachings, they seem open and public (cf. 21:5, 37).

A similar difficulty arises with the subject matter. In Luke the disciples ask what the "sign" for the destruction of the *temple* will be (21:7). However, Jesus' words also go on to speak of the future parousia of the Son of man (21:27), even though Luke means this coming of the kingdom to be understood as off in the future, far beyond A.D. 70 (cf. 21:8, 24, 28). Mark speaks more ambiguously of "when these things are all to be accom- plished" (13:4). By "these things" he means events associated with Jerusalem's fall as well as happenings at "the end of the world." Only Matthew makes clear that the sayings which follow deal with two topics: (1) "When will this [destruction of the temple] be?" and (2) "What will be the sign of your coming[15] and of the close of the age?" (24:3). One of the "fine arts" in interpreting Mark 13 and parallels is to discern what applies to A.D. 70 and what was regarded as still future when Matthew and Luke wrote.

One hardly needs to pile up examples of problems of meaning in individual verses of Mark 13. Many a reader has no doubt puzzled over them himself, and scholars still have not fathomed certain features. For example, what does "this generation" mean at Mark 13:30: "This generation will not pass away before all these things take place"? Some think it means "this world," or the "race of men." Common sense tells us, however, that the phrase ought to mean the generation of men to which Jesus be- longed. The trouble is, however, that that generation had died out by late in the first century, without the Son of man having come with his angels (13:24-27). Or did "these things" originally re- fer, not to the parousia, but to the fall of Jerusalem (cf. Luke 21:20-24), a "visitation" which did occur that generation?[16]

At Mark 13:29, in the application of the parable of the Fig Tree, what is to be made of the fact that there is a reference in Mark and Matthew to the Son of man ("*he* is near, at the very gates," Mark 13:29; cf. verse 26), whereas Luke's parallel has "*the kingdom of God* is near"? Since the verse deals with a par- able and the bulk of the parables concern the kingdom, perhaps Luke is closest to Jesus' original words.[17]

Most celebrated of the enigmas in Mark 13 is verse 14:

When you see the desolating sacrilege	When you see the desolating sacrilege spoken of by the prophet Daniel,
set up where it ought not to be (let the reader understand)	standing in the holy place (let the reader understand),
then let those who are in Judea flee. . . . (Mark 13:14)	then let those who are in Judea flee. . . . (Matthew 24:15)

The phrase "desolating sacrilege" stems from Daniel (9:27; 11:31; 12:11), as Matthew makes clear. There it meant a statue of the god Zeus which the foreign king Antiochus Epiphanes set up in 168 B.C. in the Jerusalem temple—an event which helped touch off the Maccabean revolt. This "abomination" which "made desolate" and unclean the temple of the Lord became a sort of symbol in apocalyptic for some force or person which opposes God and pollutes his holy place. The parenthetical phrase, "let the reader understand," is an attempt to call attention to this background. Most curious, however, is the fact that while Matthew refers to some object (neuter gender) "standing in the holy place," such as an idol or statute, Mark has a masculine participle and refers to a person; Mark's meaning is well brought out by the NEB, "usurping a place which is not *his*." Some students of New Testament history see here an allusion to the attempt by the Emperor Caligula in A.D. 40 to have his statue erected in the Jerusalem temple.[18] Caligula would then have been meant by the one "standing where he ought not to stand." The verse might in this case be an oracle issued around A.D. 40 in the name of the Lord Jesus by some Jewish-Christian prophet (as at Acts 11:27-28). Others say, no, the whole passage, 13:14-20, relates to the crisis of A.D. 68–70, when, it is known, the Christians fled from Jerusalem before it fell and went to a place called Pella on the other side of the Jordan, in response to a prophetic oracle.[19] Thus we would have here a "floating symbol," applied one way in 168 B.C., in another in A.D. 40, and in a third way in A.D. 68. The most surprising thing may be that Luke omits the detail entirely and substitutes a picture of Jerusalem "surrounded by armies" to show that "its desolation has come near" (21:20-24). Luke's phrases draw on Old Testament descriptions of the siege of a city[20] and his final word is of Jerusalem "trodden down by the Gentiles, until the 'times of the Gentiles' are fulfilled" (21:24).

Now it *could* be that the historical Jesus both employed Daniel's phrase about "the desolating sacrilege" and spoke of a stretch of history called "the time of the Gentiles" after A.D. 70. But here in this "speech" one has been substituted for the other. Slowly but surely the conclusion is forced upon the reader that Mark 13, Luke 21, and Matthew 24–25 are not necessarily three versions of a single speech by Jesus, but three collections of apocalyptic Jesus-material, each put together differently by each evangelist.

This conclusion is supported by one other example: each version of Jesus' speech on the last things ends differently. Mark's ending (13:33-37) emphasizes "Take heed, watch" (verses 33, 35, 37). The words echo two parables, the Talents (Matthew 25:14-30) and the Doorkeeper (Luke 12:35-36). Luke has parallels to all five verses in Mark, but scattered at different points (cf. Luke 19:12-13; 12:40, 12:38). Matthew closes with a much more systematic emphasis: disciples are to continue as good stewards until the judgment comes (cf. 24:45 ff.). Luke, too, stresses watchfulness and stewardship, but in words not found in Mark or Matthew. One can compare the tenor of these words at Luke 21:34-36 (". . . take heed to yourselves lest your hearts be weighed down with dissipation and drunkenness and cares of this life, and that day come upon you suddenly like a snare . . .") with passages in the epistles such as Romans 13:11-13 (". . . the day is at hand . . . let us conduct ourselves becomingly . . . not in reveling and drunkenness, not in debauchery and licentiousness . . ."). There are connections, of course, between "watching," stewardship, a life which avoids dissipation (Luke 21:34), and constant prayer (21:36). But the fact is that each gospel ends Jesus' discourse differently.

Of course, it could be argued, to save the historicity of each saying, that Jesus said all these different things at one time or another, on different occasions. But that would be precisely to admit that we do not have here a single discourse given on one occasion, but rather a composite, put together by the evangelists,[21] out of sayings, parables, etc., in the Jesus-material. Mark 13 is thus no more a continuous speech by the historical Jesus than is Matthew 5–7 or Matthew 13. Such a conclusion, however, frees one to seek for possible settings and meanings in Jesus' ministry for the individual sayings and parables, as well as for an overall meaning of the assembled material in the present setting which each evangelist has supplied. To illustrate: Professor Jeremias thinks the parable of the Doorkeeper (Luke 12:35-38, par. Mark 13:33-37; cf. Matthew 24:42) was originally a "crisis-parable," addressed to the crowds or perhaps specifically to the Jewish scribes, warning them that calamity was coming with the arrival of the kingdom unless they were alert.[22] As they stand in Mark 13, words of the historical Jesus have been readdressed to Christians, warning them to be alert for the Second Coming.

Thus in these problem chapters, Mark 13 and parallels, there is genuine material from Jesus but often in forms reworked and differently applied in the early church. Some of it (e.g., 13:1-4, 14-20; Luke 21:20-24) dealt with the fall of Jerusalem in A.D. 70, a tragedy which, we have maintained, Jesus the prophet might well have foreseen and on which he might have spoken. Other parts deal, however, with the "end of the age" in apocalyptic terms (e.g., Mark 13:5-8, 21-23, 24-27). Again it has been maintained that the Jesus of history might well have used such typical apocalyptic expressions, and that some of them may reflect apocalyptic interests in the church around A.D. 40 and 70 and even later on. Crises at these times provoked a new interest in such speculations. In a few cases like Luke 21:29-31 (cf. Mark 13:28-29) one can even see a saying about the nearness of the kingdom being reapplied to the coming of the Son of man.

For people today the verses about the fall of Jerusalem are past history, though they do show Jesus' prophetic concern about the world of political affairs in his day and serve as a perpetual reminder that "any one who thinks he stands must take heed lest he fall" (I Corinthians 10:12; Romans 11:20). The verses about a parousia have entered into the creeds of the church, though one suspects that many Christians nowadays do mere lip service to a Second Coming. After twenty centuries who can claim that his expectation of Jesus' coming again, is as vivid as, say, Paul's was? Yet it seems impossible to most critics to discard all such references in the Jesus-tradition as creations of the early church. The idea of a return and a presence seems stamped too deeply throughout the New Testament and in Jesus' words to be set aside completely. This future presence stands as a promise for faith, a pledge which, according to some passages, has been fulfilled by the coming of the Spirit (cf. John 14:16-17, 18-19, 20:22) according to some interpreters.

The most fruitful emphasis in the entire chapter for subsequent Christians has in many ways been that on witness (verses 9-13). "The gospel must first be preached to all nations" (Mark 13:10). According to this saying, a divine "must" stands over mission activity throughout the world.[23] Matthew had good reason to insert this section in his discourse on evangelism (10:17-22). For evangelistic witness must be added to patient endurance, watchfulness, prayer, and stewardship as hallmarks of the disciples, until "the Day" comes, the date of which no man—not even Jesus —knows (Mark 13:32).

The richest understanding of Mark 13 and the most fruitful application of its collection of Jesus-material for the church thus lay not in the apocalyptists who kept writing and rewriting their timetables about when Jesus would reappear. (The second century had such men, just as does the twentieth.) It lay with Paul and his followers and John and his pupils, who concentrated more and more not on futurist speculations but on the meaning for life now of what God had already done in Jesus' death and resurrection. The First Coming, not the Second, was the polestar for life and theology. The eighth chapter of Romans can even discuss the hope for consummation without once mentioning the parousia (8:18-39). So also in Ephesians, and by and large the Fourth Gospel. On those rare occasions when John alludes to a future coming it is only in light of the "love the Father has given us" (I John 3:1; cf. verse 2), i.e., in the earthly work of Jesus. Thus, more and more, early Christians came to concentrate on the cross, Jesus' resurrection, and the coming of the Spirit as decisive. There was, of course, for these early Christians a further fulfillment beyond, but the Second Coming was not the "tail that wags the dog." Jesus and what God wrought in him, the New Testament church decided, is central. "Heaven and earth will pass away, but my words will not pass away" (Mark 13:31).

It must be asked in a moment what, in Jesus' words and life, encouraged these first Christians to think that establishing a church somehow followed his intent or God's will. Here it remains only to add that their basic decision—in favor of a Gospel message, and against allowing apocalyptic speculation to become central— has again and again been proven right in Christian experience. Ernest Gordon describes how an initial stage of reaction among prisoners in a Japanese prisoner-of-war camp after the fall of

Singapore might be called "apocalyptic."[24] Men viewed the Bible magically and tried to derive formulas from Daniel and Revelation about when help would come. But terror, not love, ruled. Stage two, which succeeded this, was marked by hopelessness, despair, and even savagery. Only later, in a third stage, came a sort of rebirth when, he says, real Bible study proved possible. It was the Gospel, centered in what God has done, not apocalyptic formulas, which provided sustenance for life.

Jesus, the Disciples, and the Church

The view which Jesus held about the future is thus not overly specific. Some things he spoke of as going to happen soon, in "this generation," just as he sometimes spoke of the kingdom as ever so near. Other passages in the Jesus-material refer in apocalyptic language to a final end or consummation, but when, one is not told. There may be talk of signs and requests for them, but generally the references by Jesus are so general (to war, rumors of war, earthquakes, famine, suffering, eclipses, falling stars, Mark 13:7-8, 24-25) that one can scarcely claim Jesus or the evangelists compiled a timetable. Mark 13:32 and Matthew 24:36 specifically repudiate such knowledge even for Jesus. A few sections surely refer to the fall of Jerusalem, an event which for some early Christians must have seemed like the end of their world.

In view of all this, it is hard to be dogmatic about what Jesus himself believed. Some of the sayings are so vivid in their prediction of an immediate consummation that we dare not claim Jesus foresaw or talked about centuries of history ahead. On the other hand, it seems unlikely that he thought of an immediate end to everything; otherwise he would not have bothered to present an ethic for the life of disciples. Since the resurrection it has been easy to say that Jesus expected a world-shaking event soon and that this came with the cross. But during his ministry his view, at least as expressed in words, was certainly less precise than the picture could be later on. Most likely the historical Jesus, who viewed the kingdom as both present and future, envisaged at least some period of time after his death when his message and teaching would continue.[25]

While the historian today cannot be as sure as he might wish about what Jesus thought, he can be certain about what his disciples did. They formed a church,[26] a community or fellowship of those who held that God had been at work in Jesus of Nazareth and raised him from the dead and exalted him as lord. Much of this story of the beginnings and growth of the church is familiar from the account recorded some five or six decades later in the book of Acts.[27] It is also implicit in the epistles of Paul and indeed in the gospels themselves, for it was the church—the fellowship of those who believed in Christ crucified and risen—which preached the kerygma about Jesus, passed on the Jesus-material, and composed the gospels. What sort of historical ties connect Jesus and this church?

During Jesus' lifetime, as all know, he gathered disciples. There was an inner group of twelve, as well as large crowds more loosely attached to him and his teaching. After the resurrection and the coming of the Spirit, disciples became, as is also well-known, members of his community, the church. Their way of life was now marked by baptism as a means of entry into the community, the Lord's Supper as a feature of meals together, conduct which was obedient to specific "Christian" teachings (some of which went back historically to the ethic of Jesus), and above all the proclamation of the word about Jesus as the Christ.

We need not ask here whether all the followers of the historical Jesus became members of the church. (At least one of the twelve, Judas, of course, did not.) We cannot here explore how Christian faith and life developed after the resurrection in new patterns impossible during the lifetime of Jesus. Obviously much arose in new situations and new opportunities which had no parallel or precedent during Jesus' ministry. But while recognizing that earliest Christianity was based on the risen Christ and not simply on perpetuating a historical Jesus, we can ask what links there are between the disciple band of Jesus' lifetime and the church community after Easter.

The obvious starting point should be with the term "church" itself and the ideas associated therewith. We must, of course, exclude all later trappings which the intervening centuries may have added to the word "church" and take it in its simplest sense as an "assembly," for that is what the words involved in both Greek and Aramaic or Hebrew mean.[28] Even with all these allowances, however, the direct evidence in the gospels is limited to two verses, and the thread of connection is tenuous. But there are some connections from the pre-Easter to the post-Easter stages.

Two of the three references to "church" in the Synoptics occur in a single verse at Matthew 18:17. The other one is at 16:18. It is generally agreed that 18:17 refers to a local church and 16:18 to a universal or "total" church. It is also agreed by many scholars that 18:17 does not fit the lifetime of Jesus historically.[29] The context is a discussion of what to do "if your brother [i.e., fellow member of the religious group] sins against you." Three steps are proposed. (1) Go and tell him his fault privately (verse 15). (2) If that does not work, talk to him with one or two other brothers as witnesses (verse 16; cf. Deuteronomy 19:15). (3) "If he refuses to listen to them, tell it to the church; and if he refuses to listen even to the church, let him be to you as a Gentile and a tax collector" (18:17). That is, if the first two steps fail, bring the sinning brother before the local assembly, and if he refuses to heed this church assembly, let him be excommunicated, cast out as a pagan and gross sinner.

Verses 16 and 17 are found only in Matthew, in a chapter where a number of teachings on discipline among disciples are gathered together in a "discourse" (cf. 19:1) such as Matthew is fond of weaving together. It is hard to see how such elaborate machinery for solving cases where one member of the group offends another was needed during the days in Galilee, though the provisions do fit nicely into discipline for an organized church. To this day they are often cited in church constitutions. Nowhere in the gospels do we read of local assemblies organized during Jesus' ministry; such assemblies arose, and with them the need for provisions for discipline, only after the resurrection. Quite contrary to the habits of the historical Jesus, however, is the reference, "Let this sinner be regarded as a *Gentile* and a *tax collector*." Though Jesus may not have sought out Gentiles in his historical ministry, he was at least not filled with hatred for them (or for Samaritans) as "lost souls" the way some Jews were, and his attitude toward tax collectors was to welcome them into his band of followers (Mark 2:14-17). Most surprising of all is the fact that we have the same three steps of procedure in the *Manual of Discipline* for the community at Qumran.[30] One may not agree with the opinion—which, however, seems likely—that Matthew 18:15-17 is a rule for congregational discipline developed in Matthew's Jewish-Christian church, on the basis of the Old Testament and Qumran, and attributed to the risen Lord, but the reference here to "church" is a frail support on which to claim the historical Jesus established a church.

Matthew 16:18, the other verse using the word "church," is similarly disposed of by some scholars; it could not be, they say, a saying of the historical Jesus. A glance at the passage suggests their reasons for such a view.

MARK 8:29-30	LUKE 9:20-21	MATTHEW 16:16-20
Peter answered him, "You are the Christ."	And Peter answered, "The Christ of God."	Simon Peter replied, "You are the Christ, the Son of the living God." [17]And Jesus answered him, "Blessed are you, Simon Bar-Jona! For flesh and blood has not revealed this to you, but my Father who is in heaven. [18] And I tell you, you are Peter, and on this rock I will build my church, and the powers of death shall not prevail against it. [19]I will give you the keys of the kingdom of heaven, and whatever you bind on earth shall be bound in heaven, and whatever you
And he charged them to tell no one about him.	But he charged and commanded them to tell this to no one.	loose on earth shall be loosed in heaven." [20] Then he strictly charged the disciples to tell no one that he was the Christ.

In Matthew, verses 17-19 seem to intrude into the account of Peter's confession at Caesarea Philippi.[31] Mark and Luke tell the story without any reference to Jesus' blessing Simon Peter or referring to the church. The account in Matthew reads smoothly if one jumps from verse 16 to verse 20. What is more, the verses following 16:20 in Matthew do not refer to what is said in verses 17-19—unless one sees a reflection in verse 23. In that case there is a neat "pattern" in Matthew which runs thus:

Peter said, "You are the Christ, ..." (16:16)
Jesus said, "You are Peter, ..." (16:18)
Jesus said, "You are a hindrance to me; . . . ." (16:23)

But both these last two phrases seem additions to a basic account, for they occur in Matthew only. It would appear that Matthew has inserted some extra material on Peter—and the explanation rings hollow that Mark (who traditionally was Peter's "interpreter") had them but omitted them because Peter was too modest to want them included. Modesty seems not to have been Peter's greatest virtue!

It will not do, however, simply to discard Matthew 16:17-19, as scholars have sometimes seemed to, merely because of later Roman Catholic use of the verses, or because they contain the word "church," or do not fit smoothly here. We shall return to Matthew's meaning in a moment. But it is necessary first to proceed via some "indirect" evidence to show how the idea of a "church" could fit into the period of the historical ministry of Jesus.

For one thing, in Hebrew and in Aramaic there are several words which could have expressed the idea of "church," including *qahal*, *'edah*, and *kᵉnishta'*.[32] Among terms found in the Dead Sea Scrolls is one (*sodh*) in a hymn which reminds investigators of Matthew 16:18: "You [O God] will build a circle [or assembly, of men] upon the rock."[33] In the Greek translation of the Old Testament, *ecclēsia*, the very word used for "church" in the New, appears as a common rendering of the Hebrew *qahal* or "assembly";[34] it thus came to denote "God's people assembled," and that is how "church" is used in early Christian writings: God's true people, gathered together, in the last times. Such terminology might have been used by Jesus in Hebrew or Aramaic during his ministry; it was employed by the early Christians after the resurrection, in Greek.

Second, the disciples themselves constitute a major link from the time of Jesus' ministry to the early church. Those whom Jesus gathered as followers during his lifetime point forward to the church. It was the practice for prophets in the Old Testament to have disciples (Isaiah 8:16; II Kings 2:15). In Judaism teachers attracted such followers. The term meant learner, pupil, apprentice, or even adherent. In Jesus' day, the Pharisees and John the Baptist are mentioned by the gospels as having such followers (Mark 2:18). Sometimes this sort of association between rabbi and pupils or leader and friends took the more specific form of a *ḥaburah*, or religious group which came together to share common meals, such as at Passover. Thus, in view of current Jewish custom, it is completely natural that Jesus should be surrounded by a band of intimate followers and pupils, learning from him. He was teacher to his "school."

Twelve of them are mentioned as having been particularly close to the master. The precise names differ in the several lists (compare Mark 3:16-19 with Matthew 10:2-4 and Luke 6:14-16),[35] but the number "twelve" seems significant. It immediately recalls the twelve tribes of Israel in the Old Testament. The implication is that Jesus, in selecting twelve, was beginning a "New Israel" (though this phrase is nowhere used in the New Testament). Once in the Upper Room Jesus is reported as saying to the twelve, "As my Father appointed a kingdom for me, so do I appoint for you that you may eat and drink at my table in my kingdom, and sit on thrones judging the twelve tribes of Israel" (Luke 22:29-30; cf. Matthew 19:28). It will be noted that the twelve[36] are here given the kingdom and a role in the future judgment, but it must be admitted that this has to do with the "new world" when the Son of man comes (as Matthew 19:28 puts it), and not with the church in this world. The choice of twelve intimate disciples has symbolic value, pointing to a New Israel, which the church will be—but that is future, not present, in relation to Jesus' earthly ministry.

In addition to "the twelve," Jesus is also said by Luke to have had a larger circle of seventy or seventy-two[37] about him (10:1, 17) and a band of women who were with the group, providing for them out of their means (Luke 8:2-3). Beyond these were the crowds, of various degrees of loyalty, gathering here and there, sometimes following him about. One may conceive of the "Jesus-movement" in Galilee as a series of concentric circles, gathered about their leader—"the twelve," "the seventy," "the crowds." In Jerusalem there were other followers, e.g., Joseph of Arimathea (Matthew 27:57).[38]

A distinguishing feature about Jesus and his disciples, when compared with rabbis of the day and their followers, was the call which Jesus gave to certain men: "Follow me" (Mark 1:17; 2:14, etc.).[39] In spite of the fact that he preached the kingdom *of God*, the call to discipleship was in personal terms with reference to *himself*—as if (as we have seen before) there was a relation between the coming of God's reign and the person of Jesus. Also there seems more permanence to discipleship in Jesus' view. He did not train men who would one day "graduate" and be "rabbis" on their own. They continue as disciples, dependent on Jesus. They are like servants in relation to a master (Matthew

10:24-25). At the close of Matthew's Gospel it is still "the eleven *disciples*" even after the resurrection (28:16), and they are to go and "make disciples" (28:19). In the book of Acts, Christians are still described as "disciples of the Lord" (6:1-2; 9:1; 11:26, etc.).[40] Out of the original band of followers arose the church, its first leaders and members. One cannot say they were a "church" during Jesus' lifetime, but there is an obvious continuity in the persons involved.

This continuity is also suggested in a saying of Jesus where he calls his followers a "little flock": "Fear not, little flock, it is your Father's good pleasure to give you the kingdom" (Luke 12:32; cf. Matthew 26:31).[41] The same term turns up to describe the church at Acts 20:28-29. And if the theory be allowed that "Son of man" was used by Jesus in the sense of Daniel 7, then there is here another link to the church in his teachings. For in Daniel the "son of man" is a corporate figure, and there are some passages where Jesus' use of the phrase seems to couple his disciples with himself (e.g., Matthew 25:31-46, where the Son of man identifies himself with "the least of these my brethren"; perhaps Mark 2:10, 28, or 8:38).[42] Indeed, the whole notion of a "reign" of God or of a messiah includes of necessity a people to be ruled over, a people to be brought into the "new age." Thus at one point after another, Jesus' words and work presuppose a corporate group to be formed, i.e., a "church."

Having surveyed the bits and pieces of evidence which point from Jesus' ministry to a band of followers who would, after the resurrection, declare themselves his church, we may now return to the disputed verses at Matthew 16:17-19 and ask what the evangelist's intentions were in including them. It has earlier been pointed out that Matthew's Gospel especially sets forth a doctrine of the church.[43] Careful study of Matthew also shows a particular interest in discipleship.[44] In light of this, it may be suggested that Matthew intended 16:17-19 to be read so as to teach certain lessons about discipleship and the church.

There are, of course, many little changes in the passage in Matthew besides the mere insertion of verses 17-19. In Matthew Jesus seems to confirm Peter's confession, "You are the Christ," by a counter-confession, "You are Peter" (i.e., "rock," "stone"), and not just Simon (verse 17). But this is not praise for Peter on which a doctrine of his "primacy" can be built. It is not always observed that prior to chapter 16 in Matthew *all* the disciples had already confessed Jesus in a term even more significant than "Christ." For at 14:33 all the disciples in the boat *"worshiped"* Jesus and said, "Truly you are the Son of God." Thus in Matthew, Peter is not the first one to confess Jesus, and some other significance must be found for his role here than "primacy."

A likely explanation is that in chapter 16 Peter functions as a representative and model disciple. He shows us, in individual terms, what discipleship is. If we ask what the lessons are, the text suggests that (1) discipleship means confession of Jesus. (2) The confession is based on revelation, not on "flesh and blood" or human comprehension (verse 17). But (3) the disciple who confesses his lord may also deny him (16:22; 26:70-75). Peter (or any other disciple) is a "foundation stone" when he confesses Christ (16:18; cf. Isaiah 28:16), but a "stone of stumbling" and a "hindrance" when he denies him (16:23; cf. Isaiah 8:14).[45] Discipleship thus depends on revelation and God's goodness, not on man's own strength. Even Peter can fall, and lives only by the Lord's forgiveness.

As for the church here in Matthew's reference, it emerges as (1) an assembly of disciples built upon confession of Jesus Christ. The "rock" is Peter-as-confessing, not merely his confession or simply Peter as a person.[46] (2) It is, Jesus says, *"my* church"— i.e., his assembly, in contrast to the "synagogue" assembly of the Jews and in contrast to all other "assemblies" which do not make confession of his lordship. (3) "I *will* build it,"[47] Jesus is depicted as saying during his ministry; that means in the future, after the cross and resurrection. (4) That "the gates of death shall not prevail against it" is a promise of victory through the risen lord. Elsewhere Matthew puts this promise in terms of the risen lord's presence (18:20, "There am I in the midst of them"; ". . . always, to the close of the age," 28:20). Here the promise is in terms of "keys" (16:19), keys to death and Hades, keys which denote authority over these enemies and in the community (cf. 28:18).[48]

There are still other surprises which emerge when one works through the considerable literature on these verses produced in recent years. A number of scholars, including some Roman Catholics, do not think these words were spoken at Caesarea Philippi but that they stem from a later incident,[49] perhaps the appearance of the risen Christ to Peter after Easter (cf. I Corinthians 15:5; Luke 24:34), or during the "commissioning" of Peter in the Upper Room (cf. Luke 22:31-34).[50] Many scholars are also agreed that the words have no polemical thrust against Paul (as was often assumed in past Catholic-Protestant debate), but, if anything, represent an emphasis on Peter in Matthew's church at Antioch in contrast to the stress on James, the brother of Jesus, in Jerusalem.[51] But much of that is speculation. The important thing is that Matthew in this pericope has taught something about what "church" and "discipleship" should mean.

Thus, we may conclude that there was already during Jesus' ministry a group of disciples which after the resurrection could become the church. That Jesus might have spoken of this "church" in future terms and in terms of loyal confession of what he himself revealed and even what he was, is not utterly impossible, as we have seen in examining Matthew 16. For it was out of this group of followers that the church developed,[52] even if Jesus did not "found" the church before Easter, certainly not in the sense that people today generally think of it—institutional, possessing the Spirit, and with sacraments. It is not the words "holy, catholic, and apostolic" which characterize this group of disciples, but "serving, learning, and suffering." It is a "theology of the cross," and not a "theology of glory," which links the church today to the disciples of Jesus' day. It remains now to consider the sacraments and the Holy Spirit as similar links to the historical Jesus.

The Covenant—Calvary, Jordan, and the Upper Room

The sacraments of Baptism and the Lord's Supper have traditionally been regarded by Christians as links to Jesus Christ. When a person is baptized or Holy Communion celebrated, the Lord is said to be present. These two practices, it is often said in definitions of the two sacraments, were instituted by Jesus himself.

In this common understanding of the sacraments, one may note, there is already a double connection, both to the historical Jesus and to the risen Christ, similar to the twofold foci which modern study of the Synoptic Gospels brings out. The practices are said to have been instituted by the historical Jesus, but it is the risen Lord who is regarded as present.

When one looks at the actual texts in the gospels which have to do with the sacraments—and there are not many such passages —one begins to discover, however, that these two sacraments take on different meanings than later centuries of ecclesiastical tradition have often given them. There is no talk in the gospels of "substance" or "elements." "Grace" is not a metaphysical property to be infused or transmitted; the emphasis is on the coming of God himself and on personal relationships, not on a "medicine of immortality" (such as one finds in Greek Christian writers already in the early second century).[53] The "presence" of Jesus Christ (and one does not need to gild it with the adjective "real") is not confined to a communion service, but, when it is spoken of in the gospels, it applies "where two or three are gathered in my name" (Matthew 18:20) and holds "always," throughout the world (Matthew 28:20).

Moreover, careful study of the gospels has made it doubtful that Jesus ever baptized or commanded baptism during his lifetime. It has further made apparent the seemingly insurmountable difficulties in ever reconstructing historically what was said and done in the Upper Room "on the night in which Jesus was betrayed." In fact, one cannot even be sure of whether the Last Supper (which became for the church the Lord's Supper) was a Passover meal or something else. In the Upper Room, as almost nowhere else, one is confronted with the words of the early church superimposed on the voice of the historical Jesus.

In the face of the problems posed by the biblical text and by the reorientation often demanded by modern critical study, it may behoove Christians today to be a little less dogmatic about the sacraments than they have sometimes been or about supposing that one is "doing what Jesus did" by adopting this liturgical change or that. Perhaps the most important thing any study of the sacraments in the gospels can teach is that belief and practice today must spring from the Easter Gospel, and not from any presumed reconstruction of "what Jesus did" or even how "earliest Christianity" performed a rite. If one understands the Gospel aright, then Baptism and Lord's Supper are most powerful proclamations of its theme, Christ crucified and risen. But if one rests content with historical reconstruction and liturgical traditions alone, then one is ever buffeted by conflict between this theory and that. This is to suggest that the way forward in an ecumenical age may be, not to return to some form supposedly from a period of "undivided Christianity" (which doubtless ended the day after Pentecost) or even from Jesus himself, but to produce, humbly yet creatively, forms which reflect the Gospel.

One must surely grant that while there are historical ties between the lifetime of Jesus and the sacraments of the church (and in these pages we shall explore them), these ties and links do not fully explain what became normative in New Testament Christianity. After Easter something new emerged as a sacramental expression of the Gospel. And it is this Gospel, not the practices during Jesus' ministry or even the varied practices in the early church, which should shape contemporary understanding and use of the sacraments for the church today.

Of the two, Baptism and Lord's Supper, the former is in many ways the easier to deal with in the gospels. Did Jesus baptize disciples during his ministry? No, say the Synoptics. There is no statement in Mark, Matthew, or Luke that Jesus practiced such a rite. Matthew 28:19 plainly states that the command to baptize came only after the resurrection.[54] But in John the picture is more confused. Two verses, at 3:22 and 4:1, state that Jesus was baptizing in Judea, near where John the Baptist was at work (3:23), and that Jesus was actually baptizing more disciples than John. However, in the next breath, 4:2 adds, "Jesus himself did not baptize, but only his disciples."[55] The meaning seems to be that Jesus practiced baptism, though technically he did not administer the rite, his followers did.

These statements in John's Gospel have been variously assessed. Some think the Fourth Gospel has projected back into Jesus' life a later practice; others, that Jesus is portrayed as doing everything John did, only more successfully. There are scholars who regard 4:2 as a later addition (RSV has it in parentheses), but still others who regard it as a correct report of the situation. Even if this latter judgment is historically accurate, that there was baptism during Jesus' ministry, the further qualification exists that it could not as yet have been *Christian* baptism, for that arose only after Pentecost, when the Spirit was given. There is evidence in John that the fourth evangelist agrees with such a view, for 3:5-8 emphasizes that a man must be born of the Spirit, not just of water,[56] and John elsewhere stresses that the Spirit had not yet been given during the ministry (7:39; 20:22).

We may sum up by saying that Jesus seems not to have baptized —though it is not impossible that some of his followers who had previously been disciples of John the Baptist (John 1:35-42) may have performed the rite.

There were apparently a number of Jewish sects and groups in the Jordan Valley—in addition to John and his disciples—which practiced rites of immersion, ablutions, or lustrations prior to Jesus' time.[57] Such groups—and they include the "Covenanters" at Qumran—doubtless conceived of their baptisms in differing ways, but they shared the idea that baptism symbolized a break with past sin and prepared men for something startling God was about to do.

The exact origin of such a water baptism, as practiced by John, and at Qumran and elsewhere (as well as in later Christianity), is much debated. Some derive it from the symbolic actions of Old Testament prophets; for example, Ezekiel spoke of God sprinkling clean water on the people to cleanse them (Ezekiel 36:25).[58] Others point to the various washings and ablutions commanded for priests and worshipers in the Old Testament (Exodus 29:4; Leviticus 16:4, 24 ff.; Numbers 8:7; cf. Hebrews 9:10).[59] Still others see Jewish proselyte baptism as the source; this was the rite of entry for converts to the Jewish faith.[60] According to the Old Testament, the entrance requirement for a male Gentile who wanted to convert to Israel was circumcision. But for women, and as an additional entrance requirement for men, when pagans embraced the Jewish faith, baptism became common in Judaism of the first century A.D. as a rite of initiation. Such baptism was even compared with Israel's original deliverance "through water" at the Red Sea (Exodus 13:21—14:31; cf. I Corinthians 10:1-2).[61]

Since the discovery of Qumran and the Dead Sea Scrolls, a great deal has been written to claim that John's rite of baptism derived from the "monastery" there.[62] But as an explanation, the Qumran data is greatly exaggerated. True, there are many cisterns there, but these seem to have been mostly for drinking water, not baptismal rites. True, descriptions *about* the Essenes refer to water rites, but the texts themselves from Qumran have virtually no such references.[63] And it is very doubtful, though not impossible, that John the Baptist once lived at Qumran.[64] The most likely background for John's practice, therefore, seems Jewish proselyte baptism. But one must not exclude an element of originality either.

If John's practice came from Jewish rites for proselytes, there was one startling innovation which he made. The emphasis on repentance as a basis and forgiveness as a result was familiar enough from the Old Testament prophets. But completely new was the notion that such an act was necessary for Jews. John was thereby treating them just like pagans, without a claim on God: "God is able from these stones to raise up children to Abraham" (Matthew 3:9, par. Luke 3:8); pride of race will not save, repent! Along with this went a strong moral or ethical demand (Luke 3: 10-14). The act was not merely ritual but demanded "fruit that befits repentance" (Matthew 3:8, par. Luke 3:8). There was also an eschatological emphasis on judgment and salvation soon to come (Luke 3:6, 7-9, 16-17). We may add that since John had disciples (Luke 11:1), there is reason to believe that his baptism introduced men into an association or fellowship of some sort. All these are points which later characterized Christian baptism: an eschatological action initiating men into a fellowship or community where there is an ethical demand.

Perhaps the most important thing about the Baptizer's work was that John baptized Jesus. All four gospels describe or allude to this (Mark 1:9-11, par. Matthew 3:13-17; Luke 3:21-22; cf. John 1:28-34), as does the kerygma (Acts 10:37). Few facts about Jesus' career are historically more certain than that he was baptized by John. Indeed, the fact later became almost embarrassing for Christians. Since John preached a baptism for the forgiveness of sins (Mark 1:4), Jesus' baptism might imply that he was a sinner (a point, however, which no Christian writing of the New Testament intends).[65] That he was baptized by John might also imply that John was greater than Jesus or that Jesus was John's disciple (which some investigators think may have been historically the case, before Jesus began an independent ministry).[66] Matthew has handled the problem by adding 3:14-15, where Jesus explains he should be baptized as part of God's will ("to fulfil all righteousness"). Luke solves it by omitting any reference to John at the baptismal scene (3:21-22) and, in fact, by reporting John's imprisonment in the previous verses (3:19-20)!

What did John's baptism of Jesus mean? Often it has been "psychologized" as the "religious experience" which awoke the desire in Jesus' breast to be a messiah or something of that sort.

Of this there is not a word in our texts; that is the product of romantic imagination. Better is the usual theological answer, that here Jesus is identifying himself completely with the sinful people of Israel. For the evangelists and their readers the scene also serves to make known who Jesus really is: namely, the Son (Psalm 2:7) and the beloved servant of the Lord (Isaiah 42:1; 44:1)—though this knowledge was scarcely made known to Jesus' contemporaries, for even according to the oldest written account, that in Mark, only Jesus and not the bystanders heard this heavenly voice.[67] Historically, the baptism had the meaning of an acknowledgment by Jesus of God's hand in the work of John the Baptist. This is something that Jesus also stated elsewhere in his ministry, that John's baptism was "from heaven" (Mark 11:29-33; Matthew 11:11). There is also a significant connection of Jesus' baptism with his death—but more of that later. As far as the emergence of baptism as a Christian sacrament is concerned, the fact that Jesus was baptized by John may be more meaningful than attempts to prove (on slender evidence in the Fourth Gospel) that Jesus practiced baptism during his ministry.

The origins of the Lord's Supper in Jesus' ministry would appear easy enough to deal with. All one has to do, it is usually thought, is to work back to the Last Supper and describe what Jesus said and did in the Upper Room. But as anyone knows who has studied the history of Christian worship or has looked at the "words of institution" in their three Synoptic forms, this program is simple to prescribe but virtually impossible to work out historically.[68] We have already called attention to the problem of the date in connection with the chronology of the Passion.[69] The Synoptics assume that the Last Supper was a Passover meal. The Fourth Gospel states it was a gathering the day before Passover. On this decision, as to whether Jesus and his disciples were celebrating the Passover that night, or some other sort of meal, or a Passover-like gathering of their own, depends how certain details in the scene, and indeed its whole outline, are explained.

A further problem in our sources is that John not merely omits any account of how Jesus instituted a sacrament with bread and wine in the Upper Room but also has in its place something totally different, the washing of the disciples' feet by Jesus (John 13:1-30). It is not that John is ignorant of the sacrament of bread and wine, for he weaves his comments on it into a discourse after the feeding of the five thousand in chapter 6. Nor is the theory likely that he omits the words of institution as "too precious," in order to shield them from pagan eyes.[70] The theory that John is anti-sacramental does not hold either, any more than the notion that he regarded footwashing as a sacrament to be substituted for the Lord's Supper.[71] A likely explanation is that John deliberately inserted footwashing, with its lesson of humility and service, as a corrective to "magical" ideas[72] about the Lord's Supper which were gaining ground when his gospel was written toward the end of the century. Whatever his reason, we have here an example of how an evangelist might shape his material with even a scene considered so sacred as that in the Upper Room.

While John omits mention of the institution of the Lord's Supper, there is a fourth account of the institution in Paul. At I Corinthians 11:23-26 occurs what is in fact the oldest written version.[73] The introduction in verse 23 assures us that Paul is passing on an oral tradition in the Jesus-material which he has inherited from earliest Christian times (cf. I Corinthians 15:3). In verses 24b-25 he recites words which were familiar to Christians in Corinth from their mealtime celebrations of the Lord's Supper:

This is my body which is[74] for you. . . .
This cup is the new covenant in my blood. . . .

Verse 26, which states that this action proclaims "the Lord's death until he comes," seems to be part of Paul's commentary on these words.

However, the real problems come when one places this oldest written version in Paul alongside the words attributed to Jesus in each Synoptic Gospel. Mark has:

Take; this is my body.
This is my blood of the covenant, which is poured out for many.
(14:22, 24; some manuscripts have "new covenant.")

Matthew has,

Take, eat; this is my body.
Drink of it, all of you; for this is my blood of the covenant, which is poured out for many for the forgiveness of sins. (26:26-28, again with "new covenant" in some manuscripts.)

The variety of wordings is readily apparent, plus the fact that only Paul includes among Jesus' words the command to repeat each step ("Do this in remembrance of me," I Corinthians 11: 24-25), a detail which the Synoptic accounts lack. Some scholars hold that these words about repeating the two steps were an addition by the risen Christ to what the historical Jesus had said in the Upper Room; others claim that in the churches of the Synoptic evangelists this "rubric," to perform the Last Supper rite, was not stated at each Lord's Supper, but was simply obeyed without repeating the words each time.[75]

Luke's account confounds the matter even more, for here a famous textual problem enters in. As Luke 22:15-20 stands in the great majority of manuscripts, the order at the Last Supper runs, not "bread," then "cup," but "cup-bread-cup." That is, Luke's version has a second cup:

Take this [cup], and divide it among yourselves. (vs. 17)
This is my body. . . . (vs. 19)
This cup which is poured out for you is the new covenant in my blood. (vs. 20)

Luke thus has a "long text" with two cups, one before supper, one after supper (vs. 20). However, certain manuscripts, few in number but early in date, omit this second cup in vs. 20, as well as vs. 19b which describes the bread in more detail:

which is given for you. Do this in remembrance of me. (19b)

It will be noticed right away that Luke 22:19b-20, which the "shorter text" omits, agrees in many details with the Pauline version at I Corinthians 11. Hence the debate. Does Luke's "shorter text" represent a primitive form of the Lord's Supper (with the order "cup-bread")—to which an extra cup has been added to bring it into harmony with the sequence "bread-cup"? Or might "cup-bread-cup" reflect some sort of Passover practice, where several cups were passed around the table? Or has Luke combined several traditions? Modern English translations of the Bible, like the RSV, prefer to print the shorter text, with vss. 19b-20 in a footnote, though a majority of scholars probably agree that Luke wrote what we call the "longer text."[76]

Can one recover what Jesus originally said? By wading through this mass of evidence, Professor Jeremias has attempted the Herculean task of reconstructing in Aramaic what Jesus might have said in the Upper Room. While there is widespread agreement on some points of the conclusions by Jeremias, this time, it must be said, present-day scholarship has not by any means agreed with certain of his assumptions and results, notably that the last meal was a Passover and on the oldest form of the words of institution.[77] The evidence just does not allow the attainment of even relatively certain results.

A leading Canadian scholar who has studied the gospels closely concludes, "Although some account of this solemn action of Jesus at the Last Supper must have been included in the Passion Narrative from the beginning, it is no longer possible to determine exactly what was done and said, or what was the intention of Jesus."[78] It seems a further conclusion that every account we have of what was said in the Upper Room reflects liturgical usage in the early church. These words were repeated at service after service. What we have in I Corinthians, Mark, Matthew, and Luke are forms as they developed in usage at Corinth, Rome, Antioch, and elsewhere. That helps explain their differences. There can be little doubt that Jesus took bread and wine at that final meal and gave them a new meaning with reference to his death, but his precise words can no longer be discerned historically today.[79] We have them only as different early Christians employed them and the evangelists recorded them some years later.

If there are all these difficulties in recovering the words in the Upper Room as background to the Lord's Supper, it is only fair to add that modern scholarship has enriched as well as complicated our understanding of origins here. The ultimate starting point for the church's idea of a meal where God comes into fellowship with men may be not just the Upper Room, but the indelible impression which Jesus made throughout his ministry, as one who eats and drinks with sinners (Mark 2:16). Furthermore, the miracles of feeding in Galilee, like that of the five thousand, the post-resurrection meals of Jesus and his disciples (Luke 24:30-31, 35, 41-43; John 21:9-12), and the eschatological idea of a future "messianic banquet" in the kingdom (Luke 22: 29-30; 13:29; 14:15)—all doubtless played a part in developing the Christian sacrament.[80]

Here, again, with the Lord's Supper, we cannot recover precisely "what Jesus did" or even what he said, let alone re-enact the presumed sacramental celebration of the early church (there was doubtless much variety, and for some decades the sacrament was part of a regular meal, as the formula at I Corinthians 11 indicates).[81] Again, it is not historical reconstructions or liturgical traditions, even of a New Testament writer, which must be the ultimate guide for believers today (I Corinthians, Mark, and Luke are each the liturgical reflection of a single church or geographical area). It is only the Gospel which can guide, with its message that the gift in the sacrament, just as in the coming of the kingdom, is God himself in Jesus Christ.

The Synoptic texts do not leave one wholly without help, however, in discerning what Jesus meant in the Upper Room. Two clues stand out. The one is the word "covenant" which occurs in all accounts (I Corinthians 11:25; Mark 14:24; Matthew 26:28; Luke 22:20, cf. vs. 29 "I 'covenant' for you"). As is well-known, the covenant was one of the great themes of the Old Testament—perhaps *the* theme.[82] It refers to a relationship into which God enters with the people whom he has redeemed. He will be their God, they will be his people. Often such covenant agreements were sealed with a meal (cf. Exodus 24:9-11). The Old Testament is really a story of a series of such covenants, with Noah, Abraham, Moses and Israel, and of the promise of a "new covenant" (Jeremiah 31:31-34), when there will be forgiveness and perception of what God is really like. Christianity understood as the religion of the "New Testament" reflects this same idea, for "testament" and "covenant" are translations of a single Greek word, *diathēkē*.

When Jesus in the Upper Room gave a new explanation to the bread and wine, beyond what Jews were accustomed to at a Passovertime, he put it in terms of a (new) covenant.[83] It is the only time that "covenant" was ever on his lips, according to the gospel records. But this once is significant. The meaning was of a new order of salvation. Some have even said that the disciples that night in the Upper Room constituted a sort of "church in embryonic form," as the people of the new covenant.[84]

But the new order of salvation was not quite yet achieved that night. It was only envisioned. One crucial step was still future: the cross. Jesus' words also refer to "my *blood* of the covenant." This was an ancient phrase, going back to Exodus 24:8, for example, and the notion that sacrificial blood was a necessary part of making a covenant. Jesus applies it to his own blood, or life, which is about to be poured out for men on the cross (cf. Mark 14:24-25, cf. vs. 21). Paul emphasizes that bread and cup proclaim the Lord's death (I Corinthians 11:26).

Thus, at the basis of the sacrament is what Jesus said in the Upper Room and—even more—what he did at the cross. The Lord's Supper is nothing less than a personalized presentation of the Lord's death "for you" (I Corinthians 11:24) and "for many" (Mark 14:24)[85] in its meaning as forgiveness and new life for the covenant people.

Such an interpretation of "sacrament" is paralleled in the case of baptism not only by the way baptism serves to introduce men into God's covenant family, but also in the way that baptism relates to Jesus' death. He himself spoke of his death as a "baptism" (Luke 12:50; Mark 10:38-39). The epistles were later to speak of the baptism of Christians as "baptism into [Christ's] death" (Romans 6:3-4), whereby they die to sin and are to walk in "newness of life," i.e., a new kind of living, with a new relationship to God (Colossians 2:12; I Peter 3:18-21). Some theologians have even spoken of Jesus' death on the cross as a universal "baptism" for all men, the "one baptism" (Ephesians 4:5) into which each person enters when he receives his baptism.[86] In this sense, Jesus' "baptism" at the cross stands at the outset of his "wider ministry" to the world, just as his baptism by John was the start of his earthly ministry.

There is therefore a connection between things in the historical lifetime of Jesus and the church's sacraments. But the route travels not simply from Jordan Valley and the Upper Room to the churchly sacraments of baptism and the Lord's Supper. The road goes above all via Calvary, and the empty tomb. Sacraments, like the church itself, derive from the death and resurrection of Jesus. And permeating the whole, is the theme of a new covenant, with the ancient promises fulfilled. But to make the historical work of the man Jesus in his ministry and on the cross "come alive" as word of God for later generations, something more is needed: the vivifying power of God's Holy Spirit.

Jesus and the Spirit

Christian believers are accustomed to regard the Holy Spirit[87] as the most important link to Jesus Christ and to God. The Spirit is the one whom Jesus promised to send in his stead after his earthly ministry was ended, to be with his people forever (John 14:16). He is the Spirit of God himself; he leads believers (Romans 8:14) and makes God known and real to men. Indeed,

Paul says, contrasting the Old Testament revelation with the New, the Lord who manifested himself on Mount Sinai to Moses and Israel (Exodus 33–34) is now present in the Spirit in the Christian community (II Corinthians 3:7-18).[88]

Hence God's Spirit is likewise regarded as the really important, vivifying factor in sacraments. Baptism is not just a matter of water, but of the Spirit (John 3:5). With regard to "the bread from heaven," it is "the Spirit that gives life" (John 6:63). The church is said to be that fellowship where the Spirit is at work; its confession comes not by "flesh and blood" but by the Spirit (Matthew 16:17b), as does inheritance of the kingdom (I Corinthians 15:50).

There is no question but that this prominence of the Spirit was characteristic throughout the early church. One reads with regard to this man or that, that he was "full of the Holy Spirit" (Acts 6:5; 7:55). Paul says to Christians, "God has sent the Spirit of his Son into our hearts, crying, 'Abba! Father!'" (Galatians 4:6). Hence Paul can admonish all believers to "walk by the Spirit" and "live by the Spirit" (Galatians 5:16, 25). One must say of the early believers that theirs was a church of the Spirit. It was really only with the coming of the Spirit that the church could come to be.

But for all this emphasis on the Holy Spirit in the epistles, in Acts, and early Christianity generally, there are remarkably few references to the Spirit in the gospels. We ought not to be surprised at this, for it is simply the clearest and sharpest example of the difference between the period "before Easter" and the time "after Easter." The New Testament uniformly insists that it was only after the resurrection and exaltation of Jesus that the Spirit was poured out upon his followers (John 20:22; Acts 2).[89] This being so, we can expect the references to the Spirit to be only occasional and sporadic in accounts which deal with the ministry of Jesus.

One should probably also not be surprised at a difference in emphasis which appears between the Fourth Gospel and the Synoptics. The Synoptic Gospels, it has been seen, in many ways adhere more closely to the historical conditions of Jesus' ministry. John has a tendency to read back the fuller experience of the post-Easter period into his presentation of the work and words of Jesus. So here. John presents a much more developed picture of the Spirit and his role in the discourses about the Paraclete in chapters 14–16. The Paraclete (or "Comforter" or "Counselor" or "Advocate")—only John ever uses this term for the Spirit—will come, he says, and impart Christ's life, and guide Christians into fuller understanding of the truth as it is in Jesus (14:16-31; 15:26—16:15 especially). Although John has gone far beyond the Synoptics in attributing a "doctrine of the Holy Spirit" to the time of Jesus' ministry, there must be noted a qualification which holds even in the Fourth Gospel. John is quite clear that during the time of Jesus' ministry the Spirit was not yet given (7:39). That gift comes only when Jesus is glorified, via cross and resurrection. Hence during the ministry there is much the disciples do not grasp or experience (2:22) because the Spirit had not yet come to them.

In the Synoptics there are far fewer references than in John (though more in Luke than in Mark or Matthew). Indeed, some critics reckon with only two or three authentic ones in the Synoptic tradition. The few which do occur are brief, scattered, and sometimes hard to interpret. Their view of the Spirit seems "rough" and inchoate when compared with later insights. But it must be remembered that the time of the ministry of Jesus was not a period when anyone had a doctrine of "the Third Person of the Trinity." Development of "the way of love" as the finest manifestation of the Spirit (I Corinthians 13) lay in the future, after Easter. The comparison for Jesus' lifetime must be with the Old Testament, not with the early church.

It is the Old Testament, and not notions of the divine spirit in the Greek world,[90] which provides the most likely background for references by Jesus. The Hebrews spoke of "the Spirit of God," and their word (*ruah*), like the Greek word for "spirit" (*pneuma*), could denote "wind" as well as "spirit" (cf. Genesis 1:2 and John 3:8, with the RSV notes in each case). For the Old Testament, God's Spirit meant his power, power to create and recreate; the term was associated with God's presence and with the activities by which he revealed what he is like. On occasion the Old Testament even comes close to saying that God is spirit (cf. Isaiah 31:3; John 4:24), but more typical are the words of a psalmist:

Cast me not away from thy presence,
and take not thy holy Spirit away from me. (Psalm 51:11)

The Spirit here denotes God's presence.

This creative presence of God could be seen in a number of areas, according to Old Testament writers. (1) One area lay in Israel's national life, where the Spirit was regarded as endowing judges (like Gideon, Judges 6:34), kings (for example, Saul, I Samuel 10:10), and others for leadership. These were usually extraordinary cases, for crisis situations, and the endowment of the Spirit here might be called "charismatic"—that is, a gift of God's grace for a particular situation. (2) Sometimes it was considered that the gift of the Spirit had to do with some particular skill (like that of the craftsman Bezalel, Exodus 31:3) or practical wisdom (such as the elders or Joshua showed, Numbers 11:25; Deuteronomy 34:9). In later times, wisdom came to be regarded especially as an endowment of the Spirit (Proverbs 1:23). (3) The most familiar manifestation of the Spirit in the Old Testament is probably in prophecy. Prophets were regarded as speaking and acting by the power of the Spirit. They were "Spirit-bearers."[91] Micah exulted, "I am filled with power, with the Spirit of the Lord" (3:8). Ezekiel was lifted up and filled with Spirit (2:2). Isaiah's "Servant" felt the Spirit of God upon himself (42:1; 61:1).

(4) For the future there was a hope that the Spirit of God would some day be poured out even more abundantly. This hope applied to the messiah (Isaiah 11:2) but also to the whole nation. Over the centuries there had been a desire, according to a statement attributed to Moses himself, "Would that all the Lord's people were prophets, that the Lord would put his Spirit upon them" (Numbers 11:29). There were times when this hope was regarded as fulfilled (Haggai 2:4-5, "My Spirit abides among you"), but generally the expectation was future (Ezekiel 37:1-14; Joel 2:28). In the century or two prior to Jesus' day, the mood, we have already seen, was that prophets—and thus also the Spirit—were lacking. Of course, the Spirit still spoke through inspired Scripture, but the Spirit himself had departed from Israel. Rabbis hoped for his reappearance. It was held that the Spirit might be given in rare cases as the reward for a lifetime of obedience. Rabbi Hillel was said to be worthy thereof but did not attain it because the generation in which he lived was so bad![92] Hence there was a "dearth of the Spirit" even in religious circles in Jesus' day. Men looked to the future.

(5) To complete the Old Testament picture, we may add that the Spirit of God was sometimes associated with creation (Genesis 1:2; Job 26:13; Psalm 104:30, unless the meaning in these verses is "wind" rather than "spirit"). (6) The Spirit was also held to maintain or renew life, so that "if [God] should take back his Spirit, . . . all flesh would perish" (Job 34:14; Isaiah 32:14-15). Through all these passages runs the idea of the Spirit as a creative, transforming power of God—and the hope that one day God's Spirit would come upon men and be poured forth into the world.

There are, of course, times in Jesus' life when a concept of the Spirit appears very much as in one of these Old Testament uses. The really striking thing is how, on a few occasions, Jesus speaks of the long-hoped-for coming of the Spirit as being manifested in his ministry and as going to be manifested through the lives of his followers. We shall look first at the more or less routine references, which are quite in harmony with the Old Testament, and then at the sayings of Jesus which seem most significant.

A phrase like that at Mark 12:36 is obvious enough, when Jesus introduces a quotation from Psalm 110 with the words, "David himself, inspired by the Holy Spirit, declared. . . ."[93] This is the Old Testament idea of kings, prophets, and Scripture as inspired.

The birth stories, especially in Luke 1–2, are probably also to be viewed in connection with the Old Testament background. Modern readers are most struck, of course, by the references to the role of the Spirit in the birth of Jesus (Matthew 1:18, 20; Luke 1:35). They may not always notice that the narrative is heavily colored by the Old Testament, or that the concept of Spirit as "the power of the Most High" (Luke 1:35) is quite in line with the view of the Spirit of God in ancient Israel. One should probably emphasize the words of Luke 1:37 as a key to the whole section, "With God nothing will be impossible"—and these words are a quotation from Genesis 18:14, which is also a story of the wondrous birth of a child by God's promise.[94]

Even more worthy of attention is the fact that Jesus' birth is not the only example of the Spirit's activity in Luke 1–2.[95] Both Elizabeth and Zechariah, the parents of John the Baptist, were "filled with the Holy Spirit" (Luke 1:41, 67). Of the baby John it is said, "he will be filled with the Holy Spirit, even from his mother's womb" (1:15). The Holy Spirit is also expressly said to have been upon Simeon, the old man who blessed the infant Jesus in the temple (Luke 2:25-35); so probably also with the prophetess Anna (2:36-38). We must say that Luke 1–2 portrays small pious circles of Israelites and certain individual men and women as living under the Spirit, just as in the Old Testament or at Qumran. There are "outbursts," charismatically (Luke 2: 27), of the Spirit's utterance, at Jesus' birth. These examples in Luke should be viewed against their Old Testament background and as a step toward later Christian experience of the Spirit.

These examples help one see that in the gospels Jesus is undoubtedly regarded as "a man of the Spirit." This would follow from what has already been said of him as a prophet and as a "teacher of wisdom." Such men were, on Old Testament assumptions, expected to reflect the presence and power of the Spirit. The stories of his baptism and temptation (Mark 1:9-13, and parallels) both make clear that Jesus was a man on whom the Spirit had descended (Mark 1:10), a man led by the Spirit (Matthew 4:1). It has already been remarked, however, that we should be leery of attempts to read these incidents as "psychological experiences" of Jesus where the Spirit first came upon him and awoke him to his "destiny."[96] The birth stories mean to suggest that Jesus was a "bearer of the Spirit" from the very beginning,[97] not just from the time of his baptism. We ought not rashly to attempt to state when Jesus first "received the Spirit"—whether at his baptism (as Mark can be read to infer) or from birth (as in Matthew 1 and Luke 1). The important thing is that in each gospel Jesus is presented from the outset as a man of the Spirit. How did this manifest itself historically?

The outstanding example is a saying at Matthew 12:28 which we have already considered in connection with the "Beelzebul incident."[98] When Jesus denied that he cast out evil spirits by the help of the prince of demons, Beelzebul, he went on to add, "But if it is by the Spirit of God that I cast out demons, then the kingdom of God has come upon you." Here we have the familiar idea that the kingdom is already in some ways being manifested during Jesus' ministry, notably by his casting out of the spirits which oppose God's name and power. The new note to observe is that he claims to do this "by the Spirit of God." This would be an assertion that the age of the Spirit, so long and devoutly wished for, was breaking in. It is true that the Lucan parallel has instead the phrase "by the finger of God." Many biblical scholars prefer this Lucan wording as what Jesus is more likely to have spoken; they would regard Matthew's reference to "the Spirit of God" as a post-resurrection touch.[99] However, there is no reason why Jesus could not have spoken of so familiar an Old Testament concept as that of the Spirit. Moreover Luke's phrase, about "the finger of God," may be his own insertion, substituting a well-known biblical figure of speech, which denotes God's power in the miracle stories in Exodus (cf. Exodus 8:19). All in all, there is reason for assuming that Jesus himself claimed to work miracles "by the Spirit of God"—the "finger of God" being an alternate expression adopted by Luke.[100]

A similar view is found at Luke 10:21 when we read, "In that same hour Jesus rejoiced in the Holy Spirit. . . ." The context is difficult to determine, but Luke 10:17-20 states that Jesus' disciples have just reported their success in casting out demons, and Jesus has remarked, "I saw Satan fall like lightning from heaven" (10:18). The impression is that Jesus' rejoicing in the Spirit stems from the exorcism of evil spirits.[101]

We go a step further when we observe that not only Jesus' miracles but also his teaching and preaching—indeed, his entire ministry—manifest a power and authority which can only be attributed to the Spirit of God. The connection between "the Spirit" and "power" in the Old Testament has already been noted. Jesus' ministry was one which continually struck men with its assertions of power and authority (cf. Mark 6:2, 14; 1:27; Matthew 9:8). Many a contemporary must have drawn the conclusion that it was the Spirit who brought such force to what Jesus said and did. On rare occasions Jesus implied as much himself. Once, when he was asked point-blank, "By what authority are you doing these things?" he answered with a counter-question which implied that his power was "from heaven" (i.e., from God; Mark 11:27-33). In another cryptic saying at Luke 13:31-33, Jesus refers to his exorcisms and cures (which he claimed to work by the Spirit), and then, as a prophet, to the course which was leading him to Jerusalem—and martyrdom. This view of himself as a martyr-prophet also assumes he is a man of the Spirit. Knowing the Old Testament passages (like Ezekiel 37) on how the Spirit creates and re-creates, could

Jesus, in this utterance, as a man of the Spirit, have also expected vindication by God after his death? (Cf. Luke 13:32, "Behold, I cast out demons and perform cures today and tomorrow, and the third day I finish my course.") It is hard to penetrate back behind the individual verses, but it looks as if Jesus' view of the Spirit in his life tied together his concept of his miracles, his role as prophet, his anticipated martyrdom, and his future hope for God's care, even beyond death. The Spirit links these ideas and actions of Jesus together, and further provides the connection with God.

Such a view of the Holy Spirit as active in Jesus' career comes through in yet another statement, that about the "unpardonable sin." The saying is preserved in two unfortunately rather different forms:

MARK 3:28-30	MATTHEW 12:31-32 (cf. LUKE 12:10)
[28]Truly, I say to you, all sins will be forgiven the sons of men, and whatever blasphemies they utter;	[31] Therefore I tell you, every sin and blasphemy will be forgiven men, but the blasphemy against the Spirit will not be forgiven.
[29] but whoever blasphemes against the Holy Spirit never has forgiveness, but is guilty of an eternal sin—[30] for they had said, "He has an unclean spirit."	[32] And whoever says a word against the Son of man will be forgiven; but whoever speaks against the Holy Spirit will not be forgiven; either in this age or in the age to come.

To make a long—and much disputed—story short, the Q version in Matthew and Luke seems to fit best in the period after Easter. It refers (1) to a time before a man is converted to Jesus Christ ("the Son of man") and (2) to a time after conversion when he has received the gift of the Holy Spirit. The verses say that a man can be forgiven for any sin committed before conversion, even "a word against the Son of man"; but after a man becomes a follower of Christ, there is one sin which can never be forgiven: blasphemy or "speaking against" the Holy Spirit. This is usually interpreted to mean deliberate and knowing rejection of the Spirit and of the Gospel, after having once accepted it (cf. Hebrews 6:4-6 and I John 5:16b). Note that it can be committed only by a person who has received the Holy Spirit.

In Mark, on the other hand, we have a form of the saying which fits the time of Jesus' ministry: all sins are forgivable, save one—that against the Spirit. Verse 30 and the context of the

Beelzebul incident (3:22-27) tell what that unforgivable blasphemy was. It was to attribute Jesus' work, in this case his miracles, not to the Spirit of God, but to Beelzebul, prince of demons. It is the view that Jesus has "an unclean spirit," not God's Spirit. Thus, in Jesus' lifetime the "unpardonable sin" was to deny the Spirit's work through the man from Nazareth. Since Easter it has been for a Christian the sin of rejecting the Spirit who gave him his new birth. The meaning in Jesus' ministry is again that he claimed what he was doing was the work of God's Spirit. The *Q* version in Matthew gives it new meaning for Christians. Luke has given it yet another application in incorporating it in a section on "fearless confession" (12:2-12). He makes it mean, "When they bring you before the authorities, do not blaspheme the Holy Spirit, for the Spirit will be with you and teach you in that hour what you ought to say" (12:10-12).[102]

A final idea about the Spirit in Jesus' sayings is this: he related the Spirit to witnessing and promised that the Spirit would be with disciples and speak through them when they must bear witness under persecution. Mark includes the thought in his "Little Apocalypse," in connection with the troubles which followers will face; Jesus' promise is, "When they bring you to trial . . . do not be anxious beforehand what you are to say; but say whatever is given you in that hour, for it is not you who speak, but the Holy Spirit" (13:11). With certain differences in wording, Matthew has the same saying in his "discourse to disciples" (10:19-20), and Luke at 21:14-15 as well as at 12:12. Related is the promise at Luke 11:13, where the Spirit is promised from the heavenly Father to those who ask him. Jesus' sayings thus speak of the presence of the Spirit especially with regard to witness during persecution. It is against this background that one can understand the boldness of the early witnesses after the resurrection (Acts 4:13, 29), and also the Johannine theme of the Paraclete as Advocate in the witnessing of disciples (John 15:26-27).

Of all the Synoptics, Luke brings out these connections between Jesus and the Spirit most consistently and in a pronounced way.[103] His has been called "the Gospel of the Spirit," and "(Holy) Spirit" occurs twice as much in Luke as in Mark and Matthew combined. It is true that Luke omits some places where the other gospels refer to the Spirit (e.g., Luke 11:20; 21:25; and 20:42, the parallels to Matthew 12:28; Mark 13:11; and 12:36, respectively), but he adds others (e.g., Luke 11:13, cf. Matthew 7:11). All of these passages are doubtless to be explained by the theological outlook of Luke the evangelist—he had his own view of Christianity as "the time of the Spirit"; he had a concept of the Spirit strongly colored by the Old Testament (as in Luke 1–2); he makes the good news of the kingdom mean that the Spirit is upon men (Luke 4:18; Acts 1:2, 5-6, 8).[104] But all this is a way of heightening an emphasis already there. The other sources speak enough of the Spirit to make it clearly a topic to which Jesus referred at least occasionally.

It has been noted that Jesus' usages were akin to those in the Old Testament. The references in Acts are also similar in that they depict the Spirit as power, breaking in on men, charismatically endowing them for new tasks and the meeting of new tests (e.g., Acts 8:29, 39; 7:55). The developed picture of the Spirit and his ethical manifestations, such as Paul and John stressed, could come only with several decades of Christian experiences with the Holy Spirit—several decades after Pentecost.

All in all, there is thus a certain "silence of the Synoptics"[105] about the Spirit. The first three gospels, though the products of a church where the Spirit was real and dominant, say remarkably little on the theme. Surely it must have been a great temptation to read back into the lifetime of Jesus more on the Spirit than the sources provided. But the early church and the evangelists by and large did not. They held the line between "historical ministry" and "risen lord" to such a degree that a reader today is amazed how rarely the Synoptics refer to the Spirit. The most likely explanation is that Jesus actually did speak of the Spirit on only a few occasions. The fact that the gospels hew to this paucity of references helps give confidence in their general reliability, it has been argued, and a claim for the role of the Spirit in the formation of these books has even been advanced on the basis of this fact: "The Synoptic silence as to the Holy Spirit in the midst of the overwhelming evidence of His activity in the very *milieu* in which all the gospels were written is the strongest proof of the inspiration of those gospels by the Holy Spirit Himself."[106]

Jesus, the Gospel—and Us

This study of Jesus and the Spirit may be the proper one on which to end a study of Jesus in the church's gospels. For we have here seen the importance of the Old Testament as background for

references to the Spirit during Jesus' ministry. We are here confronted dramatically with the difference between "before Easter"
and afterward, the great watershed of cross and resurrection. We
observe, in this case in Luke (and John), the fact that an evangelist may well expand on certain themes which are within his
special interests. We have had to wrestle with difficult-to-deter-
mine reworkings of the Jesus-material and have had to observe
how the sayings fit into the general framework of the kerygma.
But in spite of all this, a historical picture begins to emerge of
Jesus as a man of the Spirit who asserted that his miracles, authority, and entire ministry were to be explained as the work of
God's Spirit—and nothing else. This claim—that God was acting
here—was the basis of the Gospel. In fact, it *was* the Gospel.
That this action was through the power of the Spirit provided the
link by which that Gospel was expected to go on and to remain
the Good News until the end of the age, ever fresh, ever joyous,
and ever powerful to save.

Thus it *is* possible to know some things about Jesus historically
—but never without the Gospel. For not only is the Gospel "about
Jesus," but what Jesus was about, during his years on earth, was
the making of the Gospel. We have gospel records, yes, in which
to make investigations about Jesus "as he was," but more than
that in these same documents we have Christ proclaimed to us.
The Spirit makes them speak as word of God.

It has been said that the really distinguishing criterion of Jesus
in the Synoptic Gospels is his identification with sinners, right
down to the point of death for them. The message of the word of
God is that this man, in that career of self-identification, provided
salvation and still offers life today to sinful, searching men and
women. He accepted sinners and ate with them (Mark 2:15-17).
When we grasp that God, through Jesus Christ, still accepts god-
less men as they are and enters into fellowship with them (Romans 4:5), and that this holds for us, then the New Testament
witness has done its work. Then the Spirit has made Jesus in the
church's gospels come alive, as lord, for us.

NOTES, GLOSSARY
BIBLIOGRAPHY
INDEXES

Notes

Introduction

1. Albert Schweitzer, *The Quest of the Historical Jesus: A Critical Study of its Progress from Reimarus to Wrede,* trans. W. Montgomery (London: A. & C. Black, 1910; paperback ed., New York: Macmillan, 1961), p. 326. Schweitzer made the remark with reference to the "imaginative lives of Jesus" appearing at the end of the nineteenth century, but the same thing could be said, as Maurice Goguel observed, about lives written by "Catholics, conservative Protestants, Liberals, Rationalists," and others (*Jesus and the Origins of Christianity,* trans. Olive Wyon [New York: Macmillan, 1933; paperback ed., New York: Harper Torchbooks, 1960], Vol. 1, p. 37.

2. One could, of course, also write on "Jesus in the gospels outside the church," for there are documents, also called gospels, which provide still other and different pictures of Jesus. These apocryphal gospels, as they are usually called, are also the product of Christian communities of varying sorts—Jewish-Christian, gnostic-Christian, syncretistic Christian, etc.—and are preserved sometimes only in fragments, sometimes in complete manuscripts. Cf. *Edgar Hennecke, New Testament Apocrypha,* ed. W. Schneemelcher, trans. ed. by R. McL. Wilson, Vol. 1, *Gospels and Related Writings* (Philadelphia: Westminster, 1963). A generation ago Walter Bauer assembled and discussed much material from such sources on the life and teachings of Jesus in his book, *Das Leben Jesu im Zeitalter der neutestamentlichen Apokryphen* (Tübingen: J.C.B. Mohr, 1909). We shall make occasional reference to such noncanonical documents, but a full assessment of them would require a separate volume. Judged religiously, these documents have not been accepted into either Protestant or Catholic canons of Scripture. Judged historically, they are at most points inferior as sources to the canonical gospels, especially to the Synoptics and the earliest materials underlying them. On occasion, however, we must take their evidence into consideration, e.g., on the parables as transmitted in *Thomas,* for it could be that the extracanonical version preserves an earlier form or detail than does the canonical one.

3. *The Quest of the Historical Jesus* (see above, n. 1), p. 4.

4. Published as *Jesus of Nazareth: Son of God, Son of Man* (Philadelphia: Lutheran Church Press, 1966).

1 The Man from Nazareth in Galilee

1. "The beginning of the Gospel of Jesus Christ, the Son of God, just as it is written in Isaiah the prophet . . . , was John the Baptist, preaching in the wilderness. . . ." Or: "The beginning of the Gospel of Jesus Christ, the Son of God, was just as it is written in Isaiah the prophet: . . . . John the Baptist came preaching in the wilderness." Or one can take the opening words as a title ("The Beginning of the Gospel") and then translate the opening sentence, "Just as it is written in Isaiah the prophet, . . . John the Baptist came preaching. . . ."

2. No date in Jesus' career can be fixed as to the year with absolute certainty (even the year of his death). The sixfold chronology at Luke 3:1-2 demands a date between A.D. 26 and 29, but even its most precise phrase is ambiguous: is "the fifteenth year of Tiberius" to be dated (a) from the time when Tiberius became co-regent with Augustus (A.D. 12, less likely 11 or 13) or the time when he became sole emperor (A.D. 14), and (b) by the Roman, Syro-Macedonian, or Jewish calendar, each one of which has its new year begin at a different point?

3. M. S. Enslin, *The Interpreter's Bible*, Vol. 7 (New York and Nashville: Abingdon, 1951), p. 103.

4. W. D. Davies, in *The Scrolls and the New Testament*, ed. Krister Stendahl (New York: Harper, 1957), p. 282, n. 86; Davies repeats the former phrase in *Peake's Commentary on the Bible*, ed. Matthew Black and H. H. Rowley (New York: Nelson, 1962), p. 710.

5. E. Stauffer, *Jesus and the Wilderness Community at Qumran*, trans. H. Spalteholz ("Facet Books, Biblical Series," 10 [Philadelphia: Fortress Press, 1964]), p. 21.

6. It is commonly said, on the basis of statements in the church fathers Origen and Jerome, that the Sadducees regarded as sacred only the Pentateuch, not the prophets or other writings of the Hebrew canon. Such a position would be similar to that of the Samaritans. In reality, however, the precepts which the Sadducees held binding seem to have included all written Scripture, in contrast to the oral "traditions of the elders" revered by the Pharisees.

7. T. W. Manson, *The Servant-Messiah: A Study of the Public Ministry of Jesus* (New York: Cambridge University Press, 1953), p. 11, following figures in Josephus and the modern researches of Jeremias.

8. Even geographical details sometimes have the power to impress on people the reality of Jesus and his world, for better or for worse. J. K. S. Reid tells how a British soldier, stationed in Palestine during World War II, wrote home that his "faith was shattered" when he discovered one could go from Jerusalem to Bethlehem by bus nowadays (*Our Life in Christ* [London: SCM Press, 1963], p. 57, n. 1).

2 The Gospel and Our Gospels

1. Tacitus speaks, in his *Annals* 15. 44, of the torture of Christians at Rome by Nero in the sixties A.D. and of "Christus" who "suffered the extreme penalty during the reign of Tiberius"; his knowledge of Jesus and the Christian movement is no more than what anyone in Rome could have had from common gossip of the day. Suetonius, a bit later, refers to disturbances in the Jewish quarter of Rome over one "Chrestus" in the forties; it is possible that Tacitus was his source. Josephus, a historian who had commanded Jewish forces early in the revolt against Rome and who later espoused the Roman cause, writing about A.D. 90 mentions John the Baptist and Jesus. A translation of Josephus into the Slavonic language has even more striking references to Jesus. Most scholars feel, however, that this material, especially the Slavonic version, has for the most part been inserted by later Christian hands. An interpolation at *Antiquities* 18. 63-64, the most famous reference, probably reflects the early Christian preaching or *kerygma* about Jesus and could reflect, specifically, a Christology in vogue in the late third century A.D.; such are some of the most recent theories about what Christian hands added as they copied whatever Josephus originally had about Jesus at this point in his briefer reference.

2. The analysis by the Jewish scholar, Joseph Klausner, in *Jesus of Nazareth* (New York: Macmillan, 1925), pp. 17-54, is a standard one. He concluded that there are reliable statements in rabbinical sources that Jesus expounded Scripture as the Pharisees, had five disciples, but "practiced sorcery" and led Israel astray, for which he was put to death. There are also "statements of a tendencious or untrustworthy character" that Jesus was the illegitimate child of an adulteress, and that no one would speak in behalf of Jesus at his trial (p. 46).

3. Paul tells us, for example, that Jesus was "born of woman," under Jewish law (Galatians 4:4), lived a life of poverty and service (II Corinthians 8:9), died on a cross, was raised, etc.; he knows many of Jesus' teachings—compare I Corinthians 9:14 with Luke 10:7; Romans 12:14 with Matthew 5:44; Romans 12:17 with 5:39 ff.; Romans 13:7 with Mark 12:13-17; Romans 14:14, 20 with Mark 7:15, 18-19, etc. However, Paul nowhere gives a "gospel portrait" of Jesus.

4. Cf. the examples cited of this approach (which is really a type of rationalism, in defense of Scripture taken literally) and the comments on the method by Harvey K. McArthur, *The Quest Through the Centuries: The Search for the Historical Jesus* (Philadelphia: Fortress Press, 1966), pp. 7-10.

5. The work of Jakob and Wilhelm Grimm in recovering and analyzing oral material in nineteenth-century Germany is described, e.g., in

George Kent's article, "Happily Ever After with the Brothers Grimm," *The Reader's Digest*, 87, No. 523 (January, 1965), 167-72.

6. Technically, the study of the stages of development of the material in our gospels goes under the following names: (1) the "New Quest" for the historical Jesus; (2) Form Criticism; (3) Source Criticism; and (4) *Redaktionsgeschichte* or the history of the editing process.

7. Mark 10:10-12 provides an example. (1) *Jesus* was once asked a question about divorce (Mark 10:2-9); his answer was to command "no divorce" as a principle (vss. 9, 11-12). (2) In the *oral period* this teaching was treasured and widely circulated. Matthew 19:9 reports a version which modifies the basic principle: no divorce "except for unchastity" (see also Matthew 5:32). It is unlikely that Jesus had historically taught *both* things. The "exceptive clause" in Matthew may have arisen out of Christian experience; the absolute principle, "no divorce" ever, worked a hardship in some cases, and the spirit of Jesus led Christians in that church to allow this exception. (3) The teaching apparently got into *written sources*. Luke 16:18 reports the same basic teaching, "no divorce," but without the story of how Jesus was asked a question by the Pharisees (Mark 10:2-9). (4) Each *evangelist* reports the teaching of Jesus differently. Mark 10:10 places it in a house, privately to the disciples (contrast Matthew 19:9, addressed to the Pharisees). Mark 10:12 also adds that if *a woman* "divorces her husband and marries another, she commits adultery." Jewish law forbade a woman to divorce a man; that was a Gentile practice. So unless it originally referred to a case like that of Herodias (who left her first husband), it appears that vs. 12 is an extension of Jesus' principle by Mark (or the church at Rome) to cover this Gentile practice. Matthew has reported the teaching as part of the Sermon on the Mount (5:32), in addition to the story at 19:3-9 where he adds some further *M* material about men who do not marry (19:10-12). Luke relates the saying to the law (16:16) but gives no setting. Thus a story about Jesus or a saying of his can be traced through these four stages.

8. See above, pp. viii-ix.

9. The *Acts of Pilate*, for example, tells of a highway robber, Dysmas, who met Mary and the baby Jesus during their flight into Egypt (Matthew 2). He was kind to them, and as a reward his child was cured of leprosy by being bathed in the bath water which Jesus had used. Later Dysmas reappeared in Jesus' life as the penitent thief who was forgiven at the cross. People liked (and probably still like) such stories. They were the "novels" of their day. But fiction is all they are.

10. G. Bornkamm, *Jesus of Nazareth*, trans. Irene and Fraser McLuskey with James M. Robinson (New York: Harper, 1961), p. 25: each

anecdote and story scene "contains the person and history of Jesus in their entirety."

3   "The Christ Must Suffer Many Things"

1. D. E. Nineham, *Theology* (Cambridge, England), 60 (1957), 269.

2. Emil Brunner, *The Mediator*, trans. Olive Wyon (Philadelphia: Westminster, 1947), pp. 435-36, citing the Weimar Edition of Luther's works, Vol. 25, p. 330.

3. The first one is reported just after Peter's confession at Caesarea Philippi, the second on the way through Galilee, the third as Jesus and his disciples near Jerusalem. The second one is the most brief and general (especially in the form at Luke 9:44), the third the most detailed. There is much debate whether the sayings are statements by the historical Jesus or creations of the early church. An argument in favor of the former view is the fact that the details, especially in the third Passion saying, do not completely fit with the details of the Passion as narrated in Mark 14 and 15—Mark 10:34 has "mock, spit, scourge, kill"; 15:15-20 has "scourge, spit, mock, crucify." A possible view is that the Passion sayings go back to a genuine utterance of Jesus in which he spoke of his fate at Jerusalem and of God's care for him, but that after the resurrection some of the details were sharpened in light of actual happenings.

4. There are expressions in these verses not typical of Paul; e.g., Paul usually speaks of "sin" in the singular, not "sins" as here. "He was raised" is a typically Semitic way of saying "God raised him." The emphasis that what happened is "in accordance with the scriptures," suggests that the formula comes from Jewish Christians, who naturally emphasized the Old Testament scriptures.

5. Since all sources agree that Jesus died on a Friday (in our calendar) around Passover time, it is possible, thanks to modern calendrical tables, to list the date of Fridays around Passover in each of the various years in which Jesus might have died; cf. Jack Finegan, *Handbook of Biblical Chronology* (Princeton University Press, 1964), pp. 285-98. What remains in dispute, however, because of conflicting evidence in the Synoptics and John, is the year involved.

6. Josef Blinzler, *The Trial of Jesus* (Westminster, Maryland: Newman Press, 1959), pp. 265-70.

7. The statistics compiled by the Survey Research Center of the University of California and reported by C. Y. Glock and R. Stark, *Chris-*

tian Beliefs and Anti-Semitism (New York: Harper & Row, 1966), illustrate how some connect anti-Jewish prejudice with interpretations of the crucifixion.

8. *Tosephta Sanhedrin* 9. 11; *Mishna Sanhedrin* 7. 2b; *Jerusalem Targum Sanhedrin* 7. 2. 24b. Further references on the incident, which Rabbi Eleazer ben Zadok, who was active about A.D. 100, is said to have witnessed as a child on his father's shoulders, are cited in Blinzler (see above p. 340, n. 6), p. 155.

9. The temple inscription discovered in 1871 is accessible in translation in *The New Testament Background: Selected Documents,* ed. C. K. Barrett (New York: Harper Torchbooks ed., 1961), p. 50.

10. The Syriac manuscript discovered in 1892 at the Monastery of St. Catharine at Mount Sinai by Mrs. Agnes S. Lewis, of Cambridge, has the verses of chapter 18 in the sequence 13, 24, 14, 15, 19-23, 16-18.

11. The statement at John 11:49, that Caiaphas "was high priest that year," has been interpreted to mean that under the Romans the appointment was an annual one; or that the Roman governor shuffled high priests in and out of office so frequently that it seemed annual; or that John has mistakenly confused practice at Jerusalem with pagan custom in Asia Minor, where the office was annual. Most likely John's Greek simply means "was high priest in that fateful year."

12. Cf. David Daube, *The New Testament and Rabbinic Judaism* (London: Athlone Press, 1956), p. 230.

13. Commentators have shown that there were roosters in Jerusalem; the term need not be taken as a reference to a Roman trumpet call.

14. At Luke 22:63 and 23.11. See p. 343, n. 21 below, where the various references to the mocking of Jesus during the trials are classified.

15. The Jewish writers Philo (*Legation to Caius* 38) and Josephus (*Ant.* 18.55-89; *Jewish War* 2.169-77) give a negative picture of Pilate, presenting a long catalog of his crimes. Tacitus (*Annals* 15.44) makes a more neutral reference to him.

16. *Jesus and His Story,* trans. Dorothea M. Barton (London: SCM Press, 1960), pp. 106-7; U.S. ed., trans. Richard and Clara Winston (New York: Knopf, 1960), pp. 129-30.

17. The incidents about the ensigns, the shields, and the water supply are recorded in Josephus. It is not clear to which of these incidents, if any, Luke 13:1 has reference, but Luke's depiction is in keeping with Pilate's character as presented by the Jewish sources.

18. The charges against Jesus in Luke: (1) he perverted the nation or misled it; (2) he forbade tribute to Caesar; (3) he claimed to be an anointed king (or "Christ a king," as Christians would later understand the words). The basis assumed is probably the incident about the tribute money (Mark 12:13-17). According to this story, Jesus, when asked about paying taxes, had said, "Render to Caesar the things that are Caesar's," but the rest of his answer, about giving priority to God, and his basic teaching about the kingdom of God could have given rise to the mistaken idea that he taught a rebellious attitude toward Caesar (cf. Mark 14:48, where the term "robber" or "revolutionary" is used of Jesus). His position as teacher and his popularity could have caused him to be considered able to mislead the nation of the Jews— chief priests and Roman rulers alike would keep an eye on such a man. However, that Jesus was widely regarded as a king during his lifetime, or thought of himself in such terms, is very doubtful. (Chapter 9 will discuss "messiah" or "Christ" as a title.) In the Synoptics Jesus proclaims *God* as king, not himself. According to John 6:15, the very suggestion that people might regard him as a king caused Jesus to withdraw from their midst. The word "king" would make Pilate prick up his ears, however. The chief priests seem to have regarded Jesus as a dangerous teacher and messianic pretender (Mark 15:10, they delivered him "out of envy"). Transferred into the political realm, the charges would have prompted the governor to act.

John's Gospel presents the accusation of "evildoer" against Jesus (18:29-30) and presumes the charge "he makes himself a king" too (18:33). John has Jesus amplify in private what kind of kingship his is (18:36-37). The Jews also adduce the charge that Jesus has broken their law by making himself the Son of God (19:7). At this point the religious and the political charges are being combined. The whole seems a religious disagreement among Jews transformed into political terms which Pilate would heed. The "many things" of which Jesus was further accused (Mark 15:3) are not stated. The basic charge: he poses a political threat to Rome's peace.

19. Along with most exegetes, I find unconvincing the attempt to take Luke 23:15 to mean that Pilate said to the Jews, "I did not find this man guilty of any of your charges against him. But *not so Herod*. For he has sent him back to us [to be put to death]."

20. One theory is that two men were arrested about the same time: Jesus of Nazareth, on orders from Pilate, and Jesus Barabbas. When Pilate learned of this, he asked the priests, "Which of the two do you want," and they said, "Release Barabbas, Jesus of Nazareth is the one we want crucified." Out of some such happening grew the story which

the evangelists tell. But the theory is sheer speculation. Cf. Paul Winter, *On the Trial of Jesus* ("Studia Judaica," 1 [Berlin: de Gruyter, 1961]), p. 99.

21. The Passion of Jesus includes mockings at the hands of several different groups, at various points:

(1) *Jewish*—Mark 14:65; Matthew 26:27, by members of the Sanhedrin and their servants, *after* the Jewish trial; Jesus mocked as a *prophet*.

(2) *Jewish*—Luke 22:63, onlookers by night at the high priest's house, *before* the trial (which takes place at dawn); (Luke omits a mocking after the trial).

(3) *Herod Antipas* and his soldiers—Luke 23:11 (this seems to take the place in Luke of a second mocking, by the Romans).

(4) *Roman*—by the soldiers but *before* the Roman trial ends (John 19:1-3; the scourging may be an attempt by Pilate to substitute a lighter punishment for the death penalty).

(5) *Roman*—by the soldiers of the governor *after* sentence is pronounced (Mark 15:16-20; Matthew 27:27-31). This is the place where, in Roman practice, such mockery is most to be expected. But human nature may have been to pelt a prisoner whenever the chance came.

22. There was no need for first-century preachers to do what one American evangelist is reported to have done: he nailed a lamb to a cross before the eyes of his congregation—garnering a lot of publicity, and prompt attention from the S.P.C.A.

23. *A Man Called Jesus: The Gospel Story told by J. B. Phillips in 26 short plays* (London: Geoffrey Bles, 1959; rev. ed. with stage instructions, 1962; London: Fontana Books, 1965), p. 180. [U.S. edition, *A Man Called Jesus: a Series of Short Plays from the Life of Christ* (New York: Macmillan, 1959).]

24. Plato, *The Republic* 2. 362A.

25. Cf. Mark 15:40, "There were also women looking on from afar," a detail also given in Matthew 27:55. Luke 23:49 has something startlingly different: *"all his acquaintances* and the women who had followed him from Galilee stood at a distance and saw these things." Who are "all Jesus' acquaintances"? A partial answer comes when we realize that the words at Luke 23:49 come out of Psalm 38:11, the prayer of a man in great suffering who is tormented by his enemies; he complains:

My friends and companions stand aloof from my plague,
    and my kinsmen *stand afar off.*

The original psalm blamed the acquaintances because they shunned the man. Luke, whose mind was filled with phrases from the Old Testament, uses the verse to describe how Jesus' acquaintances were there, though afar off. The problem thickens when we observe that the phrase "from afar" in Mark and Matthew is the same one as in the psalm. And the matter becomes most complicated when we ask what Luke means by Jesus' "acquaintances." The answer must be Jesus' disciples, and if one reads Luke very carefully, one finds that it is perfectly possible in the Lucan scheme of things for the disciples to be present at this point. For Luke has omitted the statement at Mark 14:50 that "they all forsook him [Jesus], and fled" (no Lucan parallel to this). It may be that when Luke says "a great multitude of the people, and of women who bewailed and lamented Jesus" followed him on the way to Calvary, he means to include the disciples among the people. Further, in Luke, the disciples do not scatter to Galilee after the crucifixion (contrast Mark 16:7); they are in Jerusalem, as a group, where the resurrection appearances will take place. All this amounts to saying that Luke has a different view from Mark and Matthew about the presence of the disciples at the cross. But how much of this is history, and how much arises from use of an Old Testament verse?

26. *The Day of His Coming: The Man in the Gospels* (Philadelphia: Fortress Press, 1963), p. 269.

27. See pp. 340, n. 5, and 319. According to Mark 14:12, 14, 16, it was Passover; according to John 19:14, it was the day before the Passover. On the morning of Nisan 15 (Passover), a faithful Jew should not be coming from work in the field. But, it is objected, Simon may not have been a Jew, or an observant one, or he may have been coming, not from work, but to pray at the temple; cf. J. Jeremias, *The Eucharistic Words of Jesus* (rev. ed.; New York: Scribner's, 1966), pp. 75-77.

28. Cf. above, p. 53. Mark's chronology seems almost too schematic, since most time references appear to be given at three-hour intervals:

14:72, "cockcrow"—3 A.M.? (third watch of the night, 12-3 A.M.);
15:1, "early"—6 A.M. (close of the Sanhedrin trial);
15:25, "third hour"—9 A.M. (they crucify him, according to Mark);
15:33, "sixth hour until the ninth hour"—noon to 3 P.M. (darkness);
15:34-37, "ninth hour"—about 3 P.M. (Jesus dies);
15:42, "when it was late" (literally)—toward 6 P.M. (burial).

Did Mark adopt this arrangement to make the chronology easy to remember? Where other gospels agree, it is natural to accept Mark's time scheme; where, as at 15:25, they differ, and Mark's artificial scheme crowds the schedule too much for all the events that are reported, then there is reason for preferring John over Mark. The chronology of the Passion is nowadays very much under discussion. A Frenchwoman, a Roman Catholic scholar, Annie Jaubert, has even proposed a sequence, based on evidence in the Dead Sea Scrolls and elsewhere, whereby Jesus was arrested on a *Tuesday* night, with the Passion events spread over three days, but the "solution" has, for good reasons, been generally rejected.

29. References to the offering of wine to Jesus at Golgotha can be charted thus:

MARK	MATT.	LUKE	JOHN	
1) 15:23	27:34	——	——	Drugged wine, given out of *compassion* to relieve pain; rejected by Jesus (to keep his mind clear?).
2) ——	——	23:36	——	Soldiers, in *mockery*, offer wine vinegar; no indication that Jesus took or rejected it.
3) 15:36	27:48	——	19:28-29	"One of them" (bystanders?) put it on a reed and "gave it to him to drink"; in John, Jesus had said, "I thirst." Hostile or helpful?

Are 2) and 3) variants of the same happening? It is very hard to tell because of the different arrangements in the gospels.

30. Luke 23:47 has instead, "Certainly this man was innocent!" Luke's wording reflects his repeated theme of Jesus' innocence.

31. G. Gloege, *The Day of His Coming* (see above, p. 344, n. 26), p. 267.

4 The Lord Taught Them to Pray

1. John 8:6, 8 preserves merely the detail that Jesus could write—unless it means simply that he doodled on the ground as he spoke with the accusers of the woman taken in adultery.

2. Cf. the titles by Harald Riesenfeld and Birger Gerhardsson listed in the Bibliography, and the summaries and rebuttal in the essays (also listed there) by Morton Smith and W. D. Davies (see p. 505, under *"Semitic Backgrounds to Jesus' Teaching and its Transmission"*).

3. On John 2:22, see above, p. 65.

4. An example of how a saying of Jesus was transmitted with considerable fidelity and yet also with a surprising amount of freedom in the early church is that now found (among other places) at Matthew 6:14-15: "For if you forgive men their trespasses, your heavenly Father also will forgive you; but if you do not forgive men their tres-

passes, neither will your Father forgive your trespasses." The thought
of this saying fits with the phrase in the Lord's Prayer, "Forgive us
our debts, as we also forgive our debtors," as well as with other sayings
of Jesus. Matthew has reported this saying right after the Lord's
Prayer (6:9-13). Originally it was not necessarily connected with the
prayer—at least Luke does not record it in connection with the prayer,
or anywhere else, for that matter. Mark has the saying, but in a different
place. At Mark 11:25, after a discussion of faith and prayer, there
appear words that sound like a slightly different Greek translation of
Matthew 6:14: "And whenever you stand praying, forgive, if you
have anything against any one; so that your Father also who is in
heaven may forgive you your trespasses." Some later scribes, when copy-
ing Mark, saw this connection with Matthew 6, for they added (in
some manuscripts) another verse, Mark 11:26 (=Matthew 6:15),
"But if you do not forgive, neither will your Father who is in heaven
forgive your trespasses." One must say that in Matthew and Mark a
saying from Jesus on forgiveness is carefully preserved, but early
Christians used it with a certain freedom, to illustrate *either* a petition
in the Lord's Prayer *or* in connection with general teachings on prayer.
There is one thing more to add. In 1891 an Anglican bishop, F. H.
Chase, made the ingenious guess that Matthew 6:14-15 (=Mark
11:25-26) originally belonged after the parable of the Unmerciful
Servant (Matthew 18:23-35), which teaches, "So also my heavenly
Father will do to every one of you, if you do not forgive your brother
from your heart." The example may be diagramed thus:

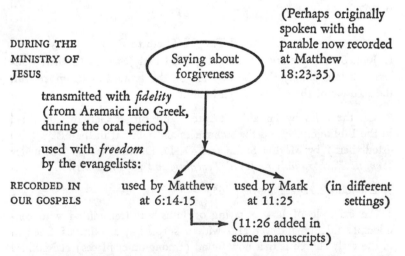

DURING THE
MINISTRY OF
JESUS

Saying about
forgiveness

(Perhaps originally
spoken with the
parable now recorded
at Matthew
18:23-35)

transmitted with *fidelity*
(from Aramaic into Greek,
during the oral period)

used with *freedom*
by the evangelists:

RECORDED IN   used by Matthew   used by Mark   (in different
OUR GOSPELS   at 6:14-15   at 11:25   settings)

(11:26 added in
some manuscripts)

We must recognize both faithfulness to what Jesus said, and new
insights as his words were applied in new ways.

5. In Matthew's Sermon on the Mount, the Lord's Prayer is part of a larger section on true piety (6:1-18) expressed in terms of almsgiving (6:2-4), prayer (6:5-15), and fasting (6:16-18). The part on prayer is built up of four separate little sections: vss. 5-6 and 7-8 (both on wrong kinds of prayer), the Lord's Prayer as an example of proper prayer (vss. 9-13), and vss. 14-15 as an admonition to forgive when you pray. Matthew slants his teachings of Jesus to people who know a lot about prayer but need bad habits corrected. In Luke the Lord's Prayer is connected with a scene where the disciples ask Jesus how to pray (11:1-4). Then follows a parable that teaches men to persist in prayer (11:5-8). Verses 9-10 repeat this theme: keep on asking God, He'll reply. The closing verses (11-13) of Luke's section on prayer emphasize that God, far more than even any human father, will be generous with his sons. Luke has chosen his teachings from Jesus on prayer to encourage men to pray, men who need confidence to make their requests known before God. Thus each gospel uses the Lord's Prayer to make a slightly different point: proper, "unwordy," forgiving prayer (Matthew); simple, confident prayer (Luke). Cf. J. Jeremias, *The Lord's Prayer*, trans. J. Reumann, ("Facet Books, Biblical Series," 8 [Philadelphia, Fortress Press, 1964]), pp. 8-9; reprinted in *The Prayers of Jesus* ("Studies in Biblical Theology," Second Series, 6 [London: SCM Press, 1967]), pp. 87-89.

6. One attempt at reconstructing the original of the Lord's Prayer in Aramaic is offered by Joachim Jeremias in *The Lord's Prayer*, (see above p. 347, n. 5), p. 15.

7. *A Man Called Jesus* (see above, p. 343, n. 23), pp. 79-80 (italics in the original).

8. Cf. the discussion and reconstruction of the "original prayer" in J. Jeremias, *The Lord's Prayer* (see above, p. 347, n. 5), p. 6-17.

9. The Matthean expansion, from "Father" to "Our Father, who art in heaven," is in line with Palestinian piety and Matthew's own views. God was regarded by Jews of the day as dwelling "in heaven," far away from the world and its corruption. Increasingly his separation from the world was emphasized, in contrast to the Old Testament idea that, for all his holiness, Yahweh is with Israel. Cf. Matthew 5:34-35, heaven is "the throne of God," the earth is his "footstool." Matthew likes this emphasis on heaven, and in fact talks of the "kingdom of heaven" as equivalent to the "kingdom of God."

10. A small detail which argues for the claim that this doxology from I Chronicles 29:11-12 must go back at least to the Palestinian church which used Aramaic and not Greek, if not to Jesus himself, is the fact

that the phrases of I Chronicles 29:11-12 in the Septuagint Greek translation of the Old Testament do not at all accord with the wording of
the doxology in Greek manuscripts of Matthew 6:13.

11. It is, of course, possible that "the evil" here is neuter, rather than
masculine—evil as a "collective force," instead of "Satan"—as the
RSV prefers to take it. But people in Jesus' day usually saw evil per-
sonified and thought in terms of a devil, not just abstract principles
(cf. John 17:15 and I John 5:18). There are other verses, though,
where the phrase is neuter or ambiguous (II Timothy 4:18; II Thessalonians 3:3). Early liturgies took it as masculine in the Lord's
Prayer; the neuter comes through the influence of Latin liturgy.

12. The version of the Lord's Prayer put together from rabbinical
materials runs like this:
    Our Father, who art in Heaven. Hallowed be Thine exalted Name
in the world which Thou didst-create according to Thy will. May
Thy Kingdom and Thy lordship come speedily, and be acknowledged
by all the world, that Thy Name may be praised in all eternity.
May Thy will be done in Heaven, and also on earth give tranquillity
of spirit to those that fear thee, yet in all things do what seemeth
good to Thee. Let us enjoy the bread daily apportioned to us. Forgive us, our Father, for we have sinned; forgive also all who have
done us injury; even as we also forgive all. And lead us not into
temptation, but keep us far from all evil. For thine is the greatness
and the power and the dominion, the victory and the majesty, yea
all in Heaven and on earth. Thine is the Kingdom, and Thou art
Lord of all beings for ever. Amen.

Cf. Israel Abrahams, *Studies in Pharisaism and the Gospels, Second
Series* (Cambridge University Press, 1924; reprinted, New York: Ktav
Publishing House, 1967), pp. 98-99, as quoted in T. W. Manson,
The Sayings of Jesus (London: SCM Press, 1949), p. 167 (American
ed., *The Mission and Message of Jesus* [New York: E. P. Dutton,
originally 1938], p. 459).

13. Gerhard Kittel, as quoted in Hans Windisch, *The Meaning of the
Sermon on the Mount,* trans. S. MacLean Gilmour, (Philadelphia:
Westminster Press, 1951), pp. 59-60.

14. A. Raymond George, *Communion with God in the New Testament*
(London: Epworth Press, 1953), p. 73.

15. Cf. Claude G. Montefiore, *The Synoptic Gospels* (2d rev. ed.,
London: Macmillan, 1927), Vol. 1, p. cxl: "whereas in the Rabbinical
literature the great things are scattered around and among a huge mass

of third and fourth rate material, in the New Testament they are found knit together in a small compass, emphasized, concentrated, and condensed."

16. As quoted in A. M. Hunter, *A Pattern for Life: An Exposition of the Sermon on the Mount* (Philadelphia: Westminster Press, 1953), p. 25.

17. Cf. T. W. Manson, "The Lord's Prayer: II," *Bulletin of the John Rylands Library* (Manchester), 38, 2 (March, 1956), 436-48.

18. A synagogue prayer, the *Qaddish*, set forth a similar hope about the kingdom: "May God rule his kingdom in your lifetime and in your days and in the lifetime of the whole house of Israel, speedily and soon. And to this, say: Amen." However, Jesus' eschatology (see chapter 6, below), about God's reign being manifested in his own day, made the accent of the petition different.

19. So J. Jeremias, *The Lord's Prayer*, (see above, p. 347, n. 5), pp. 17-21, and *The Central Message of the New Testament* (New York: Scribner's, 1965), pp. 9-30. The alternate explanation is that, since "Father" was used as a term of address for God in Hellenistic Judaism with some frequency (cf. Sirach 23:1; Wisdom of Solomon 2:16 and 14:2; Tobit 13:4; or III Maccabees 7:6), and since "Father" had been used for centuries in the Greek world to refer to God, including the usage in the phrase in the Cybele cult, *"Atte pappa"* (cf. *"Abba, patēr"* [= father] in the New Testament), therefore, Abba, father" as a term of address to God first appeared in Christian circles in the Hellenistic church. On this view, the term was then read back onto the lips of Jesus by the early church, in picturing his prayer-life. In support of the view it is noted that at Romans 8:15 and Galatians 4:6, the two places outside the gospels where "Abba, father" appears, the cry is connected with the Spirit (not the historical Jesus) and with seemingly extraordinary situations where the Spirit sets man's prayer in motion with this outcry. This alternative view depends on the extremely negative assumptions that Jesus is unlikely to have spoken in so startling a way and that we are not likely to have preserved for us much authentic material from him. Jeremias' case remains impressive, though not absolutely proven. For the alternative view, cf. J. C. G. Greig, " 'Abba' and 'Amen': the Relevance of Christology," a paper read at the Third International Congress on New Testament Studies, "The New Testament Today," Oxford, 1965, the proceedings of which will be published as *Studia Evangelica*, Vols. IV-V ("Texte und Untersuchungen"; Berlin: Akademie-Verlag). The fullest statement of Jeremias' view is now available in English in his essay "Abba," in *The Prayers of Jesus* (see above, p. 347, n. 5), pp. 11-65 and 108-15.

20. William Barclay observes, "*Abba* in ancient Palestine . . . was the word by which a little child addressed his father in the family circle. Any English translation is grotesque for the meaning is Daddy." *Flesh and Spirit: An Examination of Galatians 5:19-23* (Nashville: Abingdon, 1962), p. 90. The question for those today who wish to follow Jesus' lead in prayer is whether they can find language for God that is warm and intimate but still preserves His dignity—something between the formal idiom of collects used in church about the "Divine Majesty" and "Omnipotency" and the brashness of talk about God as a "livin' doll."

21. So E. Basil Redlich, *The Forgiveness of Sins* (Edinburgh: T. & T. Clark, 1937), p. 126: according to Jesus, God "would only forgive on condition that the offended forgave his fellow-men." Redlich finds Jesus' demand for "repentance with precedent human forgiveness" as the condition for attaining divine forgiveness the revolutionary note in Jesus' teaching.

22. This point is stressed by I. Abrahams, *Studies in Pharisaism and the Gospels, Second Series,* (see above, p. 348, n. 12), pp. 95-98. Abrahams holds that this notion, that man must first forgive his brother and only then can he go to God to seek forgiveness himself, has come into Jewish liturgy only in modern times, and then under Christian influence. He names this petition about forgiveness as the only one in the Lord's Prayer (in Matthew's form) with which a Jew feels himself out of sympathy—and it is the only one without Jewish models.

23. J. Jeremias, *The Lord's Prayer,* (see above p. 347, n. 5), p. 14.

24. This interpretation, "Forgive us as we herewith pledge forgiveness for others" (not "in proportion to the way we forgive others"), is supported by several ancient versions and comments. The *Didache,* a Jewish-Christian document (to be dated perhaps around A.D. 100) has, like Luke, "as we also forgive" (present tense). The Old Syriac translation has a future tense ("forgive us, and we also will forgive"). Polycarp (about A.D. 150) wrote to the Philippians, "If we pray to the Lord that he forgive us, we ought also to forgive." The sequence in all these cases is, "God forgives, therefore we forgive and will forgive." The full sequence, of course, assumed in the early Christian community would be, "God forgives; we forgive others; we need God's forgiveness, however; He forgives; we continue to forgive others," etc.

25. Cf. T. W. Manson, "The Lord's Prayer," *Bulletin of the John Rylands Library* (Manchester), 38, 1 (September, 1955), 99-113.

26. Luke likes to bring out the "daily" aspect of discipleship; cf. 9:23 where he adds "daily" to Mark 8:34.

27. It is often stated that a papyrus from Egypt published in 1889 and reported to the world of New Testament scholarship in 1925 (and subsequently cited in most lexicons and commentaries) establishes the meaning of the Greek word in the Lord's Prayer as "daily." Unfortunately the man who recorded the papyrus (which was a householder's list) was not always extremely accurate at reading such papyri, and he lost the original when a friend mislaid it. Hence there is doubt whether this reported example is really accurate. A second example claimed in 1954 from an inscription found on the island of Rhodes has turned out to be a case where the letters were incorrectly read and the gaps filled in improperly, so that the term from the Lord's Prayer does not appear there in actuality. Cf. Bruce M. Metzger, "How Many Times Does 'Epiousios' Occur Outside the Lord's Prayer?" *The Expository Times* 69, 2 (November, 1957), 52-54. The clues for interpretation of the term must therefore come from context, etymology (which is disputed), a gloss on the word in the "Gospel of the Nazarenes" (preserved in Jerome), and evidence such as a Latin inscription at Pompeii which suggests the sense "rations for tomorrow." (Baking might be done one day so as to make certain a supply of bread for the next.) But we cannot be positive about the meaning of the word in question.

28. The Latin version speaks of *panem nostrum supersubstantialem,* "our supersubstantial bread," i.e., the eucharistic bread. Some medieval theologians knew, of course, of the problems in the meaning of the phrase. There is a story that Abelard, who was aware of the difficulties in finding a proper Latin translation for the unusual Greek word in the Lord's Prayer, rebuked Heloise, who had introduced a new translation into her convent, that such matters were the concern of scholars, not mother superiors. Today, until scholars can find satisfactory evidence for a more accurate meaning, the traditional rendering as "daily" bread should probably stand.

29. Cf. Wisdom of Sirach 15:11-12, 20:
Do not say, "Because of the Lord I left the right way," . . .
Do not say, "It was he who led me astray"; . .
He has not commanded any one to be ungodly,
    and he has not given any one permission to sin.

30. The variant, "Thy Holy Spirit come upon us and cleanse us," occurs in the minuscule manuscripts of the Greek New Testament numbered 700 (from the eleventh century) and 162 (dated A.D. 1153) and in the church fathers Gregory of Nyssa, Maximus the Confessor,

and Tertullian; it seems also to have been used by Marcion in the second century A.D. "Hallowed be thy name upon us" is read by manuscript D, the sixth-century representative of the "Western Text." Cf. Frederic Henry Chase, *The Lord's Prayer in the Early Church* ("Texts and Studies," I, 3 [Cambridge: Cambridge University Press, 1891]), pp. 25-31. Some scholars think that such insertions were inserted into the prayer, not only to adapt it for liturgical use, but also out of a desire to have one specifically Christian petition in the prayer.

31. *Luthers Werke* (Weimar Edition), Vol. xxxvii, p. 326, as cited in C. E. B. Cranfield, *The Gospel according to Saint Mark* ("Cambridge Greek Testament Commentary" [New York: Cambridge University Press, 1959]), p. 431.

32. Cf. F. C. Grant, *Translating the Bible* (Greenwich, Connecticut: Seabury Press, 1961), p. 47.

33. Karl Barth, *Die Kirchliche Dogmatik* IV/1 (Zürich, 1953), p. 292; trans. G. W. Bromiley, *Church Dogmatics* IV/1 (Edinburgh: T. & T. Clark, 1956), p. 265: "Now he had to face the reckoning . . . the final fruit and consequence of what He had begun."

34. For those who have tended to look on history as an "objective science," with results possible which are akin to those in the life sciences or even the physical sciences, this conclusion may seem overly pessimistic. It is actually a fairly optimistic one, in view of the fact that historical study is always limited by its sources and is further, because of its necessity methodically to doubt and interrogate all source material, limited to conclusions of only relative probability. This condition applies not only to ancient history but also to modern happenings. It needs to be underscored that, even in our world of tape recorders and electronic devices, it is not always possible even for trained observers, such as newspaper reporters, to agree on details of what was said or done. The following example concerns the wedding of the actress Grace Kelly to Prince Rainier of Monaco in 1956; it was reported in *Time* for April 30, 1956, under "The Press" (the abbreviations refer to the various press services, International News Service, Associated Press, and United Press):

There were almost as many differences of opinion on what had gone on as there were newsmen.

The civil wedding took place in the palace throne room, which was described by I.N.S. as decorated with "gilded damask," by the New York *Herald Tribune* as "crimson damasked," and by the New York *Post* as "tapestried and frescoed." During the ceremony Grace Kelly had "tears in her eyes" for the U.P., but the A.P. said flatly:

"No tears." Miss Kelly, said the U.P., looked at Prince Rainier just once, with a "shy glance." The *Herald Tribune* called it "a proud romantic glance"; the New York *Times* thought it was "twice . . . distraughtly," while I.N.S. wrote that she glanced "often . . . as if to seek reassurance."

Even in their own ranks, Hearstlings managed to avoid sameness. Dorothy Kilgallen reported that "not once did the Prince look at his bride"; Bob Considine wrote that it was "only once." When the time came for the couple's responses, "both replied *'Oui'* firmly . . . Miss Kelly in husky, throaty sincerity," according to the *Herald Trib.* But in the *Times,* "each assented with a virtually inaudible *'Oui.' "* In any case, the ceremony lasted just 20 minutes (Considine), 16 minutes (Kilgallen), 40 minutes (*Post*), 15 "emotion-laden" minutes (New York *News*).

At the religious ceremony next day, Grace was "close to tears" in the *Post,* but for the U.P., "uncontrolled tears coursed down [her] cheeks." How did she make her responses this time?" *"Je veux* (I will)," said the U.P. *"Oui,"* said the *Post. "Oui, Monseigneur,"* said the *Times. "Oui, je veux,"* said the *Herald Trib.* Finessed Newshen Kilgallen: "[It was] barely audible."

5 God Raised Him from the Dead

1. G. Gloege, *The Day of His Coming* (see above, p. 344, n. 26), p. 275. Gloege, pp. 274-88, uses as an outline a helpful attempt (which is followed in the presentation above) to distinguish the Easter message, the Easter narratives, and the Easter event.

2. Both appendices to Mark are given in the RSV in smaller type; compare the footnotes in the NEB, where both endings are given in the same size type as the rest of the gospel.

The short ending to Mark, in the RSV translation, runs:
But they reported briefly to Peter and those with him all that they had been told. And after this, Jesus himself sent out by means of them, from east to west, the sacred and imperishable proclamation of eternal salvation.

The longer ending (16:9-20), familiar to many from the KJV, draws every detail which it contains from some other early Christian writing: vss. 9-11 = John 20:11-18; vss. 12-13 = Luke 24:13-35; vs. 14 = John 20:19-23; vss. 15-16 = Matt. 28:18-20; vss. 17-18 (verses which have often been made into unfortunate "tests of faith"—snake-handling, etc.—testing God in violation of the sixth petition in the Lord's Prayer), cf. Acts 28:3 ff. and stories in the apocryphal Acts of

John; vs. 19 = Luke 24:50-51; vs. 20 = the author's conclusion in this added ending. Every part becomes clear in light of some other early Christian resurrection story.

In addition to these two endings there is an insertion in one manuscript within the longer ending at the end of Mark 16:14. According to the Freer Logion, as this insertion is called, the disciples explain why they were so slow to believe about Jesus' resurrection:

And those men replied, "This age of lawlessness and unbelief is under Satan, who through evil spirits, does not permit God's truth to be perceived [the Greek is corrupt here, and most commentators follow a Latin rendering in Jerome]; therefore reveal now thy righteousness." They were speaking to the Messiah, and the Messiah said to them, "The limit of the years of the authority of Satan has been fulfilled, but other terrible things are drawing near, even for the sinners on behalf of whom I was delivered over to death, in order that they might turn to the truth and no longer sin, in order that they might inherit the spiritual and incorruptible glory of righteousness which is in heaven."

3. On the position which I have here taken, W. G. Kümmel notes in his recently translated *Introduction to the New Testament*, trans. A. J. Mattill, Jr. (New York and Nashville: Abingdon, 1966), pp. 71-72, that "scholarship in increasing measure is inclining toward the view that Mark reached his intended end with 16:8."

4. In Matthew, as this scene at the tomb is recounted, there is (compared with Mark) more emphasis on supernatural events (28:2-4, an earthquake as at the crucifixion; the angel of the Lord descends, the guards tremble). Matthew carries over the sense of awe from Mark but adds that the women ran with great joy to tell the disciples (vs. 8). The stress in Matthew vss. 9-10 is that Jesus appeared to the women and they worshiped him. The Greek clearly implies that it was the women who not only first found the tomb empty but also first worshiped the risen Christ. The command "go to Galilee" leads into Matthew's final scene there.

5. A much less well attested insertion, and surely a late one, is the detail added in one important Greek manuscript and a few other textual witnesses at Luke 23:53, that the stone at the tomb was so big that scarcely twenty men could move it. This picturesque detail reminds one of the line at Homer's *Odyssey*, 9. 241, where it is said that the stone which Cyclops put at the mouth of his cave was so big that one couldn't budge it with twenty four-wheeled wagons to help move it. On the whole, Luke tells of the empty tomb (24:1-11) somewhat differently from Mark. In his version the women do not need to buy

spices early in the morning since they had prepared them before sundown on Friday (23:56). Perplexity, not awe, marks their attitude
when they find the tomb empty (24:4), and they "remembered his
words" about the resurrection as soon as the angel reminds them
(24:8). The original sense of awe and fear in the Marcan version has
been "tamed down" in Luke just as in Matthew.

6. The other disciple with Cleopas in Luke 24 is unidentified. Vss.
33-34 say that the two returned to Jerusalem and reported their experience immediately to the eleven, who greeted them with news of their
own, "The Lord has appeared to Simon [Peter]." Only then did the
two get out their own story. But one manuscript claims that it was
Cleopas and his friend who rushed in with the news, "The Lord has
appeared to Simon"; in this case, Simon Peter was the man with
Cleopas on Emmaus Road.

7. Luke takes special pains, in the story of the appearance to the
eleven, to stress that Jesus is not a ghost (vs. 39); this emphasis seems
directed against notions of the Docetists who taught a "resurrection"
in spirit only of a none-too-human Jesus, who had not died, but had
ascended from the cross or had let someone else die in his place. Luke
also stresses scenes where the risen Christ eats with his friends (cf.
24:30-31, 42-43, Acts 1:4 in the RSV note; cf. also John 21:9-13).
It is often said that these scenes are "eucharistic" and reflect the idea
of Jesus' presence through the Lord's Supper. But the use of fish and
the absence of wine suggest links rather to the feeding miracles during
the historical ministry (Luke 9:10-17) and the emphasis that the risen
Christ is the same person as the Jesus of those experiences.

8. "O little town of Bethlehem," verse 3.

9. These individual resurrection narratives do share certain features of
form, however. Four elements regularly appear: (1) a brief description
of the situation where the disciples are in sorrow, bereft of Jesus (Luke
24:13 ff.; or 24:36); (2) the risen lord appears (24:15, 30-31, 36b);
(3) his greeting; and (4) a command from him. The greetings express
usually comfort and joy (Luke 24:38; Matthew 28:9; John 20:21).
For commands, see Mark 16:7 (from the angel); Matthew 28:10,
19-20; Luke 24:48-49; John 20:22-23; 21:15.

10. Any attempt to try to correlate the list at I Corinthians 15 with
resurrection appearances in the gospels leaves a series of unanswered
riddles. According to I Corinthians, Jesus appeared:
    15:5, to Cephas (Peter)—cf. Luke 24:34 (mentioned but not de-
        scribed) or John 21:15-19; critics think there must have been

a story of Jesus' resurrection appearance to Peter, of which
only fragments have survived;

to the twelve (really, the eleven)—Matthew 28:16-20; Mark
16:14;

15:6, to more than five hundred brethren—Pentecost, Acts 2?;

15:7, to James—there is no canonical account of the resurrection appearance by which Jesus' brother must have been converted;
to all the apostles—Luke 24:50?.

One must allow the various appearances to stand independently, without being able to integrate them into a chronological list.

11. See above, pp. 48-49. Whether the famous definition for an
apostle at Acts 1:22 represents merely a Lucan view or is characteristic
of all of primitive Christianity, it is the only one which the New
Testament really provides; here an apostle is described as ". . . a witness to his [Jesus'] resurrection" who had also been with the group
during Jesus' earthly ministry.

12. In Mark 16, the second woman is literally "Mary the ——— of
James"; translations usually supply "mother," but "wife" or "daughter"
is also possible. Which James? Probably James "the less" (or younger);
cf. the similar lists at Mark 15:40 and 47 and parallels. Salome is mentioned only in Mark, though later gnostic writings, like the *Gospel of
Thomas,* make much of her.

13. Each account, in describing the angels at the tomb, seems to some
extent to reflect the interests of the particular evangelist. Mark means
to describe an angelic messenger in human terms (16:5). Matthew has
employed the language of the Old Testament and of apocalyptic (an
"angel of the Lord," cf. Genesis 16:7; "appearance . . . like lightning,
. . . raiment white as snow"). Perhaps Luke has two angels because of
the principle that a thing should be established at the mouth of two
witnesses (Deuteronomy 19:15). We can see reasons why each writer
has what he does. We can scarcely prove historically what the "original account" said.

14. Attempts have often been made to use archeological evidence to
prove or disprove the resurrection. An inscription found at Nazareth,
the so-called Ordinance of Caesar, probably from a date after Jesus'
day, threatens death for anyone who robs a tomb. (Cf. C. K. Barrett,
The New Testament Background, [see above, p. 341, n. 9], p. 15.)
Some claim this law was instituted to keep other groups from stealing
a body and claiming a resurrection, the way Christians had. Equally
as likely is that such penalties for grave-robbery, here reiterated, would
have acted as a deterrent on Jesus' disciples from even thinking of such
a thing.

Another inscription which has stirred up a great deal of interest is the one found in a tomb at Jerusalem which was first interpreted to mean "Alas for Jesus." Further study has advanced the opposite interpretation, however, that it is a plea for the risen Jesus to help the man buried there. And still further study has led to the claim that these ossuary inscriptions reflect Christian influence on Jewish magical formulas. Here, as often, the results of archeology prove ambiguous. Cf André Parrot, *Golgotha and the Church of the Holy Sepulchre* ("Studies in Biblical Archaeology No. 6" [London: SCM Press, 1957]), pp. 113-19; B. Gustafsson, "The Oldest Graffiti in the History of the Church?" *New Testament Studies,* 3 (1956-57), 65-69; and D. Fishwick, "The Talpioth Ossuaries Again," *New Testament Studies,* 10 (1963-64), 49-61. See also above, p. 20.

One can scarcely be optimistic about the view that ossuaries found in the Kidron Valley outside Jerusalem in 1941 and possibly containing burials from a Jewish family from Cyrenaica could have included the bones of Alexander and Simon of Cyrene, who carried Jesus' cross; cf. N. Avigad, "A Depository of Inscribed Ossuaries in the Kidron Valley," *Israel Exploration Journal,* 12 (1962), 1-12.

15. A. M. Hunter, *The Work and Words of Jesus* (Philadelphia: Westminster, 1950), p. 123.

16. There are other indications in Paul's letters that he knew and accepted the idea that Jesus' resurrection had been a bodily one. At Philippians 3:21 Paul writes (or, according to some, quotes an earlier Christian formula which he takes over without change) that the Lord Jesus Christ "will change our lowly body to be like his glorious body" at the parousia. In I Corinthians 15, especially vss. 20, 35, 42-54, Paul argues that our bodies will be changed at the resurrection, just as has already happened with Christ, the first fruits of the dead. Cf. also Romans 6:3-4, where Paul states that in baptism believers are buried with Christ (and will be raised with him), and now already walk in newness of life. In these passages what has happened to Jesus Christ at Easter is used as an analogy to the bodily resurrection or renewal of believers. Cf. A. Michael Ramsey, *The Resurrection of Christ: An Essay in Biblical Theology* (Philadelphia: Westminster, 1946), pp. 43-44.

17. For theories which allow an empty tomb without a resurrection, see "explanations" b), c), d), and e), for example, on p. 119. The notion of a resurrection without an empty tomb is advanced particularly by scholars who hold that the stories of the appearances of the risen Jesus antedate those about the empty tomb, and that the earliest Easter faith therefore did not include an empty tomb. This position is also

sometimes taken for apologetic or philosophical reasons. Such a view is comprehensible on the basis of Greek views of man (where the soul is imprisoned in the body), but would a Pharisee, or any Jew, rooted in the Old Testament view of man as a psychosomatic unity, have thought in such terms?

18. D. F. Strauss, *The Life of Jesus, Critically Examined* (trans. from 4th German ed.; London: Chapman Brothers, 1846), III, 355. Cf. pp. 362-63, where Strauss wrote regarding this theory, which had already been advanced in his day.

> Jesus, we are told, seeing no other way of purifying the prevalent messianic idea from the admixture of material and political hopes, exposed himself to crucifixion, but in doing so relied on the possibility of procuring a speedy removal from the cross by early bowing his head, and of being afterwards restored by the medical skill of some among his secret colleagues; so as to inspirit the people at the same time by the appearance of a resurrection. Others have at least exonerated Jesus from such a contrivance, and have admitted that he really sank into a deathlike slumber; but have ascribed to his disciples a preconceived plan of producing apparent death by means of a potion, and thus by occasioning his early removal from the cross, securing his restoration to life. But of all this our evangelical sources give no intimation, and for conjecturing such details we have no ground. Judicious friends of the natural explanation, who repudiate such monstrous productions of a system which remodels history at will, have hence renounced the supposition of any remains of conscious life in Jesus, and have contented themselves, for the explanation of his revivification, with the vital force which remained in his still young and vigorous body, even after the cessation of consciousness; and have pointed out, instead of premeditated tendance by the hands of men, the beneficial influence which the partly oleaginous substances applied to his body, must have had in promoting the healing of his wounds, and, united with the air in the cave, impregnated with the perfumes of the spices, in reawakening feeling and consciousness in Jesus; to all which was added as a decisive impulse, the earthquake and the lightning which on the morning of the resurrection opened the grave of Jesus. Others have remarked, in opposition to this, that the cold air in a cave must have had any thing rather than a vivifying tendency; that strong aromatics in a confined space would rather have had a stupifying and stifling influence; and the same effect must have been produced by a flash of lightning bursting into the grave, if this were not a mere figment of rationalistic expositors.

After allowing that, in spite of all the improbabilities, such a view might be possible, that Jesus had not fully died on the cross, he, however, concludes (p. 365), "we must . . . doubt the reality of the resurrection rather than that of the death."

I have quoted at such length from Strauss to show the complexity of the arguments which this scholar of over a century ago had mastered in the already considerable literature which had by then appeared; but also to call attention to how theories which have been touted as the latest sensation in our own day have, to a considerable degree, been anticipated in the discussions of a century or two ago. Thus, the "secret colleagues" of Jesus (who are supposed to have revived him after his crucifixion experience) had been identified as "Essenes" in some rationalist lives of Jesus, long prior to the discoveries at Qumran and all the extreme theories promulgated in light of the Dead Sea Scrolls. Some of Strauss' arguments, it may be added, still apply to the theory recently revived by Hugh J. Schonfield in his own particular form in *The Passover Plot* (New York: Bernard Geis Associates, 1965), namely, that Jesus plotted his own death, intending, with the help of drugs, to feign that he had died; in this view, the unexpected spear wound weakened him so much, however, that he soon died after a friend had taken him from the tomb.

19. A. Michael Ramsey, *The Resurrection of Christ* (see above, p. 357, n. 16), pp. 91-101, especially emphasizes this approach, as do many other commentators.

20. The benediction at Hebrews 13:20 is the one exception and may be a later addition in the document.

21. Hans F. von Campenhausen, *Der Ablauf der Osterereignisse und das leere Grab* (Heidelberg, 1958); an English summary of his views is offered in Heinz Zahrnt, *The Historical Jesus* (New York: Harper & Row, 1963), pp. 123-38, or in Daniel P. Fuller, *Easter Faith and History* (Grand Rapids: Eerdmans, 1965), pp. 157-66. Professor von Campenhausen regards the empty tomb as the most controllable of all hypotheses historically. The empty tomb is explainable, however, he emphasizes, either on a human or a divine basis. In his reasoning, historical considerations open the door to faith but do not compel anyone to go through that door.

22. As cited in A. E. Gould, *Jesus King Most Wonderful: Studies in the Sovereignty and Saviourhood of Jesus Christ* (London: Allen & Unwin, 1965), p. 197. Cf. Karl Heim, *Jesus the World's Perfecter: The Atonement and the Renewal of the World*, trans. D. H. van Daalen (London: Oliver and Boyd, 1959; Philadelphia: Muhlenberg Press, 1961), pp. 148-49.

23. *The Day of His Coming* (see above, p. 344, n. 26), p. 118.

24. It is widely held that the Hebrew word for God, "Yahweh," was rendered in the Septuagint Greek Old Testament by *kyrios,* "lord," and that when early Christians began to speak of Jesus as lord (*kyrios*), the way was thus opened for regarding him as God (equivalent to Yahweh). It is now realized that the story of developments within early Christianity is more complicated. The Septuagint manuscripts which render "Yahweh" by *kyrios* are all copies made by *Christian* hands after the first century A.D. In recent years manuscripts of the Old Testament in Greek from *Jewish* hands have come to light, thanks to discoveries in the Judean desert. In these manuscripts the four Hebrew letters of "Yahweh" (YHWH) regularly appear in the Greek text, instead of any Greek translation or transliteration into Greek letters, thus showing that at this stage Jewish scribes did not write *kyrios* for "Yahweh." Of course, Jews reading such Greek manuscripts might have spoken the term *kyrios* every time they came to YHWH (to avoid uttering the sacred Hebrew name), but that is uncertain. We can no longer claim, however, that *kyrios* was a pre-Christian rendering of "Yahweh," which early Christians took over and applied to Christ. Cf. Paul E. Kahle, *The Cairo Geniza* ("The Schweich Lectures for the British Academy," 1941 [London: Oxford University Press, 1947]), pp. 171-72; (2d ed.; New York: Praeger, 1960), pp. 218-28. The evidence, including the more recent finds from Qumran, is summarized by P. Vielhauer, "Ein Weg zur neutestamentlichen Christologie?", *Evangelische Theologie,* 25 (1965), 29-31, where further references to the periodical literature are given. The problem is assumed in the discussion by W. Kramer, *Christ, Lord, Son of God,* trans. B. Hardy ("Studies in Biblical Theology," 50 [London: SCM Press, 1966]), pars. 18F (p. 84), 22B (p. 95), 43A-D (pp. 156-59).

25. Out of eighteen such cases in the Gospel of Luke, sixteen seem to come from Luke's special source. Therefore it is *L,* rather than Luke himself, who should probably be credited with this particular usage.

26. A further example of how the term "lord" is projected backward from the resurrection into Jesus' life and even earlier involves the way Psalm 2:7 is used in the New Testament. The psalm verse, where God says, "You are my son, today I have begotten you" (originally with reference to the king, probably, at his coronation or an enthronement festival), is applied in New Testament documents with regard to the *resurrection* (cf. Acts 13:33, noting the use here of Psalm 2:7, "You are my Son, *today* I have begotten you"—here "today" is the day of the resurrection); Jesus' *baptism* (cf. Luke 3:22, here Jesus is declared God's Son, and some manuscripts in Luke [see RSV footnote]

use Psalm 2:7, "today I have begotten you"; here Jesus' sonship, and indirectly his lordship, would be seen from the time of his baptism); and *the time prior to his earthly life,* from the very beginning of things, when he was with God (cf. Hebrews 1:10, where Jesus is called "Lord," and at 1:5 and 5:5 the same psalm verse is quoted, with the claim that Jesus was son from the very beginning; "today" in Psalm 2:7 is here referred to a day prior to creation).

27. In his book *Son of Man: The Life of Christ* (New York: E. P. Dutton, 1961), Leslie Paul entitled his final chapter on the resurrection, "The Epilogue Which Was a Prologue." This description fits the relation of the resurrection not only to the epistles and the rise of primitive Christianity, but also to the gospels which we have today and their contents: Jesus' resurrection is the prologue assumed in all the accounts of the ministry.

28. The length of time between Jesus' resurrection and his ascension varies both in "orthodox" writings and "gnostic" sources. Though Acts 1:3 says "forty days" was the length of time involved, Acts 10:41 mentions no length of time, and 13:31 simply says "many days." Other documents outside the New Testament set the period at 50 days, still others at 545 or 550 days (i.e., eighteen months). Still others, and they are usually sources which are gnostic in their tendencies, lengthen it to three and a half years (so that the post-resurrection ministry balances in length the time assumed for the pre-resurrection ministry of Jesus on earth), and twelve years or more. For references, cf. James M. Robinson, "Ascension," in *The Interpreter's Dictionary of the Bible* (New York and Nashville: Abingdon, 1962), Vol. 3, p. 246, and J. G. Davies, *He Ascended into Heaven: A Study in the History of Doctrine* (London: Lutterworth, 1958), especially pp. 69-94, 192-98.

29. John 20:17 mentions ascending to the Father, but there is no account as in Luke-Acts. Cf. also Ephesians 4:8-10.

30. The phrase comes from C. F. D. Moule, "The Ascension—Acts i.9," *Expository Times,* 68, 7 (April, 1957), 208.

31. A. Michael Ramsey, *The Resurrection of Christ* (see above, p. 357 n. 16), p. 9.

32. Recent surveys on such chronological problems are provided by J. Finegan, *Handbook of Biblical Chronology* (see above, p. 341, n. 5), pp. 280-85, and H. E. W. Turner, "The Chronological Framework of the Ministry," in *Historicity and Chronology in the New Testament* ("SPCK Theological Collections," 6 [London: SPCK, 1965]), pp. 59-74. I should agree with Turner's judgment (p. 59) that all the

gospels provide "kerygmatic history." For a recent assessment of material in John, though with properly cautious reservations about using it to reconstruct scientifically the ministry of Jesus, cf. R. E. Brown, S.S., *The Gospel according to John (i-xii)* ("The Anchor Bible," 29 [Garden City: Doubleday, 1966]), pp. xli-li.

33. The best-known recent example of an attempt to see John's Gospel in such a light, as a series of sermons based on a Jewish lectionary or series of readings for the liturgical year, is Aileen Guilding's *The Fourth Gospel and Jewish Worship* (Oxford: Clarendon Press, 1960). A summary of several such theories is provided by Leon Morris, *The New Testament and Jewish Lectionaries* (London: Tyndale Press, 1964).

34. The survey article by Vincent Taylor, "The Life and Ministry of Jesus," in *The Interpreter's Bible* (New York: Abingdon), Vol. 7 (1951), pp. 114-44, uses the Marcan outline as its framework, though Taylor's remarks in his commentary, *The Gospel according to St. Mark* (New York: St Martin's Press, 1952), pp. 145-48, seem a bit more cautious.

35. The whole argument of C. H. Dodd's famous little book, *The Apostolic Preaching and Its Developments* (London: Hodder & Stoughton, 1936), especially pp. 46-56, points in this direction.

36. *The Quest of the Historical Jesus* (see above, p. 336, n. 1), pp. 330-97.

37. See above, pp. 358-59, n. 18.

38. See below, chapter 9, pp. 256-59.

39. See below, chapter 9, pp. 260-295, with regard to Jesus' view as to certain messianic titles, or chapter 10, pp. 297-333, with regard to his possible views on eschatology and the future, discipleship and the church, and related topics.

40. Cf. Oscar Cullmann "The Origin of Christmas," in *The Early Church: Studies in Early Christian History and Theology,* ed. A. J. B. Higgins (Philadelphia: Westminster, 1956), pp. 21-38 (in abridged paperback ed., 1966, pp. 17-36).

41. Cullmann's essay, *ibid.,* especially pp. 29-32, gives some examples and detailed evidence on the matter of date.

42. *Edgar Hennecke, New Testament Apocrypha* (see above, p. 336, n. 2), 1, pp. 363-417.

43. See above, pp. 3-5.

44. In spite of many learned attempts to identify behind the "star of Bethlehem" a planetary conjunction (e.g. of Jupiter, Saturn, and Mars in 7 or early 6 B.C.), or a comet (such as Halley's in 12 B.C.), or a nova mentioned in Chinese records (cf. J. Finegan, *Handbook of Biblical Chronology* [see above, p. 340, n. 5], pp. 238-48), we must renounce all such efforts not only because of the chronological and other uncertainties involved, but because Matthew's word means an individual star, not a constellation or comet or conjunction of planets. Matthew no doubt envisioned a miraculously appearing star, and his story reflects the ancient notion that each man has a star which rises at his birth (and sets when he dies) ; hence Herod's interest in ascertaining when the star appeared, so as to discover when the child was born. The Magi represent oriental magic, forced to kneel before the Christ child. The emphasis in the story is on their homage to him and the celestial corroboration of the significance of this child. Such is the interpretation of the oldest Christian commentary on the star, in Ignatius' letter to the Ephesians, section 19, in the second century A.D.:

How was he [the child of Mary] then made manifest to the ages? A star shone in heaven above all the stars, and its light was ineffable and its newness caused amazement. All the rest of the stars, together with the sun and moon, formed a chorus about the star, but the star itself surpassed them all in its light. And there was perplexity to know whence this newness had arisen which was so unlike them [the stars]. From then on, all magic was dissolved and every spell, the ignorance which stems from evil vanished, the ancient kingdom [of the Evil One] was overthrown, because God appeared in human form to bring newness of eternal life.

There is also in Matthew's story a reflection of Old Testament verses such as Psalm 72:10-11, 15, and Isaiah 60:6.

45. The known dates for an imperial census (8 B.C., A.D. 4) do not fit other details of chronology about the birth of Jesus, and a possible provincial census in A.D. 6/7 seems too late and would not involve "all the world" (Luke 2:1). Recent discussions of the archeological and Roman legal evidence are surveyed by A. R. C. Leaney, *The Gospel according to St. Luke* ("Harper's New Testament Commentaries" [New York: Harper, 1958]), pp. 44-48, and by H. E. W. Turner, in *Historicity and Chronology in the New Testament* (see above, p. 361, n. 32), pp. 60-65, but no clear solution which satisfies all the evidence is apparent.

46. Martin Dibelius, in his famous essay "Jungfrauensohn und Krippenkind" (1932, reprinted in his collected essays, *Botschaft und*

Geschichte [Tübingen: J. C. B. Mohr, 1953], I, 1-78), has provided a starting point for all subsequent analysis of Luke 1 and 2 by showing how chapter 1 stresses Mary, the Virgin's son, and the virginal conception by the Spirit (1:26-38 especially), while chapter 2 stresses the savior-child in the manger (the phrase "in the manger" is repeated at 2:7, 12, and 16). In chapter 2 the signs and wonders center on the child, not the mother, there is no reference to the Spirit, and Joseph is mentioned more frequently. Thus chapter 2 has little direct connection with chapter 1, and A. R. C. Leaney, in his commentary on Luke (see above, p. 363, n. 45), pp. 20-27, has attempted to analyze two separate traditions here, with that in chapter 2 regarded as the earlier one. A partial summary of Dibelius' view can be found in English in Thomas Boslooper, *The Virgin Birth* (Philadelphia: Westminister, 1962) pp. 207-210. The standard conservative work on the subject, *The Virgin Birth of Christ*, by J. Gresham Machen (New York: Harper & Brothers, 1930; rev. ed., 1932; reprinted, London: James Clarke, 1958), appeared just prior to publication of Dibelius' essay.

47. On "Son" and "Son of God" in connection with Jesus in the gospels, see below, pp. 286-95. It is a confession of Luke's faith (and that of his church) that he traces Jesus' genealogy back to "Adam, the son of God" (Luke 3:38), and not just back to Abraham as does Matthew (who in his genealogy, 1:1-17, stresses Jesus as son of David and son of Abraham). Luke sees Jesus in a more universal context, not just against the background of Israel; as son of God (1:32, 35; 4:3), not just as "son of Abraham" or "son of David."

48. Krister Stendahl ("Quis et Unde? An Analysis of Mt 1-2," in *Judentum Urchristentum Kirche* [Festschrift for Joachim Jeremias; ed. W. Eltester; "Beihefte zur Zeitschrift für die neutestamentliche Wissenschaft," 26 (Berlin: Töpelmann, 1960)], pp. 94-105) writes in discussing the nativity stories in Matthew, "The tendency to *describe* what originally was *believed* is one of the creative forces in the development of Nativity Gospels" (p. 94, n. 1). He then refers to the effort by Oscar Cullmann (in his discussion of "Infancy Gospels," in the Hennecke-Schneemelcher *New Testament Apocrypha* [see above, p. 336, n. 2], Vol. 1, pp. 363-69) to distinguish the canonical nativity stories from those in the noncanonical literature on the basis of motive: those in the New Testament are marked by theological interest primarily, those in the apocrypha reflect much more a narrative and an apologetic interest. However, that belief shapes description applies already to the narratives in Matthew and Luke, and Christology, as part of the church's resurrection faith, is certainly a key to understanding

Matthew 1–2 and Luke 1–2. For interpreting these chapters, Paul Minear once remarked that it is not so important to pin down the precise sociological situation in the early church (*Sitz im Leben*) where each story was used as it is to recall that these stories were part of the faith and praise of the early church(*Sitz im Loben, Sitz im Glauben*) with regard to the earthly origins of the Lord Jesus; cf. P. Minear, *The Interpreter and the Birth Stories* ("Symbolae Biblicae Upsaliensis," 13 [Uppsala, 1950]), p. 17.

6   The Good News of the Reign of God—Preaching and Parables

1. Even the Fourth Gospel has some references to the kingdom of God; cf. John 3:3, 5, and 18:36. It is commonly recognized that John has substituted for the theme of the kingdom of God a result of what God's reign means for man: namely, eternal life. Warrant for what John has done is already found in the Jesus-material at Mark 9:43, 45, 47; in these verses there is a clear parallel between "enter life" and "enter the kingdom of God." Johannine tradition chose to develop the theme of life.

2. Typical is the statement of Rudolf Bultmann, in his *Theology of the New Testament* (New York: Scribner, 1951-55), Vol. 1, p. 4: "The dominant concept of Jesus' message is the *Reign of God*" (italics Bultmann's). A survey of opinions is given by Gösta Lundström, *The Kingdom of God in the Teaching of Jesus: A History of Interpretation from the Last Decades of the Nineteenth Century to the Present Day,* trans. Joan Bulman (Richmond: John Knox Press, 1963). A recent presentation on the topic from the conservative position is that of George E. Ladd, *Jesus and the Kingdom: The Eschatology of Biblical Realism* (New York: Harper & Row, 1964). For a Roman Catholic treatment, cf. Rudolf Schnackenburg, *God's Rule and Kingdom,* trans. J. Murray (New York: Herder & Herder, 1963). See also Norman Perrin, *The Kingdom of God in the Teaching of Jesus* (Philadelphia: Westminster, 1963). An exception to the widespread consensus on the centrality of the kingdom in the teachings of Jesus is the view of Ernst Bammel, a German scholar now teaching at Cambridge, England. In his article "Erwägungen zur Eschatologie Jesu," in *Studia Evangelica,* III, ed. F. L. Cross ("Texte und Untersuchungen," 88 [Berlin, 1964]), pp. 3-32, Bammel argues that the Son of man was Jesus' chief theme, and he emphasizes this at the expense of the passages about the kingdom.

3. "Kingdom of God" appears in the writings of the early church outside the gospels in such passages as Acts 1:3; 8:12; 28:23, 31; I

Corinthians 4:20; Colossians 4:11; Galatians 5:21; Ephesians 5:5; and I Thessalonians 2:12.

4. So L. E. Keck, "The Introduction to Mark's Gospel," *New Testament Studies*, 12 (1965-66), 352-70.

5. The point is of some importance that Jesus proclaimed not himself, but God, as king, since certain biographers of the "radical school" as well as some conservative interpreters have both sought to envision Jesus as claiming kingship during his own lifetime. On the one hand, radical biographers like Robert Eisler, in ΙΗΣΟΥΣ ΒΑΣΙΛΕΥΣ ΟΥ ΒΑΣΙΛΕΥΣΑΣ (Heidelberg: Winter, 1928-29) and *The Messiah Jesus and John the Baptist* (New York: Dial Press, 1931), have claimed that Jesus wanted to make himself a king by force and was therefore the leader of a revolutionary movement. For more recent examples of this general position, cf. Joel Carmichael, *The Death of Jesus* (New York: Macmillan, 1963; Pelican Books, 1966), where it is maintained that Jesus died for sedition, after he and his followers had seized the temple in an insurrection; and S. G. F. Brandon, *Jesus and the Zealots* (Manchester: Manchester University Press, 1967), where Jesus' involvement in his nation's cause against the Roman overlords is evaluated in light of the sedition charge and new evidence now available about the Zealots as first-century "freedom fighters." On the other hand, Christians over the centuries have been accustomed to speak of Jesus as "king" with quite other, devotional connotations, and have in their enthusiasm read this kingship back into his own lifetime. Compare the hymn entitled "O Jesus, King most wonderful," attributed to Bernard of Clairvaux, or the book by A. E. Gould, *Jesus King Most Wonderful: Studies in the Sovereignty and Saviourhood of Jesus Christ* (London: Allen & Unwin, 1965), where the theme of "King Jesus" is projected throughout.

But did Jesus view himself as a king in his own lifetime, and did his contemporaries think about him in that way prior to the resurrection and exaltation? Occasionally in studying the passion accounts one finds a few hints that some people did regard Jesus as a king. There is, for example, the charge made by the Jews to Pilate at Luke 23:2, "He says that he is an anointed king." John 6:15 is also frequently invoked: a multitude, we are told, was so impressed by how Jesus miraculously fed the five thousand that the people were going to take him by force and make him king. No doubt there were enthusiastic followers and Zealots who would have welcomed it if Jesus had aspired to kingship. They would have supported him, just as the chief priests and the Romans would naturally oppose any such move.

However, John 6:15 adds that when Jesus perceived what the crowd

was going to do, he "withdrew again to the hills by himself." He
would have none of it. And his teachings, even though they often use
the words "king" and "kingship," say virtually nothing about Jesus
as king. In fact, quite the opposite of what one might expect, Jesus'
authentic teachings are embarrassingly bare of references to Jesus as
king. He does not refer to himself but to God as king. He does not
preach about himself or make a claim for his own person as the great
theme of his ministry. Instead he talks about the kingdom of God. If
anything, this remarkable fact has constituted an embarrassment for
later Christianity. However, it is also an indication that Jesus was not
plotting to become an earthly king himself. "King Jesus" as a title
could arise only after the resurrection, as a phrase of Christian adora-
tion, when Christians honored as lord the one who had preached a
renewed message about God as king.

6. Alan Richardson, *A Theological Word Book of the Bible* (New
York: Macmillan, 1950), p. 120, col. b. The miracles will be discussed further in chapter 7.

7. *The Kingdom of God in the New Testament* (New York: Macmillan, 1931), p. 54.

8. Oscar Cullman, "The Kingship of Christ and the Church in the
New Testament," in *The Early Church* (see above, p. 362, n. 40), pp.
101-37; and in *Christ and Time: The Primitive Christian Conception
of Time and History*, trans. Floyd V. Filson (rev. ed.; Philadelphia:
Westminster, 1964), pp. 185-90. Professor Cullmann's view is that
since the resurrection Christ is king over the church (where his rule
is acknowledged) and king over the world (where his rule is not as
yet acknowledged). At the end of the world, Christ will turn over his
rule to God, the kingdom of God will be brought to completion, and
God will be "all in all" (cf. Colossians 1:13; I Corinthians 15:24-28).
With this view, which Cullmann has developed chiefly from Pauline
passages, should be compared the view of the church and "the kingdom
of the Son of man" implied in Matthew 13, discussed below, pp.
187-88.

9. "Kingdom of heaven" is a Semitic phrase which Matthew often
substitutes for "kingdom of God" which appears more generally in
the Synoptic tradition (compare Matthew 4:17 with Mark 1:15, or
Matthew 19:23-24 with Mark 10:23-25) in order to avoid saying
the name "God." Both phrases mean exactly the same thing. On a
few occasions in the New Testament simply "the kingdom" is used
(Matthew 4:23; Acts 20:25; Revelation 1:9); this was an early Christian "shorthand" expression and means the same thing as "kingdom
of God." "Kingdom of Christ" is a post-resurrection expression which

does not appear in the Synoptic Gospels. For "kingdom of the Son of man," see p. 187. That Matthew (3:2 and 4:17) has John the Baptist and Jesus both preaching verbatim the same theme, while Luke never allows John to preach the kingdom as his theme (cf. 3:3 and 4:43), probably stems from the hand of each evangelist; it is editorial arrangement based on theological motivation. Historically the relation of Jesus' message to the Baptist's no doubt lay somewhere between these extreme possibilities presented in Matthew and Luke.

10. Cf. G. Friedrich, "*euangelizomai, euangelion*," etc., in *Theological Dictionary of the New Testament,* ed. Gerhard Kittel, trans. G. W. Bromiley (Grand Rapids: Eerdmans), 2 (1964), 707-37; and G. Kleinknecht, G. von Rad, K. G. Kuhn, and Karl Ludwig Schmidt, "*basileus, basileia,*" etc., *ibid.,* 1 (1964), 564-93, also available in *Bible Key Words,* 7, *Basileia,* trans. H. P. Kingdon (London: A. & C. Black, 1957).

11. It is surely significant that in presenting the transfiguration Luke speaks of the "departure [exodus] which he [Jesus] was to accomplish at Jerusalem" (9:31)—i.e., he refers to the cross and resurrection as the New Exodus for God's people, the one which has "delivered us from the dominion of darkness and transferred us to the kingdom of his beloved Son" (Colossians 1:13).

12. Exception to the view that God's kingdom means his reign rather than his realm is taken by S. Aalen, " 'Reign' and 'House' in the Kingdom of God in the Gospels," *New Testament Studies,* 8 (1962), 215-40, and George E. Ladd, "The Kingdom of God—Reign or Realm?" *Journal of Biblical Literature,* 81 (1962), 230-38.

13. II Baruch (Syriac Apocalypse of Baruch) 29.5; English translation by R. H. Charles, *The Apocrypha and Pseudepigrapha of the Old Testament* (Oxford: Clarendon Press, 1913), Vol. 2, pp. 497-98. The imagery reappears in Christian writers with apocalyptic tendencies in the second century; cf. the fragment from Papias preserved in Irenaeus, *Against Heresies* 5. 33.3-4, where Papias and others say that John spoke of days when each vine would produce ten thousand shoots, each shoot ten thousand branches, each branch ten thousand twigs, each twig ten thousand clusters, each cluster ten thousand grapes, and each grape twenty-five measures of wine—and, as if this is not wondrous enough, when one cluster is chosen, another one will cry out, "I am a better cluster, take me. . . . "

14. Rabbinic references to the kingdom of God are neither so common nor proportionally so important as those in the teachings of Jesus. The very phrase, however, is characteristically rabbinic. Late Judaism

preferred abstract phrases like the "kingship of God" to verbal statements such as "God reigns" which were found in the Old Testament;
thus the Aramaic paraphrase or Targum of Exodus 15:18 has "The
kingship of God stands fast" for "The Lord will reign for ever and
ever." Further, by New Testament times the name of God had been
replaced by some substitute like "heaven" (as in Matthew's phrase,
"kingdom of heaven") and by the early second century A.D. the more
abstract word "the place" was even employed instead of "heaven."
Old Testament verses where God is called king were referred to as
"kingship verses."

Actual rabbinic usage of the phrase "kingdom of heaven" suggests
that God's kingship was viewed as both present in Israel and future
as a hope. It was employed on the one hand, in the phrase "to take on
oneself the yoke of the kingdom," to mean acceptance by an individual
of God as King and then confession of this in the creed of Jewish
monotheism, "God is one"; the phrase thus came to mean "recite the
Shema" (Deuteronomy 6:4). (At Matthew 11:29-30 the "yoke"
which Jesus offers is described as "light" in contrast to the burden
imposed in taking upon oneself the law of the rabbis; cf. Matthew
23:4.) On the other hand, the rabbis also used "kingdom of heaven"
to refer eschatologically to the "end" of things when God's kingship
would be decisively revealed. One may say that Jesus' use of "kingdom
of God (heaven)" is in line with rabbinic practice with regard to the
following points: the term itself ("kingdom of God" rather than
"Yahweh reigns"); association of the term with individual decision,
conversion, or confession; and the eschatological linking of the term
with the future.

15. Just as we speak of "Platonic terms" although philosophers before
Plato used the words, so we can speak of "Jesus terms" though others
employed them previously—E. F. Scott, *The Kingdom of God* (see
above, p. 367, n. 7), pp. 51-52.

16. Gloege, *The Day of His Coming* (see above, p. 344, n. 26), p. 131.

17. Cf., for example, Kenneth Clark's article on the Greek verb involved in some of the passages about the kingdom's "drawing near,"
entitled "Realized Eschatology," *Journal of Biblical Literature,* 59
(1940), 367-83; or, for a discussion of the overall problem, W. G.
Kümmel, *Promise and Fulfillment: The Eschatological Message of
Jesus,* trans. Dorothea M. Barton ("Studies in Biblical Theology," 23
[London: SCM Press, 1957]). The problem is, of course, discussed
in most recent literature on the kingdom of God such as is listed in
note 2 in this chapter.

18. Note the phrase *"inherit* the kingdom" (e.g., Matthew 25:34; I Corinthians 6:9-10); it is given, not earned. Or Luke 12:32, "It is your Father's good pleasure to give you the kingdom"; cf. Luke 22:29. When Joseph of Arimathea is described as a man who was "awaiting the kingdom of God" (Mark 15:43, par. Luke 23:51), that means, waiting for God to manifest it.

19. Cf. M. H. Pope, "Proselyte," in *The Interpreter's Dictionary of the Bible* (see above, p. 361, n. 28), Vol. 4, pp. 921-31, especially sections 5 (on the success of such Jewish efforts) and 6.c (the status of the converts).

20. Cf. T. W. Manson, *Only to the House of Israel? Jesus and the Non-Jews* ("Facet Books, Biblical Series," 9 [Philadelphia: Fortress Press, 1964]). Albrecht Alt, *Where Jesus Worked, Towns and villages of Galilee studied with the help of local history,* trans. K. Grayston (London: Epworth, 1961). Joachim Jeremias, "The Gentile World in the Thought of Jesus," in *Bulletin of the Studiorum Novi Testamenti Societas Nos. I-III* (reprinted, New York: Cambridge University Press, 1963; originally in No. III [1952]), pp. 18-28; *Jesus' Promise to the Nations,* trans. S. H. Hooke ("Studies in Biblical Theology," 24 [London: SCM Press, 1958]).

21. Other bits of evidence help support the claim that Jesus' message about the kingdom had universal implications, even though his own ministry was geographically circumscribed. For example, Jesus seems to have had a kindly attitude toward Samaritans (every one of his stories which has a Samaritan in it refers favorably to them). Jesus often speaks of a judgment on his own Jewish people but can call a publican a "son of Abraham" (Luke 19:9), and refers favorably to non-Jews (Matthew 12:41-42; 11:21-24). In line with the Old Testament and with the idea of the kingdom as God-given, it has been argued, by Jeremias, for example (see references in the previous note), that Jesus expected the coming of the Gentiles into the kingdom by an eschatological action of God; cf. Isaiah 2:2-3; 11:9-10; 25:6-7. One day, on "that day," the Day of the Lord, the nations would come to God's holy mount at Jerusalem; this is what Luke 13:28-29 is said to envision. It is God who will eventually bring the Gentiles in. A more convincing argument for a universal intent may be to appeal to the broader Old Testament background. There universal notes of Yahweh's power and kingship begin to appear as early as the prophet Amos. God is king of the earth, not just of Israel; so the rabbis also claimed. His kingship would affect the entire universe. Jesus' view of the kingdom, it can reasonably be claimed, would pick up this line of thought and carry it over, by implication. Above all, there is the fact

that Jesus, like the rabbis, sought an individual response to the kingship of God. Simply to be a son of Abraham was not automatically
enough. Everyone who hears is challenged to respond personally. All
in all, there seems to be enough evidence to warrant calling Jesus'
message "universal," even though it was heralded to a historically
limited group in Palestine.

22. Among the Old Testament links which are often invoked in discussion of a connection between the kingdom and some human figure
are the terms "son of David" (II Samuel 7:12-16) and "son of man"
(Daniel 2:44 and 7:13-27). (Contrary to what is often assumed, a
"Messiah" or "Christ" was not regularly mentioned in the Old Testament as inaugurating God's kingship and the realization of his kingdom.) "Son of man" (and "Christ") will be considered in chapter 9.
"Son of David" had, in Jesus' day, come to have a nationalistic sense
denoting a ruler from the old royal family; it plays a comparatively
small part in the New Testament picture of Jesus. It is true that II
Samuel 7:16 had promised that a member of David's family would
always rule for God. Amos 9:11-15, Isaiah 9:2-7, 11:1-9, and Micah
5:2-4 voiced this hope in later times. Even after the exile, attempts
were apparently made to reestablish a descendant of David, Zerubbabel,
on the throne (cf. Zechariah 6:9-15 and commentaries on these difficult
verses about the crowning of a messianic leader); however, the effort
failed. Yet the hope lingered on in Jesus' day. The cry at Mark 11:10
reflects such an outlook: "Blessed is the kingdom of our father David
that is coming!" (To what extent the whole story of Jesus' "triumphal
entry" into Jerusalem with its cry of "Hosanna to the Son of David"
is intended as historical report and to what extent a reflection of the
church's faith is well discussed by Eduard Lohse, *History of the Suffering and Death of Jesus Christ,* trans. Martin O. Dietrich [Philadelphia:
Fortress Press, 1967], pp. 20-27.) When suppliants addressed Jesus
as "Son of David" (Mark 10:47), such is the background in their
mind. But Jesus himself does not, via this term, construct any connection to the kingdom of God which he announces. His major reference
to "the son of David" is in the form of a riddle; see Mark 12:35-37,
discussed on p. 256. "Son of David" was not Jesus' way of showing his
connection to the coming of God's kingdom.

23. G. Bornkamm, *Jesus of Nazareth* (see above, p. 340, n. 10), p. 67.

24. Cf. the article by Kenneth Clark, and W. G. Kümmel's *Promise
and Fulfillment,* pp. 19-25, both cited above on p. 369, n. 17.

25. Cf. Kümmel, *Promise and Fulfillment* (see above, p. 369, n. 17),
pp. 25-29 especially.

26. The verb at Luke 16:16 is a difficult one to interpret; RSV has, "every one enters [the Kingdom of God] violently," NEB, "forces his way in."

27. C. H. Dodd, *The Apostolic Preaching* (se above, p. 362, n. 35), pp. 79-96, and frequently in Dodd's other books. On the term "realized eschatology" and how Dodd later came to accept Joachim Jeremias' phrase "eschatology becoming actualized" as more descriptive of what he intended, cf. my note in Joachim Jeremias, *The Lord's Prayer* (see above, p. 347, n. 5), p. 32, n. 27.

28. Cf. T. Francis Glasson, *The Second Advent: The Origin of the New Testament Doctrine* (London: Epworth, 1945), and *His Appearing and His Kingdom: The Christian Hope in the Light of Its History* (London: Epworth, 1953); and John A. T. Robinson, *Jesus and His Coming: The Emergence of a Doctrine* (New York and Nashville: Abingdon, 1957).

29. At Matthew 12:28 (par. Luke 11:20) Jesus denies that his healing miracles are works of Satan; they are works of God, and imply that the kingdom-time of salvation has come. But this argument, directed against a specific charge of his enemies, is far from the sort of "signs" or series of events that some asked for to date the coming of the kingdom. Elsewhere Jesus refuses to give signs (Mark 8:12). He refuses to give a calendar.

30. A. Rüstow, *"Entos hymōn estin.* Zur Deutung von Lukas 17, 20-21," *Zeitschrift für die neutestamentliche Wissenschaft,* 51 (1960), 197-224.

31. Cf. N. A. Dahl, "The Parables of Growth," *Studia Theologica,* 5 (1951), 132-66.

32. *Jesus of Nazareth* (see above, p. 340, n. 10), pp. 72-73.

33. Cf. Kümmel, *Promise and Fulfillment* (see above, p. 369, n. 17), pp. 151-53, especially n. 27; Cullmann, *The Early Church* (see above, p. 362, n. 40), pp. 153-54.

34. The Gnostics, for example, wanting to prove from Scripture their notion that there are thirty "aeons" or heavenly powers separating man from God, found their "proof" in the fact that the employer in the parable of the Laborers in the Vineyard went out to hire men at the third, sixth, ninth, and eleventh hours; add $3 + 6 + 9 + 11 + 1$ (the one hour which the last man worked), and the total is thirty.

35. R. C. Trench, *Notes on the Parables of our Lord* (originally 1841;

New York: Appleton, 1859; rev. ed., 1874; often reprinted, most recently by Baker Book House, Grand Rapids).

36. A. Jülicher, *Die Gleichnisreden Jesu. 1. Teil: Die Gleichnisreden Jesu im allgemeinen* (1888); *2. Teil: Auslegung der Gleichnisreden der drei ersten Evangelien* (1899) (3d ed.; Tübingen: J. C. B. Mohr, 1910; reprinted, Darmstadt: Wissenschaftliche Buchgesellschaft, 1963).

37. C. H. Dodd, *The Parables of the Kingdom* (New York: Scribner's, 1935; rev. ed., 1961).

38. J. Jeremias, *The Parables of Jesus,* trans. S. H. Hooke (New York: Scribner's, 1954; rev. ed., 1963). A simplified edition for general readers, which omits most of the footnotes and technical material, has appeared under the title *Rediscovering the Parables,* trans. adapted by Frank Clarke (New York: Scribner's, 1966). An excellent summary for laymen on much of the work on the parables is found in A. M. Hunter, *Interpreting the Parables* (Philadelphia: Westminster, 1961).

39. Hellenistic Jewish writers outside Palestine, like Philo, could be extremely allegorical in their writings, and allegorical interpretations appear in the documents from Qumran. However, at times, and perhaps under Greek influences, the rabbis too could introduce allegory into their parables. Examples were offered by the German scholar, Paul Fiebig, in his books *Altjüdische Gleichnisse und die Gleichnisse Jesu* (Tübingen: J. C. B. Mohr, 1904) and *Die Gleichnisreden Jesu im Lichte der rabbinischen Gleichnisse des neutestamentlichen Zeitalters* (Tübingen, 1912); for some examples in English, cf. *The New Testament Background,* ed. C. K. Barrett (see above, p. 341, n. 9), pp. 148-49, and A. M. Hunter, *Interpreting the Parables* (see above, p. 373, n. 38), pp. 113-16. Hence, Hunter holds that Jesus could have included a little allegory in his parables as he told them (p. 95; cf. also Eta Linnemann, *Jesus of the Parables: Introduction and Exposition,* trans. John Sturdy (New York: Harper & Row, 1967), pp. 5-8. However, other exegetes are much more strict in denying any allegory to the parables as Jesus told them; cf. Jeremias, *The Parables of Jesus* (see above, p. 373, n. 38), rev. ed., pp. 88-89, and *Rediscovering the Parables* (see above, p. 373, n. 38), p. 71. Jeremias finds the allegorizing, which he argues comes from other hands, to be heaviest in Matthew and claims it is absent in *L* and the *Gospel of Thomas.* In essence, this difference of opinion between Hunter and Jeremias reflects a difference between Fiebig and Jülicher a generation earlier in Germany. Rudolf Bultmann, *The History of the Synoptic Tradition,* trans. John Marsh (New York: Harper & Row, 1963), pp. 197-99, 417-18, decides in favor of the Jülicher-Jeremias view.

Obvious cases where allegory appears in connection with a parable of Jesus include the following. (1) At Mark 12:6, in the parable of the Wicked Tenants, there is an allegorical touch when the son is called a "beloved son," a title which was applied after the resurrection to Jesus (Colossians 1:13); Matthew (21:37), however, lacks the title, and so it is likely that we should not trace this term back to the original parable which could have been told by Jesus (other features of this parable have also been called allegorical; see pp. 255 and 291 for further discussion). In other cases allegorical explanations are attached to parables: (2) the parable of the Tares or Weeds (Matthew 13:36-43; to be discussed below, pp. 186-87, where it will be concluded that this explanation comes from the early church, not from Jesus); and (3) the Sower (Mark 4:13-20). Unfortunately, this allegorical explanation of the parable of the Sower, which has been read for centuries in liturgical churches on Sexagesima Sunday, has given many people the impression (arising from its ecclesiastical use and from its very location, namely after the first parable designated as such in Mark) that all parables should be treated that way—allegorically. There is good reason to believe, however, that this allegorical explanation, too, stems from the early church, not from Jesus; at least the reference to "persecution . . . on account of the word" (4:17) and other details suggest the situation of the early church, not that of Jesus' lifetime. But even if these verses of allegorical explanation do go back to Jesus, that is no reason to assume that all parables should be allegorized according to later tastes. On that almost all interpreters today are agreed. Cf. also below p. 380 n. 70 on authenticity in the parables.

It should be added that the "one-point" approach to each parable urged by Jülicher and followed by many exegetes since his day has recently been challenged; cf. G. V. Jones, *The Art and Truth of the Parables: A Study in their Literary Form and Modern Interpretation* (London: SPCK, 1964), and Dan Otto Via, Jr., *The Parables: Their Literary and Existential Dimension* (Philadelphia: Fortress, 1967). This aesthetic approach, which emphasizes the "concept of existence" found in parables, is exceedingly fruitful and stimulating for the subsequent preacher, but it remains to be seen whether the contentions of this approach will be accepted as a valid understanding of the original parables told by Jesus, prior to their transmission and use in the early Christian church. Eta Linnemann, *Jesus of the Parables* (see above, p. 373, n. 39), also seeks the existential meaning of the parables in the "language event" which occurred when Jesus, in telling the parable, staked all on the power of language, but she repudiates any idea of allegory in the authentic parables and holds to the one-point approach.

40. This post-resurrection meaning can derive, in some cases, from the

Christian community during the oral period; in other cases, from a (written) source (such as *L*) upon which the evangelist drew; or, in still other cases, from the evangelist himself. It is even possible that one evangelist can give a different application to a parable than some other evangelist has.

41. On rabbinic use, see note 39 above. Cf. also Linnemann, *Jesus of the Parables* (see above, p. 373, n. 39), 18-20.

42. The "conflict setting" of the parables was stressed by A. T. Cadoux, *The Parables of Jesus, their Art and Use* (New York: Macmillan, 1931) and C. W. F. Smith, *The Jesus of the Parables* (Philadelphia: Westminster, 1948), and also by C. H. Dodd, *The Parables of the Kingdom* (see above, p. 373, n. 37). The emphasis appears in most recent works on the subject, e.g., Jeremias, *The Parables of Jesus* (see above, p. 373, n. 38), rev. ed., p. 21, and Linnemann, *Jesus of the Parables* (see above, p. 373, n. 39), pp. 22, 35-41. Cf. also J. Stanley Glen, *The Parables of Conflict in Luke* (Philadelphia: Westminster, 1962).

43. Cf. Jeremias, *The Parables of Jesus* (see above, p. 373, n. 38), rev. ed., pp. 38-40; *Rediscovering the Parables* (see above, p. 373, n. 38), pp. 29-31. This is not to say, however, that the more original version of the parable may not be in Matthew 18:12-13, and that the Lucan setting in 15:1-2 may not be secondary, even though it correctly hits on the historical situation originally involved; cf. Linnemann, *Jesus of the Parables* (see above, p. 373, n. 39), pp. 65-70.

44. Luke 8:10 agrees with Mark in presenting Isaiah's words as the purpose for speaking in parables ("in order that seeing they may not see, and hearing they may not understand"). But Luke agrees with Matthew in omitting the last part of Isaiah 6:10 (which Mark added), "lest they should turn again and be forgiven."

45. Jeremias, *The Parables of Jesus* (see above, p. 373, n. 38). The revised edition of 1963, pp. 115-229, rearranges and expands the material in the first English edition (1954), pp. 89-158; *Rediscovering the Parables* (see above, p. 373, n. 38) presents the same points on pp. 89-180.

46. On the Son-of-man material, see chapter 9; some of the references to the Passion have already been noted in chapter 3. Parable material about the consummation is taken up later in this chapter (see pp. 184-85) as well as in chapter 10.

47. To illustrate Hunter's four points with parables as examples: (1) the coming of the kingdom—the Mustard Seed and the Leaven (Luke

13:18-21, par. Matthew 13:31-33, cf. Mark 4:30-32); (2) the grace of the kingdom—Luke 18:9-14, the Pharisee and the Publican (concerning which Hunter says, p. 102, that the teaching that God justifies the ungodly [Romans 4:5] was Jesus' message before it was Paul's); (3) the crisis of the kingdom—Luke 12:16-21 (Rich Fool), or 14:25-35 (decision for discipleship); and (4) the men of the kingdom—Luke 14:7-14 (on humility).

48. Cf. Jeremias, *The Parables of Jesus* (see above, p. 373, n. 38), rev. ed., pp. 124-46, especially 131 and 230; *Rediscovering the Parables* (see above, p. 373, n. 38), pp. 97-116, especially 103 and 181; Hunter, *Interpreting the Parables* (see above, p. 373, n. 38), pp. 51-63.

49. The parable of the Laborers in the Vineyard provides a useful example of how later accretions and usages lead to false clues for understanding the point of a parable and therefore result in interpretations which are different from that which the original story intended. The parable occurs in Matthew only (*M* source). No setting or context is provided by Matthew, but Jeremias is probably right that Jesus told it to rebuke critics. Jesus is defending his own actions (in graciously going to and accepting all sorts of people) and is defending his picture of God at one and the same time, because Jesus' activity and message are a reflection of the kind of God he knows. Most of the parable story is clear. Verse 15 ("Am I not allowed to do what I choose with what belongs to me? Or do you begrudge my generosity?") is literally translated in the RSV footnote, and reflects ancient views about the "evil eye"; the phrase denotes "envy" (Mark 7:22), and the RSV text gives the proper sense. Verse 16 ("So the last will be first, and the first last") is a "generalizing conclusion" which has little to do with Jesus' original story. Verse 16*b*, "for many be called, but few chosen," appears only in the KJV, because many Greek manuscripts lack it. The verse crept in from Matthew 22:14. It sets forth the idea that those called at the third hour forfeited salvation because they murmured. This makes the parable a warning, but that was not Jesus' original meaning. Verse 16*a* is in the RSV, "the last will be first, and the first last," and appears to be Matthew's addition, added as an ending just as at his previous story (see 19:30). Verse 16*a* means to make the point that God's judgment will reverse many conditions of rank and wealth on earth. But that was not Jesus' point either, originally.

Jews had a story where one rabbi praised another who had died very young, by saying that God had taken him to himself because this man was like a laborer who received a full day's wages for just two hours' work—he had accomplished more in twenty-eight years than most men do in a lifetime (quoted in Jeremias, *The Parables of Jesus* [see above,

p. 373, n. 38], rev. ed., p. 138, *Rediscovering the Parables* [see above, p. 373, n. 38], pp. 109-110; it is, he says, based on Jesus' parable). This Jewish parable emphasizes how the man had earned his full wages in a short time by working so exceptionally hard. That teaching—merit and righteousness earned through one's works—was not Jesus' point either. In the Lutheran and Roman Catholic Churches this parable is read on the First Sunday in Lent when the emphasis is supposed to be on the call into God's vineyard and patient, disciplined labor for God. But that was not Jesus' original aim either.

The original purpose of the parable was not as a warning, nor about judgment, nor righteousness by works, nor an opinion on economic practices, nor even the call to God's vineyard. The parable tells about God, as good, gracious, generous, giving the unexpected.

50. So Jeremias, *The Parables of Jesus* (see above, p. 373, n. 38), rev. ed., pp. 33-38 and 136-39, especially p. 136, n. 16; *Rediscovering the Parables* (see above, p. 373, n. 38), pp. 24-29 and 108-11, especially p. 108, n. 1. Cf. Linnemann, *Jesus of the Parables* (see above, p. 373, n. 39), pp. 81-88.

51. See above, pp. 101-4.

52. *The New English Bible* rendering, which makes clear that the woman has loved much because her sins had been forgiven, is to be preferred to the translation in both the RSV and KJV which might suggest that Jesus forgave her because of her act of love.

53. Note that this story of the Two Debtors serves as a defense for Jesus' actions as well as an expression of what God in his graciousness is like. Simon criticized *Jesus;* Jesus replies by telling him what *God* is like. In this way Jesus' ministry and the picture of God which his parables present are being drawn closer together. The comment of Morton S. Enslin, in *The Prophet from Nazareth* (New York: McGraw-Hill, 1961), p. 14, is in this connection correct: "All who heard Jesus understood him. His enemies sent him to the cross, not because they did not know what he meant, but because they did."

54. *The Parables of Jesus* (see above, p. 373, n. 38), rev. ed., p. 145; cf. *Rediscovering the Parables* (see above, p. 373, n. 38), p. 115, where only the final sentence of what is quoted above is differently translated, "You wrong both her and me, and so you are missing God's best gift."

55. Dietrich Bonhoeffer, *The Cost of Discipleship;* rev. ed., trans. R. H. Fuller with some revision by Irmgard Booth (New York: Macmillan, 1959), p. 35.

56. See above, pp. 164-66; *The Parables of Jesus* (see above, p. 373,

n. 38), rev. ed., pp. 160 ff.; *Rediscovering the Parables* (see above, p. 373, n. 38), pp. 127 ff.

57. *Interpreting the Parables* (see above, p. 373, n. 38), pp. 64-74

58. Cf. the title of A. M. Hunter's book about the Sermon on Mount, *Design for Life* (London: SCM Press, 1953); U. S. ed., *A Pattern for Life* (see above, p. 349, n. 16).

59. The word "demand" has often caused a great deal of difficulty for evangelically oriented Christians, and it is not a word which is found frequently in the gospel tradition (in the RSV, cf. Luke 12:48, however). The point involved can be made however by looking at use of the term "love" in the gospels, particularly in the Synoptics. Christians speak a great deal of "the love of God" and mean by it usually "God's love for men." John 3:16 is a sort of "little Gospel," summing up how God loved men to the extent of a cross. Dozens of other New Testament verses, especially in the epistles, echo this thought about God's love for men. I John 3:16 provides a sort of Gospel-ethic, based on God's love for us, telling how we should respond—"By this we know love, that he laid down his life for us," and then the verse goes on that by self-sacrifice and love we should respond to God's gift in Christ. "We love, because he first loved us" (I John 4:19). With this side of the matter Christians are quite familiar.

But when one turns to the teachings of Jesus it is something of a shock to discover that in the Synoptic Gospels Jesus virtually never talks about the love of God for men. (Cf. E. Stauffer, "*agapaō*," in Kittel's *Theological Dictionary* (see above, p. 368, n. 10), I, 44-48.) Instead, when he uses the term "love" (*agapē* in Greek), it is to demand love from men. You are to love God and love the neighbor (Mark 12:30-31), you are to love enemies (Matthew 5:44). If one is going to discuss "love," in terms of the Synoptic Gospels, the vocabulary must include the word "demand." For Jesus makes a new demand, through this very word.

But there is also a new situation involved. For Jesus had come preaching the kingdom of God. That means, a God-given kingdom. That means, a time of salvation. So it is that now in this new situation Jesus can speak about really fulfilling the will of God as never before. He can urge selflessness and forgiveness, since God has given men a share in his kingdom and in himself, and has forgiven men. He can call for faith in God, since God has manifested something of his power in Jesus of Nazareth. It is too early to speak of God's love being manifested in a cross; the crucifixion has not happened as yet. But already in Jesus' ministry there can be the demand for the same sort of a responsive, serving, loving life of faith for which the epistles call—in Jesus' ministry, however, it is based on the announcement of the coming kingdom rather than on what was later accomplished in the cross, which elsewhere in the New Testament provides the basis for much of what is said about ethics.

60. *The Parables of Jesus* (see above, p. 373, n. 38), rev. ed., p. 201; cf. *Rediscovering the Parables* (see above, p. 373, n. 38), p. 158.

61. Even if we allow that Matthew has here concentrated and heightened Jesus' condemnation of a religion that taught salvation by human works, we still must say there was a clash between Jesus' message and that of the Pharisees which cannot be overlooked.

62. The context of the parable of the Servant's Wages in Luke seems to address it to disciples (17:1), but it is uncertain whether that audience is meant to carry over to vss. 7-10. At 17:5 "apostles" are specified as the audience, but that is an anachronism, like Luke's use of "the Lord" to refer to Jesus prior to the resurrection. There were no apostles in any technical sense prior to the resurrection; cf. Luke's definition of an apostle at Acts 1:22. Luke likes to read the term back into this historical ministry of Jesus. It helps make the words appear to speak to Christians of his own day. At 17:20, it is not "apostles" or disciples, but Pharisees who are being addressed. The safest guide as to the original audience for this parable at 17:7-10 is to ask whom the contents best addressed. It fits well a crowd of people, friends and opponents, listening to Jesus (note the phrase "any one of you," vs. 7). Its teaching has made the parable applicable to all times, however. Indeed, some rabbis held a similar view. Antigonus of Socho said, "Be not like servants who serve their lord on condition of receiving a reward; but rather be like servants who serve their lord under no condition of receiving a reward" (*Sayings of the Fathers*, 1, 3).

63. The phrase at Luke 17:10, "We are unworthy servants" (RSV; "unprofitable servants," KJV) is difficult to translate. It does not mean to say that the servants are lazy or that their fulfillment of their duty is without value, but simply that they are poor men, mere men, not God. One Syriac version omits the term, and so does the NEB.

64. See above, pp. 101-4.

65. Jeremias, *The Parables of Jesus* (see above, p. 373, n. 38), rev. ed., pp. 210-13, and *Rediscovering the Parables* (see above, p 373, n. 38), pp. 164-66, provides much exegetical detail on this parable which is reflected in some of the remarks above.

66. Martin Doerne, *Er kommt auch noch heute: Homiletische Ausle-gung der alten Evangelien* (3d ed.; Berlin: Evangelische Verlagsanstalt, 1955), p. 149, as quoted in Jeremias, *The Parables of Jesus* (see above, p. 373, n. 38), rev. ed., p. 211; *Rediscovering the Parables* (see above, p. 373, n. 38), p. 165.

67. *Through the Valley of the Kwai* (New York: Harper & Row, 1962), p. 177.

68. *Ibid.*, pp. 221-22.

69. *Ibid.*, p. 230.

70. The statement that only Jesus told parables and that no one in the early church did, is sometimes made. However, a writing from the early second century, the *Shepherd of Hermas*, has a few parables in it. And if some critics are correct, certain of the parables attributed to Jesus in our gospels are actually creations of the early church. Rudolf Bultmann, *The History of the Synoptic Tradition* (see above, p. 373 n. 39), pp. 203-5, offers criteria for discerning genuine similitudes of Jesus (they must have no specifically Christian features, and must express "the distinctive eschatological temper which characterized the preaching of Jesus" [p. 205] in contrast to Jewish morality and piety) and cites Luke 16:19-31 (the Rich Man and Lazarus) and Mark 12:1-12 (the Wicked Husbandmen) and Matthew 25:1-13 (the Wise and Foolish Virgins) as examples of parables which the early church formulated and then placed on the lips of Jesus in the gospels. Eta Linnemann, *Jesus of the Parables* (see above, p. 373, n. 39), sees the Wise and Foolish Virgins and the Unjust Judge (Luke 18:1-8) as creations of the early church. (Jeremias argues in all these cases for a basic, authentic parable of Jesus.)

71. C. Leslie Mitton, *The Good News* ("Bible Guides," 13 [New York and Nashville: Abingdon, 1961]), p. 85.

72. A convenient translation of the *Gospel of Thomas* by W. R. Schoedel, together with introduction and discussion of each saying, is found in the book written by Robert M. Grant with D. N. Freedman, *The Secret Sayings of Jesus* (Garden City: Doubleday, 1961). The references are cited in these footnotes by Grant's numbering system which divides *Thomas* into 112 sayings; since however, many other editions and translations of the *Gospel of Thomas* divide it into 114 sections, the alternate numbering is given above in the text of this book. The English phraseology here given is my own, a composite from several renderings in English, German, and Latin. This *Gospel of Thomas* (not to be confused with a collection of legends about

Jesus' boyhood also attributed to Thomas) is one of forty-nine compositions in the thirteen volumes from a gnostic library found by Egyptian peasants in a grave at Nag Hammadi (near Luxor) in the Nile Valley. The document, copied perhaps in the fourth century and buried after A.D. 400 when that area of Egypt was being Christianized, consists of 114 (or 112) separate sayings, often introduced simply with the phrase, "Jesus said." Some of these noncanonical sayings were previously known from papyri found at Oxyrhynchus, Egypt, in the 1890's. Parables, beatitudes, little anecdotes, etc., are loosely strung together. It has reminded some scholars of the Q document. *Thomas* is in the Sahidic dialect of the Coptic language, but seems to be a translation from the Greek. Probably several smaller collections of sayings have been put together, since some sayings may occur twice in slightly different forms. Some parts are more "gnostic" than others. The best guess is that the collection was put together about A.D. 140, in Syria. Some scholars are convinced that here and there *Thomas* contains authentic material, even though other parts are obvious fabrications for unorthodox views.

73. Grant (see above, p. 380, n. 72), No. 8, pp. 121-22. The detail that "the worm ate it" is introduced into *Thomas* from Mark 9:48. The closing figures "sixty-fold and one-hundred-and-twenty-fold" continue a variation already found in the canonical versions (Mark has 30, 60, 100; Matthew has 100, 60, 30; Luke has 100).

74. Grant (see above, p. 380, n. 72), No. 65, pp. 159-61:
  Jesus said: "A man had guests, and when he had prepared the banquet, he sent his servant to summon the guests. He went to the first, he said to him, 'My master summons you.' He said, 'Some merchants owe me some money; they will come to me this evening; I will go and give them orders. I pray to be excused from the dinner.' He went to another, he said to him, 'My master has summoned you.' He said to him, 'I have bought a house, and they are requesting me for a day; I will have no leisure.' He came to another, he said to him, 'My master summons you.' He said to him, 'My friend will celebrate a wedding, and I am to direct the banquet. I will not be able to come. I pray to be excused from the banquet.' He went to another, he said to him, 'My master summons you.' He said to him, 'I have bought a village; I go to collect the rent; I will not be able to come. I pray to be excused.' The servant came, he said to his master, 'Those whom you summoned to the banquet have excused themselves.' The master said to his servant, 'Go out to the streets, bring those whom you will find, so that they may dine. The buyers and the merchants shall not come into the place of my Father.' "

On the phrase "the place of my Father," see above, pp. 368-69, n. 14.

75. Grant (see above, p. 380, n. 72), No. 104, pp. 181-82. I have added italics to call attention to the distinctive phrases in *Thomas* which are discussed above.

76. Grant (see above, p. 380, n. 72), No. 95, p. 177; and No. 112, pp. 185-86. The final saying in *Thomas*, 114 (Grant, No. 112), suggests that the obliteration of sex was a gnostic goal—not in the sense of Galatians 3:28 (in Christ there is neither male nor female), but in the sense that sex is regarded as evil, and an ascetic, monastic life is regarded as the ideal. Compare the following examples in *Thomas* on the same subject:

> His disciples said: "On what day will you be revealed to us and on what day will we see you?" Jesus said: "When you undress without being ashamed, and you take your clothing, lay them under your feet as little children, and tread on them, then you will behold the son of the Living One and you will have no fear." (37; Grant, No. 38, pp. 144-45.)
> . . . They said to him, "If we are children, shall we enter the kingdom?" Jesus said to them, ". . . when you make the male and the female into a single one, so that the male will not be male and the female will not be female, . . . then you shall enter." (22; Grant, No. 23, pp. 136-37.)
> Jesus said: "Blessed are the solitary [or monks] . . . for you shall find the kingdom. . . ." (49; Grant, No. 50, pp. 151-52.)
> Jesus said: Many are standing at the door, but the solitaries [or monks] are the only ones who will enter the bridal chamber." (75; Grant, No. 75, p. 166.)

Jesus did use the phrase "sons of the bridechamber" for his followers (Mark 2:19), but this sort of talk about "the solitary" was an emphasis on celibacy and monasticism which entered into Christianity from other sources in the early second century, when the Jesus-material was infiltrated with further ideas, and the sayings and parables were accordingly reworked. While the *Gospel of Thomas* may occasionally provide us with a more authentic insight into what Jesus said, it more often shows what happened to the sayings of Jesus under influences alien to the Gospel.

77. For example, the *L* source has no allegory in its parables; *Q* has a bit; Mark a lot in proportion to the number of parables involved; and the *M* source and the evangelist Matthew the most. Mark centers his few parables around "the mystery" (or secret) of the kingdom of God (4:11); Matthew, around judgment and his desire to instruct Christians of the day; while Luke emphasizes the setting of the par-

ables (cf. 15:1-2), and has a great many stories which serve as examples for life (Good Samaritan, 10:30-37; Rich Fool, 12:16-21; Pharisee and the Publican, 18:9-14).

78. *The Parables of Jesus* (see above, p. 373, n. 38), rev. ed., pp. 23-114; *Rediscovering the Parables* (see above, p. 373, n. 38), pp. 16-88. Hugh Montefiore has applied Jeremias' seven "laws of transformation" (or better, "tendencies towards alteration") to the parable material in the *Gospel of Thomas* and has thus confirmed the principles which Jeremias had worked out for the canonical gospels with regard to this later collection of Jesus-material; cf. "A Comparison of the Parables of the Gospel according to Thomas and of the Synoptic Gospels," in H. E. W. Turner and Hugh Montefiore, *Thomas and the Evangelists* ("Studies in Biblical Theology," 35 [London: SCM Press, 1962]), pp. 40-78. The revised edition of Jeremias, *The Parables of Jesus* (see above, p. 373, n. 38), also takes into consideration the *Thomas* parallels.

79. A reference to this version occurs in the *Theophania* (or *Divine Manifestation*), written by Eusebius of Caesarea sometime after A.D. 323, and preserved in Greek fragments and in a Syriac translation. An English translation is given in *Gospel Parallels* (New York: Thomas Nelson, 1949), p. 161, in a footnote to section 228.

80. See above, p. 163.

81. The details are quite complex as to how this parable of the Lost Sheep has come down to us in Matthew and Luke. Matthew 18:12-13 probably preserves the more original version of the parable itself. Luke's setting is secondary too, just as Matthew's is, but in this case it is likely that Luke's setting reflects the original, historical situation. Cf. Linnemann, *Jesus of the Parables* (see above, p. 373, n. 39), pp. 65-70, and p. 375, n. 43 above.

82. Jeremias, *The Parables of Jesus* (see above, p. 373, n. 38), rev. ed., p. 27; *Rediscovering the Parables* (see above, p. 373, n. 38), p. 18. A further example of "cultural adaptation" by the evangelists appears in the following parallel verses:

. . . you do not know when the master of the house will come, in the evening, or at midnight, or at cockcrow, or in the morning (Mark 13:35).	. . . the Son of man is coming at an hour you do not expect . . . in the second watch, or in the third. . . . (Luke 12:40, 38).

Luke preserves the Palestinian division of the night into three watches; Mark has the four divisions used in the Roman army. It appears as if

Mark has "translated" Jesus' figure into terms which readers in Rome (and elsewhere), familiar with Roman divisions of time, would understand.

83. Paraphrase and cultural adaptation are found frequently in missionary translations. For example, evening is in certain dialects, when "the sun is lost" or "the sitting-together time"; midnight is "the stomach of the night"; the time before sunrise, "when the world begins to get white" or "before the sky-opens-door." To render a term like "believe," modern missionary translators must use even odder expressions to get the point across in some dialects—e.g., "to join the word to the body," "to hear in the insides," "to make the heart straight for something," or "to make the mind big for something." These examples and many more are given in R. G. Bratcher and E. A. Nida, *A Translator's Handbook on the Gospel of Mark* (Leiden: Brill, 1961), pp. 38, 423. Knowledge of how modern missionary translators must work often offers insight into problems faced by the early church.

84. Technically, the term "Second Coming" is not found in the New Testament (Hebrews 9:28 comes closest). What the historical Jesus had to say about the future is a rather complicated matter; see the section in chapter 10 on "Jesus and the Future." However, the idea of a parousia or Second Coming was prominent at certain times and places in the early church.

85. The Thief in the Night (Matthew 24:43-44, par. Luke 12:39-40); the Wise and Foolish Virgins (Matthew 25:1-13); the Doorkeeper (Mark 13:33-37, and par.); the Faithful and Wise Servant (Matthew 24:45-51, par. Luke 12:41-46); and the parable of the Talents (Matthew 25:14-30; Luke 19:12-27).

86. To get the number seven, which was considered a "perfect" number in the Bible, one can either regard the closing "parable" of the Householder (13:52) as a dominical saying rather than a parable (in which case the parables in the chapter are usually introduced by some phrase like "another parable," or "again"), or one can count the related parables of the Treasure and the Pearl together as one. Or are modern commentators prone to see symbolical significance at points where Matthew never dreamed of it?

87. One curious feature is that for the explanation, Jesus "left the crowds and went into the house" (13:36). This is similar to Mark's idea that the explanation to the Sower was given only in private, when Jesus was alone with the disciples (Mark 4:10). The "house" seems to be a place of revelation, where Jesus explains what his public ministry does not expound. All the parables at the close of Matthew 13,

from 13:36 on, seem to be given in private to the disciples alone. Thus the evangelist seems to be making a distinction between public parables about the kingdom and revelations to the disciples alone which bear on the church.

If the parable of the Wheat and Tares goes back to Jesus during his historical ministry, it was very likely a reply to some Pharisee who said, "Why doesn't Jesus weed out his movement? There are too many sinners looking for 'cheap grace,' and not enough real penitents in his ranks." Jesus replied with a parable that said to have patience and let God do the weeding (13:30). This answer by Jesus was carried over and applied by Matthew to the church of his day: the answer still is, Let God do the weeding ultimately; the kingdom of the Son of man (i.e., the church) is not to make this job its own. All the evidence points to the allegorical explanation as being the work of Matthew (see p. 385, n. 89).

88. For the parables of the Treasure and the Pearl, see pp. 171-72. For the "growth parables," like the Seed Growing Secretly and the Sower, see pp. 157-58.

89. *The Parables of Jesus* (see above, p. 373, n. 38), rev. ed., pp. 81-85; *Rediscovering the Parables* (see above, p. 373, n. 38), p. 66.

90. Matthew alone, among the gospels, uses the word "church" (16:18; 18:17), and so one can expect him to have a "doctrine of the church."

91. Cf. C. W. F. Smith, "The Mixed State of the Church in Matthew's Gospel," *Journal of Biblical Literature*, 82 (1963), 149-68. In Matthew 13, note verses 47-50, the parable of the Dragnet. It teaches that the kingdom-call embraces fish ("men") of every kind; the church includes good and bad; the separation or sorting out is done only at the close of the age, by (the angels of) God. There is particular emphasis here on the Last Judgment—the coming of God's kingdom is like the sorting out of fish. Men cannot make a true judgment (13:29). God has set a time for one, at the close of the age. Until then, the church goes on preaching, even and especially to its own members who have not really gotten the message or who have fallen away.

92. C. F. D. Moule, "The Parables of the Jesus of History and the Lord of Faith," *Religion in Education*, 28 (1961), 64.

93. The Roman Missal appoints Luke 16:1-9 for the Seventh Sunday after Trinity (in the Roman Catholic reckoning, the Eighth Sunday after Pentecost). The American Book of Common Prayer (1928) inserted the Prodigal Son (Luke 15:11-32) in place of the Unjust

Steward, a change also followed by the Scottish Book of Common Prayer in listing an alternate selection.

94. See especially Joseph A. Fitzmyer, S.J., "The Story of the Dishonest Manager (Lk 16:1-13)" *Theological Studies,* 25 (1964), 23-42, and the literature cited there; and also Hans Kosmala, "The Parable of the Unjust Steward in the Light of Qumran," in *Annual of the Swedish Theological Institute* (Jerusalem), Vol. 3 (Leiden: Brill, 1964), pp. 114-21.

95. A. M. Hunter, *Interpreting the Parables* (see above, p. 373, n. 38), pp. 67-68, 104-6. J. Jeremias, *The Parables of Jesus* (see above, p. 373, n. 38), rev. ed., pp. 44-48, 181-82; *Rediscovering the Parables* (see above, p. 373, n. 38), pp. 34-36, 143-45.

96. Cf. J. Duncan M. Derrett, "Fresh Light on St Luke XVI: II. Dives and Lazarus and the Preceding Sayings," *New Testament Studies,* 7 (1960-61), 364-80; F. J. Francis, "The Parable of the Unjust Steward," *Angelican Theological Review,* 47 (1965), 103-105.

97. J. B. Phillips, *The Gospels translated into Modern English* (London: Geoffrey Bles, 1952), pp. 242-43, following the suggestion of C. C. Torrey, *The Four Gospels: A New Translation* (New York: Harper, 1933), p. 311, and *Our Translated Gospels: Some of the Evidence* (New York: Harper, 1936), pp. 56-60.

98. J. Duncan M. Derrett, "Fresh Light on St Luke XVI: I. The Parable of the Unjust Steward," *New Testament Studies,* 7 (1960-61), 198-219; a summary of his article appears in Via, *The Parables* (see above, p, 374, n. 39), pp. 157-59. Actually the solution here advanced about the steward's conduct was put forward as long ago as 1903 by an English woman, Mrs. M. D. Gibson, of Cambridge, who had traveled considerably in the Middle East, but Derrett's research into the legal aspects has made the explanation much more likely.

99. Cf. Via, *The Parables* (see above p. 374, n. 39), p. 161: "the present is a crisis . . . man by making an appropriate response to the crisis can overcome the danger." Via classes the parable as a "comic" (rather than a "tragic") one and stresses its "picaresque mood" (pp. 159-60). One may agree that the parable suggests there was in Jesus' message "an element of comic relief from dead seriousness" (p. 162), but "comic relief" is a feature in which neither the Jesus-tradition nor the gospel books abound (though irony is another matter).

100. See above, p. 126.

101. *The Parables of Jesus* (see above, p. 373, n. 38), p. 46, n. 85; *Rediscovering the Parables* (see above, p. 373, n. 38), p. 35, n. 1.

102. John Wesley's famous sermon on Luke 16:9 had three points:
(1) Gain all you can without hurting yourself or your neighbor in body
or mind; (2) Save all you can, by cutting foolish expenditures; (3)
Give all you can. How much of this, one wonders, is simply common
sense and how much springs from the text? And how might Wesley's
sermon have differed if it had started out from some other application
of the same parable?

103. Donald R. Fletcher, "The Riddle of the Unjust Steward: Is Irony
the Key?" *Journal of Biblical Literature*, 82 (1963), 15-30, observes
that many exegetes and preachers, Protestant as well as Roman Catholic,
including George Buttrick, G. Campbell Morgan, and Helmut Thielicke,
have found a "self-interested form of philanthropy" in this verse (p.
26).

104. *The Parables of Jesus* (see above, p. 373, n. 38), p. 46; *Rediscovering the Parables* (see above, p. 373, n. 38) p. 35.

105. *Anglican Theological Review*, 30 (1940), 120.

7 The Mighty Works of the Reign of God

1. Typical of the older, traditional approach is *Notes on the Miracles of
our Lord*, by R. C. Trench, originally published in 1846 as a companion
to his book on the parables (New York: Appleton, 2d American ed.,
1866; often reprinted, most recently by Baker Book House, Grand
Rapids). The later nineteenth century and the Liberal period often
sought to explain the miracles away. Among the more significant recent
treatments are the following: D. S. Cairns, *The Faith that Rebels: A
Re-examination of the Miracles of Jesus* (New York: Doubleday,
1928); C. H. Dodd, "Miracles in the Gospels," *The Expository Times*,
44 (1932-33), 504-9; Alan Richardson, *The Miracle Stories of the
Gospels* (New York: Harper, 1941); James Kallas, *The Significance of
the Synoptic Miracles* ("SPCK Biblical Monographs," 2 [London:
SPCK, 1961]); Reginald H. Fuller, *Interpreting the Miracles* (Philadelphia: Westminster, 1963); *The Miracles and the Resurrection*
("SPCK Theological Collections," 3 [London: SPCK, 1964]);
Miracles: Cambridge Studies in their Philosophy and History, ed. C. F.
D. Moule (London: Mowbray, 1965, and New York: Morehouse-Bar-
low, 1966); H. van der Loos, *The Miracles of Jesus* ("Supplements
to Novum Testamentum," 9 [Leiden: Brill, 1965]); S. Vernon Mc-
Casland, who wrote *By the Finger of God: Demon Possession and Exorcism in Early Christianity in the Light of Modern Views of Mental
Illness* (New York: Macmillan, 1951), has provided the pertinent
articles in two recent Bible dictionaries: "Miracle," in *The Interpreter's*

Dictionary of the Bible (see above, p. 361, n. 28), Vol. 3, pp. 392-402; and "Miracles," in *Hastings' Dictionary of the Bible,* rev. ed., edited by F. C. Grant and H. H. Rowley (New York: Scribner's, 1963), pp. 663-66. Like the parables, the miracle stories have had their own history of interpretation (see below, notes 2-4). An example involving a single pericope is provided by Roy A. Harrisville, "The Woman of Canaan: A Chapter in the History of Exegesis," *Interpretation,* 20 (1966), 274-87.

2. Celsus wrote his *True Discourse* against Christianity about A.D. 178. Much of the contents of his charges is preserved in the reply *Against Celsus* written by Origen in the next century. References to Jesus' miracles occur in Origen in Book 1, chapters 6, 28, 68; Book 2, chapters 49-53; and Book 3, chapters 24-25. Eng. trans. F. Crombie, in *The Ante-Nicene Fathers: Translations of The Writings of the Fathers down to A.D. 325,* ed. Alexander Roberts and James Donaldson, rev. A. Cleveland Coxe, Vol. 4 (New York: Scribner's, 1913), pp. 398-99, 408, 427, 450-53, 473-74.

3. David Hume's famous definition of a miracle was "a transgression of a law of nature by a particular volition of the Deity, or by the interposition of some invisible agent" (*An Enquiry Concerning Human Understanding* [Oxford: Clarendon Press, 2d ed. 1902], p. 115, n. 1). For a brief discussion of his "Essay on Miracles" and other views in the age of reason, cf. McCasland, "Miracle," in *The Interpreter's Dictionary of the Bible* (see above, p. 361, n. 28), Vol. 3, pp. 395-98, and G. H. Boobyer, "The Gospel Miracles: Views Past and Present," in *The Miracles and the Resurrection* (see above, p. 387, n. 1), pp. 31-49. For a broader survey of problems discussed in this period cf. H. D. McDonald, *Ideas of Revelation: An Historical Study A.D. 1700 to A.D. 1860* (London: Macmillan, 1959).

4. Matthew Arnold, *Literature and Dogma* (popular edition, 1900), chapter 5, as noted in H. D. McDonald, *Theories of Revelation: An Historical Study 1860-1960* (New York: The Humanities Press, 1963), p. 45. See also the references cited in Boobyer, "The Gospel Miracles" (see above, p. 388, n. 3), p. 33. Arnold believed that Christianity had a "boundless future," if it would only drop any idea of God acting miraculously in men's lives. McDonald, pp. 44-68 in particular, discusses views about miracles during the period of the rise of materialism. For the period of Liberalism, note in particular T. W. Manson's essay (with its charge that the Liberals in effect imprisoned God behind a soundproof, plate-glass window, cut off from the world he had made), "The Failure of Liberalism to Interpret the Bible as the Word of God," in *The Interpretation of the Bible,* ed. C. W. Dugmore (London: SPCK,

1944), pp. 92-107. For a recent examination of some aspects of the problem of science and miracles, cf. R. Hooykaas, *Natural Law and Divine Miracle: the Principle of Uniformity in Geology, Biology and Theology* (Leiden: Brill, 1963).

5. Further examples of contradictions in Synoptic retellings of the miracle stories: Mark 7:26 calls the Syrophoenician woman "a Greek," Matthew 15:22 terms her "a Canaanite." (Harrisville, "The Woman of Canaan" [see above, p. 388, n. 1], pp. 280-81, thinks that the Marcan description of the woman is political, while Matthew's is religious, designed to heighten the contrast involved in the story between Israel and the Gentiles.) At Mark 2:4 the friends of the paralytic dig through the (mud) roof (apparently as in a Palestinian house), but at Luke 5:19 they are said to take the tiles off (as one would do with a Hellenistic house.) This is an example of the sort of "cultural adaptation" noted above, pp. 182-83, in connection with the parables.

6. It is not within the scope of this book to illustrate fully the point that Jeremias' "laws of transformation" formulated with regard to the parables have application to the miracle stories, but the following examples will suggest how the principles discussed above, on pp. 181-85, are pertinent to the miracles. (The matter is worth a careful, independent investigation.)

Embellishment occurs when the number of persons healed in a miracle is doubled. For example: Matthew 8:28-34, "two demoniacs" (contrast Mark 5:2, "a man with an unclean spirit"); Matthew 20:29-34 and 9:27-31, "two blind men" (contrast Mark 10:46, "Bartimaeus, a blind beggar"); Matthew 14:21 adds to the statement in Mark 6:44 (that five thousand men were fed) that there were "about five thousand men, *besides women and children*" (this later phrase, in italics, is meant to heighten the miracle). Matthew is the evangelist most likely to add this sort of embellishment. The account of the healing of two blind men in Matthew 9:27-31 may be a doublet of the Bartimaeus story which is retold with "doubling" at Matthew 20:29-34; at 9:27 "two blind men" must be involved in order that the story may serve as fulfillment of the Old Testament verse quoted at 11:5, "the blind [plural] receive their sight" (Isaiah 35:5).

Just as the opinion has been advanced that some of the parables may be *creations of the early church,* so it can be noted that some of the miracle stories may be compositions of the Christian community. In addition to Matthew 9:27-31, just noted, cf. Luke 5:1-11 on the miraculous catch of fishes, which may have been put together from the story of the calling of the first disciples at Mark 1:16-20 and the post-resurrection narrative at John 21.

A tendency to use the miracle stories for purposes of *exhortation* can be seen as early as the versions found in Mark. Thus at Mark 1:31, when Simon's mother-in-law has been healed by Jesus, she demonstrates her cure by "serving." Some commentators have seen here a didactic emphasis on serving; cf. Richardson, *The Miracle Stories of the Gospels* (see above, p. 387, n. 1), pp. 76-80, on this and other such examples. Harrisville's article, "The Woman of Canaan" (see above, p. 388, n. 1), illustrates how the narrative at Mark 7:24-30 (par. Matthew 15:21-28) can be used to teach the nature of faith.

On *allegory* and the miracle stories, see below, p. 214. The narrative about the cursing of the fig tree, Mark 11:12-14, 20-21 (par. Matthew 21:18-21), discussed below, p. 213, may be a case where a parable was allegorized into a story in miracle form about God and Israel.

In addition to the *collections* of miracle stories noted above, one may cite Mark 1:21-34, a combination of two miracle accounts and a generalizing summary, which forms "a day in the life of Jesus" as Mark presents it. Thus while Matthew, especially, collects his miracle stories into blocks, Mark had already done this before him, and probably some of these collections existed in embryonic form in the oral period.

For examples of how the church's "new situation" *in the Gentile world* influenced the retelling of the miracle stories, see the two examples in the preceding note. It has been argued, at least since the time of Augustine, that the feeding of the four thousand (Mark 8:1-10), told after the feeding of the five thousand (Mark 6:30-44), has to do with a crowd from a Gentile region and therefore represents the revelation and salvation offered through Jesus as intended for Gentiles as well as for the Jews; cf. Richardson, *The Miracle Stories of the Gospels* (see above, p. 387, n. 1), pp. 97-98. "Missionary outreach" and concern can be seen in miracle stories at Mark 5:19-20 ("Go . . . and tell them how much the Lord has done for you . . ."), Mark 7:24-30 (the Syrophoenician woman), and Mark 1:45; cf. Richardson (*ibid.*, p. 387, n. 1) pp. 78-80, 109-11.

Additional examples might be given from the miracle stories for what Jeremias and others refer to in connection with the parables as *"reaudiencing," conflation,* and *changes in setting.* Only the influence of the delay of the parousia seems difficult to trace in the history of the transmission of the miracle stories. But the lines of development which Jeremias has worked out for the parables very obviously have application to the miracles.

7. The Jewish evidence is conveniently given in Klausner, *Jesus of Nazareth* (see above, p. 338, n. 2), pp. 18-47, especially pp. 19, 25, 27-28, 40-41, 46 (note especially *Sanh.* 107*b*; *Sota* 47*b*; *J. Hag. II* 2;

and *Sanh.* 43*a*). Ethelbert Stauffer, *Jesus and His Story* (see above, p. 342, n. 16), especially stresses this rabbinic evidence; see pp. 18-21, 161-62 (British edition), and pp. 8-12 (U.S. edition).

8. In addition to references in most of the treatments cited above in note 1 to this chapter, see the detailed study by Robert M. Grant, *Miracle and Natural Law in Graeco-Roman and Early Christian Thought* (Amsterdam: North-Holland Publishing Company, 1952).

9. Apollonius of Tyana was a Neopythagorean philosopher who died about the end of the first century A.D. An account of his life and travels, including the miracles he was said to have worked, was recorded by Flavius Philostratus in the third century A.D. At times Apollonius was set forth as a rival to Christ—a view which provoked a reply from Eusebius, the Christian historian from Caesarea in the fourth century. An English translation by F. C. Conybeare, in two volumes, exists in the "Loeb Classical Library," *Philostratus: The Life of Apollonius of Tyana* (New York: Macmillan, 1912). A few excerpts are quoted in C. K. Barrett, *The New Testament Background* (see above, p. 341, n. 9), pp. 76-79. Numerous other miracle stories have come down from the ancient world, including one where the Emperor Vespasian (A.D. 69-79) is credited with having healed a blind man in Egypt (Tacitus, *History* 4.81). One of the fullest collections of such materials, organized with reference to New Testament miracle stories, is R. Bultmann, *The History of the Synoptic Tradition* (see above, p. 373, n. 39), pp. 209-44, especially pp. 220-26, 231-38.

10. *Berakoth* 33*a Baraita*, as cited in H. L. Strack and Paul Billerbeck, *Kommentar zum Neuen Testament aus Talmud und Midrasch*, Vol. 2 (Munich: Beck, 1924), p. 169. Rabbi Hanina ben Dosa is to be dated about A.D. 70.

11. The concluding statements in the miracle accounts in the Synoptic Gospels are often rather stylized, closing with the ascription of glory to God for what he has done through Jesus of Nazareth. Occasionally, however, a flash of opposition is seen. Cf. Luke 7:16-17; Mark 1:45; 2:12; 3:6; and Matthew 9:34 as the climax of reaction to all the miracles reported in Matthew 8-9.

12. Cf. Bultmann's statement in "Is Exegesis without Presuppositions Possible?", *Existence and Faith: Shorter Writings of Rudolf Bultmann*, trans. Schubert M. Ogden (New York: Meridian, "Living Age Books," 1960), pp. 291-92: "The historical method includes the presupposition that history is a unity in the sense of a closed continuum of effects in which individual events are connected by the succession of cause and effect. . . . This closedness means that the continuum of historical hap-

penings cannot be rent by the interference of supernatural, transcendent powers and that therefore there is no 'miracle' in this sense of the word. Such a miracle would be an event whose cause did not lie within history." Bultmann does make quite clear, however, that while historical science cannot demonstrate an act of God, it can indicate that there were those who believed in such acts. Science "can only leave every man free to determine whether he wants to see an act of God in a historical event that it itself understands in terms of that event's imminent historical causes."

13. I owe the idea of these three factors as tests to Professor C. F. D. Moule, of Cambridge. They amount to asking whether the miracle story is (1) irrecoverable (from the sources available), (2) improbable or impossible (in the view of the investigator), and (3) improper (for God or Jesus as pictured in the rest of the gospel sources). To put it another way, these tests ask (1) what the investigator thinks of the gospels as sources, (2) what one conceives to be the limits of the power (*dynamis*) of God, and (3) what sort of actions are in harmony with the general conception of God involved.

14. According to Jerome's *Commentary on Matthew,* on 12:13, the *Gospel of the Nazarenes* added the detail that the man with the withered hand (Mark 3:1-6, par. Matthew 12:9-14 and Luke 6:6-11) asked Jesus for help, saying, "I was a mason and earned [my] livelihood with [my] hands; I beseech you, Jesus, to restore to me my health that I may not with ignominy have to beg for my bread." Eng. trans. in *Edgar Hennecke, New Testament Apocrypha* (see above p. 336, n. 2), pp. 147-48.

15. The phrase stems from Harvey K. McArthur, "Basic Issues: A Survey of Recent Gospel Research," *Interpretation,* 18 (1964), 47-50, where McArthur is seeking to establish criteria by which authentic material may be distinguished from inauthentic in the gospels.

16. *The Infancy Story of Thomas* (often referred to as "The Gospel of Thomas," but not to be confused with the sayings collection found in 1947 at Nag Hammadi), 2. 3-5 (Eng. trans. in *Edgar Hennecke, New Testament Apocrypha* (see above, p. 336, n. 2), 1, p. 393.

17. C. S. Lewis, *Miracles: A Preliminary Study* (London: Geoffrey Bles, 1947), p. 11.

18. G. H. Boobyer, "The Gospel Miracles" (see above, p. 388, n. 3), p. 41.

19. Only Mark has the detail that "friends" thought Jesus was "beside himself" because of the way he talked about God and his coming king-

dom (3:19b-21). According to Mark, this opinion was shared by Jesus' own brothers and by Mary, for they wanted to take him away from what he was doing, until he could "come to his senses" (3:31-35). It is only the disciples, who have faith, who discern what Jesus is really about.

20. Luke 11:15 is very indefinite about identifying these men. Mark 3:22 calls them "scribes who came down from Jerusalem." Matthew 12:24 terms them "Pharisees."

21. "Beelzebul" (or "Beelzebub" in some later manuscripts and the KJV) was regarded in Jewish apocalypses as the prince or leader of an army of demons which kept men in subjection. Originally a Philistine god, mockingly called "lord of the flies," he appears in the Dead Sea Scrolls as "Belial" (cf. II Corinthians 6:15, "Beliar"). The term refers to the same being as the word "Satan" does.

22. On Matthew 12:28 (par. Luke 11:20), see below, pp. 329-30.

23. For the most recent discussion on this verse, cf. E. Bammel, " 'John Did No Miracle,' " in Miracles: Cambridge Studies (see above, p. 387, n. 1), pp. 179-202.

24. As in the case of the parables, the exact count of how many miracles appear in each gospel varies from commentator to commentator; compare the articles in Bible dictionaries. Fuller, Interpreting the Miracles (see above, p. 387, n. 1), pp. 126-27, includes in his lists gospel miracles and also sayings about the miracles. Richardson, The Miracle Stories of the Gospels (see above, p. 387, n. 1), pp. 36-37, gives some percentage figures; e.g., in Mark almost one-third of the verses are concerned with miracles. Proportionally Mark has more miracles than any other gospel. Certain other generalizations are also possible. Matthew especially likes to group miracles in blocks, but Mark had also done this (see above, p. 390, n. 6). Luke omits certain miracles found in both Mark and Matthew, like the walking on the water and the feeding of the four thousand, but recounts certain stories which only he includes (from his L source, apparently), such as the widow's son at Nain (7:11-17), the healing of an infirm woman (13:10-17), and the ten lepers (17:11-19). Luke's stories often have a special tenderness about them. Mark's are frequently full of vivid, almost "primitive" details (cf. 7:33 or 8:23-25).

25. Cf. C. F. D. Moule, "The Classification of Miracle Stories," in Miracles: Cambridge Studies (see above, p. 387, n. 1), pp. 239-43. On the healing miracles, cf. Laurence J. McGinley, S. J., Form-Criticism of the Synoptic Healing Narratives: A Study in the Theories of Martin Dibelius and Rudolf Bultmann (Woodstock, Maryland: Woodstock College Press, 1944).

26. H. H. Farmer, *Are Miracles Possible?* (London: SPCK, 1960), p. 5. His larger book, *The World and God* (London: Nisbet, 1948; New York: Harper & Row, n.d.), especially pp. 122-27, is helpful at this point. A more typical definition of a miracle is that by C. S. Lewis: "an interference with Nature by a supernatural power" (*Miracles* [see above, p. 392, n. 17], p. 15). Gloege, *The Day of His Coming* (see above, p. 344, n. 26), pp. 150-51, emphasizes the "polemical character" involved in the miracles as Jesus "brings God's power to bear at every level of earthly existence," so that "the rule of God is attacking the powers which are opposed to it."

27. Cf. Richardson, *The Miracle Stories of the Gospels* (see above, p. 387, n. 1), p. 28.

28. The various Greek terms involved in the gospels to refer to miracles will, of course, all be discussed in Kittel's *Theological Dictionary* (see above, p. 368, n. 10). Some of these articles have not been published as yet, even in German. A summary of them is available, however, in a note by C. F. D. Moule, who as a consultant for the *Dictionary* has read these articles in advance of publication; see "The Vocabulary of Miracle," in *Miracles: Cambridge Studies* (see above, p. 387, n. 1), pp. 235-38, with a listing of the pertinent Kittel articles on pp. 244-45.

29. "Signs" (from the Greek noun *sēmeion*) is used in a negative sense in the Synoptics at Mark 8:11-12 (the Pharisees seek a sign and are rebuked for it); Luke 23:8 (Herod wants a sign); and Mark 13:22 (false prophets, it is said, will work "signs"). Jesus refuses to give that sort of evidence.

30. Gloege, *The Day of His Coming* (see above, p. 344, n. 26), p. 149. "Power" (*dynamis*) is frequently used to characterize Jesus and his work in the Synoptics. Even before the disciples knew of the resurrection, they spoke of Jesus as "a prophet mighty in deed and word before God" (Luke 24:19). Authority and power characterized his ministry (Luke 4:36). This power and authority were believed to be from God —from heaven, not from men—as Mark 11:29-33 hints. Hence it was expected that "acts of power" would be worked by Jesus in God's name. Cf. Mark 6:2: "What mighty works [literally, deeds of power] are wrought by his hands!" Part of the offense was that Jesus worked miracles.

31. See above, pp. 112 and 121-22. Related to this argument, that the miracles performed during Jesus' ministry are examples of God's power antecedent to the resurrection miracle, is the claim of the New Testament records that miracles continued for a time after the resurrection in the early church. The explanation is sometimes advanced that then,

after a time, faith grew weak and hence miracles virtually ceased. Another sort of explanation popularly heard is that the original aim of the miracles was "to help people" and that this function has been taken up by doctors and others in modern society. Still others explain that miracles accompanied the ministry of Jesus and the launching of the Christian church as a special providential phenomenon to help Christianity get a foothold in the world during the crucial early years. But such explanations are difficult to justify on the basis of the texts. More pertinent is the fact that, already by the time of Paul, when Christ was confessed as the "power of God" (I Corinthians 1:24), it was understood that Christ and the power expressed through the Spirit need not take the form of working miracles but can take the form of faith and love in life together (cf. I Corinthians 12:28-29, then Ephesians 4:11-12 as lists of what counts in Christianity; I Corinthians 13 shows a "better way" than the miracles which the Corinthians so prized—the way of self-giving love, as 13:2 emphasizes).

32. For the views in this paragraph, cf. Gerhard Ebeling, "Jesus and Faith," *Word and Faith,* trans. James W. Leitch (Philadelphia: Fortress Press, 1963), pp. 201-46.

33. It is true that the miracle stories as they are preserved in the New Testament retain Aramaic terms which Jesus used, like *"Ephphatha"* (Mark 7:34), and it may be that these were used for exorcisms in the early church (cf. Acts 16:18; I Corinthians 12:28-30). It is also true that Jesus sometimes used a physical means in a cure, such as spittle (Mark 7:33) or clay (John 9:6). But the point is, his word is what regularly effects the cure, not some secret formula. An interesting example is Mark 1:24-25. It is the demon who tries—in the language of ancient magic—to use a "formula" by unmasking the secret of who Jesus really is—"the Holy One of God" (vs. 24). Jesus rebukes him with a word of power (vs. 25). This is to admit similarities between New Testament and pagan miracle stories, but to claim that it is the demons who use magic formulas against the word. Jesus' view of God forbids magical transactions. Cf. W. Grundmann, *"dynamai/dynamis,"* in Kittel's *Theological Dictionary* (see above, p. 368, n. 10), Vol. 2 (1964), p. 302; R. Bultmann, *The History of the Synoptic Tradition* (see above, p. 373, n. 39), p. 209, n. 1.

34. Matthew may have changed Mark's phrase, she "is at the point of death," to "has just died" in order to avoid any notion that the child was not really dead but only in a faint. The phrase at Mark 5:39, "The child is not dead but sleeping," could have left the door open to the charge that she had not really died. Matthew wants to emphasize that it was a real restoration to life.

35. Cf., for example, Rudolf Bultmann, *The History of the Synoptic Tradition* (see above, p. 373, n. 39), pp. 228-29, 240-41. Such miracle stories obviously were popular in the Hellenistic world; the Greek historian Herodotus (3. 42), for instance, told a famous tale about a ring which turned up in a fish's mouth, and forms of this story were widely retold, even among the Jews; in this light cf. Matthew 17:27. What is more, the Hellenistic church at times looked on Jesus as a "divine man," in terms akin to those used in the Greek world for its heroes and deities. Early Christians of Greek background no doubt tried to enhance the Jesus they presented by the use of miracle stories about him. In this way stories originally told about some other personage could have been transferred to Jesus. It is likely that in the Hellenistic church Jesus' refusal to give signs was at times replaced by a notion that miracles do "prove" deity, or that miracles show the authority of an apostle. Thus in Acts Paul is credited with working mighty deeds of various sorts, though his own letters do not lay much weight on these. Indeed, Paul seems to have had problems with false "wonder-workers" at Corinth (see II Corinthians 12:12; 11:13-14). At Mark 16:17-18, in one of the added endings, the importance of such signs appears as an appendage in some later manuscripts.

36. Plutarch, *Caesar* 38 (726c). Cf. Cassius Dio 41. 46.

37. Aristides 2. 337 and 362.

38. Cf. Bultmann, *The History of the Synoptic Tradition* (see above, p. 373, n. 39), p. 237.

39. *Ibid.*, pp. 238-39.

40. The messianic age, according to some Old Testament passages, would be a time of many miracles; cf. Isaiah 29:18-19. A later Jewish document says of the messiah, "then shall he show them very many wonders" (IV Ezra 13:50). On Old Testament backgrounds to New Testament miracle stories, cf. Bultmann, *The History of the Synoptic Tradition* (see above, p. 373, n. 39), pp. 229-31; and Barnabas Lindars, "Elijah, Elisha and the Gospel Miracles," in *Miracles: Cambridge Studies* (see above, p. 387, n. 1), pp. 61-80.

41. See above, pp. 79-87.

42. So in Leslie D. Weatherhead's sermon, "Did Jesus Really Still a Storm?" in *When the Lamp Flickers* (New York and Nashville: Abingdon-Cokesbury, 1948), pp. 64-72. Cf. Weatherhead's treatment of Jesus' miracles in *Psychology Religion and Healing* (New York and Nashville: Abingdon; rev. ed. © 1952), pp. 29-69.

43. Thus Lloyd C. Douglas, *Those Disturbing Miracles* (New York: Harper, 1927), pp. 132-39; and in more popular terms, in his novel, *The Big Fisherman* (Boston: Houghton Mifflin, 1948), pp. 414-15. It should be recognized that this sort of explanation for the miracles had appeared a century previously in Germany in the rationalist lives of Jesus, such as that by H. E. G. Paulus, of Heidelberg, in 1828; cf. Albert Schweitzer, *The Quest of the Historical Jesus* (see above, p. 336, n. 1), pp. 51-55.

44. Cf. Paul J. Achtemeier, "Person and Sea: Jesus and the Storm-Tossed Sea," *Interpretation,* 16 (1962), 169-76; this article cites much material from the ancient Near East and from the Bible to show the attitude toward the sea in Semitic mentality.

45. Cf. G. H. Boobyer, "The Eucharistic Interpretation of the Miracles of the Loaves in St. Mark's Gospel," *Journal of Theological Studies,* New Series 3 (1952), 161-71.

46. In Matthew's presentation, Jesus is one who not only speaks for God (cf. Matthew 7:28-29) but who also acts with God's power (cf. 8:27; 9:8, 33-34).

47. Cf. Heinz Joachim Held, "Matthew as Interpreter of the Miracle Stories," in Günther Bornkamm, Gerhard Barth, and Heinz Joachim Held, *Tradition and Interpretation in Matthew,* trans. Percy Scott (Philadelphia: Westminster, 1963), pp. 165-299.

48. Cf. for this paragraph Günther Bornkamm, "The Stilling of the Storm in Matthew," *ibid.,* pp. 52-57.

49. For Matthew's stress on discipleship in this section, cf. 8:19-22 and 9:9. In this pericope on the stilling of the storm, Matthew seems to intend a contrast between disciples and other men: *"men* marveled" at the miracle (8:27) but *"disciples* followed" (8:23). There is a similar contrast at the end of Matthew's Gospel: "the eleven disciples . . . worshiped him [the risen Jesus]; but some doubted" (28:16-17).

50. Compare the programmatic scene which Luke has set at the outset of Jesus' ministry, the scene in the synagogue at Nazareth, Luke 4:16-30, as a summary of the meaning of Jesus' words and deeds. Here the use of Isaiah 61:1-2 provides the "program" for Jesus' work.

8 The New Way of Life under the Reign of God

1. See below, pp. 319-20.

2. I owe the way of putting this question and of describing the difference before and after the resurrection to lectures of Professor C. F. D. Moule, of Cambridge.

3. On the term prophet in connection with Jesus, cf. Oscar Cullmann, *The Christology of the New Testament,* trans. Shirley C. Guthrie and Charles A. M. Hall (Philadelphia: Westminster, 1959; rev. ed., 1963, adds some bibliography without changing the pagination), pp. 13-50; Ferdinand Hahn, *Christologische Hoheitstitel: Ihre Geschichte im frühen Christentum* ("Forschungen zur Religion und Literatur des Alten und Neuen Testamentes," 83 [Göttingen: Vandenhoeck & Ruprecht, 1963]), pp. 351-404; P. E. Davies, "Jesus and the Role of the Prophet," *Journal of Biblical Literature,* 64 (1945), 241-54, and "Did Jesus Die as a Martyr Prophet?" *Biblical Research,* 2 (1957), 19-30; F. W. Young, "Jesus the Prophet: A Re-examination," *Journal of Biblical Literature,* 68 (1949), 285-99; H. McKeating, "The Prophet Jesus," *The Expository Times,* 73 (1961), 4-7, 50-53; and R. H. Fuller, *The Foundations of New Testament Christology* (New York: Scribner's, 1965), pp. 125-29.

4. At John 7:52 the proper reading probably is, according to two recently discovered manuscripts, "*The* prophet does not rise from Galilee"; cf. R. E. Brown, *The Gospel according to John (i-xii)* (see above, p. 362, n. 32), p. 325.

5. Cf. also I Maccabees 14:41, where Simeon is made leader and high priest "until a trustworthy prophet should arise."

6. Cf. Helmer Ringgren, *The Faith of Qumran: Theology of the Dead Sea Scrolls,* trans. Emilie T. Sander (Philadelphia: Fortress Press, 1961), pp. 173-76, where references in the scrolls themselves are given.

7. *Antiquities* 20. 8. 6; *Jewish War* 2. 13. 4-5. Acts 21:38 speaks of leading the people out into the wilderness; Josephus says the pretender led 30,000 people out to the Mount of Olives, claiming the city walls would collapse at his command. The soldiers of the Roman governor Felix dispersed the crowd, killing or capturing over five hundred of them.

8. The *Q* saying at Matthew 23:34-36, par. Luke 11:49-51 poses numerous questions of content and origin. Cf. especially R. Bultmann, *The History of the Synoptic Tradition* (see above, p. 373, n. 39), pp. 114, 151; and T. W. Manson in H. D. A. Major, T. W. Manson, and C. J. Wright, *The Mission and Message of Jesus* (New York: E. P. Dutton, 1938), pp. 392-97, 530-32. As the passage now stands, there are some details which surely show the hand of the editors, Matthew and Luke. The basic saying in *Q* is introduced by Luke with the words "Therefore also the Wisdom of God said, 'I will send them prophets and apostles . . .'" (11:49). Some scholars feel that the quotation here comes from a lost Jewish book called *The Wisdom of God* or some-

thing like that, and that Matthew has transformed this quotation into a saying of Jesus, for Matthew 23:34 has Jesus say, "Therefore I send you prophets and wise men and scribes. . . ." (Luke's use of "apostles" here doubtless represents an anachronism, the term being read back into Jesus' lifetime from the post-resurrection period; cf. above, p. 379, n. 62. Matthew's terms, "prophets and wise men and scribes," may reflect groups familiar in his day in the church of Matthew.) The identification of "Zechariah, who perished between the altar and the sanctuary" (Luke 11:51; Matthew 23:35 adds, "the son of Barachiah") is uncertain. See T. W. Manson (see above, in this note), pp. 396-97, for a list of possible candidates. Most commonly this Zechariah is equated with the last martyr to be mentioned in the Hebrew canon, at II Chronicles 24:20-22 (though that Zechariah was a priest, the son of Jehoiada). Perhaps the most one can claim here is that Jesus' originally quoted a saying from "the Wisdom of God" and then spoke in prophet-martyr terminology about his own time and situation. Cf. Ferdinand Hahn, *Christologische Hoheitstitel* (see above, p. 398, n. 3), p. 382, n. 2.

9. Authenticity of the sayings now found at Luke 13:31-35 has often been debated. Note that, significantly, Bornkamm, *Jesus of Nazareth* (see above, p. 340, n. 10), has accepted as genuine the basic tradition in 13:31-33, and refers to the decision to go to Jerusalem as "the turning-point in Jesus' life" (p. 154); cf. p. 97, and p. 210, n. 2.

10. Cf. C. K. Barrett, "The Background of Mark 10:45," in *New Testament Essays: Studies in Memory of Thomas Walter Manson . . .*, ed. A. J. B. Higgins (Manchester: Manchester University Press, 1959), pp. 1-18. For a New Testament catalogue of prophets who suffered martyrdom, cf. Hebrews 11:32-38. If Jesus ever thought of his work as standing in any sort of sequence to that of prophets like Jeremiah or John the Baptist, then it is likely that he reckoned with the possibility of martyrdom in carrying out his task, for the office of a prophet is not only to speak but also often to suffer and to die.

11. The picture of Jesus as prophet is undergirded by the fact that he did many things characteristic of the Old Testament prophets, besides speak the will of God. He apparently made future prophecies (see below, p. 298). He engaged in intercessory prayer (Luke 22:32). He employed teaching methods like those of the ancient prophets, including "enacted prophecy" (perhaps the incident with the fig tree belongs here, or the actions in the Upper Room, including foot washing). Cf. H. McKeating, "The Prophet Jesus" (see above, p. 398, n. 3), though some of his examples ought not to be pressed.

12. On Jesus as teacher, cf. C. H. Dodd, "Jesus as Teacher and Prophet," in *Mysterium Christi: Christological Studies by British and German Theologians,* ed. G. K. A. Bell and Adolf Deissmann (New York: Longmans, Green and Co., 1930), pp. 51-66; K. H. Rengstorf, *"didaskō, didaskalos,"* in Kittel's *Theological Dictionary* (see above, p. 368, n. 10), Vol. 2 (1964), pp. 135-65; John Wick Bowman, *Jesus' Teaching in its Environment* (Richmond: John Knox Press, 1963); and F. Hahn, *Christologische Hoheitstitel* (see above, p. 398, n. 3), pp. 74-81.

13. The Hebrew adjective *rab* meant originally "great (one)" and then "master," and could be used in a variety of situations, much like the English word "chief"; there is a saying (third century A.D.) from one rabbi who had earlier lead a roving life with a robber band, "There [in the gang] they called me 'chief' [*rabbi*], and here [in the school] they call me 'chief' [*rabbi*]" (cited in Kittel's *Theological Dictionary* (see above, p. 368, n. 10), Vol. 2 (1964), p. 153, n. 37). As early as the end of the second century B.C. *rab* appeared as a term of address for teachers. In time pupils added a suffix *(rabbi)* to indicate the idea "my master, my teacher." By the middle of the first century A.D. *rabbi* was being used without any emphasis on the suffix, however, and by the end of this century numerous examples of *rabbi* as a title appear in Jewish sources, for example on gravestones, even at times in Greek transliteration. *"Rabboni"* (Mark 10:51; John 20:16) is a Palestinian Aramaic form. Since the evidence is not sufficient to establish precisely when in the first Christian century "rabbi" came into use as a title, it has been claimed that use of the word in Jesus' lifetime is an anachronism. Cf. S. S. Cohon, "Rabbi," in *Hastings' Dictionary of the Bible,* rev. ed. (see above, p. 388, n. 1), pp. 829-30, but cf. Eduard Lohse, *Die Ordination im Spätjudentum und im Neuen Testament* (Göttingen: Vandenhoeck & Ruprecht, 1951), p. 52, and the article *"rabbi,"* in Kittel's *Theologisches Wörterbuch zum Neuen Testament* (Stuttgart: Kohlhammer), Vol. 6 (1959), pp. 962-66, with further literature cited there.

In the gospels, "rabbi" occurs most frequently in John (eight times, plus "rabboni" once); three times in Mark (plus "rabboni" once), and four times in Matthew (not counting cases where "teacher" [*didaskalos*] could represent the word "rabbi" which might have stood at that point in the earlier tradition). Luke, writing for Gentiles, never uses "rabbi"; cf. 9:33, for example, where Luke substitutes another word meaning "master" *(epistatēs)* for "rabbi" which is found at Mark 9:5. Matthew, interestingly, never has the disciples address Jesus as "rabbi" but prefers to use "lord" *(kyrios)* in these situations; thus at 17:4, the parallel to Mark 9:5 and Luke 9:33, "Lord, it is well that we are here."

Matthew does allow one exception, however: Judas calls Jesus "rabbi" (26:25, 49). For Matthew, Jesus is not a teacher in the Jewish sense (a rabbi), but is lord. This usage is also behind the Matthean statement to the disciples (23:8) that in the Christian community "you are not to be called rabbi, for you have one teacher [*didaskalos*], and you are all brethren." Cf. G. Bornkamm, "End-Expectation and Church in Matthew," in *Tradition and Interpretation in Matthew* (see above, p. 397, n. 47), p. 41.

14. Cf. W. D. Davies, *The Setting of the Sermon on the Mount* (New York: Cambridge University Press, 1964), especially pp. 418-25, and *The Sermon on the Mount* (New York: Cambridge University Press, 1966), pp. 129-38; David Daube, *The New Testament and Rabbinic Judaism* (see above, p. 341, n. 12), Parts II and III; Morton Smith, *Tannaitic Parallels to the Gospels* ("Journal of Biblical Literature Monograph Series," 6 [Philadelphia: Society of Biblical Literature, 1951]). A great deal of information about rabbinic teaching methods is found in Birger Gerhardsson, *Memory and Manuscript: Oral Tradition and Written Transmission in Rabbinic Judaism and Early Christianity*, trans. E. J. Sharpe ("Acta Seminarii Neotestamentici Upsaliensis," 22 [Lund: C. W. K. Gleerup, 1961]); however, some of Gerhardsson's judgments must be qualified by criticisms voiced by W. D. Davies, "Reflections on a Scandinavian Approach to 'The Gospel Tradition,' " in *The Setting of the Sermon on the Mount* (as cited in this note), pp. 464-80, and by Morton Smith, "A Comparison of Early Christian and Early Rabbinic Tradition," *Journal of Biblical Literature*, 82 (1963), 169-76.

15. Cf. K. H. Rengstorf, "*didaskō*" (see above, p. 400, n. 12), pp. 137, 148, 153. Rengstorf sums the matter up by saying that, in the biblical view, the teacher is one who indicates God's way according to the law revealed by God.

16. Cf. G. Bornkamm, *Jesus of Nazareth* (see above, p. 340, n. 10), p. 98; W. D. Davies, *The Setting of the Sermon on the Mount* (see above, p. 401, n. 14), pp. 427-28; and Herbert Braun, *Spätjüdische-häretischer und frühchristlicher Radikalismus: Jesus von Nazareth and die essenische Qumransekte* ("Beiträge zur historischen Theologie," 24 [Tübingen: J. C. B. Mohr, 1957]).

17. It is misleading to separate Jesus' preaching, teaching, and other activities too sharply, for passages in the gospels closely associate them. At Matthew 4:23 "teaching in their synagogues and preaching the gospel of the kingdom and healing" are three expressions of the same authority and message. At Mark 1:27 the "new teaching" and "authority"

of Jesus refer to his miracles (1:23-26) and *kerygma* (1:14-15) and not just to teachings in the strict sense; actually Mark cites no teachings here (see 1:21-22).

18. Cf. the maxims on study cited by Louis Finkelstein, *Akiba: Scholar, Saint and Martyr* (1936; reprinted, Cleveland: World Publishing Company, and Philadelphia: Jewish Publication Society of America, 1962), pp. 62, 175, 260.

19. Cf. G. Bornkamm, *Jesus of Nazareth* (see above, p. 340, n. 10), pp. 57-63, 144. D. E. Nineham, in *The New Testament Gospels* (London: British Broadcasting Corporation, 1965), p. 35, sums it up:

> [Jesus] was not dependent on any support from outside himself. For example, he did not say, as the Rabbis tended to say, 'Things are thus and so because that's what the Old Testament means if properly interpreted.' Nor did he say: 'so and so's going to happen because if you add up the numbers in Daniel or Jeremiah that's how it works out.' He just boldly claimed: 'I tell you. . . .'

20. An illustration of how sayings of Jesus appear in different contexts in different gospels is provided by the following verses from Luke 11:33-36 and Matthew 5:14-15 and 6:22-23:

LUKE 11	MATTHEW 5 AND 6
	5:14 "You are the *light* of the world. A city set on a hill cannot be hid.
11:33 "No one after lighting a *lamp* puts it in a cellar or under a bushel, but on a stand, that those who enter may see the light.	15 "Nor do men light a *lamp* and put it under a bushel, but on a stand, and it gives light to all in the house.
34 "Your eye is the *lamp* of your body; when your eye is sound, your whole body is full of light; but when it is not sound, your body is full of darkness. 35 Therefore be careful lest the light in you be darkness. 36 If then your whole body is full of light, having no part dark, it will be wholly bright, as when a *lamp* with its rays gives you light."	6:22 "The eye is the *lamp* of the body. So, if your eye is sound, your whole body will be full of light; 23 but if your eye is not sound, your whole body will be full of darkness. If then the light in you is darkness, how great is the darkness!"

Matthew 5:14 has no parallel in Luke (or in any other New Testament gospel); Luke 11:36 likewise has no parallel. Within the common material, Luke 11:33-35, par. Matthew 5:15 and 6:22-23, we seem to have two separate sayings; Matthew has reported these sayings in different contexts, while Luke has linked these two sayings together with the word "lamp" (which occurs in each one; italicized above) as the link. Matthew has both sayings within the Sermon on the Mount; Luke includes

neither of them in his Sermon on the Plain. It is also to be noted that
Matthew has linked the one saying (5:15) with a context of its own
in his sermon by means of the word "light" which appears in 5:14.
In the case of his use of the other saying at 6:22-23 Matthew has no
such verbal link to the context. The relationships can be diagramed as
follows:

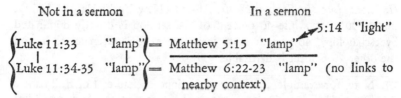

Not in a sermon   In a sermon

                                                      5:14   "light"
Luke 11:33   "lamp" = Matthew 5:15   "lamp"
Luke 11:34-35   "lamp" = Matthew 6:22-23   "lamp"   (no links to
                              nearby context)

With such varying arrangements in each gospel, it is naturally a major
problem to decide how and when—and even if—Jesus originally used
each saying during his ministry.

21. To illustrate the point of reapplication during the transmission process with regard to the verses discussed in the preceeding note, (a saying
by Jesus about a lamp), Luke 11:33 applies it to strengthen Luke's
point in 11:29-32 that Jesus is a "sign" greater than Jonah. Luke seems
to have in mind the type of house found in the Greco-Roman world,
where a lamp was placed in the vestibule to give light to those who
enter. Matthew 5:15 applies the saying to disciples and their good
works (cf. 5:16, "Let your light so shine before men, that they may see
your good works and give glory to your Father who is in heaven") and
has in mind a scene where the lamp shines for those who are within
the house. It is, of course, extremely hard to decide precisely what each
gospel means in the application it makes, let alone what any earlier
source (in this case, Q) might have meant by it, or—even more tenta-
tively—what Jesus may originally have meant by what he said. In this
case the forms in both Matthew and Luke may already be reapplications
of Jesus' words.

22. Cf. Albert Barnett, "Jesus as Theologian," in *Early Christian Origins: Studies in Honor of Harold R. Willoughby,* ed. Allen Wikgren
(Chicago: Quadrangle Books, 1961), pp. 16-23.

23. On "love" in the teaching of Jesus, see below, pp. 240-41.

24. Cf. Hans Conzelmann, "The Method of the Life-of-Jesus Research,"
in *The Historical Jesus and the Kerygmatic Christ: Essays on the New
Quest of the Historical Jesus,* trans. and ed. Carl E. Braaten and Roy A.
Harrisville (New York and Nashville: Abingdon, 1964), pp. 65-67.

25. *The Quest of the Historical Jesus* (see above, p. 336, n. 1), pp.
365-66, 398-403.

26. G. Bornkamm, *Jesus of Nazareth* (see above, p. 339, n. 10), p. 223. While, as we shall see, the beatitudes do have an eschatological orientation, and indeed the whole sermon does, it is not one which stresses a brief interim before the world goes under. It is hard to pretend that one hears the strains of *Götterdämmerung* running through the Sermon on the Mount. Cf. the conclusion in Harvey K. McArthur, *Understanding the Sermon on the Mount* (New York: Harper, 1960), pp. 84-90, that, while 40 percent of the sermon is directly dominated by eschatology, 40 percent more lacks any explicit reference to it, and the other 20 percent is debatable.

27. Note, for example, the order of sections in chapter 1 of Bultmann's *Theology of the New Testament* (see above, p. 365, n. 2), 1, pp. 4-22: "The Eschatological Message" and "Jesus' Interpretation of the Demand of God." Cf. H. Conzelmann, "The Method of the Life-of-Jesus Research" (see above, p. 403, n. 24), p. 66, and the remarks by Richard H. Hiers, "Eschatology and Methodology," *Journal of Biblical Literature*, 85 (1966), 170-84, especially 177-78.

28. So Conzelmann, "The Method of the Life-of-Jesus Research" (see above, p. 403, n. 24), 65-67.

29. C. F. Andrews, *Mahatma Gandhi's Ideas*, p. 93, as cited in A. M. Hunter, *A Pattern for Life* (see above, p. 349, n. 16), p. 100.

30. Gordon Rupp, *Principalities and Powers: Studies in the Christian Conflict in History* (New York and Nashville: Abingdon-Cokesbury, 1952), p. 43. Rupp prefaces his statement with the judgment that this conclusion will be discovered if one "will work through word by word the Sermon on the Mount with exact reference to the philological and theological background of its vocabulary, say as expounded in Kittel's great theological dictionary."

31. On theories of interpreting the Sermon on the Mount, cf. G. Bornkamm, *Jesus of Nazareth* (see above, p. 340, n. 10), pp. 221-25; G. Gloege, *The Day of His Coming* (see above, p. 344, n. 26), pp. 209-11; A. M. Hunter, *A Pattern for Life* (see above, p. 349, n. 16), pp. 95-99; Joachim Jeremias, *The Sermon on the Mount*, trans. Norman Perrin ("Facet Books, Biblical Series," 2 [Philadelphia: Fortress Press, 1963]), pp. 1-12; and Harvey K. McArthur, *Understanding the Sermon on the Mount* (see above p. 404, n. 26).

32. Hans Windisch, *The Meaning of the Sermon on the Mount* (see above, p. 348, n. 13) argued for the "fulfillability" of the sermon. Cf. Bultmann's review of the first German edition (1929) in *Deutsche Literatur-Zeitung*, 6 (1929), 985-93; Windisch refers to it on pp.

116-17 of the English translation of the second edition of his book. He admits the validity of Bultmann's two arguments against his view but holds that Jesus did not recognize such barriers to fulfillability.

33. See below, pp. 234-35.

34. McArthur, *Understanding the Sermon on the Mount* (see above, p. 404, n. 26), pp. 17-18, quotes Robert Frost's poem, "The Masque of Mercy," as a modern reflection of this view attributed to Paul as Frost understands him.

35. This approach is especially associated with the names of the Marburg theologian Wilhelm Herrmann (1846-1922), and of Max Weber (1864-1920) in his essay *Politics as a Vocation*, trans. H. H. Gerth and C. Wright Mills ("Facet Books, Social Ethics Series," 3; Philadelphia: Fortress, 1965), pp. iii, 46 ff. It appears particularly in the lectures at Yale in 1937 by the German New Testament scholar Martin Dibelius, *The Sermon on the Mount* (New York: Scribner's, 1940).

36. G. Bornkamm, *Jesus of Nazareth* (see above, p. 339, n. 10), pp. 224-25.

37. *Sabbath* 31a, freely rendered; for English translation, cf. C. G. Montefiore and H. Loewe, *A Rabbinic Anthology* (1938; Philadelphia: The Jewish Publication Society of America, 1960), p. 200, selection [539]. The context is a story about a Gentile who went first to Shammai and asked if he could teach him the whole law while he stood on one leg; Shammai chased him away. But when the Gentile asked Hillel, the rabbi summed it up with this "negative Gold Rule."

38. Especially in Luke 11–14 and 16. For some specific examples of material which Matthew has in the Sermon on the Mount and Luke places elsewhere, compare Matthew 6:19-21 with Luke 12:33-34; 6: 25-34 with Luke 12:22-31; and 7:13-14 with Luke 13:23-24. At Matthew 6:24 the saying about two masters occurs; we have already seen (above, p. 197) that Luke uses it in connection with the parable of the Unjust Steward (16:13). To reverse the line of argument, Luke sometimes includes material in his sermon which Matthew has elsewhere. For example, Luke includes four "woes" in his sermon (6:24-26), but Matthew includes "woes" only in another discourse, against the Pharisees (chapter 23). Luke refers to a "parable" in his sermon (6: 39), but Matthew uses this verse at another point and directs it against the Pharisees (15:14).

39. *The Day of His Coming* (see above, p. 344, n. 26), p. 208; cf. p. 188.

40. So Jeremias, *The Sermon on the Mount* (see above, p. 404, n. 31), pp. 25-32.

41. Luke has four beatitudes (and four woes). Matthew has nine beatitudes, though the last two are really on the same subject of persecution. All of Luke's appear in Matthew, except the third one ("weep/laugh," 6:21*b*), but Matthew often expands them (see above, p. 230-31, for two examples). Luke always has direct address to the disciples, "Blessed are you . . ."; Matthew has a third-person form, "Blessed are those who . . .," except at 5:11 where he has Luke's form. Some differences may be "translation variants," but Luke makes clearer that Jesus' words were direct address to disciples, while Matthew states them more as general principles.

42. The recent New Testament translation prepared for the American Bible Society by Robert G. Bratcher renders the beatitudes thus; e.g., "Happy are those who mourn: God will comfort them!" *Today's English Version of the New Testament* (New York: Macmillan, 1966); paperback ed., *Good News for Modern Man: The New Testament in Today's English Version* (New York: American Bible Society, 1966).

43. J. Jeremias, *The Sermon on the Mount* (see above, p. 404, n. 31), pp. 34-35.

44. See above, pp. 208-9.

45. Matthew 23:34 refers to a promise by Jesus to send "prophets and wise men and scribes" (see above, p. 398, n. 8); cf. also 13:52. One can picture, in the community where Matthew wrote, such Christian prophets and wise men and those learned in the Scriptures seeking to work out the meaning of the Gospel, while not neglecting the Old Testament heritage, for the new problems faced by Matthew's church.

46. So J. Jeremias, *The Sermon on the Mount* (see above, p. 404, n. 31), pp. 22-23; in this view, Matthew 5:21-48 reflects a contrast between Jesus and the scribes or "theologians," and 6:1-18 a contrast with the righteousness of the Pharisees. Matthew 5:20 is the conclusion of a pivotal passage in Matthew's sermon (5:17-20) which makes Jesus appear extremely legalistic. Jesus himself probably did see his work as a continuation in many ways of the Old Testament revelation in the law and the prophets (vs. 17). However, the combination of thoughts here and some details of phrasing are certainly Matthew's, and some of the sayings in vss. 17-20 (I should hold that each verse was an independent saying originally) probably arose within the Matthean community. In vs. 17, "fulfil" is a favorite theme of Matthew (e.g., "fulfil" Scripture, 1:22; 2:15, 17, 23). In 5:18 the phrase "until all is accomplished"

probably refers to God's entire will and plan. The next verse (5:19) emphasizes that in the kingdom it is not "do as you please," but do and teach according to God's will. Matthew was concerned lest Christians with the Gospel fall below the scribes and Pharisees in righteous conduct (5:20). Gloege's remarks on Jesus and the law, in *The Day of His Coming* (see above, p. 344, n. 26), especially p. 183, are helpful. For detailed analysis of the sayings in 5:17-20, cf. Wolfgang Trilling, *Das wahre Israel: Studien zur Theologie des Matthäusevangeliums* ("Erfurter Theologische Studien," 7 [Leipzig: St. Benno-Verlag, 1959]), pp. 138-59; English summary in *Journal of Biblical Literature*, 79 (1960), 378.

47. On Matthew 5:6 and 6:33, see above, p. 231. At 5:10, those to whom the kingdom belongs are persecuted "for righteousness' sake."

48. In light of Old Testament and Jewish use of the term "righteousness," there is, of course, no reason why Jesus could not have spoken of it as something related to the coming of God (cf. Isaiah 59:15*b*-17*a*) and as what God seeks in conduct. It is striking, however, that the term occurs only in Matthew, either in verses which come from the *M* source (3:15; 5:10, 20; 6:1 [RSV, "piety"]; 21:32) or in additions which Matthew has made to other sources (5:6; 6:33).

49. There is Old Testament background in the wholeness or perfection demanded of Israel as the people of God; cf. Leviticus 11:44-45 ("I am the Lord your God; consecrate yourselves therefore, and be holy, for I am holy. . . . For I am the Lord who brought you up out of the land of Egypt, to be your God; you shall therefore be holy, for I am holy") and the so-called Holiness Code in Leviticus 17–26 (note the formula at 19:2; 20:7, 8, 26; 21:6, 8, 15, 23; 22:9, 16, 32; the formula is quoted at I Peter 1:16, and some commentators have sensed an early Christian "Holiness Code" underlying some of the ethical sections in New Testament epistles). The possibility of a translation variant arises if it is assumed that Matthew has translated the Hebrew word *tamim* in a literal way, as "perfect," while Luke has interpreted it more narrowly, as "merciful," for his Greek readers. Cf. A. M. Hunter, *A Pattern for Life* (see above, p. 349, n. 16), pp. 58-59. Matthew's context implies a generous character, that of a God who sends rain on just and unjust alike and sunshine on the good and bad.

50. See above, p. 339, n. 7.

51. The formulation of the saying on divorce at Mark 10:11-12, with its reference to the possibility of a wife instituting divorce proceedings against her husband, reflects Gentile, rather than a strictly Jewish, environment.

52. Compare with Matthew's treatment of divorce the way he prese.ts his view of the church in the parable of the Wheat and the Tares (13:24-30, 36-43; see above, pp. 186-88). There his view was that the church includes "both bad and good," and while God will some day judge, man is not to undertake a weeding out process now. So likewise the Matthean church includes persons who are an exception to a strict view that no divorce should be permitted. One can suggest that Matthew's "realistic" view in each case grows out of Christian experience over the years.

53. In the antithesis of Matthew 5:43-44 ("You have heard that it was said, 'You shall love your neighbor and hate your enemy.' But I say to you, 'Love your enemies . . .' "), it is to be noted that only the first half of the saying in verse 43 comes out of the Old Testament (Leviticus 19:18, italicized above); the other half of the statement, about hating enemies, is not an Old Testament commandment, but is now found in the teachings of the Qumran sectarians. Cf. Ethelbert Stauffer, *Jesus and the Wilderness Community at Qumran* (see above, p. 337, n. 5), p. 14.

54. While Jesus speaks of love mainly as a demand on disciples, he does reflect God's continuing love for men in the beatitudes and at 6:26, 30, 32, and 7:7-11 in the Sermon on the Mount. At Mark 12:28-34 and parallels, where Jesus also speaks of love for God and for the neighbor, in answer to a scribe's question about the great commandment, the query would seemingly assume the covenant relationship brought about for Israel by God's love, in light of which the series of Old Testament commandments had followed. Cf. E. Stauffer, *"agapaō, agapē,"* in Kittel's *Theological Dictionary* (see above, p. 368, n. 10), Vol. 1, pp. 44-48.

55. Each gospel has its own features, probably redactional, in retelling the story about the great commandment. In Mark the scribe is portrayed very sympathetically (12:32-34), but this element has disappeared in Matthew's version. Matthew instead closes his version with the emphasis that these two commandments sum up "all the law and the prophets" (22:40; cf. 5:17). Luke 10:25-28 uses the incident to introduce the parable of the Good Samaritan.

56. Cf. G. Bornkamm, *Jesus of Nazareth* (see above, p. 339, n. 10), pp. 112-14.

57. The Old Testament picture of God as the judge of all the earth (Genesis 18:25) carries over into the New Testament in such verses as Hebrews 12:23 and James 4:12. Later Christian statements, such as the Apostles' and Nicene Creeds, keep the idea of judgment, but

associate it, since the resurrection, with Christ, as the agent of God; usually in such creeds judgment is viewed entirely as future. In Jesus' teaching, the Old Testament picture of God as all-powerful and just, and therefore a righteous judge, is assumed, for example in the parables at Matthew 5:25-26, par. Luke 12:57-59 (which teaches that the crisis has come, "we shall all be hauled before the Judge") and Luke 18:1-8. In the latter parable Jesus' audience must have been shocked when he compared God to an *unjust* judge, as he argued that what is true even in human affairs with a corrupt judge (that he will eventually give heed) must be true in higher matters with God the Judge. Note also the vivid description of God as "him who . . . has power to cast into Gehenna," the place of punishment (Luke 12:5, par. Matthew 10:28).

58. That men stand or fall eternally on the basis of their relation to Jesus is certainly clear in the preaching of the Christian church after the resurrection; cf. Acts 4:12 (only Jesus saves) or I Thessalonians 1:10 (Jesus delivers men from the wrath to come). But in some gospel passages the idea that how men respond to Jesus' message about the kingdom will determine their inclusion in or exclusion from the coming kingdom is already present. This connection is made, for example, in the famous Q saying at Matthew 10:32-33, par. Luke 12:8-9: to acknowledge Jesus before men means that you will be acknowledged before the Father when the Son of man comes. For further discussion on this Son-of-man saying, see below, pp. 275-76. It is clear, however the details are interpreted, that in this saying one's status at the judgment depends on one's relation to Jesus.

59. C. H. Dodd, in his several books, has emphasized "realized eschatology" in the Fourth Gospel, and Bultmann has attributed verses like 5:28-29 to an "Ecclesiastical Redactor"; cf. the discussion in R. E. Brown, *The Gospel according to John* (*i-xii*) (see above, p. 362, n. 32), pp. cxvi-cxxi, 219-20.

60. While attempts have been made to find the origins of the idea of the resurrection within the thought of ancient Israel, it is more likely that influences from Persia are responsible for developing the theme in late Judaism. The very earliest Jewish passages on the topic (and they are late, from the third or second century B.C.) seem to speak of a resurrection only of the righteous in Israel. It is the later passages which suggest a resurrection of other men—at times, of the bad as well as the good in Israel; at times, of all men, even outside Israel. Naturally pictures of the latter type raised the question of what will happen to the unrighteous at the Last Judgment—what will be their punishment? Further, if all men are raised up, what of those who have been especially loyal to God and have served him well in their lifetime? Will

they receive a further reward? Questions of this sort became especially real for Jews during the period of Maccabean persecution in the second century B.C., when some Jews were disloyal and in the eyes of the faithful community deserved punishment, and other Jews died for their faith and were deemed worthy of some sort of reward. Against this background such questions were debated in Jesus' day. In this way resurrection, judgment, and punishments and rewards are all related; cf. II Timothy 4:8 for a New Testament reflection: God is "the righteous judge," on the Day of the Lord the dead will be raised up (cf. I Thessalonians 4:16-17), and God will reward his own. (Pauline references generally say little about the fate of unbelievers.) In Jesus' teaching, his prophetic heritage as well as apocalyptic influence help account for references to the judgment, but his central theme of the kingdom of God implies it too: God will come to judge, as well as to save. The Old Testament often viewed God as saving Israel at the same time as he judged her enemies. John the Baptist and Jesus saw the meaning of judgment as judgment upon Israel too. Since it is not just a matter of being an Israelite (Luke 3:7-9, par. Matthew 3:7-10), neither race nor inherited religion will save; some other basis for salvation is needed.

61. Speculations, on the basis of the New Testament, about "eternal extinction" usually begin from obscure passages like the apocalyptic ones in Revelation concerning a "second death" (20:12-15; 21:8). Against such a notion are passages like Matthew 25:46, which refers to "eternal punishment"; but this phrase, in turn, occurs in a parable and seems but a parallel formation to "eternal life"—which means "life of the new age," not "life of endless duration." Hope for a universal salvation stems from references like John 12:32, Colossians 1:20, and I Timothy 2:4, where the word "all" occurs ("I, when I am lifted up from the earth, will draw all men to myself"). All such shreds of evidence are frail reeds on which to build dogmatic assertions, however.

62. Mark 9:44, 46 are inserted in later manuscripts as repeats of 9:48, which in turn comes from Isaiah 66:24. "There will be weeping and gnashing of teeth" is introduced a number of times in Matthew (8:12; 13:42, 50; 22:13; 24:51; and 25:30); it seems more a pet phrase of Matthew than a genuine utterance of Jesus.

63. James 5:9 may be an exception to this pattern when it admonishes Christians, "Do not grumble . . . [because] the Judge is standing at the doors."

64. On the subject of reward in the teachings of Jesus, cf. P. E. Davies, "Reward," *The Interpreter's Dictionary of the Bible* (see above, p. 361,

n. 28), Vol. 4, pp. 71-74; A. M. Hunter, *A Pattern for Life* (see above, p. 349, n. 16), pp. 37-40; especially G. Bornkamm, *Jesus of Nazareth* (see above, p. 339, n. 10), pp. 137-43; G. de Ru, "The concept of reward in the teaching of Jesus," *Novum Testamentum*, 8, 2-4 (April-October, 1966), 202-22, (= *Placita Pleiadia* [Festschrift for G. Sevenster; Leiden: Brill, 1966], pp. 202-22); and, in a sermon, C. S. Lewis, *The Weight of Glory* (New York: Macmillan, 1949), pp. 1-15.

65. It is conceivable that some of the sayings about reward attributed to Jesus in Matthew's Gospel are creations of the post-resurrection community within which Matthew wrote. At this point the community would have been trying to make Jesus' teachings sound more traditional, in harmony with the views of late Judaism. But it is to be doubted that all references to reward in the Jesus-material can be attributed to the community, and that none of them go back to Jesus himself.

66. Cf. such hymns as A. M. Toplady's "Rock of Ages" ("Nothing in my hand I bring, / Simply to thy Cross I cling; / Naked, come to thee for dress; . . . When I soar to worlds unknown, / See thee on thy judgment throne, / Rock of Ages, cleft for me, / Let me hide myself in thee") or E. Mote's "My hope is built on nothing less / Than Jesus' Blood and righteousness" ("When he shall come with trumpet sound, / O may I then in him be found, / Dressed in his righteousness alone, / Faultless to stand before the throne!").

67. See above, pp. 151, 159-69.

68. It has been observed that in the stories where Jesus calls men into discipleship, reward plays no part in the call (cf. Mark 1:16-20; 2: 13-14). Quite the contrary, Jesus insists on the demanding nature of discipleship, not the chance for rewards (cf. Matthew 8:18-22, par. Luke 9:57-62).

69. Cf. John A. T. Robinson, "The 'Parable' of the Sheep and the Goats," *Twelve New Testament Studies* ("Studies in Biblical Theology," 34 [London: SCM Press, 1962]), pp. 76-93; see below, pp. 249-50.

70. Genesis 15:1 can also be rendered, as in the KJV and the Luther Bible, "Fear not, Abram, I am thy shield and thy exceeding great reward." In the context of the Abraham story the reward God promised was originally a great number of descendants (Genesis 13:14-17). It was only after the idea of a resurrection appeared that there could be an individual, future hope for life with God. In late Judaism the view sometimes appeared that good works earn and guarantee future security. For example, "Give alms, so that you will lay up a good treas-

ure for yourself against the day of necessity; charity delivers from death" (Tobit 4:7-10; cf. Matthew 6:2-4, where such crass ideas are avoided). "Do your work before the appointed time, and in God's time he will give you your reward" (Ecclesiasticus 51:30). The rabbis sometimes debated what would become of a man whose good and bad deeds precisely balanced one another.

71. The story of the "Rich Young Ruler" (as he is usually called, thus conflating three accounts into a descriptive phrase found in no one of them; Mark 10:17-31, par. Matthew 19:16-30 and Luke 18:18-30) lends itself, because of some of its language, to a doctrine of reward for one's works. This is especially true of the saying at the end of the section (Mark 10:29-30, par. Matthew 19:28-29 and Luke 18:29-30), to the effect that those who leave home and family to follow Jesus will receive a hundredfold ("now," Mark adds) and in the age to come eternal life.

As it stands, the passage exhibits a number of variations among the Synoptic accounts which make it difficult to tell at points what the original form may have been. Thus, when the man asks Jesus what he must do to inherit eternal life, Mark and Luke have Jesus answer, "Why do you call me good? No one is good but God alone." Matthew 19:17, on the other hand, has Jesus say, "Why do you ask me about what is good?" The usual explanation is that Matthew made the change in order to avoid any notion that Jesus might be repudiating his own goodness. It is likely that the Marcan version of the story did imply a difference between Jesus in his human life and God as the "One there is who is good" (Matthew 19:17). The story falls into three parts. (1) The rich man is directed to God's will as revealed in the Old Testament commandments (cf. Romans 13:8-10). Jesus did not repudiate the Old Testament as revelation of God's will but here endorses it. Whether the man had really observed all these commandments in the spirit demanded of disciples at Matthew 5:21 ff. is not stated; however, a version in the *Gospel of the Hebrews* has Jesus upbraid him, "How can you say you have fulfilled the law of love when many of your brethren are dying of hunger and you are rich?" Jesus faces him with a demand for obedience and renunciation at a point where it hurts most; the man preferred mammon over God. "Treasure in heaven" (Mark 10:21) is language which he might have understood—but he could not respond in positive terms. Jesus' words are directed to a specific situation here, with stewardship as the goal for that particular man; the passage scarcely sets forth poverty as a universal virtue. (2) The discussion which follows with the disciples (Mark 10:23-27) centers in the saying of Jesus that "all things are possible with God" (vs. 27); God is able. (3) There is added a statement about reward for disciples—i.e., those already in the fellowship of Jesus. The first half of Jesus' statement refers to rewards in fellowship now (Mark 10:30a) ; the second half makes the life of the new age (with God) the eventual reward (10:30b). Use of the term "inherit" is to be noted (Mark 10:17; Matthew 19:29). To enter the kingdom (Matthew 19:23) is to inherit it; on this term in early Christian use, cf. Galatians 3:18; Colossians 3:24; and Ephesians 1:14.

72. John A. T. Robinson, "The 'Parable' of the Sheep and the Goats" (see above, p. 411, n. 69), p. 77.

73. Contrast the spirit of Matthew 25:37, where the righteous disclaim any knowledge of having done something significant or laudable, with the proud boast in the Egyptian "Book of the Dead," "I have given satisfaction to God by doing what he delights in: I have given bread to the hungry, water to the thirsty, clothed the naked," etc.

74. "Certainty," not "security." God's promises are certain, in the New Testament view, but he does not promise secure lives or security in the world. Response is sought. But to this response God also promises a just reward.

75. *Luther's Works*, Vol. 21, *The Sermon on the Mount (Sermons) and The Magnificat* ("American Edition" [St. Louis: Concordia, 1956]), pp. 285-94, especially pp. 290-91 ("if we are discussing the fruit that follows grace and the forgiveness of sins, we will let the terms 'merit' and 'reward' be used," p. 291).

9 Stony Ground—and the Claim of Jesus Christ

1. C. H. Dodd, *The Parables of the Kingdom* (see above, p. 373, n. 37) ; rev. ed., pp. 145-47; Vincent Taylor, *The Gospel according to St. Mark* (see above, p. 362, n. 34), pp. 250-51.

2. C. W. F. Smith, *The Jesus of the Parables* (see above, p. 375, n. 42), p. 17.

3. Gabriel Hebert, *The Christ of Faith and the Jesus of History* (London: SCM Press, 1962), p. 62.

4. A. M. Hunter jousts with the one view when he asks, "Would men have crucified a Galilean Tusitala ["Teller of Tales," a Samoan name for Robert Louis Stevenson] who told picturesque stories to enforce prudential platitudes?" (*Interpreting the Parables* (see above, p. 373, n. 38), p. 39. For the other view of Jesus, cf. Bruce Barton's *The Man Nobody Knows: A Discovery of the Real Jesus* (New York: Grosset & Dunlap, 1925), with its chapters on "The Executive," "The Sociable Man," and "The Founder of Modern Business"; such a book could have been written only in the United States in the 1920's.

5. Cf. Acts 4:28, Jesus' Passion was in accord with what God's "hand and . . . plan had predestined to take place"; it was "according to the definite plan and foreknowledge of God" (Acts 2:23).

6. Sherman E. Johnson, *Jesus in His Homeland* (New York: Scribner's, 1957), p. 69.

7. As quoted in Gloege, *The Day of His Coming* (see above, p. 344, n. 26), p. 251.

8. On Jesus' opponents, cf. S. E. Johnson, *Jesus in His Homeland* (see above, p. 414, n. 6), pp. 68-88; and G. Gloege, *The Day of His Coming* (see above, p. 344, n. 26), pp. 250-55; Paul Winter, *On the Trial of Jesus* (see above, p. 343, n. 20), pp. 111-35.

9. See above, pp. 45-67.

10. The Pharisees are mentioned in the lengthy Synoptic accounts of Jesus' Passion only at Matthew 27:62, after his death and burial, and in John only at 18:3 in the garden (a place where Mark does not mention them, cf. Mark 14:43) and at 11:46-47, 57, before the entry into Jerusalem. In other words, the Pharisees are almost never associated in our accounts with the crucifixion of Jesus.

11. The parables which Matthew adds in chapters 21 and 22 to the Marcan outline serve to emphasize the differences between Jesus and his audience (the Jews) in Jerusalem. His hearers are said to be like a son (Israel) who says he will obey his father but does not (21:30); a time will come when the people whom God has invited to the marriage feast but who have said "No" will be punished (22:1-10). Note that Matthew has omitted the favorable words about the widow and her gift at the Jerusalem temple which were found at Mark 12:41-44.

12. Cf. Otto Weber, *Ground Plan of the Bible,* trans. Harold Knight (London: Lutterworth, 1959), pp. 111-12, on the structure of the section.

13. So A. M. Hunter, *Interpreting the Parables* (see above, p. 373, n. 38), pp. 87-88, and, even more strongly, C. E. B. Cranfield, *The Gospel according to Saint Mark* (see above, p. 352, n. 31), pp. 366-68 ("an earnest appeal to the consciences of those who were plotting Jesus' death," p. 367). On the other hand, at least some details in the parable are allegorizing additions by the early church, and the use of Psalm 118:22-23 (about the "stone which the builders rejected") at the close of the parable in Mark (and parallels) as well as the addition of the harsh words at Matthew 21:43 ("the kingdom of God will be taken away from you [the Jews] and given to a nation producing

the fruits of it [that is, to the church, as the new Israel]") likewise stem from the Christian community after Easter. J. Jeremias, *The Parables of Jesus* (see above, p. 373, n. 38), rev. ed., pp. 70-77, shows how the allegorical element grew as the parable was developed in Mark and Matthew, though Luke (and the *Gospel of Thomas* even more) avoid such allegorizing. Dan O. Via, Jr., *The Parables* (see above, p. 374, n. 39), p. 134, concludes that "the parable is an original saying of Jesus," but with allegorical accretions in all versions.

As it stands, the parable employs language from Isaiah 5:2, about a vineyard. The vineyard is meant to be Israel. Its fruits should be returned to God, but the tenants (the people of Israel) have driven off the messengers (the prophets) sent by the owner and, Jesus says, reject finally his son. Mark has made it especially clear that this reference is to Jesus Christ by use of the phrase "beloved son" (12:6; cf. 1:11). The verse about the rejected stone which became the most important stone in the whole building (12:10-11 = Psalm 118:22-23) is intended to refer to Jesus, rejected by Israel but raised up by God in glory. The parable threatens punishment to those wicked tenants who say "No" to God, a point which Matthew especially emphasizes (21: 41, 43, 45).

14. Some commentators think that Jesus had already defeated the questioners when he said, "Bring me a coin," and they immediately produced a denarius. If they had been utterly sincere, they would not have had in their possession a coin which bore the image of Tiberius and the inscription ". . . Caesar, son of the deified Augustus."

15. The fantastic case posed by the Sadducees at Mark 12:20-23 might have arisen out of an actual happening. In Cambridge, England, a British naval officer married three sisters in the same church consecutively in 1924, 1930, and 1961, the first two marriages having ended in death. In the nineteenth century a German missionary sent to Ghana by the Basel Missionary Society married, one after the other, two sisters, who died in Africa from the climate; he then returned to Germany to seek the hand of the third sister in the family, but she chose instead of emigrate to America, the grandmother of the present writer.

16. The rabbis similarly sometimes taught that in heaven there would be no begetting of children, no strife, no bargaining, and so forth. The emphasis in what Jesus says is on the reality of the resurrection and the fact that at Exodus 3:6 God spoke of long-deceased patriarchs as still alive to him.

17. Jesus' answer concerning the great commandment cuts the knot in debate on a topic which had long engaged rabbinic experts. It is not

clear from the sources available whether he was the first to combine Deuteronomy 6:4 ("love the Lord your God") and Leviticus 19:18 ("love your neighbor as yourself") as an answer, for a Jewish writing, *The Testaments of the XII Patriarchs,* also combines them: "Love the Lord and your neighbor," Testament of Issachar 5:2; cf. 6:6; and Testament of Dan 5:3. However, the date of the material in this document is open to some debate. As Matthew retells the story about the great commandment, he omits the details at Mark 12:28, 32-34 which suggest a kindly and favorable attitude toward the scribe. Luke, who has the story at another point (10:25-28), describes him as a lawyer who, as in Matthew, asks his question to test Jesus.

18. A full list of Jesus' opponents during the Jerusalem ministry (Mark 11-12, and par.) is as follows:
1. The question about divine authority: chief priests, scribes, elders (11:27; cf. Matthew 21:23, 45, par. Luke 20:1, 19). This is the only set of references to the priests, scribes, and elders in these controversy stories, and may be redactional.
2. Israel's "No" to Jesus, God's "No" to Israel: the people (12:1-12; Luke 20:9).
3. "No" to the Zealots: Pharisees, Herodians, spies (12:13; Luke 20:20).
4. "No" to the Sadducees: Sadducees (12:18).
5. "No" to the Pharisees: a scribe (12:28), a Pharisee lawyer (Matthew 22:34).
6. "No" to any more questions: the Pharisees in the temple (12:35-37a; Matthew 22:41).
7. "Yes" to the faith of a poor widow: spoken to his disciples (12:43).

A list of the enemies of Jesus for the entire Gospel of Mark is given in Paul Winter's *On the Trial of Jesus* (see above, p. 343, n. 20), pp. 121-23.

19. Matthew disrupts the Marcan sequence in order to add other miracle stories in chapter 9 (they are part of his own scheme of a collection of ten miracle stories in chapters 8 and 9), a discourse to the disciples in chapter 10 (one of Matthew's "five great discourses"), and material from the *Q* source in chapter 11; but then at 12:1 he resumes the Marcan outline at the point where he had left off at 9:17.

20. Mark and Luke call the tax collector who followed Jesus "Levi," but some manuscripts of Mark have "James" as his name. Matthew has "Matthew." All sorts of theories have been advanced, but a final solution is lacking.

21. Howard M. Kuist, in his book on methods of Bible study, *These Words upon Thy Heart* (Richmond: John Knox Press, 1947), used Luke 5:17—6:11, about Jesus' controversy with the Pharisees at Capernaum, as an example to illustrate the literary law of climax in a long passage, a point especially brought out if one notes the verbs involved. However, the combination of the several brief controversy stories had been made prior to Luke, in Mark's Gospel, and very likely prior to Mark, in the pre-Marcan tradition according to form critics like Martin Dibelius and Martin Albertz; cf. V. Taylor, *The Gospel according to St. Mark* (see above, p. 362, n. 34), pp. 91-92.

22. Strictly speaking, the opponents are said to "murmur against" (Luke 5:30) or "say to" the disciples, "Why does *he* [your teacher] eat with tax collectors and sinners?" (Mark 2:16, par. Matthew 9:11); but Luke has, "Why do *you* eat and drink with tax collectors and sinners?" It is difficult to tell if the polemic is directed against Jesus or his disciples or both.

23. Cf. V. Taylor, *The Gospel according to St. Mark* (see above, p. 362, n. 34), p. 91: "compiled by Mark or an earlier collector in order to show how Jesus came to His death through conflict with the Rabbis."

24. Cf. J. C. Weber, Jr., "Jesus' Opponents in the Gospel of Mark," *The Journal of Bible and Religion,* 34 (1966), 214-22, with references there to additional literature dealing with each pertinent passage in Mark in detail.

25. Cf. Paul Winter, *On the Trial of Jesus* (see above, p. 343, n. 20), especially pp. 132-35; W. D. Davies, *Introduction to Pharisaism* ("Facet Books, Biblical Series," 16 [Philadelphia: Fortress Press, 1967]); A. T. Robertson, *The Pharisees and Jesus* (London: Duckworth, 1920); Donald W. Riddle, *Jesus and the Pharisees* (Chicago: University of Chicago Press, 1928); F. C. Burkitt, "Jesus and the Pharisees," *Journal of Theological Studies,* 28 (1927), 392-97; H. L. Ellison, "Jesus and the Pharisees," *Journal of the Transactions of the Victoria Institute,* 85 (1953), 33-46, cf. 107-14; and Asher Finkel, *The Pharisees and the Teacher of Nazareth* ("Arbeiten zur Geschichte des Spätjudentums und Urchristentums," 4 [Leiden: Brill, 1964]).

26. *The Prophet from Nazareth* (see above, p. 377, n. 53), p. 14.

27. The secondary literature on the term "Christ" ("Messiah"), as on all the other titles which are discussed in succeeding sections of this chapter, is virtually endless. One may examine these titles in their possible pre-Christian usage and backgrounds, with regard to Jesus' own usage, and then in connection with application and development in the

New Testament church and beyond. Strictly speaking, one ought to trace out the lines along which each title developed in the Aramaic-speaking church in Palestine and neighboring regions, then in the Greek-speaking church prior to Paul, then in Paul's own christological thought (and often what has been attributed to Paul is really a development in the church prior to him), and then in John, and the other early Christian writers. Such a full account on Christology is beyond the scope of this book, and we have attempted merely to indicate the possible use of each term in Jesus' own lifetime, while also indicating a bit of how the titles developed after the resurrection, particularly in the church's gospels.

On "Christ," cf. in *Hastings' Dictionary of the Bible* (see above, p. 388, n. 1), rev. ed., P. Gardner-Smith, "Christology," especially pp. 140-41; and James Barr, "Messiah," pp. 646-55 (especially good on Old Testament backgrounds). S. E. Johnson, "Christ," in *The Interpreter's Dictionary of the Bible* (see above, p. 361, n. 28), Vol. 1, pp. 563-71. G. Gloege, *The Day of His Coming* (see above, p. 344, n. 26), pp. 226-29. Vincent Taylor, *The Names of Jesus* (New York: St Martin's Press, 1953), pp. 18-24. Oscar Cullmann, *The Christology of the New Testament* (see above, p. 398, n. 3), pp. 111-36. E. Stauffer, *Jesus and His Story* (see above, p. 341, n. 16), British ed., pp. 131-32; U.S. ed., pp. 160-62. G. Bornkamm, *Jesus of Nazareth* (see above, p. 339, n. 10), pp. 227-28. F. Hahn, *Christologische Hoheitstitel* (see above, p. 398, n. 3), pp. 133-241, in connection with which should be considered the critique by P. Vielhauer, "Ein Weg zur neutestamentlichen Christologie? Prüfung der Thesen Ferdinand Hahns," *Evangelische Theologie*, 25 (1965), 24-72, on "Christos," pp. 52-61. M. de Jonge, "The Use of the Word 'Anointed' in the Time of Jesus," *Novum Testamentum*, 8, 2-4 (April—October, 1966), 132-47 (= *Placita Pleiadia* [Festschrift for G. Sevenster; Leiden: Brill, 1966], pp. 132-47). The most illuminating books in many ways for English readers are the two by Reginald H. Fuller: *The Mission and Achievement of Jesus* ("Studies in Biblical Theology," 12 [London: SCM Press, 1954]), where he argues basically in defense of the Anglo-Saxon critical view against the more radical position of Bultmann (pp. 108-11 on "Christos") ; and *The Foundations of New Testament Christology* (see above, p. 398, n. 3), where some twenty years later, he deals with the broader problem of the titles of Jesus in the "post-Bultmannian era," in a way which recognizes the insights of continental scholarship and yet which seeks to preserve much that was correct in Anglo-Saxon views (pp. 23-31, 63-64, 109-11). The latter book is the one which can be most recommended to show development of christological titles, step by step, in the early church. More detailed is Werner Kramer,

Christ, Lord, Son of God, trans. Brian Hardy, ("Studies in Biblical Theology," 50 [London: SCM Press, 1966]), pp. 19-64, 133-50, 203-14. A recent survey especially reflecting Roman Catholic scholarship is Leopold Sabourin, S.J., *The Names and Titles of Jesus: Themes of Biblical Theology,* trans. M. Carroll (New York: Macmillan, 1967).

28. To anoint with oil could, of course, have a more secular meaning than the "messianic sense" which concerns us here. It could refer to the application of olive oil or some scented ointment for a festival (Ruth 3:3; Luke 7:46). It could refer also to the anointing of sacred objects, like the tent of meeting and the altar, as well as the priests, in religious ceremonies (cf. Exodus 30:22-33, on "sacred anointing oil"). The practice of anointing existed all over the ancient Near East. There is, for example, a reference to anointing a king in the Amarna letters of the fourteenth century B.C.

29. This broad view of the importance and even cruciality of the term "Messiah" in connection with the historical Jesus and of "messianic" for the entire New Testament is to be seen in some of the older literature, e.g., Shailer Mathews, *The Messianic Hope in the New Testament* (Chicago: University of Chicago Press, 1905); H. G. Hatch, *The Messianic Consciousness of Jesus: An Investigation of Christological Data in the Synoptic Gospels* (London: SPCK, 1939). Compare the view of E. F. Scott, "That Jesus did indeed regard himself as Messiah it is only a perverted critical ingenuity tha[t] can deny" (*The Kingdom of God in the New Testament* [see above, p. 367, n. 7], p. 121), with the position of Bornkamm, who leaves the "messianic question" almost to the end of his book, *Jesus of Nazareth,* and who then takes the position that Jesus did not claim any of the traditional titles for himself (pp. 169-78, 226-31). Involved in this shift in the last generation is not simply some general change in the religious climate or even the growth of historical-critical techniques with regard to study of the gospels, but an awareness that precision is needed in treating each title separately in Christology, and not just as a collective mass, and a tendency to refer today under the heading of "eschatological" to what an earlier generation lumped together under "messianic" with regard to the historical Jesus. Cullmann is correct "that the adjective 'messianic' is almost a synonym for 'eschatological'" (*The Christology of the New Testament* [see above, p. 398, n. 3], p. 111), but most scholars today would prefer to speak of Jesus' "eschatological consciousness" rather than his "messianic consciousness."

30. "The Jews had no doctrine about the Messiah invested with the sanction of orthodoxy," George Foot Moore, *Judaism in the First Centuries of the Christian Era: The Age of the Tannaim* (Cambridge: Har-

vard University Press, 1927-30), Vol. 1, p. 90. Cf. O. Cullmann, *The Christology of the New Testament* (see above, p. 398, n. 3), p. 111, "Judaism had by no means a single fixed concept of the Messiah."

31. Scandinavian scholars particularly, chiefly those of the Uppsala School, have pursued this line of investigation. For a brief summary, cf. S. Szikszai, "King," *The Interpreter's Dictionary of the Bible* (see above, p. 361, n. 28), Vol. 3, pp. 15-16; H. Ringgren, *The Messiah in the Old Testament* ("Studies in Biblical Theology," 18 [London: SCM Press, 1956]); and R. H. Fuller, *The Foundations of New Testament Christology* (see above, p. 398, n. 3), pp. 24 and 54, with further references given in all three surveys. Probably the most important book representing this viewpoint is Sigmund Mowinckel's *He that Cometh* (New York and Nashville: Abingdon, 1954). These scholars note that in lands around Israel, such as Babylon, Ugarit, and Egypt, the anointing of the king took on a theocratic character (that is, by God). Such was the pattern of kingship that the king was regarded as a "son of God" (in Mesopotamia, a man adopted by the deity; in Egypt, the actual embodiment of Horus). Each New Year's day there would be a festival celebrating the king's coronation or anointment as the representative of the god(s). Scholars of the Uppsala School think that this common Near Eastern pattern was followed in Israel also and that the king there was likewise regarded as the "anointed representative" and "son" of Yahweh. The king would thus be "the Lord's anointed" in a special sense; cf. I Samuel 24:6, 10, where David will not slay his enemy Saul because he is the Lord's anointed. On this view, Psalm 2 is regarded as a "royal psalm," composed for the king's coronation; note vs. 2, "the Lord and his anointed," and vss. 7-9, the words used at the coronation to show that the anointed king is Yahweh's son, ". . . 'You are my son, today I have begotten you. . . .' " Many of the traditionally "messianic" passages are presumed to come from this setting (Psalm 89:1-4, 19-20, 26-29; 110:1; and Isaiah 9:6-7; 11:1-3, in particular). Since the house of David was at one point promised the throne forever (II Samuel 7:13-14), it is a "son of David" or descendant of Jesse (David's father) who is looked for in these passages as the ideal anointed king. After the last king of Judah was deposed in 586 B.C., the dream of a great future Davidic king or "anointed one" had to live on in other forms, some of which are discussed in the following paragraphs of this chapter.

32. A pertinent section of the pseudepigraphical book, *The Assumption of Moses,* is given in C. K. Barrett, *The New Testament Background* (see above, p. 341, n. 9), selection 220 (*Assumption of Moses* 10). It is possible that this document stresses the coming of the kingdom apart

from any messiah in reaction to messianic expectations in other Jewish circles in preceding decades. Some circles were looking for a Davidic messiah to inaugurate the Golden Age. They got Herod instead as king. Hence the reaction: no messiah, but only a messenger, then God himself will bring the new age. A messianic agent is also lacking in the writings of Jews of the first century A.D. like Philo and Josephus. The latter, who fought in the revolt against Rome in A.D. 68, was likely, in his later life, thoroughly disillusioned with all messianic and eschatological speculation. In his *Jewish War* 6. 312-13 he writes that the revolt had been caused by an oracle about the messiah, a "prophecy that one of their country would become ruler of the world"; Josephus himself explained this to mean the sovereignty of Vespasian, who was proclaimed emperor on the soil of Palestine.

33. The *Psalms of Solomon* represented a protest against the misrule of the Hasmonean priest-kings, the Maccabean rulers who had assumed both throne and high-priesthood, and also expressed a hope for a Davidic king-messiah. This hope that God will act and raise up such a king is most vividly expressed in Psalm of Solomon 17, a composition which has been called "the Marseillaise of the kingdom of God": "Behold, O Lord, and raise up . . . their king, the son of David, . . . that he may reign over Israel thy servant" (Barrett, *The New Testament Background* [see above, p. 341, n. 9], selection 223), But even here, God is referred to as king, just as is the son of David.

34. An interesting but obscure reflection of the situation in the Jewish community which was set up in Palestine after the Exile is reflected in Zechariah 4. The "two olive trees" (4:11) or "anointed" ones (literally "two sons of oil," 4:14), "who stand by the Lord of the whole earth," are the governor Zerubbabel, of the line of David (I Chronicles 3:17-19; Matthew 1:12; Luke 3:27), who was to be anointed king but later mysteriously disappeared, and Joshua, the anointed priest, whose name appears in chapter 3 and at 6:11. Originally the 6:11 passage, about setting a crown on someone's head, probably referred to Zerubbabel, about whom messianic expectations had arisen; but after these hopes were dashed, the text was doctored to refer to Joshua. Here is an example of how lingering hopes for a Davidic messiah were transmuted, amid the hard facts of reality, to ideas about an anointed priest.

35. On Daniel 9:25-26, cf. James Barr, in *Peake's Commentary* (see above, p. 337, n. 4), rev. ed., section 526*d*., or Norman W. Porteous, *Daniel: A Commentary* ("The Old Testament Library" [Philadelphia: Westminster, 1965]), pp. 141-42. Information on Zerubbabel will be found in the article on him by B. T. Dahlberg, in *The Interpreter's*

Dictionary of the Bible (see above, p. 361, n. 28), Vol. 4, pp. 955-56; and on Onias III in that by S. B. Hoenig, *ibid.*, Vol. 3, pp. 603-604. A further picture of Onias and his times is provided in Glanville Downey's *Ancient Antioch* (Princeton: Princeton University Press, 1963), pp. 62-63. Onias was a high priest in Jerusalem about 180 B.C. who took the Egyptian side against the Seleucid position and who (traditions vary) either fled to Egypt and founded a temple at Heliopolis which was to be a rival to that at Jerusalem, or took sanctuary at the temple of Daphne in Antioch and was killed when he left its precincts (II Maccabees 4:33-34).

36. On the references in Enoch, where, in this library of late Jewish and perhaps early Christian speculations, the terms "Messiah," "Elect One," and "Son of man" are at times lumped together to suggest a pre-existent redeemer figure who descends from heaven, and who at other times is identified with Enoch himself, see below, pp. 271-72, and also R. H. Fuller, *The Foundations of New Testament Christology* (see above, p. 398, n. 3), pp. 28, 37-41. Fuller is inclined to date the Enoch references in the pre-Christian period, but he notes some of the debate; I am inclined not to assume an early dating for chapters 37–71, and thus regard the idea of a messiah-Son-of-man figure in pre-Christian Judaism as unproven.

37. 1QS 9. 11 (the *Manual of Discipline;* C. K. Barrett, *The New Testament Background* [see above, p. 341, n. 9], selection 234).

38. Scholars might have perceived the doctrine of two messiahs, priestly and lay, some sixty years ago in documents then available such as the *Damascus Covenant Document* ("Zadokite Fragments") and the *Testaments of the XII Patriarchs,* but under the influence of R. H. Charles they were generally inclined to read these references as referring to one view of the messiah which was replaced by another, rather than as a doctrine of two anointed leaders side by side: cf. A. Richardson, *An Introduction to the Theology of the New Testament* (London: SCM Press, 1958), p. 127. Research on the Dead Sea Scrolls has corrected this misunderstanding. Cf. K. G. Kuhn "The Two Messiahs of Aaron and Israel," *New Testament Studies,* 1 (1954-55), 168-80, reprinted in *The Scrolls and the New Testament* (see above, p. 337, n. 4), pp. 54-64. Fuller, *The Foundations of New Testament Christology* (see above, p. 398, n. 3), pp. 28-30, has a brief summary; H. Ringgren, *The Faith of Qumran* (see above, p. 398, n. 6), pp. 167-82, provides more data.

39. Cf. T. W. Manson's opening chapter on "The Messianic Hope," in *The Servant-Messiah: A Study of the Public Ministry of Jesus* (see above, p. 337, n. 7), especially pp. 5, 10, 25-35. Care must be taken.

however, to exclude that sort of caricature which holds that, while the Jew expected a bloodthirsty warrior-hero, the Christian messiah was the Prince of Peace. With some justification, Claude G. Montefiore protested about some of the representations in writings early in this century: "The Jewish Messiah is depressed and depreciated, and Jesus is magnified and exalted." The former is stripped of any ethical or spiritual side and made a conquering king, "whose sole function it is to cause the Jews to triumph over their enemies and to make them the supreme world-power. . . . The *Judenmessias* would appear to be a sort of Napoleon, protected and inspired by the narrow 'Jewish' God" (*The Synoptic Gospels* [see above, p. 348, n. 15], Vol. 1, p. 75). Jewish expectations varied so much that even if some Jews, in their situation under foreign tyranny, hoped for such a Zealot leader, theirs was but one view among many in Judaism.

40. An indication of the variety of views among Jews about the messiah and the kingdom in the early Christian period can be seen in the two Jewish revolts of the period: in A.D. 68-70 there seems to have been no messianic figure involved in the Zealot revolt, for Jews could expect the new age to be ushered in without any messianic figure at all; on the other hand, in the revolt of A.D. 132-35 there were apparently two anointed leaders, a priest Eleazer, and a self-styled lay or political leader, Simon bar Kokheba—thus the pattern of two messiahs as at Zechariah 4:14 or in the Dead Sea Scrolls. Apocalyptists and pietists expected direct divine intervention; Zealots saw need for human effort, indeed armed revolt. But all sorts of variations and combinations of views must have existed.

41. Vernon Neufeld, *The Earliest Christian Confessions* ("New Testament Tools and Studies," 5 [Grand Rapids: Eerdmans, 1963]), regards this as the basic New Testament confession, taking priority even over "Jesus is lord." The two titles are used together in a sermon in Acts 2, where it is stated that, upon raising Jesus from the dead, God "has made him both Lord and Christ" (2:36).

42. According to Acts 11:26 it was at Antioch in Syria that "the disciples" (a technical term in Acts for the Christians) were first called *Christianoi*. The term suggests that pagans in Antioch by this time regarded "Christ" as a proper name, and coined this word to refer to the man's followers—probably with an invidious sense, as was the wont of the populace in Antioch. To pagans the Greek word *Christianoi* might suggest "followers of the 'Smeared One' or the 'Perfumed One.' " What started as a term of insult became, of course, in time a badge of honor, as with many other names in the history of religion; e.g., "Method-ist."

43. E. Stauffer, *Jesus and His Story* (see above, p. 342, n. 16), British ed., pp. 131-32; U.S. ed., pp. 160-62. A much more positive evaluation of the use by Jesus of the term "Messiah" is found in T. W. Manson's *The Servant-Messiah* (see above, p. 337, n. 7). One can appeal to such incidents as the feeding of the five thousand, where John 6:15 suggests the people wanted to make him king (i.e., anoint him); the cleansing of the temple, where Jesus acts with Zealot-like vigor to cleanse the temple court; and the anointing at Bethany, where the woman may have supposed she was anointing the messianic king. But many critics today find such interpretations hard to credit as the historical meanings in Jesus' lifetime. Jesus certainly seems to have removed himself from the popular desire for a warlike Zealot leader who should lead an armed revolt. There seems also to be little evidence for the traditional explanation that Jesus took over such a nationalistic notion of messiahship and "purified" or "spiritualized" it during his lifetime.

44. See below, pp. 309-10.

45. Detailed study of the pericope about Peter's Confession at Caesarea Philippi has produced a variety of theories in recent years. One of the results to be reckoned with is the view, held by some exegetes of both Protestant and Roman Catholic confessional convictions, that sections of the narrative, as it now stands in the Synoptic Gospels, cannot be historical. In addition to commentaries on each of the three gospels, see the summaries on exegesis in Francis W. Beare, *The Earliest Records of Jesus* (New York and Nashville: Abingdon, 1962), pp. 136-40; and R. H. Fuller, *The Foundations of New Testament Christology* (see above, p. 398, n. 3), p. 109.

That the pericope at Mark 8:27-33 is built up from a number of smaller units was argued by Bultmann in *The History of the Synoptic Tradition* (see above, p. 373, n. 39), pp. 257-59, and also 138-40, 427, and 405-406, who viewed the passage form-critically as a "legend of faith." The opening clause in 8:27a ("And Jesus went on with his disciples, to the villages of Caesarea Philippi") is regarded by Bultmann as the conclusion of previous pericope (8:22-26), and, he thinks, the phrase "on the way" in 27b comes from the evangelist. The basic narrative is found in verses 27b-29, though even this story, with its question about who men think Jesus is and its climax in Peter's confession, is in structure of a secondary type, for (unlike more primitive stories of this type where Jesus is asked a question, which serves to introduce a saying of his that provides the point of the story) Jesus here is depicted as taking the initiative when he asks, "Who do men say that I am?" Moreover, the disciples here seem to represent the church, serving as a medium between Jesus and the people; the confession "Thou art the Christ" is the opinion of the church—in contrast to the view of those outside—that Jesus was a prophet of some sort. Hence Bultmann's judgment that the basic narrative is a legend about Peter and Jesus, told in the interests of the Christian faith. Verse 30, about the messianic secret,[*] represents a typically Marcan motif, verse 31 is a Passion prediction composed after the resurrection in the Christian community. Verses 32-33, the "Satan saying" addressed to Peter ("Get behind me, Satan!"), grew up in the Hellenistic church and could have arisen in opposition to the claims for the Jewish-Christian leader, Peter. So Bultmann. Perhaps the most interesting detail in his treatment is the further judgment that the original ending to the story of Peter's confession is not to be found in any of these verses in Mark, but in Matthew 16:17-19 (where Jesus responds, "Blessed are you, Simon Bar-Jona! . . . you are Peter, and on this rock I will build my church . . ."). These verses, preserved only in Matthew, Bultmann attributes to old Aramaic tradition from the Palestinian church (note such Semitisms as the name "Simon Bar-Jona," not "Peter" as in Mark 8:29, and the word play on his name "Cephas" with the Aramaic word for "rock" [*cepha*], which is deemed more likely than word play on "Peter" and *"petra"* ["rock"] in Greek). Nonetheless, Bultmann regards 16:17-19 as a post-resurrection creation, not something from the lifetime of Jesus. The entire story, as it begins in Mark and is completed in Matthew 16:17-19, would be a post-Easter creation about the risen Jesus, confessed as Christ, who establishes his church on Peter who makes the confession. If such treatment of the gospel material seems cavalier, we must remember that the Fourth Evangelist did something similar centuries before Bultmann when he presented in post-resurrection scenes the verses where the risen Christ grants to the disciples power to forgive sins (John 20:22-23; cf. Matthew 16:19) and installs Peter to feed his sheep (John 21:15-19; cf. Matthew 16:18).

Much in Bultmann's analysis has, of course, been contested, especially his notion that 8:27*a* goes with the previous pericope (8:22-26), and the contention that Matthew 16:17-19 provides the original ending. Moreover, some scholars, such as Vincent Taylor and C. E. B. Cranfield, have defended the basic historicity of the pericope. But it is significant that both Stauffer and Bornkamm, in their lives of Jesus, agree that the story was originally a post-Easter one; cf. *Jesus and His Story* (see above, p. 341, n. 16), British ed., p. 122, and U.S. ed., p. 148; *Jesus of Nazareth* (see above, p. 339, n. 10), pp. 186-88.

One of the most interesting treatments of the passage has come from Oscar Cullmann, *Peter: Disciple, Apostle, Martyr: A Historical and Theological Study*, trans. F. V. Filson (Philadelphia: Westminster, 1953; rev. ed., 1962), rev. ed., pp. 164-217, and *The Christology of the New Testament* (see above, p. 398, n. 3), pp. 122-25, who, contrary to Bultmann, takes Mark 8:27-33 as a unity. This causes him to regard Matthew 16:17-19, not as the completion of the original story, but as a fragment from a separate incident, which occurred, not at Caesarea Philippi, but during the Passion week, in Jerusalem, probably in the Upper Room, in connection with the material now recorded at Luke 22:31-34 ("Simon, Simon, behold, Satan has desired . . . to sift you as wheat, but I have prayed for you . . ."). Thus both passages are historical: Matthew 16:17-19, in the Upper Room; Mark 8:27-33, at Caesarea Philippi. However, Cullmann then goes on to supply his own interpretation of Peter's "confession": it really was not a confession at all, but actually a Satanic misunderstanding of Jesus' role; hence Jesus must reprimand Peter in verse 33 ("You are not on the side of God, but of men"). Jesus didn't want the title "messiah," because of its nationalistic connotations, and therefore talked instead of a suffering Son of man (vs. 31). When Peter tries to "correct" such views (vs. 32), Jesus must rebuke him. The incident, on this reading, should be called, not Peter's confession, but "Jesus' Reprimand of Peter's Satanic Conception of Christ." Cullmann's analysis has, however, in turn been critized on a number of counts; cf., for example, K. L. Carroll, "Thou Art Peter," *Novum Testamentum,* 6 (1963), 268-76; and R. H. Gundry, "The Narrative Framework of Matthew xvi, 17-19. A Critique of Professor Cullmann's Hypothesis," *Novum Testamentum,* 7 (1964), 1-9.

To go a step further, two recent treatments in Germany have handled the passage in a slightly different way from any of the previous analyses; cf. F. Hahn, *Christologische Hoheitstitel* (see above, p. 398, n. 3), pp. 226-30, and Erich Dinkler, "Petrusbekenntnis und Satanswort: Das Problem der Messianität Jesu," in *Zeit und Geschichte,* a collection of essays presented to Bultmann on his eightieth birthday, ed. E. Dinkler (Tübingen: J. C. B. Mohr, 1964), pp. 127-53. Hahn and Dinkler agree that the Caesarea Philippi pericope, as it stands, is a post-Easter reworking of a tradition which goes back to the lifetime of Jesus. The original story connected Peter's confession of Jesus as the coming messiah (verse 29) with the "Satan saying" (verse 33), which was Jesus' response: that is, Jesus declined the messianic confession, and left it to the post-resurrection community to find an adequate title. In Hahn's analysis, the original story, a biographical one, telling about Jesus and ending in a saying of his, consisted of 8:27a and 29b (the setting and Peter's confession) and verse 33 (the rebuke of Peter as a "Satan"). This original story was retold, after Easter, within the believing community of Christians, with verses 27b-29 being added to bring out a positive christological meaning (Jesus is the Messiah, and not only a prophet). This exegesis takes seriously the resurrection as the starting point for interpretation of who Jesus really is, but also preserves a historical core and continuity between Jesus' lifetime and the new setting in the early church. It depends on the fact that the phrase "Thou art the Messiah" could have one meaning during Jesus' lifetime (in terms of Jewish nationalism, an interpretation which Jesus rejects) and another meaning worked out after the resurrection ("Messiah" is an attempt to confess him as more than a prophet; messiahship involves suffering).

Needless to say, not all passages can be treated in this book with the detailed survey of opinions such as are offered here. But when the difficulties are noted which exist in the text of the New Testament accounts then perhaps it can be seen more readily why the conclusion is proposed above that the Caesarea Philippi incident is scant evidence for assuming that Jesus used the title "Messiah." At the best, one must say that if the title was offered, the historical Jesus either rejected it or was reserved about it.

46. The Matthean version for Jesus' answer to the high priest is preferred by O. Cullmann, *The Christology of the New Testament* (see above, p. 398, n. 3), pp. 118-19, who cites A. Merx and J. Héring in support of the view. L. Sabourin, *The Names and Titles of Jesus* (see above, p. 418, n. 27), p. 33, n. 2, also regards it as "permissible" to read "Thou said [sic] it," as in Matthew; he cites X. Léon-Dufour also. R. H. Fuller, *The Foundations of New Testament Christology* (see above, p. 398, n. 3), p. 110, writes that one must "either follow Cullmann" and the Matthean form, or "suppose that Jesus actually remained silent throughout the investigation. . . . But on either view Mark 14:62 cannot be used as evidence for Jesus' own acceptance of the title Messiah." As for the textual problem at Mark 14:62, Vincent Taylor, *The Gospel according to St. Mark* (see above, p. 362, n. 34), p. 568, gives the reasons why he thinks Mark originally wrote "You say that I am," rather than the reading which the RSV renders, "I am."

47. An extreme example of making Jesus conform to a rigid doctrine of Messiahship is found in H. J. Schonfield's book, *The Passover Plot* (see above, p. 359, n. 18), especially pp. 34-47 and 89-100. It is significant that Schonfield takes Peter's confession at Caesarea Philippi as precisely the thing that Jesus wanted to hear (p. 92). On this interpretation, Jesus should have commended him, "Good for you, Peter!" instead of rebuking him as a "Satan."

48. The phrase "a son of man" occurs at Revelation 1:13 and 14:14. However, both references are quotations from Daniel 7:13, right down

to the detail that it is "*a* son of man" rather than "*the* son of man."
Hebrews 2:6 also uses the phrase in a quotation of Psalm 8:4, a verse
taken up below, p. 272.

49. Cf. E. Stauffer, *Jesus and His Story* (see above, p. 341, n. 16),
British ed., p. 133; U.S. ed., p. 162; *New Testament Theology*, trans.
John Marsh (London: SCM Press, 1955), p. 108.

50. On "Son of man," cf. *Hastings' Dictionary of the Bible* (see above,
p. 388, n. 1), rev. ed., pp. 141-42, where there is a strong position taken
against allowing too much apocalyptic influence on Jesus' usage. S. E.
Johnson, "Son of man," in *The Interpreter's Dictionary of the Bible*
(see above, p. 361, n. 28), Vol. 4, pp. 413-20. V. Taylor, *The Names of
Jesus* (see above, p. 418, n. 27), pp. 25-35. O. Cullmann, *The Christology of the New Testament* (see above, p. 398, n. 3), pp. 137-92. E.
Stauffer, *Jesus and His Story* (see above, p. 341, n. 16), British ed., pp.
133-35; U.S. ed., pp. 162-65. G. Bornkamm, *Jesus of Nazareth* (see
above, p. 339, n. 10), pp. 228-31. G. Gloege, *The Day of His Coming*
(see above, p. 344, n. 26), pp. 231-36. F. Hahn, *Christologische
Hoheitstitel* (see above, p. 398, n. 3), pp. 13-66, and the critique by P.
Vielhauer, "Ein Weg," *Evangelische Theologie* (see above, p. 418, n.
27), pp. 26-27. R. H. Fuller, *The Mission and Achievement of Jesus*
(see above, p. 418, n. 27), pp. 95-108; *The Foundations of New Testament Christology* (see above, p. 398, n. 3), pp. 34-43 and 119-24. L.
Sabourin, *The Names and Titles of Jesus* (see above, p. 419, n. 27),
pp. 195-207. H. E. Tödt, *The Son of Man in the Synoptic Tradition,*
trans. Dorothea M. Barton (Philadelphia: Westminster, 1965). A. J. B.
Higgins, *Jesus and the Son of Man* (Philadelphia: Fortress Press,
1965). N. Perrin, *Rediscovering the Teaching of Jesus* (New York:
Harper and Row, 1967), pp. 164-202 (includes a summary of a forth-
coming article on the phrase in the Kittel *Wörterbuch* by Professor
Carsten Colpe, of Göttingen). Morna D. Hooker, *The Son of Man in
Mark* (London: SPCK, 1967). There is a survey article by I. H.
Marshall, "The Synoptic Son of Man Sayings in Recent Discussion,"
New Testament Studies, 12 (1965-66), 327-51.

51. Somerset Corry Lowry (1855-1932), *Service Book and Hymnal
of the Lutheran Church in America,* No. 542, vs. 1.

52. E. Stauffer, *New Testament Theology* (see above, p. 428, n. 49),
p. 108.

53. To a Jew of the first century A.D. the term "Son of man" would
have conjured up probably more the picture of a heavenly judge with
eyes of flaming fire and feet like bronze and a sword in his mouth

(Revelation 1:13) than the notion of a gentle, "meek and mild" carpenter which many Christians have come to associate with the term. Moderns have domesticated a term which once produced a sense of awe.

54. So, for example, G. Bornkamm, *Jesus of Nazareth* (see above, p. 339, n. 10), pp. 228-29, or Alan Richardson, *An Introduction to the Theology of the New Testament* (see above, p. 422, n. 38), pp. 132-36. R. H. Fuller, *The Mission and Achievement of Jesus* (see above, p. 418, n. 27), pp. 96-97, gives a chart of the three groupings classified by sources, as do many other treatments on the subject.

55. See above, p. 51.

56. E. Stauffer, *New Testament Theology* (see above, p. 128, n. 19), p. 109.

57. See above, pp. 127-28.

58. One newly discovered manuscript, P⁷⁴, reads "Son of God," rather than "Son of man," at Acts 7:56. G. D. Kilpatrick, "Acts vii. 56: Son of Man?" *Theologische Zeitschrift*, 21 (1965), 209, thinks it possible that "Son of God" could be the original reading.

59. There have been many theories advanced as to why the Son of man is *standing* at Acts 7:56. Some think that the ascended Christ had not yet taken his seat of honor; others, that he stands, like the angels, before God; still others, that he is rising to welcome the martyr Stephen; another view is that he has arisen to make his entry at the parousia. Cf. H. E. Tödt, *The Son of Man in the Synoptic Tradition* (see above, p. 428, n. 50), pp. 303-5; and C. F. D. Moule, "From Defendant to Judge—and Deliverer: An Inquiry into the Use and Limitations of the Theme of Vindication in the New Testament," originally in the *Bulletin of the Studiorum Novi Testamenti Societas*, No. III (first published, 1952; reprinted New York: Cambridge University Press, 1963), pp. 40-53, and now reprinted as Appendix I in Professor Moule's *The Phenomenon of the New Testament: An Inquiry into the Implications of Certain Features of the New Testament* ("Studies in Biblical Theology," Second Series, 1 [London: SCM Press, 1967]), pp. 82-99; Moule, on pp. 90-91 of the most recent reprinting, argues that the Son of Man stands as a witness to give evidence for the vindication of his disciple Stephen before the angels of God.

60. D. E. H. Whiteley, *The Theology of St. Paul* (Philadelphia: Fortress Press, 1964), p. 117, regards Cullmann's suggestion that Paul reflects a Son-of-man Christology as "precarious." Cf. also Robin Scroggs, *The Last Adam: A Study in Pauline Anthropology* (Philadelphia: Fortress Press, 1966).

61. The History-of-Religions approach to the New Testament found the background to the Son-of-man concept in the myth of an *Urmensch,* a primal or heavenly man, the first Adam. Though theories vary, this Man-with-a-capital-M was usually viewed as a figure who had a place in the realm of God, perhaps in the heavenly court of the Lord. (Note that at Daniel 7:9 it is stated in the biblical account that "thrones [plural] were placed," but only one of them was occupied by the Ancient of Days. Is this a remnant of an earlier version where the-heavenly-Man figure had a throne too?) This Original Man is assumed to have occupied a place in heaven but to have come down to earth on a mission of redemption. (Cf. I Corinthians 15:49, where Christ is spoken of as "the man of heaven," or the general "plot" of Philippians 2:6-11.) He suffered among men, but then entered into glory, having shown what true man is intended to be. This sort of Son of man, far from being "just a man," partakes of deity and is a bridge between heaven and earth (cf. John 1:51: "You will see . . . the angels of God ascending and descending upon the Son of man"). Such a Son of man makes God known (cf. John 1:18 and 3:13; "No one has ascended into heaven but he who descended from heaven, the Son of man"). The very presence of such a personage implies divine judgment (cf. John 5:26-27: "The Father . . . has given him authority to execute judgment, because he is the Son of man"). This view is especially developed in Carl H. Kraeling, *Anthropos and Son of Man: A Study in the Religious Syncretism of the Hellenistic Orient* (New York: Columbia University Press, 1927). For further discussion, cf. William Manson, *Jesus the Messiah* (Philadelphia: Westminster, 1946), pp. 174-85; O. Cullmann, *The Christology of the New Testament* (see above, p. 398, n. 3), pp. 142-52; H. E. Tödt, *The Son of Man in the Synoptic Tradition* (see above, p. 428, n. 50), p. 23, n. 2; or R. H. Fuller, *The Foundations of New Testament Christology* (see above, p. 398, n. 3), p. 36.

It is worth noting that this assumed myth nowhere occurs in any one document, but must be pieced together from a variety of sources, and no one New Testament passage spells out all the details which some scholars have associated with the myth, though Philippians 2:6-11 follows the general outline. One may presume that whatever ideas of such a redeemer figure were circulating in the first-century world were used at times by Christians to help tell the meaning which they had found in the work and person of Jesus Christ.

As for Jesus' own usage of the term, it seems more likely that he derived it from the figure in Daniel 7 than from some general mythological concept, though one cannot be as certain that there was no extra-biblical influence on Jesus as William Manson was in his discussion of the matter (p. 185). The latest research, reported by N. Perrin, in *Rediscovering the Teaching of Jesus* (see above, p. 428, n. 50), pp. 164-69, suggests that there was no concept of a coming, apocalyptic Son of man in pre-Christian Judaism, in the sense of specific expectations about a pre-existent heavenly redeemer figure. Behind Daniel 7 may have been a Canaanite myth (from Ugarit or Tyre), which the author of Daniel has reworked, and that version in Daniel 7 was the source for further separate lines of development in Enoch, IV Ezra, and in early Christianity. We have assumed, as Perrin and Fuller both have concluded, that Synoptic usage in Jesus' sayings roots in Jewish apocalyptic, and specifically in Daniel 7.

62. The Ezekielic derivation has especially been supported in Anglo-Saxon scholarship, for example by Alan Richardson, *An Introduction to the Theology of the New Testament* (see above, p. 422, n. 38), pp. 145-46.

63. In support of the Ezekielic derivation, it can be argued that Jesus elsewhere seems to draw upon the book of Ezekiel. For example, Ezekiel 34:11-31 is one of the Old Testament backgrounds for the picture of the Good Shepherd at John 10:11-18, and Ezekiel 37 (the vision of the dry bones) is one of the few passages in the Old Testament which hints at a resurrection. However, the Greek version of Ezekiel always has *huios anthrōpou* (literally "son of a man"), not *ho huios tou anthrōpou* (literally, "the son of the man") which is the regular Greek form in the gospels; further, "son of (a) man" in Ezekiel occurs regularly in the vocative case, whereas in the gospels it is a term used in statements, not in direct address. Moreover, Ezekiel emphasizes the Spirit and even connects it with the phrase "son of (a) man" (for example at 11:4-5, ". . . 'prophesy, O son of man.' And the Spirit of the Lord fell upon me . . ."), whereas the Synoptics are notoriously lacking in references to the Spirit (see below, pp. 325-26). There is above all the question of whether Jesus' usage of "Son of man" is merely prophetic (and thus in line with Ezekiel) or rather apocalyptic (and therefore to be connected with Daniel). For arguments for the rejection of the Ezekielic hypothesis, cf. R. H. Fuller, *The Mission and Achievement of Jesus* (see above, p. 418, n. 27), pp. 99-102, a conclusion which he reaffirms in *The Foundations of New Testament Christology* (see above, p. 398, n. 3), pp. 42-43.

64. T. W. Manson especially championed the Danielic background; e.g., in *The Servant-Messiah* (see above, p. 337, n. 7), pp. 72-73. In recent discussion this position is supported by Fuller, *The Foundations of New Testament Christology* (see above, p. 398, n. 3), pp. 34-43, and N. Perrin, *Rediscovering the Teaching of Jesus* (see above, p. 428,

n. 50), pp. 164-99. Opinions vary as to how closely IV Ezra 13 and the Similitudes of Enoch (chapters 37—71), which also mention a Son-of-man figure, are to be taken along with Daniel 7 as background for New Testament usage. Perrin sees them as separate lines of development by Jewish seers and in midrashic imagery (p. 166) and thus denies that there is a unified doctrine of the Son of man in late Jewish apocalyptic. He points out (p. 260) that even the forthcoming article in the Kittel *Wörterbuch* by C. Colpe on *"huios tou anthrōpou"* decides that the existing sources in Daniel, I Enoch, and IV Ezra 13 are not sufficient and that a lost Jewish source must be posited. A further complicating element, which Perrin does not stress, is the fact that it is precisely the chapters in Enoch (37—71) dealing with the Son of man which seem to be lacking in the extant Greek fragments of the book and which have not turned up to date in the Semitic fragments of Enoch discovered at Qumran; hence the Son-of-man references depend on manuscripts of a later Ethiopic translation. For Jesus' own possible usage of the term "Son of man" I should therefore prefer to argue chiefly from the Danielic material, and certainly not, in our present state of knowledge, appeal to Enoch as background, though for Christian writings of the later decades of the first century there is more possibility of influence from the traditions known to us from IV Ezra and even Enoch. For a summary of the problem, cf. R. H. Fuller, *The Foundations of New Testament Christology* (see above, p. 398, n. 3), p. 37 (with further references in the notes). Fuller decides in favor of a Son-of-man figure established in pre-Christian Jewish apocalyptic as "the eschatological agent of redemption" (p. 38), but his view ought to be assessed by Perrin's arguments, noted above.

65. See below, pp. 277-78.

66. While Mark 2:27-28 can be thus interpreted, final decision depends not only on detailed examination of the verses but also one's whole position of the Son-of-man problem. It is to be noted that only Mark has 2:27, both Matthew and Luke omitting any parallel to his statement that "The sabbath was made for man, not man for the sabbath," and in fact the Western Text of Mark omits the verse too. In the parallel at Luke 6:5 the Western Text inserts the additional little story: "On the same day, seeing some one working on the sabbath, he said to him, 'Man, if indeed you know what you are doing, you are blessed; but if you do not know, you are cursed and a transgressor of the law.' " Mark 2:27-28 has fared variously in the hands of the exegetes. Liberal scholars welcomed verse 27 as a statement of Jesus that "man is the measure of all things." Subsequent scholarship has often stressed the christological aspect of verse 28: the exalted

Son of man (the risen Christ) has authority even over the sabbath, and some have suggested that verse 27 then refers to Christian man—in Christ he is free of Sabbath regulations (cf. the Western Text addition at Luke 6:5). On the other hand, F. W. Beare argues that verse 27 refers neither to Christian man nor to man in general, but to the Son of man, as a messianic title used for Jesus (the saying is not authentic, but could reflect Jesus' attitude; *The Earliest Records of Jesus* [see above, p. 424, n. 45] pp. 91-93). Both verses, 27 and 28, were originally separate sayings. It is conceivable that Jesus could have said what verse 27 reports, as part of his opposition to the Sabbath-piety found in certain areas of Judaism; verse 28 is then most likely a christological affirmation of this principle after the resurrection: Jesus, now identified as exalted Son of man, is credited with authority over even the Sabbath.

67. The view that the Aramaic phrase *bar 'enosh* ("son of man") can mean "man" or "I" has been traced back to Wellhausen in the last century. Bultmann follows it with regard to the "present" Son-of-man sayings, in his *Theology of the New Testament* (see above, p. 365, n. 2), Vol. 1, p. 30. R. H. Fuller, *The Foundations of New Testament Christology* (see above, p. 398, n. 3), p. 43 (and notes) refers to his efforts to refute this interpretation. However, it seems clear that in Aramaic the phrase could mean "I who speak." In a lecture entitled "The Use of the Term 'Son of Man' in Aramaic," delivered to the Third International Congress on New Testament Studies, "The New Testament Today," at Oxford in 1965, Geza Vermes presented additional evidence that the phrase was especially employed in situations of danger, humiliation, and embarrassment; until the revised edition of Matthew Black's *An Aramaic Approach to the Gospels and Acts* appears and the Congress proceedings are published in *Texte und Untersuchungen*, cf. the brief reference in I. H. Marshall's article in *New Testament Studies*, 12 (1965-66), 328, n. 3.

68. So J. Y. Campbell, "The Origin and Meaning of the term Son of Man," *Journal of Theological Studies*, 48 (1947), 145-55, reprinted in *Three New Testament Studies, Republished and Presented to him by his Friends with an Appreciation* (Leiden: Brill, 1965), pp. 29-40. Cf. R. H. Fuller, *The Foundations of New Testament Christology* (see above, p. 393, n. 3), p. 43.

69. See above, p. 270. One passage where the various aspects in the Synoptic picture of the Son of man (Passion and parousia) and the kingdom of God also are united is Luke 17:20-37. In verses 20-21 there is reference to the coming of the kingdom of God; verse 25 speaks of the suffering of the Son of man; verses 24 and 30 treat the parousia.

However, the passage is a composite one, made up of many small units of sayings material, from Q and L; especially to be noted is the editorial hand of Luke himself, for example in the phrase (found only here in all of the New Testament), "the days [plural] of the Son of man." The phrase is a Lucan device to refer, in Luke's theology of history, to the sequence of significant moments from the time of Jesus (his earthly ministry, which for Luke is a unique period in all human history) to the parousia (which for Luke is off in the distant future, at the end of the present "time of the church"). Cf. on the composite nature of the passage, F. W. Beare, *The Earliest Records of Jesus* (see above, p. 424, n. 45), pp. 185-87; and on "the days of the Son of man," A. R. C. Leaney, *The Gospel according to St. Luke* (see above, p. 363, n. 45), pp. 68-72, 230-31.

70. Cf. T. Francis Glasson, *The Second Advent*; and *His Appearing and His Kingdom: The Christian Hope in the Light of Its History* (see above, p. 372, n. 28). J. A. T. Robinson, *Jesus and His Coming: The Emergence of a Doctrine* (see above, p. 372, n. 28).

71. See above, pp. 184-85.

72. See above, note 70. Robinson achieves his conclusions only by an exegetical tour de force, which at times seems overly interested in proving the outlook of "realized eschatology" to be characteristic of Jesus.

73. This view is found especially in the Bultmann School, for instance in G. Bornkamm, *Jesus of Nazareth* (see above, p. 339, n. 10), p. 228. It received its most definitive and stimulating expression in H. E. Tödt, *The Son of Man in the Synoptic Tradition* (see above, p. 428, n. 50). Among Anglo-Saxon writers, the position has now been espoused by A. J. B. Higgins, *Jesus and the Son of Man* (see above, p. 428, n. 50), (who, however, manages to blunt something of Tödt's presentation by claiming that Jesus, even though he did not identify himself as the Son of man, did regard himself as God's Son in that he "believed God to be his Father in a unique and special sense" [p. 202]); and also by R. H. Fuller, *The Foundations of New Testament Christology* (see above, p. 393, n. 3), pp. 119-25, who refers frequently to Tödt.

74. For Bultmann's view, cf. his *Theology of the New Testament* (see above, p. 365, n. 2), Vol. 1, pp. 29-30. The endorsement of the position by Higgins and Fuller (references in previous note) is significant, since both of them had previously defended the position of T. W. Manson, in opposition to the Bultmannian analysis; in some of the reviews there is a note of disappointment concerning this "about-face"; cf. Vincent Taylor, on Fuller's book on Christology: many "will

be disappointed by his new work. In 1961 he spent a period of study in Germany, where he came into close contact with some of Bultmann's former pupils . . . . The impression left on my mind is that he makes far too many concessions to continental theology in his new work" (*The Expository Times*, 77, [1965-66], 141). What has been called "the psychological argument" above is found, for example, in John Knox, *The Death of Christ* (New York and Nashville: Abingdon, 1958), pp. 52-76— "Could so sane a person have entertained such thoughts about himself?" (p. 58), or, "A sane person, not to say a good person, just could not think of himself in such a way" (p. 65) —similarly, F. C. Grant, *The Gospel of the Kingdom* (New York: Macmillan, 1940), pp. 63-66, 153-61. On Jesus' psychic health, cf. also the remarks and references in M. S. Enslin, *The Prophet from Nazareth* (see above, p. 377, n. 53), pp. 145-48.

75. Against the view that Jesus used "Son of man" only with reference to someone else who would come in the future, Eduard Schweizer has argued that, contrary to what is taken for granted in most of the literature in German on the topic, there is not a single saying in the class II, parousia group, the authenticity of which is beyond doubt, but there are sayings in both classes I and III (about the Passion and about the present humble life of the speaker on earth) which are surely genuine. This is to argue that it is the parousia sayings which are critically dubious and that Jesus likely spoke about his coming suffering (and expected vindication by God) as well as about himself as the Son of man in his present life on earth. This could be termed another theory. Cf. Schweizer's article, "The Son of Man," *Journal of Biblical Literature*, 79 (1960), 119-29; and two other articles—"Der Menschensohn," *Zeitschrift für die neutestamentliche Wissenschaft*, 50 (1959), 185-209; and "The Son of Man Again," *New Testament Studies*, 9 (1962-63), 256-61—reprinted in his collected essays, *Neotestamentica* (Zurich: Zwingli-Verlag, 1963), pp. 56-84, 85-92. Another line of dissent is found in the recent book by Morna D. Hooker, *The Son of Man in Mark* (see above, p. 428, n. 50), where the apparent aim is merely to trace out how Mark has arranged his references to the Son of man. But after discovering a pattern—Jesus first uses the title openly as a claim for authority, only to have the Jewish leaders reject this claim, so that he then employs "Son of man" only among his own disciples to show that his claim must be rejected but God will vindicate him—Miss Hooker then goes on to suggest that this pattern makes sense and could well go back to Jesus' historical ministry. It is to be feared, however, that her observations tell us more about Marcan redaction than the historical Jesus. The most penetrating attack on the thesis of Tödt, it seems, comes from Norman

Perrin's attempt to show that there was no Jewish doctrine of a coming
Son of man, and that Jesus could not therefore have spoken of such
a figure as coming in the near future. On this view, the parousia sayings—whether applied to Jesus, or to some other figure by Jesus
(Tödt's view)—turn out all to be products of the early church and
not genuine sayings of Jesus (Perrin [see above, p. 428, n. 50], p. 198).

76. See above, n. 69, and the literature cited there. Luke 17:20-21
is a brief story centered in a saying about the kingdom of God. Verse
22, with its characteristically Lucan phrase, "one of the days [plural]
of the Son of man," is the product of Luke the editor. Verses 23-24
are from *Q* (par. Matthew 24:26-27). Verse 25 is unique to Luke, and
seems formed by analogy to the Passion predictions ("he must suffer
many things and be rejected by this generation"); the theme that "the
Christ must suffer" is particularly stressed by Luke (cf. Acts 3:18 and
26:23). It is also to be noted that as Luke has put these separate sayings together from their varied sources, verses 20-21 are addressed to
Pharisees, while verses 22-25 are directed to disciples. Thus, neither
in terms of Luke's presentation, nor critical analysis, can 17:20-25 be
termed a statement which combines the kingdom and the Son of man.

77. This view has been advocated by H. B. Sharman, *Son of Man and
Kingdom of God: A Critical Study* (New York: Harper's, 1943),
and more recently by Philipp Vielhauer, in his "Gottesreich und
Menschensohn in der Verkündigung Jesu," in the *Festschrift für
Günther Dehn*, ed. W. Schneemelcher (Neukirchen: Verlag der Buch-
handlung des Erziehungsvereins Neukirchen, 1957), pp. 51-79, reprinted in Vielhauer's *Aufsätze zum Neuen Testament* ("Theologische
Bücherei," Vol. 31 [Munich: Chr. Kaiser, 1965]), pp. 55-91, and in
other articles noted in Perrin, *Rediscovering the Teaching of Jesus*
(see above, p. 428, n. 50), p. 259 (also reprinted in Vielhauer's *Aufsätze*). The view has been supported by E. Käsemann and Hans Conzelmann (references in Perrin, p. 259), and Eduard Schweizer agrees in
rejecting the parousia sayings (though he accepts some in the other
two classes as genuine, see above, n. 75). The view which is the
exact reverse of that held by Sharman and Vielhauer has been set forth
by E. Bammel, namely, that the sayings about an apocalyptic Son of
man are to be regarded as genuine, and therefore the kingdom emphasis
must be questioned; see above, p. 365, n. 2.

78. Cf. Vincent Taylor, *The Names of Jesus* (see above, p. 418, n. 27),
pp. 32-35 (Jesus used Son of man apocalyptically with reference to
the parousia early in his ministry [this assumes that Mark has artificially placed all the parousia sayings at the end of the book, and that
Taylor's psychological reconstruction of Jesus' mind is to be preferred

to Mark's redaction] and that Jesus later on developed the idea of the suffering of the Son of man) ; or William Barclay, *Jesus as They Saw Him: New Testament Interpretations of Jesus* (New York: Harper and Row, 1962), pp. 68-92. E. Stauffer, *New Testament Theology* (see above, p. 428, n. 49), pp. 108-11, gives a similar impression; cf. also, however, *Jesus and His Story* (see above, p. 341, n. 16), British ed. pp. 133-35, U.S. ed. pp. 162-65, where Stauffer notes that it must be asked which sayings actually were spoken by Jesus and which developed in the early church and grants that it is source criticism and form criticism which must determine the answer (U.S. ed. omits the specific reference to these disciplines). One ought also, for a fuller picture, to examine Stauffer's latest book, *Jesus war ganz anders* (Hamburg: Friedrich Witte Verlag, 1967), where it is emphasized that Jesus historicized the mythological Son-of-man theme found in Jewish apocalyptic.

79. T. W. Manson, *The Servant-Messiah* (see above, p. 337, n. 7), pp. 72-73; *The Teaching of Jesus: Studies of its Form and Content* (New York: Cambridge University Press, 1931; paperback reprint 1963), pp. 211-34; "The Son of Man in Daniel, Enoch and the Gospels," *Bulletin of the John Rylands Library* (Manchester), 32 (1950), 171-93, reprinted in Manson's collected essays, *Studies in the Gospels and Epistles*, ed. Matthew Black (Philadelphia: Westminster, 1962), pp. 123-45. Cf. further on the general position here taken, as it must be modified today, C. F. D. Moule, "From Defendant to Judge" (see above, p. 429, n. 59) ; and N. Perrin, *Rediscovering the Teaching of Jesus* (see above, p. 428, n. 50), pp. 164-99, especially 197-98 (note the tribute to Manson in the bibliographical evaluation of his work, p. 249).

80. The four beasts are probably meant to stand for Babylon, Media, Persia, and the Seleucid Greek empire, all of which had ruled over the remnants of Israel, the people of God, in the centuries after the fall of Jerusalem in 587-86 B.C. The fantastic descriptions of the beasts, if one tries to envision them, have something in common with certain cover portrayals on *Time* magazine.

81. There is, as might be expected, much dispute over the interpretation of Daniel 7. The son-of-man figure there is obviously meant to appear in favorable contrast to the four beasts, and, as the passage now stands, appears as a frail martyr-figure, seemingly unlikely to triumph over his powerful enemies; however, from God's hand he receives dominion. Many details take on more specific meaning in light of situations in the crisis time when the book of Daniel was put together, for example, the phrase "for a time, two times, and half a time" in

verse 25 (it probably refers to the three-and-a-half year period of oppression under Antiochus Epiphanes, the Seleucid king, just prior to
his overthrow in the Maccabean revolt). For details, see such commentators as E. W. Heaton, *Daniel* ("Torch Bible Commentaries"
[London: SCM Press, 1956]), pp. 182-86; James Barr, in *Peake's
Commentary* (see above, p. 337, n. 4), rev. ed., pp. 597-98; and
Norman W. Porteous, *Daniel* (see above, p. 421, n. 35), pp. 93-117.
The chapter is a curious combination of prose and poetry (as the RSV
arrangement shows). It is not necessary for our purposes to settle the
question to what extent an ancient myth, perhaps from Ugarit, involving El and Baal, stands behind the present references to the Ancient
of Days and the son of man, nor the question of whether verses 21
and 22 may be an insertion into older material. Any expositor of New
Testament times would likely have dealt with the text as we now have
it. Barr, it may be noted, accepts the opinion of Martin Noth, that the
son of man and the "saints of the Most High" referred originally to
angels (in which case the insertion of verses 21-22 reinterprets it and
prepares the way for the reference in verse 25 to how the fourth beast
"shall wear out the saints of the Most High") ; Barr carries this opinion
through consistently, so that angels, rather than the pious of Israel are
meant. The passing remark in Porteous' exposition, p. 111, that Jesus
appropriated the title "Son of man" and combined it with the thought
of the Suffering Servant, is simply a reflection of a common British
view about Jesus' "personal Christology," and needs critical evaluation
in light of study of the Servant passages (see below, pp. 279-86).

82. Pertinent passages from IV Ezra 13 and Enoch, which develop the
Son-of-man theme from Daniel 7, are conveniently available in C. K.
Barrett, *The New Testament Background* (see above, p. 341, n. 9),
selections 216, 224, 225.

83. The theory rests on the concept of "corporate personality" (whereby
an individual can represent the group, and the group be summed up in
an individual figure) as developed for biblical thought especially by
H. Wheeler Robinson; cf. his essays reprinted in *Corporate Personality
in Ancient Israel* ("Facet Books, Biblical Series," 11 [Philadelphia:
Fortress Press, 1964]). A corporate interpretation of some of the Son-
of-man sayings, on the basis of Daniel 7, is part of T. W. Manson's
solution to the overall problem; cf. *The Servant-Messiah* (see above,
p. 337, n. 7), pp. 73-74; *The Teaching of Jesus* (see above, p. 437,
n. 79), pp. 231-34; "The Son of Man in Daniel, Enoch and the
Gospels" (see above, p. 437, n. 79), pp. 126-27, 140-45 (in the reprinted version in *Studies in the Gospels and Epistles*). Synoptic verses
which could express the corporate idea include Mark 2:28 (Christians

are free from Pharisaic laws about the Sabbath and are lord over it because their lord, Jesus, is the Son of man and lord of the Sabbath) or 2:10 (Christians have power on earth to forgive sins). The view is sometimes reflected in recent commentaries; cf. V. Taylor, *The Gospel according to St. Mark* (see above, p. 362, n. 34), p. 384 (on Mark 8:38), p. 386 (on Matthew 16:28); or A. W. Argyle, *The Gospel according to Matthew* ("The Cambridge Bible Commentary" [New York: Cambridge University Press, 1963]), pp. 8-9, 69 (on 8:20), p. 72 (on 9:6, 8; cf. 6:14-15), p. 92 (12:8), p. 185 (on 24:30).

84. Cf. C. F. D. Moule, "From Defendant to Judge" (see above, p. 429, n. 59). It is such a pattern of humiliation and exaltation, suffering and glory, which James M. Robinson has emphasized for Jesus' own message as well as for the kerygma of the early church; cf. *A New Quest of the Historical Jesus* ("Studies in Biblical Theology," 25 [London: SCM Press, 1959]), pp. 121-25, and "The Formal Structure of Jesus' Message," in *Current Issues in New Testament Interpretation: Essays in honor of Otto A. Piper,* ed. W. Klassen and G. F. Snyder (New York: Harper, 1962), pp. 91-110.

85. Cf. C. H. Dodd, *The Old Testament in the New* ("Facet Books, Biblical Series," 3 [Philadelphia: Fortress Press, 1963]), pp. 12-30; and *According to the Scriptures: The Sub-structure of New Testament Theology* (New York: Scribner's, 1953), especially pp. 62-74.

86. Two examples may illustrate some of the difficulties which cluster around the Son-of-man verses. In *Q* there was a saying about a "sign" connected with the Son of man ("the sign of Jonah"). According to Luke 11:29-30 the sign is preaching, in the cases of both Jonah and Jesus; but Matthew 12:40 identifies the sign as "three days and three nights in the heart of the earth," followed by a resurrection. There seems little doubt that an earlier form of the saying has been reapplied in the Matthean version to refer to the resurrection. Matthew 24:30, an apocalyptic passage from *M*, also refers to "the sign of the Son of man" which will appear in heaven, a symbol sometimes taken by the church fathers to mean the cross which would appear in the sky before the world's end.

An even more debated example is Matthew 10:23: ". . . you will not have gone through all the towns of Israel, before the Son of man comes." As is well-known, Matthew uses the verse in a discourse to the disciples who are being sent out on a preaching mission (10:1, 5); they, however, do return from their mission shortly thereafter (Mark 6:30). Albert Schweitzer seized upon this as an example of unfulfilled prophecy, where Jesus was wrong, and must later have changed his mind about the apocalyptic timetable (*The Quest of the Historical*

Jesus [see above, p. 336, n. 1], pp. 360-64). The older commentators have tried to refer the verse to Pentecost (the coming of the Holy Spirit is the coming of the Son of man), or to the destruction of Jerusalem in A.D. 70. Some take the phrase "all the towns of Israel" to mean every Jewish synagogue in the Roman empire or all the world; the saying would thus deal with the missionary task of the early church. A number of scholars think it originated as a saying from the risen Christ through a Jewish-Christian prophet about A.D. 40, expecting the end of the world before the evangelizing of the Jews had been completed. In this interpretation it is to be noticed that "Son of man" is obviously a title for Jesus in use in the early church. On all these verses, compare the standard commentaries, or, for example, F. W. Beare's *The Earliest Records of Jesus* (see above, p. 424, n. 45).

87. On "the Servant (of the Lord)," cf. C. R. North, "Servant of the Lord," in *Hastings' Dictionary of the Bible*, rev. ed., (see above, p. 388, n. 1), pp. 898-99, and also in *The Interpreter's Dictionary of the Bible* (see above, p. 361, n. 28), Vol. 4, pp. 292-94. V. Taylor, *The Names of Jesus* (see above, p. 418, n. 27), pp. 36-37. O. Cullmann, *The Christology of the New Testament* (see above, p. 398, n. 3), pp. 51-82. E. Stauffer, *Jesus and His Story* (see above, p. 341, n. 16); British ed., pp. 139-41; U. S. ed., 170-73. G. Bornkamm, *Jesus of Nazareth* (see above, p. 339, n. 10), pp. 226-27. G. Gloege, *The Day of His Coming* (see above, p. 344, n. 26), pp. 236-42. F. Hahn, *Christologische Hoheitstitel* (see above, p. 398, n. 3), pp. 54-66, and the critique by P. Vielhauer, "Ein Weg," *Evangelische Theologie*, 25 (1965), 27-28. R. H. Fuller, *The Mission and Achievement of Jesus* (see above, p. 418, n. 27), pp. 54, 86-95; *The Foundations of New Testament Christology* (see above, p. 398, n. 3), pp. 66, 115-19. L. Sabourin, *The Names and Titles of Jesus* (see above, p. 419, n. 27), pp. 150-60. T. W. Manson, *The Servant-Messiah* (see above, p. 337, n. 7), pp. 57-58, 64, 73. C. H. Dodd, *According to the Scriptures* (see above, p. 439, n. 85), pp. 88-103. Morna D. Hooker, *Jesus and the Servant: The Influence of the Servant Concept of Deutero-Isaiah in the New Testament* (London: SPCK, 1959; detailed bibliography). Eduard Lohse, *Märtyrer und Gottesknecht: Untersuchungen zur urchristlichen Verkündigung vom Sühntod Jesu Christi* ("Forschungen zur Religion und Literatur des Alten und Neuen Testaments," 64 [Göttingen: Vandenhoeck & Ruprecht, 1955; 2d expanded ed., 1963; bibliography]). W. Zimmerli and J. Jeremias, *The Servant of God* ("Studies in Biblical Theology," 20 [London: SCM Press, 1957]) is a translation by Harold Knight of the article in the Kittel *Wörterbuch* on *"pais theou"* ("servant of God"); the second English edition, 1965, has been revised somewhat and thus is more up-to-date than the original article in the German.

88. The "Servant poems" or " '*Ebed Yahweh* songs" (so called from the Hebrew for "servant of Yahweh"), were first isolated by Bernard Duhm in his commentary on Isaiah in 1892. Ever since then it has been fashionable to treat these poems in isolation from the rest of Second Isaiah, and even to posit a separate author for them. It is worth remembering, however, for New Testament treatment of the passages, that no one in antiquity seems to have isolated the poems in this way, and indeed current Old Testament scholarship now has come to question whether the "Servant Songs" may not after all be by the same person as the man who wrote the rest of Isaiah 40—55. For details and further literature, cf. C. R. North, *The Suffering Servant in Deutero-Isaiah: an Historical and Critical Study* (London: Oxford University Press, 1948; 2d ed., 1956), and Otto Eissfeldt, *The Old Testament: An Introduction,* trans. Peter R. Ackroyd (New York: Harper & Row, 1965), pp. 330-41, especially 340-41.

89. Compare the following verses in I Peter 2 with the underlying phrases in Isaiah: 2:22 with Isaiah 53:9*b*; 2:24 with 53:12; 2:25 with 53:5*d*-6.

90. It has been argued by Jeremias, among others, that Philippians 2:7 is best explained in light of Isaiah 53:12, which can be translated, the servant "poured out his soul unto death" or "stripped himself even unto death." If this allusion to Isaiah 53 is correct, then Philippians 2:6-11 refers not to the incarnation and birth of Jesus at this point (in the phrase "he humbled himself") but to his cross and death. So Jeremias, *The Servant of God* (see above, p. 440, n. 87), p. 97; and in "Zu Philipper 2, 7: *heauton ekenōsen,*" *Novum Testamentum,* 6 (1963), 182-88 (= *Charis kai Sophia.* Festschrift Karl Heinrich Rengstorf [Leiden: Brill, 1964], pp. 182-88), reprinted in *Abba* (essays; Göttingen, 1966), pp. 308-13. The passage is discussed in R. P. Martin's monographs, *An Early Christian Confession* (Grand Rapids: Eerdmans, 1960), pp. 24-25, and *Carmen Christi: Philippians ii. 5-11* ("Society for New Testament Studies Monograph Series," Vol. 4 [New York: Cambridge University Press, 1967]), pp. 165-96, where Martin decides in favor of a reference to the incarnation (rather than to just the cross) in vs. 7 and inclines toward E. Schweizer's view that Jesus is depicted as "the righteous sufferer." Jeremias continues to state his position in more detail in the rev. ed. of *The Servant of God* (1965), pp. 97-99.

91. The Greek term involved is *"pais"* (hence some writers like Cullmann speak of a "Paidology" here, rather than a Christology, "servantship" rather than "messiahship"). But *pais* could also be rendered "child (of God)" or "son," as the RSV footnotes at Acts 3:13, 26

indicate; the same thing occurs at 4:25, 27, and 30. It may be added
that when sermons in Acts speak of Jesus as "the Righteous One,"
there may be a reflection of Isaiah 53:11, among other passages, for
there the servant is called "the righteous one."

92. Cf. R. H. Fuller, *The Mission and Achievement of Jesus* (see
above, p. 418, n. 27), p. 56. The position is reconsidered in *The Foundations of New Testament Christology* (see above, p. 398, n. 3), pp.
118-19, where Fuller now concludes that "between them Tödt and Miss
Hooker have demolished the thesis that Jesus understood himself as
the Servant of the Lord."

93. In general, Anglo-Saxon scholarship has preferred to regard Jesus
himself as the "original mind" who first made this connection of
Servant and Son of man (so T. W. Manson and C. H. Dodd, for example), whereas much of German scholarship (especially in the Bultmann School) regards the application of Servant categories to Jesus
as a step taken after the resurrection by the early church.

94. That the Servant passages in Isaiah were interpreted messianically
in pre-Christian Judaism has been argued especially by Jeremias; cf.
The Servant of God (see above, p. 440, n. 87), pp. 41, 57-78, the
theory being advanced that Judaism in the second century A.D. tended
to excise any interpretations of a messianic nature which might give
comfort to the Christian view that Jesus was the Servant referred to
in Isaiah. Miss Hooker's examination of the evidence, *Jesus and the
Servant* (see above, p. 440, n. 87), emphasizes how little there is on
the Servant in intertestamental Judaism, pp. 53-61. The article by M.
Rese, "Überprüfung einiger Thesen von Joachim Jeremias zum Thema
des Gottesknechtes im Judentum," *Zeitschrift für Theologie und
Kirche*, 60 (1963), 21-41, finds Jeremias' arguments unconvincing that
Isaiah 53 was interpreted messianically or that Judaism of this period
looked for a messiah who would suffer. E. Lohse, *Märtyrer und Gottesknecht* (see above, p. 440, n. 87), pp. 104-110, concludes against a
background in Isaiah 53 for the notion that the death of a righteous
man can atone for sins, and doubts that a suffering messiah concept
can be documented for Judaism prior to the second Christian century.
R. H. Fuller, *The Foundations of New Testament Christology* (see
above, p. 398, n. 3), p. 66, also concludes against the view that Isaiah
53 was messianically interpreted prior to Jesus, for example in the
Septuagint (Greek Old Testament) rendering. In the revised English
edition of *The Servant of God*, Jeremias now seems inclined to trace
the designation of Jesus as *pais theou* to the custom in late Judaism
of terming eminent men of God "servants of God," rather than to

Deutero-Isaiah, though he still affirms that Jesus did apply Isaiah 53 to himself; see pp. 43 and 59-60 especially.

95. In the Old Testament, "servant" ('ebed) is used for (a) a slave (Genesis 20:14; Exodus 21:21, a slave is a man's possession); (b) the servant of a king (I Samuel 8:11, 17; 18:5; II Samuel 11:9); (c) a polite or submissive form of address ("I am your servant and your son," II Kings 16:7); and (d) temple servants (cf. Ezra 2:55, 58).

96. On the Servant songs in Isaiah, see especially the works (and literature noted) by C. R. North and O. Eissfeldt, cited above in note 88, in addition to the articles in Bible dictionaries cited above in note 87.

97. On "corporate personality," see above, note 83.

98. Possible references to the Servant of God in the literature of Late Judaism after Deutero-Isaiah, both in the Old Testament canon and in the noncanonical intertestamental writings are discussed in J. Jeremias, *The Servant of God* (see above, p. 440, n. 87), pp. 43-78, and in Morna D. Hooker, *Jesus and the Servant* (see above, p. 440, n. 87), pp. 53-61. For the Dead Sea Scrolls, cf. H. Ringgren, *The Faith of Qumran* (see above, p. 398, n. 6), pp. 196-98 (servant references seem to apply to the community, not some individual), and Matthew Black, *The Dead Sea Scrolls and Christian Doctrine* (London: Athlone Press, 1966), pp. 12-18 (a recent survey which is more optimistic about a doctrine of the atonement at Qumran which provides a background for the New Testament). In Jeremias' *The Servant of God*, rev. ed., see pp. 45-79.

Among the passages in the literature of late Judaism which must be considered are the following. Both the humble, lowly king mentioned at Zechariah 9:9 and the reference at Daniel 12:3 to wise men who will "turn many to righteousness " (cf. Isaiah 53:11) have been regarded as reflecting the Servant idea, but neither passage mentions a servant specifically, let alone his suffering. In one of the scrolls of Isaiah found at Qumran, the text of Isaiah 52:14 seems to read: "As many men were astonished at him [the Servant] . . . so did I [God] anoint his face more than man's . . . so shall he sprinkle many nations. . . ." But this textual variant seems not original but accidental. The Qumran community did view itself as serving God, and its hymns often use such phrases in the Thanksgiving Hymns as "Thou hast poured [thy] holy spirit upon thy servant" (1 QH 17. 26). However, such examples may be said merely to reflect Old Testament practice and language, and do not develop Isaiah's idea of a "suffering servant" any further. There seems no ready-made "Jewish concept of the Servant" which Jesus could have taken over.

Attention has recently been drawn to the apocryphal book, The Wisdom of Solomon, written perhaps about 30 B.C., as providing in chapters 2–5 what may be the closest of all possible references in the intertestamental literature to the Isaianic picture of a righteous servant who suffers and then is exalted by God. The enemies of this rightous servant say:

> Let us lie in wait for the righteous man,
>> because . . . he reproaches us for sins against the law. . . .
> He professes to have knowledge of God,
>> and calls himself a child [or servant] of the Lord. (2:12-13)

These adversaries go on:

> . . . he avoids our ways as unclean;
> he calls the last end of the righteous happy,
> and boasts that God is his father.
> Let us see if his words are true,
> and let us test what will happen at the end of his life;
> for if the righteous man is God's son, He will help him,
> and will deliver him from the hand of his adversaries. (2:16-18)

However, this righteous man who calls himself a servant of God keeps his trust in the Lord, well expressed in the following words:

> The souls of the righteous are in the hand of God,
>> and no torment will ever touch them. . . .
> For though in the sight of men they were punished,
>> their hope is full of immortality.
> Having been disciplined a little, they will receive good. . . .
> They will govern nations and rule over peoples,
>> and the Lord will reign over them for ever. . . .
> He watches over his holy ones. (3:1, 4, 8-9)

Two final verses complete this picture of the righteous servant whom God cares for:

> The righteous man will stand with great confidence
>> in the presence of those who have afflicted him. . . .
> When they see him, they will be shaken with dreadful fear,
>> and they will be amazed at his unexpected salvation. . . .
> They will . . . say,
>> "This is the man whom we once held in derision . . . we fools!
> We thought that his life was madness
>> and that his end was without honor." (5:1-2, 4)

To their surprise they discover that God takes care of his servant and makes him his son.

It has been suggested that these verses in The Wisdom of Solomon were composed with the Servant-figure of Deutero-Isaiah in mind, and that, further, this picture in The Wisdom of Solomon became the basis for the presentation of the Servant of God found in the pre-Pauline hymn at Philippians 2:6-11, a passage which does quote Isaiah 45:23. What seems missing in this parallel in The Wisdom of Solomon is the notion that the Servant's sufferings avail for other men and are redemptive for the world. Thus, even if the entire background here proposed in intertestamental Judaism is accepted for early Christian development, one still does not have the necessary basis for explaining the total New Testament picture. Cf. Dieter Georgi, "Der vorpaulinische Hymnus Phil 2, 6-11," in Zeit und Geschichte (see above, p. 426, n. 45), pp. 263-94; with further literature and discussion in R. P. Martin, Carmen Christi (see above, p. 441, n. 90), pp. 92-93 and 318-19.

99. The report in the Synoptics about the words addressed to Jesus by the heavenly voice at his baptism provides a case where one must examine the texts firsthand and then raise questions about what Old Testament background lies behind them (or behind each form of the words), and about whether the words come from a reliable tradition out of Jesus' own lifetime or reflect the christological views of the early church after the resurrection. The three versions read:

MARK 1:11	MATTHEW 3:17	LUKE 3:22
"Thou are my beloved Son; with thee I am well pleased."	"This is my beloved Son, with whom I am well pleased."	"Thou art my beloved Son; with thee I am well pleased."

The first half sounds like Psalm 2:7 (in Luke, some ancient manuscripts continue with Psalm 2:7 in the second line, reading "Thou art my son, today I have begotten thee," see RSV note on Luke 3:22). The second line reflects Isaiah 42:1 and 44:2. Some have even argued that behind the word "son" was originally the Greek word pais which could be rendered either "servant" or "son" (as at Acts 3:13); in that case, the two lines could reflect the Isaianic Servant idea completely, not Psalm 2:7. But it is very hard to pin down the exact words and what Old Testament allusions stand behind them. This passage from the baptism account is the major one discussed in R. H. Fuller's section on the historical Jesus and the Servant, in The Foundations of New Testament Christology (see above, p. 398, n. 3), pp. 115-17, and he concludes that "the heavenly voice must be set to the credit of the earliest Palestinian church rather than to Jesus' personal reminiscence of his baptismal experience" (p. 116).

100. Cf. C. K. Barrett, "The Background for Mark 10:45," in New Testament Essays (T. W. Manson Festschrift) (see above, p. 399,

n. 10), pp. 1-18; contrast the more common view, expressed in E. Lohse, *Märtyrer und Gottesknecht* (see above, p. 440, n. 87), pp. 117-22, that Mark 10:45 represents a short summary of Isaiah 53:10-12. Mark 10:45 has always been a much debated verse. Some scholars have viewed it simply as a Pauline-like formulation, akin to the little creed at I Timothy 2:5-6, "[I believe in] . . . one mediator between God and men, the man Christ Jesus, who gave himself as a ransom for all, ..." Traditionally Mark 10:45 has been taken as a saying of the historical Jesus based on Isaiah 53. Barrett, noting that the Greek is not so close to the Old Testament (in Greek or Hebrew) as our English translations sometimes suggest, finds a reflection instead of the Maccabean martyr theology such as is expressed in II Maccabees 7:37-38, where a Jew who is about to die for the sake of his faith in God says, "I give up my life . . . to bring to an end the wrath of the Almighty which has justly fallen on our whole nation." For further references in the sources to what E. Stauffer terms "the Old Biblical Theology of Martyrdom," cf. his *New Testament Theology* (see above, p. 428, n. 49), Appendix I, pp. 331-34. It is clear that during the time around 165 B.C. when many Jews were suffering martyrdom for their faith the idea grew up that the death of these men could atone for the sins of the entire nation. Such ideas, of atonement for others through the suffering of the righteous, could, of course, have been in the minds of Jesus' hearers —or in Jesus' own mind—during the period of his ministry, and against this background the words of Jesus, about serving, and his example, as one who served, could after his death have awakened men again to the half-forgotten ideas of Isaiah about a Servant-figure.

101. The exact relationship among the various verses in the Synoptic tradition concerning serving must remain problematical, and final agreement on which sayings are genuine and which reflect the reworkings of the early church will probably never be attained. It can perhaps be suggested, however, that Jesus did make an impression on men during his ministry of "one who serves," a picture which comes to expression particularly in the Upper Room (Luke 22:27). Some of the various Son-of-man sayings may then be seen as outgrowths of this basic impression. The foot-washing in John 13 presents Jesus as servant in a graphic, literal way. With the title "Son of man" Mark 10:45 sums up this theme of serving, together with the idea that a martyr death atones for sins ("a ransom for many"). The Passion predictions (Mark 8:31; 9:31; and 10:33-34, and par.) then further spell out the atoning work of the Son of man, while Luke 19:10 combines "Son of man" with yet another Old Testament theme, from Ezekiel 34:16, about the shepherd (originally Yahweh) seeking and saving the lost sheep.

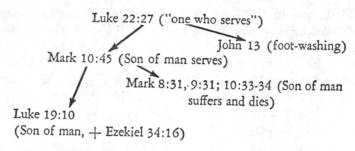

Luke 22:27 ("one who serves")

John 13 (foot-washing)

Mark 10:45 (Son of man serves)

Mark 8:31, 9:31; 10:33-34 (Son of man suffers and dies)

Luke 19:10
(Son of man, + Ezekiel 34:16)

102. Heinz Joachim Held, "Matthew as Interpreter of the Miracle Stories," in Bornkamm-Barth-Held, *Tradition and Interpretation in Matthew* (see above, p. 397, n. 47), has especially dealt with the miracles of Jesus as the fulfillment of Scripture and as the mighty works of the Servant of God on pp. 253-64. That Jesus "bore our diseases" (Isaiah 53:4 = Matthew 8:17), is meant to be illustrated in the nine healing miracle stories found in Matthew 8–9 (plus a "nature miracle" at 8:23-27); the healing miracles include: 8:1-4 (a leper), 5-13 (centurion's servant), 14-16 (Peter's mother-in-law), 28-34 (the Gadarene demoniac); 9:2-8 (paralytic), 20-22 (woman with a hemorrhage), 18-19 and 23-26 (Jairus' daughter), 27-31 (two blind men), and 32-33 (a demoniac). At Matthew 12:18-21 (= Isaiah 42:1-4), Matthew sees Jesus the Servant as having fulfilled prophecy by not arguing (12:15; cf. 12:19) and by ordering those healed to keep silent (12:16; cf. 12:19).

103. I owe this way of putting it to Professor C. F. D. Moule.

104. On "Son (of God)," cf. P. Gardner-Smith, "Christology," in *Hastings' Dictionary of the Bible,* rev. ed., (see above, p. 388, n. 1), pp. 142-43. S. E. Johnson, "Son of God," in *The Interpreter's Dictionary of the Bible* (see above, p. 361, n. 28), Vol. 4, pp. 408-13. V. Taylor, *The Names of Jesus* (see above, p. 418, n. 27), pp. 52-65. O. Cullmann, *The Christology of the New Testament* (see above, p. 398, n. 3), pp. 270-305. E. Stauffer, *Jesus and His Story* (see above, p. 341, n. 16), British ed., pp. 135-39; U.S. ed., pp. 165-70. G. Bornkamm, *Jesus of Nazareth* (see above, p. 339, n. 10), p. 226. G. Gloege, *The Day of His Coming* (see above, p. 344, n. 26), pp. 229-30. F. Hahn, *Christologische Hoheitstitel* (see above, p. 398, n. 3), pp. 280-346, and the critique by P. Vielhauer, "Ein Weg," *Evangelische Theologie,* 25 (1965), 63-70. R. H. Fuller, *The Mission and Achievement of Jesus* (see above, p. 418, n. 27), pp. 80-86; *The Foundations of New Testament Christology* (see above, p. 398, n. 3), pp. 31-33, 65, 68-72, 114-15. L. Sabourin, *The Names and Titles of Jesus* (see above, p. 419, n. 27), pp. 239-52.

B. M. F. van Iersel, *"Der Sohn" in den synoptischen Jesusworten: Christusbezeichnung der Gemeinde oder Selbstbezeichnung Jesu?* ("Supplements to Novum Testamentum," Vol. 3 [Leiden: Brill, 1961]). E. Lövestam, *Son and Saviour: A Study of Acts 13, 32-37. With an Appendix: 'Son of God' in the Synoptic Gospels* ("Coniectanea Neotestamentica," Vol. 18, trans. M. J. Petry [Lund: Gleerup, 1961]). Werner Kramer, *Christ, Lord, Son of God* (see above, pp. 418-19, n. 27), pp. 108-28, 183-194.

105. V. Taylor, *The Names of Jesus* (see above, p. 418, n. 27), pp. 174-75, has an interesting summary on how few names have really been added to the enduring stock of christological titles for Jesus since New Testament times. "Son of God" is one of the classic names; many like "the Carpenter from Nazareth" or "Our Dear Lord" reflect pietism or romanticism.

106. See above, p. 441, n. 91, and p. 283.

107. See above, pp. 100-101.

108. Acts 8:37 is rightly placed in a footnote in the RSV because it is an addition found only in some manuscripts; but it goes back at least to the second century A.D. and is an excellent example of the confession "Jesus is the Son of God" used in connection with baptism.

109. Strictly speaking, Mark has "God's son," which could simply mean "a son of God" (RSV note). Matthew 27:54 has the same thing. A Roman army officer might say "God's son" and mean "*a* son of God" or "god-like person"; a Christian reader would understand the same Greek as "*the* Son of God."

110. There is ample evidence in the first-century world for the use of Son-of-God terminology for kings and other great men, and for the notion of "divine men" or men of God who claimed to be sons and representatives of some deity and who at times received homage and worship. The Orient had long been accustomed to such language for its rulers. The Ptolemies, ruling in Egypt in the three centuries prior to the time of Jesus, for example, had claimed to be "born from the gods," or "a son of Isis and Osiris," or "son of the Sun." Alexander the Great was regarded as transformed into a deity at his death (some eastern subjects had no doubt regarded him as more than mortal even during his lifetime), and stories circulated that he was a son of Ammon (Zeus). Caligula, the Roman emperor A.D. 37-41, is said to have demanded that even his horse be regarded as divine and to have built a bridge from his palace to the temple of Jupiter "so that he might communicate with his brother god"! Evidence from coins of the New

Testament period and other sources is given in E. Stauffer's *Christ and the Caesars: Historical Sketches,* trans. K. and R. Gregor Smith (London: SCM Press, 1955). It is German scholarship in particular which has accepted the theory that the title "Son of God" as applied to Jesus arose in the early church after the resurrection, and specifically in the Hellenistic church on the basis of Greco-Roman usage for "divine men" and rulers. R. Bultmann's *Theology of the New Testament* (see above, p. 365, n. 2), Vol. 1, pp. 128-33, exemplifies this approach. Anglo-Saxon writers emphasize rather the possible Semitic background, and R. H. Fuller's assessment of "Son of God (Divine Man)" in Hellenistic *Judaism* (in contrast to simply the Greco-Roman world) should be noted (*The Foundations of New Testament Christology* [see above, p. 398, n. 3], pp. 68-72).

111. Stauffer in particular emphasizes the Semitic background as an alternative to derivation of the title "Son of God" from Greco-Roman usage; cf. *Jesus and His Story* (see above, p. 342, n. 16), British ed., pp. 135-39, and the U.S. ed., pp. 165-70. Readers of the Nativity stories may note the fact that though one may be at first reminded of some of the tales of the miraculous conception of great men or kings in the Greco-Roman world, the term "Son of God" does not occur in Matthew 1 or Luke 2, and that when it does occur in Luke 1:32 and 35, the phrases are right out of the Old Testament (Psalm 2:7, 82:6; II Samuel 7:14; Isaiah 9:6-7), where "son of God" or "son of the Most High [God]" are phrases applied to David and other kings of Israel.

112. The importance of the passage at 4Q Florilegium 10-14 is indicated by R. H. Fuller, *The Foundations of New Testament Christology* (see above, p. 398, n. 3), p. 32: ". . . evidence that "son of God" was indeed used as a Messianic title in pre-Christian Judaism." The fragment was first reported by J. M. Allegro, "Further Messianic References in Qumran Literature," *Journal of Biblical Literature,* 75 (1956), 176-77 ("Document II"), and includes, in a chain of Old Testament references about the re-establishment of the house of David in the last days, II Samuel 7:11-14, closing with a crucial phrase from the II Samuel passage (in italics below) and a comment on it: ". . . *he will be to me as a son.* He is the Branch of David who will arise with the Interpreter of the Law"—thus, II Samuel 7:14, about "my [God's] son," is taken to refer to the Davidic messiah who shall arise with the Interpreter of the Law, the leader of the Qumran community. Cf. H. Ringgren, *The Faith of Qumran* (see above, p. 398, n. 6), p. 176. The fragment is also available in translation in A. Dupont-Sommer, *The Essene Writings from Qumran,* trans. G. Vermes (Cleveland and New York: World Publishing Company, 1962), p. 313, and in G. Vermes,

The Dead Sea Scrolls in English (Baltimore: Penguin Books, 1962), p. 244. This Qumran find still does not establish the references in the document called II Esdras in the RSV Apocrypha [= IV Ezra]—7:28-29, "my son the Messiah"; "my Son," 13:32, 37, 52, and 14:9—as valid evidence for the existence of the term "Son [of God]" for the messiah in pre-Christian Judaism. For there is first of all a question of the dating of II Esdras (perhaps first written in Aramaic at the end of the first century A.D.); and secondly, while the RVS renderings are correct for the Latin (and other versions) in which the document is extant, the Latin *filius meus* here is probably a mistranslation for the underlying Hebrew, *'abhdi* ("my servant"), Greek *pais,* which has been understood to mean "son" here rather than "servant." On II Esdras, cf. Bruce M. Metzger, *An Introduction to the Apocrypha* (New York: Oxford University Press, 1957), pp. 21-30, or N. Turner, "Esdras, Books of," *The Interpreter's Dictionary of the Bible* (see above, p. 361, n. 28), Vol. 2, pp. 140-42, especially on the varied systems of reference to this document, which in the official Roman Catholic Vulgate Bible is designated as the Fourth Book of Esdras and is printed as a supplement to the New Testament, and which in scholarly circles is sometimes referred to as IV Ezra (e.g., in C. K. Barrett's *The New Testament Background* [see above, p. 341, n. 9]).

113. It is true that Luke 3:38 speaks of Adam as "the son of God," but (1) the accounts in Genesis 1—2, on which Luke bases his notions of Adam's origins, are devoid of any idea of a physical begetting; cf. Genesis 1:26-27; 2:7, 21-22—it is an act of creation, not of procreation. Moreover, (2) Luke has doubtless employed "son of God" at 3:38 in light of his general christological purpose in the genealogy, to show that Jesus is the son of God, something which has been declared in the previous scene, the baptism (3:22). Cf. F. Hahn, *Christologische Hoheitstitel* (see above, p. 398, n. 3), pp. 243-44. Even the "Virgin Birth" references at Luke 1:31-32, 35 are very delicately phrased: "You will conceive . . . and bear a son . . . the Holy Spirit will come upon you, and the power of the Most High will overshadow you"; the child is to be called "the Son of God," "the Son of the Most High." The phrases are christological testimony, the emphasis is on the power of the Spirit and the Old Testament idea of sonship. The motif of amorous adventures on the part of a deity, so common in Greek myths, is lacking.

114. See above, pp. 100-01.

115. Joachim Jeremias, *The Central Message of the New Testament* (see above, p. 349, n. 19), pp. 9-30.

116. The "I-came" sayings are a rough Synoptic counterpart to the "I-am" sayings in the Fourth Gospel ("I am the Way, the Truth, the

Life," etc.; John 6:35; 8:12, 23; 9:5; 10:7, 11; 11:25; 14:6; 15:1, 5, etc.) The "I-am" statements plainly make a christological claim. The "I-came" statements, which usually employ the Greek verb *ēlthon*, can also be read to imply a similar claim. With each of these Synoptic sayings, there is, of course, debate over their genuineness (Bultmann, for example, while admitting Jesus might have spoken of himself and his coming in the first person, generally attributes them to the creativity of the early church) and also over how much is to be read into them (e.g., does Mark 1:38 imply "came out *from heaven*"?). The "I-came" sayings are listed by R. H. Fuller, *The Foundations of New Testament Christology* (see above, p. 398, n. 3), p. 140, n. 90 (along with similar sayings which use the verb "I was sent"), and on pp. 127-28 he argues for an original nucleus of such statements from Jesus, even though the early church may have added other examples to them.

117. It could be argued that Mark's outline is constructed around the phrase "Son of God." The full list of references to it includes (1) 1:1, the title of the book. Then (2) at Jesus' baptism (1:11) the Old Testament adoption formula for a king, from Psalm 2:7, is used; in Mark it is intended as an announcement of who Jesus is and how he will function as God's obedient Son. The temptation story which follows makes clear, especially in the fuller Matthean and Lucan form, that Jesus will obey the will of God, not Satan's, whatever the cost. (3) 3:11 and 5:7 suggest that the otherworldly powers, the demons, know who Jesus is, but he bids them keep silent. (4) At the transfiguration (9:7) heaven assures the reader that God is with Jesus of Nazareth as the Passion ordeal is about to begin. (5) In a parable which, in its Marcan version, uses the phrase "beloved son" (12:6) Jesus stirs his enemies to fatal anger by hinting at his sonship. (6) In a private discourse with his disciples (13:32) he reminds them that to be the Son means limitations and does not imply complete knowledge about all details in God's plan, but rather demands profound awareness of God's ruling power and, therefore, trust in him. (7) The title is employed in Mark's version of the trial (14:61). (8) Finally there is the centurion's confession (15:39), which Mark would also want his readers to make as their own, "This man was the Son of God."

118. See above, pp. 162, 253-55.

119. A. M. Hunter, *Interpreting the Parables* (see above, p. 373, n. 38), p. 88; cf. his further discussion on pp. 116-18. The problem of authenticity and allegory in the parable has been noted above, p. 373, n. 39; p. 255; and pp. 414-15, n. 13, where Hunter, Cranfield, and Via have been cited as representative of those who see an authentic parable of Jesus involved here. The more radical scholars of the Bultmann school

take it as an allegorical creation of the early church about the history of salvation in Israel and then in the time of Jesus. A good list of commentators who espouse the various positions is given in W. G. Kümmel, *Promise and Fulfillment* (see above, p. 369, n. 17), p. 82, and he himself concludes that the parable in its present form cannot be traced back to Jesus and that we know no other form of it which can be posited as the "original." R. H. Fuller, *The Foundations of New Testament Christology* (see above, p. 398, n. 3), pp. 114, 172, takes a similar position, thinking the parable most likely to have originated in the Palestinian church. Like Dodd and Jeremias (cf. *The Parables of Jesus* [see above, p. 373, n. 38], rev. ed., pp. 70-77), B. M. F. van Iersel, *"Der Sohn" in den synoptischen Jesusworten* (see above, p. 448, n. 104), pp. 124-45, has attempted to reconstruct an original "core" parable; his effort is criticized by F. Hahn, *Christologische Hoheitstitel* (see above, p. 398, n. 3), p. 316, n. 1.

120. The phrase, which is quoted in almost every discussion, goes back in the nineteenth century, to K. A. von Hase's *Geschichte Jesu* (p. 527), as cited by V. Taylor, *The Names of Jesus* (see above, p. 418, n. 27), p. 63.

121. Claude G. Montefiore, *The Synoptic Gospels* (see above, p. 348, n. 15), Vol. 2, pp. 169, 186, as cited by A. M. Hunter, "Crux Criticorum—Matt. xi. 25-30—A Re-Appraisal," *New Testament Studies*, 8 (1961-62), 241 (reprinted in *Teaching and Preaching the New Testament* [collected essays by Hunter; Philadelphia: Westminster, 1963], p. 41).

122. See the survey article by Hunter, mentioned in the preceding note, pp. 241-49 (pp. 41-50 in the reprinted version), which defends authenticity. The passage is otherwise termed a creation of the Hellenistic church, reflecting gnostic categories, by many radical scholars, especially those of the Bultmann School. A convenient summary of the ongoing debate is provided by R. H. Fuller, *The Foundations of New Testament Christology* (see above, p. 398, n. 3), pp. 114-15, including reference to the literature in German. Fuller himself, though he opts for the view that the passage is a "church-formation," regards it as providing "an indirect witness" to the self-understanding of Jesus, on the basis of his use of "Abba." Note also Fuller's spirited argument for rooting "Son-of-God" terminology, not in the Greek world but in Hellenistic Judaism, pp. 68-72. In particular he stresses the refrences in The Wisdom of Solomon, chapters 2-5 (see above, p. 444, n. 98), about a righteous sufferer who calls himself the child (*pais*) of God and claims God is his father and that he is son (*huios*) of God; this concept Fuller further traces back to the Old Testament and specifically in part to Deutero-

Isaiah. The Jewish author of The Wisdom of Solomon, he holds, molded his presentation, not to the standards of the Greek world completely, but along lines well-known from the Old Testament.

Matthew 11:25-27 (par. Luke 10:21-22) begins with Jesus' usual term for God, "Father," plus the more usual Jewish phrase, "Lord of heaven and earth." The "wise and understanding" or "wise and clever" (Isaiah 29:14) are the scribes, who claimed wisdom. The "babes" or "simple" are Jesus' disciples, the childlike ones to whom the kingdom belongs. In order to have true knowledge of God, it is necessary to receive it by revelation, but it has been God's good pleasure to grant it now. "These things" probably referred to the message about the coming of the reign of God. Jesus claims that "all things" have been delivered to him by God; that could mean "all authority" (cf. Matthew 28:18) but more likely means "knowledge," the revelation needed for Jesus' task. The final two sentences of the passage suggest why Jesus feels qualified to reveal God's will: it is because of the exclusive and reciprocal relationship with the Father. A. M. Hunter describes this as "a personal 'I-Thou' relationship engaging heart and mind and will— a relation initiated and sustained by the Father and complemented and fulfilled by Jesus' own filial response of obedience and love . . ." ("Crux Criticorum," *loc. cit.*, p. 246; *Teaching and Preaching the New Testament* [see above, p. 452, n. 121], p. 47).

123. These Semitic parallels are especially stressed as background by Stauffer, *Jesus and His Story* (see above, p. 341, n. 16), British ed., pp. 135-37; U.S. ed., pp. 165-68. For Qumran he cites from 1 QH 4. 5-33 and 1 QS 10.9–11.22. Cf. further W. D. Davies, " 'Knowledge' in the Dead Sea Scrolls and Matthew 11:25-20," *Harvard Theological Review*, 46 (1953), 113-39, reprinted in *Christian Origins and Judaism* (Davies' collected essays; Philadelphia: Westminster, 1962), pp. 119-44.

124. Stauffer, *ibid.*, British ed., p. 137; U.S. ed., p. 168.

125. P. W. Schmiedel, "Gospels," *Encyclopaedia Biblica*, ed. T. K. Cheyne and J. S. Black (London: A. and C. Black, 1901), Vol. 2, col. 1881, produced a famous list of "absolutely credible" passages which he regarded as "the foundation-pillars for a truly scientific life of Jesus." Among them was Mark 13:32. It may be commented that many of these pillars would be assessed far differently today than in Schmiedel's time.

126. I follow here the distinctions worked out by B. M. F. van Iersel, *"Der Sohn" in den synoptischen Jesusworten* (see above, p. 448, n. 104), pp. 173-84. With our conclusion above, that Jesus could have thought and spoken in terms of sonship, cf. the assessment of R. H. Fuller, *The*

Foundations of New Testament Christology (see above, p. 398, n. 3), pp. 114-15; even though his examination of the three passages we have considered convinces him that two of them are creations of the early church (Mark 12:1-9 and Matthew 11:25-27) and that "Son of man" rather than "Son" stood originally in the other at Mark 13:32, nonetheless he concludes that "although there is no indubitably authentic logion in which Jesus calls himself the 'Son'," Jesus "was certainly conscious of a unique Sonship to which he was privileged to admit others through his eschatological ministry" and "he certainly called God his Father in a unique sense." For the interesting judgment of a Jewish scholar of Christian origins who accepts the position that "Son of God" goes back to "the self-testimony of Jesus," cf. H. J. Schoeps, *Paul: The Theology of the Apostle in the Light of Jewish Religious History*, trans. Harold Knight (Philadelphia: Westminster, 1961), pp. 158, 161, 166.

127. Underlying the conclusions summarized above is the debate pointed up in Willi Marxsen's essay, *Anfangsprobleme der Christologie* (Gütersloh: Gütersloher Verlagshaus, Gerd Mohn, 1960; 2nd ed., 1964), Eng. trans. by P. Achtemeier forthcoming in "Facet Books, Biblical Series." The question is whether Christology goes back to explicit statements and titles employed by Jesus during his historical ministry or arose only after the resurrection as the response of the early church to what Jesus had done as well as said, and to the resurrection and exaltation of Jesus by God. In outline, the answer given above amounts to this for the two stages before and after the resurrection:

Use during Jesus' lifetime:	the resurrection	Use in the confessions of the early church:
"prophet"		(little used)
"Son of man"		(some further use)
"the Son"		"the Son of God"
(one who serves)		"the Servant"
. . .		"the Christ"
"master, teacher"		"Lord"

The traditional answer has been that Jesus used all the christological titles during his lifetime, and that after the resurrection the church simply continued to employ the terms which he had taught to his disciples. The view of the radical critics has been that Jesus did not speak of himself but only of the kingdom of God, and made no claims for himself; all christological titles enter the picture only after Easter. On the former view, Christology is present in the lifetime of the man Jesus (including, in some presentations, notions that during his ministry he understood himself as the Second Person of the Trinity, in terms of the formulas of the Council of Chalcedon). On the latter view, Jesus was a non-messianic teacher who announced the kingdom of God, and Easter is the key step to making him into Christ and lord. Each side can appeal, of course, to certain texts in the New Testament. The traditional view points to the heavenly voice at the baptism and at the transfiguration, e.g., for evidence as to how Jesus understood himself, but criticism demands that these verses be historically appraised. The opposing position points, on its side, to verses like Philippians 2:9-11 (where only after the resurrection Jesus is given the name "lord") or Romans 1:4 and Acts 2:36 (Jesus is made Christ, lord, and Son of God by his resurrection from the dead). How much is the resurrection light projected back into the historical ministry in the writing of gospels? That it is can be seen simply by noting the various titles used in the various accounts of Peter's confession: "You are the Christ" (Mark 8:29); "The Christ of God" (Luke 9:20); "You are the Christ, the Son of the living God" (Matthew 16:16); "you are the Holy One of God" (John 6:69). Each variation seems to reflect the particular Christology of the individual evangelist and his community. We have even explored the possibility that none of these statements may report a verbatim, historical happening (see above, p. 265).

The "New Quest" is an attempt, in this situation and in light of modern critical scholarship, to posit some links between the historical Jesus and the Christology found in the early church. Heinz Zahrnt's report on it, *The Historical Jesus* (see above, p. 359, n. 21) was accurately titled in its German original, "It [Christology] began with Jesus of Nazareth." Some of the links which various scholars have attempted to forge have been apparent in the chapters above. One is the claim that, even though we may not be able to recover Jesus' very words (*ipsissima verba*), we can at least get back to his authentic voice (*ipsissima vox*); so J. Jeremias. Another is to claim that Jesus' authentic sayings contain the same concept of existence which comes to expression in the kerygma of the early church (so James M. Robinson, for example). A third line of approach is to argue that in those of Jesus' sayings which can pass through the critical wringer there is an implicit Christology, a "Christology *in nuce*," which becomes explicit after the resurrection, though opinions vary as to whether this connection can best be seen in certain titles, or in the eschatological orientation involved, or in Jesus' actions such as freely receiving sinners and eating with them. Marxsen himself (see above, in this note) sees the link in faith, that is, the grounding of one's existence outside of oneself: such a faith-relationship with God existed during Jesus' ministry and did not just arise after the resurrection, and so there is a connection in this way. The debate about the relationship of Jesus and Christology will no doubt continue as long as there are readers to interpret the biblical texts, and the answers of the future which are at all historically based will no doubt eschew both the extreme that Christology is veri-fiable in its fulness already in the ministry of Jesus and the extreme that the gospel records can be read without awareness of the christological dimension.

128. On "lord" as a christological title for Jesus, see above, pp. 124-26. F. Hahn, *Christologische Hoheitstitel* (see above, p. 398, n. 3), pp. 74-95, has in particular argued that there is a basis for the use of "lord" in the early church with regard to its exalted master in the usage of "my master" or "sir" (*kyrie*) during Jesus' lifetime; the position is disputed in P. Vielhauer's critique "Ein Weg" (see above, p. 418, n. 27), 31-37. On the many other christological titles applied to Jesus in the New Testament, cf. V. Taylor, *The Names of Jesus* (see above, p. 418, n. 27), for a general survey.

129. This way of posing the choice comes from Harvey K. McArthur, *Understanding the Sermon on the Mount* (see above, p. 404, n. 26), p. 154.

10 Promises and Puzzles—Jesus and His Followers

1. On Jesus' views about the future, in addition to commentaries on the pertinent Synoptic passages, such as Mark 13 and parallels, and in addition to the bibliography cited above in chapter 9 on the parousia of the Son of man, especially the books by T. F. Glasson and J. A. T. Robinson, mentioned p. 372, n. 28, see the detailed studies by G. R. Beasley-Murray, *Jesus and the Future: An Examination of the Criticism of The Eschatological Discourse, Mark 13 with Special Reference to the Little Apocalypse Theory* (New York: St Martin's Press, 1954), and *A Commentary on Mark Thirteen* (New York: St Martin's Press, 1957); further, W. G. Kummel, *Promise and Fulfillment* (see above, p. 369, n. 17), pp. 95-104; R. H. Lightfoot, *The Gospel Message of St. Mark* (Oxford: Clarendon Press, 1950), pp. 48-59; and Lars Hartman, *Prophecy Interpreted: The Formation of Some Jewish Apocalyptic Texts and of the Eschatological Discourse Mark 13 par.,* trans. N. Tomkinson ·and J. Gray ("Coniectanea Biblica, New Testament Series," 1 [Lund: Gleerup, 1966]). There is analysis of some of the pertinent passages in William Strawson's *Jesus and the Future Life:*

A Study in the Synoptic Gospels (Philadelphia: Westminster, 1959), a book which also touches on topics discussed above in previous chapters. G. Neville, *The Advent Hope: A Study of the Context of Mark 13* (London: Darton, Longman & Todd, 1961) deals with the chapter in a broader context of prophetic and apocalyptic hope. The most recent dissertation on the topic, *Die Redaktion der Markus-Apokalypse: Literarische Analyse und Strukturuntersuchung,* by Jan Lambrecht, S.J. ("Analecta Biblica," 28 [Rome: Pontifical Biblical Institute, 1967]), provides a thorough bibliography and is concerned with context and contents, as well as with Mark's own redactional contribution and the literary structure of the chapter.

2. Cf. A. Schweitzer, *The Quest of the Historical Jesus* (see above, p. 336, n. 1), pp. 360-64; see above, pp. 439-40, n. 86.

3. See above, p. 275.

4. "Armageddon" is apparently meant to stand for "Mount (*har*) Megiddo," the site for a final climactic battle between God and the forces of evil. The plain at Megiddo, in northern Palestine, was the site for a decisive battle in Old Testament times when Pharoah Neco defeated and killed King Josiah of Judah in 609 B.C. (II Kings 23: 29-30). However, there are difficulties over precisely how to interpret the term at Revelation 16:16; cf. J. W. Bowman, "Armageddon," in *The Interpreter's Dictionary of the Bible* (see above, p. 361, n. 28), Vol. 1, pp. 226-27.

5. See above, pp. 220-22.

6. I have cited brief examples from Rabbi Johanan ben Zakkai in *The Romance of Bible Scripts and Scholars: Chapters in the History of Bible Transmission and Translation* (Englewood Cliffs, N. J.: Prentice-Hall, 1965), pp. 30-32. For details, see Jacob Neusner, *A Life of Rabban Yohanan Ben Zakkai Ca. 1-80 C. E.* ("Studia Post-Biblica," 6 [Leiden: Brill, 1962]), pp. 105-10.

7. See above, p. 220.

8. 1QM; Eng. trans. in A. Dupont-Sommer, *The Essene Writings from Qumran* (see above, p. 449, n. 112), pp. 164-97, and in G. Vermes, *The Dead Sea Scrolls in English* (see above, pp. 449-50, n. 112), pp. 122-48; cf. H. Ringgren, *The Faith of Qumran* (see above, p. 398, n. 6), pp. 17-20.

9. The emphasis by Ernst Käsemann on apocalyptic as the "mother of Christian theology" is well-known, and much debated; cf. "Die Anfänge christlicher Theologie" and "Zum Thema der urchristlichen

Apokalyptik," reprinted in *Exegetische Versuche und Besinnungen*, Vol. 2 (Göttingen: Vandenhoeck & Ruprecht, 1964), pp. 82-104, 105-31.

10. Thus E. Stauffer speaks of "re-Judaizing" the Jesus-material, and thinks that in the forties and sixties it was colored by Jewish apocalyptic influence. Cf. *Jesus and His Story* (see above, p. 342, n. 16), British ed., p. 11; U.S. ed., p. xi.

11. Cf. above, p. 293.

12. On the nature of apocalyptic, cf. for a brief treatment G. Gloege, *The Day of His Coming* (see above, p. 344, n. 26), pp. 54-61; or articles such as "Apocalypticism," by M. Rist, in *The Interpreter's Dictionary of the Bible* (see above, p. 361, n. 28), Vol. 1, pp. 157-61; or, in more detail, H. H. Rowley, *The Relevance of Apocalyptic: A Study of Jewish and Christian Apocalypses from Daniel to the Revelation* (London: Lutterworth, 3d rev. ed., 1963; New York: Association Press, 1964).

13. See above, pp. 249-50.

14. G. R. Beasley-Murray, *A Commentary on Mark Thirteen* (see above, p. 456, n. 1).

15. Here at 24:3 Matthew has the Greek word *parousia*. In the discourse on the "last things," only Matthew uses the term. This vocabulary clue suggests that Matthew may have a greater interest in the Second Coming than the other gospels do.

16. Commentators vary considerably in their interpretation of what "all these things" at Mark 13:30 refers to. These varying opinions stem in part from whether the commentator is concerned merely with the verse in its present location in Mark 13 or is also interested in finding a prior setting and application, either in the early church or in Jesus' ministry. Also involved, of course, is the question of to what extent the verse reflects Mark's editorial hand and to what extent it is an authentic, unchanged saying of Jesus. Thus, G. R. Beasley-Murray notes that for some scholars the phrase "all these things" is "limited to the events leading up to and including the fall of Jerusalem" (*A Commentary on Mark Thirteen* [see above, p. 456, n. 1], p. 100), but W. G. Kümmel, *Promise and Fulfillment* (see above, p. 369, n. 17), p. 60, concludes that the phrase in the context of Mark "designates clearly the whole of the eschatological happenings including the final parousia (Mark 13.26)." However, when separated from its present Marcan context, the verse can also be understood as an isolated saying which, like Mark 9:1, states that some of the men present will witness the

eschaton in their lifetime. V. Taylor, *The Gospel according to St. Mark* (see above, p. 362, n. 34), p. 521, adopts the view that "all these things" refers in Mark to all the events described in verses 5-27, but then allows that in the original form of the saying there could have been a reference to some specific event like the fall of Jerusalem. Jan Lambrecht's minute analysis, in *Die Redaktion der Markus-Apokalypse* (see above, p. 457, n. 1), pp. 207-11, shows convincingly that 13:30 is very much the work of Mark himself, based on Matthew 23:36 ("Truly, I say to you, all this will come upon this generation") and on Mark 9:1, and on the phrase "these things" at Mark 13:29, though it is still not certain to him whether Mark means "all these things" to include the Second Coming or not. Lambrecht, however, then further conjectures (pp. 224-26) that behind Mark 13:30-31 is a form from a Marcan sayings-source (Q^{mk}) which in this instance shows affinities to the saying now found at Matthew 5:17-18, including the phrase "until all is accomplished" (Matthew 5:18). Lambrecht's work makes clear how much of the section stems from Mark, and also how precarious it is to attempt to trace much in this instance back to the historical Jesus with any certainty about its original meaning.

17. G. R. Beasley-Murray, *A Commentary on Mark Thirteen* (see above, p. 456, n. 1), reflects the quandary of the commentators: Luke "is not mistaken" in interpreting it as a reference to the kingdom, but a personal subject (such as Mark has) fits well, and perhaps "the saying originally contained a reference to the Son of man" (p. 97).

18. References to scholars who support this (and other views) are given in V. Taylor, *The Gospel according to St. Mark* (see above, p. 362, n. 34), p. 511, and G. R. Beasley-Murray, *A Commentary on Mark Thirteen* (see above, p. 456, n. 1), pp. 63-66.

19. Eusebius, *Ecclesiastical History* 3. 5. 3.

20. Cf. C. H. Dodd, "The Fall of Jerusalem and the 'Abomination of Desolation,'" *Journal of Roman Studies*, 37 (1947, Festschrift issue for Norman H. Baynes), 47-54. Dodd has sought to argue that the Marcan form (13:14-20) is secondary in comparison with Luke 21: 20-24, which uses many Old Testament phrases and is so general as a description of the fall of a city to an attacking army that it need not be cast aside as a "prophecy after the event" but could go back genuinely to Jesus. Dodd's evidence, that Luke's language here reflects the Septuagint Greek version of the Old Testament, especially in the prophetical books about the fall of Jerusalem in 587 B.C., may, however, suggest to others proof of Lucan redaction, rather than signs of authenticity.

21. Some have speculated that the material or at least some part of it was put together prior to Mark, perhaps in A.D. 40 or before A.D. 68, by Christian prophets as a sort of "fly sheet" or handbill, applying words of Jesus and commands of the risen Christ for the crisis of the day. Thus the theory is that Mark, followed by Matthew and Luke, took over such a collection of already existing apocalyptic material. But final proof for such a view is lacking. Cf. V. Taylor, *The Gospel according to St. Mark* (see above, p. 362, n. 34), pp. 498-99.

22. *The Parables of Jesus* (see above, p. 373, n. 38), rev. ed., pp. 53-55.

23. The verb "must" means "it is necessary, in accord with God's plan." Cf. the article on the Greek verb *"dei"* (which is used at Mark 13:10) by W. Grundmann, in the Kittel *Theological Dictionary* (see above, p. 368, n. 10), Vol. 2, pp. 21-25, where the frequent use of the term in Luke is especially emphasized; or the material in Tödt, *The Son of Man in the Synoptic Tradition* (see above, p. 428, n. 50), pp. 188-93. To be sure, a "plan of God" is not outlined so clearly in the teachings of Jesus as it can be in later biblical theology or as many commentators have often supposed, but the use of the verb *"dei,"* "it is necessary that . . . ," reflects this type of thinking, whether from Jesus himself or the early church. For examples, cf. Mark 8:31; Luke 22:37; 24:44; 19:5; and Acts 2:23. J. Lambrecht's treatment of Mark 13:10, *Die Redaktion der Markus-Apokalypse* (see above, p. 457, n. 1), pp. 129-30, makes clear that the preaching of the Gospel to all men as the absolute priority in the divine plan of salvation is intended.

24. *Through the Valley of the Kwai* (see above, p. 380, n. 67), pp. 58-59, 63, 77-78, 113, 116-38.

25. On Jesus' view of the kingdom as both present and future, see above, pp. 155-57. Cf. W. G. Kümmel, *Promise and Fulfillment* (see above, p. 369, n. 17).

26. Literature on the term "church" in the New Testament period is enormous and continues to grow. Many survey articles, like that by P. S. Minear in *The Interpreter's Dictionary of the Bible* (see above, p. 361, n. 28), Vol. 1, pp. 607-17, "Church, idea of," concentrate quite properly on the material in the books other than the gospels. Basic is the treatment of *ekklēsia* by Karl Ludwig Schmidt in the Kittel *Wörterbuch;* Eng. trans. by J. R. Coates in *Bible Key Words,* 1/II (New York: Harper, 1951), and by G. W. Bromiley in the *Theological Dictionary,* Vol. 3 (1965), pp. 501-36. There is a brief treatment on Jesus and the church in G. Gloege, *The Day of His Coming* (see above, p. 344, n. 26), pp. 242-50, and in G. Bornkamm, *Jesus of Nazareth*

(see above, p. 339, n. 10), pp. 186-88. Cf. in particular R. Newton Flew, *Jesus and His Church: A Study of the Idea of the Ecclesia in the New Testament* (London: Epworth, 1938); W. G. Kümmel, *Kirchenbegriff und Geschichtsbewusstsein in der Urgemeinde und bei Jesus* ("Symbolae Biblicae Upsalienses," 1 [Uppsala, 1943]); George Johnston, *The Doctrine of the Church in the New Testament* (New York: Cambridge University Press, 1943), and an article of the same title in *Peake's Commentary*, (see p. 337, n. 4), rev. ed., pp. 719-23, especially sections 627b-e; and Joseph B. Clower, Jr., *The Church in the Thought of Jesus* (Richmond: John Knox, 1959). Too often, however, in some treatments care has not been taken to distinguish elements which come from the early church from possible authentic material from Jesus. For the current approach, "End-Expectation and Church in Matthew," by Günther Bornkamm, in *Tradition and Interpretation in Matthew* (see above, p. 397, n. 47), pp. 15-51, is suggestive.

27. Many surveys are available on the growth of the early church; cf., for example, the essays on "The History of the Early Church," by E. F. Scott, W. H. P. Hatch, P. S. Minear, and Massey H. Shepherd, Jr., in *The Interpreter's Bible* (New York and Nashville: Abingdon-Cokesbury), Vol. 7 (1951), pp. 176-227; or F. V. Filson, *A New Testament History: The Story of the Emerging Church* (Philadelphia: Westminster, 1964). For an interesting attempt to view the New Testament documents in light of how the early church was coming to self-consciousness of its function and role, cf. C. F. D. Moule, *The Birth of the New Testament* ("Harper's New Testament Commentaries," Companion Volume 1 [New York: Harper and Row, 1962]). For the rise of the church our available sources are all too limited, in the eyes of the historian, to answer many of the questions which can be asked. Acts was written probably about A.D. 90-100, some thirty to sixty years after the events it describes, and is at many points tendentious. Paul's letters tell much about the churches he established, but little about their actual founding or about events between A.D. 30 and 50. The first assemblies of Christians were in Jerusalem and Galilee, then elsewhere in Palestine and Syria. By A.D. 50 or 55 there were local congregations in key cities in Asia Minor and Greece and even Rome. These churches had a sense of being bound together as "the churches of the Messiah" (Galatians 1:22); each was "the church of God" in this place or that (I Corinthians 1:2). We do not know, however, when or precisely how the new faith got to Rome or how it took root in Egypt or in what ways it advanced eastward from Palestine. As with the life of Jesus, there are many gaps in our knowledge of early Christian development.

28. On linguistic background of the biblical terms involved cf. K. L. Schmidt, *"ekklēsia,"* in *Bible Key Words* (see above, p. 460, n. 26), pp. 1-4, 24-31, 57-61; in the *Theological Dictionary* (see above, p. 460, n. 26), Vol. 3, pp. 502-504, 513-17, 530-31.

29. Matthew 18:17 seems a saying of the risen lord, addressed to his church, concerning discipline. The starting point for the development of the little section in 18:15-17 seems to have been a saying on forgiveness (vs. 15) which is also recorded at Luke 17:3. The development in verses 16-17 seems a later step. Cf. R. Bultmann, *The History of the Synoptic Tradition* (see above, p. 373, n. 39), pp. 141, 146, and F. W. Beare, *The Earliest Records of Jesus* (see above, p. 424, n. 45), p. 151, for the view that the passage in Matthew cannot be authentic. G. Gloege, *The Day of His Coming* (see above, p. 344, n. 26), pp. 243-44, reflects those commentators who see an authentic statement of Jesus behind the passage.

30. 1QS 5.25-6.1; cf. CD 9. 3; Eng. trans. in A. Dupont-Sommer, *The Essene Writings from Qumran* (see above, p. 449, n. 112), pp. 84-85, 148, and in G. Vermes, *The Dead Sea Scrolls in English* (see above, pp. 449-50, n. 112), pp. 80, 110. Cf. K. Stendahl, in *Peake's Commentary* (see above, p. 337, n. 4), rev. ed., p. 789, section 688f.

31. On the Caesarea Philippi pericope, see above, pp. 264-65 and 424, especially note 45. The little section of verses 17-19, which seems an insertion in a scene in Matthew 16 which makes good sense without these verses, begins with a beautitude on Simon, son of Jona (vs. 17). We are told that he has perceived something which can be grasped only by revelation. Then follow the commendatory words to Peter, involving a pun between the terms "rock" and "Peter," as the RSV note points out (in Greek, *Petros* and *petra;* in Aramaic, *Cephas* and *cepha*), and the statements about the church and "the keys of the kingdom of heaven." W. G. Kümmel, *Promise and Fulfillment* (see above, p. 369, n. 17), pp. 139-40, feels that verses 18-19 "cannot be considered to belong to the oldest Jesus tradition," and so there can be no question of the kingdom of God as present in a congregation during Jesus' ministry; the kingdom is present only in his person and works. On Matthew 16:17-19 as (part of) an originally independent pericope which Matthew has inserted into the Caesarea Philippi story, cf., in addition to the further references below, Willi Marxsen, *Der "Frühkatholizismus" im Neuen Testament* (Neukirchen: Neukirchener Verlag, 1958), pp. 39-54; and R. H. Fuller, "The 'Thou Art Peter' Pericope and the Easter Appearances," *McCormick Quarterly,* 20, 4 (May, 1967; Festschrift in Honor of Floyd V. Filson), 309-15. On proposals to locate this section in verses 17-19 at some other point, cf. below, pp. 313-14.

32. K. L. Schmidt's article especially stressed the possible Semitic words which might lie behind the Greek *ecclēsia*; cf. *Bible Key Words* (see above, p. 460, n. 26), pp. 46-50, and Kittel's *Theological Dictionary* (see above, p. 368, n. 10), Vol. 3, pp. 524-26. A good summary on Qumran terminology and the importance of the evidence there for establishing that a "church idea" for a group within the Jewish nation could grow up in Jesus' day is provided by G. Johnston, in *Peake's Commentary*, rev. ed. (see above, p. 337, n. 26), pp. 719-20, section 627*b*.

33. 1QH 6. 26; Eng. trans. in A. Dupont-Sommer, *The Essene Writings from Qumran* (see above, p. 449, n. 112), p. 220, and G. Vermes, *The Dead Sea Scrolls in English* (see above, pp. 449-50, n. 112), p. 171. Cf. also H. Ringgren, *The Faith of Qumran* (see above, p. 398, n. 6), p. 202.

34. It is sometimes argued that the Septuagint translators chose *ecclēsia* as a Greek rendering for the Hebrew *qahal* in the Old Testament because of a similarity of sound between the two words (something the Greek translators were at times prone to) ; further that the *qahal* of Yahweh represented the people of God assembled *for worship*, and that thus the New Testament church is to be understood as a direct parallel to the Old Testament in its term and concept of the corporate group. Considerable caution is needed here. The all too frequently overlooked study by J. Y. Campbell, "The Origin and meaning of the Christian use of the word *EKKLESIA*," *Journal of Theological Studies*, 49 (1948), 130-42, now reprinted in *Three New Testament Studies* (see above, p. 433, n. 68), pp. 41-54, has shown that while *ecclēsia* was used to render *qahal* in some Old Testament books like Deuteronomy and Chronicles, in certain other books such as Exodus, Numbers, and Leviticus, *qahal* was translated by a different Greek word, *synagogē*. Thus it is contrary to the facts to claim that Christians employed *ecclēsia* because they regarded themselves as the true people of God, in contrast to the Jewish synagogue which was designated by the term *synagogē*. There is much to be said for Campbell's view that both Greek words simply denoted a "meeting" or "assembly," and could be used by Jews or Christians without fixed meaning in the first century A.D.

35. I take it that the number twelve is what was fixed earliest in the tradition, and that the various lists of names are attempts to piece out the total with twelve names. Even within the twelve, it is to be noted, there is an inner group of three (or four) consisting of Peter (and Andrew), James, and John; cf. Mark 5:37; 9:2; 14:33; and 13:3. Some have compared the fact that at Qumran there was a council of

twelve *plus* three priests, but three within a circle of twelve is not the same as twelve plus three.

36. One ought not to apply the term "apostles" to the twelve during the period of Jesus' ministry, even though Luke has introduced this scene as one where "the apostles" sit at table with Jesus (22:14). Mark never uses the term (3:14 is a later addition). Matthew lets the word slip in just once (10:2). Luke, however, likes to read it back into the earthly ministry (6:13; 9:10; 22:14) just as he does with the term "lord" for Jesus. By New Testament definition an "apostle" is a witness to the resurrection (Acts 1:22; I Corinthians 15:3-9), and the term (which applies to more than "the twelve") can properly be used only after Easter. See above, p. 379, n. 62, and pp. 398-99, n. 8.

37. The number (which was written often in an abbreviated form and could thus more easily suffer change) varies in the manuscripts, as the RSV note on Luke 10:1 and 10:17 indicates. Cf. Bruce M. Metzger, "Seventy or Seventy-two Disciples?" *New Testament Studies,* 5 (1958-59), 299-306. To what extent the circle of seventy-(two) is a Lucan creation continues to be debated.

38. Matthew 27:57 calls Joseph of Arimathea "a disciple of Jesus," but since the parallels in Mark (15:43) and Luke (23:50) describe him simply as a member of the Sanhedrin who was a respected, good, and righteous man, it is not clear precisely how each evangelist was conceiving of his relationship to Jesus, let alone how close Joseph had actually stood to Jesus before the crucifixion.

39. As an example, however, of how complicated the analysis of a "call story" can become, cf. Wilhelm H. Wuellner's treatment on a phrase in the account of the call of Simon and Andrew at Mark 1:17, *The Meaning of "Fishers of Men"* (Philadelphia: Westminster, 1967).

40. Further references in Acts to the term "disciple" include 6:7; 9:19*b*; 13:52; and 19:1. Even in this last passage it is doubtless used in the same way as in the rest of the book, as a technical term for Christians of one sort or another. Strangely, this word which occurs 262 times in the gospels and Acts never appears in Paul, though compare the odd phrase at Ephesians 4:20 which means "learn Christian teaching as a disciple should." Apparently Paul envisioned a different and closer relationship than even that of disciple and master: the follower is now "in Christ," and discipleship has become membership in the body of "the head of the church," Jesus Christ.

41. "Little flock" is actually an Old Testament term, used for the people of Israel (cf. Zechariah 10:3; 13:7-9, the latter a messianic oracle

about a remnant of the people which will be saved). Zechariah 13:7 is cited at Mark 14:27, par. Matthew 26:31, "I will strike the shepherd, and the sheep of the flock will be scattered," but the use of the phrase at Luke 12:32 in an address to disciples remains quite striking. At I Peter 5:2-4 the figure of shepherd and flock is applied to the church. In the Old Testament, the shepherd is, of course, usually God, though at Zechariah 13:7-9 an agent for Yahweh is involved, and in a passage like I Peter 5 the usage roots in Christology. Some scholars would judge the presence of the phrase on the lips of Jesus as a reflection of early Christian usage, while others would defend genuine use by Jesus on the basis of the Old Testament background.

42. See above, p. 278.

43. See above, pp. 185-88, and also the unpublished dissertation by Dan O. Via, Jr., "The Church in Matthew." (Duke, 1955), cited by W. D. Davies, *The Setting of the Sermon on the Mount* (see above, p. 401, n. 14), pp. 98-99.

44. See above, pp. 216.

45. The figure of the "stone" or "rock" at Matthew 16:18 has a rich Old Testament background. Isaiah 28:16 speaks of God's laying a "foundation stone" (a phrase used of Christ in New Testament). Isaiah 8:14 boldly refers to God himself as a "rock of stumbling" (or "scandal"), over which people will stumble and be tripped up. At I Peter 2:6 and 8 these Isaiah verses are combined: Christ is either the foundation stone for life, or men stumble and fall because of him. Romans 9:32-33 combines the same two verses. At Matthew 16:18 and 23 we seem to have the same two images of the "stone" applied to Peter: obedient and confessing, he is a "rock" which God can use; disobedient and denying, he is a "hindrance" or "stumbling-block." These two possibilities, it is implied, always face every disciple.

46. The traditional Roman Catholic exegesis of Matthew 16:18 has been that Peter personally is the rock on which the church is built, while the traditional Protestant interpretation has held that his faith, expressed in the confession, "You are the Christ," is the rock on which the community is built. However the matter is not so simple as either side supposed, for, on the one hand, Peter the rock crumbles (verse 22), and, on the other, the community in which verses 17-19 were developed surely intended some prominence to be implied for Peter in the narrative (though Matthew has undercut this significance by having *all* the disciples make an earlier confession as to who Jesus is at 14:33). Hence the attempt to do justice to the meaning of the text in the formulation above. The rock of foundation is Peter-when-he-

confesses-Christ (the confessor and the confession being both involved), just as in verses 22-23 Peter-when-he-offends-Christ is a "rock
of stumbling" in Matthew's presentation. The dividing lines among
exegetes are by no means confessionally bounded any more; cf. G.
Bornkamm, *Jesus of Nazareth* (see above, p. 339, n. 10), p. 214, n. 12.
There are, of course, those who still view Christ as the rock on which
the church is built; cf. O. J. F. Seitz, "Upon this Rock: A Critical
Re-examination of Matt 16:17-19," *Journal of Biblical Literature*, 69
(1950), 329-40, and *One Body and One Spirit: A Study of the Church
in the New Testament* (Greenwich, Connecticut: Seabury, 1960), pp.
78-83; or G. A. F. Knight, " 'Thou Art Peter,' " *Theology Today*, 17
(1960), 168-80. Contrast the position of other Protestants, however,
like E. Stauffer: Peter "is the rock, and he alone" (*New Testament
Theology* [see above, p. 428, n. 49], p. 33). Of great influence in molding a change in attitude in this matter has been the work of Oscar
Cullmann, especially in his book *Peter* (see above, p. 425, n. 45). Cullmann's position has been that Peter is himself the rock, but that his is
a unique position as the first person to confess Jesus as Christ and there
are no successors to Peter in his role as eyewitness or first confessor,
for the testimony of the eyewitnesses passes into the New Testament
scriptures, and each disciple who makes the confession "You are the
Christ" is then built by God into his own historical position in the
church. So far as Peter's leadership role went, Cullmann contends, Peter
turned this over to James in Jerusalem when he left the Holy City to
engage in missionary work; there was no primacy which Peter could
carry with him to Rome or anywhere else (pp. 212-17).

47. Note that it is Jesus, not men, who will do the building, and that
he speaks of "my church" (based on revelation and the confession of
what has been revealed) in contrast to all other groups. But what he
will build, Jesus does not describe as a "temple" (which would be built
of stone) or even as a "house" (built on rock as at Matthew 7:24),
but in terms of an "assembly" or "community"—that is, something
living and developing. The term is sociological and shifts from the
metaphor of rock and building. Perhaps such a combination of figures
of speech helps account for a passage like Ephesians 2:19-22, where
the church is likened to a temple, built on the foundation of apostles
and prophets, with Christ as cornerstone, but with the entire structure
described as "growing," like a body or organism. A final figure in verse
18 which attracts attention is "the powers of death" which, Jesus says,
will not prevail against his church. The phrase is literally the "gates of
Hades." The abode of the dead is regarded as having doors—to which
Jesus, crucified and risen, is regarded as holding the keys (cf. Revelation 1:18). It is not clear in Matthew 16:18 whether Hades is regarded

as still on the "offensive" against God's people, as the NEB rendering suggests, or on the defensive against the church (so J. B. Phillips), but the victory is assured by Jesus.

48. So Cullmann, *Peter* (see above, p. 425, n. 45), pp. 209-12, who suggests that verse 19*a* (about the keys; see the previous note) and 19*b* (about binding and loosing) may once have been separate sayings which are here in a new context. On "keys," cf. J. Jeremias, *"kleis,"* in Kittel's *Theological Dictionary* (see above, p. 368, n. 10), Vol. 3, pp. 744-53; and on "binding and loosing," cf. C. H. Dodd, "Some Johannine 'Herrenworte' with Parallels in the Synoptic Gospels," *New Testament Studies*, 2 (1955-56), 75-86. Usually to "bind" and to "loose" denote, against the background in rabbinic usage, juridical authority, to forbid and permit, or the imposition and removal of a ban. But the reference here can also be, in light of 19*a*, to the keys to the underworld which Jesus is depicted (in Revelation 1:18) as having taken from death and Hades. Hence the power of the keys would seem to be not legislative or judicial authority but exclusion or admission to membership on the basis of the community's confession; cf. John 20:23: "If you forgive the sins of any, they are forgiven; if you retain the sins of any, they are retained." To "loose" or forgive sins is to admit to the community; to bind or retain them has to do with excluding a man from the fellowship of the church. R. H. Fuller, "The 'Thou Art Peter' Pericope (see above, p. 462, n. 31), pp. 312-13, argues that in these verses there was originally a kerygmatic reference which Matthew has transformed into a disciplinary one.

49. Cullmann, *Peter* (see above, p. 425, n. 45), p. 186, n. 84, lists some of the scholars, Roman Catholics among them, who have accepted all or part of his view on this point. One reason for sensing that 16:17-19 did not originally belong in its present context is the fact that in the Greek of verse 17, "flesh and blood has not revealed *this* to you," there is no word for "this." In the Matthean context the revelation refers to what Peter has just confessed (verse 16, "You are the Christ"), but the revelation may originally have been something else—for example, that Jesus was risen and alive (cf. Luke 24:34).

50. Cf. above, pp. 425-26, n. 45. E. Stauffer, *New Testament Theology* (see above, p. 428, n. 49), p. 31, suggested that the verses belonged originally to a story of the risen Jesus' first Easter appearance; cf. Cullmann, *Peter* (see above, p. 425, n. 45), pp. 186-87, and, in a popular vein, James McLeman, *The Birth of the Christian Faith* (Edinburgh: Oliver and Boyd, 1962) and *Resurrection Then and Now* (Philadelphia: Lippincott, 1967). A post-Easter setting for the verses is also assumed by Bultmann and Bornkamm, among others. Cullmann himself has

championed a setting for the verses in the Upper Room. Behind Matthew 16:17-19, Luke 22:31-34; John 6:66 ff., and some of the content
in John 21 he conjectures a common source, now lost, which told of
how at the Last Supper or immediately thereafter Peter confessed
Jesus as Son of God and promised to follow him to the death; Jesus
answered that God had given Peter this revelation concerning himself, and he then foretold Peter's denial but at the same time added
that Peter would be given a special task to fulfill with disciples who
would fall into the same temptation (*Peter* [see above, p. 425, n. 45],
pp. 188-91). W. Trilling, *Das wahre Israel* (see above, p. 407, n. 46),
pp. 131-37, assumes that Matthew 16:17-19 has been taken over from
earlier tradition and inserted at its present point by Matthew, but
Trilling does not go into the question of any "original" setting. He
does, however, stress the connection of Matthew's idea of the church
in these verses with his theme at 21:43 that the people of God (the
church) must be a nation bringing forth fruits of the kingdom, and
also the fact that Peter is a "type" presentation of the disciple.

51. So E. Stauffer, *New Testament Theology* (see above, p. 428, n. 49),
p. 34; *Jesus and His Story* (see above, p. 341, n. 16), British ed. pp.
122-23, U.S. ed. pp. 147-50. That the traditions in Matthew stem
from Jewish-Christianity in many cases, including this one, is obvious.
Whether the tradition about Peter at 16:17-19 came from some unknown community in northern Palestine, Phoenicia, or Syria, or developed in Antioch itself, where, it may be presumed (for want of
better evidence) Matthew's Gospel was composed, we cannot say.
What is to be emphasized is that the thought in these verses, wherever
they arose, was treasured in the community of Matthew and was directed, not against Paul or in favor of Rome, but against James and in
behalf of the apostle revered in Matthew's church (in Antioch).
Stauffer probably goes too far in his picture of James—Paul is
hounded by "secret agents" from James and must "eat crow" when
he appears before James, much as Henry IV had to at Canossa before
Pope Hildebrand—but Stauffer's references to a "Christian caliphate,"
whereby the family of Jesus set up a dynasty in the Jerusalem church
(references to ancient sources in *The Interpreter's Dictionary of the
Bible* article on "James," Vol. 2, p. 793) deserve some consideration.
Cf. H. von Campenhausen, "The Authority of Jesus' Relatives in the
Early Church," in H. von Campenhausen and H. Chadwick, *Jerusalem
and Rome* ("Facet Books, Historical Series," 4 [Philadelphia: Fortress
Press, 1966]), pp. 1-19, who reaches a negative conclusion on the
point, however. In Matthew, Peter is being projected into prominence
against the leadership of James. One indirect reflection of a rivalry
between Peter and James may be seen in I Corinthians 15, where there

seem to be two separate lists of resurrection appearances, the first headed by the solo epiphany to Cephas (Peter, 15:5), and the other headed by an appearance to James (15:7).

52. Space does not permit consideration of the varieties of structure and life which grew up in the early church and their possible connections with the historical ministry of Jesus. Cf., however, Eduard Schweitzer, *Lordship and Discipleship* ("Studies in Biblical Theology," 28 [London: SCM Press, 1960]) ; and *Church Order in the New Testament* ("Studies in Biblical Theology," 32 [London: SCM Press, 1961]).

53. Ignatius, *Ephesians* 20. 2.

54. Mark 16:16 in the "Long Ending" takes the same view as Matthew 28, that baptism is a post-Easter institution. The fact that at Matthew 28:19 baptism is commanded to be "in the name of the Father and of the Son and of the Holy Spirit" suggests that the formulation here is the result of experience and development considerably after Easter, for according to the book of Acts the earliest baptisms were simply "in the name of Jesus Christ" (Acts 2:38; 10:48). At first, apparently, only the distinctive Christian feature, "the name of Jesus Christ," was stressed; eventually the full formula reported by Matthew at 28:19 became normative. Cf. G. R. Beasley-Murray, *Baptism in the New Testament* (New York: St Martin's Press, 1962), pp. 77-92.

55. Unless one wishes to posit an Aramaic source underlying John 4:2 which said something such as "Jesus did not baptize [any] but his disciples," which was then taken to mean, "Jesus did not baptize, but his disciples did." R. E. Brown, *The Gospel according to John* (*i-xii*) (see above, p. 362, n. 32), p. 164, sees in 4:2 evidence for the presence of several hands in the Fourth Gospel: 4:2 is an attempt to undo any notion possibly arising from 3:22 that Jesus was merely imitative of John the Baptist at this point. Cf. further G. R. Beasley-Murray, *Baptism in the New Testament* (see above, p. 469, n. 54), pp. 67-72.

56. See R. E. Brown, *ibid.*, p. 151, for the view that such baptisms during Jesus' ministry were not yet Christian baptism, and pp. 141-44 for discussion of 3:5, including Bultmann's theory that the passage referred originally only to birth from the Spirit, the words "of water" being a later insertion.

57. The standard treatment is Joseph Thomas, *Le Mouvement Baptiste en Palestine et Syrie* (*150 avant Jesus-Christ—300 après Jesus-Christ*) (Catholic University of Louvain Dissertations, Series II, Vol. 28 [Gembloux, Belgium, 1935]).

58. A background for baptism in the symbolic actions of the Old Testament prophets has been suggested by H. Wheeler Robinson, for example; references and summary in W. F. Flemington, *The New Testament Doctrine of Baptism* (London: SPCK, 1948), pp. 20-22.

59. Cf. N. Dahl, "The Origin of Baptism," *Norsk Teologisk Tidsskrift*, 56 (1955), 36ff. (as noted in G. Bornkamm, *Jesus of Nazareth* [see above, p. 339, n. 10], p. 198, n. 32), reprinted in *Interpretationes ad Vetus Testamentum Pertinentes Sigmundo Mowinckel septuagenario missae* (Oslo, 1955), pp. 36-52.

60. For descriptions of proselyte baptism from the sources, cf. W. F. Flemington, *Baptism* (see above, p. 470, n. 58), pp. 4-11; and K. Lake in *The Beginnings of Christianity* (London: Macmillan) Vol. 5 (1933), pp. 78-79. The relation of proselyte baptism to John's baptism is discussed in Flemington, pp. 15-20. Among scholars who seem to have preferred this background are C. H. Kraeling, T. W. Manson, H. G. Marsh, J. Jeremias, and O. Cullmann, and especially, even since the discovery of the Qumran material, H. H. Rowley (references in the notes below).

61. Cf. J. Jeremias, "Der Ursprung der Johannestaufe," *Zeitschrift für die neutestamentliche Wissenschaft*, 28 (1929), 312-20.

62. For example, W. H. Brownlee, "John the Baptist in the New Light of Ancient Scrolls," *Interpretation*, 9 (1955), 71-90, reprinted with revision in *The Scrolls and the New Testament* (see above, p. 337, n. 4), pp. 33-53; or J. A. T. Robinson, "The Baptism of John and the Qumran Community," *Harvard Theological Review*, 50 (1957), 175-91, reprinted in *Twelve New Testament Studies* (see above, p. 411, n. 69), pp. 11-27. Contrast H. H. Rowley, "The Baptism of John and the Qumran Sect," in *New Testament Essays* (T. W. Manson volume) (see above, p. 399, n. 10), pp. 218-29; and "Jewish Proselyte Baptism and the Baptism of John" (originally in the *Hebrew Union College Annual*, 15 [1940], pp. 313-34), and "The Qumran Sect and Christian Origins" (*Bulletin of the John Rylands Library*, 44 [1961-62], pp. 119-56), now in *From Moses to Qumran: Studies in the Old Testament* (New York: Association Press, 1963), pp. 211-35, 239-79. Cf. H. Ringgren, *The Faith of Qumran* (see above, p. 398, n. 6), p. 245. Further: O. Betz, "Die Proselytentaufe der Qumransekte und die Taufe im Neuen Testament," *Revue de Qumrán*, 1 (1958-59), 213-34. On the archeological evidence at Qumran, including photos and full data on the cisterns, cf. R. North, S. J., "The Qumran Resevoirs," in *The Bible in Current Catholic Thought*, ed. J. L. McKenzie, S.J. (M. J. Gruenthaner memorial volume; New York: Herder and Herder, 1962), pp. 100-32.

For a recent summary and assessment, cf. G. R. Beasley-Murray, *Baptism in the New Testament* (see above, p. 469, n. 54), pp. 1-44.

63. While there are references concerning initiatory baths in the ancient sources *about* the Essenes, for example in Josephus, *Jewish War*, 2. 137-38 (in Barrett's *The New Testament Background* [see above, p. 341, n. 9], p. 125), the Qumran texts themselves, apparently *by* the Essenes, provide few such references. That at 1QS 5. 13 is the one usually cited, for example by J. A. T. Robinson (see above, p. 470, n. 62). This reference, to "entering into water," is equated by many with "entering into the covenant," 5. 8, and thus is regarded as an initiation rite. H. H. Rowley, "The Baptism of John and the Qumran Sect" (see above, p. 470, n. 62), pp. 219-23, objects that (1) the context of 5. 13 makes repentance, not a water rite, decisive when it says, "No one is to go into water, . . . men cannot be purified except they repent of their evil"; and (2) there are significant differences between what existed at Qumran and what John the Baptist instituted—John's baptism seems to have been unrepeatable, while the ablution at Qumran was merely one in a series of washings; at Qumran the candidate presumably washed himself, whereas John's baptism was administered by the Baptizer; John's rite was public, Qumran's private; and John seems to have had no period of probation, while Qumran required a long and formal one. Rowley's arguments, coupled with North's careful examination of the archeological evidence (see above, p. 470, n. 62), should make one think twice before accepting some of the popular pictures which have been disseminated depicting Qumran as the direct source for baptism by John or in early Christianity.

64. Again, some of the popular accounts have gone far beyond the evidence. For substantial treatment on John, cf. (prior to the Qumran finds) Carl H. Kraeling, *John the Baptist* (New York: Scribner's, 1951); since Qumran: Jean Steinmann, *St. John the Baptist and the Desert Tradition*, trans. Michael Boyes (New York: Harper, 1958), which seeks to link Qumran with later Christian monasticism; Jean Daniélou, *Jean-Baptiste: Témoin de l'Agneau* (Paris: Editions du Seuil, 1964); and Charles H. H. Scobie, *John the Baptist* (Philadelphia: Fortress Press, 1964), now the most convenient presentation for the average reader. John and the baptism he practiced are, of course, treated in such standard handbooks as O. Cullmann, *Baptism in the New Testament*, trans. J. K. S. Reid ("Studies in Biblical Theology," 1 [London: SCM Press, 1950]); H. G. Marsh, *The Origin and Significance of Baptism* (Manchester: Manchester University Press, 1941); and G. R. Beasley-Murray, *Baptism in the New Testament* (see above, p. 469, n. 54). [Daniélou's treatment has been translated by J. A. Horn, under

the title, *The Work of John the Baptist* (Baltimore: Helicon, 1966).]

65. Hebrews 4:15 describes Jesus as "tempted as we are, yet without sinning." Mark's prologue scarcely means to suggest that Jesus was a sinner who needed to be baptized, for Mark has presented him as the Son of God (verse 1), with whom God is well pleased (1:11). The *Gospel of the Hebrews* felt the problem of Jesus' baptism so keenly, however, that it has Jesus say, "In what have I sinned that I should go and be baptized by him [John]? Unless, perhaps, what I have just said is a sin of ignorance."

66. The fact that Jesus was baptized by John "embarrassed the early Church" (C. E. B. Cranfield, *The Gospel according to Saint Mark* [see above, p. 352, n. 31], p. 51). O. Cullmann has dealt with the problem in his essay on the phrase "he who comes after me," entitled (from the Greek of Matthew 3:11) *"ho opisō mou erchomenos," The Early Church* (see above, p. 362, n. 40), pp. 175-82. Another solution for the relationship between the Baptist and Jesus has been advanced by J. A. T. Robinson, in "Elijah, John, and Jesus: An Essay in Detection," *New Testament Studies*, 4 (1957-58), 263-81, reprinted in *Twelve New Testament Studies* (see above, p. 411, n. 69), pp. 28-52. Robinson supposes that (1) John the Baptist, following the sort of sequence advanced in Malachi 4:5 (according to which Elijah the messenger would one day appear, whereupon would follow the "Day of Yahweh"), identified Jesus as the Elijah figure whose appearance heralded the coming of God, while identifying himself as a mere voice in the wilderness (Isaiah 40); but (2) Jesus opened John's eyes to see that he, the Baptist, was really the Elijah figure, and that Jesus' coming therefore was a claim to something greater: Jesus is no mere Elijah but represents the eschatological coming of the Day of the Lord itself. Thus, in showing John who he was, Jesus was also making a claim for himself. The view depends on the historicity of Matthew 11:14-15, where Jesus identifies John as Elijah.

67. On the baptism, cf. further above, p. 283, especially p. 445, n. 99.

68. There are, of course, innumerable treatments of the Lord's Supper in the New Testament, many of them concerned with aspects outside the gospels and apart from the question of origins in Jesus' ministry. The most important recent treatments for our purpose are probably Joachim Jeremias, *The Eucharistic Words of Jesus*, trans. Norman Perrin (rev. ed.; New York: Scribner's, 1966), with extensive bibliography in the footnotes; and Eduard Schweizer, *The Lord's Supper According to the New Testament*, trans. James M. Davis (a revision of the article "Abendmahl im Neuen Testament," in the third edition of *Die Religion*

in Geschichte und Gegenwart; "Facet Books, Biblical Series," 18 [Philadelphia: Fortress Press, 1967]), with lengthy bibliography on pp. 39-45.

69. Cf. above, p. 53. In general the nineteenth century preferred the view of the Synoptics that Jesus and his disciples ate a Passover meal together and that Jesus died after that. More recent scholarship has often inclined to the view of John's Gospel, that Jesus died just as the Passover lambs were being sacrificed at the temple and thus prior to the eating of the Passover meal. The book by Professor Jeremias, *The Eucharistic Words of Jesus* (see above, p 472, n. 68), has persuaded some scholars back to the Synoptics' view; cf. A. J. B. Higgins, *The Lord's Supper in the New Testament* ("Studies in Biblical Theology," 6 [London: SCM Press, 1952]). There has, of course, always been a desire to harmonize the Synoptic and Johannine chronologies, and since the discovery of the Dead Sea Scrolls there have been weighty theories advanced which would explain the differences on the basis of the use of two calendars, one solar and the other lunar; on this reading of the evidence, Jesus would have celebrated a "Passover" of his own that night in the Upper Room (perhaps Tuesday evening, according to a calendar also used at Qumran) but he would have died on Passover eve (on Friday afternoon) according to the official calendar (so John). Cf. J. Finegan, *Handbook of Biblical Chronology* (see above, p. 340, n. 5), pp. 285-301, especially section 449; and George Ogg, "The Chronology of the Last Supper," in *Historicity and Chronology in the New Testament* ("SPCK Theological Collections," 6 [London: SPCK, 1965]), pp. 75-96. There is no completely satisfactory solution of this chronological problem. One is left with the fact that the Synoptics equate the *meal* with the Passover and John parallels Jesus' *death* with the Passover; both see symbolic meaning, but along different lines.

70. Jeremias, *Eucharistic Words* (see above, p. 472, n. 68), pp. 125-37, deals with "the protection of the sacred formula," and espouses the view that John omits any account of the institution in order to protect the sacred text (p. 136). But in his own way John tells far more about the sacrament and its meaning than any repetition of the words of institution would; cf. C. K. Barrett, *The Gospel according to St John* (London: SPCK, 1955), pp. 42, 71.

71. Cf. E. C. Colwell and E. L. Titus, *The Gospel of the Spirit* (New York: Harper, 1953), and E. L. Titus, *The Message of the Fourth Gospel* (New York: Abingdon, 1957). This emphasis does balance, however, the tendency in O. Cullmann, *Early Christian Worship*, trans. A. S. Todd and J. B. Torrance ("Studies in Biblical Theology," 10

[London: SCM Press, 1953]), to see sacraments throughout the Fourth Gospel. R. E. Brown, *The Gospel According to John* (*i-xii*) (see above, p. 362, n. 32), pp. cxi-cxiv, offers a mediating view.

72. Ignatius, *Ephesians* 20. 2, cited above, p. 469, n. 53. Cf. E. L. Titus, *The Message of the Fourth Gospel* (see above, p. 473, n. 71), pp. 26 and 182-87.

73. I Corinthians 11:23-26 should be read in light of the problem in Corinth discussed in verses 17-22, and of the concluding advice, especially in verses 33-34. Verses 23-25 embody a pre-Pauline tradition, often similar to the tradition later written down in the Synoptic accounts, but also with features not found in the Synoptics, including the words "Do this in remembrance of me" (verses 24-25) and the connection with the cross and the parousia (verse 26).

74. Later scribes, disturbed by this rough formula, often added some word such as "broken for" (RSV note) or "given for you."

75. The commandment, "Do this in remembrance of me," could go back to Jesus or could have arisen out of the actual performance of the rite in the early church, the formulation then being read back onto the lips of Jesus. Cf. Jeremias, *Eucharistic Words* (see above, p. 472, n. 68), pp. 237-55, and also the discussion on the institution of the Lord's Supper in E. Lohse, *History of the Suffering and Death of Jesus Christ* (see above, p. 371, n. 22), pp. 35-54. The reply is often made that the Synoptics omit these clauses because one does not recite a rubric, one performs it. Jeremias has adduced reasons for tracing the clauses back to Palestine, rather than attributing it to development in the Hellenistic church as a parallel to formulas employed at commemorative meals for the dead, but I do not find myself convinced by his theory that the words mean "Do this in order that God may remember me"; on that point, cf. D. Jones, *"Anamnēsis* in the LXX and the Interpretation of 1 Cor. xi. 25," *Journal of Theological Studies,* New Series 6 (1955), 183-91. There is doubtless development in the early church of the words of institution and the rubrics and comments attached to them, but it is rash to believe that we can always pinpoint the origin of each phrase, either with the historical Jesus or in some particular segment of the church.

76. So Jeremias, *Eucharistic Words* (see above, p. 472, n. 68), pp. 139-59, and E. Schweizer, *The Lord's Supper* (see above, p. 472, n. 68), p. 19. The preference of the RSV and NEB for the "shorter text" gives at this point a somewhat reverse picture of the scholarly consensus. An interesting example of what this position can lead to, when the shorter text is championed vigorously, is the conclusion of

R. D. Richardson, that not only Luke 22:19b-20 but also I Corinthians 11:23-26 are interpolations from the second century; see his "Supplementary Essay. A Further Inquiry into Eucharistic Origins with Special Reference to New Testament Problems," in the English edition of Hans Lietzmann's *Mass and Lord's Supper,* trans. Dorothea H. G. Reeve (Leiden: Brill, 1953-   ), pp. 217 ff.

77. E. Schweizer's essay, *The Lord's Supper* (see above, p. 472, n. 68), provides a convenient place to check, through the references in its footnotes, the degree of acceptance accorded by scholars to the various views advanced in Jeremias' *Eucharistic Words.* For a specific example, see below, note 79.

78. F. W. Beare, *The Earliest Records of Jesus* (see above, p. 424, n. 45), pp. 224-25. Beare's position is by no means self-evident, however, that the Passion narrative from the beginning, let alone the kerygma, included an account of the Upper Room. Cf. above, pp. 46-47, 50-52, and 54. We have preferred the position of the form critics, that "the tradition about the Last Supper . . . was preserved and passed down by the early Christians in connection with the celebration of the Lord's Supper in the worship services of the church" and not in the framework originally of a full Passion account (E. Lohse, *History of the Suffering and Death of Jesus Christ* [see above, p. 371, n. 22], p. 35).

79. Various solutions have been advanced as to precisely what Jesus said in the Upper Room. Some see "the covenant" as the basic idea, others the phrase "for you," others a precise parallelism involving "This is my body" and "This is my blood" as the oldest form of the words of institution. Jeremias, *Eucharistic Words* (see above, p. 472, n. 68), concludes that there are two independent versions in the New Testament, the Marcan and the Pauline-Lucan, derived from a common eucharistic tradition which was formulated in Aramaic or Hebrew; the Marcan form he pronounces to be nearest to the original Semitic tradition which goes back to the first decade after the death of Jesus (pp. 186-89). The oldest form of the tradition which Jeremias regards as attainable runs, "(Take), this is my body (or flesh), this (is) my blood of the covenant (or the covenant in my blood) which . . . for many" (p. 173). On pp. 218-37 he attempts to expound what Jesus meant in these words. Schweizer, *The Lord's Supper* (see above, p. 472, n. 68), pp. 12-17, decides that the Pauline form is closer than the Marcan to the original.

80. It is beyond the scope of this book to attempt to deal with the development of the Lord's Supper after Easter in the early church.

However, the following broad survey may be helpful in further suggesting how there was development which grew out of facets of Jesus' ministry, amplified after the resurrection. The disciples had been accustomed to meals with Jesus during his ministry, meals not only involving their own small group, but also larger crowds (cf. the feeding miracles), and fellowship meals where outcasts, publicans, and sinners of all sorts were freely accepted. Then the last meal together before his death when Jesus gave a new meaning to the idea of redemption and covenant made an especial impression on them. After the resurrection, meals with the risen lord are also reported. The earliest Christians seem to have regarded each meal as a time of rejoicing with the exalted Christ (Acts 2:42, 46-47). The practice grew up of having common meals together, at which special prayers recalled Jesus' death, invoked his presence, and looked forward to his coming again. Salvation and judgment were brought home to each participant. In the forties and fifties the form of service involved one "word" of Jesus over the bread before supper, another over the cup after the meal (I Corinthians 11:25). In time the meal dropped out and the words over bread and cup were spoken side by side. This abbreviation of the original setting within a meal led to a concentration on "elements" of bread and wine and eventually, in the Greek world, on theories to explain "what happened" in philosophical terms. Among the recent discussions which emphasize a variety of origins and influences from the ministry of Jesus and the work of the risen Christ on eucharistic development, besides the traditional approach which traces everything to the Upper Room, cf. O. Cullmann and F. J. Leenhardt, *Essays on the Lord's Supper*, trans. J. G. Davies ("Ecumenical Studies in Worship," 1 [Richmond: John Knox Press, 1958]); R. H. Fuller, "The Double Origin of the Eucharist," *Biblical Research*, 8 (1963), 3-15; and C. W. Dugmore, "The Study of the Origin of the Eucharist: Retrospect and Revaluation," in *Studies in Church History*, Vol. 2, ed. G. J. Cuming (New York: Nelson, 1965), pp. 1-18.

81. Note the phrase at I Corinthians 11:25 (between the bread and cup words), "after supper."

82. On "covenant," cf. G. Quell and J. Behm, *"diatithēmi, diathēkē,"* in the Kittel *Theological Dictionary* (see above, p. 368, n. 10), Vol. 2, pp. 104-34; G. E. Mendenhall, "Covenant," *The Interpreter's Dictionary of the Bible* (see above, p. 361, n. 28), Vol. 1, pp. 714-23; and W. Eichrodt, *Theology of the Old Testament*, trans. J. A. Baker (Philadelphia: Westminster, 1961), Vol. 1, pp. 36-69. For a theme so common in the Old Testament, "covenant" is, however, comparatively rare in the New. It is featured in Hebrews (cf. 8:6-13;

9:11-22) and by Paul at Galatians 3:15-18; 4:21-28; and II Corinthians 3:4-18 (where the argument is that Christ has fulfilled the promises made to Abraham and has replaced the old "dispensation" made with Moses by a new "arrangement" brought about through grace and characterized by the presence of the Spirit). Perhaps the fact that the term "covenant" had legal and legalistic connotations in the world of the day caused New Testament writers to shy away from it.

83. Cf. above, pp. 321-23, especially p. 475, n. 79, where it has been indicated how difficult it is to be sure about precisely what Jesus said in the Upper Room. The adjective "new" with "covenant" occurs only in I Corinthians 11, the long text of Luke, and in some later manuscripts of Mark and Matthew (RSV note), and stems from Jeremiah 31:31-34; it is likely an accretion to the words of institution in the early church's development of the meaning of the sacrament, in light of the Old Testament scriptures. Though Jeremias stresses the atoning death of Jesus in connection with the words of institution ("for many"; *Eucharistic Words* [see above, p. 472, n. 68], pp. 220-31), he does see the covenant as a part of the oldest formula (pp. 173, 225). Schweizer, *The Lord's Supper* (see above, p. 472, n. 68), emphasizes the covenant to a much greater degree (pp. 2, 12, 16) and cites other commentators who make it central (p. 16, n. 42).

84. F. J. A. Hort wrote, "the Twelve sat that evening as representatives of the Ecclesia at large," and he added, "they were disciples more than they were Apostles" (*The Christian Ecclesia* [London: Macmillan, 1900], p. 30). K. L. Schmidt: "the so-called institution of the Lord's Supper can be shown to be the formal founding of the Church" (*Bible Key Words, The Church* [see above, p. 460, n. 26], p. 40); Kittel *Theological Dictionary* (see above, p. 368, n. 10), Vol. 3, p. 521. A list of scholars who have traced the formation of the Christian community to Jesus' last meal with his disciples is given by W. G. Kümmel, *Promise and Fulfillment* (see above, p. 369, n. 17), p. 138 n, 121, though Kümmel himself rejects the idea that Jesus saw a formal congregation in the circle of disciples (p. 139).

85. The accounts in all four gospels about the Upper Room depict Jesus announcing his coming death (Mark 14:21, 25; Matthew 26:24, 29; Luke 22:15; John 13:33). The Last Supper thus looks forward to the cross, while the Lord's Supper looks back to it in the New Testament records. Hebrews 9:18-20 and 13-14 show how one New Testament writer connected the themes of cross and covenant. Some expositors, notably Cullmann in *Early Christian Worship* (see above, p. 473 n. 71) think that John has woven a reference to the two sacraments into the crucifixion scene itself: namely, that the "blood and

water" which come forth from Jesus' side on the cross symbolize the Lord's Supper and baptism (19:34). Cf. on the point E. Schweizer, *The Lord's Supper* (see above, p. 472, n. 68), pp. 7-9.

86. O. Cullmann, *Baptism in the New Testament* (see above, p. 471, n. 64), p. 23. J. A. T. Robinson, "The One Baptism," *Scottish Journal of Theology,* 6 (1953), 257-74, reprinted in *Twelve New Testament Studies* (see above, p. 411, n. 69), pp. 158-75.

87. On "the Spirit," cf. E. W. Winstanley, *Spirit in the New Testament* (Cambridge: Cambridge University Press, 1908), for a convenient assembly of passages and statistics; H. B. Swete, *The Holy Spirit in the New Testament* (London: Macmillan, 1909), pp. 11-62, 113-28; E. F. Scott, *The Spirit in the New Testament* (New York: George H. Doran Company, 1923); J. E. Fison, *The Blessing of the Holy Spirit* (New York: Longmans, Green and Company, 1950); William Barclay, *The Promise of the Spirit* (London: Epworth, 1960); C. K. Barrett, *The Holy Spirit and the Gospel Tradition* (London: SPCK, 1947), probably the most important study in English for the topic at hand; the Kittel *Wörterbuch* article by Eduard Schweizer and others, trans. with some omissions by A. E. Harvey, *Bible Key Words, 9: Spirit of God* (London: A. & C. Black, 1960); and G. W. H. Lampe, "Holy Spirit," *The Interpreter's Dictionary of the Bible* (see above, p. 361, n. 28), Vol. 2, pp. 626-39.

88. The NEB interpretation of II Corinthians 3 is to be preferred over that implied in the RSV. Examined in light of Exodus 33-34, the NEB rendering suggests that the "Lord" who "is the Spirit" now for the Christian community is to be identified with Yahweh who appeared on the mountain to Israel; a flat equation of Jesus with the Holy Spirit is not intended in the II Corinthians passage.

89. Luke makes it quite clear that Jesus promised to send the Spirit (Acts 1:4-5), but it is not completely clear when Jesus made this promise. Luke 24:49 attributes it to the risen Christ on Easter day. A saying at Luke 11:13 says "the heavenly Father will give the Holy Spirit to those who ask [in prayer]"; that statement is placed during the historical ministry, though the parallel in Matthew 7:11 omits any reference to the Holy Spirit at this point. John 14-16 has the promise made during the ministry but in private to the disciples in the Upper Room, not in the course of public teaching. A conclusion is that Jesus Christ promised the Spirit to his disciples, probably in private, perhaps only after the resurrection. The Spirit's coming was not, then, part of Jesus' public teaching, though some contemporaries might have inferred, on the basis of the Old Testament background, that the Spirit was about to come or was beginning to be active through Jesus.

90. Some scholars have argued for a background in the Hellenistic world for the New Testament doctrine of the Holy Spirit. H. Leisegang, for example, in his book *Pneuma Hagion* ("Veröffentlichungen des Forschungsinstituts für vergleichende Religionsgeschichte an der Universität Leipzig," 4 [1922]) held that the concept of the Spirit in the Synoptic Gospels should be traced back to Greek mysticism. Hans Windisch, "Jesus und der Geist nach synoptischer Überlieferung," in *Studies in Early Christianity*, ed. Shirley Jackson Case, presented to F. C. Porter and B. W. Bacon (New York: The Century Company, 1928), pp. 209-36, claimed that the Synoptic tradition originally contained much more material which portrayed Jesus as a "man of the Spirit," a *Pneumatiker*, but that the church removed many such references from the tradition, while inserting its own ideas about the Spirit; thus Windisch held that sayings about the Spirit as they now stand in the gospels are not authentic. In general, Anglo-Saxon scholarship has refused to go along with such radical positions; cf. C. K. Barrett, *The Holy Spirit* (see above, p. 478, n. 87), pp. 3-4, 117. The Qumran texts, with their frequent references to "spirit," "Spirit of God," or even "holy spirit," have put the matter in a far different light than previously, and the case for Semitic backgrounds is now greatly strengthened. On the Dead Sea scrolls, cf. H. Ringgren, *The Faith of Qumran* (see above, p. 398, n. 6), pp. 87-90; and E. Schweizer, *Spirit of God* (see above, p. 478, n. 87), pp. 15-18. Schweizer's arrangement of material and conclusions in the *Wörterbuch* article are to be especially noted: under the New Testament heading he treats first the Synoptic Gospels and only later Paul and the other New Testament writers. As a background for Paul, Schweizer is well aware of Hellenistic notions of "spirit" as "material substance" and "celestial matter" (pp. 55-56), and he articulates the case for Hellenistic influences in the Pauline references quite clearly. Synoptic usages, however, are determined, he believes, by the Old Testament concept of the Spirit (pp. 25, 36), even those in Luke-Acts (p. 36); Windisch's hypothesis is termed "unlikely" (p. 34). For details on Windisch's view, see *The Spirit-Paraclete in the Fourth Gospel*, trans. James W. Cox ("Facet Books, Biblical Series," 20 [Philadelphia: Fortress Press, 1968]).

91. The Greek translation of Hosea 9:7 actually coins the term "Spirit-bearer" (*pneumatophoros*) for the prophet.

92. References and further examples in the *Wörterbuch* article, *Spirit of God* (see above, p. 478, n. 87), p. 13 (this section on Rabbinic Judaism is by E. Sjöberg).

93. This sort of reference at Mark 12:36 (par. Matthew 22:43) to David as an inspired author of Scripture (a quotation from Psalm 110

then follows), can be paralleled in the rabbinic writings of the day. The verse is often cited to show "Jesus' own view of inspiration" (and authorship) for the Old Testament books, but it is to be noted that this verse is actually a quite singular example in the Synoptics. C. K. Barrett (*The Holy Spirit* [see above, p. 478, n. 87], pp. 107-12) may be correct in contrasting the rabbis and the New Testament at this point where they seem to be so close: the rabbis regularly talked of the inspired authors of Scripture but made no claim about a similar inspiration or work of the Spirit for themselves; early Christians (and Jesus) seldom use this phrase with regard to Scripture but they were conscious of the work of the Spirit in their own lives. Just because they knew what it was to be a prophet under the Spirit of God they may have been sparing about references to the Spirit and the ancient prophets. It is also to be observed that Luke, who normally abounds in references to the Spirit, has omitted any such note here; the parallel at Luke 20:42 reads simply, "David himself says in the Book of Psalms, ..." It is suggested by Hans Conzelmann that there may be implied here a contrast between the (mere) statements of Scripture and Jesus' inspired words, for Luke regularly stresses the presence of the Spirit throughout Jesus' ministry (cf. *The Theology of St. Luke*, trans. Geoffrey Buswell [New York: Harper's, 1960], p. 180, n. 1).

94. On the birth stories, cf. above, pp. 138-41, and the literature there cited by J. G. Machen, M. Dibelius, P. Minear, and T. Boslooper; further: C. K. Barrett, *The Holy Spirit* (see above, p. 478, n. 87), pp. 5-24.

95. Barrett, *ibid.*, p. 125, speaks of Luke 1–2 as "an island of the Old Testament, surrounded by the New." A good example of Old Testament coloring can be seen if one reads the account of Hannah and the birth of Samuel in I Samuel 1–2 (especially 1:11-18 and 2:1) alongside the references to the Spirit and the birth of John and Jesus in Luke (especially 1:46-47). Luke's references to the work of the Spirit give an underlying unity to these chapters, not only the two about the birth and infancy, but also those which follow about the beginnings of Jesus' ministry; cf. 1:35 (birth announced); 3:22 (baptism); 4:1, 14 (temptation); 4:18 (ministry begun in the synagogue at Nazareth).

96. See above, pp. 283 and 291.

97. This is true even though Luke 2:40 describes Jesus with the words, "The child grew and became strong, *filled with wisdom,*" while the parallel verse at 1:80 has said of John the Baptist, "The child grew and became strong *in spirit.*" These verses do not mean to infer that the Baptist was under the Spirit as a child while Jesus was not, but they rather stem from Luke's view that Jesus was not *"under* the Spirit"

but had the Spirit "under him," as it were. One ought to compare Mark 1:12 and its vigorous picture of the Spirit's role in the tempta- tion ("The Spirit immediately drove him out into the wilderness") and Matthew 4:1 which depicts Jesus as a passive figure under the Spirit ("Jesus was led up by the Spirit into the wilderness") with Luke 4:1 where Jesus is the active agent functioning in the sphere of the Spirit (literally, "Jesus was guided in the Spirit"; cf. 4:14, "Jesus returned in the power of the Spirit," something said in Luke with respect only to Jesus). On the point, cf. H. Conzelmann, *The Theology of St. Luke* (see above, p. 480, n. 93), p. 180. At Luke 2:40 note the addition of the words "filled with wisdom" as an Old Testament way of expressing the Spirit's presence in Jesus, even as a boy. Jesus does not need to grow "in spirit," he is the bearer of the Spirit from the outset in Luke.

98. See above, pp. 201-2, 204.

99. So C. K. Barrett, *The Holy Spirit* (see above, p. 478, n. 87), pp. 62-63, and E. Schweizer, *Spirit of God* (see above, p. 478, n. 87), p. 26. I disregard the sort of "solution" which claims that Jesus used both forms of the saying on different occasions; so William Barclay, *The Promise of the Spirit* (see above, p. 478, n. 87), p. 24.

100. "Finger of God" is used in connection with creation at Psalm 8:3, and with revelation from God at Exodus 31:18 (cf. Daniel 5:5). It was well enough known to be found in magic incantations in Egypt. Luke has a fondness for "biblical" expressions like this. Moreover, it suited his purpose to employ the phrase here, rather than "Spirit," since (1) Luke normally does not associate the Spirit with healing miracles but (2) rather connects miracles with God's "power" (8:46). Further, Luke's change fits his view that for the church the kingdom is still off in the distant future, though the Spirit is present now. Cf. H. Conzelmann, *The Theology of St. Luke* (see above, p. 480, n. 93), pp. 113-19. He does not alter Jesus' words that the "kingdom of God has come upon you," but he does avoid connecting this with the Spirit. An additional reason for preferring Matthew's wording is the fact that he has here "the kingdom of God" instead of his usual phrase, "kingdom of heaven." He seems to have preserved the saying intact. These are reasons for differing with the many scholars who prefer Luke over Matthew at this point. Admittedly an argument against the origi- nality of Matthew here is the fact that his phrase "Spirit of God" could have been influenced by the reference to the Spirit from Isaiah 42:1 which is quoted at 12:18, "I will put my spirit upon him." Nat- urally, it seems out of the question that Jesus could have used both expressions in the same sentence in his discussion with the Pharisees.

101. Matthew lacks the phrase in his parallel (11:25) and has a different context. All we can claim, therefore, is that Luke indirectly links the Spirit with the expulsion of demons here, as Matthew did in his gospel at 12:28.

102. In treating the difficult verses at Mark 3:28-30 and the Q parallel at Matthew 12:32, par. Luke 12:10, I have in general followed the solution adopted by C. K. Barrett, *The Holy Spirit* (see above, p. 478, n. 87), pp. 103-7, 133-34; cf. G. Bornkamm, *Jesus of Nazareth* (see above, p. 339, n. 10), pp. 170, 212, n. 1. One clue for interpretation turns on the fact that the Marcan version has the unusual phrase "sons of men" (plural), while the Q version refers to the Son of man (a christological title). It has been argued that the original statement read, "all sins will be forgiven the son of man [singular, as an expression for mankind or men in general]". In order to retain this meaning, the Marcan version has employed a plural form, "sons of men," but the Q version misunderstood it christologically, and interpreted it to be a reference to Jesus, the Son of man—hence the distinction, "all sins [prior to conversion], against the Son of man will be forgiven, but those against the Holy Spirit [after conversion] will not be." For a somewhat different analysis, cf. H. E. Tödt, *The Son of Man in the Synoptic Tradition* (see above, p. 428, n. 50), pp. 118-20, 312-18. Tödt agrees that the Q version (Matthew 12:32, par. Luke 12:10) reflects a notion of two periods in history: the one is the period of Jesus' activity on earth as Son of man, and the other is a later period of activity by the Spirit. A person "who did not follow the earthly Jesus may nevertheless find forgiveness when following the exalted Lord, i.e., if he does not blaspheme against the Spirit" (p. 119). However, Tödt differs about the Marcan version, regarding it as a later form of the Q saying, not an original one reflecting Jesus' lifetime when the Spirit was active.

103. In addition to the literature cited above, cf. G. W. H. Lampe, "The Holy Spirit in the Writings of St. Luke," in *Studies in the Gospels* (in Memory of R. H. Lightfoot [Oxford: Basil Blackwell, 1955]), pp. 159-200.

104. Hans Conzelmann's well-known analysis of the theological view of history held by Luke as a sequence of two periods, the period of Israel and the period of the church, separated by a unique epoch, the midpoint of time (when Jesus was on earth), the whole pointing toward an eventual coming of the kingdom, off in the future, can be applied with regard to the view of the Spirit involved for each period in the following way:

AGE OF ISRAEL	THE TIME	THE AGE OF THE	THE KINGDOM
(Old Testament)	OF JESUS	CHURCH AND	(to come, in
the Spirit oc-	(a unique epoch)	SPIRIT	the future)
casionally active	the Spirit present	(cf. Acts)	fulfillment
	(still depicted in	the Spirit	
	Old Testament	mightily at	
	terms)	work	

105. J. E. Fison, *The Blessing of the Holy Spirit* (see above, p. 478, n. 87), p. v, speaks of "the Synoptic silence" and devotes a chapter to "The Silence of the Synoptists" (pp. 81-103). C. K. Barrett concludes his book, *The Holy Spirit* (see above, p. 478, n. 87), pp. 140-62, with a chapter entitled, "Why Do the Gospels Say So Little About the Spirit?"

106. J. E. Fison, *The Blessing of the Holy Spirit* (see above, p. 478, n. 87), p. 107. Luke, who multiplies references to the Holy Spirit, is something of an exception to this Synoptic "silence" about the Spirit, but significantly his references usually reflect the Old Testament, not the post-Easter outlook. Naturally all sorts of theories have been put forth to explain this silence in the Synoptics as a whole. The traditional answer is to appeal to the Fourth Gospel and to claim that while Jesus may not have offered much public teaching about the Spirit he must have provided private instruction to the disciples on the subject (John 14–16). Cf. George Johnston, "Spirit," in *A Theological Word Book of the Bible,* ed. Alan Richardson (New York: Macmillan, 1950), p. 238.

A theory which is almost certainly wrong is the notion that Jesus never mentioned the Spirit because "Spirit" implies a great gulf between God and man (which the Spirit bridges) and that Jesus rejected any such "God-man gap." So E. F. Scott, *The Spirit in the New Testament* (see above, p. 478, n. 87), pp. 77-80. Scott to the contrary, however, Jesus seems to have been quite at home in the first-century view of angels, demons, etc., and the gulf they inhabit between God and man. Barrett, *The Holy Spirit* (see above, p. 478, n. 87), pp. 140-41, indicates why this theory is to be rejected.

A third view is that the Spirit was so "self-evident" and obvious to early Christians that they did not bother to record what Jesus said on this topic. Though Vincent Taylor advanced this argument on a form-critical basis in "The Spirit in the New Testament," in *The Doctrine of the Holy Spirit* ("Headingley Lectures" [London: Epworth Press, 1937]), pp. 53-55, Barrett (see above, p. 478, n. 87), p. 141, declares it "not entirely satisfactory," for the early church included in its tradition many other things which must also have seemed obvious to it, such as the command to love the neighbor.

A fourth approach is to claim that Jesus found it necessary to reinterpret the Old Testament idea of the Spirit dominant then and that this reinterpretation could only be achieved by living it out in the course of his ministry (R. Newton Flew, *Jesus and His Church* [see above, p. 461, n. 26], pp. 70-71). Jesus had to show in his life that the abnormal and ecstatic had now become normal and controlled. Flew associates the matter with the Messianic secret: just as Jesus could disclose who he was, the Messiah, only by reinterpreting that term, and ultimately only by death, so here. Hence he spoke little about the Spirit, but he laid the groundwork for a reinterpretation later on. One must ask, however, what evidence there is that Jesus radically changed the Old Testament view of the Spirit during his lifetime. Perhaps just as "Messiah" was used for Jesus only after the resurrection (see chapter 9), so here the doctrine (and, to a great extent, the experience) of the Spirit developed, only after Pentecost.

A fifth explanation appeals to a sort of analogy between the two testaments (cf. J. E. Fison [see above, p. 478, n. 87], pp. 83-86); it sees three periods of development in each testament:

Old Testament	abnormal and ecstatic examples— Judges, I Samuel	the "great prophets," 8/7th centuries B.C.— few direct references	a great outburst of the Spirit's power— Ezekiel, II Isaiah
New Testament	Luke 1-2, John the Baptist, opening chapters of Acts	few references by Jesus or in the Synoptic tradition	Paul and John show what the Spirit really means

The observation may be termed more homiletically than historically satisfying.

C. K. Barrett's own elaborate explanation is that (a) the Spirit is an eschatological phenomenon, like the kingdom and Jesus' messiahship (which he kept a secret); (b) just as the kingdom is to be regarded as present and future, so the Spirit is to be thought of as present (but hidden) in Jesus' ministry and destined to come fully only in the future; (c) the messianic secret demanded that Jesus therefore keep the presence and power of the Spirit "under wraps," as it were: to have allowed the full power of the Spirit to be manifest during the ministry would have betrayed the secret of who Jesus really was. Only on rare occasions during the ministry did the mask slip (for example, at Matthew 12:28, "If it is by the Spirit of God that I cast out demons, then the kingdom of God has come upon you"); by and large it was only after the cross and resurrection that the Spirit as the eschatological inbreaking of God's reign and power was really known. The weak point in this theory seems its handling of the messianic secret, but it is in harmony with the theology of Luke, Paul, and John to see the Spirit after the resurrection as the power of the new age. As for the historical Jesus, we have been content simply to conclude above that he spoke little of the Spirit, and that the gulf between "before Easter" and "after the resurrection" must be taken seriously here.

Glossary

Some Technical Terms Used in This Book

ABBA A term for "father" in Aramaic, see pp. 100-101.

ALLEGORY A prolonged metaphor or way of presenting one subject under the figure of another, with a series of correspondences between terms in the metaphor and various aspects of the subject, as in John 15:1 ff., where Jesus talks of discipleship in terms of a vine. See pp. 160-61 and the notes there, and 214.

APOCALYPTIC A type of ESCHATOLOGY found in the literature of late Judaism and early Christianity, stressing an "apocalypse" or "unveiling" of events soon to come to pass. Apocalyptic literature was usually written in dark times of trouble but looked forward to a bright future with God. Vivid imagery is used, as in the books of Daniel and Revelation. See pp. 85, 145, 150, 269-70, 275, 299-306.

APOSTLE Literally, one "sent forth" on a mission; a technical term in early Christianity for certain persons commissioned as witnesses of the risen Jesus; see pp. 172-73 and 464 n. 36.

ARAMAIC The Semitic language, related to Hebrew, which was spoken by Jesus, his disciples, and the earliest Christians.

ATONEMENT The doctrine of how man has been reconciled or made "at one" with God through the work of Jesus Christ; see p. 50.

BEATITUDE A declaration beginning with the word "blessed"; see p. 233.

BLASPHEMY Speech or action regarded as an offense against God; in Jewish law, cursing or reviling him.

CHARISMATIC Pertaining to spiritual gifts, granted by God's grace; thus, a person who possesses such gifts of the Spirit, particularly inspiration and prophecy; see pp. 327 and 329.

CHRIST Greek translation of "Messiah," meaning "anointed one"; see pp. 260-67.

CHRISTOLOGY The expression in doctrines and titles of the meaning of the work and person of Christ; see pp. 146, 294-95.

CONSUMMATION The climax and completion of God's purpose and plan for his people and the world.

"CORPORATE PERSONALITY" A Semitic, Old Testament way of thinking, whereby a group of people is conceived of as a single person and where one figure or person may "sum up" and represent the group; see p. 278, especially n. 83; 282; 312.

COVENANT In ancient times, a relationship or pact entered into by two parties; in the Old Testament, used especially of the relation between God and his people Israel; presupposed are (1) God's goodness as the basis and (2) certain obligations as part of man's response; see p. 323, especially p. 476 n. 82.

DEAD SEA SCROLLS Ancient documents, mostly in Hebrew, found since 1947 at QUMRAN, the remains of the library of a Jewish sect which existed from about 150 B.C. to A.D. 70. Included are copies of most Old Testament books, in fragments or sometimes complete manuscripts, commentaries on these books, and other religious writings.

DEUTERO-ISAIAH Chapters 40-66 of the book of Isaiah; see SECOND ISAIAH.

"ELECT," ELECTION "Chosen," according to God's choice, to carry out his purpose; implied are both blessings and duties.

ESCHATOLOGY The study of the "last things" in God's program, such as death, resurrection, judgment, and the life of the new age; in the New Testament, these "ultimate things" are regarded as breaking into the present, through Jesus. APOCALYPTIC is one form of eschatology. "Realized eschatology" is a method of interpreting the references to the "last things" so that promises relating to the future are viewed as already fulfilled. See pp. 25-26, 40-41, 145, 369 n. 17, 156-57, 226-27.

ESSENES The name given in ancient accounts from Philo, Josephus, and others to a group within Judaism at the time of Jesus which was characterized by a communal life, piety and devotion to Scripture, asceticism, etc. The name itself is usually taken to mean "the pious" or "the holy ones." Discovery of the DEAD SEA SCROLLS has led many scholars to identify the people at QUMRAN with the Essenes. However, there are enough differences between the Qumran community and the Essenes (as indeed there are differences among the ancient accounts about the Essenes on some details) that others have hotly contested the identification. It

now appears that at least the adjective "Essenic" can be used
to cover both the Qumran group and the Essenes known
from the ancient writers, provided one is aware that not all
features reported by these ancient sources conform with the
actual Qumran finds. Cf. H. Ringgren, *The Faith of Qumran* (see above, p. 398, n. 6), pp. 233-42.

EXILE   The period when Israel was in captivity in Babylon, 586-
538 B.C.; "pre-exilic" and "post-exilic" denote the periods
before and after this.

GNOSTIC   Referring to a movement in the first and second centuries A.D., found in Judaism, Christianity, and the pagan
world, which stressed knowledge which comes by revelation
to a few "ELECT"; some elements in the various forms of
gnosticism are akin to biblical thought, other features came
to be judged as heretical by orthodox Christianity—e.g.,
the denial that Jesus Christ had come in the flesh or had
died; or certain types of asceticism; see pp. 81, 131-32, 361
n. 28, 168.

GOSPEL OF THOMAS   A collection of sayings attributed to Jesus,
compiled probably in the second century A.D., some of
which seem GNOSTIC; see pp. 179-181.

GOSPEL, THE   The basic Christian message of the New Testament, the Good News, found in the epistles and in the four
gospels.

GOSPEL TRADITION   Material about what Jesus did and said,
handed down orally in the early decades along with the
KERYGMA, and later included in our gospels and other early
Christian writings; = JESUS-MATERIAL; see pp. 26-29.

GRACE   God's graciousness or love in action; not a substance or
a quality of God, but God's basic nature made known in
his deeds; see pp. 166-67.

HASMONEAN   The family and dynasty which led the Jewish state
165-63 B.C.; = MACCABEAN; see p. 7.

INTERTESTAMENTAL PERIOD   The decades between the events
covered in the Old Testament and the happenings reported
in the New; roughly the two centuries before Christ.

JESUS-MATERIAL   Reports about what Jesus did and said, circulating as a supplement to the KERYGMA; = GOSPEL TRA-
DITION; see pp. 26-29.

KERYGMA   A Greek word for the act of proclaiming a message
and for the contents of what is proclaimed. Thus, Jesus

had a *kerygma* about the kingdom. But as usually employed, the *kerygma* denotes the message about Jesus set forth by the earliest Christian witnesses; see pp. 24-25, cf. pp. 21-24, 45-46.

KINGDOM OF GOD   Jesus' central message about the kingship of God; see chapter 6. "Kingdom of heaven," a term often used by Matthew, has the same meaning; see p. 367, n. 9.

KYRIOS   Greek term for "lord," see pp. 125-26.

L (SOURCE)   Modern designation for material found in Luke's Gospel only, perhaps from a special source or sources which this evangelist had; see pp. 33-34, 40.

LITTLE APOCALYPSE   The long apocalyptic discourse by Jesus in the gospels, in Mark 13 and its parallels; it is "little" in comparison with the Apocalypse or Revelation of St. John the Divine, the last book in the New Testament; see pp. 270, 300-305, 332.

M (SOURCE)   Modern designation for material in Matthew only, perhaps from a special source or sources used by this evangelist alone; see pp. 33-34 and 40.

MACCABEAN   Pertaining to the family of leaders (or the period when they were active) who freed the Jews in 165 B.C. from their Greek-Syrian rulers and set up a Maccabean state; = HASMONEAN; see pp. 7, 278, 302.

MESSIAH   Hebrew, "anointed one"; = CHRIST; see pp. 260-67.

"MESSIANIC BANQUET"   The idea, found in Jewish apocalyptic and the New Testament, of a future glorious time with God and his "messiah," which will be joyous like a wedding feast, with all good things in abundance; see pp. 183-84.

MK   Designation used sometimes for a supposed earlier version of Mark's Gospel; see p. 40.

NEW AGE   The future "age to come," eagerly expected in Jewish apocalyptic, joyfully proclaimed in the New Testament message as present and not just future; see p. 220.

NEW QUEST (OF THE HISTORICAL JESUS)   An approach developed in the last fifteen years, in light of previous efforts, to recover what can be known about Jesus in the church's gospels; see p. 41.

"NON-ORIGINALITY" OF JESUS   A phrase to describe the fact that many of Jesus' teachings are not original with him but can be paralleled in Jewish and other teachers of the day; see pp. 97-99.

ORAL PERIOD　A time in early Christianity when the message of Jesus and all reports about Jesus were passed on entirely or chiefly by word of mouth, and not just in written form; see pp. 30-33, 88-89.

PARABLE　A comparison or extended simile where one thing is said to be like another in a specific way; often used by Jesus in conflicts with his opponents; see pp. 159-98.

PARACLETE　A term in John for the Holy Spirit; see p. 326.

PAROUSIA　Greek word for "coming" and "being present," usually applied in the early church to a future or "Second Coming" of Jesus; see p. 184.

PASSOVER　An Old Testament, Jewish festival, in the spring, commemorating the deliverance of Israel from Egypt at the Exodus.

PENTATEUCH　The first five books of the Old Testament: Genesis, Exodus, Leviticus, Numbers, Deuteronomy.

Q (SOURCE)　Modern designation for material, mostly sayings of Jesus, found in Matthew and Luke, but not in Mark; often a source or written document is assumed to lie behind this material; see pp. 33-34.

QUEST FOR THE HISTORICAL JESUS　The scholarly search in the last two centuries or so to recover Jesus "as he was"; see pp. 39-41.

QUMRAN　A site southeast of Jerusalem, in rugged country, on the shore of the Dead Sea, where the DEAD SEA SCROLLS and the ruins of buildings from a Jewish sect of the time of Jesus have been found. Most scholars identify the sect with the ESSENES, a group known from other sources; sometimes the sectarians are called "Covenanters (of Damascus)" from references in their writings. "Qumran" is used to refer to the group and its views.

SECOND COMING　The future parousia of Jesus Christ at the end of history, eagerly hoped for in some New Testament passages; see pp. 184, 297, 301 n. 15, and 303-5.

SECOND ISAIAH　The designation by critics for the second part of the book of Isaiah, chapters 40–66 (or just 40–55); stems from the end of the EXILE, about 540 B.C. as distinguished from the oracles of Isaiah himself (Isaiah 1–39, about 742-687 B.C.). Some scholars divide Second Isaiah into further sources. Deutero-Isaiah = Second Isaiah.

SEMITIC Referring to the Semites (descendants of Shem), among which peoples were the Israelites of the Old Testament and their descendants, the Jews. Sometimes "Semitic" refers to the family of languages, including Hebrew, spoken by these peoples.

SHEMA Hebrew, "Hear," the opening word of Deuteronomy 6:4, "Hear, O Israel: The Lord our God is one Lord," the great confession of the Old Testament and the rallying cry of the Jewish faith.

SYNOPTIC GOSPELS Matthew, Mark, and Luke.

TEACHER OF RIGHTEOUSNESS A title or description ("the righteous or correct teacher") given in the DEAD SEA SCROLLS to the leader (or a series of leaders) at QUMRAN; he was thought to be *the* interpreter of Scripture; see p. 292-93.

"THEOLOGY OF THE CROSS" A Christian outlook, in faith and life, which stresses the death (and resurrection) of Jesus as central, the need to accept humbly the salvation which God offers, and the necessity of a life of service; in contrast to a "theology of glory" which stresses the "rights" and power of man or the church, exalting self and glory now and not service under God. See pp. 127-28, 314.

TORAH Hebrew, "teaching, instruction, law," specifically the law of Moses, as found in the PENTATEUCH (therefore called "the Torah"); see p. 8.

TRADITION Literally, "that which is handed down," often in oral (rather than written) form, as the GOSPEL TRADITION in the ORAL PERIOD; see p. 26. This New Testament usage, referring to material about Jesus which passed into the New Testament writings, is to be distinguished from a later sense (e.g., in the Roman Catholic pronouncements at the Council of Trent) where "tradition" denoted written or unwritten teachings of the church in contrast (or even opposition) to the New Testament.

"TRANSLATION VARIANTS" The various ways a phrase in one language can be rendered in another language; e.g., an Aramaic word may be translated one way in Matthew and another way in Luke; see pp. 101, 239.

Bibliography

Some Books for Further Reading:
Basic Sources, Surveys, and Treatments for the General Reader

The following list is intended to suggest books and occasionally articles where the nonspecialist can find (1) primary source material on Jesus in English translation, and discussion of such material; and (2) surveys on topics which are treated in the chapters of this book. This listing is not, however, always as definitive or detailed as that in the notes, which the advanced student in particular should be sure to consult. The criteria of selection for the titles which follow include readability and accessibility in English, but not always strict agreement with positions taken in this book. Brief comments, characterizing many of the items, have been appended to aid the general reader.

I. SOURCES AND SURVEYS

THE BIBLICAL DOCUMENTS

For the canonical books of the Old and New Testaments, including the Synoptic Gospels, the *Revised Standard Version* (RSV; New Testament, 1946; Old Testament, 1952; revised, 1959), the English translation probably most widely used today, has usually been cited in this book; it continues the mainstream of English Bible translation and its language heritage (from the long-familiar King James Version of 1611 and the century preceding it, via the English Revised Version of 1881–85 and the American Standard Revised Version of 1901) and yet incorporates many results of modern scholarship. RSV editions with introductions and notes are particularly helpful, such as *The Oxford Annotated Bible*, ed. H. G. MAY and B. M. METZGER (New York: Oxford University Press, 1962) or (by the same editors and publisher) *The Oxford Annotated Bible with the Apocrypha* (1965) which includes late Jewish writings not usually classed as canonical by Protestants but long recognized as valuable historically for the Intertestamental Period. The RSV is now available in editions officially approved for Roman Catholic use: *The Oxford Annotated Bible with Apocrypha* in an "Imprimatur" printing (1966), and the *Holy Bible*, RSV Catholic Edition (Camden: Thomas Nelson, 1966), the latter embodying slightly more changes by a British Catholic committee.

For readers who wish fresh renderings which depart from the "Authorized Version heritage of language" in favor of a modern idiom—often quite free and likely to suggest new meanings in familiar passages, but not always as precise as necessary for detailed study—the following are among the best known examples:

PHILLIPS, J. B. *The New Testament in Modern English*. New York: Macmillan, 1958; paperback editions available.

The New English Bible, New Testament. New York: Oxford and Cambridge University Presses, 1961. (The Old Testament volume is forthcoming.) A radical departure from the Authorized Version heritage, by a committee of British scholars, under the general directorship of C. H. DODD.

Today's English Version of the New Testament. New York: Macmillan, 1966. Paperback edition, *Good News for Modern Man*. New York: American Bible Society, 1966. A fresh translation made for the Society by ROBERT G. BRATCHER, particularly to reach those who need a version in simplified English.

The Jerusalem Bible. Garden City: Doubleday, 1966. An English rendering of the French Bible prepared by the Dominicans in Jerusalem, with notes that are often excellent.

GOSPEL HARMONIES

Of particular importance for study of the biblical material about Jesus is a harmony of the gospels which prints the Synoptics or all four gospels in parallel columns so as to facilitate word-for-word comparison. Among the most important harmonies in English are the following:

Gospel Parallels: A Synopsis of the First Three Gospels. New York: Nelson, 1949. Prepared by BURTON H. THROCKMORTON, JR., along the lines of the well-known Huck-Lietzmann synopsis in Greek. The third, revised edition (1967) refers to some parallels from the *Gospel of Thomas*.

A Synopsis of the Gospels: The Synoptic Gospels with the Johannine Parallels. Philadelphia: Fortress Press, 1964. Prepared by H. F. D. SPARKS.

As can be seen, Sparks includes some material from John, while *Gospel Parallels* does not (though it does quote some noncanonical parallels). Throckmorton uses RSV; Sparks, the English Revised Version of 1881, which is a notoriously wooden translation but excellent for close study because it parallels the Greek text so exactly.

A commentary designed to be used with *Gospel Parallels* (or the Greek harmony on which it is based) is that by FRANCIS WRIGHT BEARE, *The Earliest Records of Jesus* (New York and Nashville: Abingdon, 1962). It treats the Synoptic material by sections in the order in which the passages are arranged in the synopsis.

INTRODUCTION TO THE NEW TESTAMENT BOOKS

There are any number of handbooks which treat the origin of each New Testament document. Some representative ones include:

HUNTER, A. M., *Introducing the New Testament*. 2d ed., rev.; Philadelphia: Westminster, 1957. Popular in style.

PRICE, J. L., *Interpreting the New Testament*. New York: Holt, Rinehart and Winston, 1961. Especially for college use.

KEE, H. C., F. W. YOUNG, and K. FROEHLICH, *Understanding the New Testament*. 2d ed., rev.; Englewood Cliffs: Prentice-Hall, 1965. A comprehensive treatment of the writings and their background, for college courses.

GRANT, R. M., *A Historical Introduction to the New Testament*. New York: Harper and Row, 1963. Includes a section on "The Problem of the Life of Jesus."

KÜMMEL, W. G., *Introduction to the New Testament*. Translated by A. J. MATTILL, JR. New York and Nashville: Abingdon; 1966. The standard German introduction, thorough in its bibliographies and balanced in its judgments.

WIKENHAUSER, A., *New Testament Introduction*. Translated by J. CUNNINGHAM. New York: Herder & Herder, 1960; available in paperback edition. A Roman Catholic work, especially detailed on the Synoptics.

In a class of its own is *The Birth of the New Testament, by* C. F. D. MOULE ("Harper's New Testament Commentaries," Companion Volume 1 [New York: Harper & Row, 1962]), which falls somewhere between an introduction and a New Testament theology, as it presents how the early church came to self-conscious expression of its position in the New Testament documents. An excursus by G. M. STYLER on "The Priority of Mark," pp. 223-32, provides an introduction to some current re-examination of the Synoptic problem, as does O. E. EVANS, "Synoptic Criticism since Streeter," *The Expository Times,* 72 (1960-61), 295-99. For a spirited presentation of the view that Matthew is prior to Mark, see WILLIAM R. FARMER, *The Synoptic Problem: A Critical Analysis* (New York: Macmillan, 1964), on which, see my review in *Dialog,* 4 (1965), 308-11.

COMMENTARIES

Among the many commentaries on the four gospels, the following in English are noteworthy:

In One Volume:

Peake's Commentary on the Bible, ed. MATTHEW BLACK and H. H. ROWLEY. New York: Thomas Nelson, 1962. A. S. Peake was a British scholar who produced a commentary in 1919 which made his name a household word. In 1962 it was completely redone, based on the RSV. Technical at times and hard to read because of the small print and compressed style, it is often a significant treatment even for advanced scholars. It includes excellent introductory chapters, such as "The Life and Teachings of Jesus," by J. W. Bowman, and succinct comments on Matthew by K. Stendahl, Mark by R. McL. Wilson, Luke by G. W. H. Lampe, and John by C. K. Barrett.

Major, H. D. A., T. W. Manson, and C. J. Wright. *The Mission and Message of Jesus.* New York: E. P. Dutton, 1938. Reflects the modern critical approach but not the criticism or theological interests of more recent times. The section by Manson, on *Q, M,* and *L* material, was published separately in 1949 as *The Sayings of Jesus* (London: SCM Press).

Kraeling, Emil G. H. *The Clarified New Testament,* Volume I, *The Four Gospels.* New York: McGraw-Hill, 1962. Intended as a college text, the book often reflects recent German scholarship as well as insights from the history of religions.

Popular Treatments, including Series:

The Cambridge Bible Commentary. New York: Cambridge University Press. Available in both hard-cover and paperback editions. The first such series employing the NEB, it prints that rendering and provides brief comments on difficult phrases; for teachers and others who know neither Greek nor theology. *Matthew* is by A. W. Argyle (1963); *Mark,* by C. F. D. Moule (1965); *Luke,* by E. J. Tinsley (1963); and *John,* by A. M. Hunter (1965).

Daily Study Bible. Philadelphia: Westminster. A series of volumes, written originally in the 1950's, by William Barclay, who provides his own translation and vivid illustrations from the classical and modern worlds which make for lively reading and an edifying tone. Two volumes on Matthew, one each on Mark and Luke.

Layman's Bible Commentary. Richmond: John Knox Press, 1959-64. More detailed than most series which aim at the layman. *Matthew* is by Suzanne de Dietrich (a French woman famed as a Bible study leader); *Mark,* by Paul Minear; *Luke,* by Donald Miller; *John,* by Floyd V. Filson.

Nelson's Bible Commentary. New York: Thomas Nelson. Volume 6, by F. C. Grant (1962), covers Matthew-Acts, printing RSV, with notes at the lower half of each page, similar to those which Professor Grant wrote for the *Harper's Annotated Bible* a decade earlier.

Pelican Gospel Commentaries. Baltimore: Penguin Books. Reasonably detailed paperbacks, but intended for laymen without special theological knowledge. *Matthew,* by J. Fenton, *Mark,* by D. E. Nineham, and *Luke,* by G. B. Caird, appeared in 1963.

Torch Bible Commentaries. New York: Macmillan. These volumes pro-

vide an introduction to each book and comment on each section
or verse. G. E. P. Cox did *Matthew* (1952); A. M. HUNTER,
Mark (1949); and W. R. F. BROWNING, *Luke* (1960).

The Century Bible, New Edition. New York: Thomas Nelson. This
   series has only just begun to appear with *The Gospel of Luke*, by
   E. EARLE ELLIS (1966). Brief introduction, lengthy notes at the
   bottom of the page, with the RSV translation printed above.

Shorter than any of these is the volume in the "Bible Guides" series,
The Good News, by C. L. MITTON (New York and Nashville: Abingdon, 1961); and that in the series "Westminster Guides to the Bible,"
Jesus and God's New People, by HOWARD KEE (Philadelphia: Westminster, 1959). Not part of any series is *The Gospel of Luke*, by BO
REICKE (Richmond: John Knox Press, 1964, "Chime Paperbacks"),
which offers the basic ideas and features of the Third Gospel in 89
pages.

More Advanced:

The Interpreter's Bible. New York and Nashville: Abingdon, 1951–57.
   Treats the entire Bible in twelve volumes. The format consists of
   survey articles (often excellent) in volumes 1, 7, and 12, and
   then the KJV and RSV (in parallel columns) with exegetical and
   homiletical comments below on the biblical text, book by book.
   The exegesis on Matthew is by S. E. JOHNSON, that on Mark by
   F. C. GRANT, and that on Luke by S. MACLEAN GILMOUR.

Harper's New Testament Commentaries. New York: Harper and Row.
   Each volume prints a full translation of the biblical book (often
   by the commentator himself) and a concise discussion on important
   matters of content. *Luke*, by A. R. C. LEANEY appeared in 1958;
   Matthew, by F. V. FILSON, and *Mark* by S. E. JOHNSON, in 1960.

Definitive English Commentaries:

Often the most detailed commentaries are not part of any series, and
in some cases we simply lack an up-to-date scholarly commentary in
English. For Matthew, for example, such a work is much needed today.
For Mark, VINCENT TAYLOR'S *The Gospel according to St. Mark*
(New York: St Martin's Press, 1952; reprinted with a few additions,
1966) is an obvious choice (though the comments by MORTON SMITH
in the *Harvard Theological Review*, 48 [1955], 21-64, should be
heeded), and the treatment by C. E. B. CRANFIELD, *The Gospel according to Saint Mark* (New York: Cambridge University Press, 1959) in
the "Cambridge Greek Testament Commentary" series ought to be examined too. For Luke the situation is almost as bad as for Matthew,
with J. M. CREED'S *The Gospel according to St. Luke* (New York:
Macmillan, 1930) probably the best available. For John, the situation
is better; cf. C. K. BARRETT, *The Gospel according to St John* (Lon-

don: SPCK, 1955), and RAYMOND E. BROWN, S.S., *The Gospel according to John* (*i-xii*) (Garden City: Doubleday, 1966; second volume forthcoming) in the "Anchor Bible" series. Though the Anchor Bible is directed to "the general reader with no special formal training in biblical studies" (and will eventually provide commentaries on the other gospels as well), Brown's volume is extremely detailed and surveys a wide range of opinions on most topics.

Not a commentary in the formal sense, but definitely to be considered on Synoptic passages (in spite of an English translation which leaves much to be desired and a compressed format which demands almost meditation and not just reading of the book) is RUDOLF BULTMANN's *The History of the Synoptic Tradition*, trans. J. Marsh (New York: Harper and Row, 1963).

BIBLE DICTIONARIES

Hastings' Dictionary of the Bible. An old favorite, originally edited by JAMES HASTINGS over fifty years ago and recently revised under the editorship of F. C. GRANT and H. H. ROWLEY (New York: Scribner's, 1963).

The Interpreter's Dictionary of the Bible. 4 vols. New York and Nashville: Abingdon, 1962. Provides in many cases the best short treatment anywhere available on biblical persons, places, and history. Some articles are quite technical, but there are photos, sketches, maps, and color plates.

A Theological Word Book of the Bible, ed. ALAN RICHARDSON. New York: Macmillan, 1950; paperback, 1962. Deals with many key terms. The most important survey of New Testament concepts, however, often is provided in the renowned *Theologisches Wörterbuch zum Neuen Testament,* which began to appear from the hands of German and other scholars in 1933 under the editorship of GERHARD KITTEL (later GERHARD FRIEDRICH). The articles treat Greek terms in their alphabetical order and can run to small monographs of a hundred pages. Fourteen such articles were translated in the series *Bible Key Words* (London: A. & C. Black), several of them often being reissued in a single volume later (New York: Harper and Row). The entire *Wörterbuch* is now being translated by G. W. BROMILEY under the title, *Theological Dictionary of the New Testament* (Grand Rapids: Eerdmans), Vol. 1 (1964), Vol. 2 (1965), Vol. 3 (1965), Vol. 4 (1967), covering through the letter *nu* in the Greek alphabet.

THE APOCRYPHA AND PSEUDEPIGRAPHA

The Apocrypha, the fifteen or so documents and additions to the canonical books of the Old Testament, appear in some editions of the

Bible (see above under "The Biblical Documents") or may be printed separately (e.g., *The Apocrypha: Revised Standard Version of the Old Testament* [New York: Nelson, 1957]). In addition, there are other writings from this period not included in any religious canon, the "Pseudepigrapha." The standard collection in English of both groups of documents is *The Apocrypha and Pseudepigrapha of the Old Testament*, ed. R. H. CHARLES (2 vols.; Oxford: Clarendon Press, 1913; reprinted 1963).

For a discussion of each document in the Apocrypha cf. (in addition to articles in Bible dictionaries):

METZGER, BRUCE M. *An Introduction to the Apocrypha.* New York: Oxford University Press, 1957.

PFEIFFER, ROBERT H. *History of New Testament Times: With an Introduction to the Apocrypha* (New York: Harper, 1941).

THE DEAD SEA SCROLLS

Today an edition of the Pseudepigrapha might conceivably include all Qumran finds. However, the Dead Sea Scrolls material is generally published separately. A number of English translations exist. References in this book have regularly been to those in paperback editions by A. DUPONT-SOMMER, *The Essene Writings from Qumran,* trans. G. VERMES (Cleveland and New York: World Publishing Company, "Meridian Books," 1962), and by GEZA VERMES, *The Dead Sea Scrolls in English* (Baltimore: Penguin Books, 1962). Translations are also available in MILLAR BURROWS, *The Dead Sea Scrolls* (New York: Viking, 1955) and *More Light on the Dead Sea Scrolls* (New York: Viking, 1958); and T. H. GASTER, *The Dead Sea Scriptures* (Garden City: Doubleday "Anchor Books," 1957; rev. ed., 1964). On questions of content, constant reference has been made to *The Faith of Qumran: Theology of the Dead Sea Scrolls,* by HELMER RINGGREN, trans. EMILIE T. SANDER (Philadelphia: Fortress Press, 1963), where an outstanding survey of views and an extensive bibliography are given.

JOSEPHUS

This Jewish historian's *Jewish War* and *Antiquities of the Jews,* written between A.D. 70 and his death about the year 100, provide primary source material on the New Testament period—though through the eyes of a man who had been a leader in the revolt against the Romans in Galilee and yet later espoused the Roman cause and thus writes with a certain tendentiousness. His works are available in several English editions:

Josephus. Translated by H. ST. J. THACKERAY, R. MARCUS, and A. WIKGREN. ("Loeb Classical Library.") Cambridge: Harvard University Press, 1926–1965. Provides the Greek text on verso pages and an English translation on the facing pages.

Works of Josephus. Translated by WILLIAM WHISTON. This old (1737) translation by the unorthodox Cambridge theologian and mathematician has often been reprinted, most recently in paperback (Grand Rapids: Kregel).

Other paperback editions:

The Jewish War and Other Selections from Flavius Josephus. Edited by M. I. FINLEY. The Loeb Classical Library translation by H. ST. J. THACKERAY and R. MARCUS. New York: Washington Square Press.

The Great Roman-Jewish War and The Life of Josephus. WHISTON'S translation as revised by D. S. MARGOLIOUTH, 1909. Introduction by W. R. FARMER. New York: Harper Torchbooks, 1960.

Jerusalem and Rome: The Writings of Josephus. Edited by NAHUM N. GLATZER. Whiston's translation, considerably revised. Cleveland: Meridian Books, 1960.

The Jewish War. Baltimore: Penguin Books, 1959. A fresh translation by G. A. WILLIAMSON, who has also written a biography, *The World of Josephus* (Boston: Little, Brown and Company, 1964).

OTHER SOURCES ON THE JEWISH AND ROMAN WORLDS IN JESUS' DAY

Primary source material pertinent to the time of Jesus and Christian origins is preserved in a number of rabbinic, Greek, and Latin writers. Selections from these sources will be found in collections such as C. K. BARRETT, *The New Testament Background: Selected Documents* (London: SPCK, 1956; New York: Harper Torchbooks, 1961); and the following volumes in "The Library of Religions" (New York: Liberal Arts Press): S. W. BARON and J. L. BLAU, *Judaism: Postbiblical and Talmudic Period* (1954); F. C. GRANT, *Hellenistic Religions: The Age of Syncretism* (1953), and *Ancient Roman Religion* (1957).

SURVEYS OF NEW TESTAMENT TIMES

"*Zeitgeschichte*" is the German term for a discipline in which sources on a period are brought together and analyzed. The various books in this area may include in their purview economic, cultural, and religious factors, as well as geographical ones. R. H. PFEIFFER'S *History of New Testament Times* has already been noted (above, under "Apocrypha and Pseudepigrapha").

Some other volumes:

ENSLIN, MORTON S. *Christian Beginnings, Parts I and II.* New York: Harper, 1938; paperback, 1956. Extremely lucid introduction to the period.

FOERSTER, W. *From the Exile to Christ: A Historical Introduction to*

Palestinian Judaism. Translated by G. E. HARRIS. Philadelphia: Fortress Press, 1964. Covers the Jewish background.

BONSIRVEN, J., S.J. *Palestinian Judaism in the Time of Jesus Christ.* Translated by WILLIAM WOLF. New York: Holt, Rinehart and Winston, 1963. Greater emphasis on exposition of Jewish thought.

REICKE, BO. *The New Testament Era.* Translated by DAVID E. GREEN. Philadelphia: Fortress Press, 1968. Concentrates on the political, economic and social background, Roman as well as Jewish.

Two readable books which treat persons and events in Palestine are those by STEWART PEROWNE:

The Life and Times of Herod the Great. London: Hodder and Stoughton, 1956. Covers the period down to 4 B.C.

The Political Background of the New Testament. London: Hodder and Stoughton, paperback, 1965 (originally published as *The Later Herods,* 1958). Continues the story into the first century A.D.

NEW TESTAMENT APOCRYPHA

For early Christian gospels, epistles, etc., not included in the canon, the collection compiled by M. R. JAMES, originally in 1924, *The Apocryphal New Testament* (Oxford: Clarendon Press, corrected reprint, 1953) has now been superseded by the *New Testament Apocrypha* originally assembled in German by a scholarly parish pastor, EDGAR HENNECKE (succeeded after his death by W. SCHNEEMELCHER), and now translated under the editorship of R. McL. WILSON (2 vols.; Philadelphia: Westminster, 1963, 1965). Volume 1, *Gospels and Related Writings,* is of special importance for the study of Jesus.

LIVES OF JESUS

Based on such sources as those listed above, literally hundreds of "lives" have been written over the centuries, particularly in the last hundred years. The following are among those significant as representatives of a type or as recent examples:

RENAN, ERNEST. *The Life of Jesus.* Originally published in French in 1863, it presents a warm, romantic picture of the man Jesus. Conveniently available in "Everyman's Library" and the "Modern Library."

SCHWEITZER, ALBERT. *The Quest of the Historical Jesus: A Critical Study of its Progress from Reimarus to Wrede.* Translated by W. MONTGOMERY. Preface by F. C. BURKITT. London: A. & C. Black, 1910; paperback ed., New York: Macmillan, 1961. Originally published in German in 1906, the study provides an engrossing survey of previous lives, presented so as to provide a platform for Schweitzer's own proposal of a Jesus who was consistently an apocalyptist, expecting an imminent end to the course of the world.

GOGUEL, MAURICE. *Jesus and the Origins of Christianity*. Translated by OLIVE WYON. New York: Macmillan, 1933; paperback ed., with an introduction by C. LESLIE MITTON, New York: Harper Torchbooks, 1960. The original appeared in French in 1932 and represented a lucid attempt, quite aware of the new problems raised for traditional lives by source criticism and form criticism, to state what might be said historically about each incident in Jesus' life and about his teachings. The introduction to the new edition indicates how the Anglo-Saxon world was by and large unprepared for such a critical approach in the 1930's.

BULTMANN, RUDOLF. *Jesus and the Word*. Translated by LOUISE PETTIBONE SMITH and ERMINIE HUNTRESS. New York: Scribner's, 1934; available in paperback, "Scribner Library." Written in 1926 for a popular German series on "The Immortals: Spiritual Heroes of Mankind in their Life and Work." it reflects the critical attitude that no bibliography is really possible, though one may still try to state certain scant facts which can be recovered with high probability about Jesus and his teachings.

BORNKAMM, GÜNTHER. *Jesus of Nazareth*. Translated by IRENE and FRASER McLUSKEY with JAMES M. ROBINSON. New York: Harper, © 1960. The outstanding life produced as part of the "New Quest," somewhat in reaction to Bultmann's view but certainly in line with his general method. Prepared for a popular audience in Germany, where it was published as a paperback, the book seeks to tell more about Jesus than Bultmann did but repudiates the biographical approach of the Old Quest.

GLOEGE, GERHARD. *The Day of His Coming: The Man in the Gospels*. Translated by STANLEY RUDMAN. Philadelphia: Fortress, 1963. Written by a professor of systematic theology who is quite conversant with critical scholarship, this volume was intended as a companion piece to CLAUS WESTERMANN's *A Thousand Years and a Day: Our Time in the Old Testament*, trans. STANLEY RUDMAN (Philadelphia: Fortress, 1962) which treats the Old Testament. Both volumes are concerned with theological values for men today, though not at the expense of the historical approach.

STAUFFER, ETHELBERT. *Jesus and His Story*. British ed., translated by DOROTHEA M. BARTON (London: SCM Press, 1960). U.S. ed., translated by RICHARD and CLARA WINSTON (New York: Knopf, 1960). The second volume in a German paperback trilogy on Jesus' world, life, and teaching, the presentation has much in common with the Old Quest but strikes some distinctive notes of its own.

ENSLIN, MORTON S. *The Prophet from Nazareth*. New York: McGraw-

Hill, 1961. This and the next two would claim to reflect the Liberal tradition in life-of-Jesus scholarship.

McCASLAND, S. VERNON. *The Pioneer of Our Faith: A New Life of Jesus.* New York: McGraw-Hill, 1964.

ROBINSON, D. F. *Jesus, Son of Joseph: A Re-examination of the New Testament Record.* Boston: Beacon, 1964.

CONNICK, C. MILO. *Jesus—the Man, the Mission and the Message.* Englewood Cliffs: Prentice-Hall, 1963. Like the next title, intended especially for use in college religion courses.

SAUNDERS, ERNEST W. *Jesus in the Gospels.* Englewood Cliffs: Prentice-Hall, 1967.

II. TREATMENTS OF TOPICS TAKEN UP IN THIS BOOK

CHAPTER 1: THE MAN FROM NAZARETH IN GALILEE

On the world of Jesus and its backgrounds, see above, under "Surveys on New Testament Times," and also:

SCHÜRER, EMIL. *A History of the Jewish People in the Time of Jesus Christ.* Translated by JOHN MACPHERSON, S. TAYLOR, and P. CHRISTIE. Edinburgh: T. & T. Clark, 1890. 5 vols. A standard work of nineteenth-century German scholarship, it is still valuable for its compilation of source material, though in need of supplementation from more recent finds and of correction on some interpretations. A one-volume paperback abridgement of the First Division, on political history in Palestine, 175 B.C.—A.D. 135, has been published under the title *A History of The Jewish People in the Time of Jesus* [sic], ed. NAHUM N. GLATZER, with a new nine-page introduction (New York: Schocken Books. 1961).

RUSSELL, D. S. *Between the Testaments.* Philadelphia: Muhlenberg Press, 1960. A brief treatment on the Intertestamental Period, for the general reader who needs orientation on the period.

———. *The Method and Message of Jewish Apocalyptic, 200 BC—AD 100.* Philadelphia: Westminster, 1964. A more advanced treatment of this sort of literature from the Interestamental Period, including discussion of its themes, such as "messiah" and "Son of man." Extensive bibliography.

GRANT, F. C. *The Economic Background of the Gospels.* New York: Oxford University Press, 1926. Stresses the significance of economic factors in the development of Jewish messianism.

——— "The Economic Background of the New Testament," in *The Background of the New Testament and its Eschatology: in Honour of Charles Harold Dodd,* ed. W. D. DAVIES and D. DAUBE. New York: Cambridge University Press, 1954. Pp. 96-114. Provides a more recent supplement.

SIMON, MARCEL. *Jewish Sects at the Time of Jesus.* Translated by
JAMES H. FARLEY. Philadelphia: Fortress Press, 1967. An up-to-
date, nontechnical discussion of such groups, within Palestine and
outside; much additional bibliography included.

DAVIES, W. D. *Introduction to Pharisaism.* ("Facet Books, Biblical
Series," 16.) Philadelphia: Fortress Press, 1967. Brief but helpful
in offering a more favorable assessment of the Pharisees than is
common. Bibliography lists further standard literature.

JOHNSON, SHERMAN E. *Jesus in His Homeland.* New York: Scribner's,
1957. Commended for the general reader. Especially good on the
groupings in Palestine in Jesus' day.

STAUFFER, ETHELBERT. *Jesus and the Wilderness Community at Qumran.* Translated by HANS SPALTEHOLZ. ("Facet Books, Biblical
Series," 10.) Philadelphia: Fortress Press, 1964. Emphasizes differences as well as likenesses between Jesus and Qumran.

JEREMIAS, JOACHIM. *Jesus' Promise to the Nations.* Translated by S. H.
HOOKE. ("Studies in Biblical Theology," 24.) London: SCM
Press, 1958. Treats Jesus' relation to non-Jews during his ministry,
as does the next title.

MANSON, T. W. *Only to the House of Israel? Jesus and the Non-Jews.*
("Facet Books, Biblical Series," 9.) Philadelphia: Fortress Press,
1964.

CHAPTER 2: THE GOSPEL AND OUR GOSPELS

On the term "Gospel":

STRACHAN, R. H. "The Gospel in the New Testament," in *The Interpreter's Bible* (New York and Nashville: Abingdon-Cokesbury),
Vol. 7 (1951), pp. 3-31.

PIPER, OTTO. "Gospel (Message)," in *The Interpreter's Dictionary of
the Bible* (New York and Nashville: Abingdon, 1962), Vol. 2,
pp. 442-48.

BARR, ALLAN. "Gospel," in *Hastings' Dictionary of the Bible,* rev. ed.,
ed. F. C. GRANT and H. H. ROWLEY (New York: Scribner's,
1963), p. 340.

FRIEDRICH, GERHARD. *"euangelizomai, euangelion,"* in *Theological Dictionary of the Bible,* ed. G. KITTEL. Translated by G. W. BROMILEY
(Grand Rapids: Eerdmans), Vol. 2 (1964), pp. 707-37. More
detailed than any of the other surveys listed above.

KRODEL, GERHARD. "The Gospel according to Paul," *Dialog,* 6 (1967),
95-107. Much information on and analysis of recent discussion.

On Sources about Jesus outside the Gospels:

M. GOGUEL, *Jesus and the Origins of Christianity* (see above, p. 501),
Vol. 1, pp. 70-104. Provides a helpful survey.

DUNKERLEY, RODERIC. *Beyond the Gospels.* Baltimore: Penguin Books, 1957. A convenient survey of documents and archeological evidence bearing on Jesus. Dunkerley includes Islamic evidence, on which cf. also the notes in STAUFFER, *Jesus and His Story* (see above, p. 501).

KLAUSNER, JOSEPH. *Jesus of Nazareth: His Life, Times, and Teaching.* New York: Macmillan, 1925; Boston: Beacon Press, paperback reissue. Perhaps the most convenient collection and analysis of possible rabbinic references to Jesus.

JEREMIAS, JOACHIM. *Unknown Sayings of Jesus.* Translated by R. H. FULLER. London: SPCK, and New York: Seabury, 1959; rev. ed., 1964. Treats sayings attributed to Jesus outside the gospels, for example, that at Acts 20:35, and those in the church fathers, gnostic sources, or in an Arabic inscription at a mosque in India.

On the Talpioth ossuary inscriptions, cf. A. PARROT, *Golgotha and the Church of the Holy Sepulchre* ("Studies in Biblical Archaeology," 6 [London: SCM Press, 1957]), pp. 113-19; and BERNDT GUSTAFSSON, "The Oldest Graffiti in the History of the Church?" *New Testament Studies,* 3 (1956-57), 65-69.

The Kerygma:

DODD, C. H. *The Apostolic Preaching and Its Developments.* London: Hodder and Stoughton, 1936. For some of the subsequent literature and opinions, cf. my article, "The Kerygma and the Preacher," *Dialog,* 3 (1964), 27-35.

Critical Study of the Gospels:

The following articles in *Peake's Commentary,* rev. ed. (see above, p. 495-96), and the bibliography there listed give some idea of the current status in modern biblical study, though for *Redaktionsgeschichte* or "editorial criticism" one must turn to periodical literature or technical monographs, often in German: K. W. CLARK, "The Textual Criticism of the New Testament," pp. 663-70; C. S. C. WILLIAMS, "The Synoptic Problem," pp. 748-55; and E. DINKLER, "Form Criticism of the New Testament," pp. 683-85.

BULTMANN, RUDOLF, and KARL KUNDSIN. *Form Criticism: Two Essays on New Testament Research.* Translated by F. C. GRANT. New York: Harper Torchbooks, 1962.

FULLER, REGINALD H. *The New Testament in Current Study.* New York: Scribner's, 1962; paperback ed., 1966. Designed to give a picture of "what's going on" in each segment of New Testament study.

LADD, GEORGE ELDON. *The New Testament and Criticism.* Grand Rapids: Eerdmans, 1967. Though written from a conservative standpoint, this book seeks to explain how the various kinds of critical approach function, and to elucidate their values.

Semitic Backgrounds to Jesus' Teaching and its Transmission:

BURNEY, C. F. *The Poetry of Our Lord: An Examination of the Formal Elements of Hebrew Poetry in the Discourses of Jesus Christ.* Oxford: Clarendon Press, 1925. A standard discussion, arguing that Jesus' teachings in Aramaic had poetic structure and that this can be recovered.

GERHARDSSON, BIRGER. *Memory and Manuscript: Oral Tradition and Written Transmission in Rabbinic Judaism and Early Christianity.* Translated by E. J. SHARPE. ("Acta Seminarii Neotestamentici Upsaliensis," 22.) Lund and Copenhagen, 1961. An attempt to analyze oral transmission of material in Judaism and Christianity so as to show that Jesus was like a rabbi in that he drilled his teachings into his disciples by rote and that they then transmitted them intact over the years—that is, immune from the factors in the church which the form critics maintain greatly influenced the teachings. Such a thesis, which thus seeks to undercut form criticism, had previously been advanced by HARALD RIESENFELD, *The Gospel Tradition and its Beginnings: A Study in the Limits of Formgeschichte* (London: Mowbray, 1957). For a criticism of this view, cf. W. D. DAVIES, "Reflections on a Scandinavian Approach to 'The Gospel Tradition,'" in *Neotestamentica et Patristica* (*Novum Testamentum Supplement,* 6 [Leiden, 1962]), pp. 3 ff., reprinted in DAVIES' *The Setting of the Sermon on the Mount* (New York: Cambridge University Press, 1964), pp. 464-80; and, more sharply, MORTON SMITH, "A Comparison of Early Christian and Early Rabbinic Tradition," *Journal of Biblical Literature,* 82 (1963), 169-76. GERHARDSSON has issued a rejoinder to his critics in *Tradition and Transmission in Early Christianity,* trans. E. J. SHARPE ("Coniectanea Neotestamentica," 20 [Lund and Copenhagen, 1964]).

The History of Life-of-Jesus Study:

JEREMIAS, JOACHIM. *The Problem of the Historical Jesus.* Translated by NORMAN PERRIN. ("Facet Books, Biblical Series," 13.) Philadelphia: Fortress Press, 1964. A brief survey, from the time of Reimarus to the present, written from the viewpoint that the kerygma is a response to what is primary, Jesus and his message.

GRANT, ROBERT M. *The Earliest Lives of Jesus.* New York: Harper, 1961. This volume shows how a "Quest for the historical Jesus" already existed in its own way in the church fathers of the early Christian centuries.

McArthur, Harvey K. *The Quest Through the Centuries: The Search for the Historical Jesus.* Philadelphia: Fortress Press, 1966. Of particular interest for the medieval and Reformation periods, and the rise of gospel harmonies, as well as for suggestions about the current period.

Zahrnt, Heinz. *The Historical Jesus.* Translated by J. S. Bowden. New York: Harper and Row, 1963. An ably written account by a theologian-journalist, paying particular attention to work in Germany since 1896 and especially in the last fifteen years.

See also "Lives of Jesus" above. The lives specifically mentioned in chapter 2, available in paperback reissues, are Fulton J. Sheen, *Life of Christ* (New York: Popular Library) ; and Fulton Oursler, *The Greatest Story Ever Told* (Garden City: Doubleday "Image Books"; New York: Pocket Books).

CHAPTER 3: "THE CHRIST MUST SUFFER MANY THINGS"

Chronology:

Ogg, George. "Chronology of the Life of Jesus," in *Peake's Commentary,* rev. ed. (see above, p. 494), pp. 728-30. (Most Bible dictionaries include articles on the topic.)

Historicity and Chronology in the New Testament. ("SPCK Theological Collections," 6.) London: SPCK, 1965. Provides up-to-date surveys by H. E. W. Turner on "The Chronological Framework of the Ministry," pp. 59-74; and by G. Ogg, on "The Chronology of the Last Supper," pp. 75-96, where there is a discussion of the proposal by Annie Jaubert and others (see above, p. 473, n. 69) to date the Last Supper on the Tuesday, rather than the Thursday, evening before Jesus died.

Finegan, Jack. *Handbook of Biblical Chronology: Principles of Time Reckoning in the Ancient World and Problems of Chronology in the Bible.* Princeton: Princeton University Press, 1964. The most detailed treatment available in this area, with magnificent tables and bibliographies on each topic, though some conclusions are open to debate.

The Passion and Trial of Jesus:

Dibelius, Martin. *From Tradition to Gospel.* Translated by Bertram Lee Woolf. New York: Scribner's, 1935. Now reprinted in paperback ("Scribner's Library"), this standard form-critical account includes a chapter on the Passion story (pp. 178-217).

Lohse, Eduard. *History of the Suffering and Death of Jesus Christ.* Translated by Martin O. Dietrich. Philadelphia: Fortress Press, 1967. Now perhaps the best survey for the general reader on how current scholarship treats the Passion story.

KILPATRICK, G. D. *The Trial of Jesus.* New York: Oxford University Press, 1953. Pamphlet publication of a 1952 lecture which concludes that Mark 14:55-65, the Jewish trial, need not a be fiction of the early church, and that Lietzmann's theory (that the account of the Jewish trial was unhistorical) is thus wrong.

SHERWIN-WHITE, A. N. "The Trial of Christ," in *Historicity and Chronology in the New Testament* (see above, p. 506), pp. 97-116, a summary and reworking of part of his Sarum Lectures, published as *Roman Law in the New Testament* (Oxford: Clarendon Press, 1963). An expert in Roman law concludes, against Lietzmann and Paul Winter (see below), that Jesus' trial does reflect accurately Roman practices.

BLINZLER, JOSEF. *The Trial of Jesus: the Jewish and Roman proceedings against Jesus Christ described and assessed from the oldest accounts.* Translated by ISABEL and FLORENCE McHUGH. Cork: Mercier Press, 1959. In some ways, for the general reader the most comprehensive treatment of the trials, this book is the work of a German Roman Catholic scholar, who concludes for the historicity of a Sanhedrin trial which operated according to Sadducean, rather than Pharisaic, rules. U.S. edition, Westminster, Maryland: Newman Press, 1959.

ZEITLIN, SOLOMON. *Who Crucified Jesus?* New York: Bloch Publishing Company, 1964. Originally published in 1942, this book, by a Jewish scholar who is expert in rabbinic sources (but who regards the Qumran documents as medieval and/or forgeries), is strong on its appeal to redress libels against the Jews, but leaves something to be desired in its handling of the gospel material.

WINTER, PAUL. *On the Trial of Jesus.* ("Studia Judaica," 1.) Berlin: de Gruyter, 1961. A series of essays on aspects of the trial by a scholar well versed in form criticism, who takes up the position of Lietzmann.

Most of these books cite additional references to the literature, including the studies by Lietzmann (in German) and Juster (in French).

CHAPTER 4: THE LORD TAUGHT THEM TO PRAY

The Lord's Prayer:

JEREMIAS, JOACHIM. *The Lord's Prayer.* Translated by J. REUMANN. ("Facet Books, Biblical Series," 8.) Philadelphia: Fortress Press, 1964. Brief but attractive analysis of both background and content of the prayer, with a concern to reconstruct in the original Aramaic Jesus' own prayer as well as to account for later changes. Bibliography included. The essay is reprinted with minor revisions in a collection of articles by Jeremias, *The Prayers of Jesus* ("Studies in Biblical Theology," Second Series, 6 [London: SCM Press, 1967]), pp. 82-107.

HUNTER, A. M. *A Pattern for Life.* Philadelphia: Westminster, 1953. Popularly written for the general reader; the prayer is presented (pp. 64-74) in the context of Jesus' general teachings. Cf. also Hunter's remarks in "The Lord's Prayer" in his *Teaching and Preaching the New Treatment* (Philadelphia: Westminster, 1963), pp. 93-96.

SCOTT, E. F. *The Lord's Prayer: Its Character, Purpose, and Interpretation.* New York: Scribner's, 1951. An older treatment by the American writer who was in some ways as popular with many readers in his generation as A. M. Hunter has been more recently.

LOHMEYER, ERNST. *"Our Father": An Introduction to the Lord's Prayer.* Translated by J. BOWDEN. New York: Harper and Row, 1965. A detailed analysis by a German scholar, originally published in 1946. Lohmeyer's Aramaic reconstruction of the prayer has been criticized by Jeremias.

CHAPTER 5: GOD RAISED HIM FROM THE DEAD

The Resurrection of Jesus:

RAMSEY, A. MICHAEL. *The Resurrection of Christ: An Essay in Biblical Theology.* Philadelphia: Westminster, 1946. Theological as well as historical in orientation, this treatment, by the present Archbishop of Canterbury, represents the approach of "biblical theology."

MORISON, FRANK. *Who Moved the Stone?* New York: Century Company, 1930; reprinted, New York: Barnes and Noble, "University Paperback." A famous apologetic account, written by a man who started out a skeptic, but ended arguing that the tomb was empty. Presented in the style of a detective story, the book includes some points to which professional scholars would take exception.

KEPLER, THOMAS S. *The Meaning and Mystery of the Resurrection.* New York: Association Press, 1963. A popular treatment that deals with resurrection in general as well as with the resurrection of Jesus.

CLARK, NEVILLE. *Interpreting the Resurrection.* Philadelphia: Westminster, 1967. Nontechnical, intended as a companion to Hunter's *Interpreting the Parables* and Fuller's *Interpreting the Miracles.*

The Miracles and the Resurrection. ("SPCK Theological Collections," 3.) London: SPCK, 1964. Seeks to relate the miracles of Jesus to the resurrection as the Miracle.

NIEBUHR, RICHARD R. *Resurrection and Historical Reason: A Study of Theological Method.* New York: Scribner's, 1957. On a more advanced level; a significant study of method, history, and the resurrection narratives.

For reflections of the extensive German literature, including both the radical critical treatments and the recent emphasis on the historicity of the resurrection in the so-called Pannenberg School, cf. the work by a German systematic theologian, WALTER KÜNNETH, *The Theology of the Resurrection,* trans. JAMES W. LEITCII (St. Louis: Concordia, 1966; first German ed. published in 1933), and, for more recent views: H. ZAHRNT. *The Historical Jesus,* (see above, 506), pp. 120-38.

GOPPELT, L., H. THIELICKE, and H. R. MÜLLER-SCHWEFE, *The Easter Message Today.* Translated by S. ATTANASIO and D. L. GUDER. New York: Nelson, 1964.

FULLER, DANIEL P. *Easter Faith and History.* Grand Rapids: Eerdmans, 1965.

BRAATEN, CARL E. *History and Hermeneutics.* ("New Directions in Theology Today," 2.) Philadelphia: Westminster, 1966, pp. 78-102.

Some of the most penetrating analyses have not been translated.

On the term "Lord":

JOHNSON, S. E. "Lord (Christ)," in *The Interpreter's Dictionary of the Bible* (see above, p. 498), Vol. 3, p. 151. A brief survey.

TAYLOR, VINCENT. *The Names of Jesus.* New York: St Martin's Press, 1953. Pp. 38-51. For the general reader.

CULLMANN, OSCAR. *The Christology of the New Testament.* Translated by S. C. GUTHRIE and C. A. M. HALL. Philadelphia: Westminster, 1959; rev. ed., 1963. Pp. 195-237. More detailed.

HAHN, FERDINAND. *Christologische Hoheitstitel: Ihre Geschichte im frühen Christentum.* ("Forschungen zur Religion und Literatur des Alten und Neuen Testamentes," 83.) Göttingen: Vanderhoeck & Ruprecht, 1963. Pp. 67-132. The attempt here, an important one in German scholarship, is to trace use of the term *kyrios* ("lord") back to its use during Jesus' ministry as a polite term of address (*kyrie,* "sir"). A similar argument, according to which Jesus' ministry thus provided "raw material" for the Christology of the early church, appears in REGINALD H. FULLER, *The Mission and Achievement of Jesus* ("Studies in Biblical Theology," 12 [London: SCM Press, 1954]), pp. 111-14, and *The Foundations of New Testament Christology* (New York: Scribner's, 1965), pp. 50, 67-68, 119, 155-58.

The Transfiguration:

RAMSEY, A. MICHAEL. *The Glory of God and the Transfiguration of Christ.* New York: Longmans, Green, 1949.

The "Outline" of Jesus' Life and the Nativity:
See the footnotes to this section, and also p. 480, note 94.

CHAPTER 6: THE GOOD NEWS OF THE REIGN OF GOD
— PREACHING AND PARABLES

The Kingdom of God:
In addition to Bible dictionary articles, cf. the following:

SCOTT, E. F. *The Kingdom of God in the New Testament.* New York: Macmillan, 1931. An older but readable survey.

PERRIN, NORMAN. *The Kingdom of God in the Teaching of Jesus.* Philadelphia: Westminster, 1963. A more detailed and much more recent treatment. It can in turn be further updated through Professor Perrin's exegetical treatment of some passages on the kingdom in *Rediscovering the Teaching of Jesus* (New York: Harper and Row, 1967), pp. 54-108; on pp. 255-56 he notes recent literature in German.

LUNDSTRÖM, GÖSTA. *The Kingdom of God in the Teaching of Jesus: A History of Interpretation from the Last Decades of the Nineteenth Century to the Present Day.* Translated by JOAN BULMAN. Richmond: John Knox Press, 1963. Translation of a 1947 Swedish book, representing especially the viewpoint of Scandinavian scholarship, with an appendix bringing the story of interpretation since 1947 down to the time of the English edition.

LADD, GEORGE ELDON. *Jesus and the Kingdom: The Eschatology of Biblical Realism.* New York: Harper and Row, 1964. From the viewpoint of informed conservative scholarship.

SCHNACKENBURG, RUDOLF. *God's Rule and Kingdom.* Translated by J. MURRAY. New York: Herder & Herder, 1963. An analysis originally published in German in 1959, by one of the most able Roman Catholic exegetes.

KÜMMEL, W. G. *Promise and Fulfillment: The Eschatological Message of Jesus.* Translated by DOROTHEA M. BARTON. ("Studies in Biblical Theology," 23.) London: SCM Press, 1957. Detailed examination of passages which bear on the present and future aspects of Jesus' message.

The Parables:

DODD, C. H. *The Parables of the Kingdom.* New York: Scribner's, 1935; rev. ed., 1961. A standard work, arguing for "realized eschatology."

JEREMIAS, JOACHIM. *The Parables of Jesus.* Translated by S. H. HOOKE, New York: Scribner's, 1954; rev. ed., 1963. Detailed, especially on Palestinian background; uses critical methods to recover what Jesus said.

————. *Rediscovering the Parables*. Translated by S. H. HOOKE, adapted by FRANK CLARKE. New York: Scribner's, 1966. A popular version of the previous book, omitting the technical details.

HUNTER, A. M. *Interpreting the Parables*. Philadelphia: Westminster, 1961. An attractively written survey of how the parables have been interpreted and how they are being handled in some scholarly circles today. Either this or the previously mentioned title by Jeremias is the best starting point for the average reader on the parables.

LINNEMANN, ETA. *Jesus of the Parables: Introduction and Exposition*. Translated by JOHN-STURDY. New York: Harper and Row, 1967. More demanding, but rewarding. Miss Linnemann's concern is to let the parables speak again as "language event," in accord with the hermeneutical theory of Gerhard Ebling and Ernst Fuchs.

JONES, G. V. *The Art and Truth of the Parables: A Study in their Literary Form and Modern Interpretation*. London: SPCK, 1964. Reflects a growing literary interest in the parables.

VIA, DAN OTTO, JR. *The Parables: Their Literary and Existential Dimension*. Philadelphia: Fortress, 1967. Combines the interests observed in the two preceding titles, interests which some consider to be the next emphasis in the exposition of the parables.

SMITH, C. W. F. *The Jesus of the Parables*. Philadelphia: Westminster, 1948. Recommended for the general reader.

GLEN, J STANLEY. *The Parables of Conflict in Luke*. Philadelphia: Westminster, 1962. Popular, concentrating on one gospel and the use of parables there in Jesus' debates with his opponents.

CHAPTER 7. THE MIGHTY WORKS OF THE REIGN OF GOD

LEWIS, C. S. *Miracles: A Preliminary Study*. London: Geoffrey Bles, 1947; New York: Macmillan, paperback ed. A minor classic, this book by a renowned apologist for Christianity seeks to put readers in a position to consider miracles fairly and historically.

RICHARDSON, ALAN. *The Miracle Stories of the Gospels*. New York: Harper, 1941. Contains much material on terms and themes connected with Jesus' miracles; also reflects a theological and apologetical concern.

FULLER, REGINALD H. *Interpreting the Miracles*. Philadelphia: Westminster, 1963. Similar in format to HUNTER's *Interpreting the Parables*. Probably the best single introductory volume for the English reader.

MOULE, C F. D., editor. *Miracles: Cambridge Studies in their Philosophy and History*. London: Mowbray, 1965, and New York: Morehouse-Barlow, 1966. Thirteen essays on miracles in the Old Testament, late Judaism, the Greco-Roman world, and early Christianity, by members of the New Testament seminar at Cambridge, with some attention to modern problems concerning the miracles.

McCASLAND, S. VERNON. "Miracle," *The Interpreter's Dictionary of the Bible* (see above, p. 497), Vol. 3, pp. 392-402. A general survey by a writer long interested in the relation of miracles to modern psychology.

KALLAS, JAMES. *The Significance of the Synoptic Miracles.* ("SPCK Biblical Monographs," 2.) London: SPCK, 1961. A vigorous argument in favor of the importance of the "demonic" in understanding the miracles.

CHAPTER 8: THE NEW WAY OF LIFE
UNDER THE REIGN OF GOD

Jesus' Teachings in General:

BOWMAN, JOHN WICK. *Jesus' Teaching in its Environment.* Richmond: John Knox, 1963. For the general reader.

MANSON, T. W. *The Teaching of Jesus: Studies in its Form and Content.* New York: Cambridge University Press, 1931; paperback ed., 1963. An older but still valuable work by an astute observer, many of whose comments remain valid. The contents of Jesus' teaching are treated thematically. For a treatment of materials in their canonical sequence, cf. MANSON's *The Sayings of Jesus* (see above, p. 495).

PERRIN, NORMAN. *Rediscovering the Teaching of Jesus* (see above, p. 510). An important study which seeks to combine the best in the Anglo-Saxon and German approaches. A number of gospel passages are examined in considerable detail.

FLEW, R. NEWTON. *Jesus and His Way: A Study of Ethics in the New Testament.* London: Epworth, 1963. Less critical, but helpful for the general reader.

SCHNACKENBURG, RUDOLF. *The Moral Teaching of the New Testament.* Translated by J. HOLLAND-SMITH and W. J. O'HARA. New York: Herder & Herder, 1965. This survey, by a German Roman Catholic, includes the material in the gospels.

The Sermon on the Mount:

JEREMIAS, JOACHIM. *The Sermon on the Mount.* Translated by NORMAN PERRIN. ("Facet Books, Biblical Series," 2.) Philadelphia: Fortress Press, 1963. A brief, useful survey on how this sermon developed.

HUNTER, A. M. *A Pattern for Life.* Philadelphia: Westminster, 1963. Jesus' teachings in the sermon, popularly expounded.

McARTHUR, HARVEY K. *Understanding the Sermon on the Mount.* New York: Harper, 1960. Especially good on the history of interpretation.

DAVIES, W. D. *The Sermon on the Mount.* New York: Cambridge University Press, 1966. A paperback edition, summarizing and popularizing views found in his larger work, *The Setting of the Sermon on the Mount* (New York: Cambridge University Press, 1964).

DIBELIUS, MARTIN. *The Sermon on the Mount.* New York: Scribner's, 1940. An older treatment by the German form critic, whose insights, however, may still be new for some readers.

CHAPTER 9: STONY GROUND—AND THE CLAIM
OF JESUS CHRIST

Extensive literature on the christological titles is cited in the notes. For the general reader the following books offer surveys which are quite readable, though not always as critical as some scholars would wish.

TAYLOR, VINCENT. *The Names of Jesus.* New York: St Martin's Press, 1953. Summaries, each one to ten pages in length, on forty-two titles used for Jesus in the New Testament.

BARCLAY, WILLIAM. *Jesus As They Saw Him: New Testament Interpretations of Jesus.* New York: Harper and Row, 1962. Forty-two articles on titles for Jesus, amplified with illustrative anecdotes.

CULLMANN, OSCAR. *The Christology of the New Testament* (see above, p. 510). More detailed; representative of a conservative critical position.

FULLER, R. H. *The Foundations of New Testament Christology* (see above, p. 509). For the advanced student, the most scientifically oriented and rigorous treatment available in English.

CHAPTER 10: PROMISES AND PUZZLES—
JESUS AND HIS FOLLOWERS

The Church:

FLEW, R. NEWTON. *Jesus and His Church: A Study of the Idea of the Ecclesia in the New Testament.* London: Epworth, 1938. An older treatment, oriented to the ecumenical movement then emerging, but still worth reading. See pp. 460-61, note 26, for additional titles.

Baptism:

FLEMINGTON, W. F. *The New Testament Doctrine of Baptism.* London: SPCK, 1948. A good survey of the many aspects of this area. Briefer but more recent is Flemington's article "Baptism," in *The Interpreter's Dictionary of the Bible* (see above, p. 497), Vol. 1, pp. 348-53. For the advanced student, a standard treatment is now G. R. BEASLEY-MURRAY, *Baptism in the New Testament* (New York: St Martin's Press, 1962).

The Lord's Supper:

SCHWEIZER, EDUARD. *The Lord's Supper According to the New Testament.* Translated by JAMES M. DAVIS. ("Facet Books, Biblical Series," 18.) Philadelphia. Fortress Press, 1967. A highly compressed treatment of a complex question. Extensive bibliography.

JEREMIAS, JOACHIM. *The Eucharistic Words of Jesus.* Translated by NORMAN PERRIN. New York: Scribner's, rev. ed., 1966. For the advanced student; comprehensive, with some striking hypotheses.

The Spirit:

BARCLAY, WILLIAM. *The Promise of the Spirit.* London: Epworth, 1960. For the beginning student; a survey which informs and at times inspires.

BARRETT, C. K. *The Holy Spirit and the Gospel Tradition.* London: SPCK, 1947. More critical, detailed, and advanced. There is a paperback edition (1966), which reprints the 1947 presentation without change.

Indexes

References to Scripture and Other Ancient Sources

References to Authors and Other Persons

General Index

Prodigal Son, 385 n. 93
Rich Farmer (Fool), 165, 376 n. 47,
383 n. 77
Rich Man and Lazarus, 166, 191, 380
n. 70
Seed Growing Secretly, 158, 186, 385
n. 88
Servant's Wages (Reward), 172, 248,
379 n. 62
Sheep and the Goats, 248-50
Sower, 158, 180, 186, 251, 374 n. 39,
381 n. 73, 384 n. 87, 385 n. 88
Talents, 181, 249, 303, 384 n. 85
Thief at Midnight (in the Night),
179, 185, 384 n. 85
Treasure, 171, 186, 384 n. 86, 385 n.
88
Two Debtors, 168, 377 n. 53
Two Sons, 253
Unjust Judge, 380 n. 70
Unjust Steward, see "Dishonest Steward"
Unmerciful Servant, 103, 173-74
Wheat and Tares, 166, 186, 243, 374
n. 39, 385 n. 87, 408 n. 52
Wicked Tenants (Husbandmen), 254-
55, 291-92, 294, 373-74 n. 39, 380
n. 70, 414-15 n. 13, 451 n. 117,
451-52 n. 119
Wise and Foolish Virgins (Ten Maidens), 179, 249, 380 n. 70, 384 n. 85
collection of, 186
comic and tragic, 386 n. 99
connected with Jesus' death, 251
definition of, 160, 162
delay of parousia and, 184-85
double setting of, 161, 162, 179, 189
creations of the early church, 380 n. 70
expanded in a miracle story, 213, 390
n. 6
generalizing conclusions to, 376 n. 49
history of interpretation of, 159-61
interpretation of the Sower, 186, 189,
374 n. 39; of the Wheat and the
Tares, 186-87, 189, 243, 374 n. 39,
385 n. 87
in early church, 380 n. 70
in Gospel of Thomas, 179-81
in Old Testament, 161-62
kingdom in, 144, 153, 159, 161, 164-76,
190
laws of transmission for, 163
literature on, 511-12
new applications of, 178, 191-98
number of, 159
of growth or contrast, 157-58, 165, 372
n. 31
public and private, 384-85 n. 87
purpose of, 163-64, 186
reaudiencing of, 182, 189, 304
response to, 165, 170-76
reworking of, 163, 178, 179-85
transmission and transformation of,
178-85, 191, 383 n. 78
parousia, 132, 184-85, 188, 269, 275, 299,
300, 301, 304, 305, 357 n. 16, 384 n.
84, 429 n. 59, 433-34 n. 69, 436 n. 78,
456 n. 1, 458 n. 15, n. 16, 474 n.
73, 490
Passion, 27, 30, 33, 42, 43, 44-87, 88,
114, 128, 129, 135, 138, 220, 252, 256,
258, 269, 280, 282, 319, 322, 340 n.
3, 343 n. 21, 375 n. 46, 414 n. 5, n.
10, 451 n. 117, 475 n. 78, 507-08;
predictions on the, 46, 51-52, 128,
265, 269, 275, 340 n. 3, 425 n. 45,
436 n. 76, 446 n. 101
Peter, 22, 61, 64, 78, 106, 107, 118, 128,
129, 130, 131, 136, 212, 220, 221,
280, 287, 296, 300, 309-10, 314, 353
n. 2, 355-56 n. 10, 424-27 n. 45, 462
n. 31, 463 n. 35, 468 n. 51
as a model disciple, 313, 468 n. 50
as the rock, 465 n. 45, 465-66 n. 46
confession of, 128, 264-65, 269, 270,

309-10, 312-14, 340 n. 3, 424-27 n.
45, 427 n. 47, 455 n. 127, 462 n. 31,
468 n. 50
primacy of, 312-13, 466 n. 46
Pharisees, 14, 15, 16-17, 30, 64, 67, 94,
117, 152, 157, 162, 165, 167, 168, 172,
191, 192, 219, 227, 232, 237, 238, 239,
240, 242, 245, 253, 254, 255, 256, 258,
259, 260, 262, 338 n. 2, 339 n. 7,
358 n. 17, 379 n. 61, n. 62, 385 n.
87, 393 n. 20, 394 n. 29, 405 n. 38,
406-07 n. 46, 414 n. 10, 417 n. 21, n.
25, 436 n. 76, 439 n. 83, 481 n. 100,
503, 507
"pillar" passages, 293, 299, 453 n. 125,
490
Pontius Pilate, 8, 30, 44, 52-56, 62, 66-
77, 80, 82, 83, 341 n. 15, n. 17, 342
n. 18, n. 19, n. 20, 343 n. 21, 366
n. 5
prophet-martyr terms, theology, 221, 222,
330, 399 n. 8

Q (source), strata, 33-34, 35, 37, 40, 42,
93, 139, 152, 185, 201, 202, 204, 216,
221, 224, 231, 232, 239, 264, 267, 269,
270, 287, 292, 300, 331, 332, 381 n.
72, 382 n. 77, 398 n. 8, 403 n. 21,
409 n. 58, 416 n. 19, 434 n. 69, 436
n. 76, 439 n. 86, 482 n. 102, 490, 495
Qmk (source), 459 n. 16
"Quest for the historical Jesus, 40-41, 490,
see "Old Quest," "New Quest"
Qumran, 8, 14-15, 16, 94, 151, 169,
175, 205, 220, 263, 289, 292, 293, 299,
308, 317, 329, 359 n. 18, 360 n. 24,
373 n. 39, 386 n. 94, 408 n. 53, 432
n. 64, 443 n. 98, 449-50 n. 112, 463
n. 32, 463-64 n. 35, 470 n. 60, n. 62,
471 n. 63, n. 64, 473 n. 69, 479 n.
90, 490, 499, 504, 507, see "Dead Sea
Scrolls"

rabbinic (Judaism), 17, 259, 401 n. 13,
467 n. 48, 479 n. 92
"radical school," scholars, 293, 366 n. 5,
451 n. 119, 452 n. 122, 454-55 n. 127,
479 n. 90
realized eschatology, 155-56, 157, 158, 369
n. 17, 372 n. 27, 409 n. 59, 434
n. 72, 487, 510
Redaktionsgeschichte, redactional features,
339 n. 6, 408 n. 55, 435 n. 75, 437 n.
78, 457 n. 1, 459 n. 20, 504
reign of God, 134, 142, 149, 151, 153, 154,
156, 159, 170, 188, 199, 204, 210, 218,
225, 226, 234, 251, 260, 262, 292, 293,
296, 311, 312, 349 n. 18, 365 n. 1, n.
2, 368 n. 12, 453 n. 122, 484 n. 106
see "kingdom of God"
resurrection, future, general, 244, 245,
254-56, 409-10 n. 60, 411 n. 70, 415
n. 16, 431 n. 63
"resurrection light" in Jesus' life, 123-34,
138, 139, 260
in christological titles, 260-94, 360-61
n. 26, 455 n. 127
resurrection of Jesus, 1, 19, 20,
22, 23, 24, 25, 27, 30, 47, 50, 51, 61,
65, 78, 85, 86, 87, 88, 91, 96, 98, 100,
109, 110-34, 136, 142, 146, 153, 154,
163, 169, 178, 179, 194, 199, 202, 207,
210, 212, 216, 217, 219, 221, 227, 234,
235, 241, 271, 276, 280, 281, 291, 293,
294, 296-97, 305, 306, 307, 308, 310,
312, 313, 314, 316, 324, 326, 334, 340
n. 3, 360 n. 26, 361 n. 27, 366-67 n.
5, 367 n. 8, 368 n. 11, 374 n. 39, 379
n. 62, 394 n. 30, 397 n. 2, 409 n. 57,
n. 58, 425-27 n. 45, 439 n. 86, 445 n.
99, 449 n. 110, 454-56 n. 127, 464 n.
36, 476 n. 80, 478 n. 89, 484-85 n.
106
appearances after the, 39, 47, 113, 114-
15, 116, 117, 118, 120, 130-33, 220,

Type, 11 on 13 and 10 on 11 Garamond
Display, Garamond